# Empirical Corporate Finance
## Volume III

# The International Library of Critical Writings in Financial Economics

*Series Editor:* Richard Roll

*Allstate Professor of Economics*
*The Anderson School at UCLA, USA*

This major series presents by field outstanding selections of the most important articles across the entire spectrum of financial economics – one of the fastest growing areas in business schools and economics departments. Each collection has been prepared by a leading specialist who has written an authoritative introduction to the literature.

1.  The Theory of Corporate Finance (Volumes I and II)
    *Michael J. Brennan*

2.  Futures Markets (Volumes I, II and III)
    *A.G. Malliaris*

3.  Market Efficiency: Stock Market Behaviour in Theory and Practice (Volumes I and II)
    *Andrew W. Lo*

4.  Microstructure: The Organization of Trading and Short Term Price Behavior (Volumes I and II)
    *Hans R. Stoll*

5.  The Debt Market (Volumes I, II and III)
    *Stephen A. Ross*

6.  Options Markets (Volumes I, II and III)
    *George M. Constantinides and A.G. Malliaris*

7.  Empirical Corporate Finance (Volumes I, II, III and IV)
    *Michael J. Brennan*

Future titles will include:

Continuous Time Finance
*Stephen M. Schaefer*

International Securities
*George C. Philippatos and Gregory D. Koutmos*

Emerging Markets

Behavioral Finance
*Harold M. Shefrin*

Asset Pricing Theory and Tests
*Robert Grauer*

International Capital Markets

Wherever possible, the articles in these volumes have been reproduced as originally published using facsimile reproduction, inclusive of footnotes and pagination to facilitate ease of reference.

For a list of all Edward Elgar published titles visit our site on the World Wide Web at
http://www.e-elgar.co.uk

# Empirical Corporate Finance
# Volume III

*Edited by*

# Michael J. Brennan

*Goldyne and Irwin Hearsh Professor of Banking and Finance,*
*University of California, Los Angeles, USA and Professor of Finance,*
*London Business School, UK*

THE INTERNATIONAL LIBRARY OF CRITICAL WRITINGS IN FINANCIAL ECONOMICS

**An Elgar Reference Collection**
Cheltenham, UK • Northampton, MA, USA

Published by
Edward Elgar Publishing Limited
Glensanda House
Montpellier Parade
Cheltenham
Glos GL50 1UA
UK

Edward Elgar Publishing, Inc.
136 West Street
Suite 202
Northampton
Massachusetts 01060
USA

A catalogue record for this book is available from the British Library.

**Library of Congress Cataloguing in Publication Data**

Empirical corporate finance / edited by Michael J. Brennan.
      p. cm. — (The international library of critical writings in financial economics; 7)
    Includes bibliographical references and index.
    1. Corporations—Finance. I. Brennan, Michael J. II. Series.

    HG4026 .E475 2001
    658.15—dc21                                                                                              00–066245

ISBN   1 85898 484 X (4 volume set)

Printed and bound in Great Britain by MPG Books Ltd, Bodmin, Cornwall

# Contents

# Acknowledgements

The editor and publishers wish to thank the authors and the following publishers who have kindly given permission for the use of copyright material.

American Economic Association for article: Judith A. Chevalier (1995), 'Capital Structure and Product Market Competition: Empirical Evidence from the Supermarket Industry', *American Economic Review*, **85** (3), June, 415–35.

Blackwell Publishers for articles: Mitchell A. Petersen and Raghuram G. Rajan (1994), 'The Benefits of Lending Relationships: Evidence from Small Business Data', *Journal of Finance*, **XLIX** (1), March, 3–37; Tim Loughran and Jay R. Ritter (1995), 'The New Issues Puzzle', *Journal of Finance*, **L** (1), March, 23–51; Rafael La Porta, Florencio Lopez-de-Silanes, Andrei Shleifer and Robert W. Vishny (1997), 'Legal Determinants of External Finance', *Journal of Finance*, **LII** (2), July, 1131–50; Philip G. Berger, Eli Ofek and David L. Yermack (1997), 'Managerial Entrenchment and Capital Structure Decisions', *Journal of Finance*, **LII** (4), September, 1411–38; Tim Loughran and Jay R. Ritter (1997), 'The Operating Performance of Firms Conducting Seasoned Equity Offerings', *Journal of Finance*, **LII** (5), December, 1823–50; Joel F. Houston and Michael D. Ryngaert (1997), 'Equity Issuance and Adverse Selection: A Direct Test Using Conditional Stock Offers', *Journal of Finance*, **LII** (1), March, 197–219; John R. Graham, Michael L. Lemmon and James S. Schallheim (1998), 'Debt, Leases, Taxes, and the Endogeneity of Corporate Tax Status', *Journal of Finance*, **LIII** (1), February, 131–62; Luigi Zingales (1998), 'Survival of the Fittest or the Fattest? Exit and Financing in the Trucking Industry', *Journal of Finance*, **LIII** (3), June, 905–38; Mark Carey, Mitch Post and Steven A. Sharpe (1998), 'Does Corporate Lending by Banks and Finance Companies Differ? Evidence on Specialization in Private Debt Contracting', *Journal of Finance*, **LIII** (3), June, 845–78; Assem Safieddine and Sheridan Titman (1999), 'Leverage and Corporate Performance: Evidence from Unsuccessful Takeovers', *Journal of Finance*, **LIV** (2), April, 547–80.

Elsevier Science Ltd for articles: Larry Lang, Annette Poulsen and René Stulz (1995), 'Asset Sales, Firm Performance, and the Agency Costs of Managerial Discretion', *Journal of Financial Economics*, **37** (1), January, 3–37; Michael J. Alderson and Brian L. Betker (1995), 'Liquidation Costs and Capital Structure', *Journal of Financial Economics*, **39** (1), September, 45–69; John J. McConnell and Henri Servaes (1995), 'Equity Ownership and the Two Faces of Debt', *Journal of Financial Economics*, **39** (1), September, 131–57; Steven A. Sharpe and Hien H. Nguyen (1995), 'Capital Market Imperfections and the Incentive to Lease', *Journal of Financial Economics*, **39** (2 & 3), October–November, 271–94; John R. Graham (1996), 'Debt and the Marginal Tax Rate', *Journal of Financial Economics*, **41** (1), May, 41–73; Kooyul Jung, Yong-Cheol Kim and René M. Stulz (1996), 'Timing, Investment Opportunities, Managerial Discretion, and the Security Issue Decision', *Journal of Financial Economics*, **42** (2), October, 159–85.

MIT Press Journals for article: Takeo Hoshi, Anil Kashyap and David Scharfstein (1991), 'Corporate Structure, Liquidity, and Investment: Evidence from Japanese Industrial Groups', *Quarterly Journal of Economics*, **106** (1), February, 33–60.

Oxford University Press for articles: Mitchell A. Petersen and Raghuram G. Rajan (1997), 'Trade Credit: Theories and Evidence', *Review of Financial Studies*, **10** (3), Fall, 661–91; Dan Kovenock and Gordon M. Phillips (1997), 'Capital Structure and Product Market Behavior: An Examination of Plant Exit and Investment Decisions', *Review of Financial Studies*, **10** (3), Fall, 767–803.

University of Chicago Press for article: Mark Hoven Stohs and David C. Mauer (1996), 'The Determinants of Corporate Debt Maturity Structure', *Journal of Business*, **69** (3), July, 279–312.

Every effort has been made to trace all the copyright holders but if any have been inadvertently overlooked the publishers will be pleased to make the necessary arrangement at the first opportunity.

In addition the publishers wish to thank the Marshall Library of Economics, Cambridge University and the Library of Indiana University at Bloomington, USA, for their assistance in obtaining these articles.

# Part I
# Corporate Financial Policy

# A
# The Role of the Legal Framework

# [1]

THE JOURNAL OF FINANCE • VOL. LII, NO. 3 • JULY 1997

# Legal Determinants of External Finance

RAFAEL LA PORTA, FLORENCIO LOPEZ-DE-SILANES, ANDREI SHLEIFER,
and ROBERT W. VISHNY*

## ABSTRACT

Using a sample of 49 countries, we show that countries with poorer investor protections, measured by both the character of legal rules and the quality of law enforcement, have smaller and narrower capital markets. These findings apply to both equity and debt markets. In particular, French civil law countries have both the weakest investor protections and the least developed capital markets, especially as compared to common law countries.

WHY DO SOME COUNTRIES have so much bigger capital markets than others? Why, for example, do the United States and the United Kingdom have enormous equity markets, while Germany and France have much smaller ones? Why do hundreds of companies go public in the United States every year, while only a few dozen went public in Italy over a decade (Pagano, Panetta, and Zingales (1995))? Why do Germany and Japan have such extensive banking systems, even relative to other wealthy economies? If we look at a broader range of countries, why in fact do we see huge differences in the size, breadth, and valuation of capital markets? Why, to take an extreme example, do Russian companies have virtually no access to external finance and sell at about one hundred times less than Western companies with comparable assets (Boycko, Shleifer, and Vishny (1993))?

In our earlier article (La Porta, Lopez-de-Silanes, Shleifer, and Vishny (1996), henceforth LLSV (1996)), we have conjectured that the differences in the nature and effectiveness of financial systems around the world can be traced in part to the differences in investor protections against expropriation by insiders, as reflected by legal rules and the quality of their enforcement. We presented evidence indicating that legal rules protecting investors and the quality of their enforcement differ greatly and systematically across countries. In particular, these rules vary systematically by legal origin, which is either English, French, German, or Scandinavian. English law is common law, made by judges and subsequently incorporated into legislature. French, German, and Scandinavian laws, in contrast, are part of the scholar and legislator-made civil law tradition, which dates back to Roman law (David and Brierley (1985)). Most countries have adopted their legal systems through occupation or colo-

* La Porta, Lopez-de-Silanes, and Shleifer are from Harvard University, and Vishny is from the University of Chicago. We are grateful to Alex Chang, Mark Chen, and Magdalena Lopez-Morton for research assistance, to Ed Glaeser, Stewart Myers, and Luigi Zingales for helpful comments, and to the HIID and the National Science Foundation for support of this research.

nization by one of the European powers to which they owe the origin of their laws. Some other countries, such as those in Latin America, have adopted their legal systems after attaining independence, but have still typically chosen the laws of their former colonizers.

By comparing legal rules across 49 countries, we showed that legal rules from the different traditions differ in content as well as in the history of their adoption. In the area of protection against expropriation by insiders, common law countries protect both shareholders and creditors the most, French civil law countries the least, and German civil law and Scandinavian civil law countries somewhere in the middle. We also showed that richer countries enforce laws better than poorer countries, but, controlling for per capita income, French Civil law countries have the lowest quality of law enforcement as well. In our earlier article, we did not pursue the consequences of differences in legal environments at great length, except to show that countries with poor investor protections have more highly concentrated ownership of shares. The broader question, of course, is whether they also have inferior opportunities for external finance and thus smaller capital markets.

Accordingly, in this article we try to assess the ability of firms in different legal environments to raise external finance through either debt or equity. Presumably, the willingness of an entrepreneur to sell his equity, or to assume debt, depends to a large extent on the terms at which he can obtain external finance. For equity, these terms are reflected by valuation relative to the underlying cashflows; for debt, they are reflected by the cost of funds. If the terms are good, an entrepreneur would sell more of his shares or raise more debt. Countries whose financial systems offer entrepreneurs better terms of external finance would then have both higher valuations of securities and broader capital markets in the sense that more firms would access them. To the extent that better legal protections enable the financiers to offer entrepreneurs money at better terms, we predict that the countries with better legal protections should have more external finance in the form of both higher valued and broader capital markets.

Measuring the size of financial markets—whether debt or equity—is a bit tricky. The values of these markets are dominated by the largest firms. To address this problem, we supplement an aggregate stock market valuation measure with the number of domestic listed firms as well as the number of Initial Public Offerings (IPOs). We also focus on a debt measure that includes all private debt and bond market borrowing. Finally, we examine a sample of all firms from the WorldScope database, a subset consisting of the largest listed firms.

We compare external finance across 49 countries as a function of the origin of their laws, the quality of legal investor protections, and the quality of law enforcement. We find strong evidence that the legal environment has large effects on the size and breadth of capital markets across countries.

Our article is related to several recent strands of research. Shleifer and Vishny (1997) and LLSV (1996) focus on the legal solutions to agency problems between entrepreneurs and investors, and in particular emphasize the cross-country differences in these solutions. Modigliani and Perotti (1996) also focus on contract enforcement as a determinant of external finance, and in particular stress the choice between bank loan and equity finance. Rajan and Zingales (1995) look at G-7 evidence on the determinants of capital structure, or debt and equity choice, although they do not emphasize investor protection. It is possible that the relative legal treatment of shareholders and creditors affects capital structure as well as the availability of either kind of finance, but we do not focus on this issue here. Finally, a growing literature surveyed by Levine (1996), and including recent contributions by King and Levine (1993) and Rajan and Zingales (1996), examines the consequences of developed financial markets for investment and growth. Our article, in contrast, focuses on the determinants of financial development, but does not follow through on its "real" consequences. Unlike the rest of the literature, then, our article aims to empirically establish the link between the legal environment and financial markets.

Section I describes our data. Section II presents the results, and Section III concludes.

## I. Data

We are interested in the ability of companies in different countries to raise external funds in the form of either equity or debt. Since we do not have direct measures of external financing for smaller companies, we use primarily aggregate data, which partly capture the breadth of various markets. Table I summarizes the data we use and the sources they come from.

We use three measures of equity finance. Our first variable looks at the ratio of stock market capitalization to GNP in 1994, scaled by a rough measure of the fraction of the stock market held by outside investors. Conceptually, it is not appropriate to look at just the ratio of stock market valuation to GNP. For example, if 90 percent of a firm's equity is held by the insiders and 10 percent is held by the outsiders, then looking at the market capitalization of the whole firm gives a tenfold overestimate of how much has actually been raised externally. For each country, we roughly estimate the average fraction of equity held by the insiders by looking at the country's 10 largest publicly traded nonstate firms, finding the combined ownership stake of the three largest shareholders in each of these firms, and averaging that stake over the 10 firms (see LLSV (1996)). Since we made this calculation for only the largest firms, and since we do not take account of cross-holdings, this procedure probably overestimates the share of equity held by the true outsiders. With all the roughness, this procedure is still conceptually preferred to looking at the uncorrected ratio of market capitalization to GNP. We also note that the results presented below hold for that uncorrected ratio as well, although with lower explanatory power.

We look at two further measures of the extent of equity finance that focus more specifically on market breadth. The first is the number of listed domestic firms in each country relative to its population. The second is the number of

**Table I**

## Description of the Variables

| | |
|---|---|
| Origin | Identifies the legal origin of the Company Law or Commercial Code of each country. Source: Reynolds and Flores (1989) and La Porta *et al.* (1996). |
| External cap/ GNP | The ratio of the stock market capitalization held by minorities to gross national product for 1994. The stock market capitalization held by minorities is computed as the product of the aggregate stock market capitalization and the average percentage of common shares not owned by the top three shareholders in the ten largest non-financial, privately-owned domestic firms in a given country. A firm is considered privately owned if the State is not a known shareholder in it. Source: *Moodys International, CIFAR, EXTEL, WorldScope, 20-Fs, Price-Waterhouse*, and various country sources. |
| Domestic firms/ Pop | Ratio of the number of domestic firms listed in a given country to its population (in millions) in 1994. Source: *Emerging Market Factbook* and *World Development Report 1996*. |
| IPOs/Pop | Ratio of the number of initial public offerings of equity in a given country to its population (in millions) for the period 1995:7–1996:6. Source: *Securities Data Corporation, AsiaMoney, LatinFinance, GT Guide to World Equity Markets*, and *World Development Report 1996*. |
| Debt/GNP | Ratio of the sum of bank debt of the private sector and outstanding non-financial bonds to GNP in 1994, or last available. Source: *International Financial Statistics, World Bondmarket Factbook*. |
| GDP growth | Average annual percent growth of per capita gross domestic product for the period 1970–1993. Source: *World Development Report 1995*. |
| Log GNP | Logarithm of the Gross National Product in 1994. Source: *World Development Report 1996*. |
| Rule of law | Assessment of the law and order tradition in the country. Average of the months of April and October of the monthly index between 1982 and 1995. Scale from 0 to 10, with lower scores for less tradition for law and order. Source: *International Country Risk Guide*. |
| Antidirector rights | An index aggregating shareholder rights. The index is formed by adding 1 when: (1) the country allows shareholders to mail their proxy vote; (2) shareholders are not required to deposit their shares prior to the General Shareholders' Meeting; (3) cumulative voting is allowed; (4) an oppressed minorities mechanism is in place; or (5) when the minimum percentage of share capital that entitles a shareholder to call for an Extraordinary Shareholders' Meeting is less than or equal to 10% (the sample median). The index ranges from 0 to 5. Source: Company Law or Commercial Code and La Porta *et al.* (1996). |
| One-share = one-vote | Equals one if the Company Law or Commercial Code of the country requires that ordinary shares carry one vote per share, and 0 otherwise. Equivalently, this variable equals one when the law prohibits the existence of both multiple-voting and non-voting ordinary shares and does not allow firms to set a maximum number of votes per shareholder irrespective of the number of shares she owns, and 0 otherwise. Source: Company Law or Commercial Code and La Porta *et al.* (1996). |

*Legal Determinants of External Finance* 1135

**Table I—Continued**

| | |
|---|---|
| Creditor rights | An index aggregating creditor rights. The index is formed by adding 1 when: (1) the country imposes restrictions, such as creditors' consent or minimum dividends, to file for reorganization; (2) secured creditors are able to gain possession of their security once the reorganization petition has been approved (no automatic stay); (3) the debtor does not retain the administration of its property pending the resolution of the reorganization; (4) secured creditors are ranked first in the distribution of the proceeds that result from the disposition of the assets of a bankrupt firm. The index ranges from 0 to 4. Source: Company Law or Bankruptcy Laws and La Porta *et al.* (1996). |
| Market cap/ sales | The median ratio of the stock market capitalization held by minorities to sales in 1994 for all nonfinancial firms in a given country on the *WorldScope* database. Firm's *j* stock market capitalization held by minorities is computed as the product of the stock market capitalization of firm *j* and the average percentage of common shares not owned by the top three shareholders in the ten largest nonfinancial, privately-owned domestic firms in a given country. A firm is considered privately owned if the State is not a known shareholder in it. Source: *WorldScope*. |
| Market cap/ cash-flow | The median ratio of the stock market capitalization held by minorities to cash flow in 1994 for all nonfinancial firms in a given country on the *WorldScope* database. Firm's *j* stock market capitalization held by minorities is computed as the product of the stock market capitalization of firm *j* and the average percentage of common shares not owned by the top three shareholders in the ten largest nonfinancial, privately-owned domestic firms in a given country. A firm is considered privately owned if the State is not a known shareholder in it. Source: *WorldScope*. |
| Debt/sales | Median of the total-debt-to-sales ratio in 1994 for all firms in a given country on the *WorldScope* database. Source: *WorldScope*. |
| Debt/cash flow | Median of the total-debt-to-cash-flow ratio for all firms in a given country on the *WorldScope* database. Source: *WorldScope*. |

initial public offerings of shares in each country between mid-1995 and mid-1996 (the period for which we have been able to obtain the data), also relative to the population. These two variables obviously reflect the stock and the flow of new companies obtaining equity finance. It may make sense to look at both of them because the development of financial markets has accelerated greatly in the last decade, and hence the IPO evidence provides a more recent glance at external equity financing.

Finding data on debt finance that do not just focus on the largest companies is more difficult, since bank financing information is not readily available. However, we do have data on the total bank debt of the private sector in each country, as well as on the total face value of corporate bonds in each country. The aggregate of these two variables relative to the GNP is a plausible measure of the overall ability of the private sector to access debt finance. The fact that we are looking at the whole private sector rather than just corporations may actually be an advantage, since in many countries entrepreneurs raise money on their personal accounts to finance their firms (for example, by mortgaging their properties).

Although the principal focus of our analysis is on the aggregate data, we devote some attention to the microdata on the largest firms, obtained from the WorldScope Database for 1996. For this sample, we also develop measures of equity and debt finance in different countries. For each country, we use four measures of access of their WorldScope companies to capital markets. The first equity variable is the median ratio of market capitalization to sales of the companies in the WorldScope sample for that country, corrected as in the aggregate data by the estimated share of equity of large companies held by outsiders. (We use the exact same correction here as for the aggregate data rather than assembling outside ownership data for all companies.) The second variable for each country is the median ratio of market capitalization to cash flow, again corrected for outside ownership. The first of these two variables is roughly the analog of the aggregate equity valuation variable, and the second is just a different—but perhaps more easily interpretable—normalization.

For debt, we also define two variables for each country. The first is the median ratio of total debt to sales of all the firms in the WorldScope database in that country. The second is the median ratio of total debt to cash flow. The first variable in particular is roughly parallel to our aggregate debt measure.

Our measures of investor protection draw on our earlier work, which has developed measures of shareholder and creditor protections in different legal regimes (LLSV (1996)). Theoretically, we are interested in the legal rights that shareholders and creditors have that enable them to extract a return on their investment from the insiders. For equity, these rights are most importantly the voting rights in the election of directors and other important corporate matters, as well as the rights to make specific claims against the corporation. For debt, these rights cover the liquidation and reorganization procedures when the borrower defaults. In LLSV (1996), we quantified many of these rights for a sample of 49 countries from around the world.

In this article, we use some of the summary variables from the earlier article. First, we know for each country the legal origin of its laws. Second, we have a survey-based estimate of the quality of law enforcement, called "rule of law," which is an assessment by investors in different countries of the law and order environment they operate in. Third, we have measures of how well legal rules themselves protect investors in different countries. For shareholders, we have constructed an antidirector rights index described in detail in Table I. The index aggregates such elements of minority shareholder rights as the ability to vote by mail, the ability to retain control of shares during the shareholders' meeting, the possibility of cumulative voting for directors, the ease of calling an extraordinary shareholder meeting, and perhaps most importantly, the availability of mechanisms of allowing oppressed minority shareholders to make legal claims against the directors (e.g., the possibility of class action suits). We also use another shareholder rights variable, namely the requirement that each ordinary share carry only one vote in the country's commercial law.

For creditors, we use a creditor rights index that aggregates the various rights that secured creditors might have in liquidation and reorganization. Restrictions on the managers' ability to seek unilateral protection from creditors, mandatory dismissal of management in reorganization, lack of automatic stay on assets, and absolute priority for secured creditors all contribute to this index. Again, the precise definition of the index is presented in Table I.

## II. Results

### A. Presentation of the Data

Table II presents the aggregate data used in this study, with countries organized by origin of their legal system. It also presents comparisons across legal origins. Several interesting results jump out. First, on all measures, common law countries provide companies with better access to equity finance than civil law countries, and particularly French civil law countries. Common law countries have the average ratio of outsider held stock market to GNP of 60 percent, compared to 21 percent for the French civil law countries, 46 percent for the German civil law countries, and 30 percent for the Scandinavian countries. The United States, incidentally, is below the common law average in this sample, which is not entirely surprising given that it is growing much slower than Hong Kong, Malaysia, or Singapore. Common law countries have 35 listed firms per one million people (on average), compared to 10 for the French civil law countries, 17 for the German civil law countries, and 27 for the Scandinavian countries. It is actually quite striking to see that France has 8 listed firms per million people, Italy has 4, and Germany has 5, compared to 36 in the United Kingdom, 30 in the United States, and 128 in Israel. Finally, during the year we look at, common law countries averaged 2.2 IPOs per million people, compared to 0.2 of an IPO for the French origin, 0.12 of an IPO for German origin, and 2.1 IPOs for the Scandinavian origin. During that year, Germany had 7 IPOs, France had 10, while the United States had 803 and India had 1114. On all the equity measures, the differences in means between the English and the French origin are statistically significant.

As Table II indicates, our antidirector rights measure is by far the highest in common law countries, intermediate in Scandinavian and German civil law countries, and the lowest in the French civil law countries. In contrast, there is not much difference in the incidence of one-share-one-vote rules. These results give a preliminary indication that low shareholder protection may be the reason why some legal origins have smaller equity markets as well as lower access of firms to equity finance.

Aggregate debt as a share of GNP is 68 percent for common law countries, 45 percent for the French civil law countries, 97 percent for the German civil law countries, and 57 percent for the Scandinavian countries. Again, debt finance is more accessible in the English than in the French origin. However, indebtedness is even higher in the German civil law countries—also sometimes described as countries with bank-focused financial systems. The creditor rights

## Table II
## External Capital Markets

This table classifies countries by legal origin. Definitions for each of the variables can be found in Table I. Panel B reports tests of means for the different legal origins.

| Country | External Cap/GNP | Domestic Firms/Pop | IPOs/Pop | Debt/GNP | GDP growth | Log GNP | Rule of Law | Antidirector Rights | One-Share = One-Vote | Creditor Rights |
|---|---|---|---|---|---|---|---|---|---|---|
| | | | | Panel A: Means | | | | | | |
| Australia | 0.49 | 63.55 | — | 0.76 | 3.06 | 12.64 | 10.00 | 4 | 0 | 1 |
| Canada | 0.39 | 40.86 | 4.93 | 0.72 | 3.36 | 13.26 | 10.00 | 4 | 0 | 1 |
| Hong Kong | 1.18 | 88.16 | 5.16 | — | 7.57 | 11.56 | 8.22 | 4 | 1 | 4 |
| India | 0.31 | 7.79 | 1.24 | 0.29 | 4.34 | 12.50 | 4.17 | 2 | 0 | 4 |
| Ireland | 0.27 | 20.00 | 0.75 | 0.38 | 4.25 | 10.73 | 7.80 | 3 | 0 | 1 |
| Israel | 0.25 | 127.60 | 1.80 | 0.66 | 4.39 | 11.19 | 4.82 | 3 | 0 | 4 |
| Kenya | — | 2.24 | — | — | 4.79 | 8.83 | 5.42 | 3 | 0 | 4 |
| Malaysia | 1.48 | 25.15 | 2.89 | 0.84 | 6.90 | 11.00 | 6.78 | 3 | 1 | 4 |
| New Zealand | 0.28 | 69.00 | 0.66 | 0.90 | 1.67 | 10.69 | 10.00 | 4 | 0 | 3 |
| Nigeria | 0.27 | 1.68 | — | — | 3.43 | 10.36 | 2.73 | 3 | 0 | 4 |
| Pakistan | 0.18 | 5.88 | — | 0.27 | 5.50 | 10.88 | 3.03 | 4 | 1 | 4 |
| Singapore | 1.18 | 80.00 | 5.67 | 0.60 | 1.68 | 11.68 | 8.57 | 3 | 1 | 3 |
| South Africa | 1.45 | 16.00 | 0.05 | 0.93 | 7.48 | 10.92 | 4.42 | 4 | 0 | 4 |
| Sri Lanka | 0.11 | 11.94 | 0.11 | 0.25 | 4.04 | 9.28 | 1.90 | 2 | 0 | 3 |
| Thailand | 0.56 | 6.70 | 0.56 | 0.93 | 7.70 | 11.72 | 6.25 | 3 | 0 | 3 |
| UK | 1.00 | 35.68 | 2.01 | 1.13 | 2.27 | 13.86 | 8.57 | 4 | 0 | 4 |
| US | 0.58 | 30.11 | 3.11 | 0.81 | 2.74 | 15.67 | 10.00 | 5 | 0 | 1 |
| Zimbabwe | 0.18 | 5.81 | — | — | 2.17 | 8.63 | 3.68 | 3 | 0 | 4 |
| **English origin avg** | **0.60** | **35.45** | **2.23** | **0.68** | **4.30** | **11.41** | **6.46** | **3.39** | **0.22** | **3.11** |
| Argentina | 0.07 | 4.58 | 0.20 | 0.19 | 1.40 | 12.40 | 5.35 | 4 | 0 | 1 |
| Belgium | 0.17 | 15.50 | 0.30 | 0.38 | 2.46 | 12.29 | 10.00 | 0 | 0 | 2 |
| Brazil | 0.18 | 3.48 | 0.00 | 0.39 | 3.95 | 13.03 | 6.32 | 3 | 1 | 1 |
| Chile | 0.80 | 19.92 | 0.35 | 0.63 | 3.35 | 10.69 | 7.02 | 3 | 1 | 2 |
| Colombia | 0.14 | 3.13 | 0.05 | 0.19 | 4.38 | 10.82 | 2.08 | 1 | 0 | 0 |
| Ecuador | — | 13.18 | 0.09 | — | 4.55 | 9.49 | 6.67 | 2 | 0 | 4 |
| Egypt | 0.08 | 3.48 | — | — | 6.13 | 10.53 | 4.17 | 2 | 0 | 4 |
| France | 0.23 | 8.05 | 0.17 | 0.96 | 2.54 | 14.07 | 8.98 | 2 | 0 | 0 |
| Greece | 0.07 | 21.60 | 0.30 | 0.23 | 2.46 | 11.25 | 6.18 | 1 | 1 | 1 |
| Indonesia | 0.15 | 1.15 | 0.10 | 0.42 | 6.38 | 11.84 | 3.98 | 2 | 0 | 4 |
| Italy | 0.08 | 3.91 | 0.31 | 0.55 | 2.82 | 13.94 | 8.33 | 0 | 0 | 2 |
| Jordan | — | 23.75 | — | 0.70 | 1.20 | 8.49 | 4.35 | 1 | 0 | — |
| Mexico | 0.22 | 2.28 | 0.03 | 0.47 | 3.07 | 12.69 | 5.35 | 0 | 0 | 0 |
| Netherlands | 0.52 | 21.13 | 0.66 | 1.08 | 2.55 | 12.68 | 10.00 | 2 | 0 | 2 |
| Peru | 0.40 | 9.47 | 0.13 | 0.27 | 2.82 | 10.92 | 2.50 | 2 | 1 | 0 |
| Philippines | 0.10 | 2.90 | 0.27 | 0.10 | 0.30 | 10.44 | 2.73 | 4 | 0 | 0 |
| Portugal | 0.08 | 19.50 | 0.50 | 0.64 | 3.52 | 11.41 | 8.68 | 2 | 0 | 1 |
| Spain | 0.17 | 9.71 | 0.07 | 0.75 | 3.27 | 13.19 | 7.80 | 2 | 0 | 2 |
| Turkey | 0.18 | 2.93 | 0.05 | 0.15 | 5.05 | 12.08 | 5.18 | 2 | 0 | 2 |
| Uruguay | — | 7.00 | 0.00 | 0.26 | 1.96 | 9.40 | 5.00 | 1 | 1 | 2 |
| Venezuela | 0.08 | 4.28 | 0.00 | 0.10 | 2.65 | 10.99 | 6.37 | 1 | 0 | — |
| **French origin avg** | **0.21** | **10.00** | **0.19** | **0.45** | **3.18** | **11.55** | **6.05** | **1.76** | **0.24** | **1.58** |
| Austria | 0.06 | 13.87 | 0.25 | 0.79 | 2.74 | 12.13 | 10.00 | 2 | 0 | 3 |
| Germany | 0.13 | 5.14 | 0.08 | 1.12 | 2.60 | 14.46 | 9.23 | 1 | 0 | 3 |
| Japan | 0.62 | 17.78 | 0.26 | 1.22 | 4.13 | 15.18 | 8.98 | 3 | 1 | 2 |
| South Korea | 0.44 | 15.88 | 0.02 | 0.74 | 9.52 | 12.73 | 5.35 | 2 | 1 | 3 |
| Switzerland | 0.62 | 33.85 | — | — | 1.18 | 12.44 | 10.00 | 1 | 0 | 1 |
| Taiwan | 0.88 | 14.22 | 0.00 | — | 11.56 | 12.34 | 8.52 | 3 | 0 | 2 |
| **German origin avg** | **0.46** | **16.79** | **0.12** | **0.97** | **5.29** | **13.21** | **8.68** | **2.00** | **0.33** | **2.33** |
| Denmark | 0.21 | 50.40 | 1.80 | 0.34 | 2.09 | 11.84 | 10.00 | 3 | 0 | 3 |
| Finland | 0.25 | 13.00 | 0.60 | 0.75 | 2.40 | 11.49 | 10.00 | 2 | 0 | 1 |
| Norway | 0.22 | 33.00 | 4.50 | 0.64 | 3.43 | 11.62 | 10.00 | 3 | 0 | 2 |
| Sweden | 0.51 | 12.66 | 1.66 | 0.55 | 1.79 | 12.28 | 10.00 | 2 | 0 | 2 |
| **Scandinavian origin avg** | **0.30** | **27.26** | **2.14** | **0.57** | **2.42** | **11.80** | **10.00** | **2.50** | **0.00** | **2.00** |
| **Sample average** | **0.40** | **21.59** | **1.02** | **0.59** | **3.79** | **11.72** | **6.85** | **2.44** | **0.22** | **2.30** |

*Legal Determinants of External Finance* 1139

### Table II—Continued

| Country | External Cap/GNP | Domestic Firms/Pop | IPOs/Pop | Debt/GNP | GDP growth | Log GNP | Rule of Law | Antidirector Rights | One-Share = One-Vote | Creditor Rights |
|---|---|---|---|---|---|---|---|---|---|---|
| | | | Panel B: Tests of Means (*t*-statistics) | | | | | | | |
| Common vs civil law | 3.12 | 3.16 | 3.97 | 1.33 | 1.23 | −1.06 | −0.77 | 5.24 | −0.03 | 3.61 |
| English vs French origin | 3.29 | 3.16 | 4.50 | 2.29 | 1.97 | −0.28 | 0.51 | 5.13 | −0.11 | 3.61 |
| English vs German origin | 0.68 | 1.24 | 2.34 | −1.88 | −0.78 | −2.31 | −1.82 | 3.66 | −0.52 | 1.43 |
| English vs Scand. origin | 1.25 | 0.44 | 0.08 | 0.71 | 1.81 | −0.44 | −15.57 | 2.14 | 2.20 | 1.71 |
| French vs German origin | −2.38 | −1.85 | 0.78 | −3.39 | −1.96 | −2.48 | −2.55 | −0.47 | −0.45 | −1.29 |
| French vs Scand. origin | −0.91 | −3.31 | −5.45 | 0.82 | 0.97 | −0.33 | −20.80 | −1.25 | 2.50 | −0.60 |
| German vs Scand. origin | 0.94 | −1.21 | −2.76 | 2.71 | 1.32 | 2.11 | −11.29 | −0.98 | 1.58 | 0.63 |

index is the highest in common law countries, intermediate in German and Scandinavian civil law countries, and the lowest in the French civil law countries. Again, low rights line up with small markets when we compare French and English origin, but German civil law countries are somewhat of a mystery. A possible explanation of this mystery is suggested by Rajan and Zingales (1995), who find that German companies have high overall liabilities, though not necessarily high debt per se. Overall, the results on debt, like those on equity, suggest that legal rules influence external finance.

Table III abstracts away from origin and examines in more detail the determinants of external financing. It suggests that stronger antidirector rights (and perhaps also one-share-one-vote rules) are associated with larger and broader equity markets. The association between creditor rights and indebtedness is more tenuous. Better law enforcement, as measured by rule of law, is associated with more domestic firms and IPOs per capita, as well as a greater ratio of private sector debt to GNP. There is also some weak evidence that larger countries have higher debt. Table III confirms our preliminary impressions from Table II, points to the importance of law enforcement as well as of the legal rules, and indicates the need for more systematic testing in a regression framework.

### B. Regression Analysis

Tables IV–VII present a series of regressions of capital market size measures on various controls as well as estimates of the quality of investor protection. We include several control variables in all the regressions. First, we control for historical GDP growth because growth is likely to affect both valuations and market breadth. Second, we control for the (logarithm of) real GNP on the theory that setting up capital markets might be an increasing returns to scale activity, and therefore larger economies might have larger capital markets. Third, because all the regressions include our rule of law measure, and the correlation between rule of law and GDP per capita is 0.87, we do *not* include GDP per capita as a control. Including it does not have much of an effect on the coefficients on legal rights variables, but does eliminate the significancè of rule of law. In a sense, rule of law is a theoretically more appropriate variable.

**Table III**

## Investor Rights and External Finance

This table classifies countries according to their ranking in: (a) Antidirector Rights; (b) One-Share = One-Vote; (c) Creditor Rights; (4) Rule of Law; (5) GDP Growth; and (5) Log GNP. For each panel, the table shows the average value of different external finance measures for the bottom quartile, the middle two quartiles, and the top quartile. The last row of each panel shows the *t*-statistic for a test of means between the bottom and the top quartiles.

| | External Cap/ GNP | Domestic Firms/Pop | IPOs/Pop | Debt/GNP |
|---|---|---|---|---|
| Means by antidirector rights | | | | |
| Bottom 25% | 0.19 | 12.05 | 0.14 | 0.44 |
| Mid 50% | 0.39 | 20.03 | 0.97 | 0.63 |
| Top 25% | 0.58 | 35.68 | 2.05 | 0.63 |
| Test of means (*t*-statistic) | | | | |
| Bottom 25% vs. Top 25% | −2.50 | −2.35 | −2.55 | −1.22 |
| Means by one-share = one-vote | | | | |
| Not One Vote | 0.32 | 20.10 | 0.87 | 0.59 |
| One Vote | 0.65 | 26.76 | 1.48 | 0.56 |
| Test of means (*t*-statistic) | | | | |
| One Vote vs Not One Vote | −2.61 | −0.76 | −1.08 | 0.29 |
| Means by creditor rights | | | | |
| Bottom 25% | 0.27 | 18.43 | 0.85 | 0.49 |
| Mid 50% | 0.40 | 18.25 | 0.62 | 0.66 |
| Top 25% | 0.59 | 31.30 | 2.37 | 0.65 |
| Test of means (*t*-statistic) | | | | |
| Bottom 25% vs. Top 25% | −2.09 | −1.11 | −1.95 | −1.15 |
| Means by rule of law | | | | |
| Bottom 25% | 0.28 | 8.51 | 0.28 | 0.34 |
| Mid 50% | 0.47 | 22.36 | 0.89 | 0.63 |
| Top 25% | 0.36 | 33.08 | 1.85 | 0.70 |
| Test of means (*t*-statistic) | | | | |
| Bottom 25% vs. Top 25% | −0.73 | −4.11 | −2.30 | −3.84 |
| Means by GDP growth | | | | |
| Bottom 25% | 0.42 | 22.83 | 0.74 | 0.54 |
| Mid 50% | 0.28 | 15.90 | 0.86 | 0.60 |
| Top 25% | 0.62 | 30.43 | 1.64 | 0.62 |
| Test of means (*t*-statistic) | | | | |
| Bottom 25% vs. Top 25% | −1.05 | −0.61 | −1.20 | −0.56 |
| Means by log GNP | | | | |
| Bottom 25% | 0.25 | 15.36 | 0.27 | 0.43 |
| Mid 50% | 0.46 | 26.12 | 1.33 | 0.50 |
| Top 25% | 0.39 | 19.82 | 0.98 | 0.82 |
| Test of means (*t*-statistic) | | | | |
| Bottom 25% vs. Top 25% | −1.31 | −0.63 | −1.24 | −3.26 |

Table IV looks at the ratio of our estimate of externally held market capitalization to GNP. Not surprisingly, the results show that faster growing economies have higher capitalization stock markets: a 1 percent faster growth rate between 1970 and 1993 raises the ratio by about 4 to 6 percentage points (where the worldwide mean is 40 and the standard deviation is 37 percentage

### Table IV
## External Market Capitalization of Equity/GNP Regressions

Ordinary least squares regressions of the cross-section of 49 countries around the world. The dependent variable is "External Cap." The independent variables are (1) GDP Growth; (2) Log GNP; (3) Rule of law; (4) French origin; (5) German origin; (6) Scandinavian origin; (7) Antidirector Rights; (8) One-share = One-Vote. Standard errors are shown in parentheses.

| Independent Variables | Dependent Variable: External Cap/GNP | | | | |
|---|---|---|---|---|---|
| GDP growth | $0.0617^b$ | $0.0544^b$ | $0.0584^b$ | $0.0562^b$ | $0.0441^b$ |
| | (0.0232) | (0.0201) | (0.0238) | (0.0242) | (0.0209) |
| Log GNP | $-0.0129$ | $-0.0168$ | 0.0038 | $-0.0053$ | 0.0091 |
| | (0.0333) | (0.0334) | (0.0386) | (0.0382) | (0.0324) |
| Rule of law | $0.0378^c$ | $0.0455^b$ | 0.0417 | $0.0424^b$ | $0.0437^c$ |
| | (0.0206) | (0.0203) | (0.0250) | (0.0243) | (0.0231) |
| French origin | | | $-0.3225^a$ | $-0.2142^c$ | $-0.3341^a$ |
| | | | (0.1131) | (0.1194) | (0.1084) |
| German origin | | | $-0.2962^c$ | $-0.1849$ | $-0.3230^b$ |
| | | | (0.1497) | (0.1599) | (0.1438) |
| Scandinavian origin | | | $-0.3391^b$ | $-0.2816^c$ | $-0.3056^b$ |
| | | | (0.1373) | (0.1479) | (0.1218) |
| Antidirector rights | $0.1171^a$ | | | $0.0675^c$ | |
| | (0.0353) | | | (0.0354) | |
| One-share = one-vote | | $0.2745^b$ | | | $0.2890^b$ |
| | | (0.1235) | | | (0.1111) |
| Intercept | $-0.2437$ | $0.0100^b$ | 0.0336 | $-0.0860$ | $-0.0475$ |
| | (0.2880) | (0.3063) | (0.3677) | (0.3629) | (0.3066) |
| Observations | 45 | 45 | 45 | 45 | 45 |
| Adjusted $R^2$ | 0.2936 | 0.2347 | 0.2867 | 0.3016 | 0.3801 |

[a] Significant at 1%; [b] Significant at 5%; [c] Significant at 10%.

points). Country size does not matter. The coefficient on the rule of law is around 4 in all specifications: raising rule of law from the sample average of 6.85 to a perfect 10 increases outsider held market capitalization by about 13 percent of the GNP.

The five specifications in Table IV look at the different combinations of origin dummies and shareholder rights variables. We find that individually, both the antidirector rights score and the one-share-one-vote dummy have a relatively large effect on the market capitalization ratio. Raising the antidirector rights score from its French origin average of 1.76 to its common law average of 3.39 raises the market capitalization to GNP ratio by 19 percentage points—half of the difference between the French and the English means. Countries with mandatory one-share-one-vote rules have a 27 percentage points higher ratio. Each of the three civil law families has an about 30 percentage points lower outsider held market capitalization relative to GNP than the common law family does. The reason that these results looked less pronounced in the raw data in Table II is that German and Scandinavian origin countries have extremely high rule of law scores, which contribute to larger stock markets. Once these scores are controlled for, all civil law families have much smaller stock markets than those in common law countries, presumably because of inferior investor protections.

The last two columns of Table IV include both the origin dummies and the two shareholder rights variables, included one at a time. The coefficients on all variables fall relative to their values when included in isolation. Taken on face value, the estimates suggest that our shareholder rights variables account for some of the difference between relative market capitalizations of different legal families, but that the family effects are also significant.

The results on the number of listed domestic firms per (million) capita are presented in Table V. Here, higher GDP growth is not associated with a statistically significantly higher number of listed firms, suggesting that the result of Table IV is explained by a higher valuation of listed firms in faster growing economies rather than by a higher number of listed firms. The results also show that countries with bigger economies have fewer listed firms per capita, other things equal. Rule of law again comes in very significantly: a move from the world mean of 6.85 to a perfect score of 10 is associated with 15 more domestic listed firms per million people (the world mean is 22). When included alone, our antidirector rights score is highly significant: a move from the French to the English mean in that score raises the number of listed domestic firms per million people by 12. The one-share-one-vote dummy is no longer significant, although it has a relatively large estimated effect of the predicted sign.

The dummies for civil law origins again point to much narrower stock markets for countries in the French, German, and Scandinavian legal families than in common law countries. The parameter estimates of about $-20$ indicate that civil law countries have about 20 fewer listed firms per million people. This is 0.8 of a standard deviation, and is a pretty impressive estimate given that the sample-wide mean of the dependent variable is 21. When the antidirector rights score is included together with origin dummies, the coefficient estimates on the dummies fall only slightly, while the coefficient on the antidirector score falls sharply. As far as market breadth is concerned, there is more to the difference between legal families than is captured by our antidirector rights score.

Our last, and relatively direct, measure of firms' access to capital markets is the number of IPOs between mid-1995 and mid-1996, again per million people. In Table VI, the GDP growth rate has a statistically significant effect on the number of IPOs in specifications that control for legal origin; the coefficient

Table V

## Domestic Firms/Population Regressions

Ordinary least squares regressions of the cross-section of 49 countries around the world. The dependent variable is "Domestic Firms/Pop." The independent variables are (1) GDP growth; (2) Log GNP; (3) Rule of law; (4) French origin; (5) German origin; (6) Scandinavian origin; (7) Antidirector rights; (8) One-share = one-vote. Standard errors are shown in parentheses.

| Independent Variables | Dependent Variable: Domestic Firms/Pop | | | | |
|---|---|---|---|---|---|
| GDP growth | 1.0767 | 1.3461 | 1.0111 | 0.8950 | 0.5763 |
| | (1.4000) | (1.3318) | (1.2661) | (1.2733) | (0.9884) |
| Log GNP | $-4.3181^b$ | $-4.0659^b$ | $-2.9126$ | $-3.3073^b$ | $-2.7979$ |
| | (1.6588) | (1.7697) | (1.7698) | (1.8165) | (1.6816) |
| Rule of law | $4.5093^a$ | $4.8584^a$ | $4.8422^a$ | $4.8577^a$ | $4.9582^a$ |
| | (1.2579) | (1.4023) | (1.3616) | (1.3377) | (1.3356) |
| French origin | | | $-21.9069^a$ | $-17.5313^b$ | $-22.5204^a$ |
| | | | (7.4014) | (8.9183) | (7.2884) |
| German origin | | | $-25.1485^a$ | $-20.5611^b$ | $-26.3007^a$ |
| | | | (8.4882) | (9.7216) | (7.8639) |
| Scandinavian origin | | | $-22.2680^b$ | $-19.9575^c$ | $-21.3009^b$ |
| | | | (10.1744) | (10.0144) | (10.0541) |
| Antidirector rights | $7.3034^a$ | | | 2.7304 | |
| | (1.8052) | | | (1.6591) | |
| One-share = one-vote | | 8.1382 | | | 10.0675 |
| | | (7.5228) | | | (6.3165) |
| Intercept | 19.3863 | $29.0780^c$ | 33.0485 | 28.6987 | 30.6212 |
| | (15.4445) | (17.0108) | (20.6317) | (21.4015) | (20.2510) |
| Number of observations | 49 | 49 | 49 | 49 | 49 |
| Adjusted $R^2$ | 0.2198 | 0.1153 | 0.2197 | 0.2495 | 0.2681 |

[a] Significant at 1%; [b] Significant at 5%; [c] Significant at 10%.

estimates indicate that a one percentage point higher historical growth rate raises the number of IPOs by about 0.2, or less than one-tenth of a standard deviation. The size of the economy is again insignificant. Rule of law has a large positive effect on the number of IPOs: the move from the world mean to a perfect 10 in the rule of law raises the number of IPOs by 0.8, where the world mean is 1 per million people per year. The antidirector rights score is highly significant (just as in Table V): moving from the French to the English origin mean raises the number of IPOs by 0.8. In contrast, one-share-one-vote is not significant when included alone, just like what we found in Table V.

The results on the effects of the legal origin are a bit different than before. The French and German civil law countries average 2 fewer IPOs (per million

*Empirical Corporate Finance III*

*The Journal of Finance*

## Table VI
## Initial Public Offerings/Population Regressions

Ordinary least squares regressions of the cross-section of 49 countries around the world. The dependent variable is "IPOs/Pop." The independent variables are (1) GDP growth; (2) Log GNP; (3) Rule of law; (4) French origin; (5) German origin; (6) Scandinavian origin; (7) Antidirector rights; (8) One-share = one-vote. Standard errors are shown in parentheses.

| Independent Variables | Dependent Variable: IPOs/Pop | | | | |
|---|---|---|---|---|---|
| GDP growth | 0.1222 | 0.1320 | 0.1937[b] | 0.1916[c] | 0.1633[b] |
| | (0.1281) | (0.1193) | (0.1012) | (0.1037) | (0.0744) |
| Log GNP | −0.1672 | −0.1225 | 0.0662 | 0.0452 | 0.1255 |
| | (0.1453) | (0.1692) | (0.1086) | (0.1129) | (0.1002) |
| Rule of law | 0.2549[a] | 0.2943[a] | 0.2122[b] | 0.2108[b] | 0.2127[a] |
| | (0.0889) | (0.0926) | (0.0842) | (0.0830) | (0.0731) |
| French origin | | | −1.5982[a] | −1.2949[a] | −1.6677[a] |
| | | | (0.3552) | (0.3696) | (0.3132) |
| German origin | | | −2.8118[a] | −2.5450[a] | −3.027[a] |
| | | | (0.5698) | (0.5909) | (0.5543) |
| Scandinavian origin | | | −0.3123 | −0.1421 | −0.1367 |
| | | | (0.8666) | (0.8486) | (0.8414) |
| Antidirector rights | 0.5352[a] | | | 0.1937[c] | |
| | (0.1364) | | | (0.0989) | |
| One-share = one-vote | | 0.6359 | | | 1.0287[a] |
| | | (0.5422) | | | (0.3450) |
| Intercept | −0.5546 | −0.2720 | −0.9201 | −1.3071 | −1.7268 |
| | (1.3472) | (1.7534) | (1.3233) | (1.3204) | (1.2088) |
| Number of observations | 41 | 41 | 41 | 41 | 41 |
| Adjusted $R^2$ | 0.3082 | 0.1571 | 0.4907 | 0.4927 | 0.5643 |

[a] Significant at 1%; [b] Significant at 5%; [c] Significant at 10%.

people) than the common law countries—more than a standard deviation of the IPO variable. Scandinavian countries, however, do not appear to have fewer IPOs in any of the specifications. The adverse effects of the French and German origin on IPOs remain once we include the antidirector rights score and the one-share-one-vote dummy. Both of our rights measures are significant after controlling for origin. Overall, the results in this table, like those of the previous one, show that our shareholder rights measures explain some of the variation in equity finance across countries, but that there is more to the origin effect than is captured by these measures. The regressions also confirm all our earlier results that civil law—particularly of the French or German

*Legal Determinants of External Finance*                    1145

**Table VII**
## Debt/GNP Regressions

Ordinary least squares regressions of the cross-section of 49 countries around the world. The dependent variable is "Debt/GNP." The independent variables are (1) GDP growth; (2) Log GNP; (3) Rule of law; (4) French origin; (5) German origin; (6) Scandinavian origin; (7) Creditor rights. Standard errors are shown in parentheses.

| Independent Variables | Dependent Variable: Debt/GNP | | |
|---|---|---|---|
| GDP growth | 0.0310[c] | 0.0251[c] | 0.0197 |
| | (0.0171) | (0.0134) | (0.0152) |
| Log GNP | 0.0667[b] | 0.0370 | 0.0404 |
| | (0.0252) | (0.0255) | (0.0250) |
| Rule of law | 0.0615[a] | 0.0698[a] | 0.0694[a] |
| | (0.0132) | (0.0147) | (0.0148) |
| French origin | | −0.1516[b] | −0.1163 |
| | | (0.0740) | (0.0825) |
| German origin | | 0.1080 | 0.1082 |
| | | (0.1010) | (0.0982) |
| Scandinavian origin | | −0.2764[b] | −0.2618[b] |
| | | (0.1037) | (0.1075) |
| Creditor rights | 0.0518[c] | | 0.0270 |
| | (0.0267) | | (0.0298) |
| Intercept | −0.8621[a] | −0.3496 | −0.4414 |
| | (0.2579) | (0.2524) | (1.341) |
| Number of observations | 39 | 39 | 39 |
| Adjusted $R^2$ | 0.5522 | 0.5191 | 0.5984 |

[a] Significant at 1%; [b] Significant at 5%; [c] Significant at 10%.

variety—reduces the breadth of the stock markets. In Scandinavian countries, the IPOs picture is brighter than that for the number of listed issues.

Table VII presents the results for our aggregated indebtedness measure. Note a somewhat smaller sample owing to the lack of data. In the specification that does not include origin dummies, both the level of the nation's GNP and the historical growth of GDP are associated with higher total debt relative to GNP; however, the statistical significance of these results does not carry over once origin is controlled for. In the specification without origin dummies, the coefficient on the creditor rights index is also statistically significant, but this result loses significance, and the coefficient falls sharply once origin is controlled for. The effect of rule of law is more robust, as before. Rule of law yet again has a large and statistically significant effect on the size of the capital market: the move from world mean to a perfect 10 is associated with a 20 percentage point increase in debt to GNP ratio, or 0.7 of a standard deviation.

The origin effects are interesting. Relative to common law countries, French legal origin countries have a lower ratio of debt to GNP (which becomes insignificant when creditor rights are also included, perhaps because of a high negative correlation between creditor rights and the French dummy). French origin countries have a 12 to 15 percentage point lower ratio of debt to GNP, where the overall sample mean is 59 percent. German origin countries again have a higher ratio of debt to GNP, but the effect is not statistically significant. Finally, Scandinavian origin countries have a hugely (almost one standard deviation) lower ratio of debt to GNP, a difference not much diminished by the inclusion of the creditor rights index. In sum, French and Scandinavian civil law countries do have more narrow debt markets than common law countries, a difference not adequately captured by our creditor rights index.

The overall results of Tables IV to VII are straightforward to summarize. We find that good law enforcement has a large effect on the valuation and breadth of both debt and equity markets. We also find large systematic differences between countries from different legal origins in the size and breadth of their capital markets. Whether measured by capitalization of equity held by outsiders, by the number of listed firms, or by IPOs, common law countries have larger equity markets than civil law, and particularly French civil law, countries, and at least part of the differences is captured by the differences in shareholder protections *that we measure*. Common law countries also have larger aggregate liabilities than do the French civil law and Scandinavian, though not German, countries. Our measure of creditor rights is less effective in capturing the difference between origins than our measure of shareholder rights. The results add up to a rather consistent case that the quality of the legal environment has a significant effect on the ability of firms in different countries to raise external finance.

### C. Who gets External Finance?

Our analysis has focused on aggregate measures of the valuation and breadth of markets. An alternative approach is to look at microdata. The key issue about these data is that they cover primarily large firms that may have exposure to international capital markets, access to government finance, and captive banks. In this section, we attempt a very preliminary investigation of whether large firms are different, and in what ways.

To this end, we examine the WorldScope Database for 1996, which provides data for 38 of our 49 countries. The exclusion of smaller firms is pronounced both in that only a fraction of listed firms is included from each country, and in that relatively fewer firms are included from the emerging markets. For rich countries, WorldScope appears to cover 30–50 percent of the listed firms, whereas for developing countries, the share may be just a couple of percentage points (see the last column of Table VIII). For example, we have 2161 firms for the United States compared to nearly 7,770 listed firms, 93 firms for Italy compared to 223 listed firms, and 54 firms for India compared to 7,000 listed firms.

**Table VIII**

## External Funding at the Firm Level

The sample of thirty-eight countries includes all the firms on the Worldscope database for 1996. The table shows median values for all the firms in each country. Panel A show the medians based on a classification by legal origin. The definition for each of the variables can be found in Table I. Panel B gives the tests of means for the different legal origins. Panel C shows mean of medians and *t*-tests for countries sorted by levels of "External Cap/GNP." Panel D shows mean of medians and *t*-tests for countries sorted by "Debt/GNP."

| Country | Market Cap/Sales | Market Cap/ Cash-Flow | Debt/ Sales | Debt/Cash- Flow | WorldScope Firms/ Domestic Firms |
|---|---|---|---|---|---|
| *Panel A: Median Values by Legal Origin* | | | | | |
| Australia | 0.75 | 6.15 | 0.19 | 1.42 | 0.12 |
| Canada | 0.76 | 4.66 | 0.30 | 2.07 | 0.26 |
| Hong Kong | 0.66 | 4.01 | 0.31 | 2.50 | 0.12 |
| India | 0.73 | 8.75 | 0.47 | 4.26 | 0.01 |
| Ireland | 0.75 | 3.51 | 0.16 | 0.74 | 0.29 |
| Israel | 0.34 | 3.79 | 0.17 | 1.41 | 0.03 |
| Malaysia | 1.46 | 6.82 | 0.24 | 1.45 | 0.23 |
| New Zealand | 0.38 | 4.26 | 0.23 | 2.74 | 0.11 |
| Pakistan | 0.50 | 4.18 | 0.33 | 2.34 | 0.05 |
| Singapore | 0.83 | 5.68 | 0.07 | 0.83 | 0.19 |
| South Africa | 0.40 | 3.23 | 0.29 | 2.06 | 0.22 |
| Thailand | 0.71 | 4.65 | 0.54 | 3.45 | 0.32 |
| UK | 0.64 | 5.77 | 0.11 | 1.06 | 0.51 |
| US | 0.67 | 6.70 | 0.18 | 1.86 | 0.28 |
| **Average English origin** | **0.69** | **5.16** | **0.26** | **2.01** | **0.20** |
| Argentina | 0.63 | 4.18 | 0.28 | 1.78 | 0.10 |
| Belgium | 0.16 | 2.28 | 0.25 | 2.52 | 0.39 |
| Brazil | 0.24 | 1.97 | 0.18 | 1.52 | 0.11 |
| Chile | 1.68 | 8.15 | 0.29 | 1.59 | 0.13 |
| France | 0.29 | 4.28 | 0.19 | 2.36 | 0.67 |
| Greece | 0.25 | 5.99 | 0.21 | 2.55 | 0.04 |
| Indonesia | 0.48 | 3.03 | 0.37 | 3.25 | 0.23 |
| Italy | 0.17 | 2.21 | 0.32 | 3.04 | 0.44 |
| Mexico | 0.47 | 4.06 | 0.66 | 1.54 | 0.29 |
| Netherlands | 0.27 | 3.93 | 0.11 | 1.33 | 0.42 |
| Philippines | 1.61 | 5.17 | 0.29 | 0.86 | 0.14 |
| Portugal | 0.19 | 2.48 | 0.33 | 3.73 | 0.17 |
| Spain | 0.27 | 3.28 | 0.25 | 2.33 | 0.15 |
| Turkey | 0.46 | 2.87 | 0.11 | 0.50 | 0.12 |
| **Average French origin** | **0.51** | **3.85** | **0.27** | **2.06** | **0.24** |
| Austria | 0.21 | 2.29 | 0.24 | 2.38 | 0.17 |
| Germany | 0.21 | 3.29 | 0.10 | 1.24 | 0.55 |
| Japan | 0.63 | 13.80 | 0.34 | 6.99 | 0.50 |
| South Korea | 0.29 | — | 0.58 | — | 0.09 |
| Switzerland | 0.26 | 3.06 | 0.30 | 3.14 | 0.36 |
| Taiwan | 2.21 | 14.94 | 0.26 | 2.16 | 0.20 |
| **Average German origin** | **0.63** | **7.48** | **0.30** | **3.18** | **0.31** |
| Denmark | 0.30 | 3.30 | 0.22 | 1.88 | 0.38 |
| Finland | 0.30 | 2.90 | 0.31 | 2.58 | 0.80 |
| Norway | 0.49 | 3.70 | 0.36 | 3.62 | 0.46 |
| Sweden | 0.40 | 3.10 | 0.21 | 1.59 | 0.82 |
| **Average Scandinavian origin** | **0.37** | **3.25** | **0.28** | **2.42** | **0.61** |
| **Sample average** | **0.58** | **4.77** | **0.27** | **2.24** | **0.28** |

*The Journal of Finance*

**Table VIII—Continued**

| Country | Market Cap/Sales | Market Cap/ Cash-Flow | Debt/ Sales | Debt/Cash-Flow | WorldScope Firms/ Domestic Firms |
|---|---|---|---|---|---|
| | Panel B: Tests of Means (*t*-statistics) | | | | |
| Common vs. civil law | 1.04 | 0.64 | −0.60 | −0.87 | |
| England vs. France | 1.10 | 2.11 | −0.36 | −0.14 | |
| England vs. Germany | 0.20 | −1.33 | −0.71 | −1.61 | |
| England vs. Scandinavia | 2.17 | 2.38 | −0.32 | −0.73 | |
| France vs. Germany | −0.42 | −2.04 | −0.43 | −1.59 | |
| France vs. Scandinavia | 0.54 | 0.69 | −0.06 | −0.68 | |
| Germany vs. Scandinavia | 0.64 | 1.32 | 0.30 | 0.64 | |

| | Panel C: Sorted by External Cap/GNP | | Panel D: Sorted by Debt/GNP | |
|---|---|---|---|---|
| Means | | | | |
| Bottom 25% | 0.29 | 3.23 | 0.26 | 1.94 |
| Mid 50% | 0.53 | 4.31 | 0.29 | 2.17 |
| Top 25% | 0.97 | 7.28 | 0.24 | 2.52 |
| Test of means | | | | |
| Bottom 25% vs. Top 25% | −3.03 | −2.68 | 0.33 | −0.80 |

Table VIII presents the results for the two debt and two equity variables developed for each country, and described in Section I and in Table I. To begin, Panel A presents the data on country medians, and Panel B shows the *t*-tests of comparison between families. For the outsider held market capitalization to sales ratio (which is closest to the variable in Table IV), we get the same pattern of results as before: common law countries have a higher outsider-held capitalization of the largest companies than does any other group, with the difference being most pronounced for the Scandinavian and the French origin. However, the statistical significance of the results is considerably lower. When we normalize by cash flow rather than sales, we actually get that the German legal origin countries have the highest capitalization, in part because of extremely high market valuations in Japan and Taiwan. Basically, the picture on equity for the largest firms is similar to the aggregate picture, but less pronounced. These results, incidentally, continue to hold if we consider, for each country, the median market capitalization to sales and to cash flow ratios, without correcting for the share of equity held by insiders.

For both measures of debt, the differences between the English law, the French, and the Scandinavian origins essentially disappear, although debt of large companies in German origin countries remains the highest, especially relative to cash flow. Still, the similarity of these debt numbers across origins is remarkable, and suggests to us—albeit somewhat indirectly—a potentially important conclusion: large publicly traded firms get external debt finance in almost all countries, regardless of legal rules. A possible reason for this is debt financing *of the largest publicly traded firms* comes from the government and its banks. The countries whose large companies have unusually high debt levels compared to these countries aggregate ratio of liabilities to GNP are Mexico, India, and South Korea—all with heavy state intervention in banking. We cannot be sure given the available data that this is the right interpretation.

Still, the focus on large, publicly-traded firms in assessing the ability of firms in different countries to raise external funds may be misleading.

Panels C and D focus even more directly on the comparison of the results for large firms with our earlier results. In Panel C, we sort countries into bottom 25 percent, middle 50 percent, and top 25 percent by their aggregate ratio of external market capitalization to GNP (the variable in Table IV). For each of these three groups, we compute the average of the market capitalization to sales ratio and the average market capitalization to cash flow ratio for the countries in that group, from Panel A. The results in Panel C confirm the consistency of the aggregate and large firm data for equity: countries with high aggregate outsider held market capitalization are also the countries with the relatively high relative valuation of the largest firms. In Panel D, we make the same calculation for the two debt variables used in Panel A. The striking result is that our debt measure for large firms does not vary nearly as much as the aggregate measure: large publicly traded firms in countries with low aggregate debt do not have unusually low debt levels. The largest firms appear to get external finance even in countries where smaller listed firms do not.

## III. Conclusion

The results of this article confirm that the legal environment—as described by both legal rules and their enforcement—matters for the size and extent of a country's capital markets. Because a good legal environment protects the potential financiers against expropriation by entrepreneurs, it raises their willingness to surrender funds in exchange for securities, and hence expands the scope of capital markets.

Our results show that civil law, and particularly French civil law, countries, have both the weakest investor protections and the least developed capital markets, especially as compared to common law countries. Our measures of investor protection capture some, though not all, of the difference between legal environments across origins. It is interesting to note in this regard that our earlier article (LLSV (1996)) has been criticized for choosing measures of investor protection that paint a selectively bleak picture of investor protection in the French civil law family. If anything, the results of this article show the reverse: our measures of investor protection do not fully account for outside investors' predicament in these countries.

While this article has further developed the theme that legal environments differ across countries, and that these differences matter for financial markets, we have again refrained from answering the deeper question: what is it about the civil law family, and particularly about the French civil law subfamily, that accounts for the relative unfriendliness of laws to investors? Is it just by coincidence that these countries have investor-unfriendly laws? Or, have the laws been designed to keep investors relatively weak, and to assure family firms and the state a larger role in economic development? Alternatively, are poor laws just a proxy for an environment that is hostile to institutional development, including that of capital markets? In this connection, we have found some evidence (La Porta, Lopez-de-Silanes, Shleifer, and Vishny (1997)) that public and private institutions are less effective in countries exhibiting low levels of trust among citizens. It is possible that some broad underlying factor, related to trust, influences the development of all institutions in a country, including laws and capital markets. We cannot resolve these issues now, but hope to address them in future work.

## REFERENCES

Boycko, Maxim, Andrei Shleifer, and Robert W. Vishny, 1993, Privatizing Russia, *Brookings Papers on Economic Activity* 2, 139–192.

David, Rene, and John Brierley, 1985, *Major Legal Systems in the World Today*, (Stevens and Sons, London, U.K.).

King, Robert and Ross Levine, 1993, Finance and growth: Schumpeter might be right, *Quarterly Journal of Economics* 108, 717–738.

La Porta, Rafael, Florencio Lopez-de-Silanes, Andrei Shleifer, and Robert W. Vishny, 1996, Law and Finance, NBER Working paper 5661.

La Porta, Rafael, Florencio Lopez-de-Silanes, Andrei Shleifer, and Robert W. Vishny, 1997, Trust in large organizations, *American Economic Review Paper and Proceedings* 87, 333–338.

Levine, Ross, 1996, Financial development and economic growth, *Journal of Economic Literature*, forthcoming.

Modigliani, Franco, and Enrico Perotti, 1996, Protection of minority interest and development of security markets, Mimeo, MIT.

Pagano, Marco, F. Panetta, and Luigi Zingales, 1995, Why do companies go public?: An empirical analysis, NBER Working paper 5367.

Rajan, Raghuram, and Luigi Zingales, 1995, What do we know from capital structure: Some evidence from the international data, *Journal of Finance* 50, 1421–1460.

Rajan, Raghuram, and Luigi Zingales, 1996, Financial dependence and growth, NBER Working paper 5758.

Reynolds, Thomas, and Arturo Flores, 1989, *Foreign Law: Current Sources of Basic Legislation in Jurisdictions of the World*, (Rothman and Co., Littleton, CO).

Shleifer, Andrei, and Robert W. Vishny, 1997, A survey of corporate governance, *Journal of Finance*, 52, 737–783.

# B
# The Role of Taxation and Security

# [2]

Journal of Financial Economics 41 (1996) 41–73

# Debt and the marginal tax rate

## John R. Graham

*David Eccles School of Business, University of Utah, Salt Lake City, UT 84112, USA*

(Received October 1994; final version received August 1995)

### Abstract

Do taxes affect corporate debt policy? This paper tests whether the incremental use of debt is positively related to simulated firm-specific marginal tax rates that account for net operating losses, investment tax credits, and the alternative minimum tax. The simulated marginal tax rates exhibit substantial variation due to the dynamics of the tax code, tax regime shifts, business cycle effects, and the progressive nature of the statutory tax schedule. Using annual data from more than 10,000 firms for the years 1980–1992, I provide evidence which indicates that high-tax-rate firms issue more debt than their low-tax-rate counterparts.

*Key words*: Debt; Capital structure; Marginal tax rate; Taxes
*JEL classification*: G32; H20

## 1. Introduction

The marginal tax rate plays an important role in many topics in finance, including cost of capital calculations, debt policy and corporate compensation decisions, and relative pricing between taxable and nontaxable securities. Given its importance, it is surprising that the marginal tax rate ($MTR$) is almost never explicitly calculated. Instead, proxies are used to gauge a firm's tax status

I would like to thank Jennifer Babcock, Jim Brickley, Rick Green, Jack Hughes, Avner Kalay, Pete Kyle, Mike Lemmon, Craig Lewis, Gordon Phillips, Terry Shevlin, Tom Smith, Jerry Zimmerman, and participants of the Duke, Harvard, Rochester, Utah, and 1995 AFA seminars for helpful comments. I am also grateful to the editor, Richard Ruback, and two referees, Henry Reiling and Robert Taggart, for suggestions that helped improve the paper. I am responsible for all remaining errors. The Semiconductor Research Corporation provided financial support during the time much of this paper was written as a chapter in my doctoral dissertation at Duke University.

42              *J.R. Graham/Journal of Financial Economics 41 (1996) 41–73*

although these proxies are at best indirect and can be misleading.[1] This could explain why most financial research fails to find that tax considerations are an important factor in corporate financial decisions.[2]

Recent work by MacKie-Mason (1990), Shevlin (1990), and Scholes and Wolfson (1992) suggests that there are shortcomings with the manner in which tax effects have been tested in the past. The main thrust of this paper is to address these shortcomings by i) explicitly calculating company-specific marginal federal income tax rates and ii) using these rates to examine incremental financing choices, thus allowing for a direct test of whether tax status influences corporate debt policy.

Financial theory is clear that the *marginal tax rate* is relevant when analyzing incremental financing choices. However, the $MTR$ is rarely, if ever, explicitly calculated because doing so requires the use of complex tax-code formulas at the federal, state, and international levels. In this paper, company-specific tax-code-consistent marginal tax rates are explicitly calculated, using an expanded version of the method first employed by Shevlin (1990), who simulates marginal tax rates over a forecasted stream of taxable income to account for the carryforward and carryback tax opportunities related to net operating losses; I extend this approach to incorporate the effect of investment tax credits and the alternative minimum tax. The simulated tax variable calculated here appears to offer a more refined measure of tax status than other tax proxies.

To appropriately capture the relation between debt and taxes, it is also important to analyze *incremental* financing decisions. To see why, imagine a company with a high marginal tax rate and virtually no debt. Suppose that this firm issues substantial debt to exploit the interest-deduction benefit offered by a high marginal tax rate. Such an action implies a positive relation between the tax rate and the choice of debt as financial instrument. However, increasing a firm's fixed debt obligation can lower its expected $MTR$ by shifting the company to a lower tax bracket or by increasing the probability that the firm will pay no taxes. As a result, a time series of this company's financial data could contain high-$MTR$/low-debt and low-$MTR$/high-debt observations. A standard approach would be to regress this company's debt/equity ratio on its tax

---

[1]Tax proxies include nondebt tax shields (Bradley, Jarrell, and Kim, 1984; Titman and Wessels, 1988; Mackie-Mason, 1990; Kale, Noe, and Ramirez, 1991), taxes paid over pre-tax income (Fisher, Heinkel, and Zechner, 1989; Givoly, Hahn, Ofer, and Sarig, 1992), or dummy variables equal to one if a firm has a net operating loss carryforward and equal to zero otherwise (Scholes, Wilson, and Wolfson, 1990; analogously, most cost of capital calculations effectively use an net operating loss dummy equal to either the top statutory rate or zero).

[2]See, for example, Myers (1984), Bradley, Jarrell, and Kim (1984), Titman and Wessels (1988), Smith and Watts (1992), and Gaver and Gaver (1993). Fisher, Heinkel, and Zechner (1989) have mixed results for the tax hypothesis.

*J.R. Graham/Journal of Financial Economics 41 (1996) 41–73* 43

status, yielding a negative coefficient – exactly the wrong inference. Therefore, examining *cumulative* measures of financial policy, such as the debt/equity ratio, to test whether tax status affects financing choice can lead to a misinterpretation of the relation between taxes and corporate policy. This paper examines changes in debt, rather than levels, to focus on incremental financing and documents a positive relation between tax rates and the use of debt as a financing instrument.

MacKie-Mason (1990) studies incremental financing decisions by converting the choice of debt over equity into a zero–one event, considering only registered security offerings and using a proxy for the marginal tax rate. I look at changes in debt levels, appropriately scaled; my approach incorporates changes in debt due to sinking-fund payments, conversion of equity into debt, etc., as well as registered offerings. We both conclude that high-tax firms are more likely to finance with debt than are low-tax firms. Givoly, Hahn, Ofer, and Sarig (1992) also use change in debt as the dependent variable. They use the lagged average of taxes paid divided by taxable income as an independent variable to measure tax status. Their tax variable is consistent with, although cruder than, using the level of the marginal tax rate as an explanatory variable; however, the variable is also consistent with their interpretation of it as a proxy for the *change* in the marginal tax rate associated with the reduction in statutory corporate tax rates resulting from the Tax Reform Act of 1986. (Note that it is possible to explicitly calculate the change in the marginal tax rate using the tax variable derived in the present paper.) Their results also indicate a positive relation between the tax variable and the change in debt.

The $MTR$ calculation incorporates the effects of tax deductions and tax credits. If a company has enough nondebt tax shields ($NDTS$) to lower its expected $MTR$, the company will issue less debt than an identical firm without the shields. This is consistent with the claim by DeAngelo and Masulis (1980) that debt substitutes can lead to a firm-specific optimal leverage decision. However, my results indicate that the impact on debt policy of traditional measures of $NDTS$, such as depreciation expense and the investment tax credit, appears to be small in comparison to the influence of net operating losses.

The debt policy equation is estimated on a pooled cross-section of differenced time series data for a collection of over 10,000 Compustat firms. In testing the relation between tax status and financing choice, it is necessary to control for other factors which affect debt policy. By including control variables, it is possible to determine that the marginal tax rate is not proxying for another explanatory effect and that tax effects account for about 15% of our ability to explain debt policy. The control factors indicate that firms with high free cash flows *decrease* their debt holdings on average, firms which are growing larger or increasing research and development expenditures are likely to use debt financing, and that the usual measure of a company's growth status (book value over market value of the firm) has an ambiguous effect on incremental debt policy.

44                  *J.R. Graham/Journal of Financial Economics 41 (1996) 41–73*

The rest of the paper proceeds as follows. Section 2 discusses how to explicitly calculate the marginal tax rate and presents its empirical distribution. Section 3 describes tax theories of capital structure. Section 4 discusses the data, while Section 5 presents the econometric techniques and results. Section 6 concludes the paper.

## 2. The marginal tax rate

The marginal tax rate is defined as the present value of current and expected future taxes paid on an additional dollar of income earned today. Explicit calculation of the $MTR$ involves two essential features: 1) reasonably mimicking the federal tax code treatment of net operating losses ($NOLs$), investment tax credits ($ITCs$), and the alternative minimum tax ($AMT$),[3] and 2) measuring managers' tax rate expectations at the time debt policy choices are made. The following discussion on losses and credits follows that in Altshuler and Auerbach (1990, pp. 63–65).

### 2.1. Losses, credits, and the AMT

Each year a firm calculates its current-year taxable income, $TI_t$, before credits; if the result is positive, the firm determines its pre-credit tax bill and proceeds to the credit calculations. If taxable income is negative, the firm has a net operating loss. The loss can be 'carried back' and used to offset taxable income in the preceding three years, starting with $TI_{t-3}$. If $TI_{t-3}$ is completely offset, the firm next applies the losses to $TI_{t-2}$, and likewise to $TI_{t-1}$. The tax bill is recalculated for any year in which losses are carried back; the firm receives a refund if any previous-year tax bill is lowered.

If current-year losses more than offset the total taxable income from the preceding three years, the losses are then 'carried forward' and used to offset taxable income for up to 15 years into the future (changed from five years by the Economic Recovery Act of 1981). The term *carryforward* thus applies only when

---

[3]Ideally, the effect of foreign tax credits should also be considered because firms can receive a domestic tax credit for taxes paid overseas. I ignore foreign tax credits because Compustat does not provide data on company-specific repatriated foreign income. I also ignore state income taxes, even though they can be as high as 10%, because 1) gathering the data necessary to examine state taxes would be a formidable task, as the tax rules vary widely by state, and 2) assigning a state of operation to each company using Compustat data would likely be a very noisy procedure because many companies have operations in multiple states and Compustat only provides information about the state in which the company is headquartered. For more details on the federal tax code, see Courdes and Sheffrin (1983), Altshuler and Auerbach (1990), Shevlin (1990), or Scholes and Wolfson (1992).

*J.R. Graham/Journal of Financial Economics 41 (1996) 41–73*          45

carryback potential has been fully exhausted. If a company experiences losses in more than one year, the incremental losses are added to any unused losses from previous years; the carryback and carryforward procedures are then applied to taxable income, net of any previously taken losses, with the oldest losses applied first. Although the tax-code allows firms to bypass the carryback feature and choose to only carry losses forward, I assume that firms never bypass the carryback feature.

When available the Compustat net operating loss carryforward figure is used for net operating losses. Otherwise, I follow the lead of Altshuler and Auerbach (1990) and Shevlin (1990) and assume that the *NOL* carryforward is zero in 1972 and begin accumulating *NOL*s in 1973.

The relation between operating losses and the *MTR* is not always obvious. For example, a firm with a current-period loss could have a high marginal tax rate. Suppose that current-period losses exactly offset taxable income in the previous three periods. In this case, earning an extra dollar of income today results in the firm's tax refund decreasing by the amount $\tau_c$, where $\tau_c$ is the applicable statutory tax rate. Thus, the firm's *MTR* is $\tau_c$, so that the marginal tax rate can be high even when a firm has negative current-period income.

Alternatively, the effective *MTR* of a firm earning positive income today can be low if there is a positive probability that current taxes will be refunded. For example, suppose that we expect *NOL*s to occur next year as well as in all years in the foreseeable future, and that the amount of carried-back losses will more than offset current taxable income; this leads to a tax refund next year. In this case, the *MTR* today equals $\tau_c$ minus $\tau_c$ discounted one period, a relatively low rate even though current-period taxable income is positive. Thus, all else equal, a firm which is more likely to incur losses in the future will have a lower *MTR*.

These examples demonstrate that the tax treatment of losses can render some *MTR* proxies ineffective. For example, consider the *effective tax rate* equal to taxes paid (which are negative if there is a refund) divided by taxable income. The effective tax rate can be negative, or even greater than one. Typically, extreme effective tax rate estimates are truncated at arbitrary limits to make them more 'reasonable'. The approach used to model marginal tax rates in this paper explicitly models the tax-code treatment of net operating losses, calculates a *MTR* according to the statutory tax schedule, and always results in marginal tax rates between zero and the top statutory rate.

Once operating losses have been netted out against income, a company calculates its investment tax credits. Until the Tax Reform Act of 1986, firms could accumulate investment tax credits of approximately 7% of capital investment. These credits can be used to offset the first $25,000 of taxes and 85% of taxes in excess of $25,000 (50% before 1978) and they can be carried forward (back) up to 15 (3) years. The investment tax credit was repealed and accumulated *ITC* carryforwards were reduced by 17.5% in both 1987 and 1988 in association with the Tax Reform Act of 1986, although *ITC*s remained on the books of some companies as recently as 1994 (and some firms may have $ITC$ carryforwards on their books through the end of the century). As will be discussed in the next section, my analysis concentrates on the period 1980–1992; therefore, the $ITC$ is a potentially important consideration for this paper.

Finally, the Tax Reform Act of 1986 introduced an alternative minimum tax $(AMT)$ in response to some highly publicized cases in which profitable firms paid no federal taxes. The $AMT$ is designed to ensure that companies with positive income pay at least some federal income taxes. The $AMT$ is calculated by broadening the tax base (i.e., adding back some tax preference items such as accelerated depreciation to taxable income) and calculating an alternative tax based on a flat $AMT$ rate. This rate is 20% but can be reduced to an effective 15% of the pre-tax $AMT$ base by using $ITCs$ or to an effective 2% by using $NOL$ carryforwards (or foreign tax credits). An add-on minimum tax existed prior to 1987, but I ignore it in my analysis because, as noted by Altshuler and Auerbach, it had less bite than the $AMT$.

Taxes owed are the maximum of taxes determined from the regular formulas and those from the $AMT$ formulas. If the $AMT$ causes additional taxes to be paid due to adding back tax preference items to the tax base, the additional amount can be carried forward indefinitely as a tax credit. Thus, for the most part, the $AMT$ affects the timing of tax payments on tax preference items and not the total nominal bill, although it can affect the total bill in certain circumstances. Companies that are highly profitable or consistently experience losses will not likely be affected by the $AMT$. Companies that cycle between losses and profits and companies with high levels of accelerated depreciation are most likely to be affected. See Manzon (1992) for an excellent discussion on the $AMT$.

The Compustat tapes do not provide much information about the tax preference items that are added back to the tax base to determine the alternative minimum tax. Therefore, I use the regular tax base but calculate the tax bill using the $AMT$ tax rate. While the total tax bill may be inaccurate (because I use an incorrect tax base), the marginal impact of earning an extra dollar should reflect the true $MTR$. Finally, for ease of computer programming, I only allow an 18-year $AMT$ carryforward period rather than the indefinite carryforward period stated in the tax code.

## 2.2. Simulating expected marginal tax rates

The ability to carry losses and credits forward and backward makes it unlikely that examining current-period financial statements will provide an accurate assessment of a company's $MTR$. Instead, it is desirable to estimate the $MTR$ by supplementing historical data with a forecasted stream of future taxable income and then calculate the tax bill over the entire horizon in a manner consistent with the tax rules.

J.R. Graham/Journal of Financial Economics 41 (1996) 41–73          47

Given the 15-year carryforward feature associated with NOLs and ITCs, predictions of taxable income at least 18 years into the future should be considered when calculating the current-period MTR. For example, the tax consequences of earning an extra dollar of income today may not be realized for 15 years if a firm is not expected to have net taxable income for the next 14 years. Furthermore, $TI_{t+15}$ can be affected by $TI_{t+18}$ due to NOL and ITC carryback rules; therefore, 18 years of future income streams should be forecasted for each current-period MTR simulation. AMT carryforward rules allow an indefinite carryforward period; however, the impact beyond 18 years in the future is negligible due to discounting.

To forecast taxable income, I use Shevlin's (1990) main model which states that firm $i$'s taxable income follows a random walk with drift:

$$\Delta TI_{it} = \mu_i + \varepsilon_{it},$$  (1)

where $\Delta TI_{it}$ is the first difference in taxable income, $\mu_i$ is the sample mean of $\Delta TI_i$, and $\varepsilon_{it}$ is distributed normally with mean zero and variance equal to that of $\Delta TI_i$ over the sample. Taxable income is estimated from the Compustat tapes as pre-tax book income minus deferred tax expense, with the latter term divided by the appropriate statutory corporate tax rate so that it is expressed on a pre-tax basis.

When estimating $MTR_{it}$ for, say, $t = 1980$, forecasts of firm $i$'s taxable income for the years 1981–1998 are obtained by drawing 18 random normal realizations of $\varepsilon_{it}$ and using Eq. (1). Next, the present value of the tax bill from 1977 (to account for carrybacks) through 1998 (to account for carryforwards) is calculated. Taxes paid in the years 1981–1998 are discounted using the average corporate bond yield, as gathered from Moody's Bond Record; taxes for the years 1977–1980 are not discounted or grossed-up because, for all practical purposes, tax refunds are not paid with interest.[4] The tax bill is calculated using the entire corporate tax schedule, and not just the top statutory rate, as gathered from Commerce Clearing House publications. Next, a dollar is added to 1980's income and the present value of the tax bill is recalculated. The difference between the two tax bills represents the present value of taxes owed on an extra dollar of income earned by firm $i$ in year $t = 1980$ (i.e., a single simulated estimate of $MTR_{it}$).

---

[4] An area for future research might be to incorporate firm-specific discount rates, including an equity component. Such an approach would reduce the size of the sample, perhaps considerably, in the process of obtaining firm-specific bond and equity information. Furthermore, this is a delicate issue because i) there is a circularity between weighted average after-tax discount rates and marginal tax rates, and ii) the appropriate firm-specific rate should reflect the tax status and investment choices of the marginal investor. Using the economy-wide bond rate sidesteps these issues (but does incorporate the economy-wide time value of money). Abstracting from uncertainty, using the bond yield is correct if the marginal investor between equity and corporate debt is a tax-free entity (e.g., a pension fund).

The simulation procedure just described is repeated 50 times to obtain 50 estimates of 1980's $MTR$; each simulation is based on a new forecast of 18 years of taxable income. The 50 estimates of the marginal tax rate are averaged to determine the expected $MTR_{it}$ for firm $i$ in year $t = 1980$. This provides a single expected $MTR_{it}$ for a single firm-year. The standard deviation of the $MTR_{it}$ across the 50 simulations, $\sigma_{mtr, it}$, measures the precision with which firm $i$ estimates its $MTR$ in year $t$.

Next, the procedure is repeated 50 times for 1981 using historical data up to 1981 and predicting taxable income for 1982–1999; this produces estimates of $MTR_{it}$ and $\sigma_{mtr, it}$, for firm $i$ in year $t = 1981$. This technique is repeated for each company in the sample, for each year between 1980 and 1992.

Each forecast of taxable income is based upon the firm-specific sample mean and variance of changes in taxable income. Thus, a company with volatile earnings will experience $NOLs, ITC$ deferment, etc., more frequently in its group of 50 estimates than will a company with stable positive earnings. Averaging over the 50 estimates should reflect management's *expectation* of the impact of $NOLs$, etc., on the firm's marginal tax rate better than would using *ex post* data.

As an example of the simulation procedure, consider the single forecast of taxable income represented by the thick solid line in Fig. 1. If the company under consideration earns an extra dollar of income today, it pays taxes of $0.34 immediately. In the thick-solid-line scenario, the firm does not expect to experience $NOLs$ at any time during the next 18 years, so its marginal tax rate for this simulation is 34%. In the dashed-line scenario, the firm pays taxes of $0.34 on the extra dollar earned in period $t$, but anticipates getting a refund of $0.34 in period $t + 1$, paying $0.34 in taxes in period $t + 5$, and then remaining profitable from period $t + 6$ onward. Using a discount rate of 10%, the present value of taxes paid in this simulation is $0.242. In the thin-solid-line scenario, the firm pays taxes at 34% in period $t$ but expects to obtain a tax refund in period $t + 1$ because it experiences a net operating loss; the firm does not expect to pay taxes again during the next 18 years. Using a discount rate of 10%, the firm's $MTR$ is 3.1% in this simulation ($0.031 = 0.34 - (0.34/1.10)$). The expected marginal tax rate for this firm in period $t$ is 20.4% (which is the average of 34%, 24.2%, and 3.1%). The cross-sectional standard deviation of the rates ($\sigma_{mtr, it}$) in the three scenarios is 15.8%. The actual simulation procedure used in the paper performs 50, rather than three, simulations per $MTR_{it}$ and considers the interplay of the $ITC$ and $AMT$ in addition to influence of net operating losses.

## 2.3. The empirical distribution of the MTR

Fig. 2 presents the distribution of simulated marginal tax rates for the firms in the sample for 1980, 1984, 1988, 1992, and an aggregation across all years in the sample (See Section 4 for details on sample selection). The data indicate that there is substantial variation in the marginal tax rate across firms and through

*J.R. Graham/Journal of Financial Economics 41 (1996) 41–73*          49

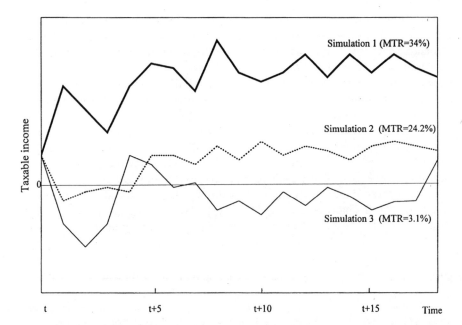

Fig. 1. An example of simulated marginal tax rates, assuming a statutory tax rate of 34%.

The three lines show a firm's forecasted taxable income streams for three different simulations, where taxable income follows a random walk with drift. In simulation 1, the firm pays $0.34 in taxes on an extra dollar of income earned in period $t$, is profitable from period $t + 1$ to period $t + 18$, and therefore has a marginal tax rate of 34% in period $t$. In simulation 2, the firm pays $0.34 in taxes in period $t$, receives a $0.34 refund in period $t + 1$, and then pays $0.34 in taxes in period $t + 5$. Assuming a discount rate of 10%, the present value of taxes owed on the extra dollar of income earned in period $t$, and hence the firm's marginal tax rate, is 24.2% in simulation 2. In simulation 3, the firm pays taxes of $0.34 in period $t$, receives a refund in $t + 1$, does not pay taxes again through period $t + 18$, and has a marginal tax rate of 3.1%. In simulation 3, the firm does earn positive taxable income in periods $t + 4$, $t + 5$, $t + 7$, and $t + 18$ but does not pay taxes in any of those periods because it has a net operating loss carryforward. The firm's expected marginal tax rate in period $t$ is 20.4% (i.e., the average of 35%, 24.2%, and 3.1%).

time. In any given year, about one-third of the firms have $MTR$s equal to the top statutory tax rate, about one-fifth have $MTR$s of zero, and the rest have $MTR$s ranging between zero and the highest rate. The cross-sectional variation in tax rates occurs because of the carryforward and carryback features of the federal tax code, as well as the progressive nature of the corporate tax rate schedule (i.e., some firms are not subject to the highest statutory tax rate). The relatively large percentage of low tax rates results because over 25% of the observations in the sample represent firms with negative taxable income.

A large percentage of $MTR$s are in the 30–35% range for 1988 and 1992; this reflects the reduction of the top statutory corporate tax rate to 34% starting in

50             *J.R. Graham/Journal of Financial Economics 41 (1996) 41–73*

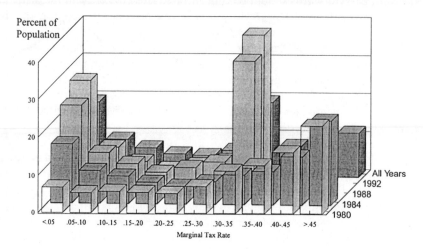

Fig. 2. The empirical distribution of the marginal tax rate.

The distribution of the marginal tax rate for all firms on the Compustat tapes with nonmissing taxable income data, a total sample of 10,240 firms. The distributions are shown for the years 1980, 1984, 1988, and 1992, and aggregated across all years from 1980–1992. The marginal tax rate is calculated for a given year as the present value of additional taxes owed from earning an extra dollar of income in that year. The tax calculation considers the effect of net operating losses, the investment tax credit, the alternative minimum tax, and other nondebt tax shields such as depreciation.

1988 (from 46% prior to the Tax Reform Act of 1986). Also, a much larger percentage of firms have $MTRs$ near zero in 1988 and 1992 than in the other years. This is probably because approximately 35% percent of the firms in the sample experienced losses in the late 1980s and early 1990s, while fewer than 20% experienced losses in the early 1980s. Overall, corporate marginal tax rates vary considerably through time due to changes in the tax code and business cycle effects. The annual equally weighted average $MTRs$ from 1980–1992 are 33.2%, 32.3%, 30.4%, 29.8%, 28.9%, 26.1%, 25.1%, 22.2%, 19.5%, 19.2%, 19.1%, 19.3%, and 20.0%, respectively. The value-weighted $MTRs$ for the same years are 41.1%, 40.5%, 39.5%, 39.3%, 39.7%, 39.3%, 39.3%, 32.8%, 30.0%, 30.0%, 29.8%, 29.4%, and 27.8%.

One tax status proxy which has been used with some degree of success in the past is a dummy variable equal to zero if a company has a net operating loss carryforward and equal to one otherwise (Scholes, Wilson, and Wolfson, 1990). *NOL* status is potentially important because 25% of the observations in the sample are from firms with *NOL* carryforwards, and over 50% of the firms in the sample had *NOL* carryforwards at some point during the period 1980–1992. For a *NOL* dummy variable to be most effective, the distribution of $MTRs$ for firms

*J.R. Graham/Journal of Financial Economics 41 (1996) 41–73* 51

with *NOL* carryforwards should be concentrated close to zero and the distribution for firms with no *NOL* carryforwards should be concentrated near the top statutory rate. Using the simulated tax rate data, we can directly examine whether these conditions are realized. Panels A and B in Fig. 3 indicate that the conditional distributions are skewed in the appropriate manner; however, less than half the population lies near the appropriate extreme in most years. This suggests that the *NOL* dummy variable does a good job of partitioning tax status, but that simulated tax rates offer a finer partition. (This issue will be examined further in Section 5.3.)

Finally, past empirical research indicates that many corporate policies are correlated with firm size, notwithstanding the frequent absence of theoretical justification for this result. This suggests that it may be worthwhile to examine the empirical distribution of marginal tax rates for groups of small and large firms. To accomplish this, I divided the sample into the smallest and largest size quartiles, based on the year-by-year market value of the firm. Panel C (D) in Fig. 3 indicates that small (large) firms have relatively low (high) marginal tax rates; that is, there is a positive correlation between firm size and marginal tax rates. Therefore, researchers should be careful to separate out tax effects from 'size effects' (see also Zimmerman, 1983; Omer, Molloy, and Ziebart, 1993). Also, the relatively small cross-sectional variation in tax rates among large companies indicates that it may be difficult to identify tax effects among, say, Fortune 500 firms. Finally, panel D indicates that large firms were somewhat insulated from the surge of near-zero marginal tax rates that occurred during the late 1980s and early 1990s.

The next section describes how the tax variables are used in the debt policy regression.

## 3. Explaining debt policy

The numerator for the dependent variable in the debt policy equation, *ΔDEBT*, is the first difference in the book value of long-term debt. The change in debt level captures the effect of incremental financing; it also measures changes due to sinking fund payments or security-holder conversion of convertible securities. It is unclear if changes associated with the second group of effects represent *intentional* debt policy or are simply artifacts due to imperfect capital markets. For example, if there were no transaction costs, a firm might offset each 'artifact' with an intentional action; however, nontrivial transaction costs encourage companies to allow artifacts to accumulate before eventually acting to reinstate the optimal debt policy. Therefore, in an effort to isolate intentional changes in debt, an alternative debt policy variable is also examined which represents changes in debt worth at least 2% of lagged capital structure.

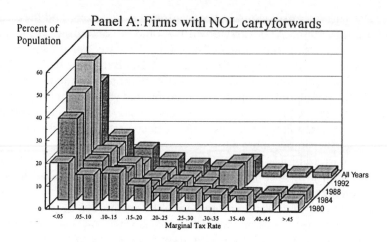

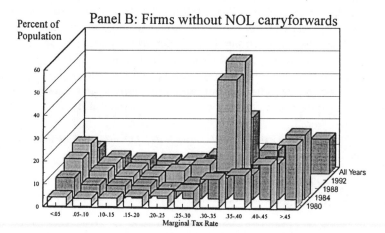

Fig. 3. The empirical distribution of the marginal tax rate given *NOL* carryforward status or firm size.

Panel A (B) shows the distribution of the marginal tax rate for all Compustat firms with nonmissing taxable income data which have (do not have) net operating loss carryforwards; firms with (without) *NOL* carryforwards comprise approximately 25% (75%) of the sample. Panel C (D) shows the distribution of the marginal tax rate for all Compustat firms with nonmissing taxable income data in the smallest (largest) quartile of firms, where size is defined by market value of the firm. The data are presented for the years 1980 (1981 for size conditioning), 1984, 1988, and 1992, and aggregated across all years from 1980–1992. The total sample contains tax rates for 10,240 firms. The marginal tax rate is calculated for a given year as the present value of additional taxes owed from earning an extra dollar of income in that year. The tax calculation considers the effect of net operating losses, the investment tax credit, the alternative minimum tax, and other nondebt tax shields such as depreciation.

*J.R. Graham/Journal of Financial Economics 41 (1996) 41–73* 53

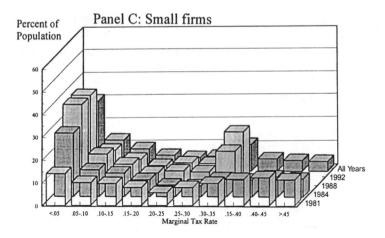

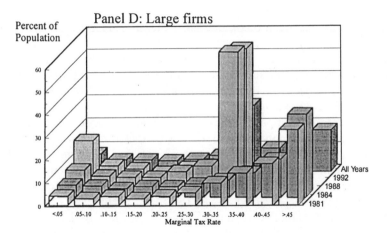

Fig. 3 (continued)

The value of $\Delta DEBT$ is deflated by the lagged market value of the firm, defined as the book value of debt plus the market value of equity. This is a common adjustment which standardizes the unit of measurement across firms. Note that the dependent variable is not the change in the debt/value ratio; it is defined as the first difference in $DEBT$ (performed first) divided by lagged firm value (performed second). This definition helps attenuate possible mismeasurement of debt policy due to large variation in the market value of equity. For example, suppose that a firm does not raise capital in a given year but that the value of its existing equity increases due to a booming stock market. This may cause the firm's debt/equity ratio to shrink considerably. Thus, a variable measuring the change in the debt/equity ratio cannot distinguish between debt retirement and increases in the market value of equity. $\Delta DEBT$ can distinguish between these events because it does not vary unless the book value of debt changes. The explanatory variables are discussed next.

### 3.1. Explanatory variables

#### 3.1.1. Tax status

A firm with a high marginal tax rate has greater incentive to issue debt, relative to a low-$MTR$ firm, to take advantage of interest deductibility; this implies a positive relation between firm $i$'s tax rate, $MTR_i$, and its debt issuance. Note clearly that the association is between the *level* of the marginal tax rate and *incremental* debt policy.

Consider an alternative specification which is sometimes used: regressing the level of debt on the level of the $MTR$. The debt level represents years of cumulative financial policy. The current $MTR$ may not reflect the incentives associated with past decisions which led to the current level of debt, but instead represents the tax incentive associated with the next dollar of income earned or shielded. Scholes, Wilson, and Wolfson (1990) point out that the tax status explanatory variable should be the $MTR$ in effect at the time a financing instrument is chosen (in their words, the 'but-for' $MTR$). When examining incremental debt financing, the contemporaneous $MTR$ is not 'but-for' because it already reflects the impact of the choice of financial instrument. For example, an increase in fixed debt obligations lowers the $MTR$ because the interest deduction reduces taxable income, possibly moving the firm to a lower tax bracket, and makes it more likely that a firm will experience a current or future $NOL$; on average, this defers the tax obligation due to earning an extra dollar today and lowers the expected $MTR$. To at least partially accommodate these considerations, I relate the one-period lag of the $MTR$ to $\Delta DEBT$ because these variables are both consistent with decisions made at the margin.[5]

Although $MTR_{it-1}$ is probably a very reasonable proxy for management's perception of the 'true' $MTR$ as they make decisions in period $t$, it may suffer two limitations as a but-for tax measure. The true tax rate to gauge the tax advantage of interest deductibility should probably i) be an average of future expected $MTR$s (matching the life of the debt instrument) and ii) reflect the impact of deducting the total amount of interest and not just one dollar's worth. However, correcting for these issues is beyond the scope of this paper because doing so would require issue-specific information on principal and coupon rates (not available from Compustat) and a much more complicated $MTR$ simulation algorithm.

---

[5]Rather than using a lagged tax variable, Graham, Lemmon, and Schallheim (1995) measure but-for tax status with a simulated variable based on contemporaneous earnings *before* interest and taxes.

*J.R. Graham/Journal of Financial Economics 41 (1996) 41–73*          55

It is sometimes argued that firms with volatile income streams issue less debt than firms with stable streams. However, this argument is not very persuasive when comparing a firm with profits which vary between, say, three and nine million dollars each year versus a firm which makes six million dollars each year. The impact of volatility on debt issuance is much more important if the volatility jeopardizes the firm's ability to take interest tax deductions. Recall that volatility reduces the expected $MTR$ for firms which cannot take interest deductions in every state of nature (because of carryforwards, etc.); in fact, it may seem that for a risk-neutral firm volatility is only relevant to the degree that it lowers the expected $MTR$. However, if the $MTR$ is an increasing function of taxable income (i.e., if the function mapping taxable income into tax liability is convex), then a firm with a large value of $\sigma_{mtr}$ will have a larger expected tax bill than a firm with an identical $MTR$ but a lower $\sigma_{mtr}$, and therefore issue debt more aggressively. If this hypothesis is true, the coefficient on $\sigma_{mtr}$ should be positive. (Recall that $\sigma_{mtr,\,it}$ is the standard deviation of the estimated $MTR_{it}$ for firm $i$ across 50 tax simulations associated with year $t$.)

Finally, the simulated tax rate provides a mechanism for estimating a firm's 'true' $MTR$; however, in a large cross-section of firms, is it reasonable to expect that *all* managers make leverage decisions based on the simulated rate? If some managers make decisions based on their firm's current statutory tax status, then estimated regression coefficients should indicate that, on average, firms with statutory rates above (below) the expected $MTR$ will issue more (less) debt than firms for which the statutory rate equals the expected rate. That is, $\tau_{stat,\,it-1} - MTR_{it-1}$ should be positively related to debt usage, where $\tau_{stat,\,it-1}$ is firm $i$'s statutory tax rate in period $t-1$. According to this hypothesis, the coefficient on this variable will be zero if firms make tax-based leverage decisions based solely on simulated rates.

### 3.1.2. The relative cost of debt and equity

In the spirit of Miller (1977), DeAngelo and Masulis (1980), and Scholes and Wolfson (1992), it can be argued that the relation between the personal tax rate on interest payments, the personal tax rate on equity, and the corporate tax rate can influence the choice between debt and equity financing. In particular, suppose that there is a marginal investor who is indifferent between the after-tax returns from debt and equity. For a given level of risk, this determines the equilibrium relation between debt and equity prices which in turn defines $MTR^*$ for which some marginal corporation is indifferent between the after-corporate-tax proceeds from issuing debt or equity. Corporations with a marginal tax rate above (below) $MTR^*$ have an incentive (disincentive) to issue debt relative to issuing equity. If so, the relative tax advantage associated with debt, $ADVDEBT$ (defined as $(1 - \tau_{debt})/[(1 - \tau_{equity})(1 - MTR_{it-1})]$), should be positively related to debt issuance. This variable primarily captures the effect of the Tax Reform Act of 1986 on the relative tax advantage of debt. The average annual values of *ADVDEBT* for the years 1981–1992 are 0.97, 0.99, 1.03, 0.99, 0.99, 1.01, 1.08, 1.33, 1.28, 1.27, 1.28, and 1.29, respectively. Given that $MTR_{it-1}$ is already included in the regression, an alternative specification which excludes $(1 - MTR_{it-1})$ from the denominator of *ADVDEBT*, and thereby examines only the effect of relative personal tax rates on debt and equity, will also be examined.

The personal tax rate on interest for the marginal investor, $\tau_{debt}$, is inferred from the lagged difference between the one-year yield on municipal and taxable bonds, as published in Salomon Brother's Bond Market Roundup. The personal tax rate on equity income, $\tau_{equity}$, is equal to the lagged tax rate on long-term capital gains.

### 3.1.3. Probability of bankruptcy

If bankruptcy is costly, many theories argue that debt usage should be a dcreasing function of the probability of bankruptcy (e.g., Bradley, Jarrell, and Kim, 1984; MacKie-Mason, 1990). Like MacKie-Mason, I use a variant of Altman's (1968) *ZPROB* to measure the probability of bankruptcy. *ZPROB* equals total assets divided by the sum of 3.3 times earnings before interest and taxes plus sales plus 1.4 times retained earnings plus 1.2 times working capital. My measure is the inverse of MacKie-Mason's. The theory implies a negative coefficient on *ZPROB*. Recall that $MTR_{it}$ already measures the expected effect of entering non-tax-paying status (such as bankruptcy) on the interest deductibility incentive to issue debt. Therefore, *ZPROB* may empirically capture other direct and indirect costs of bankruptcy, such as legal fees, soured relations with suppliers and creditors, the drain on management time, agency costs associated with debt, etc.

An alternative approach to measuring non-interest-deduction incentives to avoid financial distress is also available. For the most part, companies which have *NOL* carryforwards are currently, or have recently been, experiencing some level of financial distress. It is likely that creditors and suppliers for these firms will be 'on alert' and will threaten to withhold future supplies, or only provide them at a very high cost, if there is any indication that the firm cannot meet its fixed obligations. This can create a disincentive to issue debt for a firm currently experiencing a net operating loss, relative to a firm not currently experiencing a loss, even if both firms have the same *expected* marginal tax rate (because the expected *MTR* reflects the tax implications of bankruptcy, but not the costs associated with suppliers, legal fees, etc.). If so, firms currently in *NOL* carryforward status might issue debt less aggressively than firms without carryforwards because of the offsetting effect of expected bankruptcy costs. This hypothesis can be tested by interacting $MTR_{it-1}$ with dummy variables indicating whether a firm has an *NOL* carryforward: $MTR_{NOL,it-1}$ ($MTR_{nonNOL,it-1}$) is equal to $MTR_{it-1}$ if firm $i$ had (did not have) an *NOL* carryforward in period $t - 1$, and equals zero otherwise. If the expected bankruptcy cost hypothesis is

*J.R. Graham/Journal of Financial Economics 41 (1996) 41–73*          57

true, firms with $NOLs$ will issue debt less aggressively than firms without $NOLs$ (i.e., the estimated coefficient on $MTR_{NOL, it-1}$ should be less than the coefficient on $MTR_{nonNOL, it-1}$). Note that this hypothesis must be tested in a separate regression from a specification which includes $MTR_{it-1}$ as a stand-alone variable.[6] Another possibility would be to include, say, $MTR_{it-1}$ and $MTR_{NOL, it-1}$ in the same regression. I use $MTR_{NOL, it-1}$ and $MTR_{nonNOL, it-1}$ to facilitate comparison between simulated tax rates and the $NOL$ dummy variable. For example, the coefficient on $MTR_{NOL, it-1}$ ($MTR_{nonNOL, it-1}$) is associated with the sample of data shown in panel A (B) of Fig. 3.

### 3.1.4. Nondebt tax shields

DeAngelo and Masulis (1980) argue that nondebt tax shields are a substitute for the interest deduction associated with debt; therefore, the optimal amount of debt in a firm's capital structure is a decreasing function of $NDTS$. It follows that an increase in $NDTS$ should, all else equal, be accompanied by a reduction in debt. $NDTS$ are measured as the sum of book depreciation and $ITC$. The variable included in the regression is first differenced and then deflated by the lagged market value of the firm to be consistent with the dependent variable. The change in research and development ($\Delta RD$) and advertising expenses ($\Delta AD$) can also be viewed as $NDTS$ and should be negatively related to debt usage if they serve as tax substitutes (Bradley, Jarrell, and Kim, 1984).

MacKie-Mason argues that an extra dollar of $NDTS$ does not crowd out interest deductibility for profitable firms; e.g., a company with large $NDTS$ may be profitable, have a high $MTR$, and issue a lot of debt. On the other hand, a company experiencing 'tax exhaustion' (e.g., a firm which has exhausted all contemporaneous tax write-off opportunities because it has $NDTS$ that more than offset operating income) is likely to avoid debt financing because the associated interest deduction is crowded out by $NDTS$. Therefore, $NDTS$ should have a negative influence on debt usage for firms with a high value for $ZPROB$ (because these companies are close to tax exhaustion and most likely cannot fully exploit the deductibility of interest). That is, a high value of $ZPROB$ is consistent with a low $MTR$, according to this argument, and implies that debt can be crowded out by $NDTS$. MacKie-Mason conjectures a negative

---

[6]There could, of course, be $NOL$ (non$NOL$) firms which issue debt aggressively (cautiously) because they anticipate that their $NOL$ status will change in the near future; this would offset the effect cited in the text. It is an empirical question as to which effect dominates. It is also difficult to empirically distinguish the test of whether managers simulate tax rates from the test of whether expected bankruptcy costs matter. For example, the coefficient for $MTR_{NOL, it-1}$ will be lower than the coefficient for $MTR_{nonNOL, it-1}$ if not all managers simulate tax rates because $NOL$ (non$NOL$) firms have low (high) statutory tax rates, on average. This is the same relation as hypothesized in the expected bankruptcy cost argument; that is, the two arguments are empirically similar. Analogously, $\tau_{stat, it-1} - MTR_{it-1}$ may be positively related to debt usage if firms with high (low) expected bankruptcy costs have a lower (higher) statutory rate than their expected rate.

coefficient on his 'debt substitution' variable ($NDTS$ times $ZPROB$). In summary, MacKie-Mason separates the 'profitability' and 'debt substitution' aspects of nondebt tax shields by using $NDTS$ and $NDTS$ interacted with $ZPROB$ as two separate variables; his results are consistent with the profitability (debt substitution) component being positively (negatively) related to debt usage.

MacKie-Mason's approach has strong intuitive appeal. However, the ability of a firm to carry losses and $NDTS$ backward or forward is only modeled indirectly, through the interaction with $ZPROB$, and is not reflective of the tax code. In contrast, my simulated $MTR$ calculation directly measures the effect of $NDTS$ on the marginal tax rate in a manner which is consistent with the federal tax code. As noted by MacKie-Mason (p. 1474), 'tax shields should matter only to the extent that they affect the marginal tax rate on interest deductions'. Thus, the predominant tax effect of $NDTS$ should be captured by the simulated $MTR$.

Finally, the general point of the DeAngelo and Masulis article is that company-specific optimal debt policies may arise because companies have varying abilities to deduct interest expense. This is consistent with the tax hypothesis stated above, given the explicit modeling of the tax code in the simulated $MTR$ calculation.

### 3.1.5. Control variables

While the primary focus of this paper is to investigate whether leverage decisions are affected by tax status, it is important to control for competing explanations of debt policy. Otherwise, it is possible that the tax variables do not really test tax hypotheses but instead proxy for other explanations of debt policy, such as firm quality. Including control factors also allows us to determine the relative contribution of tax variables to the debt policy specification. Briefly, the regression equations estimated below include control variables to proxy for each firm's free cash flow, investment opportunity set, size, R&D and advertising expense, and asset tangibility. When appropriate, the control variables are expressed in difference form to be consistent with the specification of the dependent variable, although $ZPROB$ and $ZPROB$ interacted with $NDTS$ are not differenced because using these variables in level form allows for a more direct comparison of the results derived here with those in MacKie-Mason's article (first-differenced forms of these variables do not change the conclusions drawn about the other explanatory variables). A detailed explanation of the capital structure theories related to each control variable is available from the author upon request. (An abbreviated description of the variables appears in the footnotes to Table 2.)

## 4. The data sample

The data are gathered from the annual Compustat Full-Coverage (NASDAQ, OTC, some NYSE, and regional-exchange firms which file 10-K forms with the SEC), Primary, Secondary, and Tertiary (large NYSE companies) and merged

*J.R. Graham/Journal of Financial Economics 41 (1996) 41–73*          59

industrial research (firms which have dropped off the other tapes because of mergers, LBOs, liquidation, etc.) tapes. These tapes contain information from 1973 through 1992. The *MTR* simulations require a start-up period to accumulate *NOLs*. Data from 1973–1979 are used as the start-up period and from 1980–1992 to simulate marginal tax rates. There are 88,282 observations, representing 12,197 companies, available over the 1980–1992 period. This total is misleading, however, because a firm which exists for one year is assigned 20 observations, one with data and 19 with missing values, by Compustat. After deleting observations with missing values for the control variables, the sample contains 64,445 observations covering 10,865 companies.

Financial firms (with two-digit SIC codes between 60 and 64) are deleted from the sample because they follow a different set of tax rules. This eliminates 2,610 observations and 468 firms. Observations are also eliminated if the absolute value of the change in debt, or the absolute change in other variables deflated by market value, is greater than the lagged market value of the firm. This helps eliminate outliers such as firms in severe financial distress or perhaps data coding errors on the Compustat files and deletes an additional 658 observations and 44 firms.

The analysis of debt policy is limited to 1981–1992 because the *MTR* lagged one period is used as an explanatory variable. This requirement results in the deletion of an additional 6,990 observations and 113 companies. The final sample has 10,240 firms and 54,181 firm-year observations.

$\Delta DEBT$ has a mean of 0.008 and a standard deviation of 0.139 indicating that the average firm had a 0.8% annual increase in debt usage over the sample period. Sample statistics for the tax variables are included in Table 1. The *MTR* ranges between zero and 0.46, with a mean of 0.241 and a standard deviation of 0.154. The other variables also exhibit a reasonable amount of variation across the sample. Note that the effective tax rate has a mean of 0.196, but that it ranges from $-620.9$ to 623.3. Also, both *NDTS* interacted with *ZPROB* and the effective tax rate are essentially uncorrelated with the other tax variables.

There is a modest degree of collinearity across the proposed tax variables. To investigate possible effects of multicollinearity, I drop the variables with cross-correlations greater than 0.10 from the regression, one at a time. The results for the remaining variables are essentially unchanged, with the exception that the sign of *ADVDEBT* (representing the relative tax advantage of debt) changes when *MTR* was dropped from the regression specification. (This exception will be discussed below.)

## 5. Empirical results

### 5.1. Econometric technique and primary findings

Coefficients for the proposed independent variables are estimated in a linear regression. The standard errors are obtained using White's (1980) technique and

60     *J.R. Graham/Journal of Financial Economics 41 (1996) 41–73*

Table 1
Descriptive statistics of the tax variables

| | Mean | Std. dev. | Minimum | Maximum |
|---|---|---|---|---|
| $MTR_{t-1}$ [a] | 0.241 | 0.154 | 0.000 | 0.460 |
| $\sigma_{mtr,t-1}$ [b] | 0.071 | 0.058 | 0.000 | 0.203 |
| $\tau_{stat,t-1} - MTR_{t-1}$ [c] | 0.026 | 0.188 | -0.460 | 0.460 |
| $MTR_{NOL,t-1}$ [d] | 0.039 | 0.095 | 0.000 | 0.460 |
| $MTR_{nonNOL,t-1}$ [e] | 0.202 | 0.174 | 0.000 | 0.460 |
| $ADVDEBT_{t-1}$ [f] | 1.130 | 0.257 | 0.638 | 1.726 |
| $NDTS_t * ZPROB_t$ [g] | 0.043 | 2.215 | -141.6 | 312.6 |
| Effective tax rate [h] | 0.196 | 7.769 | -620.9 | 623.3 |
| NOL dummy variable [i] | 0.264 | 0.441 | 0.000 | 1.000 |

Cross-correlations

| | $\sigma_{mtr}$ | $\tau_{stat} - MTR$ | $MTR_{NOL}$ | $MTR_{nonNOL}$ | $ADVDEBT$ | $NDTS*ZPROB$ | Effective tax rate | $NOL$ dummy |
|---|---|---|---|---|---|---|---|---|
| $MTR$ | -0.098 | -0.301 | 0.078 | 0.841 | 0.563 | 0.005 | 0.012 | -0.370 |
| $\sigma_{mtr}$ | 1.000 | 0.130 | 0.058 | -0.117 | -0.344 | -0.006 | 0.005 | 0.008 |
| $\tau_{stat} - MTR$ | | 1.000 | -0.110 | -0.211 | -0.094 | -0.007 | 0.051 | -0.013 |
| $MTR_{NOL}$ | | | 1.000 | -0.474 | -0.026 | 0.011 | -0.002 | 0.696 |
| $MTR_{nonNOL}$ | | | | 1.000 | 0.512 | -0.001 | 0.012 | -0.681 |
| $ADVDEBT$ | | | | | 1.000 | -0.005 | 0.006 | -0.286 |
| $NDTS*ZPROB$ | | | | | | 1.000 | -0.001 | 0.003 |
| Effective tax rate | | | | | | | 1.000 | -0.009 |

[a] One-period lag of the simulated marginal tax rate.

[b] One-period lag of the standard deviation of the simulated marginal tax rate.

[c] One-period lag of the difference between a firm's statutory and simlated marginal tax rates.

[d] One-period lag of the simulated $MTR$ for firms with net operating loss carryforwards; zero for firms without $NOL$ carryforwards.

[e] One-period lag of the simulated $MTR$ for firms without net operating loss carryforwards; zero for firms with $NOL$ carryforwards.

[f] One-period lag of the ratio (one minus the marginal investor's personal tax rate on interest income) over the quantity (one minus the personal tax rate on long-term capital gains) times (one minus $MTR_t$). The personal tax rate on interest income is inferred from the yield differential on taxable and tax-free one-year bonds.

[g] Nondebt tax shields divided by lagged market value of the firm, the quantity multiplied by the probability of bankruptcy.

[h] Taxes paid divided by taxable income.

[i] Equal to one if a firm has a $NOL$ carryforward, equal to zero if the firm does not have a $NOL$ carryforward.

are thus heteroscedastic-consistent. The results for the regression using all 54,181 observations are shown in the leftmost columns of Table 2. In Table 2, $\Delta$ indicates a first difference and each variable is denoted with a time subscript, $t$. The firm subscript, $i$, is suppressed in the table, and throughout the remainder of the text, for notational simplicity. First consider the results for the specification which appear in the leftmost column of the table, which I will refer to as the 'main regression' of the paper. The adjusted $R^2$ is 0.050, and the $F$-value of 205.1 ($p$-value $< 0.01$) confirms the significance of the overall regression equation. With the exception of $ZPROB$, the $t$-statistics for all of the proposed tax variables are statistically significant at a 5% confidence level. The estimated coefficient of 0.069 on the marginal tax rate confirms a positive relation between tax rates and debt usage. This finding holds for subsamples of firms with high growth and low growth (results not reported), confirming that the $MTR$ does not just proxy for future growth. The coefficient of 0.044 on $\tau_{stat,t-1} - MTR_{t-1}$ indicates that, on average, statutory tax status affects debt decisions; this can occur because either i) not all firms simulate tax rates or ii) expected bankruptcy costs matter (see footnote 6). The positive coefficient on $\sigma_{mtr}$ is consistent with the notion that firms with larger expected tax bills issue more debt than firms with smaller tax bills, but the same expected $MTR$.

The coefficient for $ADVDEBT$ has a sign opposite from that hypothesized, possibly because the relative advantage of issuing debt may already be captured in the coefficient on $MTR_{t-1}$. To investigate this issue further, I run an alternative regression in which $MTR_{t-1}$ is dropped from the specification (results not shown in Table 2); in this case, $ADVDEBT$ is positive, although the overall adjusted $R^2$ dropped to 0.0466. Finally, to more directly examine the contribution of personal-tax considerations on corporate debt policy, the main regression is rerun after dropping $(1 - MTR_{t-1})$ from the denominator of $ADVDEBT$ [i.e., $ADVDEBT = (1 - \tau_{debt})/(1 - \tau_{equity})$]. The estimated coefficient is negative and significant (results not reported in Table 2). The overall implication of these results is that the relative taxation of debt and equity at the personal level does not seem to affect corporate debt policy in the manner anticipated.

The sign on $ZPROB$ is negative, as hypothesized, but insignificant. Finally, the coefficient on the change in $NDTS$ times $ZPROB$ is negative, as hypothesized, and weakly significant. This is consistent with the notion that not all firms simulate marginal tax rates, or perhaps that the simulation procedure does not model the effect of $NDTS$ perfectly. (The relative explanatory power of the change in $NDTS$ times $ZPROB$ will be compared to that of the simulated tax rate in Section 5.4.)

The third column of Table 2 repeats the regression for observations in which the absolute change in debt is at least 2% of market value. This should eliminate debt changes which are unintentional artifacts due, perhaps, to transactions costs and should also cut down on the noise in the data. This change eliminates almost one-half of the observations and increases the adjusted $R^2$ to 0.113. Paring down the data does not change the qualitative results regarding the individual variables. The estimated coefficient on $MTR_{t-1}$ almost doubles to 0.127. These results should be interpreted cautiously, however. Because the intentional debt policy regressions eliminate observations based on the magnitude of the dependent variable, it is possible that the observed increase in coefficients and adjusted $R^2$ has been spuriously induced. I am unable to distinguish between the 'eliminate unintentional debt policy' and 'spuriously induced' explanations. I thank Jim Brickley for pointing this out.

Table 2 also contains results for regressions in which $MTR_{t-1}$ is replaced by $MTR_{NOL,t-1}$ and $MTR_{nonNOL,t-1}$ to analyze the possibility that firms which are currently experiencing $NOL$ carryforwards will act differently than non$NOL$ firms with the same expected marginal tax rate. Given the 0.032 (0.071) coefficient for $NOL$ (non$NOL$) firms, it appears that $NOL$ firms pursue interest deductibility less aggressively than non$NOL$ firms. The differing coefficients for $NOL$ and non$NOL$ firms could be interpreted as implying either that not all firms expend the resources necessary to simulate marginal tax rates or that $NOL$ firms have higher expected bankruptcy costs.

## 5.2. Cross-sectional analysis

The results so far are based on a pooled cross-section of time series data. To determine if the results hold for nonpooled data, a cross-sectional regression is run for each year in the sample and for an aggregation of the data over three-year and 12-year horizons (see Table 3).

The positive influence of $MTR$, $\tau_{stat,t-1} - MTR_{t-1}$, and $\sigma_{mtr,t-1}$ on debt policy is relatively robust to purely cross-sectional analysis, although there is a noticeable deterioration in the relation between debt policy and $MTR$ in 1986 and 1987, possibly due to the Tax Reform Act of 1986. The effects of $MTR$ and $\tau_{stat,t-1} - MTR_{t-1}$ are generally more significant when the data are aggregated over three or 12 years. This may indicate that equilibrating movements in debt policy take more than one year to occur.

## 5.3. Sensitivity analysis

I repeat the analysis in Table 2 modifying the definition of the dependent variable so that it measures 1) long-term plus short-term debt and 2) total debt (long-term plus short-term plus convertible debt). The overall results do not change for these alternative specifications. The results are also robust to dropping the data from the merged industrial research tape; this confirms that the observed relations hold for a sample of firms which have not gone out of business or otherwise disappeared from the public record.

Table 2
The results of pooled time-series, cross-sectional regressions estimating the empirical factors which cause debt policy

The full data sample consists of all firms with nonmissing Compustat observations for the dependent and independent variables. The regressions use annual data from 1981–1992. Statistical significance is determined with White (1980) standard errors to correct for heteroskedasticity. The dependent variable in the regressions is the change in debt: $\Delta DEBT_t$.

| | Estimated coefficients | | | |
|---|---|---|---|---|
| | All observations | | Intentional debt policy $(\|\Delta DEBT\| > 0.02)$[a] | |
| *Tax variables* | | | | |
| $MTR_{t-1}$[b] | 0.069* | | 0.127* | |
| $\sigma_{mtr,t-1}$[c] | 0.050* | 0.054* | 0.046** | 0.050* |
| $\tau_{stat,t-1} - MTR_{t-1}$[d] | 0.044* | 0.042* | 0.070* | 0.067* |
| $MTR_{NOL,t-1}$[e] | | 0.032* | | 0.068* |
| $MTR_{nonNOL,t-1}$[f] | | 0.071* | | 0.133* |
| $ADVDEBT_{t-1}$[g] | −0.008** | −0.009* | −0.015* | −0.017* |
| $ZPROB_t$[h] (×1000) | −0.002 | −0.002 | −0.009 | −0.009 |
| $NDTS_t*ZPROB_t$[i] | −0.001** | −0.001** | −0.001* | −0.001* |
| *Control variables* | | | | |
| $\Delta MATURITY_t$[j] (×1000) | 0.001** | 0.001* | −4.441 | −4.495 |
| $FREE_t$[k] (×1000) | −0.003** | −0.003** | −0.046* | −0.046* |
| $\Delta SIZE_t$[l] | 0.038* | 0.038* | 0.061* | 0.061* |
| $\Delta RD_t$[m] (×100) | 0.008** | 0.008* | 0.009* | 0.009* |
| $\Delta AD_t$[n] (×10) | 0.004 | 0.004* | 0.138* | 0.139* |
| $\Delta NDTS_t$[o] | 0.227* | 0.229* | 0.482* | 0.482* |
| $\Delta PLANT_t$[p] (×1000) | 0.003* | 0.003* | 0.004* | 0.004* |
| $\Delta INTAN_t$[q] | 0.359* | 0.358* | 0.445* | 0.444* |
| Intercept | −0.006 | −0.004 | −0.005 | −0.024 |
| Adjusted $R^2$ | 0.050 | 0.051 | 0.113 | 0.114 |
| $F$-value | 205.1* | 194.2* | 273.4* | 258.0* |
| Durbin–Watson $d$ | 2.068 | 2.068 | 2.137 | 2.138 |
| Number of obs. | 54181 | 54181 | 29835 | 29835 |
| Mean ($\Delta DEBT$) | 0.008 | 0.008 | 0.017 | 0.017 |

[a] $\Delta DEBT$ is the change in long-term book value of debt divided by the lagged level of the market value of the firm.

[b] One-period lag of the simulated marginal tax rate.

[c] One-period lag of the standard deviation of the simulated marginal tax rate.

[d] One-period lag of the difference between a firm's statutory and simulated marginal tax rates.

[e] One-period lag of the simulated $MTR$ for firms with net operating loss carryforwards; zero for firms without $NOL$ carryforwards.

[f] One-period lag of the simulated $MTR$ for firms without net operating loss carryforwards; zero for firms with $NOL$ carryforwards.

As mentioned earlier, the effect of foreign tax credits should be incorporated into the domestic marginal income tax rate calculation; however, Compustat does not provide information on repatriated foreign income. To verify if excluding foreign credits could be biasing the results, the regressions were run on a sample of domestic-only firms, i.e., companies which had no foreign income (as determined by annual Compustat variable 273). The results are essentially unchanged on the domestic-only subsample.

The estimates are also robust with respect to estimation on other subsets of the data. For example, no substantial change occurs if the data is restricted to 1981–1986 or 1987–1992. The results are also essentially unchanged when the simulated 1987 $MTRs$ are replaced with rates which accurately anticipate the change in the statutory schedule associated with the Tax Reform Act of 1986. Likewise, the results hold on a subset of firms making products that require specialized servicing and also on a subset of firms that do not require such servicing (see Titman, 1984). Finally, eliminating data for companies that have been involved with a merger or acquisition, as indicated by Compustat footnotes, does not alter the findings.

It was previously noted that $NDTS$ times $ZPROB$ is a weakly significant measure of tax status. This is also true if the variables associated with the simulated tax rate are dropped from the specification. To further gauge the relative value of simulating tax rates, two other commonly used proxies for the

Table 2 (continued)

[g]One-period lag of the ratio (one minus the marginal investor's personal tax rate on interest income) over the quantity (one minus the personal tax rate on long-term capital gains) times (one minus $MTR_t$). The personal tax rate on interest income is inferred from the yield differential on taxable versus tax-free one-year bonds.

[h]Probability of bankruptcy, defined as total assets divided by the sum of 3.3 times earnings before interest and taxes plus sales plus 1.4 times retained earnings plus 1.2 times working capital.

[i]Nondebt tax shields divided by lagged market value of the firm, the quantity multiplied by the probability of bankruptcy.

[j]Change in investment opportunity set: change in book value of assets divided by market value of the firm.

[k]Free cash flows: pre-tax, pre-interest-expense cash flow, net of investments and funds from debt and equity issuance or retirement.

[l]Change in the log of real sales.

[m]Change in research and development expenses as a percentage of sales.

[n]Change in advertising expenses as a percentage of sales.

[o]Change in nondebt tax shields divided by market value of the firm.

[p]Change in fixed plant and equipment divided by total assets.

[q]Change in intangible assets divided by total assets.

Superscript asterisks indicate significance at $p < 0.01$ (*) and $p < 0.05$ (**).

Table 3
Cross-sectional regressions

The first twelve rows contain the coefficients on the tax variables estimated over a cross-section of firms for one year. The control variables are also included in the regressions but their estimated coefficients are not reported. All firms on the Compustat tapes which do not have missing values for the explanatory variables are included in the regressions. The next four rows show the results for cross-sectional regressions over three-year aggregates of the variables. The last row contains the results from a single cross-sectional regression in which the data are aggregated over the 12-year period 1981–1992. The dependent variable in each regression is $\Delta DEBT$, the change in long-term book value of debt divided by the lagged level of the market value of the firm.

| | $MTR^a$ | $\sigma_{mtr}{}^b$ | $\tau_{stat} - MTR^c$ | $ADV\,DEBT^d$ | $ZPROB^e$ | $\Delta NDTS* \\ ZPROB^f$ | Adjusted $R^2$ |
|---|---|---|---|---|---|---|---|
| *Annual regressions* | | | | | | | |
| 1981 | 0.034* | 0.023 | 0.042* | n.a. | 0.0001** | − 0.001 | 0.057 |
| 1982 | 0.021 | 0.040** | 0.013** | n.a. | 0.0001 | − 0.010** | 0.635 |
| 1983 | 0.072 | 0.054 | 0.020** | n.a. | − 0.0001* | − 0.003* | 0.108 |
| 1984 | 0.046 | 0.108* | 0.027* | n.a. | − 0.0001 | 0.002 | 0.100 |
| 1985 | 0.119* | 0.060*** | 0.036* | n.a. | 0.0001 | − 0.0004 | 0.083 |
| 1986 | 0.013 | 0.035 | 0.023** | n.a. | − 0.0045 | 0.003 | 0.102 |
| 1987 | − 0.025 | 0.091* | 0.033* | n.a. | − 0.0001 | − 0.0002* | 0.099 |
| 1988 | 0.106* | 0.051 | 0.076* | n.a. | 0.0001** | − 0.007* | 0.095 |
| 1989 | 0.012 | 0.084*** | 0.061* | n.a. | 0.0002** | − 0.004 | 0.085 |
| 1990 | 0.108*** | − 0.085** | 0.098* | n.a. | − 0.0001 | − 0.003 | 0.049 |
| 1991 | 0.080 | − 0.050 | 0.021 | n.a. | 0.0005** | − 0.009* | 0.025 |
| 1992 | 0.138* | − 0.055 | 0.033** | n.a. | − 0.0007 | − 0.001 | 0.030 |

J.R. Graham/Journal of Financial Economics 41 (1996) 41–73

*Three-year aggregates*

|  |  |  |  |  |  |  |  |
|---|---|---|---|---|---|---|---|
| 1981–1983 | 0.093* | 0.351* | 0.033** | −0.001 | −0.001* | 0.002 | 0.070 |
| 1984–1986 | 0.094* | 0.262* | 0.063* | 0.032 | −0.002* | 0.065* | 0.104 |
| 1987–1989 | 0.055*** | 0.316* | 0.106* | 0.052* | −0.001 | 0.002 | 0.091 |
| 1990–1992 | 0.234* | −0.148** | 0.152* | −0.076* | −0.0004 | −0.004 | 0.058 |

*Twelve-year aggregates*

|  |  |  |  |  |  |  |  |
|---|---|---|---|---|---|---|---|
| 1981–1992 | 0.263* | 0.657* | 0.145* | −0.016* | 0.0002 | −0.002 | 0.099 |

[a] One-period lag of the simulated marginal tax rate.

[b] One-period lag of the standard deviation of the simulated marginal tax rate.

[c] One-period lag of the difference between a firm's statutory and simulated marginal tax rates.

[d] One-period lag of the ratio (one minus the marginal investor's personal tax rate on interest income) over the quantity (one minus the personal tax rate on equity income) times (one minus the corporate income tax rate). The personal tax rate on interest income is inferred from the yield differential on taxable versus tax-free one-year bonds. The personal tax rate on equity income is the capital gains tax rate.

[e] Probability of bankruptcy.

[f] Nondebt tax shields divided by lagged market value of the firm, the quantity multiplied by the probability of bankruptcy.

Superscript asterisks indicate significance at $p < 0.05$ (*), $p < 0.10$ (**), and $p < 0.15$ (***).

n.a. stands for not applicable.

marginal tax rate are examined. In particular, $MTR_{t-1}$, $\tau_{stat,t-1} - MTR_{t-1}$, $\sigma_{mtr,t-1}$, and $ADVDEBT_{t-1}$ are replaced in the main regression by the one-period lag of 1) a dummy variable equal to one when a company has a $NOL$ carryforward and, separately, 2) the effective tax rate, i.e., taxes paid divided by taxable income. Both these measures have the correct sign in their respective regressions (results not reported), although only the $NOL$ dummy variable is statistically significant. The fact that all of the tax measures have the correct sign in their respective regressions attests to the importance of examining incremental financing policy. The relative explanatory power of the various tax measures is explored more fully below.

Additional unreported regressions are run to determine if $MTR_{t-1}$ measures tax status for two subsets of data: i) firms that do not have a net operating loss carryforward and ii) firms that do. The estimated coefficients are positive and significant in both subsamples, implying that $MTR_{t-1}$ provides a finer partition of corporate tax status than does the $NOL$ carryforward categorization (recall panels A and B from Fig. 3).

The estimated coefficient on $NDTS$ interacted with $ZPROB$ implies that firms near tax exhaustion may decrease their use of debt to avoid losing the tax shield provided by $NDTS$, although the relation is fairly weak statistically. However, recall that the effect of $NDTS$ is also directly measured in the simulated marginal tax rate. This suggests that an alternative way to gauge the importance of $NDTS$ is to compare the simulated $MTR$ to an alternative simulated $MTR$ which is identical except that it ignores $NDTS$. To accomplish this, I simulate tax rates based on pre-tax book income *plus depreciation*, and exclude the effect of the $ITC$;[7] this procedure produces a tax rate which is not affected by $NDTS$. If $NDTS$ significantly influences marginal tax rates, then we can expect the tax rates which exclude the effect of $NDTS$ to i) vary considerably from the simulated tax rates previously derived in the paper and ii) be less significant in explaining debt policy than the $MTR$ that includes the effects of $NDTS$. However, the simulated $MTR$ and the non$NDTS$ simulated $MTR$ have a correlation coefficient of 0.85. Furthermore, the estimated coefficient for the tax variable that excludes the effect of $NDTS$ is of the same level of significance as the simulated $MTR$ used in the main regression (both variables are significant at $p$-value $< 0.001$). Taken together, these results confirm that traditional measures of $NDTS$ play a fairly minor role in determining the corporate marginal tax rate.

---

[7]Technically, $NOL$ carryforwards are nondebt tax shields. However, the definition of $NDTS$ used throughout the paper applies only to depreciation and $ITC$ to remain consistent with the previous literature. To save on computer resources, the analysis in this paragraph only examines firms on the Compustat Primary, Secondary, and Tertiary tape.

## 5.4. Significance of the estimated coefficients

A statistically significant relation between leverage decisions and tax status has been documented in the previous sections. But how important is tax status as a determinant of debt policy, relative to the explanatory power of other factors causing debt policy (i.e., relative to the control variables)? And how much extra explanatory power do the variables associated with the simulated $MTR$ add beyond that in other proxies for the marginal tax rate?

To answer these questions, first note that the adjusted $R^2$ from a regression using only the control variables and $ZPROB$ on the full sample is 4.36%. Although not particularly impressive, an $R^2$ of 4.36% is in line with results from many cross-sectional studies and/or first-difference specifications. Still, the number is lower than might be expected given the strong tax and other incentives associated with debt financing, probably due to a relatively noisy dependent variable. The question as to why we cannot explain more than 5% of the variation in debt policy is a future challenge for financial researchers. For the time being, any improvements in the adjusted $R^2$ from including various tax variables in the specification are relative to a fairly low starting point.

With this caveat in mind, and to answer the first question above, consider the ratio of the adjusted $R^2$ from the full regression (5.00%) to the adjusted $R^2$ from the control regression (see panel A of Table 4). This ratio implies that the tax variables add about 14.7% to the explanatory power of the debt policy equation $(0.147 = (0.0500/0.0436) - 1)$. The percentage of increased explanatory power is 16.3% when $MTR$ is replaced by $MTR_{NOL}$ and $MTR_{nonNOL}$. Considering a regression including just $MTR$ and $\tau_{stat} - MTR$, the simulated tax variables add 13.3% to the explanatory power of the debt policy equation. To the extent that the tax variables are correlated with other explanations of debt policy such as firm size (see Fig. 3), these estimates may represent lower bounds.

To answer the second question about the explanatory power of various proxies for tax status, consider the adjusted $R^2$ after replacing the simulated tax variables with the other tax proxies used in the finance literature: the $NOL$ dummy variable, the effective tax rate, and the interaction of the change in $NDTS$ with the probability of bankruptcy.[8] (The $NOL$ dummy variable is equal to one if the firm has a $NOL$ carryforward and equal to zero otherwise.) The enhanced explanatory power of these specifications are 7.6%, 0.0%, and 0.02%, respectively (see Table 4). (Using an alternative $NOL$ specification, perhaps better referred to as a non$NOL$ variable, equal to the highest statutory tax rate (0.46 prior to 1987, 0.395 in 1987, 0.34 after 1987) if the firm did not have $NOL$ carryforwards and zero otherwise, improves the adjusted $R^2$ to 0.0479, an

---

[8]Graham (1995) provides a detailed analysis of the relative merit of various proxies for the marginal tax rate.

Table 4
Significance of tax variables in explaining debt policy

Panel A shows the significance of tax variables relative to the explanatory power from using just the control variables (from Table 2) and the probability of bankruptcy as independent variables. Relative significance is measured by comparing the adjusted $R^2$ of the control regression to $R^2$s from regressions which include tax variables. For example, the adjusted $R^2$ of the control regression, using only the control variables and the probability of bankruptcy, is 0.0436. The adjusted $R^2$ of a regression which includes the tax variables which are related to the simulated $MTR$, in addition to the control variables and the probability of bankruptcy, is 0.0500. Thus, the tax variables related to the simulated $MTR$ offer an improvement of approximately 14.7% in the explanatory power of the of debt policy specification $(0.147 = (0.0500/0.0436) - 1)$. Also shown are the relative importance of alternative tax specifications.

Panel B shows the percentage increase in the dependent variable from the 'main regression' (i.e., the regression reported in the leftmost column of Table 2), and the analogous regression for 'intentional debt policy', for a hypothetical firm which moves from the average marginal tax rate (0.24) to the top marginal tax rate in the sample (0.46), all else equal.

*Panel A*

| Included tax variables | Adjusted $R^2$ | Added explanatory power |
|---|---|---|
| None[a] | 0.0436 | N.A. |
| $MTR$, $\sigma_{mtr}$, $\tau_{stat} - MTR$, $ADVDEBT$[b] | 0.0500 | 14.7% |
| $MTR_{NOL}$, $MTR_{nonNOL}$, $\sigma_{mtr}$, $\tau_{stat} - MTR$, $ADVDEBT$[c] | 0.0507 | 16.3% |
| $MTR$, $\tau_{stat} - MTR$[d] | 0.0494 | 13.3% |
| $NOL$ dummy variable[e] | 0.0469 | 7.6% |
| Effective tax rate[f] | 0.0436 | 0.0% |
| $NDTS * ZPROB$[g] | 0.0437 | 0.02% |

*Panel B*

| Shocked tax variable | Percentage change in the dependent variable: $\Delta DEBT$ | |
|---|---|---|
| | All observations | Intentional debt policy ($|\Delta DEBT| > 0.02$) |
| $MTR$ | 1.52% | 2.79% |

[a] This specification regresses the dependent variable, $\Delta DEBT$, on the control variables from Table 2 as well as $ZPROB$, where $ZPROB$ is the probability of bankruptcy, defined as total assets divided by the sum of 3.3 times earnings before interest and taxes plus sales plus 1.4 times retained earnings plus 1.2 times working capital.

[b] This specification regresses the dependent variable, $\Delta DEBT$, on the control variables from Table 2 as well as $ZPROB$, the lagged simulated marginal tax rate, the lagged difference between the statutory and simulated marginal tax rates, and the relative tax advantage of debt.

[c] This specification regresses the dependent variable, $\Delta DEBT$, on the control variables from Table 2 as well as $ZPROB$, a variable equal to the lagged simulated marginal tax rate for $NOL$ firms or zero for other firms, a variable equal to the lagged simulated marginal tax rate for non$NOL$ firms or zero for other firms, the lagged difference between the statutory and simulated marginal tax rates, and the relative tax advantage of debt.

[d] This specification regresses the dependent variable on the control variables as well as the probability of bankruptcy, the lagged simulated marginal tax rate, and the lagged difference between the statutory and simulated marginal tax rates.

*J.R. Graham/Journal of Financial Economics 41 (1996) 41–73* 71

improvement in predictive power of 9.9%.) Thus, in a relative sense, the *NOL* dummy variable explains roughly one-half of the variance in debt policy explained by the simulated tax variables, while the other tax measures explain virtually nothing. In conclusion, simulating tax rates appears to offer the most refined measure of corporate tax status, although the *NOL* dummy variable also provides a reasonable proxy. It is surprising, however, that taxes do not explain a larger portion of debt policy.

To gauge the economic significance of the estimated coefficient of 0.069 on $MTR_{t-1}$ reported in Table 2, consider the impact on leverage policy resulting from a movement from the average $MTR$ of 0.24 (see Table 1) to the maximum for this sample period (0.46). All else equal, a hypothetical firm with a tax rate of 46% would *annually* issue 1.52% more debt, measured as a percent of capital structure, than an identical firm with a tax rate of 24% $(0.0152 = 0.069(0.46-0.24)$; see panel B of Table 4). If the coefficient from the intentional debt policy equation is used (0.127), a 46% $MTR$ firm would annually issue 2.79% more debt than a 24% $MTR$ firm.

## 6. Conclusion

It is hard to imagine that the ability to deduct interest payments from taxable income does not contribute to the decision to issue corporate debt. This implies that tax status affects corporate debt policy, although much previous academic research fails to validate this hypothesis. This paper simulates marginal tax rates that are consistent with the federal tax code. These explicitly calculated marginal tax rates are used to empirically document a positive relation between tax status and incremental debt policy. This result is consistent with a growing body of research (MacKie-Mason, 1990; Scholes, Wilson, and Wolfson, 1990; Givoly, Hahn, Ofer, and Sarig, 1992) that finds that tax status affects corporate decision-making. Two common themes running through this research are the use of incremental financing and/or an appropriately specified measure of tax status.

The tax-code-consistent marginal tax rates calculated in this paper indicate that there is substantial variation in marginal tax rates across time and across

Table 4 (continued)

---

[e]This specification regresses the dependent variable $\Delta DEBT$ on the control variables as well as the probability of bankruptcy and a dummy variable equal to one if the firm has *NOL* carryforwards and zero otherwise.

[f]This specification regresses the dependent variable on the control variables plus the probability of bankruptcy and the lagged effective tax rate (taxes paid divided by taxable income).

[g]This specification regresses the dependent variable on the control variables plus the probability of bankruptcy and the lag of *NDTS* times the probability of bankruptcy.

firms. There is also variation for subsets of the data which include just large (small) firms, as well as for firms with (without) *NOL* carryforwards. With respect to *NOL* status, firms do not appear to be as responsive to the tax incentives associated with debt when they have *NOL* carryforwards, relative to when they do not. This suggests that expected bankruptcy costs are relatively high when a firm is in the *NOL* state, dampening the intensity of debt usage.

The results suggest that a net operating loss dummy variable is a reasonable tax status proxy. However, the *NOL* dummy variable only accounts for approximately one-half of the explanatory power of the simulated tax variables. Simulating marginal tax rates provides a finer partition of tax status than simply conditioning on whether a company has a net operating loss carryforward.

Finally, the following two questions pose future challenges to financial researchers: 1) given the large number of theories available to explain the use of debt, why is our ability to empirically explain debt policy not much better than it is, and 2) given the strong tax incentives associated with debt issuance, why do taxes not explain a larger portion of debt policy than that documented here?

## References

Altman, Edward, 1968, Financial ratios, discriminant analysis, and the prediction of corporate bankruptcy, Journal of Finance 23, 589–609.

Altshuler, Rosanne and Alan Auerbach, 1990, The significance of tax law asymmetries: An empirical investigation, Quarterly Journal of Economics CV, 61–86.

Auerbach, Alan, 1985, Real determinants of corporate leverage, in: B.M. Friedman, ed., Corporate capital structures in the United States (University of Chicago Press, Chicago, IL).

Bradley, Michael, Gregg A. Jarrell, and E. Han Kim, 1984, On the existence of an optimal capital structure, Journal of Finance 39, 857–878.

Courdes, Joseph and Steven Sheffrin, 1983, Estimating the tax advantage of corporate debt, Journal of Finance 38, 95–105.

DeAngelo, Harry and Ronald Masulis, 1980, Optimal capital structure under corporate and personal taxation, Journal of Financial Economics 8, 3–29.

Fisher, Edwin, Robert Heinkel, and Josef Zechner, 1989, Dynamic capital structure choice: Theory and tests, Journal of Finance 44, 19–40.

Gaver, Jennifer and Kenneth Gaver, 1993, Additional evidence on the association between the investment opportunity set and corporate financing, dividend and compensation policies, Journal of Accounting and Economics 16, 125–160.

Givoly, D., C. Hahn, A. Ofer, and O. Sarig, 1992, Taxes and capital structure: Evidence from firms' response to the tax reform act of 1986, Review of Financial Studies 5, 331–355.

Graham, John, 1995, Proxies for the marginal tax rate, Working paper (University of Utah, Salt Lake City, UT).

Graham, John, Michael Lemmon, and James Schallheim, 1995, An empirical investigation of debt, leases, and taxes, Working paper (University of Utah, Salt Lake City, UT).

Kale, Jayant, Thomas Noe, and Gabriel Ramirez, 1991, The effect of business risk on corporate capital structure: Theory and evidence, Journal of Finance 16, 1693–1715.

MacKie-Mason, Jeffrey, 1990, Do taxes affect corporate financing decisions?, Journal of Finance 45, 1471–1493.

Manzon, Gil, 1992, Earning management of firms subject to the alternative minimum tax, Journal of the American Taxation Association 14, 88–111.

Miller, Merton, 1977, Debt and taxes, Journal of Finance 32, 261–275.

Myers, Stewart, 1984, The capital structure puzzle, Journal of Finance 39, 572–592.

Omer, Thomas, Karen Molloy, and David Ziebart, 1993, An investigation of the firm size-effective tax rate relation in the 1980s, Journal of Accounting, Auditing and Finance 8, 167–182.

Scholes, Myron, G. Peter Wilson, and Mark Wolfson, 1990, Tax planning, regulatory capital planning, and financial reporting strategy for commercial banks, Review of Financial Studies 3, 625–650.

Scholes, Myron and Mark Wolfson, 1992, Taxes and business strategy: A planning approach (Prentice-Hall, Englewood Cliffs, NJ).

Shevlin, Terry, 1990, Estimating corporate marginal tax rates with asymmetric tax treatment of gains and losses, Journal of the American Taxation Association 12, 51–67.

Smith, Clifford and Ross Watts, 1992, The investment opportunity set and corporate financing, dividend and compensation policies, Journal of Financial Economics 32, 263–292.

Titman, Sheridan, 1984, The effect of capital structure on a firm's liquidation decision, Journal of Financial Economics 13, 137–151.

Titman, Sheriden and Roberto Wessels, 1988, The determinants of capital structure choice, Journal of Finance 43, 1–19.

White, Halbert, 1980, A heteroskedastic consistent covariance matrix and a direct test for heteroskedasticity, Econometrica 48, 817–838.

Zimmerman, Jerold, 1983, Taxes and firm size, Journal of Accounting and Economics 5, 119–149.

# [3]

THE JOURNAL OF FINANCE • VOL LIII, NO. 1 • FEBRUARY 1998

# Debt, Leases, Taxes, and the Endogeneity of Corporate Tax Status

JOHN R. GRAHAM, MICHAEL L. LEMMON,
and JAMES S. SCHALLHEIM*

## ABSTRACT

We provide evidence that corporate tax status is endogenous to financing decisions, which induces a spurious relation between measures of financial policy and many commonly used tax proxies. Using a forward-looking estimate of *before-financing* corporate marginal tax rates, we document a negative relation between operating leases and tax rates, and a positive relation between debt *levels* and tax rates. This is the first unambiguous evidence supporting the hypothesis that low tax rate firms lease more, and have lower debt levels, than high tax rate firms.

MANY THEORIES OF CAPITAL STRUCTURE imply that, all else equal, the incentive to use debt financing increases with a firm's marginal tax rate due to the tax deductibility of interest expense (e.g., Modigliani and Miller (1963), DeAngelo and Masulis (1980)). Conversely, leasing models generally predict that firms with low marginal tax rates employ relatively more leases than do firms with high marginal tax rates. The logic behind the leasing prediction is that leases allow for the transfer of tax shields from firms that cannot fully utilize the associated tax deduction (lessees) to firms that can (lessors) (e.g., Myers, Dill, and Bautista (1976), Smith and Wakeman (1985), Ross, Westerfield, and Jaffe (1996)).

Despite these straightforward predictions, empirically testing for tax effects is difficult because a spurious relation exists between the financing decision and many commonly used tax proxies. Specifically, both interest expense and lease payments are tax deductible. Thus, a firm that finances its operations with debt or leases reduces its taxable income, potentially lowering its expected marginal tax rate. If not properly addressed, this endogeneity of the tax rate can bias an experiment in favor of finding a negative

*Graham is from the Fuqua School of Business, Duke University, Schallheim is from the David Eccles School of Business, The University of Utah, and Lemmon is from the College of Business, Arizona State University. We thank Jennifer Babcock, Hank Bessembinder, Charles Cuny, Eugene Fama, Avner Kalay, Uri Loewenstein, Stewart Myers, Mitch Petersen, Steven Sharpe, Terry Shevlin, Alex Triantis, and seminar participants from the 1997 American Finance Association conference, the Arizona Finance Symposium, the National Bureau of Economic Research, Duke, Penn State, Vanderbilt, and the Universities of Maryland, Utah, and Virginia for helpful comments. We also thank René Stulz (the editor) and an anonymous referee for detailed suggestions. All errors are our own. The simulated tax rates used in this paper (or an updated version thereof) can be found in a file on Graham's home page, http://www.duke.edu/~jgraham, or on the *Journal of Finance* home page.

relation between leasing and taxes and against finding a positive relation between debt and taxes. We document that the endogeneity of the marginal tax rate is a very real problem that may confound the interpretation of tax-related effects in previous studies.

In this paper, we construct a direct measure of the corporate marginal tax rate (based on taxable income *before-financing*) that is not endogenously affected by financing decisions.[1] Using an experiment designed to correct for many of the confounding influences in previous studies, we document evidence consistent with the tax effects predicted by theories of debt and lease financing.

We believe that our leasing result is the first definitive evidence supporting the hypothesis that, all else being equal, low tax rate firms lease more than high tax rate firms. Indeed, most empirical work fails to find a negative correlation between leasing and the tax rate (e.g., Flath (1980), Ang and Peterson (1984), and Krishnan and Moyer (1994)), although some recent research does find a negative relation. Among the recent work, Barclay and Smith (1995) and Sharpe and Nguyen (1995) show that the level of leasing is positively correlated with a tax-loss carryforward dummy variable, where the existence of tax losses implies a low marginal tax rate.[2] We argue that their tax findings are difficult to interpret because they are largely based on the relation between taxes and capital leases, which are not necessarily classified as *true* (tax-advantaged) leases by tax authorities. Instead, capital leases are likely a mixture of *true* leases and *nontrue* leases (the latter are sometimes referred to as conditional-sales contracts and are treated as debt by the IRS). On the one hand, the findings by Barclay and Smith and Sharpe and Nguyen show a positive relation between the use of capital leases and tax-loss carryforwards, which seems to support the expected negative relation between leases and tax rates. On the other hand, their tax results may be spuriously caused by the endogeneity of corporate tax status because using leases or debt can lower a firm's observed tax rate.

In this study, we focus on operating leases, which are likely to be classified as *true* tax-advantaged leases by the IRS, in addition to using the before-financing measure of corporate tax status mentioned above. As predicted by the theory, we document a negative relation between a firm's use of operating leases and its marginal tax rate. We find little relation between a firm's use of capital leases and its tax status, which we interpret as evidence that

---

[1] In the terminology of Scholes, Wilson, and Wolfson (1990), our tax variable is a "but for financing" (or *before-financing*) marginal tax rate. It measures a firm's marginal tax rate net of all financing decisions. Our tax variable accounts for the endogeneity problem and also incorporates many features present in the tax code, such as tax-loss carryforwards and carrybacks, the investment tax credit, and the alternative minimum tax.

[2] The Barclay and Smith and Sharpe and Nguyen papers do not focus on tax issues but do include proxies for the marginal tax rate in their analysis. Instead, they focus on the priority structure of corporate liabilities and contracting cost incentives to lease, respectively. Sharpe and Nguyen examine both operating and capital leases. A recent paper by O'Malley (1996) finds that tax-exhausted firms, and similarly firms with substantial net operating losses, use leases to finance a relatively large share of their incremental investments.

capital leases are indeed a mixture of true and nontrue leases.[3] At the same time, we document another important empirical regularity, namely a positive relation between debt levels and the before-financing measure of the marginal tax rate.

The implications of our result confirming the positive relation between debt levels and taxes are twofold. First, we believe this is the first unambiguous evidence linking high debt *levels* with high tax rate firms. As such, it reconciles the tax findings found in studies of incremental debt policy with those from studies using debt levels, and provides important insight into what Myers (1984) calls "the capital structure puzzle." Many previous studies examining the correlation between debt levels (e.g., the ratio of long-term debt to firm value) and tax rates do not find a positive relation, possibly due to the endogeneity problem described above (e.g., see Titman and Wessels (1988), and Gaver and Gaver (1993)). Studies that do find a positive relation between debt usage and tax rates (such as MacKie-Mason (1990), Givoly et al. (1992), Rajan and Zingales (1995), and Graham (1996a)) examine *incremental* debt policy, thereby avoiding the spurious negative relation induced by the endogeneity of corporate tax status. Given the predictable tax effects documented in studies of incremental financing, the puzzle has remained as to why similar tax effects have not been found using cumulative measures of leverage such as debt *levels*. By using our before-financing tax measure, we avoid the endogeneity problem and document a positive relation between debt levels and tax rates.

The second contribution of documenting a positive correlation between levels of debt and tax rates is related to the leasing analysis. We are unable to directly investigate the effect of taxes on nontrue leases because they do not appear separately on corporate financial statements. However, because nontrue leases receive the same tax-treatment as debt contracts, the relation between nontrue leases and taxes should be identical to the relation between debt and taxes. At the same time, the effect of taxes on the use of true leases should be opposite that for debt. Our debt results thus provide a proper benchmark for evaluating the tax effects associated with leasing.

The organization of the remainder of the paper is as follows. Section I reviews the predicted relations between explanatory variables and financing policy. Section II describes data and measurement issues. Section III presents the empirical results, which include evidence that personal taxes affect corporate financing decisions. Section IV concludes with a brief summary and suggestions for future research.

## I. Determinants of Leasing and Debt Policies

In this section we describe how tax and nontax incentives affect a firm's choice between debt and lease financing.

---

[3] Unfortunately, it is not possible to disaggregate a firm's capital leases into *true* and *nontrue* leases using publicly available financial statements.

## A. Tax Incentives

Leasing is a financial transaction that separates the costs and benefits of ownership from the costs and benefits of asset use. In the presence of taxes, the ability to transfer ownership rights can create value for both parties in a leasing contract. Specifically, conventional wisdom holds that the leasing activity of a firm should be inversely related to its tax rate because leasing allows low tax rate firms to sell tax shields to high tax rate lessors, who value the tax benefits more highly. A portion of the savings generated from the sale of tax shields can be passed along to the lessee in the form of lower lease payments.[4]

In practice, the ability to transfer tax benefits is limited by tax authorities. The IRS classifies leases as *true* leases (tax transfers allowed) or *conditional-sales contracts* (hereafter *nontrue* leases: tax transfers not allowed). Unfortunately, the IRS classifications are not publicly available. In public financial statements, leases are classified as capital leases (on the balance sheet) or operating leases (off the balance sheet, but disclosed in footnotes). In many cases, the criteria that define a capital lease do *not* qualify the lease as a true lease under IRS law (the Appendix contains the criteria that define capital leases according to generally accepted accounting principles and the guidelines for tax qualification).[5] However, there are exceptions because it is common practice for a firm to maintain financial statements separate from tax reporting records. Therefore, a capital lease can qualify as a true lease if different assumptions are used in financial versus tax accounting; e.g., it is fairly easy to make different assumptions about the economic life of the asset, discount rate, residual value, and residual value guarantees (see Schallheim (1994)). Thus, capital leases are likely comprised of both true and nontrue leases. The tax and accounting guidelines suggest that operating leases are predominantly *true* leases.

### A.1. Tax Incentives to Use True Leases

True leases allow the transfer of tax benefits from lessees to lessors. The lessor supplies the initial capital to purchase the asset and then rents the asset to the lessee. Models by Miller and Upton (1976) and Lewellen, Long, and McConnell (1976) show that, in a competitive leasing market, lease payments must be structured to compensate the lessor for the opportunity cost of capital plus the loss of value due to economic depreciation. This implies that the equilibrium single-period lease payment at time $t$ can be expressed as

---

[4] This tax motivation for leasing is the basis for the examples presented in most corporate finance texts (e.g., see Brealey and Myers (1991) and Ross, Westerfield, and Jaffe (1996)). Myers, Dill, and Bautista (1976) and Lewis and Schallheim (1992) also provide models motivating the tax incentive to lease.

[5] Following FASB 13 guidelines, capital lease payments are divided into interest expense and capital lease amortization. The interest expense from capital leases is usually included as part of total interest expense in financial statements. For example, in COMPUSTAT the interest expense from capital leases is included as "interest capitalized" in annual data item 15 (interest expense), and the amortization is included in data item 14 (depreciation and amortization).

$$L_t = [E(r) + E(d)]A_t, \tag{1}$$

where $A_t$ is the cost of the asset at time $t$, $E(r)$ is the expected rate of return on capital, and $E(d)$ captures the expected rate of economic depreciation. The expression for the lease payment can be further expanded to include any additional capital flows provided by, or tax subsidies provided to, the lessor (e.g., maintenance expenditures, investment tax credits, or accelerated depreciation).

Given the schedule of lease payments, Smith and Wakeman (1985) summarize the present value difference in the total tax bill between purchasing and leasing as

$$(T_0 - T_b)[(\text{Dep} + \text{Debt} + \text{Maint}) - (\text{Lease} + \text{Gain})], \tag{2}$$

where $T_0$ is the tax rate of the owner/lessor, $T_b$ is the tax rate of the user/lessee, Dep is the present value of depreciation, Debt is the present value of the interest tax shields associated with borrowing to purchase the asset, Maint is the present value of expected maintenance costs if these expenses are covered by the lease, Lease is the present value of the lease payments, and Gain is the present value of the taxable capital gain from the eventual sale of the asset. Leasing by low tax rate firms ($T_b < T_0$) will produce net tax benefits when the present value of depreciation, interest expense, and maintenance costs exceeds the present value of lease payments and the capital gains from the eventual sale of the asset. Leasing by the low tax rate firm is favored when (i) the depreciation tax shield is received early in the lease term, (ii) the taxable gain on the sale of the asset is relatively small, (iii) larger lease payments occur later in the lease term, or (iv) the before-tax discount rate is high. Although it is possible to devise situations in which the high tax rate firm is the lessee, the conditions are atypical, such as a lease with large payments early in the term and depreciation tax shields occurring later in the term. In general, the tax guidelines for leasing (see the Appendix) and the use of accelerated depreciation schedules tend to favor conditions under which the low tax rate firm is the lessee.

### A.2. Tax Incentives to Use Nontrue Leases or Debt

Tax-based theories of optimal capital structure predict a positive relation between the use of debt financing and the corporate marginal tax rate (e.g., Modigliani and Miller (1963), DeAngelo and Masulis (1980)). This well-known association follows directly from the fact that U.S. tax law favors debt through the tax deductibility of interest payments. Because nontrue leases do not allow the transfer of tax benefits, their tax treatment is identical to that for debt. Thus, we predict that the use of nontrue leases is positively related to a firm's tax rate. It is not possible to directly test for the effect of taxes on the use of nontrue leases because nontrue leases are not publicly available as a separate data item (they are included in the capital

### Table I
### Sign of the Predicted Tax Effects for Leasing
### Based on Accounting and IRS Classifications

True leases allow for the transfer of tax shields from firms that cannot fully utilize the associated tax deduction to firms that can; thus, the use of true leases is expected to be negatively related to a firm's tax rate. Nontrue leases do not allow for the transfer of tax shields because they are treated as debt by the IRS, and therefore their use is expected to be positively related to a firm's tax rate. As indicated by the classification rules in the Appendix, leases that have an accounting classification of operating leases are likely to be recognized as true leases by the IRS; thus, the use of operating leases is expected to be negatively related to a firm's tax rate. Capital leases are likely a mixture of true and nontrue leases, and hence the relation of their use to a firm's tax rate is ambiguous.

|  | IRS Classification | | Accounting Classification | |
|---|---|---|---|---|
|  | True Leases | Nontrue Leases | Operating Leases | Capital Leases |
| Relation to marginal tax rate | − | + | − | ? |

lease category). Instead, we use the estimated relation between taxes and debt as a benchmark for evaluating the effect of taxes on leasing behavior.

### A.3. Summary of the Tax Incentives to Lease

Based on IRS classifications, the use of true leases should be negatively related to the firm's tax rate, and the use of nontrue leases, which are treated like debt, should be positively related. Unfortunately, the IRS classifications are not publicly available and hence we cannot directly estimate the relation between taxes and nontrue leases. Instead, we observe public financial statements that categorize leases as operating or capital leases. Operating leases should be predominantly true leases and hence we expect their use to be negatively related to the firm's tax rate. The expected relation between capital leases and taxes is ambiguous because capital leases are likely a mix of true and nontrue leases. The predicted relations between leasing intensity and the marginal tax rate, based on the accounting and IRS classifications, are summarized in Table I.

### B. Financial Distress

A leasing contract represents a commitment to make a series of fixed payments over the life of the lease. Relative to debt, leasing contracts have high priority in bankruptcy (Krishnan and Moyer (1994), Barclay and Smith (1995)). Within bankruptcy, if the lease is affirmed by the court then the lessee is required to continue to make scheduled lease payments to the lessor, giving the lease priority on par with administrative expenses. In contrast, bankruptcy proceedings grant the debtor a stay on the payment of most other financial claims, including those of secured debtholders, until the bank-

*Empirical Corporate Finance III*

ruptcy is resolved. Thus, a firm with a high probability of entering financial distress is likely to be able to ex ante arrange lease financing on more favorable terms than other forms of financing, such as issuing bonds. Therefore, firms likely to enter distress will have a greater proportion of deductible financing costs arising from leases, which we expect to detect as a positive relation between leasing and ex ante measures of financial distress. With respect to debt policy, the trade-off theory of capital structure suggests that firms will ex ante balance the tax benefits of debt against the expected costs of financial distress. This implies that, ceteris paribus, firms with higher ex ante expected costs of financial distress should use less debt.

Ex post, the occurrence of financial distress can potentially obscure the empirical relation between financial policy and taxes. As an illustration of how this might occur, consider a firm that was financially healthy when it issued debt, but that, due to exogenous factors, is presently experiencing financial distress. Because of the decline in equity value associated with distress, this firm will currently have a high observed debt ratio, as well as a low expected marginal tax rate (because of the loss carryback and carryforward provisions in the tax code). A similar argument applies to lease financing. Thus, we predict that distressed firms are likely to display an ex post positive relation between financial distress and measures of debt and leasing, thereby confounding our ability to detect tax effects. It is therefore important to control for ex post financial distress.

## C. Contracting Costs

### C.1. The Investment Opportunity Set

Myers (1977) argues that shareholders of a firm with risky fixed claims in its capital structure will potentially forgo positive NPV investments if project benefits accrue to the firm's existing bondholders. Myers suggests that the incentive to underinvest (resulting from the conflict between bondholders and stockholders) can be mitigated by reducing the amount of debt in the firm's capital structure, by including restrictive covenants in the debt contracts, or by shortening the maturity of the firm's debt obligations. Stulz and Johnson (1985) further suggest that these incentive problems can be reduced if the firm retains the ability to finance new investments with high priority claims, such as secured debt and leases.[6] These arguments suggest that firms with more growth options in their investment opportunity sets should have a lower proportion of fixed claims in their capital structure.

In their analysis of leasing, Sharpe and Nguyen (1995) suggest that leasing may economize on transaction costs for firms facing a high cost of external funds. They use several proxies to measure the severity of financial constraints facing the firm and find that, for the most part, these variables

---

[6] The asset substitution problem (e.g., Jensen and Meckling (1976)) suggests that the presence of debt may provide incentives to transfer wealth from bondholders to shareholders by increasing the risk of the firm's projects. Secured debt and lease financing can alleviate the asset substitution problem.

are related to leasing intensity in the manner predicted. We contrast their results and ours in Section III.

## C.2. Collateral

The leasing contract, by definition, is tied to a specific fixed asset. Therefore, all else equal, firms that use more fixed assets in the production process should use more lease financing. We also expect to find a positive relation between the use of fixed assets and debt usage because, relative to intangible assets, fixed assets are more valuable in liquidation and hence support a higher debt capacity.

## C.3. Regulation

Leasing can be disadvantageous for regulated firms. The return for utility shareholders is calculated from the firm's capital base. Operating leases do not count as part of the capital base. Capital leases may or may not "count" as part of the capital base depending on the application of accounting rules by state regulators or rate commissions. Debt does not have this problem; it always counts as part of the capital base. Therefore, we expect regulated firms to use less leasing and more debt.

Smith (1986) suggests that greater debt also prohibits regulators from transferring wealth from investors to customers. Alternatively, causation can run in the reverse direction, with regulated industries having more stable cash flows and, therefore, a lower probability of financial distress and commensurately more debt in their capital structure. Regardless of the direction of causality, we expect a positive correlation between debt and degree of regulation.

## C.4. Firm Size

Size-based theories suggest that large firms are more likely to be debt financed than their smaller counterparts. This may be true because large companies are more diversified and, thus, have more stable cash flows. Additionally, large firms may be able to exploit economies of scale in issuing securities. Because of information asymmetries, smaller firms also are likely to face higher costs for obtaining external funds. Sharpe and Nguyen (1995) suggest that leases mitigate these information problems and provide lower financing costs. Thus, lease usage should be inversely related to firm size.

## II. Data and Measurement Issues

### A. Measuring Debt and Leasing Policies

Our data consist of all COMPUSTAT firms with SIC codes between 2000 and 5999 and cover the years 1981 through 1992. The full sample has 18,193 firm-year observations. To gauge debt policy we use the ratio of the book

**Table II**
## Percentage of Firm-Years with Debt or Leases
## in Their Capital Structure

The sample consists of 18,193 firm-year observations for firms on COMPUSTAT with SIC codes between 2000 and 5999 over the period 1981 through 1992.

| Long-Term Debt | Capital Leases | Operating Leases |
|---|---|---|
| 88.1% | 52.6% | 99.9% |

value of total long-term debt net of capital leases to the market value of the firm, where the market value of the firm is the book value of total assets minus the book value of equity plus the market value of equity plus the present value of operating leases.[7] Firm value thus includes the effect of operating leases, which are not reported on the balance sheet. The use of capital leases is recorded as the ratio of capital leases reported on the balance sheet to the market value of the firm. The use of operating leases is measured as the ratio of the present value of current-year rental expense plus rental commitments over the next five years (discounted at 10 percent) to the market value of the firm. Because this operating lease variable could be biased if different firms have different costs of lease capital, we also examine an alternative variable in which lease payments are discounted using the firm's average short-term borrowing rate as reported in COMPUSTAT. The short-term borrowing rate has many missing observations and reduces the sample size to 11,637 observations.[8] However, the use of this alternative measure (not reported) does not change the qualitative nature of our results. Because lease payments, like debt, represent a fixed payment obligation, it is also useful to examine the division of the firm's total fixed claims among debt and leases. To do so, we calculate the usage of debt and leases as a fraction of the firm's total fixed claims, where total fixed claims are defined as the book value of long-term debt plus the book value of capital leases plus the present value of operating leases.

Table II reports the fraction of observations for which each of the three financial instruments is employed. It is interesting that although only 53 percent of the firm-years report nonzero levels of capital leases, 88 percent have nonzero levels of long-term debt, and nearly all indicate usage of operating leases. The high incidence of operating leases reflects the fact that most firms lease at least some items, such as office equipment or automobiles. Panel A of Table III reports summary statistics for the financing variables. Long-term debt accounts for 14.2 percent of firm value on average;

---

[7] Similarly, the book value of the firm is measured by the book value of total assets plus the present value of operating leases.

[8] The average short-term borrowing rate for the sample is 9.6 percent, which is close to our choice of 10 percent for the discount rate.

### Table III
## Summary Statistics for Variables Associated
## with Debt and Leasing Policy

The sample consists of 18,193 observations for firms on COMPUSTAT with SIC codes between 2000 and 5999 over the period 1981 through 1992. Debt is the book value of total long-term debt net of capital leases. Capital leases are the book value of capital leases. Operating leases are current rental expense plus the present value of operating lease commitments for the next five years discounted at 10 percent. The market value deflator is defined as the book value of total assets minus the book value of equity plus the market value of equity plus the present value of operating leases. The fixed claim deflator is defined as the book value of long-term debt plus the book value of capital leases plus the present value of operating leases. The before-financing marginal tax rate is simulated based on income after depreciation but before interest expenses are deducted. ECOST is the standard deviation of the first difference in the firm's earnings before depreciation, interest, and taxes divided by the mean level of the book value of total assets multiplied by the sum of research and development and advertising expenses divided by assets. Z-Score is a modified version of Altman's (1968) Z-Score. OENEG is a dummy variable equal to one if the book value of common equity is negative. Market-to-book is the market value of the firm divided by the book value of the firm, where the book value of the firm is total assets plus the present value of operating leases. Collateral is equal to net property, plant, and equipment divided by the book value of total assets. Telephone dummy is equal to one if the firm is in the telecommunications industry through 1982 (SIC codes 4812 and 4813). Utilities dummy is equal to one if the firm is a gas or electric utility (SIC codes 4900–4939). Size is the natural log of the market value of the firm.

| Panel A: Summary Statistics for Financial Policy Variables | | | | |
|---|---|---|---|---|
| Variable | Mean | Std. Dev. | Min. | Max. |
| Debt-to-value | 0.142 | 0.134 | 0.00 | 0.84 |
| Capital leases-to-value | 0.016 | 0.037 | 0.00 | 0.54 |
| Operating leases-to-value | 0.080 | 0.086 | 0.00 | 0.74 |
| Debt-to-fixed claims | 0.524 | 0.316 | 0.00 | 1.00 |
| Capital leases-to-fixed claims | 0.063 | 0.123 | 0.00 | 1.00 |
| Operating leases-to-fixed claims | 0.412 | 0.308 | 0.00 | 1.00 |

| Panel B: Summary Statistics for Explanatory Variables | | | | |
|---|---|---|---|---|
| Variable | Mean | Std. Dev. | Min. | Max. |
| Corporate Tax Rate Variable | | | | |
| Before-financing marginal tax rate | 0.331 | 0.143 | 0.00 | 0.46 |
| Financial Distress Variables | | | | |
| ECOST | 0.008 | 0.089 | 0.00 | 11.10 |
| Z-score | 2.049 | 3.344 | −202.14 | 150.30 |
| OENEG | 0.047 | 0.212 | 0.00 | 1.00 |
| Contracting Costs Variables | | | | |
| Market-to-book | 1.444 | 1.251 | 0.19 | 67.32 |
| Collateral | 0.313 | 0.187 | 0.00 | 0.96 |
| Telephone dummy | 0.001 | 0.037 | 0.00 | 1.00 |
| Utilities dummy | 0.005 | 0.071 | 0.00 | 1.00 |
| Size (log of firm value) | 5.059 | 2.034 | −1.38 | 11.78 |

capital and operating leases account for 1.6 percent and 8.0 percent of firm value, respectively. In the division of fixed claims among debt and leases, long-term debt represents 52.4 percent of total fixed claims on average; capital and operating leases account for 6.3 percent and 41.2 percent of fixed claims, respectively. On average, operating leases are a much more important part of firms' capital structures than are capital leases. This conclusion is further supported by noting that the mean dollar value of operating (capital) leases is $627,000 ($250,000) for the lowest operating-lease quintile of firms and $287,000,000 ($60,500,000) for the highest quintile. For ease of exposition our subsequent analysis focuses on the use of debt and leases as a fraction of firm value; however, in Section III we also discuss results for the division of fixed claims.

In the remainder of this section, we describe the variables we use to explain financing policy. The variable definitions and summary statistics for these variables are presented in Panel B of Table III.

## B. Measuring the Corporate Marginal Tax Rate

As important as the marginal tax rate is to theories of financing policy, the task of constructing a tax variable is nontrivial because of the complexity of the tax code and the fact that corporate tax status is endogenous.

### B.1. Endogeneity of Corporate Tax Status

Most empirical studies of capital structure regress some measure of a firm's debt (or leasing) ratio on several control variables, including a proxy for the firm's marginal tax rate. Unfortunately, many of the tax proxies used in the extant literature bias the experiment against finding the anticipated positive relation between the debt level and the corporate marginal tax rate (and in favor of finding the anticipated negative relation between leasing and taxes). One problem is that a firm's current debt and leasing positions are the cumulative result of many past financial decisions. Because most measures of tax status are affected by earlier financing decisions, these measures can induce a spurious relation between the measured debt or leasing position and the tax proxy. To see this, consider two firms with identical distributions of future cash flows, both of which are, prior to financing, in the highest marginal tax bracket. Suppose that one of the firms increases its debt level to the extent that, because of interest deductibility, its expected marginal tax rate declines; the reduction in the tax rate may occur because the firm moves to a lower tax bracket or because it is more likely to obtain a refund of taxes paid today (because it is more likely to experience a loss in the future).[9] In this case, the firm with a large amount of debt is associated with a low observed marginal tax rate, while the

[9] This is not a "general equilibrium" example in that we do not explain why two identical firms pursue different debt policies. The example is intended simply to clarify the endogeneity problem.

142                          *The Journal of Finance*

firm with no debt has a high marginal tax rate. A regression across these two firms of debt levels on a measure of the ex post marginal tax rate will produce a negative coefficient, opposite to the sign predicted by theory. We provide empirical evidence in Section III that is consistent with this description of the endogeneity problem.

### B.2. Avoiding the Endogeneity Problem by Using Before-Financing Tax Rates

To avoid the problems that can be caused by the endogeneity of corporate tax status, the tax rate needs to be, in the words of Scholes, Wilson, and Wolfson (1992), "but-for financing" decisions. In addition, recent research indicates that tax status can be measured more precisely with a measure of the marginal tax rate that is both backward- and forward-looking (Shevlin (1987, 1990), Graham (1996a, 1996b)). We address both these concerns by using a version of Graham's simulated marginal tax rate.

Briefly, the simulated tax rate is calculated by assuming that taxable income follows a random walk with drift and forecasting a firm's taxable income eighteen years into the future (which makes the variable forward-looking in that it accounts for a fifteen-year net operating loss (NOL) carryforward period and an additional three years in which NOL and investment tax credit carrybacks can affect the tax bill in year $t + 15$). The present value of the total tax bill is then calculated from year $t - 3$ to year $t + 18$, with Moody's corporate bond yield used as the economy-wide discount rate. Next, the present value of the total tax bill is recalculated after adding one dollar to taxable income in year $t$. The difference between these two total tax bills represents an estimate of expected marginal taxes owed on an extra dollar of income or, in other words, the marginal tax rate. A total of 50 simulations (based on 50 separate forecasts of taxable income) are performed for each firm in each year, with the average across the simulations taken to represent the expected marginal tax rate for firm $i$ in year $t$. The simulation procedure accounts for net operating loss carryforwards and carrybacks, the investment tax credit, and the alternative minimum tax.[10] In additional research on this topic, Graham (1996b) demonstrates that the simulated tax rate is a better proxy for the marginal tax rate than other variables that have been used in previous studies, such as a tax-loss carryforward dummy variable.

We adopt Graham's simulated tax rate, but modify the variable to account for the fact that we use cumulative measures of financial policy (i.e., levels of debt and leasing). In his study of incremental financing, Graham's (1996a) measure is "but-for" because he uses the lagged marginal tax rate (based on pretax income, *after* deductions for depreciation, interest and leasing expenses) to ex-

---

[10] The effects of net operating losses on the firm's marginal tax rate can be significant. For example, if a firm currently has NOL carryforwards that are expected to shield taxable income for five years (and ignoring alternative minimum tax considerations) earning an extra dollar of income today leads to an expected marginal rate of 21.7 percent, assuming a discount rate of 10 percent ($0.217 = 0.35/1.1^5$).

amine current-period debt policy.[11] Therefore, his tax rate is measured before the effect of the *current year's* financing decisions. In our study (and in many other capital structure papers), we examine cumulative financial policy, and therefore our before-financing tax variable must be measured before the effects of *aggregate* financing decisions. In particular, we examine the marginal tax rate that the firm faces after making the investment decision, but prior to making the lease versus purchase decision. To calculate our measure of before-financing tax status we begin with the firm's operating income after depreciation (including the depreciation component of the lease payment—see below), but *before* interest expenses are deducted. Thus, our tax rate reflects the firm's anticipated nondebt tax-shields, but not the additional tax-shields associated with the aggregate financing decision.

It is straightforward to determine taxable income before debt and capital lease financing by simply adding back interest expense to earnings before taxes. However, operating leases are represented in financial statements (and in COMPUSTAT) as "rental expense," a figure that aggregates the lessor's required rate of return on capital (analogous to interest expense had the asset been purchased) and the economic rate of asset depreciation.[12] Thus, there is no explicit accounting for the interest component of operating lease payments available to "add back" to earnings before taxes to determine income "but-for operating leases." Instead, using the relation from the leasing model of Miller and Upton (1976) from equation (1), we estimate the proportion of the lease payment attributable to the return on capital versus that for asset depreciation.

Assuming that economic depreciation is equal to depreciation for tax purposes, the dollar value of depreciation expense, $D_t$, is equal to $E(d)A_t$, where $A_t$ is the cost of the asset and $E(d)$ is the expected rate of economic depreciation; therefore, the proportion of the lease payment attributable to depreciation is given by $D_t/L_t = 1/(E(r)/E(d) + 1)$. Assuming that the rate of depreciation is $E(d) = 20$ percent and that the cost of capital is $E(r) = 10$ percent, the proportion of the lease payment attributable to depreciation is two-thirds, implying that the remaining one-third is analogous to interest expense.[13] Thus, for firms with operating leases, we add back one-third of

---

[11] Plesko (1994) uses a but-for measure appropriate for examining incremental decisions. In his study of research and development limited partnerships, Shevlin (1987) uses the converse of the but-for approach. Shevlin examines the tax status of firms that funded research and development expenses via partnerships "as-if" they instead had used debt financing, and compares these firms to others that actually used debt financing.

[12] We thank Steven Sharpe for bringing this point to our attention.

[13] Schallheim et al. (1987) document that the average lease term is five years, which implies an average annual depreciation rate of approximately 20 percent, assuming straight line depreciation. The average short term borrowing rate for the firms in our sample is approximately 10 percent as reported in COMPUSTAT. In unreported sensitivity tests, we calculate alternative tax rates based on adding back (i) one-half of the rental payment as interest expense to taxable income, and (ii) not adding back any portion of the rental payment as interest expense. Our conclusions with respect to the tax incentives to lease and use debt financing are unchanged when we use these alternative tax variables.

144                         *The Journal of Finance*

the firm's rental expense to earnings before taxes (in addition to adding back any interest expense from debt and capital lease financing, as mentioned above) as our proxy for earnings after depreciation, but prior to the lease versus purchase decision. This measure of earnings is the basis for the simulations of the firm's marginal tax rate.

The simulated tax rate is "but-for" in our context because it measures the tax incentives a firm faces after making the investment decision but before choosing between leasing or purchasing with debt financing; that is, our tax rate measures the marginal benefit of additional tax shields arising from the tax deductibility of interest expense (or from lease payments). This measure of the tax rate should be largely free of the endogeneity problems described above.[14]

The before-financing marginal tax rate ranges between 0 to 46 percent in our sample, with an average of 33.1 percent and a standard deviation of 14.3 percent (see Panel B of Table III). As a basis for comparison, and to provide some initial evidence on whether the endogeneity problem described above is empirically important, we also calculate a simulated marginal tax rate based on operating income *after* depreciation and interest expense. The average value of the after-financing marginal tax rate is 27.0 percent (the standard deviation is 15.6 percent), significantly lower than the before-financing measure of the marginal tax rate. As shown in Figure 1, there is substantial cross-sectional and time-series variation in both tax variables, with the distribution for the before-financing rate (Panel A) containing more mass at higher values than the distribution for the after-financing rate (Panel B).

## C. Nontax Variables Used to Explain Debt and Leasing Policies

### C.1. Financial Distress

To gauge the ex ante expected costs of financial distress (*ECOST*), we interact a measure related to the coefficient of variation of the firm's earnings (to proxy for the likelihood of financial distress) with the firm's level of asset intangibility (to proxy for the proportion of firm value likely to be lost in liquidation). To measure the coefficient of variation in earnings, we use the standard deviation of the first difference in the firm's historical earnings before depreciation, interest, and taxes (*EBDIT*) divided by the mean level of the book value of total assets as a proxy for the level of earnings.[15] We gauge asset intangibility by the sum of research and development (R&D) and

---

[14] The tax variable is measured before the interest component of debt and lease financing. It is not free of all decisions that can endogenously affect and be affected by tax status (and that may be intertwined with the debt and leasing decisions), such as entering into a research and development partnership. Our tax measure also assumes that the relative importance of nondebt tax shields remains unchanged in the future.

[15] We divide by the mean level of assets rather than the mean level of earnings to circumvent the problem in interpreting the coefficient of variation when the mean level of earnings is negative. In general, the level of earnings and the level of book assets are positively correlated. This measure of earnings variability is also used by MacKie-Mason (1990).

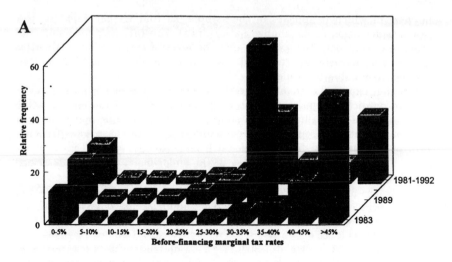

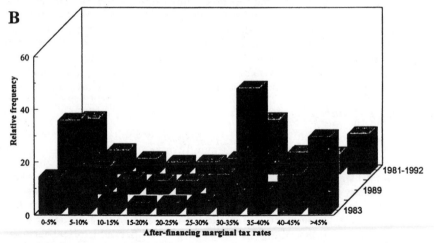

**Figure 1. Histograms for simulated marginal federal corporate income tax rates.** These histograms show the distribution of marginal tax rates for 1983, 1989, and an aggregation across all years 1981 to 1992. The before-financing tax rates in Panel A are based on taxable income before financing expenses are deducted. The after-financing tax rates in Panel B are based on taxable income after financing expenses are deducted, and are therefore endogenously affected by the choice of financing.

advertising expenses divided by assets. (Our results are unchanged when we measure asset intangibility as one minus the proportion of fixed assets.) In constructing this ex ante measure of financial distress, we require that a firm has at least five nonmissing observations for *EBDIT* prior to the year in which it appears in the sample (so that we can calculate the standard deviation of the change in earnings). The rationale for using this measure is that both the variance and the level of earnings determine the likelihood of financial distress, and that intangible assets are likely to lose most of their value in liquidation. The trade-off theory predicts that firms with higher expected costs of financial distress will use less debt and, therefore, we predict a negative relation between *ECOST* and the level of debt. Because leased assets have relatively high priority in bankruptcy proceedings, we expect the proportion of lease financing to increase with expected costs of distress, and hence be positively related to *ECOST*. The mean value of *ECOST* for the sample is 0.008 and the standard deviation is 0.089.

We use two measures of ex post financial distress. One is the contemporaneous value of a modified version of Altman's Z-score,[16] the other is a dummy variable (*OENEG*) set equal to one if the book value of common equity is negative. A large value of *Z-Score* indicates a low level of financial distress. The second variable proxies for firms that are likely to have experienced prolonged distress. We expect the debt and leasing ratios to be negatively related to *Z-score*, and positively related to *OENEG*. The *Z-Score* averages about 2.0 for all firm-year observations, and there is a very large dispersion around this number (standard deviation of 3.3). Approximately 5 percent of the firm-years in our sample report book value of owners' equity of less than zero (*OENEG* = 1).

## C.2. Contracting Costs

We use the *market-to-book* ratio as our proxy for the firm's investment opportunity set, which we expect to be negatively related to both debt and leasing intensity. Among others, Smith and Watts (1992), Barclay and Smith (1995), and Rajan and Zingales (1995) use market-to-book as a measure of investment opportunities. Regulated firms are expected to use more debt and less lease financing and we measure regulation with a dummy variable equal to one for firms in regulated industries. Following Barclay and Smith (1995), we define regulated industries as telecommunications (SICs 4812 and 4813) through 1982, and gas and electric utilities (SICs 4900–4939). We measure *collateral* as net property, plant, and equipment divided by total

---

[16] Our measure of the *Z-score* is given by

$$3.3 \frac{\text{EBIT}}{\text{Total Assets}} + 1.0 \frac{\text{Sales}}{\text{Total Assets}} + 1.4 \frac{\text{Ret. Earnings}}{\text{Total Assets}} + 1.2 \frac{\text{Working Capital}}{\text{Total Assets}}.$$

Altman's (1968) Z-score also includes the ratio of market value of equity to book value of debt. We do not include this variable because a similar term enters our regression separately as a measure of the investment opportunity set, as well as in the dependent variable of the debt equation. MacKie-Mason (1990) first uses the modified Z-score.

assets, and we expect both debt and leases to be positively related to this measure of fixed asset usage.[17]

The average market-to-book ratio for all firm-year observation is 1.44, with a standard deviation of 1.25. The percentage of sample firm-years in regulated industries is small, with only 0.1 percent of the firm-year observations coming from the telecommunications industry and 0.5 percent from utilities. Fixed assets (i.e., *collateral*) constitute 31.3 percent of total assets with a standard deviation of 18.7 percent.

We define firm size as the natural logarithm of the market value of the firm.[18] The mean size of firms in the sample is 5.06 (or without taking the natural logarithm, $1,366 million), with a standard deviation of 2.03 ($5,557 million). Larger firms are expected to use more debt financing while smaller firms are more likely to use leases.

### C.3. Other Control Variables

Several researchers have documented industry effects associated with debt and leasing policy. For example, Bradley, Jarrell, and Kim (1984) document persistent interindustry differences in leverage ratios, even after controlling for other explanatory variables. Ang and Peterson (1984) show that the use of capital leases also varies across industries, and Sharpe and Nguyen (1995) document interindustry differences in the use of operating leases. To control for industry effects in our regressions, we include dummy variables for each one-digit SIC code grouping. Additionally, because of the change in the tax code due to the 1986 Tax Reform Act, we include two dummy variables in our regressions to control for time series variation in financial policies related to the change in the tax code that are not captured perfectly by our estimated tax rate variable. The first tax reform dummy is set equal to one in 1986, and equal to zero otherwise; the second dummy variable equals one for the years 1987–1992, and equals zero otherwise.[19]

## III. Results

### A. Univariate Results

In Panel A of Table IV we report correlations between our measures of financial policy and the explanatory variables. The largest correlations are those between the marginal tax rate and size, and those involving the ex

---

[17] Presuming that operating leases are tied to fixed assets, we examine an alternative definition of collateral by adding operating leases to both the numerator and denominator of the variable. The unreported results using this definition are qualitatively identical to those reported in the text.

[18] Our results are essentially unchanged if we use total book assets (adjusted for operating leases), or total sales as a measure of firm size.

[19] Our results are essentially unchanged if we use two-digit SIC code groupings to define industries, or if we use annual dummies for all years.

**Table IV**

**Pearson Correlation Coefficients for Variables Associated with Debt and Leasing Policy**

The correlations in Panel A are based on 18,193 observations for firms on COMPUSTAT with SIC codes between 2000 and 5999 over the period 1981 through 1992. Debt-to-value is defined as the ratio of the book value of total long-term debt net of capital leases to the market value of the firm, where market value is the book value of total assets minus the book value of equity plus the market value of equity plus the present value of operating leases. Capital leases-to-value is the ratio of the book value of capital leases to the market value of the firm. Operating leases-to-value is the ratio of current rental expense plus the present value of operating lease commitments for the next five years discounted at 10 percent to the market value of the firm. The before-financing marginal tax rate is simulated based on income after depreciation but before interest expenses are deducted. ECOST is the standard deviation of the first difference in the firm's earnings before depreciation, interest, and taxes divided by the mean level of the book value of total assets multiplied by the sum of research and development and advertising expenses divided by assets. Z-score is a modified version of Altman's (1968) Z-Score. OENEG is a dummy variable equal to one if the book value of common equity is negative. Market-to-book is the market value of the firm divided by the book value of the firm, where the book value of the firm is total assets plus the present value of operating leases. Collateral is equal to net property, plant, and equipment divided by the book value of total assets. Size is the natural log of the market value of the firm. The correlations in Panel B are based on 18,190 observations for no dividend, 18,193 observations for cash flow-to-sales and average tax rate, and 16,146 observations for large tax-loss carryforward and small tax-loss carryforward. No dividend is a dummy variable equal to one if the firm does not pay dividends. Cash flow-to-sales is the ratio of earnings before interest, depreciation, rent, and taxes to sales, and is truncated at zero. Large tax-loss CF is a dummy variable equal to one if the book value of tax-loss carryforwards is greater than the firm's earnings before interest, depreciation, and taxes. Small tax-loss CF is a dummy variable equal to one if the book value of tax-loss carryforwards is less than or equal to the firm's earnings before interest, depreciation, and taxes. Average tax rate is the ratio of tax expense to pretax income. The variable is truncated so as to fall between zero and one, is set equal to zero for all firms with nonpositive tax expense, and is set to one for firms that have positive taxes and negative pretax income.

Panel A. Simple Correlations of Financial Policy and Explanatory Variables

| Variable | Market-to-Book | Size | Collateral | Marginal Tax Rate | Z-Score | OENEG | ECOST |
|---|---|---|---|---|---|---|---|
| Debt-to-value | -0.214* | 0.100* | 0.225* | 0.017* | -0.052* | 0.096* | -0.038* |
| Cap. leases-to-value | -0.110* | -0.015 | 0.245* | 0.091* | 0.067* | -0.008 | -0.021* |
| Op. leases-to-value | -0.190* | -0.209* | 0.015 | -0.083* | 0.047* | 0.025* | 0.007 |
| Market-to-book | — | 0.046* | -0.086* | -0.120* | -0.365* | 0.141* | 0.299* |
| Size (in firm value) | | — | 0.356* | 0.306* | 0.154* | -0.082* | -0.074* |
| Collateral | | | — | 0.131* | 0.009 | -0.038* | -0.039* |
| Marginal tax rate | | | | — | 0.375* | -0.273* | -0.096* |
| Z-score | | | | | — | -0.292* | -0.574* |
| OENEG | | | | | | — | 0.074* |
| ECOST | | | | | | | — |

Panel B. Simple Correlations between Explanatory Variables Used in This Study and Those Used by Sharpe and Nguyen (1995)

| Variable | Market-to-Book | Size | Collateral | Marginal Tax Rate | Z-Score | OENEG | ECOST |
|---|---|---|---|---|---|---|---|
| No dividend | 0.076* | -0.514* | -0.257* | -0.425* | -0.224* | 0.194* | 0.065* |
| Cash flow-to-sales | 0.118* | 0.405* | 0.264* | 0.465* | 0.118* | -0.137* | -0.049* |
| Large tax-loss CF | 0.109* | -0.369* | -0.174* | -0.604* | -0.414* | 0.300* | 0.224* |
| Small tax-loss CF | -0.045* | 0.047* | -0.011 | 0.083* | 0.021* | -0.036* | -0.017* |
| Average tax rate | -0.058* | 0.170* | -0.012* | 0.257* | 0.143* | -0.044* | -0.045* |

*Statistically significant at the 1 percent level.

post financial distress measures. As argued in Section II, these correlations highlight the need to control for financial distress in the empirical tests, and also
suggest that firms with tax incentives to lease may also have nontax reasons.
Nevertheless, the simple correlations between the marginal tax rate and both
operating leases and debt are significant and have the predicted signs.

In Panel B we report correlations between our explanatory variables and
those used by Sharpe and Nguyen (1995) (except that we do not examine
their measure of debt rating). Note that our tax measure is highly correlated
with the variables used to proxy for asymmetric information costs by Sharpe
and Nguyen (no dividend and cash flow-to-sales).[20] Our tax variable is also
highly correlated with their large tax-loss carryforward, but less correlated
with their measure of the average tax rate.[21] These results are consistent
with our contentions that (i) we use a more precise measure of the marginal
tax rate than has been employed in previous leasing research, and (ii) firms
with the largest tax-related leasing benefits are also the firms likely to use
leasing to attenuate high contracting costs. Thus, we view our findings as
complementary to those of Sharpe and Nguyen.

To provide some initial evidence on whether capital leases are a debt-like financing instrument, Table V presents a two-way classification of the mean values of our financial policy variables based on the usage of debt and capital leases.
Firms that use no debt or use no capital leases have higher market-to-book ratios, smaller size, higher expected costs of financial distress, and lower marginal tax rates.[22] The debt results are consistent with the trade-off theory of
capital structure. The capital leasing results mirror those for debt, suggesting
that capital leases and debt are similar financial instruments. Firms with no
debt use operating leases more intensely than firms with debt (which is consistent with the hypothesis that debt and leases are substitutes), while the opposite relation holds between capital leases and operating leases.

## B. Capital Structure Regressions

### B.1. Determinants of Financial Policy

In Table VI, we present results from pooled time-series cross-sectional censored (Tobit) regressions of the capital structure measures on the explanatory variables. The dependent variables in these regressions are the value of

---

[20] For *no dividend*, Sharpe and Nguyen use a dummy variable equal to one for nondividend-
paying firms; for cash flow, they use operating income before interest, depreciation, rent, and
taxes (truncated at zero).

[21] Sharpe and Nguyen estimate the *average tax rate* as tax expense divided by pretax income
(truncated to fall between zero and one). The ratio is set equal to zero for all firms with nonpositive tax expense, and is set to one for firms that have positive taxes and negative pretax
income. The *large* and *small tax-loss carryforward* are dummy variables indicating whether the
amount of the tax-loss carryforward exceeds operating earnings (high) or not (low).

[22] The result that firms with capital leases have higher marginal tax rates than those without differs from the finding of Krishnan and Moyer (1994), who find no difference in *average* tax
rates across leasing and nonleasing firms.

Table V

## Two-way Classifications for the Use of Debt and the Use of Capital Leases

The samples consist of 18,193 observations for firms on COMPUSTAT with SIC codes between 2000 and 5999 over the period 1981 through 1992. Debt-to-value is defined as the ratio of the book value of total long-term debt net of capital leases to the market value of the firm, where market value is the book value of total assets minus the book value of equity plus the market value of equity plus the present value of operating leases. Capital leases-to-value is the ratio of the book value of capital leases to the market value of the firm. Operating leases-to-value is the ratio of current rental expense plus the present value of operating lease commitments for the next five years discounted at 10 percent to the market value of the firm. The before-financing marginal tax rate is simulated based on income after depreciation but before interest expenses are deducted. ECOST is the standard deviation of the first difference in the firm's earnings before depreciation, interest, and taxes divided by the mean level of the book value of total assets multiplied by the sum of research and development and advertising expenses divided by assets. Z-score is a modified version of Altman's (1968) Z-Score. OENEG is a dummy variable equal to one if the book value of common equity is negative. Market-to-book is the market value of the firm divided by book value of the firm, where the book value of the firm is total assets plus the present value of operating leases. Collateral is equal to net property, plant, and equipment divided by the book value of total assets. Size is the natural log of the market value of the firm.

### Panel A: Sample Means of Variables Based on Usage of Debt

| Variable | No Debt (N = 2,171) | With Debt (N = 16,022) |
|---|---|---|
| Debt-to-value | 0.000 | 0.161 |
| Capital leases-to-value | 0.008 | 0.017 |
| Operating leases-to-value | 0.094 | 0.078 |
| Before-financing marginal tax rate | 0.253 | 0.341 |
| ECOST | 0.023 | 0.006 |
| Z-score | 1.122 | 2.175 |
| OENEG | 0.074 | 0.043 |
| Market-to-book | 2.044 | 1.362 |
| Collateral | 0.190 | 0.330 |
| Size (log of firm value) | 3.698 | 5.244 |

### Panel B: Sample Means of Variables Based on Usage of Capital Leases

| Variable | No Capital Leases (N = 8,612) | With Capital Leases (N = 9,581) |
|---|---|---|
| Debt-to-value | 0.133 | 0.150 |
| Capital lease-to-value | 0.000 | 0.030 |
| Operating lease-to-value | 0.074 | 0.085 |
| Before-financing marginal tax rate | 0.314 | 0.345 |
| ECOST | 0.010 | 0.006 |
| Z-score | 1.823 | 2.253 |
| OENEG | 0.058 | 0.037 |
| Market-to-book | 1.558 | 1.341 |
| Collateral | 0.276 | 0.346 |
| Size (log of firm value) | 4.726 | 5.359 |

## Table VI
## Censored (Tobit) Regressions of Financial Claims as a Fraction of Firm Value

The table summarizes the results from three separate pooled time-series cross-sectional regressions. The value of the financial claim as a fraction of the firm's total market value is used as the dependent variable in each regression where total market value is defined as the book value of total assets minus the book value of common equity plus the market value of common equity plus the present value of operating lease commitments over the next five years. The before-financing marginal tax rate is simulated based on income after depreciation but before interest expenses are deducted. ECOST is the standard deviation of the first difference in the firm's earnings before depreciation, interest, and taxes divided by the mean level of the book value of total assets multiplied by the sum of research and development and advertising expenses divided by assets. Z-score is a modified version of Altman's (1968) Z-Score. OENEG is a dummy variable equal to one if the book value of common equity is negative. Market-to-book is the market value of the firm divided by book value of the firm, where the book value of the firm is total assets plus the present value of operating leases. Collateral is equal to net property, plant and equipment divided by the book value of total assets. Telephone dummy is equal to one if the firm is in the telecommunications industry through 1982 (SIC codes 4812 and 4813). Utilities dummy is equal to one if the firm is a gas or electric utility (SIC codes 4900–4939). Size is defined as the natural log of the market value of the firm. One-digit SIC code industry dummies and year dummies for 1986 and 1987 through 1992 are included. The sample consists of 18,193 observations for firms with SIC codes between 2000 and 5999 over the period 1981 through 1992. *p*-values are in parentheses.

| Variable | Debt-to-Value | Capital Leases-to-Value | Operating Leases-to-Value |
|---|---|---|---|
| Intercept | 0.1205 | 0.0135 | 0.2068 |
| | (0.0001) | (0.0001) | (0.0001) |
| Before-financing marginal tax rate | 0.0740 | −0.0037 | −0.0339 |
| | (0.0001) | (0.3317) | (0.0001) |
| ECOST | −0.1032 | 0.0260 | 0.0626 |
| | (0.0001) | (0.0007) | (0.0001) |
| Z-score | −0.0118 | 0.0005 | 0.0005 |
| | (0.0001) | (0.0399) | (0.0439) |
| OENEG | 0.0741 | 0.0018 | 0.0036 |
| | (0.0001) | (0.4330) | (0.2014) |
| Market-to-book | −0.0549 | −0.0069 | −0.0127 |
| | (0.0001) | (0.0001) | (0.0001) |
| Telephone dummy | 0.0728 | −0.0679 | −0.0643 |
| | (0.0074) | (0.0001) | (0.0001) |
| Utilities dummy | 0.0706 | −0.0350 | −0.0652 |
| | (0.0001) | (0.0001) | (0.0001) |
| Collateral | 0.1269 | 0.0793 | 0.0074 |
| | (0.0001) | (0.0001) | (0.0301) |
| Size (log of firm value) | 0.0081 | −0.0006 | −0.0088 |
| | (0.0001) | (0.0169) | (0.0001) |
| Dummy for SIC codes 2000–2999 | 0.0139 | −0.0250 | −0.0814 |
| | (0.0001) | (0.0001) | (0.0001) |
| Dummy for SIC codes 3000–3999 | −0.0010 | −0.0251 | −0.0851 |
| | (0.6994) | (0.0001) | (0.0001) |
| Dummy for SIC codes 4000–4999 | 0.0155 | −0.0256 | −0.0313 |
| | (0.0011) | (0.0001) | (0.0001) |
| Dummy for 1986 | 0.0016 | −0.0130 | 0.0015 |
| | (0.6841) | (0.0001) | (0.4909) |
| Dummy for 1987–1992 | 0.0027 | −0.0210 | 0.0103 |
| | (0.2428) | (0.0001) | (0.0001) |
| $R^2$ from OLS regression | 0.130 | 0.143 | 0.253 |

### Endogeneity of Corporate Tax Status                   153

claims in each class expressed as a fraction of total firm value. Although the statistical significance is likely to be overstated because of serial dependence in the error terms (which we address in Section *B.2*), the results are very supportive of the tax hypothesis. Specifically, operating leases are negatively related to the tax variable (*p*-value of 0.0001), and debt usage is positively associated with the firm's marginal tax rate (*p*-value of 0.0001). The relation between capital leases and the marginal tax rate is negative and not statistically significant (*p*-value of 0.3317). More importantly, the absolute value of the coefficient on the tax rate for capital leases is more than eight times smaller than the tax coefficient for operating leases. Our results indicate that a change in the marginal tax rate from 0 to 46 percent will, on average, result in a 19.6 percent increase in the firm's debt-to-value ratio, a 17 percent decrease in the firm's ratio of operating leases to firm value, and a 5.1 percent decrease in the ratio of capital leases to firm value.[23]

Finding a positive relation between debt levels and tax rates helps resolve "the capital structure puzzle" (Myers (1984)). Myers states that he "knows of no study clearly demonstrating that a firm's tax status has predictable, material effects on its debt policy. I think the wait for such a study will be protracted" (p. 588). Starting with MacKie-Mason (1990), and continuing with Givoly et al. (1992), Rajan and Zingales (1995), and Graham (1996a), empirical research has demonstrated that taxes have predictable, material effects on a firm's *incremental* debt policy; until now, however, this effect had not been documented unambiguously in studies of debt *levels*. Our debt result provides the first evidence that high tax rate firms have high debt levels. We provide evidence in Section B.3 consistent with the hypothesis that our ability to document the positive relation between debt levels and taxes follows because we use before-financing tax rates, thereby avoiding the endogeneity problem.

The operating lease result is the first definitive evidence that low tax rate firms lease more than high tax rate firms. The tax findings for leasing are consistent with the hypothesis that operating leases are predominantly true leases but that capital leases are a mix of both true and nontrue leases. With respect to the latter implication, the finding that debt levels are positively related to the tax rate implies that, due to their identical tax treatment, the use of nontrue leases is positively related to the corporate marginal tax rate; thus, if capital leases are a combination of true and nontrue leases, their estimated relation with tax rates should lie between the debt and operating lease results, as documented.

Our measure of the ex ante expected costs of financial distress (*ECOST*) is negatively related to debt usage, thus supporting the trade-off theory of capital structure. The use of both operating and capital leases is positively related to the expected costs of financial distress, which is supportive of the notion that firms with large expected costs of financial distress are likely to

---

[23] The percentage change in the dependent variable is calculated as the Tobit-adjusted change in the dependent variable associated with a change in the tax rate, divided by the sample mean of the dependent variable.

finance with leases. Debt is associated with the ex post financial distress variables (*Z-Score* and *OENEG*) in the manner expected, which confirms our prediction that firms in financial distress are likely to have high debt ratios because of the deterioration in equity value. The evidence about the relation between leases and ex post financial distress is inconclusive.

Consistent with the contracting cost hypotheses, the findings in Table VI show that the use of all three financial instruments is negatively related to growth opportunities (market-to-book) and positively related to asset tangibility (collateral). The use of debt is positively correlated with regulation and size, while both capital and operating leases are negatively related. The latter result supports the notion that regulated firms have incentives to build up their capital base and that leases may not "count" in these rate-base calculations.

In line with the findings of previous studies, all three financial policy variables exhibit significant interindustry differences. The level of capital leases appears to decline in the post-tax-reform period, and the use of operating leases increases during this time period. We detect no significant ceteris paribus change in the use of debt over the sample period.

### B.2. Robustness of Tax Results

Our previous results (in Table VI) are based on the division of total market value into debt and leasing. As a robustness check, we estimate regressions similar to those in Table VI, but use the value of claims in each class as a fraction of the book value of total assets as the dependent variables. The inferences from these regressions are qualitatively identical to those reported in Table VI, and strongly support the tax hypothesis.

Because the lease versus purchase decision is generally motivated by a comparison between debt and lease financing, some leasing models investigate the division of fixed claims into debt and leasing. Tax hypotheses from these models predict that low tax rate firms should have a greater proportion of their fixed claims in the form of operating leases; high tax rate firms should have a greater proportion of their fixed claims in the form of debt. To explore this proposition, we estimate regressions similar to those in Table VI, but use the value of claims in each class as a fraction of total fixed claims as the dependent variables. The signs and statistical significance levels of the tax and ex ante financial distress variables in these regressions are qualitatively identical to those reported in Table VI.[24]

To address the issue of autocorrelated errors we perform year-by-year cross-sectional regressions (not tabulated) for each of the financial policy vari-

---

[24] In the book value and total fixed claims analyses, the use of operating leases is positively related to market-to-book. This suggests that firms with more growth opportunities use more operating leases. Alternatively, this finding could reflect induced correlation between the dependent variables and market-to-book. Details of the book value and fixed-claims analyses are available from the authors upon request.

ables.[25] The results from the cross-sectional regressions are similar to those in Table VI. As a fraction of firm value, the relation between operating leases and the tax rate is negative in 11 of the 12 years, and 8 of the 11 negative coefficients are statistically significant at the 10 percent level. The relation between debt and the tax rate is positive in 10 of the 12 years, and 8 of the 10 positive coefficients are statistically significant. The coefficient on the tax variable in the capital leasing regressions is negative in 10 of the 12 years, and two of the negative coefficients are statistically significant. The results using the book value of assets as the deflator are similar. When expressed as a fraction of fixed claims, the relation between operating leases and the tax rate is negative and statistically significant in 11 of the 12 years, and the relation between debt and tax rate is positive and significant in 11 of the 12 years. The coefficient on the tax variable in the capital leasing regressions is negative in 11 of the 12 years, and four of the negative coefficients are statistically significant.

For each set of year-by-year regressions, we test whether the time-series mean of the tax coefficients is different from zero (analogous to Fama and MacBeth (1973)), using a $t$-test corrected for first-order autocorrelation. Although the tests are based on only 12 observations, the findings support those documented above. For operating leases, the time-series mean of the tax coefficients is negative and different from zero at the 1 percent level or better in all specifications. For debt, the mean is positive and different from zero at the 5 percent level. For capital leases, the mean is negative and is significantly different from zero at 5 percent, but the magnitude is quite small ($-0.008$ as a fraction of firm value).

Income volatility affects both the benefits (tax rates) and costs (e.g., expected bankruptcy costs) associated with debt and lease financing. For example, firms with volatile income streams typically have low expected marginal tax rates and relatively high probabilities of financial distress. Our tax and distress cost measures are designed to capture the direct effects of volatility on the benefits and costs of financial policy. Nevertheless, to ensure that our results are not driven by any unmeasured effect of volatility, we estimate regressions identical to those in Table VI, except the new regressions include an extra term measuring the volatility of income (and in separate regressions, the coefficient of variation of volatility). The results are qualitatively identical to those shown in Table VI. The conclusions are also unchanged in regressions estimated separately for each quintile of income volatility.

We also investigate whether personal taxes affect the use of debt. (We do not consider the effect of personal taxes in our leasing analysis. Most theoretical

---

[25] As an alternative method of controlling for serial correlation, we also estimate a between-firms regression in which the time series means of the variables for each firm are treated as a single observation. The results are very similar to those reported in Table VI and provide strong support for the tax hypotheses for debt and operating leases. However, the coefficient on the tax rate for capital leases becomes positive and marginally significant, which is consistent with the tax incentives for capital leases being more like those for nontrue leases than for true leases, on average.

156                              *The Journal of Finance*

models do not incorporate the effect of personal taxes, and those that do only
include their effect on lease payments through the lessor's debt decision (Lewis
and Schallheim (1992)). The theories of Miller (1977) and DeAngelo and Masulis (1980) imply that some portion of the corporate tax advantage of interest
deductions is offset at the personal level. To test for the effect of personal taxes,
we replace the marginal tax variable in the specification reported in Table VI
with a variable defined as $(1 - T_{personal})/(1 - T_{capital\ gains})(1 - T_{corporate})$, where
$T_{personal}$ is inferred from the difference between the one-year yield on municipal and taxable bonds, as published in Salomon Brother's Bond Market Roundup.
The results (not tabulated) from this alternative specification are qualitatively identical to those shown in Table VI, except that the tax variable is more
significant in the sense that it has a "larger $t$-score," which is consistent with
the hypothesis that personal taxes matter. The results in Table VI are reported using just $T_{corporate}$ as an explanatory variable to allow for a more direct
comparison between the debt and leasing regressions.

### B.3. The Endogeneity of Corporate Tax Status

Next we conduct an experiment to explore whether the tax variable is
endogenous to the financing decision. In two separate specifications, we regress the financial policy variables on our control variables and two alternative measures of the marginal tax rate, both of which are endogenously
affected by the firm's past financing decisions.[26] The first measure is a simulated tax variable based on operating income *after* interest deductions (i.e.,
the *after-financing* marginal tax rate). This is the tax rate used in Graham
(1996a) to examine incremental financing decisions. The second measure is
a non-NOL carryforward dummy variable equal to one when a firm does not
have book tax-loss carryforwards (and is also an after-financing decision variable). A version of the second measure of tax status is used in many studies
including Barclay and Smith (1995) and Sharpe and Nguyen (1995). The
signs of the estimated coefficients for the tax variables are summarized in
Table VII. The top row of the table reviews the results from Table VI for the
before-financing tax rate.

With respect to debt policy, the estimated coefficient on the after-financing
tax rate is negative, as is the coefficient on the non-NOL carryforward variable, and both are significantly different from zero. In contrast to results
using the before-financing tax measure, both of these variables have incorrect signs based on the theoretical relation between debt and taxes. This

---

[26] The concept of whether a tax variable is "endogenous" is specific to the experiment. For
example, the after-financing simulated rate and NOL dummy are endogenous for our specification because we examine cumulative financing choice. If we were instead to lag the variables
and study incremental financing choice, the tax measures would not be endogenous. One of the
points of our paper is that many past studies of capital structure have (i) examined aggregate
financing choices, and (ii) failed to document the expected sign on the tax coefficient. We provide evidence in the text implying that the failure to document tax effects in the past may have
been due to inappropriate measurement of tax status, that is, the use of endogenously affected
tax rates.

**Table VII**

## Estimated Relations between Measures of Financial Policy and Alternative Tax Variables

The table summarizes the estimated relations between the three measures of financial policy and alternative tax variables from a total of nine separate censored (Tobit) regressions. The value of the financial claim as a fraction of the firm's total market value is used as the dependent variable in each regression. The before-financing marginal tax rate is simulated based on income after depreciation but before interest expenses are deducted. The after-financing marginal tax rate is simulated based on income after depreciation and interest expenses are deducted. The Non-NOL carryforward is a dummy variable equal to one when the firm does not have book tax-loss carryforwards. Each regression also includes the following control variables (not shown): ECOST is the standard deviation of the first difference in the firm's earnings before depreciation, interest, and taxes divided by the mean level of the book value of total assets multiplied by the sum of research and development and advertising expenses divided by assets. Z-score is a modified version of Altman's (1968) Z-Score. OENEG is a dummy variable equal to one if the book value of common equity is negative. Market-to-book is the market value of the firm divided by book value of the firm, where the book value of the firm is total assets plus the present value of operating leases. Collateral is equal to net property, plant, and equipment divided by the book value of total assets. Telephone dummy is equal to one if the firm is in the telecommunications industry through 1982 (SIC codes 4812 and 4813). Utilities dummy is equal to one if the firm is a gas or electric utility (SIC codes 4900–4939). Size is the natural log of the market value of the firm. One-digit SIC code industry dummies and year dummies for 1986 and 1987 through 1992 are included. The sample consists of 18,193 observations for firms with SIC codes between 2000 and 5999 over the period 1981 through 1992. p-values are in parentheses.

| Variable | Debt-to-Value | Capital Leases-to-Value | Operating Leases-to-Value |
|---|---|---|---|
| Before-financing marginal tax rate | 0.0740 | −0.0037 | −0.0339 |
| | (0.0001) | (0.3317) | (0.0001) |
| After-financing marginal tax rate | −0.1327 | −0.0434 | −0.0642 |
| | (0.0001) | (0.0001) | (0.0001) |
| Non-NOL carryforward dummy variable | −0.0212 | −0.0091 | −0.0155 |
| | (0.0001) | (0.0001) | (0.0001) |

finding supports our hypothesis that measuring income after interest deductions induces a spurious negative relation between debt usage and after-financing tax rates.

With respect to both capital and operating leases, the after-financing tax coefficients have the same signs as those in the debt regressions. For example, the relation between capital leases and the after-financing tax rate is negative and significant. We argue that the capital leasing result is difficult to interpret because it could be caused by (i) the endogeneity of corporate tax status (i.e., the use of capital leases, whether they are classified as true or nontrue leases by the IRS, lowers the after-financing tax rate, biasing the regression coefficient downward), (ii) by the expected negative relation between taxes and true leases (to the extent that capital leases are classified as true leases), or (iii) a combination of both reasons. Similarly, a portion of the negative relation between operating leases and after-financing tax rates could be spuriously induced (because the tax deductibility of rental expense can lower a firm's marginal tax rate); the fact that the coefficient on the after-financing tax rate is more negative than the coefficient on the before-financing tax rate is consistent with this hypothesis. These results are consistent with the notion that corporate tax status is endogenous, but also that the problem can be avoided through careful measurement of tax variables.[27] We believe that using the before-financing simulated tax rate allows us to unambiguously confirm the expected relations between debt, leases, and tax rates.

## IV. Conclusion

We provide evidence consistent with theory regarding the relation between debt policy, leasing policy, and taxes. Using a forward-looking measure of firms' marginal tax rates before financing decisions, we show that the corporate marginal tax rate is positively related to debt usage, but negatively related to the use of operating leases. Our results for capital leases are less clear regarding the tax effect, suggesting that capital leases represent a mixture of *true* leases and *nontrue* leases. One possible direction for future research is to document the tax status of capital leases directly. In the process of testing for tax effects, we find that corporate tax status is endogenous to financial policy and argue that tax incentives must therefore be measured carefully. We also find that (i) the propensity to lease (use debt) increases (decreases) with the expected costs of financial distress, (ii) the use of leases and debt are consistent with contracting cost explanations of financial policy, and (iii) personal taxes affect debt financing decisions.

## Appendix: Accounting and Tax Rules for Leases

*Definition of Capital and Operating Leases*

Following is a brief list of the accounting rules that define capital and operating leases. *Statement of Financial Accounting Standards (SFAS) No. 13* provides the detailed criteria for a lease contract to be specified as a capital or operating lease. Four criteria apply to lessees; a capital lease is defined as a lease that meets any one or more of the four criteria.

(1) **Transfer of Ownership.** If the lease agreement transfers ownership to the lessee before the lease expires, without payment of additional compensation to the lessor, the lease is considered a purchase financing arrangement, similar to an installment purchase.

(2) **Bargain Purchase Option.** The lessee can purchase the asset for a bargain price when the lease expires. A bargain purchase option requires comparing the option's purchase price to the leased asset's expected residual

---

[27] An unreported Hausmann test provides statistically significant evidence consistent with the after-financing tax rate being endogenous to the financing decision. Details are available from the authors upon request.

value at the maturity of the lease. If the purchase option is well below the expected residual value, the lessee is not expected to pass up the savings, and the probability is high that the lessee will buy the asset at maturity.

(3) **75 Percent of Economic Life.** The lease lasts for at least 75 percent of the asset's expected economic life. A bargain renewal option, an option to renew the lease at a rental rate below the expected fair market rental at the time of the exercise of the option, is considered to lengthen the lease life used in this determination.

(4) **90 Percent of Asset's Value.** The present value of the minimum lease payments is at least 90 percent of the asset's fair value. The minimum lease payments is defined by *SFAS No. 13* to mean "the payments that the lessee is obligated to make or can be required to make in connection with the leased property." Of course, the minimum lease payments consist mainly of the periodic payments. However, minimum lease payments also include such items as the bargain purchase option or bargain renewal option payments. Some leases contain additional provisions that are included as minimum lease payments such as a guaranteed residual value by the lessee or a penalty payment for failure to renew if it is expected that the renewal option will be rejected by the lessee.

*IRS Guidelines for True Leases*

The IRS set forth six guidelines for advance rulings to determine true ownership and lease validity. A lease satisfying these requirements is called a true lease, but is also known as a "guideline" lease or a tax-oriented lease. If the lease does not satisfy the IRS guidelines, it is classified as a conditional-sales contract.

**Guideline (1): Minimum At-Risk Requirement.** This guideline requires that at inception and throughout the lease term the lessor must have an investment equal to at least 20 percent of the total acquisition cost of the property. The investment made is considered to be only the consideration paid and personal liability of the lessor. The lessor must have net worth sufficient to cover such obligation. This investment must be unconditional, with no provisions for return, although provisions for reimbursement from outside groups for failure of the equipment to meet quality standards is permissible. The investment must be maintained at all times throughout the lease term with the sum of the lease payments to be made never to exceed the excess of the initial investment over the 20 percent minimum investment plus the cumulative pro rata portion of the projected profit.

**Guideline (2): Minimum Estimated Residual Value.** The second requirement is that the leased property must have a reasonably estimated residual value equal to at least 20 percent of the initial cost of the property at the end of the lease term. The lease term is defined to include any extension periods except those before which the lessee may renegotiate rental payments.

At the beginning of the lease, the lessor can obtain an appraisal confirming the estimated residual value of 20 percent or more of cost at the end of the lease term. For pricing purposes, the lessor might use a residual value of less than 20 percent on the basis of liquidation value or quick sale price, for example. However, this fact, if it applies, does not invalidate the 20 percent estimated residual value for tax purposes.

**Guideline (3): Minimum Remaining Life for Asset.** The third requirement for advanced ruling states that the remaining life of the property at the end of the lease term equal the longer of one year or 20 percent of its originally estimated life. The Internal Revenue Service requires that representations that these requirements have been met be made by the lessor.

**Guideline (4): No Bargain Purchase Option.** There may also be no bargain purchase option (for any member of the lessee group) nor may there be any requirement that any party purchase the property at any price. To prove the validity of the lease the lessor must be required to dispose of the property at the end of the lease term, thus bearing the risk of ownership. In similar fashion, the lessee is restricted from providing any of the cost of the property or the cost of any improvements made to such property (with the exception of those readily removable from the property or routine maintenance). If the lease does not prohibit the lessee from paying for improvements then the lessor must recognize as income the value of such improvements.

**Guideline (5): No Loan from Lessee to Lessor.** The fifth requirement for advance ruling purposes is that no member of the lessee group may loan the lessor the money necessary to purchase the leased property nor may they guarantee loans the lessor incurs to purchase such property. This does not preclude other members of the lessee group from guaranteeing the performance of the lessee.

**Guideline (6): Lessor Must Demonstrate Expectation of Profits.** Lastly, the IRS requires that the lessor be able to demonstrate the expectation of profits to be derived from the lease. Tax benefits from such transactions are not considered to be "profits" sufficient to demonstrate that expectation. But residual value of the equipment does count as part of the profit.

*Comparison of Accounting and Tax Rules for Leasing*

The four criteria that define a capital lease in most cases will *not* qualify the lease as a true lease for tax purposes. Consider the four accounting criteria for a capital lease as discussed at the beginning of this appendix:

(1) **Transfer of Ownership.** Any transfer of ownership prior to the maturity of the lease will not qualify as a true lease for tax purposes. This violates Guideline (1) for minimum at-risk requirement on the part of the lessor.

(2) **Bargain Purchase Option.** There can be no bargain purchase option for a lease to qualify as a true lease, which is Guideline (4).

(3) **75 Percent of Economic Life.** For economic life criteria, there is a slight difference between the accounting rule and the tax rule. The tax rule requires a remaining economic life for the asset at the end of the lease of at least one year or 20 percent of the originally estimated life, Guideline (3). However, the concept of "economic life" leaves a great deal of room for subjective assumptions.

(4) **90 Percent of Asset's Value.** Guideline (2) for tax deductible lease payments requires that the lessor maintain a minimum of 20 percent of the asset's cost throughout the life of the lease. Therefore, if a lease qualifies as a capital lease under criteria 4, it would not qualify as a true lease. Here again, however, there is room for subjectivity based on assumptions about the proper discount rate to compute the present value of the (minimum) lease payments.

## REFERENCES

Altman, Edward, 1968, Financial ratios, discriminant analysis, and the prediction of corporate bankruptcy, *Journal of Finance* 23, 589–609.

Ang, James, and Pamela P. Peterson, 1984, The leasing puzzle, *Journal of Finance* 39, 1055–1065.

Barclay, Michael J, and Clifford W. Smith, 1995, The priority structure of corporate liabilities, *Journal of Finance* 50, 899–917.

Bradley, Michael, Gregg A. Jarrell, and E. Han Kim, 1984, On the existence of an optimal capital structure, *Journal of Finance* 39, 857–887.

Brealey, Richard, and Stewart Myers, 1991, *Principles of Corporate Finance* (McGraw-Hill, New York, N.Y.).

DeAngelo, Harry, and Ronald Masulis, 1980, Optimal capital structure under corporate and personal taxation, *Journal of Financial Economics* 8, 3–29.

Fama, Eugene, and James MacBeth, 1973, Risk, return, and equilibrium: Empirical tests, *Journal of Political Economy* 71, 607–636.

Fiscal Federalism, 1981–92 (U.S. Advisory Commission on Intergovernmental Relations, Washington, DC).

Flath, David, 1980, The economics of short-term leasing, *Economic Inquiry* 18, 247–259.

Gaver, Jennifer, and Kenneth Gaver, 1993, Additional evidence on the association between the investment opportunity set and corporate financing, dividend and compensation policies, *Journal of Accounting and Economics* 6, 125–160.

Givoly, Dan, Carla Hahn, Aharon Ofer, and Oded Sarig, 1992, Taxes and capital structure: Evidence from firms' response to the tax reform act of 1986, *Review of Financial Studies* 5, 331–355.

Graham, John, 1996a, Debt and the marginal tax rate, *Journal of Financial Economics* 41, 41–73.

Graham, John, 1996b, Proxies for the corporate marginal tax rate, *Journal of Financial Economics* 42, 187–221.

Jensen, Michael C., and William H. Meckling, 1976, Theory of the firm: Managerial behavior, agency costs, and ownership structure, *Journal of Financial Economics* 3, 305–360.

Krishnan, V. S., and R. Charles Moyer, 1994, Bankruptcy costs and the financial leasing decision, *Financial Management* 23, 31–42.

Lewellen, Wilbur G., Michael S. Long, and John J. McConnell, 1976, Asset leasing in competitive capital markets, *Journal of Finance* 31, 787–798.

Lewis, Craig, and James Schallheim, 1992, Are debt and leases substitutes?, *Journal of Financial and Quantitative Analysis* 27, 497–511.

MacKie-Mason, Jeffrey, 1990, Do taxes affect corporate financing decisions?, *Journal of Finance* 45, 1471–1493.

Miller, Merton, 1977, Debt and taxes, *Journal of Finance* 32, 261–275.

Miller, Merton H., and Charles W. Upton, 1976, Leasing, buying, and the cost of capital services, *Journal of Finance* 31, 761–786.

Modigliani, Franco, and Merton H. Miller, 1963, Corporate income taxes and the cost of capital: A correction, *American Economic Review* 53, 433-443.

Myers, Stewart C., 1977, Determinants of corporate borrowing, *Journal of Financial Economics* 3, 799–819.

Myers, Stewart C., 1984, The capital structure puzzle, *Journal of Finance* 39, 572–592.

Myers, Stewart C., David A. Dill, and Alberto J. Bautista, 1976, Valuation of financial lease contracts, *Journal of Finance* 31, 799–819.

O'Malley, Michael P., 1996, The effects of taxes on leasing decisions: Evidence from panel data, Working paper, Board of Governors of the Federal Reserve System.

Plesko, George, 1994, The tax advantage of corporate debt after tax reform: A direct test of the effect of tax rate changes on corporate leverage, Working paper, Northeastern University.

Rajan, Raghuram G., and Luigi Zingales, 1995, What do we know about capital structure choice? Some evidence from international data, *Journal of Finance* 50, 1421–1460.

Ross, Stephen, Randolph Westerfield, and Jeffrey Jaffe, 1996, *Corporate finance* (Irwin, Chicago, Ill.).

Schallheim, James, 1994, *Lease or Buy: Principles for Sound Corporate Decision Making* (Harvard Business School Press, Boston, MA).

Schallheim, James, Ramon Johnson, Ronald Lease, and John McConnell, 1987, The determinants of yields on financial leasing contracts, *Journal of Financial Economics* 19, 45–67.

Scholes, Myron, G. Peter Wilson, and Mark Wolfson, 1990, Tax planning, regulatory capital planning, and financial reporting strategy for commercial banks, *Review of Financial Studies* 3, 625–650.

Sharpe, Steven A., and Hien H. Nguyen, 1995, Capital market imperfection and the incentive to lease, *Journal of Financial Economics* 39, 271–294.

Shevlin, Terry, 1987, Taxes and off-balance sheet financing: Research and development limited partnerships, *The Accounting Review* 62, 480–509.

Shevlin, Terry, 1990, Estimating corporate marginal tax rates with asymmetric tax treatment of gains and losses, *The Journal of the American Taxation Association* 12, 51–67.

Smith, Clifford, 1986, Investment banking and the capital acquisition process, *Journal of Financial Economics* 15, 3–29.

Smith, Clifford, and L. MacDonald Wakeman, 1985, Determinants of corporate leasing policy, *Journal of Finance* 40, 895–908.

Smith, Clifford, and Ross Watts, 1992, The investment opportunity set and corporate financing, dividend and compensation policies, *Journal of Financial Economics* 32, 263–292.

Stulz, René, and Herb Johnson, 1985, An analysis of secured debt, *Journal of Financial Economics* 14, 501–521.

Titman, Sheridan, and Roberto Wessels, 1988, The determinants of capital structure choice, *Journal of Finance* 43, 1–19.

**[4]**

Journal of Financial Economics 39 (1995) 45–69

# Liquidation costs and capital structure

Michael J. Alderson[a], Brian L. Betker*[,b]

[a]*School of Business Administration, Saint Louis University, St. Louis, MO 63108, USA*
[b]*Max M. Fisher College of Business, Ohio State University, Columbus, OH 43210, USA*

(Received May 1994; final version received November 1994)

### Abstract

We investigate the relation between liquidation costs of assets and composition of capital structure for firms that reorganized under Chapter 11 of the Bankruptcy Code. Firms with high liquidation costs emerge from Chapter 11 with relatively low debt ratios. The debt of these firms is more likely to be public and unsecured, and to have less restrictive covenant terms; these firms are also more likely to raise new equity capital. Assets with high liquidation costs thus lead firms to choose capital structures that make financial distress less likely.

*Key words:* Capital structure; Liquidation costs
*JEL classification:* G32

## 1. Introduction

We examine the relation between liquidation costs and capital structure for 88 firms that completed reorganizations under Chapter 11 of the Bankruptcy Code. Firms emerging from Chapter 11 have an opportunity to select a completely

---

* Corresponding author.

This work was completed while Alderson was at the University of Missouri–St. Louis. We appreciate helpful comments from Nasser Arshadi, David T. Brown, David Dubofsky, Tom George, Jean Helwege, Scott Lee, Richard Marcus, David Mayers, Wayne Mikkelson (the editor), Tim Opler, John Persons, Raghuram Rajan, Gabriel Ramírez, Michael Ryngaert (the referee), René Stulz, Paul Torregrossa, Michael Vetsuypens, Ralph Walkling, and seminar participants at Illinois, Marquette, Missouri, Ohio State, and SMU. We thank the many attorneys and corporate officers who provided us with information about their bankruptcy cases. Betker thanks the Dice Center for Research in Financial Economics for financial support.

46       *M.J. Alderson, B.L. Betker/Journal of Financial Economics 39 (1995) 45–69*

new capital structure, and we observe firms at the point when this choice is made. We investigate the leverage ratio as well as the mix of public and private debt and the terms of the restrictive covenants in the debt contracts.

Firms that reorganize in bankruptcy must disclose their post-bankruptcy financial structure as well as estimates of going-concern and liquidation values of their assets. We use these estimates to define the cost of liquidation as the excess of going-concern value over liquidation value, and interpret this difference as a measure of asset specificity and asset illiquidity. Firms have low liquidation costs if the value of their assets in liquidation is nearly as great as their value in current use. Liquidation costs are high if the value of assets in liquidation is substantially less than their value in current use. High liquidation costs may occur if asset specificity is high or the secondary market for the assets is thin. Asset characteristics influence financial leverage because high debt levels can lead to the realization of liquidation costs in financial distress.

Myers (1977), Williamson (1988), Harris and Raviv (1990), and Shleifer and Vishny (1992) link asset characteristics and capital structure by comparing the benefits of financial leverage to the costs of liquidation. Their models suggest that high leverage is discouraged if assets are either firm-specific and hence not easily liquidated or trade in illiquid secondary markets. While these models focus on the choice between debt and equity, they are also consistent with the idea that firms may move from highly restrictive to less restrictive debt contracts as liquidation costs increase. We thus consider the mix of public and private debt and the nature of the restrictive covenants that govern the sample firms.

We find that firms with high liquidation costs have lower debt levels with less restrictive covenant terms, and are more likely to raise new equity capital as part of the reorganization process. The debt of firms with high liquidation costs is also more likely to be public and unsecured. Firms with high liquidation costs thus choose capital structures that make future financial distress less likely. These results confirm the importance of liquidation costs in determining the capital structure of the firm.

Previous research has obtained mixed results in relating a firm's intangible assets to its financial leverage.[1] These studies employ variables such as the book value of fixed assets, advertising and R&D expense, industry classification, and market-to-book assets to measure cross-sectional differences in asset tangibility or liquidation value, although Myers (1977) argues that it is the low liquidation

---

[1] Harris and Raviv (1991) review this literature, and cite Marsh (1982), Bradley, Jarrell, and Kim (1984), Long and Malitz (1985), Kester (1986), Kim and Sorenson (1986), Friend and Hasbrouck (1988), Friend and Lang (1988), Titman and Wessels (1988), and Chaplinsky and Niehaus (1990). More recent evidence is provided by Kale, Noe, and Ramírez (1991), Smith and Watts (1992), Gaver and Gaver (1993), Opler and Titman (1993), and T.A. John (1993).

*M.J. Alderson, B.L. Betker/Journal of Financial Economics 39 (1995) 45–69*      47

value of an asset, not its intangible nature, that discourages financial leverage. While these studies use different time periods, different measures of asset characteristics, and different leverage measures, they generally find that leverage increases with fixed assets and nondebt tax shields, and decreases with advertising and R&D expense and market-to-book assets. However, some individual studies (e.g. Kale, Noe, and Ramirez, 1991) come to opposite conclusions.[2]

Our paper is distinct from prior studies in three ways. First, we observe the selection of new capital structures by established firms that are free of the holdout and hidden information problems that might otherwise restrict a complete capital structure rearrangement.[3] Second, because our study employs a value-based measure of liquidation costs, rather than an accounting-based measure of intangibility, we provide a more direct test of capital structure models that highlight liquidation costs. Finally, we look beyond leverage ratios and examine capital structure in a broader context, including restrictiveness of covenants and the mix of public and private debt.

## 2. Theory and testable implications

This section reviews some of the theories that relate liquidation costs to capital structure and discusses their testable implications. These models are based on asset characteristics such as firm specificity and secondary-market liquidity. The testable implications of these theories are then discussed.

### 2.1. Liquidation costs and capital structure theory

Myers (1977) argues that assets consisting primarily of growth options discourage debt because of the potential for underinvestment. Underinvestment

---

[2]Gilson (1993) also examines the capital structure of reorganized firms. Gilson examines changes in leverage during financial distress, whereas we relate post-bankruptcy capital structure to the firm's asset characteristics. Gilson finds that post-distress leverage ratios are positively related to pre-distress leverage and pre-distress bank debt to total debt and negatively related to the firm's nondebt tax shields. He also finds that after restructuring firms have fewer long-term debt contracts and covenants that allow more flexibility in servicing fixed claims.

[3]Asymmetric information should be less of an influence on capital structure in newly reorganized firms. During the Chapter 11 proceedings, creditor committees have the right to investigate, at the firm's expense, any aspect of the firm's business or financial condition. Giammarino (1989) argues that information asymmetries between managers and creditors may cause workouts to fail. If debtholders are uncertain about the firm's true value, it may be optimal for them to obtain better information about the firm through a costly bankruptcy proceeding, rather than accept the firm's initial workout offer.

48        M.J. Alderson, B.L. Betker/Journal of Financial Economics 39 (1995) 45–69

occurs when stockholders of distressed firms reject projects with positive net present values because the value created would accrue primarily to the debtholders. Since higher leverage results in the rejection of more positive NPV projects, firms with assets that require large amounts of discretionary investment, or growth options, will use less debt.

Myers notes that the existence of growth options is only a necessary condition for linking financial leverage to asset characteristics. The constraints on debt capacity imposed by the firm's asset characteristics are binding only if the growth options are not easily transferred to an alternative use, as can occur if the options are firm-specific or trade in an illiquid secondary market. In either case it is the option's low liquidation value, not its intangibility, that makes low debt levels optimal. Myers (1977, p. 163) argues that 'one can think of real options that are separable, objectively identifiable, relatively long-lived, and for which reasonable secondary markets exist ... Such options should 'support' debt to the same extent as otherwise similar real assets'.

Williamson (1988) assumes that firm-specific assets, which have high liquidation costs, are more likely to require discretionary investment. As in Myers' (1977) model, debt financing may prevent firms from making the investment necessary to realize the full value of firm-specific assets. Unlike Haugen and Senbet (1978), Williamson does not allow arbitrage to preclude suboptimal liquidation in bankruptcy. Thus, in this model debt financing may force the liquidation of the assets at a discount to their going-concern value. The use of debt financing therefore creates the potential not only for underinvestment but for the realization of liquidation costs when firm-specific assets are redeployed in bankruptcy. In contrast, equity financing allows greater managerial discretion and is the preferred financing method for assets with high liquidation costs.

Shleifer and Vishny (1992) consider the effect of illiquid secondary markets on liquidation costs. In their model, profitability within an industry and across the economy affects the price at which assets can be transferred to their next best use. For example, liquidation costs may be high in a depressed industry even if assets are not firm-specific, because the buyers with the expertise to use the assets, primarily other firms in the industry, cannot obtain the financing to purchase them. Assets with illiquid secondary markets support less debt because, like firm-specific assets, they impose greater liquidation costs in default.

Harris and Raviv (1990) argue that firms with low liquidation costs should have high leverage because for these firms the probability is high that liquidation is more efficient than continuing current operations. Harris and Raviv assume that managers are reluctant to liquidate the firm, perhaps to preserve the benefits of control, so investors use debt to monitor managers and gather information. If the firm defaults, debtholders can use their legal rights to obtain information and implement the efficient liquidation or continuation decision.

*M.J. Alderson, B.L. Betker/Journal of Financial Economics 39 (1995) 45–69*          49

The optimal amount of debt balances the value of limiting managerial discretion with the costs of liquidating or reorganizing when the firm defaults.[4]

## 2.2. Testable implications

The theories of capital structure reviewed here assign a central role to liquidation costs in the firm's use of debt financing. Debt is a less attractive source of financing for assets with high liquidation costs because it imposes conditions that can trigger default. Default can lead to the realization of liquidation costs by forcing divestiture or by causing assets with high liquidation costs to decline in value during financial distress. As Myers (1984) and Williamson (1988) note, assets with high liquidation costs, such as growth opportunities or firm-specific assets, are more likely to lose value in financial distress because distress prevents the firm from making the discretionary investment needed to preserve the assets' value.

For a given level of business risk, debt with restrictive covenant provisions will lead to default more often than less restrictive debt contracts. Financial claims therefore lie on a continuum ranging from borrowing agreements with specific security arrangements and strict covenants to claims such as unsecured debentures, preferred stock, and in the extreme, common equity.

The empirical implications are straightforward. Companies with easily redeployed assets that trade in liquid secondary markets will tend to be financed by debt. Firms which face high liquidation costs, either because their assets are firm-specific or the secondary market for their assets is illiquid, will employ debt with less restrictive covenants or preferred or common stock. K. John (1993) reaches a similar conclusion after surveying the theoretical literature.

We examine the effects of liquidation costs on capital structure formation using direct estimates of liquidation costs from information contained in bankruptcy reorganization plans. Two firms, American Healthcare Management and Maxicare, provide an example of how these costs can differ. Both firms have the same three-digit SIC code, and both bankruptcies took place during the period 1988–1990. American Healthcare primarily owns hospital buildings and land. The value of land or a building in one city should not depend greatly on the value of a similar asset in a different location, so American Healthcare should

---

[4]Titman (1984) relates debt levels to asset characteristics by considering a different type of liquidation cost. Liquidation imposes costs on customers if it limits the availability of additional products, parts, or service. These costs will be high for firms that produce a unique or durable product and low for firms with generic products. Titman's main empirical implication is that firms that can impose high costs on customers if they liquidate choose relatively low debt ratios. However, these firms do not necessarily have assets with high going-concern value relative to liquidation value. Thus we do not directly test Titman's theory in this paper.

have low liquidation costs. In contrast, Maxicare owns little tangible property; it is a health maintenance organization, which is a network of contracts between physicians, hospitals, and employers for delivery of health care services to enrollees. A single contract would have little value outside of this network, so Maxicare's liquidation costs should be relatively high.

The estimated going-concern value of American Healthcare's assets was $198 million, with the liquidation value estimated at $175 million. The estimated going-concern value of Maxicare's assets was $154 million and the estimated liquidation value was $37 million. (Details on how these estimates are obtained are contained in Section 3.) These figures imply that only 12% of the value of American Healthcare would be lost in liquidation, compared to 76% for Maxicare. These estimated liquidation costs reflect both the firm-specific nature of the assets and the liquidity of the secondary market for the assets. We expect to see differences in the amount and type of debt used by the reorganized firms. In fact, American Healthcare reorganized with a ratio of long-term debt to assets of 88.8%; new debt was 85% secured bank debt and 15% secured public debt. Maxicare reorganized with long-term debt to assets of 43.5%; new debt consisted entirely of unsecured, public debentures.

The appendix contains additional case studies of liquidation costs, asset composition, and capital structure for ten sample firms.

# 3. Data

## 3.1. Sample selection and empirical methods

We begin with a list of 201 firms that completed Chapter 11 bankruptcies during the period 1982–1993. The list was compiled from the samples in Altman and Nammacher (1985), Betker (1995), Eberhart, Moore, and Roenfeldt (1990), Franks and Torous (1989), Gilson, John, and Lang (1990), Lang and Stulz (1992), LoPucki and Whitford (1990), and from the Bankruptcy DataSource. We obtained disclosure statements of bankruptcy plans for 128 firms, either from the firms or their attorneys or in exhibits to 8Ks or 10Ks. The disclosure statement for a bankruptcy plan contains details of the firm's post-bankruptcy business plan, financial projections, and other pertinent information. It is mailed to all claimholders and is used to solicit votes on the bankruptcy plan. Under Section 1125(a) of the 1978 Bankruptcy Code, the disclosure statement must contain 'adequate information...that would enable a hypothetical reasonable investor...to make an informed judgment about the plan'.

We dropped 11 of the 128 firms because they either liquidated or were acquired in Chapter 11, and thus had no post-bankruptcy capital structures to analyze.

*M.J. Alderson, B.L. Betker/Journal of Financial Economics 39 (1995) 45–69*        51

To emerge from bankruptcy a firm must show that its reorganization plan is in the best interests of all claimants; that is, each creditor class must get at least as much as they would under the absolute priority rules in a Chapter 7 liquidation (§1129(a) of the 1978 Bankruptcy Code). Thus, every firm must estimate what its assets would sell for in liquidation. Going-concern values were estimated in one of three ways. Some firms presented their going-concern value side-by-side with their liquidation value, to facilitate comparisons between reorganization and liquidation. Other firms adopted fresh-start or quasi-reorganization accounting, in which all assets and liabilities on the balance sheet are restated to their fair market value.[5] In either case, the market value of the firm's assets and liabilities is generally estimated by investment bankers or valuation consultants, who use standard techniques such as discounted cash flows, multiples of cash flow, and comparable firm valuations. For nine other firms all of the claims on the reorganized firm were publicly traded, and we used the market value of these claims as an estimate of each firm's value.[6]

We dropped firms whose liquidation values were not well documented, or which did not estimate the going-concern value of their assets. Typically these firms would simply state that they estimated their liquidation value to be lower than their going-concern value, without divulging any details of their analysis. Our final sample of 88 firms provided estimates of both liquidation value and going-concern value.

We define the liquidation cost of the firm as the ratio of going-concern value less liquidation value to going-concern value. Liquidation cost thus measures the percentage of going-concern value that would be lost if the firm liquidated. As noted earlier, firms with low liquidation costs have low asset specificity and

---

[5]Under American Institute of Certified Public Accountants Statement of Position 90-7, 'Financial Reporting by Entities in Reorganization under the Bankruptcy Code', firms are required to adopt fresh-start accounting if they are insolvent and they experience an ownership change as a result of the bankruptcy. A firm is insolvent if the face value of its liabilities exceeds the fair market value of its assets. An ownership change occurs if pre-bankruptcy shareholders own less than half of the reorganized firm's equity. Under fresh-start accounting, total assets are recorded as the firm's going-concern value. This value is then allocated to specific assets. Each liability is recorded at its estimated market value (the present value of promised cash flows). Shareholder's equity is the difference between total assets (going-concern value) and market value of liabilities.

[6]For these nine firms, going-concern value is not observed until after the firm emerges from bankruptcy, while liquidation value is estimated several months before the firm emerges. For the other firms, going-concern value and liquidation value are estimated simultaneously. This might cause a problem if estimated and actual going-concern values systematically differ; as shown below, however, they do not. Furthermore, results in the paper do not differ if these nine firms are dropped from the sample.

liquid assets, since the value of the assets if liquidated is nearly as great as the value of the assets in current use. Firms with high liquidation costs have illiquid assets, either because asset specificity is high or the secondary market for those assets is thin.

### 3.2. Sample characteristics

Table 1 reports mean and median liquidation costs, post-bankruptcy total assets, and net operating loss carryforwards for the full sample of 88 firms as well as for quartiles formed on the basis of liquidation costs. Net operating loss carryforwards are expressed as a percentage of total assets. We later consider net operating loss carryforwards since nondebt tax shields may affect debt ratios. All else constant, firms with high net operating loss carryforwards might choose low debt ratios to ensure that they can use the net operating loss carryforwards in the future, as argued by DeAngelo and Masulis (1980).

Mean liquidation costs are 36.5% (median 34.7%), suggesting that about one-third of the typical firm's going-concern value would be lost in liquidation. Liquidation costs do not appear to be a function of firm size; the mean and median total assets of the high and low quartiles are not significantly different at the 10% level. Firms with low liquidation cost have significantly higher net operating loss carryforwards than firms with high liquidation costs.

The sample firms belong to 56 different industries, based on three-digit SIC codes. The quartile of firms with the lowest liquidation costs is dominated by oil and gas firms; 10 of the 22 firms are in this industry. OXOCO, the sample firm with the lowest liquidation costs (3.1%), was an oil drilling firm. Other firms with low liquidation costs are businesses like food processors, shoe companies, and steel producers. The top quartile includes high-tech and service firms, which should have a high degree of asset specificity. These companies include computer makers, drug companies, movie producers, and health care providers.

Median industry debt ratios are commonly used as proxies for determinants of optimal debt ratios. However, some SIC codes appear in both the high and low liquidation cost quartiles, such as codes for oil and gas field services, grocery stores, and hospitals. Industry classification is not always a good proxy for liquidation costs, as demonstrated by the earlier discussion of Maxicare and American Healthcare Management.

We examine the correlation between our measure of liquidation costs and several accounting proxies used in previous investigations of capital structure, including fixed assets, inventory, capital expenditures, depreciation and amortization, intangible assets, research and development expense, and advertising expense. These data were collected for the year prior to entering bankruptcy and from the pro forma financial statements in the firms' disclosure statements. We focus on the pro forma variables since they, like the liquidation cost data, reflect the nature of the firm that emerges from bankruptcy, not the firm that entered

*M.J. Alderson, B.L. Betker /Journal of Financial Economics 39 (1995) 45–69*    53

Table 1

Selected characteristics of 88 firms that reorganized in Chapter 11 during the period 1982–1993. Firms are divided into quartiles based on their liquidation costs, defined as the ratio of going-concern value less liquidation value to going-concern value. Going-concern value is the market value of the firm's assets, while liquidation value is what the assets would sell for in a Chapter 7 liquidation; both are estimated from information in the firms bankruptcy disclosure statements. Net operating loss carryforwards are obtained from the firm's disclosure statement or their first post-bankruptcy 10K.

| | | All firms (N = 88) | Firms with low liquidation costs (N = 22) | Quartile 2 firms (N = 22) | Quartile 3 firms (N = 22) | Firms with high liquidation costs (N = 22) | t (Z) for difference in means (medians) of high and low quartile firms |
|---|---|---|---|---|---|---|---|
| Liquidation costs | Mean | 0.365 | 0.128 | 0.276 | 0.437 | 0.618 | 21.28[a] |
| | Median | 0.347 | 0.151 | 0.269 | 0.452 | 0.577 | (5.69)[a] |
| Post-bankruptcy total assets | Mean | 339.3 | 331.3 | 336.1 | 320.0 | 370.1 | 0.27 |
| | Median | 163.5 | 156.5 | 205.9 | 138.8 | 143.1 | (0.18) |
| Net operating loss carry forwards/ total assets | Mean | 0.705 | 1.198 | 0.680 | 0.418 | 0.433 | 1.79[b] |
| | Median | 0.348 | 0.457 | 0.520 | 0.304 | 0.201 | (1.32) |

[a]Significant at the 1% level.
[b]Significant at the 10% level.

bankruptcy. No historical accounting variable was significantly correlated with our measure of liquidation costs, and the only pro forma accounting variable that was significantly correlated with liquidation costs was the ratio of fixed assets to total assets, with an estimated correlation coefficient of $-0.26$ (p-value 0.02). Only 19 sample firms reported intangible assets, with only three reporting R&D expense and two reporting advertising expense. We are thus unable to make reliable inferences about the relation between liquidation costs and these three variables.

### 3.3. Data quality

The quality of the data is an important consideration. The going-concern value and liquidation value of the firm are estimated by investment bankers hired by the firm and are based on information provided by the firm in many cases. In order to emerge from Chapter 11, a firm must demonstrate that its going-concern value exceeds its liquidation value. Hotchkiss (1995) finds that managers systematically overestimate the firm's post-bankruptcy performance. In order to sell the plan to creditors management may push for a low liquidation value and a high going-concern value. However, creditor committees can hire their own consultants at the firm's expense and can challenge the accuracy of any estimate in the plan. A successful challenge would be grounds for throwing the disclosure statement out of court. Bankruptcy attorneys with whom we conferred observe that the estimates of going-concern value and liquidation value are closely scrutinized by creditor committees, and that they are the best estimates available.

One way to judge the accuracy of estimates for going-concern value is to compare the market value of equity implied by estimates of the going-concern value and the market value of liabilities with the observed market value of the firm's equity after it emerges from bankruptcy. Post-bankruptcy stock prices were available for 66 sample firms; 37 of these firms underestimated the actual value of their equity, while 29 firms overestimated it. We define the firm's estimation error as the estimated value minus the actual market value of equity, expressed as a fraction of the actual equity value. The mean estimation error is 0.18, while the median is $-0.01$. Neither the mean nor median is significantly different from zero at the 10% level. The mean and median unsigned errors are 0.49 and 0.23. Furthermore, the correlations between estimation errors and liquidation costs, firm size, and the post-bankruptcy ratio of long-term debt to assets are $-0.05$, $-0.01$, and $-0.04$, respectively, and have p-values exceeding 0.50. Thus, although firms' estimates of their market value are noisy, they are unbiased, and estimation errors are unrelated to liquidation costs, firm size, or observed leverage ratios.

We cannot tell if firms accurately estimate their going-concern value but underestimate their liquidation value. Firms may have an incentive to provide liquidation values less than the face value of old debt outstanding, since if liquidation value exceeds total debt, creditors can demand payment in full. However, for 80 of the 88 sample firms, the amount owed to creditors in bankruptcy exceeded the firm's going-concern value. These firms would not need to lower their estimate of liquidation value in order to justify offering creditors an amount less than the face value of their claims. In what follows we are less interested in the absolute value of liquidation costs and more interested in cross-sectional variation in these numbers. Even systematic underestimation of liquidation values should not bias cross-sectional tests.

## 4. Empirical results

### 4.1. Amount and type of new debt

Table 2 reports evidence concerning the ratios of long-term debt to assets, total liabilities to assets, and specific types of debt to total debt. The table includes estimated coefficients from regressions of debt ratios on liquidation costs, firm size, and net operating loss carryforwards. Summary statistics for debt ratios are also provided for each liquidation cost quartile.

Debt ratios are obtained from the pro forma balance sheets in firms' disclosure statements. Under fresh-start accounting, total assets are equal to the firm's going-concern value, as noted earlier, while each liability is recorded at its estimated market value, i.e., the present value of promised cash flows. Debt ratios are thus based on estimated market values, which for newly reorganized firms are the same as book values. Debt is classified as either private or public. Private debt includes bank debt and debt placed with insurance companies or other institutions. Debt may be straight or convertible and secured or unsecured. Debt is also classified by the degree of security. Some debt is secured by a first lien on all of the firm's assets, while other secured debt may have specific assets as collateral.

The ratio of long-term debt to assets is significantly negatively related to liquidation costs. The regression coefficient of $-0.505$ indicates that an increase in liquidation costs of 0.10 decreases the long-term debt ratio by 0.05. Firms in the low quartile of liquidation costs have a mean long-term debt to assets ratio of 0.579, compared to 0.347 for firms with high liquidation costs. Total liabilities to total assets follows a similar pattern, although the statistical significance of the relationship is weaker. The mean ratio of liabilities to assets for the full sample is 0.68, which is lower than Gilson's (1993) average of 0.81, although Gilson also finds that post-distress debt ratios are lower for bankrupt firms than for firms that complete workouts, and our sample contains only bankrupt firms.

Table 1 reports that firms with low liquidation costs have higher nondebt tax shields (net operating loss carryforwards), which should push them towards having less debt. Firms with high liquidation costs should have more debt. However, neither long-term debt nor total liabilities is significantly related to net operating loss carryforwards. Gilson (1993) finds that the post-reorganization leverage ratio, after controlling for pre-distress leverage, is negatively related to tax loss carryforwards; that is, firms with high tax loss carryforwards

Table 2
Regressions of amount and type of debt on liquidation costs, log of post-bankruptcy total assets, and net operating loss carryforwards (NOLs)

Liquidation costs are defined as the ratio of going-concern value less liquidation value to going-concern value. Debt ratios are obtained from pro-forma balance sheets in firm's bankruptcy disclosure statements. The sample is 88 firms that reorganized in Chapter 11 during the period 1982–1993.

| Dependent variables | Independent variables Coefficient estimates ($p$-values) | | | | |
|---|---|---|---|---|---|
| OLS regression | Intercept | Liquidation costs | Log of total assets | NOLs/ Total assets | $R^2$ ($p$-value of regression model) |
| Long-term debt/ Total assets | 0.718 (0.00) | − 0.505 (0.01) | 0.002 (0.95) | − 0.030 (0.33) | 0.066 (0.04) |
| Total liabilities/ Total assets | 0.593 (0.00) | − 0.182 (0.10) | 0.036 (0.03) | − 0.031 (0.12) | 0.101 (0.01) |
| Private debt/ Total debt | 0.931 (0.00) | − 0.506 (0.02) | − 0.017 (0.58) | | 0.044 (0.07) |
| Convertible debt/ Total debt | 0.128 (0.06) | 0.042 (0.61) | − 0.021 (0.08) | | 0.017 (0.16) |
| Secured debt/ Total debt | 1.000 (0.00) | − 0.358 (0.07) | 0.012 (0.65) | | 0.021 (0.19) |
| Logit regressions | | | | | |
| No secured debt | − 2.045 (0.15) | 3.882 (0.03) | − 0.323 (0.16) | | 0.116[a] (0.02) |
| Debt secured by first lien on all assets | 2.107 (0.05) | − 4.721 (0.00) | − 0.013 (0.94) | | 0.123[a] (0.00) |
| Debt secured by specific assets | − 2.980 (0.01) | 3.032 (0.02) | 0.197 (0.26) | | 0.062[a] (0.04) |

*M.J. Alderson, B.L. Betker/Journal of Financial Economics 39 (1995) 45–69* 57

Table 2 (continued)

| Dependent variables | Summary statistics for dependent variable Mean (Median) | | | |
|---|---|---|---|---|
| OLS regression | Low liquidation cost firms (N = 22) | Quartile 2 firms (N = 22) | Quartile 3 firms (N = 22) | High liquidation cost firms (N = 22) |
| Long-term debt/ Total assets | 0.579 (0.584) | 0.615 (0.652) | 0.572 (0.549) | 0.347 (0.342) |
| Total liabilities/ Total assets | 0.717 (0.768) | 0.675 (0.727) | 0.754 (0.796) | 0.565 (0.597) |
| Private debt/ Total debt | 0.816 (1.000) | 0.704 (0.882) | 0.543 (0.504) | 0.531 (0.632) |
| Convertible debt/ Total debt | 0.042 (0.000) | 0.010 (0.000) | 0.008 (0.000) | 0.075 (0.000) |
| Secured debt/ Total debt | 0.845 (1.000) | 0.923 (1.000) | 0.714 (0.986) | 0.630 (0.900) |
| Logit regressions | Number of firms | | | |
| No secured debt | 2 | 0 | 3 | 6 |
| Debt secured by first lien on all assets | 18 | 14 | 12 | 6 |
| Debt secured by specific assets | 2 | 8 | 7 | 10 |

[a]Pseudo-$R^2$ from logit regression, defined at one minus the log-likelihood ratio at convergence over the log-likelihood ratio at zero.

reduce their debt ratio more than firms with low tax loss carryforwards, which does not contradict our finding that post-bankruptcy carryforwards are unrelated to the *level* of debt ratios.

Distinct differences between firms with high and low liquidation costs also appear when we compare the type of debt in the capital structure. Table 2 reports the results of ordinary least-squares regressions on the type and amount of debt for the sample firms. The dependent variable is the percentage of total debt represented by a specific debt type. The explanatory variables are liquidation costs and firm size. Net operating loss carryforwards are not included in these regressions since there is no reason to expect the type of debt to depend on the firm's tax attributes.

Liquidation costs are significantly negatively related to the proportions of both private and secured debt. One possible reason for the higher percentage of private debt held by firms with low liquidation costs is that they are small firms. However, the higher incidence of secured private debt in these firms is not a function of firm size. Liquidation cost has significant explanatory power in the regressions, while size does not. The summary statistics indicate that the debt of the median firm in the low liquidation cost quartile consists entirely of secured private debt. In contrast the median firm in the high liquidation cost quartile has more than one-third of its debt in public hands.

This finding contrasts with the common presumption that private debt contracts are more easily renegotiated in financial distress and may therefore be more appropriate for firms with *high* liquidation costs. However, our finding is consistent with Asquith, Gertner, and Scharfstein (1991) and Brown, James, and Mooradian (1994) who find that banks are more likely to force liquidation of assets than public debtholders. Our result may also be explained by Harris and Raviv (1990), who argue that, when liquidation costs are low, it is optimal to allow lenders to make frequent liquidation or continuation decisions. Although Harris and Raviv do not consider the choice between public and private debt, it is likely that private lenders, who should have an informational advantage over public lenders, can make the correct liquidation or continuation decision at lower cost than public lenders. Rajan (1992) argues that assets which require large discretionary investment should be financed with public rather than private debt. He notes that informed banks can prevent projects from going awry, but also have bargaining power over the firm's profits once projects have begun, reducing the firm's incentive to make the discretionary investment needed to maintain the project's value. If assets that require large amounts of discretionary investment also tend to have high liquidation costs, as argued by Williamson (1988), then our finding that private debt is more often used when liquidation costs are low is consistent with Rajan's model as well.

The nature of the collateral for secured debt also differs between the high and low quartiles of liquidation costs. Of the 20 firms with low liquidation costs and secured debt, 18 pledged all of their assets as collateral for debt. In contrast, only six of the 16 firms with high liquidation costs and secured debt pledged all the firm's assets; the other ten firms pledged only specific assets. The results of logit regressions reported in Table 2 confirm the statistical significance of the relation between collateral and liquidation costs: firms with low liquidation costs are more likely to have secured debt and are more likely to put up the entire firm up as collateral for the debt. Assets with low liquidation values make poor collateral for secured debt.

Finally, sample firms rarely issue convertible debt upon emerging from bankruptcy, and the existence of convertible debt is unrelated to liquidation costs. Stein (1992) argues that convertible debt can be used as 'backdoor equity financing' when informational asymmetries are high. The lack of convertible

*M.J. Alderson, B.L. Betker/Journal of Financial Economics 39 (1995) 45–69*          59

financing in the sample firms is consistent with our earlier argument that there should be little hidden information about a firm that has spent the last few years under court supervision. In summary, the results in this section support the conclusion that firms with high liquidation costs choose claims such as unsecured public debt and equity that reduce the probability of future distress.[7]

### 4.2. Raising new equity capital

Of the 88 sample firms, 27 sold equity to new investors as they emerged from bankruptcy. Panel A of Table 3 reports summary statistics for the number of firms raising equity, the number of shares purchased by new investors, and the amount of new capital raised for each quartile of liquidation costs.

Only two of the 22 firms with the lowest liquidation costs raised new equity, compared to 11 of the 22 firms with the highest liquidation costs. Note that liquidation costs are computed without including the value of the equity injection in the estimate of going-concern value. Thus, the observed relation between liquidation costs and new equity financing is not due to the fact that injecting equity raises the firm's going-concern value. Firms with low liquidation costs sold an average of 39% of their equity to new investors, while firms with high liquidation costs sold 61% of their equity on average. The average amount of new capital raised was 8% of assets for firms with low liquidation costs, and 22% of assets for firms with high liquidation costs. These results are consistent with capital structure models that predict a move towards equity financing as liquidation costs increase. Interestingly, Myers (1984, p. 590) notes that if 'information asymmetry disappears from time to time, then the firm should stock up with equity before it reappears'. We argue that information asymmetries, which should be greatest in firms with high liquidation costs, are reduced for firms emerging from Chapter 11. The greater frequency of equity injections for firms with high liquidation costs is consistent with Myers' observation.

To confirm that the relation between raising new equity and liquidation costs is not driven by firm size or tax status, we estimate two regressions. The dependent variable in the first regression is equal to one if the firm

---

[7]Average debt maturity does not differ among liquidation cost quartiles. Myers (1977) notes that the underinvestment problem may be reduced by shortening debt maturity. Since assets with high liquidation costs are more susceptible to underinvestment, we might expect to see these assets financed with shorter-term debt. However, average debt maturities (weighted by the value of the debt) for low, second, third, and high quartiles of liquidation costs are 7.3 years, 8.0 years, 6.3 years, and 6.9 years, respectively. Measurement of effective debt maturity is complicated by sinking fund and call provisions. However, we later show that firms with low liquidation costs are more likely to have covenants specifying mandatory debt prepayments.

raised new equity capital and zero otherwise, while in the second regression the dependent variable is the value of the equity raised as a percentage of the firm's assets. The independent variables are liquidation costs, log of total assets, and net operating loss carryforwards divided by total assets. We estimate the two regressions using logit and tobit techniques, and the results are in panel B of Table 3. Firms with high liquidation costs are

Table 3
Summary statistics for amount and value of new equity capital raised, and estimated coefficients from regressions relating equity issues to liquidation costs, firm size, and net operating loss carryforwards

Panel A shows the number of firms raising new equity capital as part of their plan to emerge from bankruptcy. Also shown are the percentage of shares in the post-bankruptcy firm owned by the new investors, and the value of the new investment as a proportion of total assets. Firms are divided into quartiles based on their liquidation costs, defined as the ratio of going-concern value less liquidation value to going-concern value. Panel B contains estimated coefficients from two regressions. The dependent variables are (1) new equity raised, which is one if the firm raised new equity capital and zero otherwise, and (2) the value of the new equity investment as a proportion of total assets. The independent variables are liquidation costs, log of total assets, and net operating loss carryforwards (NOLs) divided by total assets. The two regressions are estimated using logit and tobit techniques. The sample is 88 firms that reorganized in Chapter 11 during the period 1982–1993.

Panel A: Summary statistics

|  |  | Low liquidation cost firms $(N = 22)$ | Quartile 2 firms $(N = 22)$ | Quartile 3 firms $(N = 22)$ | High liquidation cost firms $(N = 22)$ |
|---|---|---|---|---|---|
| Number of firms raising new equity |  | 2 | 6 | 8 | 11 |
| Percentage of shares owned by new investors | Mean | 39.4% | 61.8% | 45.0% | 60.8% |
|  | Median | 39.4% | 67.4% | 41.1% | 62.5% |
| Value of shares purchased/ Total assets | Mean | 0.084 | 0.166 | 0.155 | 0.222 |
|  | Median | 0.084 | 0.152 | 0.110 | 0.167 |

Panel B: Regression coefficient estimates (p-values)

| Dependent variable | Intercept | Liquidation costs | Log of total assets | NOLs/ assets | Pseudo-$R^2$ (p-value of regression model) |
|---|---|---|---|---|---|
| New equity raised (logit) | 0.87 (0.50) | 2.55 (0.07) | − 0.44 (0.04) | − 0.92 (0.08) | 0.130[a] (0.01) |
| Value of shares purchased/ Total assets (tobit) | 0.14 (0.29) | 0.25 (0.05) | − 0.06 (0.01) | − 0.11 (0.06) | 0.397[a] (0.00) |

[a]Pseudo-$R^2$ is defined as one minus the log-likelihood ratio at convergence over the log-likelihood ratio at zero.

more likely to raise equity and raise a larger fraction of firm value than firms with low liquidation costs. Holding liquidation costs constant, smaller firms are more likely to raise new equity capital than larger firms. Net operating loss carryforwards have the opposite sign than would be expected if raising new equity were merely an attempt to ensure usage of the firm's tax attributes.

## 4.3. Restrictive debt covenants

Most capital structure theories do not directly address the terms of debt covenants, focusing instead on the determinants of the leverage ratio. These models suggest that equity financing is preferred when liquidation costs are high to reduce the probability of incurring these costs. However, these models are also consistent with the idea that firms with high liquidation costs should use debt with less restrictive covenant terms, since relaxing the terms of the debt contract also lowers the probability of default.

Table 4 contains a summary of the debt covenants that affect the sample firms. This information is missing for 14 firms. We focus on covenants that restrict discretionary investment, new financing, and use of excess cash. We hypothesize that firms with high liquidation costs will have fewer covenants that restrict their actions along these dimensions. Table 4 reports the number of firms in each liquidation cost quartile with a debt issue that includes a covenant of the specified type as well as the results of a logit regression of covenant type on liquidation cost. The dependent variable in the logit regression is one if a covenant of the specified type appears in a debt contract and zero otherwise. Including firm size as a control variable in unreported regressions does not change any conclusions regarding liquidation costs and covenants.

We observe distinct differences between the covenants of firms with high and low liquidation costs. Debt covenants that limit capital expenditures affect 75% of the firms in the lowest quartile of liquidation costs, while 44% are prohibited from changing their corporate structure via mergers, acquisitions, and changes in the firm's line of business. In contrast, 26% of the firms in the highest quartile of liquidation costs are affected by covenants that limit capital expenditures and 5% are prohibited from changing corporate structure.

There are no distinct differences between firms with high and low liquidation costs regarding covenants restricting new financing. However, four firms with low liquidation costs are prohibited from raising either new debt or new equity capital, and 69% of firms with low liquidation costs are prohibited from paying dividends, compared to 11% of firms with high liquidation costs. (All firms have covenants *restricting* dividends, and in some cases these constraints might be binding, but we only consider those cases in which the debt covenant prohibits dividends under any circumstances.)

Table 4

Logit regression of covenant type on liquidation cost, and the percentage of firms in each liquidation cost quartile with a debt issue that includes a covenant of the specified type

The dependent variable in the logit regression is one if a covenant of the specified type appears in a debt contract and zero otherwise. Covenants are identified from descriptions in the firms bankruptcy disclosure statements or from the debt indenture itself. Liquidation costs are defined as the ratio of going-concern value less liquidation value to going-concern value and are estimated from information in the firms' bankruptcy disclosure statements. The sample is 88 firms that reorganized in Chapter 11 during the period 1982–1993.

| Type of covenant | Estimated coefficient from logit regression of covenant type on liquidation cost | p-value of regression coefficient | Summary statistics: Firms with specified covenant type | | | |
|---|---|---|---|---|---|---|
| | | | Low liquidation cost firms ($N = 16$) | Quartile 2 firms ($N = 20$) | Quartile 3 firms ($N = 19$) | High liquidation cost firms ($N = 19$) |
| Prohibit asset sales | −2.13 | 0.41 | 18.8% | 0.0% | 5.3% | 5.3% |
| Limit capital expenditures | −4.64 | 0.00 | 75.0 | 70.0 | 68.0 | 26.3 |
| Prohibit change in corporate structure[a] | −2.89 | 0.05 | 44.0 | 30.0 | 47.0 | 5.3 |

M.J. Alderson, B.L. Betker/Journal of Financial Economics 39 (1995) 45–69    63

| | | | | | | |
|---|---|---|---|---|---|---|
| Issuance of new debt | Prohibited | −2.47 | 0.30 | 12.5 | 5.0 | 15.8 | 0.0 |
| | Restricted | −3.06 | 0.02 | 68.8 | 75.0 | 47.4 | 36.8 |
| Issuance of new equity | Prohibited | −6.91 | 0.13 | 12.5 | 5.0 | 0.0 | 0.0 |
| | Restricted | −2.37 | 0.68 | 0.0 | 5.0 | 0.0 | 0.0 |
| Prohibit payment of dividends | | −4.62 | 0.00 | 68.8 | 60.0 | 57.9 | 10.5 |
| New debt must be amortized[b] | | −2.19 | 0.10 | 81.3 | 90.0 | 78.9 | 57.9 |
| Debt prepayment out of proceeds of asset sales | | −1.50 | 0.22 | 43.8 | 70.0 | 68.4 | 31.6 |
| Debt prepayment out of proceeds of security issues | | −2.61 | 0.10 | 25.0 | 30.0 | 21.1 | 15.8 |
| Debt prepayment out of excess cash flow[c] | | −4.41 | 0.00 | 81.3 | 60.0 | 57.9 | 15.8 |

[a]Changes in corporate structure include mergers, acquisitions, and changes in the firm's line of business.

[b]Includes mandatory prepayments of private debt at specified intervals, and sinking fund provisions in public debt contracts.

[c]Excess cash flow is usually contractually specified as all cash in excess of working capital needs, or in excess of some fixed dollar amount.

Of the 16 firms with the lowest liquidation costs, 13 (81%) have debt that must be prepaid out of excess cash flow, as defined in the debt contract. This amount is usually specified as all cash in excess of working capital needs, or in excess of a specified dollar amount. In contrast, only 21% of the firms with the highest liquidation costs face this restriction on their use of free cash flow.

The results in Table 4 are consistent with the idea that firms with high liquidation costs choose capital structures that place fewer restrictions on their ability to make discretionary investments and are less likely to lead to future default.

## 5. Summary

We examine the relation between liquidation costs and capital structure for 88 firms that reorganized under Chapter 11 of the 1978 Bankruptcy Code. Firms that reorganize in bankruptcy must disclose estimates of the going-concern and liquidation values of their assets. We use these estimates to define the cost of liquidation as the excess of going-concern value over liquidation value.

We find that firms with high liquidation costs use less debt than firms with low liquidation costs. Furthermore, the debt of these firms is more likely to be public and unsecured. Firms with high liquidation costs are less likely to be constrained by debt covenants that prohibit dividends, restrict capital expenditures, and prohibit changes in corporate structure. These firms are also less likely to have to prepay their debt out of excess cash flow. Firms with high liquidation costs are also much more likely to attract new equity capital as part of their reorganization process. These results do not appear to be driven by either firm size or the amount of nondebt tax shields. We thus provide support for the common predictions of models that relate liquidation costs to capital structure.

## Appendix

This appendix summarizes estimates of liquidation costs, asset composition, and post-bankruptcy capital structure for ten sample firms. Five firms are randomly chosen from both the top and bottom liquidation cost quartiles.

### A.1. Firms with low liquidation costs

*Allegheny International*
Going-concern value = $635.29 million. Liquidation value = $530.02 million. Liquidation costs = 16.57%. Allegheny International is engaged in the

manufacture and sale of consumer products, including kitchen appliances, outdoor furniture, barbecue grills, electric blankets, clocks, and timers. The firm's products are marketed directly to retail stores. Assets consist primarily of manufacturing facilities and inventory. The firm (which changed its name to Sunbeam/Oster) emerged from bankruptcy with long-term debt consisting of $250 million in secured seven-year floating-rate bank debt, and $34.9 million of debt and capital leases left unimpaired by the bankruptcy plan. The ratio of long-term debt to assets is 44.8%. Covenants prohibit dividend payments and require bank approval of managers' employment contracts.

### Doskocil Companies

Going-concern value = $213 million. Liquidation value = $180.7 million. Liquidation costs = 15.16%. Doskocil sells processed meat products for use in cafeterias and in the food service industry. Customers include pizza restaurants, hotels, hospitals, school systems, and the military. Assets consist primarily of meat processing plants. The reorganized firm's long-term debt consists of secured bank debt of $141.6 million, and the debt-to-assets ratio is 66.3%. Debt covenants prohibit dividend payments, new debt issuance, and changes in the firm's line of business. The firm is required to prepay the debt using 90% of their excess cash flow each year.

### Global Marine

Going-concern value = $560 million. Liquidation value = $512 million. Liquidation costs = 8.57%. Global Marine primarily operates offshore oil and gas drilling rigs, and also engages in exploration and development of oil and gas. The firm's assets consist primarily of 30 offshore drilling rigs. The firm reorganized with long-term debt of $395.86 million, for a debt-to-assets ratio of 70.7%. Debt consists entirely of 12% eight-year bank notes each secured by a particular drilling rig. Covenants prohibit payment of dividends and changes in the firm's line of business. Each series of notes must be prepaid out of the net cash flow (revenues minus allowed expenses) of the rig securing the debt.

### Kinder-Care Learning Centers

Going-concern value = $348.92 million. Liquidation value = $295.57 million. Liquidation costs = 15.29%. Kinder-Care operates over 1,200 day-care centers in 39 states. The firm's assets consist primarily of land and the buildings housing the day-care centers. The reorganized firm's long-term debt consists of $107.5 million in eight-year floating-rate bank notes and $104.4 million in ten-year 12% bank notes. The long-term debt-to-assets ratio is 60.7%. The debt is secured by a first lien on all the firm's assets. Covenants prohibit asset sales, dividends, and changes in lines of business. The debt is prepayable annually from 75% of the firm's excess cash flow.

## TGX Corp.

Going-concern value = $50.00 million. Liquidation value = $41.54 million. Liquidation costs = 16.92%. TGX provides natural gas transportation and marketing services to producers, operates intrastate natural gas production and transmission facilities, and engages in exploration for natural gas. Assets consist almost entirely of oil and natural gas wells. Long-term debt in the reorganized firm consists of a five-year $24.88 million term loan secured by a first lien on all of the firm's assets. The long-term debt-to-assets ratio 49.8%. Debt covenants prohibit asset sales, changes in the firm's line of business, and dividends (unless paid using the proceeds from the sale of equity).

### A.2. Firms with high liquidation costs

## Chyron Group

Going-concern value = $43.19 million. Liquidation value = $19.52 million. Liquidation costs = 54.80%. Chyron designs, manufactures, and distributes high-performance digital titling and graphics equipment for use by the television industry and video production studios, and manufactures computer-assisted videotape editing systems. The firm notes that its future success depends on proprietary technology and the technical competence of its personnel to develop and introduce new products. Long-term debt consists of $5 million in five-year unsecured variable-rate convertible notes, so the long-term debt-to-assets ratio is 11.6%. The notes are free of any covenants restricting the firm's operations or use of cash flow. Chyron also received $10 million in exchange for 81% of the reorganized firm's common stock.

## In-Store Advertising

Going-concern value = $7.98 million. Liquidation value = $2.70 million. Liquidation costs = 66.16%. In-Store Advertising delivers advertising messages to shoppers in over 5,400 stores through a network of in-store electronic signs. Proprietary software and hardware allow the firm to provide up-to-the minute pricing information, company logos, and animation on the signs. The firm's primary asset is their sign network; an individual sign has minimal liquidation value, since the signs are designed to operate in a network. The firm (now called Emarc) reorganized with no long-term debt. Pre-bankruptcy creditors received convertible preferred stock in the reorganized firm. The reorganized firm also sold 60% of its common stock to its managers.

## Storage Technology

Going-concern value = $980.42 million. Liquidation value = $423.16 million. Liquidation costs = 56.84%. Storage Technology designs, manufactures, and markets computer peripheral and retrieval subsystems such as tape and disk storage units. Assets consist primarily of manufacturing facilities, inventory, and

*M.J. Alderson, B.L. Betker/Journal of Financial Economics 39 (1995) 45–69*          67

spare parts for field service. More than 10% of the firm's employees are engaged in engineering and new product development. The reorganized firm's long-term debt consists of $285 million in 13.25% ten-year unsecured debentures, $25 million in 12% five-year secured notes, and a $50 million secured revolving credit line. The ratio of long-term debt to assets is 36.7%. Covenants limit but do not prohibit payment of dividends, asset sales, and new financing.

*Tracor Inc.*

Going-concern value = $173.06 million. Liquidation value = $46.00 million. Liquidation costs = 73.42%. Tracor was spun off from Tracor Holdings after that firm emerged from bankruptcy. Reorganized Tracor provides products, systems, and service to the U.S. Department of Defense. Products include radar-avoidance materials and systems, electronic surveillance equipment, and encryption systems. Much of their business is classified. Assets consist primarily of plant and equipment and receivables. Long-term debt consists of $60 million in variable-rate seven-year secured bank notes. The ratio of long-term debt to assets is 34.7%. The bank debt is prepayable annually from 50% of the firm's excess cash flow. Covenants restrict but do not prohibit dividends and new financing. (The other firm spun off from Tracor Holdings reorganized as Littlefuse, Inc., a maker of fuses for the automotive and electronics industry. Littlefuse had liquidation costs of 21.4% and reorganized with a ratio of long-term debt to assets of 61.6%.)

*Zale Corporation*

Going-concern value = $1,143.25 million. Liquidation value = $396.67 million. Liquidation costs = 65.30%. Zale is the nation's largest retailer of fine jewelry. The firm purchases all of its merchandise in finished form from an established network of suppliers. Assets consist primarily of customer receivables, inventory, and stores. Liquidation cost estimates were based on the firm's historical experience in liquidating its stores. The reorganized firm's long-term debt consists of $60 million in 11% seven-year secured bank notes, $10 million in 8% five-year secured notes, and a $175 million secured revolving credit line. The ratio of long-term debt to assets is 21.4%. Covenants limit but do not prohibit payment of dividends, asset sales, and new financing.

**References**

Altman, Edward I. and Scott A. Nammacher, 1985, The default rate experience on high-yield corporate debt, Financial Analyst's Journal 41, 25–41.

Asquith, Paul, Robert Gertner, and David Scharfstein, 1991, Anatomy of financial distress: An examination of junk bond issuers, Working paper (Massachusetts Institute of Technology, Cambridge, MA).

Betker, Brian L., 1995, Management's incentives, equity's bargaining power and deviations from absolute priority in Chapter 11 bankruptcies, Journal of Business 68, 161–183.

Bradley, Michael, Gregg Jarrell, and E. Han Kim, 1984, On the existence of an optimal capital structure: Theory and evidence, Journal of Finance 39, 857–878.

Brown, David T., Christopher M. James, and Robert M. Mooradian, 1994, Asset sales by financially distressed firms, Journal of Corporate Finance 1, 233–258.

Chaplinsky, Susan and Greg Niehaus, 1990, The determinants of inside ownership and leverage, Working paper (University of Michigan, Ann Arbor, MI).

DeAngelo, Harry and Ronald W. Masulis, 1980, Optimal capital structure under corporate and personal taxation, Journal of Financial Economics 8, 3–30.

Eberhart, Allan C., William T. Moore, and Rodney L. Roenfeldt, 1990, Security pricing and deviations from the absolute priority rule in bankruptcy proceedings, Journal of Finance 45, 1457–1469.

Franks, Julian R. and Walter N. Torous, 1989, An empirical investigation of U.S. firms in reorganization, Journal of Finance 44, 747–769.

Friend, Irwin and Joel Hasbrouck, 1988, Determinants of capital structure, in: Andrew Chen, ed., Research in finance, Vol. 7 (JAI Press, New York, NY) 1–19.

Friend, Irwin and Larry H.P. Lang, 1988, An empirical test of the impact of managerial self-interest on corporate capital structure, Journal of Finance 43, 271–281.

Gaver, Jennifer J. and Kenneth M. Gaver, 1993, Additional evidence on the association between the investment opportunity set and corporate financing, dividend and compensation policies, Journal of Accounting and Economics 16, 125–160.

Giammarino, Ronald, 1989, The resolution of financial distress, Review of Financial Studies 2, 25–48.

Gilson, Stuart C., 1993, Debt reduction, optimal capital structure, and renegotiation of claims during financial distress, Working paper (Harvard University, Cambridge, MA).

Gilson, Stuart C., Kose John, and Larry H.P. Lang, 1990, Troubled debt restructurings: An empirical study of private reorganization of firms in default, Journal of Financial Economics 27, 315–354.

Harris, Milton and Artur Raviv, 1990, Capital structure and the informational role of debt, Journal of Finance 45, 321–349.

Harris, Milton and Artur Raviv, 1991, The theory of capital structure, Journal of Finance 46, 297–355.

Haugen, Robert and Lemma Senbet, 1978, The insignificance of bankruptcy costs to the theory of optimal capital structure, Journal of Finance 33, 383–393.

Hotchkiss, Edith, 1995, The post-bankruptcy performance of firms emerging from Chapter 11, Journal of Finance 50, 3–22.

John, Kose, 1993, Managing financial distress and valuing distressed securities: A survey and a research agenda, Financial Management 13, 60–78.

John, Theresa A., 1993, Accounting measures of corporate liquidity, leverage, and costs of financial distress, Financial Management 13, 91–100.

Kale, Jayant R., Thomas H. Noe, and Gabriel G. Ramirez, 1991, The effect of business risk on corporate capital structure: Theory and evidence, Journal of Finance 46, 1693–1716.

Kester, Carl W., 1986, Capital and ownership structure: A comparison of United States and Japanese manufacturing corporations, Financial Management 6, 5–16.

Kim, Wi Saeng and Eric H. Sorenson, 1986, Evidence on the impact of the agency costs of debt in corporate debt policy, Journal of Financial and Quantitative Analysis 21, 131–144.

Lang, Larry H.P. and René Stulz, 1992, Contagion and competitive intra-industry effects of bankruptcy announcements: An empirical analysis, Journal of Financial Economics 32, 45–60.

Long, Michael and Ileen Malitz, 1985, The investment-financing nexus: Some empirical evidence, Midland Corporate Finance Journal 3, 53–59.

LoPucki, Lynn M. and William C. Whitford, 1990, Bargaining over equity's share in the bankruptcy reorganization of large, publicly held companies, University of Pennsylvania Law Review 139, 125–196.

Marsh, Paul, 1982, The choice between equity and debt: An empirical study, Journal of Finance 37, 121–144.

Myers, Stewart C., 1977, Determinants of corporate borrowing, Journal of Financial Economics 5, 147–175.

Myers, Stewart C., 1984, The capital structure puzzle, Journal of Finance 39, 575–592.

Opler, Tim and Sheridan Titman, 1993, The determinants of LBO activity, Journal of Finance 48, 1985–1999.

Rajan, Raghuram G., 1992, Insiders and outsiders: The choice between informed and arm's-length debt, Journal of Finance 47, 1367–1400.

Shleifer, Andre and Robert W. Vishny, 1992, Liquidation values and debt capacity: A market equilibrium approach, Journal of Finance 47, 1343–1366.

Smith, Clifford W., Jr. and Ross L. Watts, 1992, The investment opportunity set and corporate financing, dividend and compensation policies, Journal of Financial Economics 32, 263–292.

Stein, Jeremy C., 1992, Convertible bonds as backdoor equity financing, Journal of Financial Economics 32, 3–22.

Titman, Sheridan, 1984, The effect of capital structure on a firm's liquidation decision, Journal of Financial Economics 13, 137–151.

Titman, Sheridan and Roberto Wessels, 1988, The determinants of capital structure choice, Journal of Finance 43, 1–19.

Williamson, Oliver, 1988, Corporate finance and corporate governance, Journal of Finance 43, 567–592.

# [5]

**Mark Hoven Stohs**
*University College Dublin*

**David C. Mauer**
*University of Miami*

*G32*

## The Determinants of Corporate Debt Maturity Structure*

### I. Introduction

Since the 1960s, a tremendous amount of theoretical and empirical research has focused on the determinants of corporate capital structures. The interplay between theory and empirical verification or rejection has progressed in a lockstep fashion, in large part due to readily accessible machine-readable accounting data. Unfortunately, we know little about the empirical determinants of corporate debt maturity structure, because readily available and detailed information about a firm's debt and debtlike obligations is difficult and time-consuming to collect. Accordingly, the papers that have attempted to examine the empirical determinants of debt maturity structure focus on either the term-to-maturity of public debt issues (Mitchell 1991; and Guedes and Opler 1994) or measures of the proportions

We examine the empirical determinants of debt maturity structure using a maturity structure measure that incorporates detailed information about all of a firm's liabilities. We find that larger, less risky firms with longer-term asset maturities use longer-term debt. Additionally, debt maturity varies inversely with earnings surprises and a firm's effective tax rate, but there is only mixed support for an inverse relation with growth opportunities. We find strong support for the prediction of a nonmonotonic relation between debt maturity and bond rating; firms with high or very low bond ratings use shorter-term debt.

* Helpful comments and suggestions have been provided by James Ang, Doug Diamond (the editor), Doug Emery, Mark Flannery, Jed Frees, Tom Noe, Tim Opler, Henri Servaes, René Stulz, Howard Thompson, Alex Triantis, Arthur Warga, an anonymous referee, and seminar participants at Indiana University, University of Kentucky, University of Miami, University of New Orleans, and University of Wisconsin—Madison. An earlier version of this article was presented at the 1994 Financial Management Association meeting and the 1994 Eastern Finance Association meeting.

(*Journal of Business*, 1996, vol. 69, no. 3)

of short- and long-term debt in firm's capital structures (Titman and Wessels 1988; and Barclay and Smith 1995).[1]

Mitchell (1991) finds that a firm is more likely to issue shorter-term debt (terms less than 20 years) if the firm is not traded on the New York Stock Exchange (NYSE) (or in the Standard and Poor's [S&P] 400), has a high retention ratio, and has convertible debt in its capital structure. She argues that her findings are consistent with the hypothesis that firms facing a high degree of information asymmetry choose shorter-term debt to minimize adverse selection costs. She finds no support for the notion that firms choose the maturity of debt issues to match their asset maturities. In a similar study of debt issues, Guedes and Opler (1994) find that large investment grade firms are more likely to issue short-term debt (terms less than 10 years) and long-term debt (terms of 30 years or more), while firms with relatively high growth prospects tend to issue shorter-term debt. They argue that their findings are consistent with agency cost explanations for debt maturity choice (e.g., Myers 1977) and with Diamond's (1991a) prediction that higher-rated firms are more active participants in short-term credit markets, while lower-rated firms have a tendency to avoid short-term debt to minimize refinancing risk.

In contrast to these studies, Titman and Wessels (1988) use balance sheet measures of debt maturity and find that smaller firms have a higher proportion of short-term debt. They argue that smaller firms rely more heavily on short-term debt to minimize flotation costs of issuing long-term debt. Barclay and Smith (1995) use a slightly more refined measure of debt maturity, the proportion of a firm's debt with maturities exceeding three years.[2] Their major finding is that smaller firms with more growth opportunities have a smaller proportion of debt that matures in more than 3 years. They argue that this evidence is consistent with Myers's (1977) view that firms use debt maturity to control conflicts of interest between equityholders and debtholders.

Although these papers provide useful insights into firms' debt maturity structure choices, their debt maturity structure measures have several limitations. First, the term-to-maturity of an individual debt issue provides information only about incremental financing choices. Since the maturity of an individual debt issue may be vastly different from the average of the maturities of the firm's existing liabilities, the power of tests that relate the term-to-maturity of debt issues to balance

---

1. One exception is Morris (1992). Similar to our study, Morris collects data from *Moody's* manuals to construct a measure of the average maturity of a firm's debt obligations.

2. Barclay and Smith's maturity measure, like that of Titman and Wessels, is computed using Compustat data. The maturity-related information in Compustat for a firm in a given year includes the amount of current debt (debt repayable within 1 year), the amount of long-term debt, and the amount of long-term debt repayable in 1–5 years.

sheet variables, for example, asset maturity, is substantially reduced.[3] Second, focusing on samples of public debt issues excludes many types of debt, including bank debt, commercial paper, and private placements, which are important components of firms' liability structures. Finally, balance sheet proportions of short- and long-term debt provide only crude approximations of the actual average maturity of a firm's debt obligations.[4]

In this article, we test the theoretically grounded debt maturity structure hypotheses with a panel data set of 328 industrial firms over the 10-year period from 1980 to 1989. Using data collected from *Moody's Industrial Manuals,* we measure a firm's debt maturity structure in a given sample year as the weighted average maturity of its entire liability structure, including all debt (e.g., debentures, notes, and commercial paper), debtlike obligations (e.g., capital and operating leases), and current liabilities. Our measure of debt maturity structure overcomes the limitations associated with individual debt issues and maturity structure approximations based on proportions of short- and long-term debt by explicitly incorporating maturity information for all of a firm's debt obligations.

We find that proxies for signaling, tax, and maturity-matching hypotheses are generally significant determinants of debt maturity structure choice. The empirical analysis reveals that debt maturity structure is inversely related to earnings surprises (a proxy for firm quality), a firm's effective tax rate and its risk and directly related to asset maturity. We also find strong evidence in support of Diamond's (1991*a*) liquidity risk theory that predicts a nonmonotonic relation between bond ratings and debt maturity structure; firms with high or very low bond ratings have shorter average maturity structures than other firms in the sample. However, the empirical analysis is less supportive of agency cost hypotheses. Although smaller firms tend to have shorter average debt maturities, there is only mixed support for the prediction that debt maturity is inversely related to proxies for growth opportunities.[5]

3. Public debt issues are probably better suited to test theories of debt maturity choice that focus on resolving short-run and/or time-varying information asymmetries. An example of such a setting is a signaling model where maturity choice signals future prospects. However, a proper test requires splitting security issue samples into those debt issues whose use is to finance incremental assets and those whose use is to refinance existing debt. Presumably, the latter type of issue conveys little information about a firm's future prospects, or at least not the type of information that extant signaling models (e.g., Flannery 1986) claim debt maturity choice conveys.

4. For example, as noted above, Barclay and Smith use the proportion of a firm's debt due in more than 3 years as their proxy for debt maturity structure. Unfortunately, such a measure cannot distinguish, for instance, between firms with 5- and 20-year debt maturity structures.

5. As noted above, Morris (1992) also examines the determinants of debt maturity structure for a sample of 140 firms in 1985. Similar to our results, he finds little evidence that debt maturity structure is inversely related to proxies for growth opportunities.

Our data also allow for an analysis of the relation between the type of debt contract that a firm uses and its credit quality. Diamond (1991*b*) argues that highly rated firms with established reputations will tend to use directly placed debt (e.g., debentures and commercial paper), while medium-rated firms will tend to use bank debt. The distribution of debt contract types across sample firms is roughly consistent with Diamond's prediction. For example, we find that bank loans are more heavily used by firms with intermediate credit ratings, whereas the heaviest concentration of commercial paper issuers is among firms with the highest credit ratings.

We develop the various hypotheses in Section II, and describe our data in Section III. The empirical analysis is in Section IV. Section V concludes.

## II.  Debt Maturity Structure Hypotheses

The literature includes four types of hypotheses about the determinants of corporate debt maturity structure: agency cost hypotheses, signaling and liquidity risk hypotheses, maturity matching hypothesis, and tax hypotheses. We consider each in turn.

### A.  Agency Costs

Myers (1977) argues that risky debt financing may engender suboptimal investment incentives when a firm's investment opportunity set includes growth options. Managers acting on behalf of equityholders may fail to exercise profitable investment options because risky debt captures a portion of equityholders' benefit in the form of a reduction in the probability of default. Myers argues that this underinvestment incentive can be controlled by issuing short-term debt that matures before the growth options are exercised. The empirical hypothesis is that firms whose assets have a large proportion of growth options use shorter-term debt.[6]

Firms with relatively large amounts of future investment opportunities tend to be smaller. Indeed, as Smith and Warner (1979) argue, smaller firms are more likely to face other potential conflicts of interest between shareholders and bondholders, including risk shifting and claim dilution. Barnea, Haugen, and Senbet (1980, 1985) argue that these agency conflicts, like Myers's (1977) underinvestment problem, can be controlled by decreasing the maturity of debt. Consequently, smaller firms who likely face more severe agency conflicts than large,

---

6. Barnea, Haugen, and Senbet (1980) and Ho and Singer (1984) argue that call and sinking fund provisions can also mitigate investment incentive effects of risky debt financing by reducing the effective maturity of debt. Empirically, adjusting the maturity of a callable bond for the possibility of a call is difficult, although it is straightforward to account for a sinking fund schedule on a bond.

well-established firms may use shorter-term debt to alleviate these conflicts.[7] The empirical hypothesis is that debt maturity varies directly with firm size.

Although smaller firms with more growth options are predicted to use shorter-term debt to mitigate agency conflicts, these predictions presume that debt is risky. However, the capital structure literature argues that these same firms use moderate amounts of leverage to reduce the risk of financial distress. As such, firms with little leverage and therefore a small probability of financial distress would likely be indifferent to using debt maturity structure to control agency conflicts, all else being the same. We therefore control for leverage in the empirical tests.

### B. Signaling and Liquidity Risk

Flannery (1986) argues that a firm's choice of debt maturity structure can signal insiders' information about firm quality when firm insiders are systematically better informed than outside investors. If a debt issue is costless, only a pooling equilibrium is possible, because low-quality firms can costlessly mimic high quality firms' debt maturity choices. As such, the market undervalues high-quality firms and overvalues low-quality firms. With positive transaction costs, however, a separating equilibrium is possible. If lower-quality firms cannot afford the cost of rolling over short-term debt, they will self-select into the long-term debt market. In the resulting separating equilibrium, high-quality firms signal their type by issuing short-term debt.[8]

Signaling models are notoriously difficult to test because the firm's "type" is private information. In Flannery's model a firm uses short-term debt to signal insiders' anticipated change in firm quality given present outward signs of quality, for example, size, bond rating, and leverage. We use the future change in earnings as a proxy for insiders' information and predict an inverse relation between it and debt maturity structure choice.

Diamond (1991a) develops a model that focuses on the liquidity risk associated with short-term debt. Given a firm's private information, short-term debt allows for a reduction in borrowing costs when a firm receives good news and the debt is refinanced. However, short-term debt exposes the firm to liquidity risk, that is, loss of unassignable control rents if lenders will not allow refinancing and the firm is liqui-

---

7. Indeed, as Whited (1992) argues, one of the most basic premises of agency theory is that small firms are generally precluded from accessing long-term debt markets, because their tangible (collateralizable) assets are small relative to future investment opportunities.

8. Kale and Noe (1990) show that a separating equilibrium in which high-quality firms issue short-term debt and low-quality firms issue long-term debt can exist without transaction costs.

284                                                                      **Journal of Business**

dated. This trade-off leads to interesting cross-sectional predictions about the type and maturity of debt that firms employ conditional on their credit rating.

Very low rated borrowers with a high probability of having insufficient cash flows to support long-term debt have no choice but to borrow short-term.[9] They do so via private placements and/or borrowing through intermediaries such as banks. Intermediate credits, who have a choice, tend to issue long-term publicly traded debt because they face a higher liquidity risk than do very high rated borrowers. Finally, very high credits, who face little liquidity risk, are active issuers of short-term directly placed debt such as commercial paper.[10] The empirical prediction is that there is a nonmonotonic relation between debt maturity and bond rating; firms with high or very low bond ratings use shorter-term debt, although the type of contract will be different for the two groups of borrowers.[11]

Note that this prediction presumes that leverage is held constant. In particular, firms with low levels of leverage would face little liquidity risk and thereby would have no incentive to shun short-term debt, for example, intermediate credits with low leverage may not be pushed into long-term debt markets. Thus, as leverage increases so does liquidity risk, and so firms with higher leverage are expected to use more long-term debt, all else being equal.[12]

In a related paper, Diamond (1991*b*) analyzes the effectiveness of monitoring and reputation as ways to deal with moral hazard in the context of a borrower's choice between bank loans (with monitoring)

---

9. Of course, in practice very low rated borrowers do issue long-term debt. However, firms that have lower ratings pay higher interest costs because the rating is a measure of the risk that the firm will not be able to meet interest and principal payments. As a result, firms with lower ratings, although not formally precluded from participating in the directly placed long-term debt market, tend to be actively involved in privately placed debt and/or borrowing through intermediaries such as banks. This type of borrowing tends to be short-term, allowing lenders to revise the terms of the debt contract or call in the loan if and when the financial condition of the borrower deteriorates.

10. This is not to say that intermediate and/or very high rated borrowers would not choose a mixture of short- and long-term debt. For example, intermediate credits, whose optimal choice is long-term debt given an either/or decision, may optimally choose a mixture of short- and long-term debt otherwise. This could allow lower borrowing costs should good news arrive without undue exposure to excessive liquidity risk.

11. In a model with temporal information asymmetry, Goswami, Noe, and Rebello (1995) argue that firms will generally prefer long-term debt because it minimizes asymmetric information induced mispricing of debt. This result contrasts with Diamond (1991*a*) and Flannery (1986) wherein dissipative costs of short-term debt (in the form of loss of control rights in Diamond and refinancing costs in Flannery) are required to motivate any use of long-term debt.

12. However, note that all else is likely not held equal, since credit rating and leverage are inversely related. This would imply that intermediate credits would likely not have low levels of leverage and liquidity risk for them would not be insignificant. Alternatively, very high credits would likely have lower leverage, suggesting that liquidity risk would not be much of an issue for them.

and public debt issues (without monitoring).[13] Although this model makes no distinction between short- and long-term debt, a key implication is that highly rated firms with established reputations rely on directly placed debt (e.g., debentures and commercial paper), while medium-rated firms tend to rely on bank loans.[14] Monitoring may not be effective for very low rated borrowers, but when monitoring costs are not too high, these borrowers also attempt to borrow from banks. We investigate these predictions by examining the distribution of debt contract types across firms in our sample.

## C. Matching Principle

A common prescription in the literature is that a firm should match the maturity of its liabilities to that of its assets. If debt has a shorter maturity than assets, there may not be enough cash on hand to repay the principal when it is due. Alternatively, if debt has a longer maturity, then cash flows from assets cease, while debt payments remain due. Maturity matching can reduce these risks and is therefore a form of corporate hedging that reduces expected costs of financial distress. In a similar vein, Myers (1977) argues that maturity matching can control agency conflicts between equityholders and debtholders by ensuring that debt repayments are scheduled to correspond with the decline in the value of assets in place. In a model of this phenomenon, Chang (1989) demonstrates that maturity matching can minimize agency costs of debt financing.[15] The empirical hypothesis is that debt maturity varies directly with asset maturity.

## D. Taxes

Kane, Marcus, and McDonald (1985) develop a continuous-time model that allows for the endogenous determination of optimal debt maturity, incorporating both corporate and personal taxes, bankruptcy costs, and debt issue flotation costs. The optimal debt maturity involves a trade-off between the per-period tax-advantage of debt and bankruptcy and debt issue flotation costs. They establish that optimal debt maturity increases as the flotation cost increases, as the tax advantage of debt decreases, and as the volatility of firm value decreases. The firm

13. Also see Rajan (1992) for a model that analyzes the choice between bank debt and arm's-length debt.

14. Disregarding the admonition that the current model ignores maturity, the prediction that intermediate credits rely on bank loans appears inconsistent with Diamond (1991a), wherein liquidity risk encourages intermediate credits to issue long-term debt. However, it is reasonable to assume that liquidity risk as well as monitoring and reputation issues are important in practice, leading to the implication that intermediate credits use a mixture of short- and long-term debt with bank debt comprising the bulk of the short-maturity debt.

15. Also see Goswami, Noe, and Rebello (1993) and Hart and Moore (1994) for alternative explanations for why firms match the maturities of assets and liabilities.

lengthens maturity as flotation costs increase to spread refinancing costs over a longer time period. The firm lengthens debt maturity as the tax advantage of debt decreases to ensure that the remaining tax advantage of debt, net of bankruptcy costs, is not less than amortized flotation costs. Finally, optimal debt maturity increases as firm value volatility decreases, because the firm does not have to rebalance its capital structure as often to moderate expected bankruptcy costs. [16] Kane, Marcus, and McDonald's analysis suggests two empirically testable hypotheses. The first is that a firm's debt maturity increases as its effective tax rate decreases. The second is that a firm's debt maturity increases as firm value volatility decreases.

Brick and Ravid (1985) also provide a tax-based rationale for an optimal maturity structure. Assuming a tax advantage to corporate borrowing and a nonflat term structure of interest rates, they demonstrate that firm value is increasing in the amount of long-term debt when the term structure is increasing.[17] The reason is that the interest tax shield on debt is accelerated by increasing the proportion of debt payments allocated to long-term debt. The result is reversed when the term structure is decreasing. The testable hypothesis is that debt maturity varies directly with the slope of the term structure.[18]

As with the other debt maturity structure hypotheses, the predictions of the tax-based models require that leverage is held constant. This is especially important when dealing with tax effects, because cross-sectional differences in leverage (and associated debt tax shields) may accompany cross-sectional differences in debt maturity structure. Accordingly, we control for this effect by including a measure of leverage in our empirical tests.

### E. Summary of Empirical Predictions

A firm's agency costs of debt, signals about quality, liquidity risk, asset maturity, and tax status provide reliable predictions about its

---

16. Wiggins (1990) demonstrates that higher firm value volatility may induce the firm to lengthen debt maturity. The reason is that the default risk premium on debt is more sensitive to volatility at longer maturities, and therefore the tax shield from interest payments on long-term debt is incrementally higher than that on short-term debt. A potential problem with Wiggins's analysis is that he does not endogenously derive the optimal debt maturity structure, and so it is not clear whether this comparative static result holds at the optimum. For a discussion of this issue, see Leland (1994).

17. Kim, Mauer, and Stohs (1995) also argue that firms should lengthen debt maturity as the slope of the term structure increases. However, their analysis focuses on how corporate debt maturity policy affects investor tax-timing options to tax-trade corporate securities.

18. Lewis (1990) argues that debt maturity structure is irrelevant when taxes are the only market imperfection. However, Brick and Ravid (1991) note that Lewis's result is driven by his assumption that payments to satisfy bondholder claims in bankruptcy are first treated as taxable interest income. This feature of the model ensures that the promised interest payment on debt is independent of debt maturity, which in turn ensures that debt maturity structure has no effect on firm value.

debt maturity structure. The agency cost explanations suggest that a firm's debt maturity decreases (1) the larger the proportion of growth opportunities in its investment opportunity set, and (2) the smaller its size. The signaling and liquidity risk arguments predict that (1) high-quality firms (firms with larger ex post abnormal earnings) use shorter-term debt, and (2) firms with high or very low credit ratings use shorter-term debt, while other firms use longer-term debt. The matching hypothesis predicts that debt maturity is positively related to asset maturity. Finally, the tax hypotheses predict that debt maturity increases as (1) a firm's effective tax rate decreases, (2) firm value volatility decreases, and (3) the slope of the term structure increases.

The various debt maturity structure theories provide a mixture of cross-sectional and time-series predictions. For example, the agency cost and maturity-matching predictions are primarily cross-sectional, whereas the signaling and term structure slope predictions are naturally time series. Fortunately, our data set (discussed next) contains observations on firms' debt maturity structures across time.

## III. Data and Descriptive Statistics

We first describe the selection procedure for the firms in the sample and the information about debt collected for these firms. We then define the debt maturity structure measure that we employ in the empirical tests and the proxies for the debt maturity structure hypotheses. Finally, we discuss descriptive statistics for the sample and examine the distribution of debt contract types across credit quality.

### A. Sample of Firms

Of the firms in the 1989 Compustat Industrial Annual File, we select those that have (1) complete data for the independent variables (discussed below) over the period from 1980 to 1989, and (2) adequate data in *Moody's Industrial Manuals* throughout the 10-year sample period to construct our measure of debt maturity structure.[19] Imposi-

---

19. Although these criteria may induce some survivorship bias in the sample, this is unavoidable given the amount of data required to calculate an accurate measure of the average maturity of a firm's liability structure. An analysis of variance on key variables of firms in and out of the sample reveals that there is no significant difference between the size (defined below) of in-sample and out-of-sample firms. However, in-sample firms have a significantly larger average market-to-book ratio (defined below) than out-of-sample firms. We investigate whether this difference influences our regression results by splitting sample firms into two groups based on the median value of this ratio for the sample. The coefficient estimates on the market-to-book ratio for the two groups have the same sign and roughly the same significance level as the coefficient estimate for the full sample.

tion of these criteria yields the final sample of 328 nonregulated firms.[20] Of these, 292 (89%) are manufacturing firms within the 2,000–3,999 range of Standard Industrial Classification (SIC) codes, 18 (5.5%) are mining firms, and 18 (5.5%) are wholesalers, retailers, or service firms. Appendix A lists the industries represented in the sample and their corresponding SIC codes.

For each firm and for each year in the sample period, we collect information about debt maturity structure from *Moody's Industrial Manuals*. *Moody's* provides relatively detailed information about the debt instruments outstanding at a firm's fiscal year-end. We define a debt instrument as an obligation that is listed as a separate item in *Moody's* for a firm in a given sample year. For instance, we record a bond issued in 1980 and still outstanding in 1989 as 10 (separate) debt instruments. Using this counting procedure, the 328 firms in the sample have a total of 21,976 debt instruments outstanding during the sample period.[21] The average number of debt instruments for a firm is 6.7 per year, with an average book value of $60 million for each instrument.

Table 1 lists the different types of debt instruments used by sample firms, their average remaining maturity, and the relative proportion of each type in the sample.[22] Notes are the most widely represented, comprising 30.9% of the 21,976 observations and 37.2% of the total dollar amount of the book value of these observations. The next most prominent instrument in the sample is debentures, with 22.2% and 29.2% of the observations and dollar value, respectively. A short-list of the other types of debt instruments in the sample includes: capital leases, revolving credit, promissory notes, subsidiary debt, and commercial paper.

The amount of information that *Moody's* provides for each debt instrument ranges from a minimal amount for the category "other debt" to an extensive amount for debentures, including issue date, maturity date, coupon rate, dollar amount outstanding, and any call and/or sinking fund features and schedules.[23] When *Moody's* does not report a maturity date for a debt instrument, we substitute a default

20. We do not include regulated firms since it is not clear whether the various debt maturity structure predictions apply to such firms.

21. This number understates the actual number of debt instruments, since all of a given type of debt may be consolidated in *Moody's* as one debt instrument. In addition, most of the firms in the sample have a category of debt labeled "other debt" by *Moody's*, which may be a large collection of individual debt items.

22. For convenience, we only list the broad categories of debt instrument types in table 1. There are over 100 different debt types reported by *Moody's* for our sample of 328 firms over the period 1980–89. For example, the table 1 category "Bonds" includes: bearer bonds, Euro bonds, German bonds, Swiss bonds, perpetual bonds, project bonds, convertible bonds, serial bonds, and silver index bonds. Obviously, firms issue an incredibly rich variety of debt instruments.

23. The category "other debt" typically includes only the amount outstanding and the due date.

TABLE 1     Distribution of Debt Instrument Types for 328 Firms during the Period 1980–89

| Type of Instrument | Average Remaining Maturity (Years) | Number | % of Total Number | Dollar Amount ($M) | % of Total Dollar Amount | Instruments with No Reported Maturity Information | | |
|---|---|---|---|---|---|---|---|---|
| | | | | | | Number | % of Number of Type | % of Dollar Amount of Type |
| Notes | 5.52 | 6,792 | 30.91 | 493,553 | 37.22 | 344 | 5.06 | 2.37 |
| Debentures | 9.46 | 4,870 | 22.16 | 387,780 | 29.24 | 5 | .10 | .01 |
| Industrial revenue bonds | 12.64 | 2,089 | 9.51 | 49,948 | 3.77 | 14 | .67 | 7.57 |
| Other debt | 7.95 | 1,755 | 7.99 | 46,833 | 3.53 | 1,199 | 68.32 | 77.90 |
| Capital leases | 6.80 | 1,313 | 5.97 | 48,692 | 3.67 | 101 | 7.69 | 4.75 |
| Mortgage bonds | 7.67 | 905 | 4.12 | 23,707 | 1.79 | 48 | 5.30 | 2.28 |
| Bank loans | 4.32 | 902 | 4.10 | 39,467 | 2.98 | 99 | 10.98 | 14.52 |
| Revolving credit | 2.90 | 691 | 3.14 | 76,396 | 5.76 | 33 | 4.78 | 2.95 |
| Promissory notes | 4.91 | 667 | 3.04 | 22,247 | 1.68 | 5 | .75 | .14 |
| Bonds | 9.44 | 526 | 2.39 | 39,137 | 2.95 | 4 | .76 | .76 |
| Pollution control bonds | 16.03 | 487 | 2.22 | 20,724 | 1.56 | 0 | .00 | .00 |
| Subsidiary debt | 7.34 | 412 | 1.87 | 38,678 | 2.92 | 103 | 25.00 | 14.08 |
| Other obligations | 7.97 | 266 | 1.21 | 9,445 | .71 | 34 | 12.78 | 11.95 |
| Commercial paper | .24 | 188 | .86 | 28,300 | 2.14 | 57 | 30.32 | 27.19 |
| Equipment leases | 6.90 | 113 | .51 | 1,112 | .08 | 0 | .00 | .00 |
| Total | | 21,976 | 100.00 | 1,326,019 | 100.00 | 2,046 | 9.31 | 5.84 |

NOTE.—A debt instrument is defined as a debt obligation that is listed as a separate item in *Moody's Industrial Manuals* for a firm in a given sample year. The dollar amounts (in millions) are for book value of outstanding debt.

value, contingent on the type of instrument. For instance, if the maturity date for a note is not reported, it is assigned 5.25 years remaining to maturity. These default values are calculated from a random sample of debt issues listed in *S&P's Bond Guide* during March 1985, the midpoint of the sample period, and are reported in appendix B.[24]

The far right columns of table 1 report the number of each debt instrument type with no maturity information and the corresponding proportions (by number of instruments and dollar amount) in the sample. Of the 21,976 debt instruments in the sample, 2,046 (9.3%) have no reported maturity date. These instruments represent only 5.8% of the total amount of debt in the sample.[25]

### B. Debt Maturity Structure Measure

We construct a measure of the maturity of the firm's total liability structure that includes all debt, debtlike obligations (e.g., capital leases), and current liabilities. It is important to include current liabilities, since these are obligations that the firm must meet and are analogous to short-term debt. This is particularly clear for the matching hypothesis. Under that hypothesis, a firm would consider the amount and maturity of its current liabilities when calculating the maturity of its entire liability structure to match with its asset maturity.[26]

We compute the average maturity of a firm's liabilities in a given sample year as

$$
\text{DEBTMAT} = \left[ \left( \frac{CL - OneYrDebt}{CL + TLTD} \right) \times MCL \right] \\
+ \left[ \left( \frac{TLTD + OneYrDebt}{CL + TLTD} \right) \times MDT \right], \tag{1}
$$

where *CL* is current liabilities, *OneYrDebt* is the amount of debt due within 1 year,[27] *TLTD* is the total amount of long-term debt outstanding (which includes long-term debtlike instruments), *MCL* is the maturity of current liabilities, and *MDT* is the (book) value-weighted average maturity of the debt and debtlike obligations outstanding as calculated

---

24. The default maturities were originally computed and reported in Morris (1992).

25. Our empirical results are not sensitive to using default values for debt instruments with no reported maturity information. When these observations are excluded from the sample, the results reported in Sec. IV are unaffected.

26. Consider two shoe companies in the sample, The 10-year sample period average long-term debt is approximately zero for both Penobscot Shoe Co. and Shaer Shoe Corp., and their sample period averages for our debt maturity structure measure (defined below) are 0.16 and 0.11 years, respectively. These values are due almost solely to their current liabilities and are well below the average debt maturity structure value of 3.38 years for the entire sample of 328 firms. Their 10-year averages for asset maturity (defined below) of 1.45 and 0.91 years are also well below that for the entire sample of 4.70 years.

27. Note that Compustat includes *OneYrDebt* in current liabilities (*CL*).

according to equation (2) below. Note that *MDT* includes all of the categories listed in table 1.

The maturity of current liabilities (*MCL*) is an estimate of the average time a firm's current liabilities are outstanding over a year. We view current liabilities as financing investment in production, with the amount of production equal to the cost of goods sold. As such, dividing the cost of goods sold by current liabilities gives the number of times in a year that a firm *refinances* its current liabilities, and the inverse of this ratio (*MCL*), is the proportion of a year that these short-term obligations are outstanding.[28]

We compute *MDT* for a firm in a given sample year as

$$MDT = \sum_{j}^{J} D_j M_j \Big/ \sum_{j}^{J} D_j, \qquad (2)$$

where *J* is the number of debt instruments outstanding, $D_j$ is the dollar amount of debt instrument *j*, and $M_j$ is the *remaining* maturity of debt instrument *j*. In cases where debt instrument *j* requires principal prepayments (e.g., sinking fund debentures), $M_j$ is calculated as

$$M_j = \sum_{k}^{K} P_k N_k \Big/ \sum_{k}^{K} P_k, \qquad (3)$$

where

$$\sum_{k}^{K} P_k = D_j, \qquad (4)$$

and where *K* is the number of principal repayments, $P_k$ is the dollar amount of principal repayment *k*, and $N_k$ is the time in years (from the current fiscal year-end) until principal repayment *k*.[29]

Note that our debt maturity structure measure does not adjust for the impact of call provisions on the maturity of long-term bonds and debentures. A call provision is expected to reduce the effective maturity of these types of instruments. Although it is desirable to adjust for this effect, reasonably accurate adjustments are difficult to make with-

---

28. Boise Cascade, for instance, had $2,378 million in cost of goods sold and $420 million in current liabilities as of December 31, 1980. It refinanced these short-term obligations 5.66 (2378/420) times during the year, giving a maturity of current liabilities of 0.18 (1/5.66) years, or approximately 2 months.

29. For example, a $1,000 par bond with 10 years of remaining maturity and no sinking fund will have $K = 1$ and $N_k = 10$ years, giving $M_j = 10$ years. In comparison, an otherwise equivalent bond with principal repayments of $200 at the end of each of the last 5 years of its remaining maturity will have $M_j = 8$ years. From (3), the calculation is: $M_j = (200 \times 6 + 200 \times 7 + 200 \times 8 + 200 \times 9 + 200 \times 10)/(1000) = 8$ years, with $K = 5$, each $P_k = \$200$, $N_k$ ranging from 6 to 10 years, and the sum of principal payments equal to $1,000.

out information about whether a particular call provision is in or out of the money. Unfortunately, attempting to gather this information for the large number of debt instruments in our sample is infeasible.[30]

### C. Proxies for Maturity Structure Hypotheses

#### 1. Agency Cost Hypotheses

*Growth options.* Growth options are proxied by the ratio of the market value of the firm's assets to the book value of its assets (MV/BV), where the market value of assets is estimated as the book value of assets plus the difference between the market and book values of equity. Smith and Watts (1992) argue that the more growth options in the firm's investment opportunity set, the larger is the ratio of the firm's market value to its book value. We expect an inverse relation between DEBTMAT and MV/BV.[31]

*Firm size.* Firm size (SIZE) is measured by the natural logarithm of the estimate of its market value (MV) in constant 1982 dollars. The Producer Price Index serves as the deflator. We expect a positive relation between DEBTMAT and SIZE.

#### 2. Signaling and Liquidity Risk Hypotheses

*Firm quality.* Insiders' anticipated change in firm quality is proxied by the future change in earnings, $\Delta$EPS, which is the difference between next year's and this year's earnings per share, scaled by this year's stock price.[32] Use of the simple change in earnings is motivated by evidence in the accounting and finance literature that annual earnings are well described by a random walk (see Kleidon 1986; Watts and Zimmerman 1986).[33] Flannery's (1986) signaling model predicts a negative relation between DEBTMAT and $\Delta$EPS.

*Firm bond rating.* Diamond (1991a) argues that firms with high and very low bond ratings use shorter-term debt, while other firms use longer-term debt. To test this prediction of a nonmonotonic relation between bond rating and debt maturity, we construct a cardinalized bond rating variable (BONDRATE) based on a firm's S&P bond rating, where AAA = 1, . . . , CCC = 7, and unrated firms receive a code

---

30. However, we have tried several ad hoc approaches to adjusting for the impact of call provisions. For example, we have used the maturity to the first call date and the maturity to the midpoint of the call schedule of the bond. These adjustments to our debt maturity structure measure have virtually no impact on the regression results reported below.

31. As an alternative proxy for intangible and discretionary investments, we also use the sum of advertising and research and development expenses scaled by total assets.

32. To construct this variable in 1989, we use the earnings-per-share figure from the 1990 Compustat tapes.

33. However, as a check of the robustness of this variable, we also use the unexpected component of next year's earnings, where earnings are forecasted using a time-series model of earnings.

of 8. We perform two types of tests. The first uses BONDRATE and the square of the variable (SQBRATE) to test the general notion that debt maturity increases as bond ratings deteriorate, but at a decreasing rate, that is, firms with very low bond ratings tend to use less long-term debt. Thus, we expect a positive relation between DEBTMAT and BONDRATE, and a negative relation between DEBTMAT and SQBRATE. The second test uses bond-rating dummy variables: LOW-BOND equals one if the firm has a rating of CCC or is unrated, and zero otherwise; and HIGHBOND equals one if the firm is rated AA or higher, and zero otherwise. We expect negative relations between DEBTMAT and both LOWBOND and HIGHBOND.[34]

Note that these tests assume that unrated firms fall into Diamond's class of firms with very low bond ratings, that is, a high probability of not meeting interest and principal payments. Although this would appear to be a reasonable assumption, we nevertheless include a dummy variable for rated firms in both test specifications. Thus, RATEDUM equals one if the firm has a bond rating and is zero otherwise.

### 3. Matching Hypothesis

The matching hypothesis predicts that firms match the maturity of their liabilities with that of their assets. We measure asset maturity (ASSETMAT) as the (book) value-weighted average of the maturities of current assets and net property, plant and equipment. We measure the maturity of current assets as current assets divided by the cost of goods sold. The rationale for this measure is based on the notion that current assets (e.g., inventory) support production, where production is measured by the cost of goods sold. The maturity of net property, plant, and equipment is that amount divided by annual depreciation expense. The rationale for this proxy is that straight-line depreciation, which is used for balance sheet reporting, provides a better approximation of economic depreciation than do the accelerated schedules that firms use for tax purposes. We expect a positive relation between DEBTMAT and ASSETMAT.

### 4. Tax Hypotheses

*Firm tax rate.* The firm's effective tax rate (TAXRATE) is measured by the ratio of income tax expense to pretax income. Recall that the tax-based debt maturity structure literature predicts a negative relation between DEBTMAT and TAXRATE.

*Firm asset variability.* The Kane, Marcus, and McDonald (1985) model predicts that debt maturity varies inversely with the volatility of firm asset value. Our proxy for asset volatility (VAR) is the standard

---

34. Although one may quibble with our low and high bond rating classifications, as discussed later, our results are robust to alternative classification schemes.

deviation of the first difference in earnings before interest, taxes and depreciation, scaled by the average book value of assets. Note that VAR is a purely cross-sectional variable since there is only one observation per firm in the panel. We expect a negative relation between DEBTMAT and VAR.

*Term structure.* The slope of the term structure (TERM) is measured by the difference between the month-end yields on a 10-year government bond and a 6-month government bond, matched to the month of a firm's fiscal year-end. Yields are from the *Economic Report of the President*. The Brick and Ravid (1985) model predicts a positive relation between DEBTMAT and TERM.

## 5. Leverage

We include a measure of leverage as a control variable. However, one might reasonably expect a positive relation between debt maturity structure and leverage. For example, Diamond's (1991*a*) analysis predicts that liquidity risk increases with leverage, and so firms with higher leverage would be expected to use more long-term debt, all else being equal. Alternatively, a positive relation could be partly mechanical, since a large proportion of long-term debt in a firm's capital structure inevitably produces a higher value for average debt maturity. We measure leverage (LEVERAGE) as the ratio of total debt (the sum of long-term debt, long-term debt due within 1 year, and short-term debt) to the estimate of the market value of the firm, that is, MV.[35]

## D. Descriptive Statistics

Table 2 reports descriptive statistics for DEBTMAT, MV/BV, SIZE, ΔEPS, ASSETMAT, TAXRATE, VAR, TERM, and LEVERAGE. Note that the statistics for SIZE are in billions of constant 1982 dollars. We use the logged value of this variable in the regressions. Panel A contains descriptive statistics across firms, using the time-series mean for each variable. Panel B contains descriptive statistics for the pooled time-series cross-sectional data, that is, 3,280 (328 firms × 10 years) firm-year observations for each variable. The average firm in the sample has a weighted average debt maturity of 3.38 years, a market-to-book ratio of 1.34, a market value of $2.89 billion, an asset maturity of 4.70 years, a tax rate of 36%, and a debt-to-firm value ratio of 20%.

An examination of the frequency distributions for each variable reveals that there are some extreme observations for ΔEPS and TAXRATE. Consider first the ΔEPS variable. Rather than employ arbitrary cut-off points to discard extreme observations, we run a pooled time-series cross-sectional regression of DEBTMAT on the various exoge-

---

35. Our results are similar when leverage is measured as the ratio of long-term debt to firm value.

TABLE 2       Descriptive Statistics of Debt Maturity, Market-to-Book Ratio, Firm
Size, Change in Earnings per Share, Asset Maturity, Tax Rate,
Earnings Variability, Term Structure, and Leverage for 328 Firms
during the Period 1980–89

| Variable | Mean | Standard Deviation | Minimum | Median | Maximum |
|---|---|---|---|---|---|
| A. Descriptive statistics across firms ($N$ = 328): | | | | | |
| DEBTMAT | 3.38 | 1.93 | .08 | 2.97 | 10.89 |
| MV/BV | 1.34 | .45 | .68 | 1.21 | 3.27 |
| SIZE ($ B) | 2.89 | 6.53 | .01 | .84 | 83.31 |
| $\Delta$EPS | .01 | .29 | −4.66 | .00 | 1.59 |
| ASSETMAT | 4.70 | 3.09 | .91 | 3.78 | 25.99 |
| TAXRATE | .36 | .55 | −6.99 | .39 | 3.87 |
| VAR | .05 | .03 | .01 | .04 | .24 |
| TERM (%) | 1.61 | .08 | 1.51 | 1.61 | 1.86 |
| LEVERAGE | .20 | .12 | .00 | .19 | .61 |
| B. Descriptive statistics across firms and over time ($N$ = 3,280): | | | | | |
| DEBTMAT | 3.38 | 2.36 | .06 | 2.92 | 15.80 |
| MV/BV | 1.34 | .55 | .49 | 1.18 | 6.51 |
| SIZE ($ B) | 2.89 | 6.78 | .01 | .76 | 112.19 |
| $\Delta$EPS | .01 | 1.29 | −63.23 | .00 | 22.09 |
| ASSETMAT | 4.70 | 3.43 | .49 | 3.71 | 53.04 |
| TAXRATE | .36 | 1.72 | −72.65 | .39 | 35.60 |
| TERM (%) | 1.65 | 1.36 | −1.93 | 2.17 | 3.17 |
| LEVERAGE | .20 | .15 | .00 | .18 | .90 |

NOTE.—The variables are defined as follows: DEBTMAT is the (book) value-weighted average of the maturities of the firm's debt; MV/BV is the market value of the firm (proxied by the sum of the book value of assets and the market value of equity less the book value of equity) scaled by the book value of assets; SIZE is the estimate of firm value measured in billions of constant 1982 dollars using the Producer Price Index (PPI) deflator; $\Delta$EPS is the difference between next year's earnings per share and this year's earnings per share, scaled by this year's common stock price per share; ASSETMAT is the (book) value-weighted average of the maturities of current assets and net property, plant, and equipment; TAXRATE is the ratio of income taxes paid to pretax income; VAR is the ratio of the standard deviation of the first difference in earnings before interest, depreciation, and taxes to the average of assets over the period 1980–89; TERM is the difference between the long-term and short-term yields on government bonds; and LEVERAGE is the ratio of total debt (the sum of long-term debt, long-term debt due within 1 year, and short-term debt) to the market value of the firm. Panel A contains descriptive statistics across firms, where the variables for each firm are averages of their respective yearly observations. Panel B contains descriptive statistics for the pooled time-series cross-sectional data, i.e., 3,280 (328 firms × 10 years) firm-year observations for each variable.

nous variables to check whether any of the extreme observations for $\Delta$EPS have an undue influence on the regression results.[36] As a result of that analysis, only one of the firm-year observations for $\Delta$EPS is

36. We use Cook's (1977) distance measure, Cook's $D$, which indicates whether the least squares point estimates calculated using all observations differ substantially from the least squares point estimates calculated using all observations except for a given extreme observation. Critical values of the $F$-distribution are used to determine whether the calculated value for Cook's $D$ for each extreme observation falls outside of an acceptable range, thereby indicating that the observation is influential.

determined to be influential, and therefore we do not include it in our empirical tests. When this observation is included, the estimated coefficient for $\Delta$EPS is not significantly different from zero. Discarding the observation, however, has little effect on the coefficient estimates of the other variables in the regression equations.

There are a number of economically unreasonable observations for TAXRATE. Following the approach in Fischer, Heinkel, and Zechner (1989), rather than delete these observations from the panel, we split TAXRATE into two variables, GTAXRATE and BTAXRATE. For each TAXRATE observation, GTAXRATE = TAXRATE and BTAX-RATE = 0 if TAXRATE is between zero and one, and GTAXRATE = 0 and BTAXRATE = TAXRATE otherwise. When TAXRATE is not split, the coefficient estimate on it is never significantly different from zero. Splitting the variable has no effect on the coefficient estimates of the other variables in the regression equations.

Table 3 reports correlations between the variables for the pooled time-series cross-sectional data. Observe that the signs of the correlations between DEBTMAT and the various explanatory variables are generally consistent with the empirical predictions. Further note that the correlations between the various explanatory variables are generally quite small. However, there are at least two noteworthy exceptions. First, the large correlations between the bond-rating variables (BONDRATE, RATEDUM, LOWBOND, and HIGHBOND) and SIZE indicate that larger firms have higher-quality bond ratings. This is consistent with previous findings in the literature (see, e.g., Iskandar and Emery 1994). Second, LEVERAGE is strongly inversely related to MV/BV (correlation of $-0.46$), indicating that firms with a larger proportion of growth opportunities use less leverage, all else being equal. A possible implication is that management of debt maturity structure may be of little importance to firms with large amounts of growth options, because such firms have little debt. This points to the importance of including leverage as a control variable in our regression tests.[37]

Figure 1 displays cross-sectional average debt and asset maturity by sample year for the 328 firms in the sample. Note that we show debt maturity structure adjusted for sinking fund provisions (DEBTMAT) and unadjusted for sinking fund provisions (DEBTMAT*). There are several interesting patterns evident in the figure. First, observe that DEBTMAT* and ASSETMAT are virtually equal in every sample year. In comparison, DEBTMAT is always below ASSETMAT

---

37. In particular, since LEVERAGE is strongly positively correlated with DEBTMAT (correlation of 0.46) and strongly negatively correlated with MV/BV, *not* controlling for leverage will tend to bias *downward* the regression coefficient estimates on MV/BV. Such a specification error could lead us to falsely support the prediction of an inverse relation between DEBTMAT and MV/BV.

**TABLE 3    Correlation Matrix of Dependent and Independent Variables for 328 Firms during the Period 1980–89**

| Variable | 1 | 2 | 3 | 4 | 5 | 6 | 7 | 8 | 9 | 10 | 11 | 12 | 13 | 14 |
|---|---|---|---|---|---|---|---|---|---|---|---|---|---|---|
| 1. DEBTMAT | | | | | | | | | | | | | | |
| 2. MV/BV | -.14 | | | | | | | | | | | | | |
| 3. SIZE | .27 | .26 | | | | | | | | | | | | |
| 4. ΔEPS | -.05 | .00 | -.02 | | | | | | | | | | | |
| 5. BONDRATE | -.29 | -.07 | -.73 | .03 | | | | | | | | | | |
| 6. RATEDUM | .41 | -.05 | .63 | .02 | -.88 | | | | | | | | | |
| 7. LOWBOND | -.39 | .03 | -.65 | .04 | .91 | -.95 | | | | | | | | |
| 8. HIGHBOND | -.05 | .22 | .46 | -.02 | -.60 | .35 | -.36 | | | | | | | |
| 9. ASSETMAT | .40 | .05 | .24 | -.03 | -.16 | .19 | -.18 | .07 | | | | | | |
| 10. TAXRATE | .00 | .02 | .01 | -.01 | -.02 | .01 | -.02 | .01 | -.03 | | | | | |
| 11. GTAXRATE | -.11 | .09 | .07 | -.13 | -.07 | -.04 | -.03 | .10 | -.08 | .09 | | | | |
| 12. BTAXRATE | .01 | .01 | .00 | .00 | -.01 | .02 | -.01 | .00 | -.02 | .96 | .00 | | | |
| 13. VAR | -.06 | -.11 | -.42 | .03 | .33 | -.22 | .25 | -.23 | .09 | -.01 | -.20 | .01 | | |
| 14. TERM | -.02 | -.03 | -.01 | -.02 | .00 | .01 | -.01 | .00 | .01 | -.01 | .02 | -.01 | .00 | |
| 15. LEVERAGE | .46 | -.46 | -.10 | -.03 | .05 | .18 | -.11 | -.22 | .19 | -.02 | -.23 | .00 | .13 | -.01 |

NOTE.—The correlations are for the pooled time-series cross-sectional data. Numbers in the first row correspond to numbers in col. 1. The variables are defined as follows: DEBTMAT is the (book) value-weighted average of the maturities of the firm's debt; MV/BV is the market value of the firm (proxied by the sum of the book value of assets and the market value of equity less the book value of equity) scaled by the book value of assets; SIZE is the natural logarithm of the estimate of firm value measured in 1982 dollars using the PPI deflator; ΔEPS is the difference between next year's earnings per share and this year's earnings per share, scaled by this year's common stock price per share; BONDRATE is the firm's cardinalized S&P bond rating, where AAA = 1, . . . , CCC = 7 and unrated firms receive a code of 8; RATEDUM equals one if the firm has a bond rating, and zero otherwise; LOWBOND equals one if the firm has an S&P bond rating of CCC or is unrated, and zero otherwise; HIGHBOND equals one if the firm's S&P bond rating is AA or higher, and zero otherwise; ASSETMAT is the (book) value-weighted average of the maturities of current assets and net property, plant, and equipment; TAXRATE is the ratio of income taxes paid to pretax income; GTAXRATE = TAXRATE if TAXRATE is between zero and one, and GTAXRATE = 0 otherwise; BTAXRATE = 0 if TAXRATE is between zero and one, and BTAXRATE = TAXRATE otherwise; VAR is the ratio of the standard deviation of the first difference in earnings before interest, depreciation, and taxes to the average of assets over the period 1980–89; TERM is the difference between the long-term and short-term yields on government bonds; and LEVERAGE is the ratio of total debt (the sum of long-term debt, long-term debt due within 1 year, and short-term debt) to the market value of the firm.

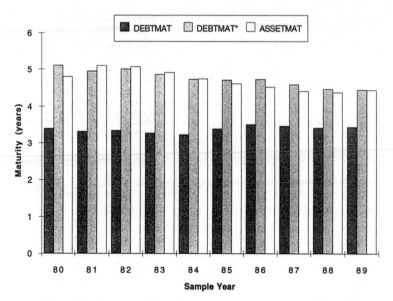

Fᴉɢ. 1.—Debt maturity and asset maturity by year for 328 firms during the period 1980–89. The maturity structure variables are defined as follows: DEBTMAT is the (book) value-weighted average of the maturities of the firm's debt adjusted for sinking fund provisions; DEBTMAT* is the (book) value-weighted average of the maturities of the firm's debt ignoring sinking fund provisions; and ASSETMAT is the (book) value-weighted average of the maturities of the firm's current assets and net property, plant, and equipment.

throughout the sample period. Clearly, adjusting the maturity of debt for sinking fund provisions has a nontrivial impact on debt maturity structure measures. Second, observe that DEBTMAT is very stable over the decade, with no systematic upward or downward drift in average debt maturity. Third, notice that the difference between ASSETMAT (and DEBTMAT*) and DEBTMAT has narrowed over the decade.[38]

Table 4 and figure 2 show the relation between debt maturity (DEBT-MAT) and bond rating for the pooled time-series cross-sectional data. The relation is strikingly nonmonotonic, illustrating that firms with high and low ratings have the shortest average debt maturities. Starting with a value of 2.34 years for AAA-rated firms, average maturity increases for each subsequent lower rating classification, reaching a maximum of 4.92 years for B-rated firms. Thereafter, average maturity

38. We find similar patterns when we compute value-weighted averages instead of equally weighted averages. For the value-weighted averages, we use the ratio of the book value of a firm's debt (assets) to the total book value of debt (assets) in the sample to compute sample year cross-sectional average debt (asset) maturity.

TABLE 4    Debt Maturity by Bond Rating for 328 Firms during the Period 1980–89

| Bond Rating | AAA | AA | A | BBB | BB | B | CCC | NR |
|---|---|---|---|---|---|---|---|---|
| DEBTMAT | 2.34 | 3.31 | 4.52 | 4.60 | 4.77 | 4.92 | 3.88 | 2.31 |
| N | 97 | 325 | 596 | 307 | 195 | 210 | 89 | 1,461 |

NOTE.—DEBTMAT is the (book) value-weighted average of the maturities of the firm's debt. For each bond rating, the table reports the average debt maturity structure for the pooled time-series cross-sectional data. There is a total of 3,280 firm-year observations; i.e., the sum of the bond rating sample sizes equals 3,280.

falls to 3.88 years for CCC-rated firms and is only 2.31 years for un-rated (NR) firms. This pattern accords with Diamond's (1991*a*) prediction that a desire to go short-term moderated by refinancing risk induces a nonmonotonic relation between debt maturity and credit quality.

Notice in table 4 that 44.5% of the 3,280 firm-year observations do not have an S&P bond rating.[39] This is not unusual. For example, in

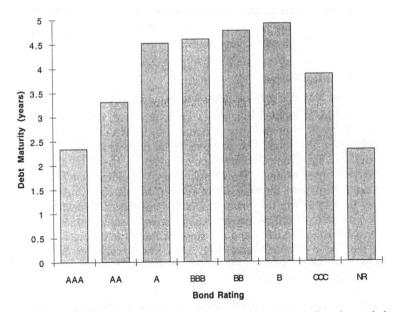

FIG. 2.—Debt maturity by bond rating for 328 firms during the period 1980–89. For each bond rating, the figure displays the average debt maturity structure for the pooled time-series cross-sectional data.

39. There are a small number of cases where *Moody's* assigned a rating when S&P did not. For these cases, we use the *Moody's* rating by converting it to the corresponding S&P rating category.

a sample of 325 firms from the Compustat database, Whited (1992) reports that only 119 have bond ratings. The primary reason for the large number of unrated observations is that S&P does not assign a firm a bond rating when it uses only privately placed debt or when its public debt issues are less than $25 million. Of course, these conditions are highly correlated with firm size, as evidenced by the correlation of 0.63 between SIZE and RATEDUM reported in table 3.

Table 5 reports the distribution of debt instrument types by bond rating for the debt categories in table 1. Several features of the data stand out. Firms with the highest credit ratings (i.e., AAA and AA) tend to rely on directly placed debt such as debentures and commercial paper. In comparison, although intermediate credits (i.e., A, BBB, and BB) are also active in public debt markets, they tend to be the heaviest users of bank debt (i.e., notes, bank loans, revolving credit, and promissory notes) among rated firms.[40] Finally, observe that unrated firms use little long-term debt (e.g., debentures and bonds), and instead tend to rely most heavily on bank debt. These findings are roughly consistent with Diamond's (1991b) prediction that firms with intermediate credit ratings will tend to rely on bank debt for their short-term financing needs, while those firms with the highest credit ratings will rely on public debt markets.

## IV.   Empirical Evidence

To jointly test the debt maturity structure hypotheses we estimate cross-sectional, pooled time-series cross-sectional, and fixed effects regressions of debt maturity structure (DEBTMAT) on the various explanatory variables. The cross-sectional regression uses 328 time-series averages (one per firm per variable) as based on the 3,279 firm-year observations.[41] The cross-sectional specification is useful because it eliminates the problem of serially correlated residuals which may tend to inflate the $t$-statistics of the coefficient estimates in the pooled and fixed effects regressions. However, we do not include abnormal earnings ($\Delta$EPS) and the slope of the term structure (TERM) in the cross-sectional regression, since these variables proxy for hypotheses that are primarily concerned with time-series variation in debt maturity structure.[42]

---

40. The category "Notes" incorporates a wide variety of intermediate-term obligations, i.e., debt instruments with original maturities of between 1 and 10 years. However, a large proportion of these instruments are bank notes.

41. Recall that we delete one firm-year observation because it has an influential value for $\Delta$EPS.

42. In particular, Flannery's (1986) signaling model predicts that firms decrease debt maturity structure to signal insiders' anticipated change in future earnings ($\Delta$EPS), while Brick and Ravid's (1985) tax-based model predicts that firms lengthen debt maturity when the term structure (TERM) is upward-sloping.

TABLE 5    Debt Instrument Type by Bond Rating for 328 Firms during the Period 1980–89

| Type of Instrument | Number of Debt Instruments for Bond Rating of: | | | | | | | | | Average Bond Rating (AAA = 1, . . . , NR = 8) | |
| --- | --- | --- | --- | --- | --- | --- | --- | --- | --- | --- | --- |
| | AAA | AA | A | BBB | BB | B | CCC | NR | Row Total | Including NR | Excluding NR |
| Notes | 193 | 824 | 1,575 | 1,181 | 461 | 446 | 173 | 1,939 | 6,792 | 4.86 | 3.60 |
| Debentures | 185 | 635 | 1,891 | 902 | 303 | 425 | 165 | 364 | 4,870 | 3.87 | 3.54 |
| Industrial revenue bonds | 12 | 156 | 660 | 251 | 172 | 129 | 40 | 669 | 2,089 | 5.06 | 3.68 |
| Other debt | 80 | 257 | 400 | 240 | 85 | 118 | 26 | 549 | 1,755 | 4.82 | 3.37 |
| Capital leases | 28 | 70 | 265 | 186 | 97 | 106 | 57 | 504 | 1,313 | 5.53 | 3.99 |
| Mortgage bonds | 2 | 46 | 54 | 113 | 118 | 103 | 14 | 455 | 905 | 6.16 | 4.48 |
| Bank loans | 12 | 77 | 203 | 97 | 52 | 58 | 39 | 364 | 902 | 5.49 | 3.80 |
| Revolving credit | 0 | 20 | 86 | 106 | 49 | 83 | 46 | 301 | 691 | 6.07 | 4.58 |
| Promissory notes | 11 | 67 | 152 | 92 | 47 | 38 | 0 | 260 | 667 | 5.27 | 3.52 |
| Bonds | 13 | 51 | 212 | 79 | 35 | 40 | 27 | 69 | 526 | 4.23 | 3.66 |
| Pollution control bonds | 17 | 4 | 258 | 58 | 93 | 0 | 0 | 57 | 487 | 4.01 | 3.48 |
| Subsidiary debt | 30 | 79 | 60 | 78 | 33 | 21 | 14 | 97 | 412 | 4.48 | 3.39 |
| Other obligations | 0 | 34 | 28 | 76 | 5 | 13 | 22 | 88 | 266 | 5.33 | 4.01 |
| Commercial paper | 31 | 53 | 51 | 32 | 14 | 6 | 1 | 0 | 188 | 2.83 | 2.83 |
| Equipment leases | 0 | 0 | 10 | 3 | 3 | 29 | 9 | 59 | 113 | 6.78 | 5.44 |
| Column total | 614 | 2,373 | 5,905 | 3,494 | 1,567 | 1,615 | 633 | 5,775 | 21,976 | 4.79 | 3.64 |

NOTE.—A debt instrument is defined as a debt obligation that is listed as a separate item in *Moody's Industrial Manuals* for a firm in a given sample year. The average bond rating for each type of debt instrument is the average cardinalized bond rating, where AAA = 1, . . . , NR = 8.

In contrast, the pooled and fixed effects regressions exploit both the cross-sectional and time-series variation in the data. The difference between these two specifications is that the fixed effects model allows for firm-specific regression intercepts. This allows for shifts in the regression line provided that the firms differ significantly in any omitted variables or in their sensitivity to the included variables (which are constrained to have the same slope across all firms).[43] Since adding a separate intercept for each firm to the pooled regression is computationally inefficient, the same effect is achieved by subtracting the firm-specific mean for each variable from each observation. As a result, earnings variability (VAR) does not enter the fixed effects regression since there is only one observation per firm.

## A.  Regression Results

Table 6 reports the cross-sectional, pooled, and fixed effects regressions of DEBTMAT on the relevant explanatory variables (i.e., $\Delta$EPS and TERM are not included in the cross-sectional specification, and VAR does not enter the fixed effects specification). The first column of the table lists the independent variables, and the second column displays the hypothesized signs for the coefficient estimates. White's (1980) heteroscedasticity-consistent $t$-statistics are reported in parentheses below the parameter estimates.

Inconsistent with the agency cost hypothesis, the coefficient estimates on the market-to-book ratio (MV/BV) are either insignificant or have the wrong sign. Thus, we find no support for the prediction that debt maturity structure decreases as the proportion of growth options (as proxied by the market-to-book ratio) in the firm's investment opportunity set increases.[44]

However, we find some evidence that larger firms have longer debt maturity structures; the coefficient estimates on SIZE are positive in all three regressions and are significant in the pooled and fixed effects regressions. To gauge the economic significance of the influence of firm size on debt maturity structure, consider the coefficient estimate

43. An alternative to the fixed effects model is the random effects model, where differences across firms are modeled with an additional firm-specific disturbance term. However, the random effects model has the disadvantage that it assumes that firm effects are uncorrelated with the explanatory variables. As a result, the estimates from the random effects model may suffer from a lack of consistency due to omitted variable bias (see, e.g., Chamberlain 1978).

44. In contrast, Barclay and Smith (1995) find strong support for the prediction that debt maturity structure (as proxied by the percentage of debt that matures in more than 3 years) is inversely related to growth options (as proxied by the market-to-book ratio). However, they do not control for leverage in their regressions. When we do not control for leverage in our regressions (i.e., LEVERAGE is excluded), the coefficient estimates on MV/BV are negative as predicted and highly significant in all three regressions. Since LEVERAGE is positively correlated with DEBTMAT and negatively correlated with MV/BV (see table 3), the significant negative coefficient estimates on MV/BV when LEVERAGE is not in the regressions suggest the presence of a left-out-variables bias.

TABLE 6    Cross-Sectional, Pooled, and Fixed Effects Regressions of Debt Maturity Structure on Explanatory Variables for 328 Firms during the Period 1980–89

| Independent Variable | Hypothesized Sign | Cross-Sectional Regression | Pooled Regression | Fixed-Effects Regression |
|---|---|---|---|---|
| Intercept | | .578 | −.141 | N.A.[a] |
| | | (.59) | (−.38) | |
| MV/BV | − | −.220 | .159 | .223 |
| | | (−1.03) | (2.07)** | (2.68)* |
| SIZE | + | .075 | .102 | .160 |
| | | (.99) | (3.55)* | (2.15)** |
| ΔEPS | − | | −.178 | −.135 |
| | | | (−3.34)* | (−3.92)* |
| BONDRATE | + | .482 | 1.436 | .657 |
| | | (1.82)*** | (10.63)* | (3.68)* |
| SQBRATE | − | −.062 | −.176 | −.074 |
| | | (−2.09)** | (−10.05)* | (−3.54)* |
| RATEDUM | N.A. | .136 | −1.143 | .557 |
| | | (.33) | (−3.52)* | (1.81)*** |
| ASSETMAT | + | .221 | .182 | .095 |
| | | (6.59)* | (10.57)* | (6.46)* |
| GTAXRATE | − | −.220 | −.560 | −.215 |
| | | (−.41) | (−2.59)* | (−2.13)** |
| BTAXRATE | N.A. | .186 | .011 | −.006 |
| | | (1.62) | (1.42) | (−.44) |
| VAR | − | −3.989 | −3.181 | |
| | | (−1.45) | (−2.47)** | |
| TERM | + | | −2.699 | −2.615 |
| | | | (−1.20) | (−1.62) |
| LEVERAGE | + | 5.663 | 6.242 | 6.337 |
| | | (5.73)* | (19.80)* | (22.26)* |
| Adjusted $R^2$ | | .49 | .43 | .72 |
| F | | 31.9* | 203.6* | 26.2* |
| No. of observations | | 328 | 3,279 | 3,279 |

NOTE.—The regressions are estimated by ordinary least squares using White's (1980) correction for heteroscedasticity. The dependent variable (DEBTMAT) is the (book) value-weighed average of the maturities of the firm's debt. The explanatory variables are defined as follows: MV/BV is the market value of the firm (proxied by the sum of the book value of assets and the market value of equity less the book value of equity) scaled by the book value of assets; SIZE is the natural logarithm of the estimate of firm value measured in 1982 dollars using the producer price index deflator; ΔEPS is the difference between next year's earnings per share and this year's earnings per share scaled by this year's common stock price per share; BONDRATE is the firm's cardinalized Standard & Poor's bond rating, where AAA = 1, . . . , CCC = 7 and unrated firms receive a code of 8; SQBRATE is the firm's squared cardinalized bond rating; RATEDUM equals one if the firm has a bond rating, and zero otherwise; ASSETMAT is the (book) value-weighted average of the maturities of current assets and net property, plant, and equipment; GTAXRATE = TAXRATE if TAXRATE is between zero and one, and GTAXRATE = 0 otherwise; BTAXRATE = 0 if TAXRATE is between zero and one, and BTAXRATE = TAXRATE otherwise; VAR is the ratio of the standard deviation of the first difference in earnings before interest, depreciation, and taxes to the average of assets over the period 1980–89; TERM is the difference between the long-term and short-term yields on government bonds; and LEVERAGE is the ratio of total debt (the sum of long-term debt, long-term debt due within 1 year, and short-term debt) to the market value of the firm. Heteroscedasticity-consistent *t*-statistics are reported in parentheses below the parameter estimates. N.A. = no answer.

[a] Firm-specific intercepts.
* Significant at the 1% level.
** Significant at the 5% level.
*** Significant at the 10% level.

on SIZE in the pooled regression. All else being equal, a 1 standard deviation increase in SIZE increases debt maturity structure by 5.7%.

Consistent with the signaling hypothesis, the coefficient estimates on abnormal earnings ($\Delta$EPS) are significantly negative. However, the economic significance of this result is questionable. For example, the estimated coefficient from the pooled regression implies that a 1 standard deviation increase in $\Delta$EPS reduces debt maturity structure by only 3.5%.

The regressions provide strong support for the liquidity risk hypothesis, as captured in the relation between debt maturity structure and bond rating. The coefficient estimates on bond rating (BONDRATE) and the square of bond rating (SQBRATE) are significantly positive and negative, respectively. The interpretation is that firms with lower-quality bond ratings tend to lengthen debt maturity structure, but that this trend diminishes as credit standing deteriorates.[45] The pooled regression's coefficient estimates indicate that a one-letter deterioration in S&P bond rating increases debt maturity structure by 1.44 years; however, the rate of increase in debt maturity structure decreases by 0.18 years for each consecutive lower grade.

The regressions also provide strong support for the maturity-matching hypothesis. The coefficient estimates on asset maturity (ASSETMAT) are significantly positive in all three regression specifications. For example, the coefficient estimate in the cross-sectional regression indicates that all else being equal, debt maturity structure increases by 0.22 years for a 1-year increase in asset maturity.

The tax-based hypotheses receive mixed support. On the one hand, the coefficient estimates on tax rate (GTAXRATE) and earnings variability (VAR) are negative as predicted, and significant in the pooled and fixed effects regressions. However, these coefficient estimates do not appear to be economically significant. From the pooled regression, a 10-percentage-point increase in the tax rate decreases debt maturity structure by only 1.7%, and a 1 standard deviation increase in earnings variability decreases debt maturity structure by only 3.1%. On the other hand, there is no evidence that debt maturity structure is positively related to the slope of the term structure (TERM). Indeed, the coefficient estimates on TERM are negative, although not significant.

Finally, there is a significant positive relation between debt maturity structure and leverage (LEVERAGE) in all three regressions. For example, the pooled regression's coefficient estimate indicates that a 1 standard deviation increase in leverage (from the sample mean of 20%–35%) increases debt maturity structure by 27.7%. The positive

---

45. Note that the nonmonotonic relation between debt maturity structure and bond rating is *not* driven by nonrated firms in the sample (i.e., those firms with a coded value for BONDRATE of 8). Our regressions dummy-out the effect of nonrated firms by including the variable RATEDUM (a dummy variable equal to one if the firm is rated and zero otherwise).

relation between debt maturity structure and leverage is consistent with the hypothesis that firms lengthen debt maturity as leverage increases to offset the higher probability of a liquidity crisis.

## B. Robustness Tests

Table 7 presents estimates for a number of alternative regression specifications for the pooled cross-section and time-series data. Model 1 includes the same independent variables as before, except the dummy variables LOWBOND and HIGHBOND replace BONDRATE, SQBRATE, and RATEDUM. Recall that LOWBOND equals one if the firm is rated CCC or is not rated, and zero otherwise; and HIGHBOND equals one if the firm is rated AA or AAA, and zero otherwise. Model 2 is equivalent to model 1, except that model 2 also includes RATEDUM to dummy-out the effect of nonrated firms who as a group have the shortest average debt maturity structure in the sample. The dummy variables LOWBOND and HIGHBOND provide an alternative test of the liquidity risk hypothesis that firms with high and very low bond ratings have shorter debt maturity structures than firms with intermediate bond ratings.

Consistent with that hypothesis, the coefficient estimates on LOWBOND and HIGHBOND are significantly negative in model 1 and model 2. All else being equal, the coefficient estimates in model 2 indicate that firms rated CCC (AA or AAA) have an average debt maturity structure that is 1.38 (1.08) years shorter than that of firms rated B, BB, BBB, and A in the sample.[46] Thus, there is strong evidence of a nonmonotonic relation between debt maturity structure and credit standing for firms with public debt ratings.

Model 3 in table 7 reestimates the pooled regression in table 6 with the addition of industry dummy variables to assess the relative importance of firm-specific and industry-specific determinants of debt maturity structure. (Appendix A reports the industries represented in the sample and their SIC codes.) A test of the null hypothesis that industry dummy variable coefficients are equal to zero is easily rejected. However, industry classification provides little additional explanatory power; the adjusted $R^2$ of the regression increases from 0.43 to 0.47. The coefficient estimates and significance levels for the other explanatory variables in the equation are essentially unaltered.

We find no support for the prediction that debt maturity structure is inversely related to growth opportunities, where growth opportunities are proxied by the firm's market-to-book ratio (MV/BV). An alternative proxy for growth opportunities that is often used in the literature

---

46. These results are quite robust to alternative rating cutoff points to classify low- and high-rated firms. One exception is when we include firms with a rating of B in LOWBOND. For this case, the coefficient estimate on LOWBOND is significantly negative only when RATEDUM is not in the equation. Recall from table 4 that B-rated firms have the longest average debt maturity structure in the sample.

**TABLE 7**    **Alternative Regression Specifications for 328 Firms during the Period 1980–89 (No. of Observations = 3,279)**

| Independent Variable | Hypothesized Sign | Model 1 | Model 2 | Model 3 | Model 4 | Model 5 | Model 6 |
|---|---|---|---|---|---|---|---|
| Intercept | | 1.444 (5.45)* | 1.478 (4.06)* | −.531 (−1.32) | .066 (.18) | −.032 (−.09) | −.200 (−.54) |
| MV/BV | − | .109 (1.41) | .109 (1.41) | .103 (1.21) | ... | .183 (2.36)** | .156 (2.04)** |
| ADVRD | − | ... | ... | ... | −1.023 (−1.98)** | −1.306 (−2.45)** | ... |
| SIZE | + | .126 (4.23)* | .127 (4.24)* | .165 (4.85)* | .125 (4.55)* | .106 (3.68)* | .104 (3.61)* |
| ΔEPS | − | −.173 (−3.33)* | −.172 (−3.08)* | −.183 (−3.60)* | −.177 (−3.31)* | −.179 (−3.35)* | ... |
| UEPS | − | ... | ... | ... | ... | ... | −.188 (−4.11)* |
| BONDRATE | + | ... | ... | 1.384 (9.63)* | 1.344 (10.03)* | 1.390 (10.23)* | 1.409 (10.43)* |
| SQBRATE | − | ... | ... | −.166 (−9.17)* | −1.64 (−9.50)* | −.171 (−9.81)* | −.171 (−9.79)* |
| RATEDUM | N.A. | ... | −.040 (−.15) | −1.035 (−3.23)* | −1.038 (−3.16)* | −1.127 (−3.48)* | −1.054 (−3.24)* |
| LOWBOND | − | −1.341 (−13.27)* | −1.377 (−4.98)* | ... | ... | ... | ... |
| HIGHBOND | − | −1.076 (−10.32)* | −1.075 (−10.33)* | ... | ... | ... | ... |

| | Predicted sign | | | | | | |
|---|---|---|---|---|---|---|---|
| ASSETMAT | + | .187 (10.52)* | .187 (10.53)* | .166 (8.56)* | .181 (10.41)* | .177 (10.28)* | .182 (10.58)* |
| GTAXRATE | − | −.467 (−2.11)** | −.501 (−2.38)** | −.472 (−2.17)** | −.538 (−2.48)** | −.565 (−2.61)* | −.567 (−2.62)* |
| BTAXRATE | N.A. | .012 (1.56) | .012 (1.59) | .012 (1.52) | .013 (1.55) | .011 (1.45) | .012 (1.52) |
| VAR | − | −3.761 (−2.94)* | −3.755 (−2.93)** | −2.662 (1.98)** | −3.111 (−3.111) | −3.172 (−3.172) | −3.167 (−3.167) |
| TERM | + | −2.587 (−1.16) | −2.580 (−1.15) | −2.647 (−1.20) | −2.741 (−1.22) | −2.535 (−1.13) | −2.462 (−1.10) |
| LEVERAGE | + | 5.967 (18.76)* | 5.978 (19.25)* | 6.093 (19.52)* | 5.939 (19.98)* | 6.223 (19.74)* | 6.238 (19.92)* |
| Industry $F$-statistic | | | | 7.81* | | | |
| Adjusted $R^2$ | | .43 | .43 | .47 | .43 | .43 | .43 |
| $F$ | | 225.6* | 206.7* | 80.2* | 203.2* | 188.5* | 204.2* |

NOTE.—The regressions are estimated by ordinary least squares using White's (1980) correction for heteroscedasticity. The dependent variable (DEBTMAT) is the (book) value-weighted average of the maturities of the firm's debt. The explanatory variables not previously defined in table 6 are defined as follows: ADVRD is advertising and research and development expenses scaled by total assets; UEPS is the unexpected component of next year's earnings per share scaled by this year's common stock price per share; LOWBOND equals one if the firm has a Standard & Poor's (S&P) bond rating of CCC or is unrated, and zero otherwise; and HIGHBOND equals one if the firm's S&P bond rating is AA or higher, and zero otherwise. The industry $F$-statistic tests the null hypothesis that a set of industry dummy variable coefficients equals zero. Heteroscedasticity-consistent $t$-statistics are reported in parentheses below the parameter estimates.

\* Significant at the 1% level.

\*\* Significant at the 5% level.

\*\*\* Significant at the 10% level.

(see, e.g., Smith and Watts 1992) is advertising and research and development expenses scaled by total assets (ADVRD).[47] To investigate the performance of ADVRD by itself and relative to MV/BV, model 4 replaces MV/BV with ADVRD, and model 5 includes both MV/BV and ADVRD.

Consistent with Myers's (1977) agency cost hypothesis, the coefficient estimates on ADVRD in models 4 and 5 are significantly negative.[48] In comparison, the coefficient estimate on MV/BV in model 5 continues to be significantly positive. As noted earlier, the problem with MV/BV is that it is highly negatively correlated with LEVERAGE (correlation of −0.46), suggesting that firms with large amounts of growth opportunities have little leverage, and therefore little incentive, to moderate debt maturity structure to alleviate conflicts of interest between equityholders and debtholders. In contrast, ADVRD is only moderately negatively correlated with LEVERAGE (correlation of −0.20),[49] and as such it is a more problem-free proxy for growth opportunities in the context of our study. Nevertheless, a conservative interpretation of our results is that we find only mixed support for growth opportunities as an important determinant of debt maturity structure choice for our sample of firms.

To test Flannery's (1986) signaling hypothesis, we use ΔEPS (i.e., the difference between year $t + 1$ and year $t$ earnings per share, scaled by year $t$ stock price) as a proxy for insiders' anticipated change in firm quality. However, ΔEPS is subject to the criticism that it measures the growth in earnings rather than the surprise in earnings. To investigate the robustness of ΔEPS, we forecast year $t + 1$ earnings per share using two forecasting models separately estimated for each firm in the panel: (1) earnings regressed on a time trend, and (2) earnings regressed on lagged earnings. The unexpected component of the future change in earnings UEPS is then computed as year $t + 1$ earnings per share minus the respective forecasted value for year $t + 1$ earnings per share, scaled by year $t$ stock price.

Model 6 in table 7 reports the results for the time-trend forecasting model. As seen there, the coefficient estimate on UEPS is significantly negative, with virtually the same magnitude as the coefficient estimate on ΔEPS. The results are similar when UEPS is computed using the lagged earnings forecasting model and when using the fixed effects regression specification (not reported in the table). The implication is that ΔEPS is a robust proxy for the unexpected component of the future change in earnings.

---

47. For the pooled data, the average (median) value for ADVRD is 0.04 (0.02), with a minimum value of zero, a maximum value of 0.46, and a standard deviation of 0.05.

48. However, note that the coefficient estimates on ADVRD are probably not economically significant. For example, the estimate in model 5 indicates that a 1 standard deviation increase in ADVRD decreases debt maturity structure by only 1.9%.

49. The correlation between MV/BV and ADVRD is 0.28.

## V. Conclusion

In this article we examine the empirical determinants of a firm's debt maturity structure for a sample of 328 industrial firms over the period from 1980 to 1989. Our measure of debt maturity structure is the weighted average maturity of a firm's debt, debtlike obligations, and current liabilities. This measure incorporates detailed information about the maturities of the firm's debt, including debentures, capital leases, bank loans, and commercial paper. We test the primary theories of debt maturity structure suggested in the literature. These include agency cost hypotheses, signaling and liquidity risk hypotheses, the maturity matching hypothesis, and tax hypotheses. Our analysis is unique in the respect that no previous test of the maturity hypotheses utilizes such extensive and reliable information about firms' debt maturity structures across time.

We find only moderate support for the agency cost perspective that debt maturity is used to control conflicts of interest between equityholders and debtholders. Although smaller firms in the sample tend to use shorter-term debt, there is only mixed support for Myers's (1977) prediction that debt maturity is inversely related to proxies for growth options in firms' investment opportunity sets. The latter result conflicts with Barclay and Smith's (1995) finding of a strong inverse relation between debt maturity and proxies for growth options. Since this article and their article use different samples and debt maturity structure measures, it is difficult to pinpoint the source of the discrepancy accurately. However, we suspect that the Barclay and Smith regressions are misspecified because they do not control for leverage. Our results suggest that firms with large amounts of growth options have little leverage, and hence little incentive to moderate debt maturity structure to minimize conflicts of interest over the exercise of those options.

Our results provide more support for predictions from theories based on private information. First, consistent with Flannery's (1986) signaling model, firms with larger earnings surprises tend to use shorter-term debt. Second, consistent with Diamond's (1991a) prediction, we find strong evidence of a nonmonotonic relation between debt maturity structure and credit quality for firms with public debt ratings. Finally, consistent with Diamond (1991b), we find that firms with intermediate credit ratings tend to rely more heavily on bank debt for their short-term financing needs, while firms with the highest credit ratings tend to rely on directly placed debt such as debentures and commercial paper.

We also find strong support for the standard textbook prescription that firms should match the maturity of their debt to that of their assets. Our tests indicate that asset maturity is an important factor in explaining both cross-sectional and time-series variation in debt matu-

*Empirical Corporate Finance III*

rity structure. However, we find only modest support for the tax hypotheses. Although the estimated coefficients on the tax and earnings variability variables are significantly negative, the economic significance of these variables is questionable. Furthermore, we find no evidence that firms adjust debt maturity structure in response to the shape of the term structure to accelerate the tax shield on debt.

Our empirical analysis focuses only on the factors predicted to influence debt maturity structure choice. However, the choice of debt maturity is only one of several decisions that comprise corporate financial policy, which also includes the choice between debt and equity, the priority structure of debt, the covenants and optionlike features associated with the debt, and whether to issue public or private debt. An important extension of our work would be to conduct joint tests of the determinants of corporate financial policy using a simultaneous equations framework. Although a challenging next step, such an investigation may yield important new insights into the determinants of corporate financial policy.

## Appendix A

TABLE A1    Sample Firms by Industry

| Industry | SIC Codes | DEBTMAT Mean (Years) | No. of Firms |
|---|---|---|---|
| Printing and publishing | 2711–96 | 1.93 | 12 |
| Transportation equipment | 3721–60 | 2.08 | 11 |
| Footwear | 3140 | 2.12 | 8 |
| Rubber and miscellaneous plastic products | 3011–89 | 2.27 | 8 |
| Fabricated metals | 3411–90 | 2.44 | 22 |
| Search and navigation equipment | 3812 | 2.52 | 10 |
| Chemicals | 2840–90 | 2.54 | 13 |
| Electronic components | 3670–90 | 2.64 | 11 |
| Textile mill products | 2200–2253 | 2.80 | 9 |
| Pharmaceuticals | 2834 | 2.90 | 11 |
| Apparel and other textile products | 2300–2340 | 2.95 | 8 |
| Industrial machinery and equipment | 3510–85 | 3.00 | 28 |
| Electronic equipment | 3613–63 | 3.23 | 14 |
| Food and kindred products | 2000–2090 | 3.46 | 23 |
| Instruments | 3822–3990 | 3.50 | 13 |
| Motor vehicle parts | 3714 | 3.68 | 10 |
| Wholesale, retail, and services | 5051–8711 | 3.70 | 18 |
| Petroleum refining | 2911 | 3.97 | 17 |
| Primary metal industries | 3310–90 | 4.02 | 22 |
| Inorganic chemicals and plastics | 2800–2821 | 4.40 | 14 |
| Mining | 1040–1400 | 4.54 | 18 |
| Stone, clay, and glass products | 3241–90 | 4.58 | 9 |
| Lumber, furniture, and paper products | 2430–2670 | 5.68 | 19 |
| Total | | | 328 |

# Appendix B

TABLE B1    Default Maturities

| Type of Debt Instrument | Average Years Remaining to Maturity |
|---|---|
| Bonds and debentures | 12.40 |
| Notes and other debt and obligations | 5.25 |
| Leases | 2.80 |
| Term loans, bank loans, foreign loans, and subsidiary debt | 2.08 |
| Revolving credit | 1.50 |
| Commercial paper | .24 |

NOTE.—The default values for remaining time-to-maturity (in years) for the debt instruments in our sample are taken from Morris (1992) and are based on a March 1985 random sample of debt issues listed in *Standard and Poor's Bond Guide*, the midpoint of our sample period, from 1980 to 1989. The default maturity for commercial paper is the average of the maturities that are reported by sample firms.

# References

Barclay, M. J., and Smith, C. W., Jr. 1995. The maturity structure of corporate debt. *Journal of Finance* 50 (June): 609–31.

Barnea, A.; Haugen, R. A.; and Senbet, L. W. 1980. A rationale for debt maturity structure and call provisions in the agency theoretic framework. *Journal of Finance* 35 (December): 1223–43.

Barnea, A.; Haugen, R. A.; and Senbet, L. W. 1985. *Agency Problems and Financial Contracting.* Englewood Cliffs, N.J.: Prentice-Hall.

Brick, I. E., and Ravid, S. A. 1985. On the relevance of debt maturity structure. *Journal of Finance* 40 (December): 1423–37.

Brick, I. E., and Ravid, S. A. 1991. Interest rate uncertainty and the optimal debt maturity structure. *Journal of Financial and Quantitative Analysis* 26 (March): 63–81.

Chamberlain, G. 1978. Omitted variable bias in panel data: Estimating the returns to schooling. *Annales de l'Insee* 30 (April–September): 49–82.

Chang, C. 1989. Debt maturity structure and bankruptcy. Working paper. Minneapolis: University of Minnesota.

Cook, R. D. 1977. Detection of influential observations in linear regression. *Technometrics* 19 (February): 15–18.

Diamond, D. W. 1991a. Debt maturity structure and liquidity risk. *Quarterly Journal of Economics* 106 (August): 709–37.

Diamond, D. W. 1991b. Monitoring and reputation: The choice between bank loans and directly placed debt. *Journal of Political Economy* 99 (August): 689–721.

*Economic Report of the President.* 1993. Washington, D.C.: U.S. Government Printing Office.

Fischer, E. O.; Heinkel, R.; and Zechner, J. 1989. Dynamic capital structure choice: Theory and tests. *Journal of Finance* 44 (March): 19–40.

Flannery, M. J. 1986. Asymmetric information and risky debt maturity choice. *Journal of Finance* 41 (March): 19–37.

Goswami, G.; Noe, T. H.; and Rebello, M. J. 1993. Asset maturity, debt maturity, and asymmetric information. Working paper. Atlanta: Georgia State University.

Goswami, G.; Noe, T. H.; and Rebello, M. J. 1995. Debt financing under asymmetric information. *Journal of Finance* 50 (June): 633–59.

Guedes, J., and Opler, T. 1994. The determinants of the maturity of new corporate debt issues. Working paper. Columbus: Ohio State University.

Hart, O., and Moore, J. 1994. A theory of debt based on the inalienability of human capital. *Quarterly Journal of Economics* 109 (November): 841–79.

Ho, T. S. Y., and Singer, R. F. 1984. The value of corporate debt with a sinking-fund provision. *Journal of Business* 57 (July): 315–36.

Iskandar, M. E., and Emery, D. R. 1994. An empirical investigation of the role of indenture provisions in determining bond ratings. *Journal of Banking and Finance* 18 (January): 93–111.

Kale, J. R., and Noe, T. H. 1990. Risky debt maturity choice in a sequential equilibrium. *Journal of Financial Research* 13 (Summer): 155–65.

Kane, A.; Marcus, A. J.; and McDonald, R. L. 1985. Debt policy and the rate of return premium to leverage. *Journal of Financial and Quantitative Analysis* 20 (December): 479–99.

Kim, C. S.; Mauer, D. C.; and Stohs, M. Hoven. 1995. Corporate debt maturity policy and investor tax-timing options: Theory and evidence. *Financial Management* 24 (Spring): 33–45.

Kleidon, A. W. 1986. Variance bounds tests and stock price valuation models. *Journal of Political Economy* 94 (October): 953–1001.

Leland, H. E. 1994. Corporate debt value, bond covenants, and optimal capital structure. *Journal of Finance* 49 (September): 1213–52.

Lewis, C. M. 1990. A multiperiod theory of corporate financial policy under taxation. *Journal of Financial and Quantitative Analysis* 25 (March): 25–43.

Mitchell, K. 1991. The call, sinking fund and term-to-maturity features of corporate bonds: An empirical investigation. *Journal of Financial and Quantitative Analysis* 26 (June): 201–22.

Morris, J. R. 1992. Factors affecting the maturity structure of corporate debt. Working paper. Denver: University of Colorado.

Myers, S. C. 1977. Determinants of corporate borrowing. *Journal of Financial Economics* 5 (November): 147–75.

Rajan, R. G. 1992. Insiders and outsiders: The choice between informed and arm's-length debt. *Journal of Finance* 47 (September): 1367–1400.

Smith, C. W., Jr., and Warner, J. B. 1979. On financial contracting: An analysis of bond covenants. *Journal of Financial Economics* 7 (June): 117–61.

Smith, C. W., Jr., and Watts, R. L. 1992. The investment opportunity set and corporate financing, dividend, and compensation policies. *Journal of Financial Economics* 32 (December): 263–92.

Titman, S., and Wessels, R. 1988. The determinants of capital structure choice. *Journal of Finance* 43 (March): 1–19.

Watts, R. L., and Zimmerman, J. 1986. *Positive Accounting Theory.* Englewood Cliffs, N.J.: Prentice-Hall.

White, H. 1980. A heteroskedasticity-consistent covariance matrix estimator and a direct test for heteroskedasticity. *Econometrica* 48 (May): 817–38.

Whited, T. M. 1992. Debt, liquidity constraints, and corporate investment: Evidence from panel data. *Journal of Finance* 47 (September): 1425–60.

Wiggins, J. B. 1990. The relation between risk and optimal debt maturity and the value of leverage. *Journal of Financial and Quantitative Analysis* 25 (September): 377–85.

# C
# The Role of Private Incentives and Agency

# [6]

THE JOURNAL OF FINANCE • VOL. LII, NO. 4 • SEPTEMBER 1997

# Managerial Entrenchment and Capital Structure Decisions

PHILIP G. BERGER, ELI OFEK, and DAVID L. YERMACK*

### ABSTRACT

We study associations between managerial entrenchment and firms' capital structures, with results generally suggesting that entrenched CEOs seek to avoid debt. In a cross-sectional analysis, we find that leverage levels are lower when CEOs do not face pressure from either ownership and compensation incentives or active monitoring. In an analysis of leverage changes, we find that leverage increases in the aftermath of entrenchment-reducing shocks to managerial security, including unsuccessful tender offers, involuntary CEO replacements, and the addition to the board of major stockholders.

MUCH CAPITAL STRUCTURE RESEARCH follows Jensen and Meckling (1976) in using agency theory to argue that managers do not always adopt capital structures with the value-maximizing level of debt. Some managers appear to entrench themselves considerably against pressures from internal and external corporate governance mechanisms, and our article tests whether the degree of this entrenchment impacts firms' choices about capital structure. We find empirical support for this theory in a panel of 434 firms studied between 1984 and 1991.

We define entrenchment as the extent to which managers fail to experience discipline from the full range of corporate governance and control mechanisms, including monitoring by the board, the threat of dismissal or takeover, and stock- or compensation-based performance incentives. Entrenched managers by definition have discretion over their firms' leverage choices. Managers may prefer less leverage than optimal because of a desire to reduce firm risk to protect their underdiversified human capital (e.g., Fama (1980)) or their dislike of performance pressures associated with commitments to disgorge large amounts of cash (e.g., Jensen (1986)).[1] Conversely, Harris and Raviv (1988), Stulz (1988), and others suggest that entrenchment motives may cause man-

---

* Berger is from the University of Pennsylvania, and Ofek and Yermack are from New York University. The authors appreciate helpful comments from René Stulz (the editor), two anonymous referees, and seminar participants from Boston College, Columbia University, New York University, University of Notre Dame, and the Financial Management Association. Berger acknowledges the financial support of Coopers & Lybrand.

[1] Jensen's (1986) view that high debt levels constrain managers from diverting "free" cash flow to pursue personal goals at the expense of value maximization underlies the models of Grossman and Hart (1982), Stulz (1990), Hart and Moore (1990), and Hart (1993). Related models by Williamson (1988) and Harris and Raviv (1990) consider the possibility that debt may force managers to reduce the size of the firm by liquidating inefficient operations. See Harris and Raviv (1991) for an extensive survey of capital structure models.

agers to increase leverage beyond the optimal point, in order to inflate the voting power of their equity stakes and reduce the possibility of takeover attempts. A third possibility is that entrenched managers sometimes adopt excess leverage as a transitory device that signals a commitment to sell assets or otherwise restructure, thereby preempting takeover attempts by outsiders who might have different plans for increasing firm value.

Our empirical analysis has two goals. First, we explore whether significant associations exist between patterns of firm leverage and variables that are associated with managerial entrenchment. Second, we evaluate how closely our findings support each of the three theories advanced above about how entrenchment might affect managers' leverage choices.

We begin by documenting cross-sectional relations between the levels of various corporate governance variables and firms' debt to equity ratios. After controlling for nonagency determinants of leverage, we find significantly lower leverage in firms whose CEOs have several characteristics of entrenchment, including a long tenure in office and compensation that has low sensitivity to performance. Leverage is also significantly lower when CEOs do not appear to face strong monitoring, as is the case when the board of directors is large or has a low fraction of outside directors, and when the firm has no major stockholders. We recognize that many of these cross-sectional levels results are also consistent with other theories of corporate governance and capital structure. Therefore, we undertake further analysis to explore the impact on firms' capital structures of large, discrete changes in corporate governance parameters. We find that in the aftermath of events that represent negative shocks to CEO security, including attempts to acquire the firm, the involuntary departure of the prior CEO, and the arrival of a major stockholder-director, firms' subsequent capital structures exhibit significantly greater leverage. We also find that leverage increases after CEOs are subjected to greater performance incentives in the form of increased inventories of stock options. Our results strongly suggest that the degree of managerial entrenchment has influence on firms' observed capital structures, and these findings represent the major contribution of the article.

We extend our analysis by examining news stories about our sample firms around the time of entrenchment shocks, seeking confirmation of a direct link between the events and the leverage changes. We also seek to evaluate three possible explanations for why managers might be motivated to change leverage when their security is threatened: to increase the firm's value by moving toward a more beneficial, although less comfortable, capital structure; to increase their personal voting control; or to commit to a defensive restructuring that, while not necessarily optimal, creates sufficient value to keep raiders away. These three theories are not mutually exclusive, and we find that each has some explanatory power.

After unsuccessful takeovers, we find net debt issued and equity repurchased both increase markedly, while new equity issued also increases, albeit less substantially. We find that the increase in net debt is generally used to finance large special dividends, equity repurchase offers, or restructuring of operations. Consistent with empirical findings by Safieddine and Titman (1996) of large and significant improvements in operating and stock performance following leverage increases, and with arguments by Grossman and Hart (1982), Jensen (1986), and Stulz (1990), these uses of funds suggest that debt generally helps firms remain independent by committing them to undertake operating improvements that the potential acquirer would otherwise make.

Forced CEO replacements and the addition of blockholders to the board are both followed by leverage increases that, while substantial, are not as large as those following unsuccessful takeovers. Both of these leverage changes arise almost exclusively from a substantial issuance of new debt. An examination of the events following forced CEO replacements shows that the new debt usually finances special dividends or operational restructuring.

Since we find that special dividends and restructurings often occur after leverage rises, our results are superficially consistent with the theory that managers use leverage as a defensive device to commit to value-increasing changes. However, we observe this pattern of events not just after failed attempts to acquire the firm, but also after entrenchment-reducing events that are not necessarily related to takeover threats, including the dismissal of the prior CEO and the arrival of a major stockholder on the board of directors. Therefore, we think the sample-wide results cannot be explained completely as temporary tactical moves to deter outside raiders. Rather, our findings also seem consistent with a conjecture that most firms have less leverage in their capital structure than optimal, and that managers who sense threats to their security increase leverage permanently as a value-enhancing action that they would otherwise prefer to avoid. Our parallel finding that leverage increases after managers receive large incentive compensation awards also seems to support this view. We further explore this possibility by analyzing how leverage changes after entrenchment shocks as a function of a firm's apparent leverage deficit or surplus at the start of each year. We find that firms with leverage deficits react to threats to entrenchment by levering themselves beyond the predicted level, whereas no significant changes are observed for firms with leverage surpluses.

However, some of our results are also consistent with the theory that managers take on excessive leverage in order to bolster their entrenchment, since we observe a positive cross-sectional association between leverage and managerial voting power, consistent with Stulz (1988).

Section I elaborates on the effect of entrenchment on managers' leverage decisions. Section II presents our analysis of leverage levels, including sample selection, variable construction, and empirical results. Section III presents similar information for the changes analysis. We summarize the results and offer conclusions in Section IV.

## I. Managerial Entrenchment and Leverage

A large literature has followed Grossman and Hart (1982) by using an ex ante efficiency perspective to derive predictions about a firm's financing decisions in an agency setting. Theories in these articles emphasize debt's role in lowering agency problems between managers and shareholders, but they ignore the agency problem to which the leverage choice itself is subject. Conflicts of interest over financing policy arise between managers and shareholders because of such factors as managers' preference for lower firm risk due to their underdiversification (Fama (1980) and Amihud and Lev (1981)), managers' disutility from being subject to the performance pressure that large fixed interest payments entail (Jensen (1986)), and managers' preference for job retention when others are better qualified (Harris and Raviv (1988) and Stulz (1988)).

Models using the ex ante efficiency perspective generally adopt the viewpoint of an initial entrepreneur seeking to maximize firm value, with some disciplinary mechanism forcing the entrepreneur to choose the value-maximizing debt level. Novaes and Zingales (1995) show, however, that the efficient choice of debt (optimal for shareholders) generally differs from the entrenchment choice (optimal for managers whose objective is to maximize tenure). Moreover, if the disciplinary mechanism (in their case takeover pressure) has high costs, managers underlever, whereas if takeovers are cheaper than debt as a disciplinary device, managers overlever to block takeovers. Jung, Kim, and Stulz (1996) find some support for entrenchment affecting leverage decisions. They show that a significant portion of equity issuers are firms with poor investment opportunities that have not exhausted their debt capacity. These firms also invest more than similar firms issuing debt. The Jung, Kim and Stulz results thus support the notion that agency costs of managerial discretion lead certain firms to issue equity when debt issuance would have better consequences for firm value.

Theoretical arguments and some empirical evidence thus point to the possibility that managers can become entrenched, and that they may deviate from choosing optimal leverage as a result of the agency costs of managerial discretion. These arguments do not, however, resolve whether entrenched managers tend to take on too little or too much debt,[2] and an important goal of our research is to cast more light on this issue.

## II. Analysis of Capital Structure Levels

In this section we analyze companies' relative levels of leverage as a function of corporate governance variables. If entrenched managers systematically make suboptimal decisions about capital structure, we should observe significant cross-sectional associations between leverage and variables that indicate greater entrenchment. Prior studies by Friend and Lang (1988) and Mehran (1992) present some evidence consistent with this view. We extend their results in this section as a prelude to our inquiry in Section III, in which we

---

[2] For example, Zwiebel (1994) presents a model in which entrenchment is determined endogenously. His predictions are that managers of the best-performing firms engage in the greatest degree of empire building, and that managers adopt increasing debt levels as their tenure increases.

*Managerial Entrenchment and Capital Structure Decisions*     1415

investigate whether large changes in entrenchment-related governance variables lead to major changes in leverage.

Section II.*A* discusses the sample selection. Section II.*B* describes the main dependent and control variables. Many of our controls are similar to those used in the study of cross-sectional leverage by Titman and Wessels (1988). Section II.*C* describes our empirical results.

## A. Sample Selection

Our analysis uses a dataset of 452 industrial companies between 1984 and 1991 assembled by Yermack (1996). The panel is drawn from annual *Forbes* magazine rankings of the 500 largest U.S. public corporations based on sales, total assets, market capitalization, and net income. The sample selection rule requires each company to qualify for at least one *Forbes* list during at least four years of the 1984 to 1991 period, with companies allowed to enter and exit the panel over time. We merge corporate governance and equity ownership data gathered from company proxy statements with accounting data drawn from the COMPUSTAT database. We exclude financial firms (Standard Industrial Classification (SIC) codes 6000 through 6999) and utilities (SIC codes 4900 through 4999) due to the marked differences in leverage and corporate governance between those industries and other sectors of the economy. Because some companies have missing values or have been deleted from recent releases of the COMPUSTAT database, our sample consists of 3,085 observations for 434 firms over eight years.

Our sample selection criteria limit our analysis to large firms only. While this approach enables us to economize on the time and cost for data collection, the conclusions of our analysis do not necessarily apply to smaller firms. But because the large companies in our sample represent a substantial fraction of the market capitalization of all U.S. public companies, the results should illuminate significant links between capital structure choices and managerial entrenchment.

## B. Variables for Analysis of Leverage Levels

Table I lists the major dependent and explanatory variables for our analysis of company leverage levels. We measure the level of leverage at the end of each fiscal year using two continuous variables that take values between 0 and 1:

$$Leverage(book\ value) = \frac{total\ debt(book\ value)}{total\ assets(book\ value)} \qquad (1)$$

$Leverage(market\ value)$

$$= \frac{total\ debt(book\ value)}{total\ debt(book\ value) + common\ equity(market\ value)} \qquad (2)$$

To assess the influence of CEO entrenchment and control upon capital structure choice, we estimate a variety of regression models of these two

**Table I**

**Variables for Analysis of Capital Structure Levels**

Definitions and descriptive statistics for variables used in analysis of capital structure levels. The sample consists of 3,085 observations for 434 companies in the 1984 to 1991 period. Financial statement variables were obtained from COMPUSTAT, with balance sheet items defined as of the end of each fiscal year. Corporate governance and stock ownership variables were obtained from proxy statements generally filed by each company during the third or fourth month of its fiscal year.

| Dependent Variable | Definition | Mean | Std. Dev. |
|---|---|---|---|
| Leverage (book value) | Total debt (book value) ÷ total assets | 0.247 | 0.169 |
| Leverage (market value) | Total debt (book value) ÷ (total debt (book value) + equity (market value)) | 0.265 | 0.202 |

| Explanatory variable | Definition | Mean | Std. Dev. | Correlation with Leverage (Book Value) |
|---|---|---|---|---|
| CEO stock ownership | Shares owned directly ÷ shares outstanding | 0.027 | 0.079 | 0.009 |
| CEO option holdings | Exercisable options held ÷ shares outstanding | 0.0017 | 0.0052 | 0.098*** |
| Presence of at least one 5% blockholder (indicator variable) | =1 if company has at least one 5% stockholder (excluding ESOPs) | 0.517 | 0.500 | 0.041** |
| CEO tenure | Log (years in CEO position) | 1.843 | 0.969 | −0.047** |
| Board composition | % of outside directors | 0.539 | 0.192 | 0.061*** |
| Board size | Log (number of directors) | 2.466 | 0.290 | 0.081*** |
| Return on assets | Earnings before interest, taxes, and depreciation ÷ total assets | 0.188 | 0.098 | −0.246*** |
| Noninterest tax shields | Investment tax credits ÷ total assets | 0.0014 | 0.0065 | 0.037** |
| Asset collateral value | (Net property, plant & equipment + inventory) ÷ total assets | 0.575 | 0.184 | 0.032* |
| Company size | Log (total assets) | 7.766 | 1.139 | 0.262*** |
| Asset uniqueness (1) | Research & development expense ÷ sales | 0.020 | 0.038 | −0.207*** |
| Asset uniqueness (2) | Selling, general & admin. expense ÷ sales | 0.156 | 0.138 | −0.196*** |

Correlations significant at the 10 percent (*), 5 percent (**), and 1 percent (***) levels.

variables, using as regressors several variables that appear widely in corporate governance studies. Our data are gathered from proxy statements filed in advance of firms' annual shareholder meetings, which usually occur in the fourth or fifth month of each fiscal year.

## Managerial Entrenchment and Capital Structure Decisions　　1417

Jensen and Meckling (1976) and other authors have identified managerial equity ownership as an important influence upon firm value, and we therefore include in our model the CEOs' direct stock ownership, measured as a percentage of common equity. We expect that CEOs will have more powerful incentives to make value-maximizing decisions about capital structure when their stock ownership is high, although, as claimed in Mørck, Shleifer, and Vishny (1988), this may not hold true over all ranges since high ownership may insulate managers against other disciplinary forces. Therefore, we cannot make an unambiguous prediction about the association between CEO ownership and leverage.

Our models also include a variable measuring the CEOs' holdings of stock options exercisable within 60 days, again as a percentage of common shares (data is unavailable for unexercisable options). While this variable should further help us measure the interaction between CEO ownership and leverage, it probably serves a more important purpose in providing a measure of the CEOs' performance-based incentive compensation, which usually depends heavily on stock options (Jensen and Murphy (1990) and Yermack (1995)). We view a CEO as entrenched if his compensation is not sensitive to performance; if entrenched CEOs prefer low (high) leverage, we expect to observe positive (negative) coefficient estimates for the stock option variable.

A related characteristic of entrenched CEOs should be a high level of fixed compensation, since one might expect entrenched managers to extract excessive resources from the firm. We use cash salary and bonus payments as a proxy for fixed compensation since estimates in Jensen and Murphy (1990), replicated by Yermack (1996) using our data, indicate that CEOs' salary and bonus compensation has extremely low sensitivity to changes in firm value. We define excess fixed compensation as the residual in the ordinary least squares (OLS) regression:

$$\log(Salary_{it} + Bonus_{it})$$

$$= \beta_1 \log(Sales_{it}) + \beta_2(CEO\ Stock + Option\ Ownership(\%)_{it}) + \beta_3(Age_{it})$$

$$+ \beta_4(Years\ as\ CEO_{it}) + \beta_5(Return\ on\ Assets_{it}) + \beta_6(Return\ on\ Assets_{it-1})$$

$$+ \beta_7(\log(1 + Stock\ Return_{it}) - \log(1 + Market\ Return_{it})) \qquad (3)$$

$$+ \beta_8(\log(1 + Stock\ Return_{it-1}) - \log(1 + Market\ Return_{it-1}))$$

$$+ \gamma'(Industry\ dummies_i) + \theta'(Year\ Dummies_t) + \varepsilon_{it}$$

The subscripts $i$ and $t$ represent firms and years, respectively, and all dollar values are adjusted for inflation. If entrenched CEOs prefer low (high) leverage, we expect to observe negative (positive) estimates for this variable.

We use a variable measuring the CEOs' years in office to reflect the likelihood that a CEO's control over internal monitoring mechanisms increases as his tenure lengthens. An entrenched CEO who is insulated from the threat of dismissal will also exhibit a large number of years in office. We use the natural log of this variable, in the belief that CEO power over corporate governance will cumulate over time at a decreasing rate.

Our models include several variables related to the strength of monitoring faced by the CEO, since a further characteristic of entrenchment is the absence of effective monitors. We use an indicator variable that equals one if the company reports having one or more holders of at least 5 percent of the common stock (we ignore company-sponsored employee stock ownership (ESOP) plans), since large blockholders have large, direct incentives to monitor managers actively. Several studies, such as Weisbach (1988), indicate that top managers face more vigorous monitoring when the board of directors is controlled by independent or outside directors. To capture the importance of this effect, we include a variable measuring the percentage of the board comprised of outside directors. The variable excludes "grey" directors who have personal business relationships with the company or are relatives of current or former officers. A related variable in our models measures the size of the board in a log specification. Board size has been identified as an important determinant of corporate governance effectiveness in theoretical articles by Lipton and Lorsch (1992) and Jensen (1993). An empirical study by Yermack (1996) shows a significant association between board size and firm value, and also presents results indicating that CEO disciplinary mechanisms related to compensation and the threat of dismissal lose power as board size increases.

In addition to these corporate governance variables, we include in our models standard control variables for other firm attributes expected to influence leverage. To control for company profitability, we use a return on assets (ROA) variable defined as earnings before depreciation, interest, and taxes, divided by total assets at the start of the year. We measure company size by using the book value of assets in place (the log of total assets).[3] We control for nondebt tax effects by using the ratio of investment tax credits over total assets. The collateral value of assets is measured by the ratio of net property, plant, and equipment plus inventory over total assets. Two variables are included to measure the uniqueness of assets: research & development (R&D) expense over sales (which also proxies for the presence of growth opportunities), and selling, general, and administrative (SGA) expenses over sales.

Table I gives the definitions of dependent and explanatory variables, along with sample-wide means and standard deviations. The table also shows sample correlations between the explanatory variables and one of our leverage measures; the majority of these correlations have the same sign as regression coefficient estimates presented in the next section.

---

[3] No material change occurs in our results if we reestimate our models using a market value measure of firm size (the log of the sum of the market value of equity plus the book value of total debt).

Managerial Entrenchment and Capital Structure Decisions 1419

### Table II
# Regression Coefficient Estimates: Determinants of Capital Structure Levels

OLS regression coefficients for models of capital structure levels. The sample consists of 3,085 observations for 434 companies in the 1984 to 1991 period. The absolute values of $t$-statistics appear in parentheses below each coefficient estimate. For each of the two specifications of the dependent variable, the table shows ordinary least squares (OLS) estimates as well as between-firm and within-firm estimates calculated using standard panel data techniques.

| Dependent Variable | Leverage (Book Value) | | | Leverage (Market Value) | | |
| --- | --- | --- | --- | --- | --- | --- |
| | OLS Estimates | Between Estimates | Within Estimates | OLS Estimates | Between Estimates | Within Estimates |
| CEO direct stock ownership (% of common shares) | 0.156*** (3.84) | 0.153 (1.63) | 0.143 (1.62) | 0.258*** (6.11) | 0.217** (2.21) | 0.249*** (2.89) |
| CEO vested option holdings (% of common shares) | 2.883*** (5.32) | 3.106** (2.13) | 0.804 (1.22) | 3.382*** (5.99) | 3.100** (2.03) | 1.410** (2.18) |
| Presence of at least one 5% blockholder (indicator variable) | 0.018*** (3.14) | 0.017 (0.98) | 0.009 (1.50) | 0.033*** (5.57) | 0.043** (2.41) | 0.003 (0.57) |
| CEO tenure (log (years in office)) | −0.005 (1.54) | −0.011 (1.14) | −0.001 (0.40) | −0.011*** (3.51) | −0.017* (1.77) | −0.008*** (3.02) |
| Board composition (% outside directors) | 0.006 (0.41) | −0.028 (0.71) | 0.058** (1.98) | 0.035** (2.11) | −0.010 (0.25) | 0.077*** (2.69) |
| Board size (log (number of directors)) | −0.036*** (2.96) | −0.033 (1.08) | −0.051*** (2.72) | −0.027** (2.10) | −0.024 (0.73) | −0.062*** (3.41) |
| Excess compensation (actual − predicted log (salary + bonus)) | 0.001 (0.15) | 0.005 (0.33) | −0.021*** (2.66) | −0.004 (0.65) | 0.0001 (0.00) | −0.036*** (4.68) |
| Return on assets (EBDIT/ total assets) | −0.346*** (10.95) | −0.347*** (3.83) | −0.230*** (6.75) | −0.805*** (24.42) | −0.953*** (9.98) | −0.489*** (14.65) |
| Noninterest tax shields (investment tax credits ÷ total assets) | −3.750*** (6.72) | −3.564** (2.24) | −0.734 (1.05) | −1.112* (1.92) | −0.650 (0.39) | 0.925 (1.35) |
| Asset collateral value ((net PPE + INVENTORY) ÷ total assets) | 0.008 (0.43) | 0.050 (1.04) | −0.146*** (4.92) | −0.021 (1.03) | 0.009 (0.18) | −0.143*** (4.95) |
| Company size (log of total assets) | 0.036*** (10.01) | 0.034*** (3.69) | 0.066*** (8.59) | 0.047*** (12.57) | 0.039*** (4.02) | 0.130*** (17.14) |
| Asset uniqueness (R&D expense ÷ sales) | −0.632*** (6.85) | −0.726*** (3.10) | −0.296* (1.72) | −0.825*** (8.59) | −0.860*** (3.50) | −0.364** (2.16) |
| Asset uniqueness (SGA expense ÷ sales) | −0.086*** (3.32) | −0.087 (1.30) | −0.074** (2.02) | −0.164*** (6.05) | −0.165** (2.34) | −0.134*** (3.73) |
| Industry indicator variables (2-digit SIC) | Yes | Yes | No | Yes | Yes | No |
| Year indicator variables | Yes | Yes | Yes | Yes | Yes | Yes |
| Observations | 3,085 | 434 | 3,085 | 3,083 | 434 | 3,083 |
| R-squared | 0.293 | 0.419 | 0.124 | 0.464 | 0.576 | 0.251 |
| F-statistic | 18.38 | 3.87 | 0.84 | 38.37 | 7.29 | 1.98 |
| P-value | 0.00 | 0.00 | 0.99 | 0.00 | 0.00 | 0.00 |

Significant at 1 percent (***), 5 percent (**), and 10 percent (*) levels.

## C. Regression Results

Table II presents regression estimates of models of leverage levels. The table shows three types of estimates: OLS, "between" estimates based on the variation of the intrafirm means of all variables, and "within" estimates based on variation of the data within each firm. Between estimates are presented to address concerns that observations drawn repeatedly from the same sample of firms may not be independent. Within estimates adjust for the possibility that unobservable, firm-specific factors influence the level of leverage in each individual company; the within estimates are equivalent to estimating OLS models and including indicator variables for each of the 434 firms. The left side of Table II shows the three estimates based on models using our book value specification of leverage, while the right side of the table shows estimates based on a market value specification. Indicator variables for individual years are included in all models, and two-digit SIC industry indicators appear in all models except the within estimates.

Results in Table II generally support the hypothesis that entrenched CEOs seek to avoid leverage. However, we are hesitant to draw strong conclusions from our levels analysis alone, since competing theories about corporate governance lead to similar predictions about how companies should design their capital structures in order to reduce agency costs and increase firm value. Moreover, many of the variables in our models of leverage levels are likely determined simultaneously, making it difficult to ascertain cause-and-effect relations from estimated regression coefficients. Few substantive differences appear to exist between the models using the book value and market value estimates of the dependent variable, but the method of estimation does affect the significance of certain explanatory variables. Most of our financial control variables generally have signs in line with accepted theories of capital structure, and to conserve space we confine our discussion to those variables related to the hypotheses about the relation between leverage and managerial entrenchment.

Our regressions show a positive and generally significant association between firm leverage and CEO direct stock ownership. These findings are consistent with an interpretation that managers whose financial incentives are more closely tied to stockholder wealth will pursue more levered capital structures to raise the value of the company. However, the findings also support the conjecture of Stulz (1988) that managers might increase leverage as a means of consolidating their own voting control. Regardless of the interpretation, the economic significance of these estimates appears low; the estimates in the range of 0.1 to 0.2 imply only modest changes in leverage in relation to reasonable changes in the fraction of the equity held by a CEO, which exhibits a mean of 0.027 and standard deviation of 0.079.

Estimates for executive compensation variables also point to an inverse association between leverage and managerial entrenchment. Our results show a significantly positive relation between leverage and CEO vested option holdings. This finding suggests that CEOs who are not entrenched, because they face financial pressure from compensation tied to firm value, will take on greater debt. However, the option result is also consistent with arguments by Haugen and Senbet (1981) and Smith and Watts (1982, 1992), as well as empirical evidence in DeFusco, Johnson, and Zorn (1990), that stock options

*Managerial Entrenchment and Capital Structure Decisions*     1421

may motivate managers to increase firm risk. It is also difficult to evaluate the importance of the option holdings variable since we have no data about the unexercisable options held by CEOs. Interestingly, however, the option variable appears to have far greater economic significance than the variable for direct stock ownership, as its estimated coefficients are an order of magnitude larger. We do not have a clear explanation for this difference.

Our measure of the CEOs' excess fixed compensation has near zero association with leverage in the OLS and between models, but a significantly negative estimated association in the within models. These latter results are consistent with entrenched CEOs taking on less debt, if one assumes that entrenched CEOs also succeed in becoming overcompensated. However, these estimates are not robust to the specification of the excess compensation variable; if one includes the Black-Scholes value of stock options as part of the CEOs' annual compensation, the estimates are no longer significant.

The CEOs' tenure in office has a negative estimated association with the level of leverage, although estimates are significant only for the dependent variable based on market values. The estimates are consistent with entrenched CEOs pursuing capital structures with lower leverage, perhaps to reduce the performance pressures that accompany high debt. However, as is the case for many of the variables in this model, the result supports alternative interpretations. For example, it is possible that CEO tenure is positively correlated with managerial quality or skill. High-quality CEOs may have presided over many years in which their firms' stock prices rose at an above average rate, resulting in capital structures with a high market value of equity. Again, the variable has modest economic significance; the estimate of $-0.008$ in the right column implies that leverage decreases by about 0.5 percent of assets as CEO tenure doubles.

Variables associated with stronger monitoring also have positive connections with leverage, reinforcing our interpretation that entrenched CEOs attempt to avoid debt. Our results indicate that leverage rises in the presence of a significant blockholder, as the indicator variable for the presence of a 5 percent stockholder is uniformly positive and significant in three out of six models, and the estimates suggest that firms with blockholders have leverage 1 to 4 percent higher than other firms. This finding suggests that managers are forced to take on more debt when an influential monitor is present, and that board blockholders and debtholders act as monitoring complements rather than substitutes. Board size has a consistently negative estimated association with leverage across all six models and is significant in four out of six estimations. If CEOs with small boards are less entrenched due to superior monitoring by these bodies, an inverse association between board size and leverage is consistent with the prediction that entrenched CEOs pursue lower leverage. The coefficient estimate of $-0.062$ in the right column implies an increase in leverage on the order of 4 percent if board size is halved. The presence of outside directors on the board seems to lead to greater leverage, although the strength of this assertion relies on the significant estimates for our two within models and the OLS model of market leverage. We conjecture that boards with more outside directors monitor CEOs more actively, causing these managers to adopt capital structures with more leverage.

Several of the results from our analysis of capital structure levels are similar to those reported by Mehran (1992), who examines a sample of 124 manufacturing firms during 1973–1983. Mehran reports OLS estimates of regressions of the level of book leverage against ownership, board structure, and control variables. Using similar measures, he documents OLS results qualitatively the same as our Table II book leverage OLS results with respect to the effects of CEO direct stock ownership, asset collateral value, and the ratio of R&D to sales. Mehran also finds that the percentage of the CEOs' total compensation awarded as stock options (as opposed to the percentage of common shares held in options that we report) has a marginally positive association with book leverage.

## III. Analysis of Changes in Capital Structure

As noted in the preceding discussion, many variables related to capital structure, firm performance, and corporate governance are likely determined simultaneously, making any analysis of cross-sectional levels difficult to interpret. Further, as MacKie-Mason (1990) notes, debt-to-equity ratios represent the cumulative result of years of separate decisions, meaning that tests based on a single aggregate of different decisions are likely to have low power. For these reasons we feel that agency-based models of leverage may be better studied by analyzing decisions to change leverage, rather than the cross-sectional variation in debt to equity ratios.[4] Our research strategy is to study whether leverage changes significantly after events that appear to represent exogenous shocks to companies' governance structures.

Section III.A discusses the variables used in our analysis. Section III.B presents estimates for regression models of changes in leverage. Section III.C explores how changes in leverage differ for firms that appear ex ante to have low and high levels of leverage.

### A. Variables for Analysis of Changes in Leverage

Key dependent and explanatory variables for our analysis of changes in leverage appear in Table III. We measure changes in the debt and equity components of leverage with the following variables, all based on annual flow of funds data obtained from COMPUSTAT:

$$Net\ issuance\ of\ debt = \frac{debt\ issued - debt\ retired}{total\ assets} \tag{4}$$

---

[4] See Jung, Kim, and Stulz (1996) for an elaboration of this view.

## Managerial Entrenchment and Capital Structure Decisions    1423

### Table III

## Variables for Analysis of Capital Structure Changes

Definitions and descriptive statistics for variables used in analysis of capital structure changes. The sample consists of 2,196 observations for 409 companies in the 1984 to 1991 period. Financial statement variables were obtained from COMPUSTAT. Corporate governance and stock ownership variables were obtained from proxy statements generally filed by each company during the third or fourth month of its fiscal year. Stock return variables were obtained from Center for Research on Security Prices (CRSP).

| Dependent Variable | Definition | Mean | Std. Dev. |
|---|---|---|---|
| Net debt issued | (Debt issued − debt retired) ÷ total assets | 0.022 | 0.132 |
| Equity issued | New equity issued ÷ total assets | 0.015 | 0.055 |
| Equity repurchased | Equity repurchased ÷ total assets | 0.020 | 0.046 |
| Change in leverage | (Net debt issued − equity issued + equity repurchased) ÷ total assets | 0.027 | 0.150 |

| Explanatory Variable | Definition | Mean | Std. Dev. |
|---|---|---|---|
| Unsuccessful tender offer (indicator variable) | = 1 if tender offer made for company during year without control change | 0.013 | 0.114 |
| First year of new CEO (indicator variable) | = 1 if CEO is serving in first fiscal year of six months or more | 0.097 | 0.296 |
| First year of new CEO following involuntary departure of predecessor (indicator variable) | = 1 if new CEO indicator = 1 and prior CEO was age 62 or less and did not remain as member of board of directors | 0.015 | 0.121 |
| Addition of 5% blockholder to board of directors (indicator variable) | = 1 if number of 5% stockholders on board of directors increases | 0.029 | 0.168 |
| Market-to-book ratio (start of year) | (Equity (market value − book value) + total assets) ÷ total assets | 1.294 | 0.919 |
| Stock return | Stock return during prior fiscal year | 0.193 | 0.361 |
| Tax status (start of year) | Net operating loss carry-forward ÷ total assets | 0.015 | 0.074 |

$$Equity\ issued = \frac{new\ equity\ issued}{total\ assets} \qquad (5)$$

$$Equity\ repurchased = \frac{equity\ repurchased}{total\ assets} \qquad (6)$$

The variables in equations (4, 5, and 6) are combined into a single variable measuring the net change in leverage over the course of a fiscal year. The variable is constructed so that a positive value indicates an increase in leverage:

$Net\ leverage\ change$

$$= \frac{net\ debt\ issued - equity\ issued + equity\ repurchased}{total\ assets} \qquad (7)$$

Total assets are measured at the start of the year for all of the dependent variables. We lose about 30 percent of our observations from the levels analysis, because some of our explanatory variables for changes in leverage are based on first differences within our eight-year panel data, and also because of missing values on COMPUSTAT for one or more of the flow-of-funds variables. Our sample for analysis of leverage changes therefore has 2,196 observations from 409 companies. We also analyze three alternative specifications of our main dependent variable, equation (7). The first alternative dependent variable uses the same net issuances numerator but replaces the denominator with the market value rather than the book value of total assets. The other two alternative dependent variables are annual changes in leverage based on both book value and market value debt ratios. Results from all of these models are qualitatively similar, and we do not report them in order to conserve space.

Related prior studies of capital structure changes have relied on data from the SEC's Registered Offerings Statistics (ROS) tape. For several reasons we use COMPUSTAT flow-of-funds data instead.[5] The ROS tape does not capture important events related to changes in leverage, such as stock repurchases, retirements of debt, issuances of nonpublic debt (especially bank debt), and issuances of new equity for such events as mergers and acquisitions. It is also difficult to construct continuous variables from data on the ROS tape, since the amount of funds actually raised from the offerings listed on the tape are generally less than the amount registered with the SEC. Finally, time lags of varying length exist between the dates on which securities issues are registered with the SEC and the dates they are actually sold to the public. Although the flow-of-funds data from COMPUSTAT overcome many of these problems, they also raise some concerns. Some capital structure changes occur as the result of actions by outside claim holders, such as the exercise of stock options or warrants, or the conversion of convertible debt into equity. Because our analysis seeks to isolate capital structure changes that occur because of managerial choices, the COMPUSTAT data capture some extraneous information that we would have liked to ignore.

To investigate whether leverage changes are related to exogenous changes in the degree of managerial entrenchment, we require explanatory variables that one would expect to be associated with discrete, meaningful changes in the security of top management. We identify several corporate governance events that typically indicate a significant threat to managerial security: an outside offer to acquire the firm, the replacement of the company's CEO, and the addition to the board of directors of a major stockholder.

We expect that managers feel great pressure to raise the value of the firm in the aftermath of failed acquisition attempts, and we use the Lexis/Nexis data retrieval system to search the database of *Investment Dealer's Digest* for reports of unsuccessful tender offers made between 1984 and 1991 for our

---

[5] Opler and Titman (1996) also use COMPUSTAT flow of funds data to identify changes in leverage. Their study does not, however, use continuous dependent variables, but rather indicator variables that equal one if a firm's annual debt or equity issuance exceeds 5 percent of total assets.

sample companies. We construct an indicator variable for unsuccessful tender offers and set it equal to one if an offer that subsequently fails is made during a fiscal year (when the offer occurs in the final month of a fiscal year, the variable is set equal to one for the following year's observation instead).

A new CEO should have relatively low job security, particularly in those cases when the board has acted to remove his predecessor. We create an indicator variable for new CEOs that equals one if the predecessor CEO left during the last six months of the prior year or the first six months of the current year. We also consider a more narrow specification of the CEO turnover variable, setting the indicator variable equal to one only for cases where the prior CEO's departure was likely forced or involuntary. We place turnover episodes into this involuntary category if the exiting CEO is age 62 or less and does not remain a member of the company's board of directors. We then check news stories about each CEO's departure to ensure that we do not misclassify departures that are actually voluntary, resulting in the exclusion of two cases in which the CEO left voluntarily for a similar position at another firm. For analysis using this involuntary turnover variable, we set equal to missing all other observations where the CEO leaves his position.

The addition to the board of a major stockholder may portend pressure for management to undertake value-increasing changes or face the threat of replacement. We create an indicator variable equal to one if the number of 5 percent stockholder-directors, as reported in the midyear proxy statement, rises by at least one compared to the prior year's value. We also test specifications of the variable based on the number of 5 percent stockholders, regardless of whether they are members of the board, but obtain no significant results.

Figure 1 shows graphically how leverage changes around each of the three events that we study. The graph shows mean values of the ratio of total debt to total assets for the subsamples of firms affected by each event, in a time series beginning three years before the event year and extending until three years after (the event year occurs between years $t$ and $t + 1$ on the graph). Leverage increases substantially during the event year and appears to remain permanently higher in each of the three subgroups; the event-year changes in mean leverage are +11.9 percent for firms subject to unsuccessful tender offers, +6.1 percent for firms whose CEO leaves involuntarily, and +5.0 percent for firms in which a major stockholder joins the board. The dotted line, representing all other observations, has a gentle upward slope, representing a secular increase in leverage of about +0.5 percent per year for our sample firms between 1984 and 1991. Data for sample medians (not shown) exhibit a similar pattern with lower magnitude: the changes in median leverage are +4.6 percent for firms subject to unsuccessful tender offers, +1.2 percent for firms whose CEO leaves involuntarily, and +1.9 percent for firms in which a major stockholder joins the board, compared to a change in median leverage of +0.7 percent for all other firm-year observations in the sample. Not much overlap exists among the three events that we analyze: 86 percent of the

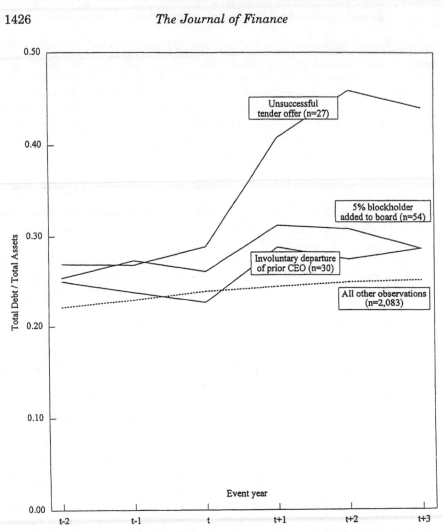

**Figure 1. Changes in leverage after shocks to managerial security.** The figure shows mean levels of the ratio of (total debt/total assets) for sample firms that experience one of three types of shocks: an unsuccessful tender offer, the addition of a 5 percent stockholder to the board of directors, or the departure of the company's prior CEO under circumstances that appeared involuntary (the CEO was age 62 or less and did not remain on the board of directors). Observations represent subsets of a sample of 2,196 observations for 409 firms in the 1984 to 1991 period. We include in this figure only those observations with data available three years before and after the event year.

unsuccessful tender offers, 73 percent of the forced CEO replacements, and 89 percent of the new stockholder-director episodes occur in the absence of either of the other two, although less formal corporate control activity may have coincided with some events in the latter two categories. The seemingly permanent change in leverage after entrenchment shocks seems to argue against the theory that managers increase debt transitorily to commit to a defensive strategy of generating cash by selling assets or restructuring operations.

Control variables for our regressions analyzing changes in leverage are similar to those used to study the level of leverage. We take first differences of our governance variables related to CEO stock ownership and board composition. We add several additional explanatory variables so that our model's specification is similar to those of two other studies: MacKie-Mason's (1990) investigation of how changes in leverage are related to differences in marginal tax rates, and Jung, Kim, and Stulz's (1996) study of how financing decisions are related to investment opportunities and agency considerations. Our additional control variables are the ratio of a firm's market value over book value at the start of the year, its leverage at the start of the year, its stock return during the preceding year, and the ratio of net operating loss carryforwards (as reported by COMPUSTAT) over total assets. We define the market-to-book ratio as the market value of equity, plus the book value of total assets, minus the book value of equity, all divided by the book value of total assets. We also include indicator variables for each year in our model in order to capture macroeconomic influences.

## B. Regression Results

Table IV presents OLS estimates for our model of net year-to-year changes in leverage. We show estimates for models separately using each of our explanatory variables that are intended to reflect sudden, significant threats to managerial security.

We find sizeable, significant increases in leverage occurring in years that firms face unsuccessful tender offers. As shown by the estimated regression coefficient in the first column of Table IV, unsuccessful tender offers are followed the next year by increases in book leverage on the order of 12.9 percent of total assets. Table V provides a more detailed look at how the components of leverage change. The table shows estimated regression coefficients for models where the dependent variables are the net change in debt, issuances of new equity, and repurchases of equity, all scaled by total assets. Estimates in the first row of Table V suggest that firms that defeat takeover attempts become heavy purchasers of their own stock, at an average level of 4.7 percent of total assets, with these buybacks apparently financed by new debt, which is issued in an average amount of 12.0 percent of total assets. The rise in debt after an unsuccessful offer is consistent with Ofek's (1994) finding that debt increases after unsuccessful management buyouts. Interestingly, some of the firms experiencing unsuccessful tender offers also appear to issue equity, as the estimated coefficient for equity issuances is positive and significant at 2.9 percent of total assets, which represents a lower magnitude than the coefficients for the other two leverage components.

The results provide evidence of increases in leverage after unsuccessful takeover attempts, but several explanations of the pattern are possible.

**Table IV**

## Regression Coefficient Estimates: Determinants of Capital Structure Changes

Ordinary least squares (OLS) regression coefficients for models of capital structure changes. The total sample consists of 2,196 observations for 409 companies in the 1984 to 1991 period. The absolute values of $t$-statistics appear in parentheses below each coefficient estimate.

| Dependent Variable: (Net Debt Issued − Equity Issued + Equity Repurchased) ÷ Total Assets | | | | | |
|---|---|---|---|---|---|
| | Estimate | Estimate | Estimate | Estimate | Estimate |
| Year following unsuccessful tender offer | 0.129*** (4.73) | | | | 0.121*** (3.91) |
| First year of new CEO | | 0.007 (0.67) | | | |
| First year of new CEO following involuntary departure of predecessor | | | 0.088*** (3.27) | | 0.071** (2.35) |
| Year following addition of 5% blockholder to board of directors | | | | 0.069*** (3.29) | 0.071*** (3.16) |
| Change in CEO stock ownership (% of common shares) | −0.066 (0.69) | −0.071 (0.76) | −0.067 (0.70) | −0.130 (1.24) | −0.117 (1.10) |
| Change in CEO exercisable option holdings (% of common shares) | 4.324*** (4.91) | 4.153*** (4.84) | 3.947*** (4.47) | 4.460*** (4.85) | 4.346*** (4.62) |
| Change in board composition (% outside directors) | 0.056 (1.10) | 0.062 (1.24) | 0.049 (0.92) | 0.053 (0.92) | 0.034 (0.55) |
| Change in board size | −0.003 (1.18) | −0.003 (1.35) | −0.003 (1.13) | −0.003 (1.07) | −0.002 (0.91) |
| Return on assets during prior year (EBDIT ÷ total assets) | 0.059 (1.33) | 0.064 (1.47) | 0.073 (1.59) | 0.083* (1.71) | 0.091* (1.78) |
| Stock return during prior year | −0.002 (0.25) | −0.003 (0.29) | −0.004 (0.40) | −0.008 (0.72) | −0.011 (0.89) |
| Leverage (book value) at start of year (total debt ÷ total assets) | −0.127*** (6.32) | −0.124*** (6.33) | −0.108*** (5.03) | −0.107*** (4.70) | −0.089*** (3.54) |
| Market-to-book ratio (start of year) | 0.013*** (2.65) | 0.012*** (2.45) | 0.012*** (2.44) | 0.015*** (2.53) | 0.017*** (2.71) |
| Tax status (net op. loss carry-fwd. ÷ total assets) | −0.075* (1.71) | −0.075* (1.76) | −0.072 (1.62) | −0.097* (1.95) | −0.090* (1.73) |
| Non-interest tax shields (investment tax credits ÷ total assets) | −0.500 (0.93) | −0.462 (0.88) | −0.441 (0.79) | −0.403 (0.71) | −0.295 (0.49) |
| Asset collateral value ((net PPE + inventory) ÷ total assets) | −0.023 (1.30) | −0.026 (1.52) | −0.023 (1.25) | −0.029 (1.46) | −0.029 (1.34) |
| Company size (log of total assets) | 0.007** (2.19) | 0.007** (2.21) | 0.007** (2.14) | 0.007** (2.14) | 0.006 (1.59) |
| Asset uniqueness (R&D expense ÷ sales) | −0.542*** (5.36) | −0.543*** (5.50) | −0.515*** (4.84) | −0.630*** (5.39) | −0.584*** (4.65) |
| Asset uniqueness (SGA expense ÷ sales) | 0.0002 (0.01) | 0.006 (0.21) | 0.011 (0.40) | 0.001 (0.03) | 0.003 (0.10) |
| Year indicator variables | Yes | Yes | Yes | Yes | Yes |
| Observations | 2,196 | 2,191 | 2,008 | 1,854 | 1,695 |
| R-squared | 0.072 | 0.064 | 0.065 | 0.067 | 0.076 |
| F-statistic | 8.05 | 7.11 | 6.55 | 6.62 | 6.24 |
| P-value | 0.00 | 0.00 | 0.00 | 0.00 | 0.00 |

Significant at 1 percent (***), 5 percent (**), and 10 percent (*) levels.

If managers carry a suboptimal amount of debt because of their dislike of risk and performance pressure, the leverage increases we observe may simply represent moves in the direction of a value-increasing debt to equity mix that managers otherwise would like to avoid. This interpretation appears consistent with Saffieddine and Titman's (1996) analysis of 573 firms that were

*Managerial Entrenchment and Capital Structure Decisions*     1429

**Table V**

**Regression Coefficient Estimates: Entrenchment Variables and Capital Structure Changes**

Ordinary least squares (OLS) regression coefficients for models of capital structure changes. The entire sample consists of 2,196 observations for 409 companies in the 1984 to 1991 period. The absolute values of $t$-statistics appear in parentheses below each coefficient estimate.

Each cell in the table represents the outcome for a separate OLS regression. The dependent variable for each regression appears at the top of each column. The explanatory variables for each regression include a measure of CEO entrenchment listed in the left column, as well as the entire set of control variables used in the models of leverage changes.

| Dependent Variable | Net Debt Issued | New Equity Issued | Equity Repurchased |
|---|---|---|---|
| Variables representing shocks to managerial security | (debt issued − debt retired) ÷ total assets | new equity issued ÷ total assets | equity repurchased ÷ total assets |
| Year following unsuccessful tender offer | 0.120*** (5.09) | 0.029** (3.25) | 0.047*** (6.03) |
| First year of new CEO | −0.001 (0.07) | −0.0004 (0.12) | 0.004 (1.37) |
| First year of new CEO following involuntary departure of predecessor | 0.082*** (3.46) | −0.0004 (0.04) | 0.015* (1.80) |
| Year following addition of 5% blockholder to board of directors | 0.100*** (5.55) | 0.009 (1.21) | −0.008 (1.25) |

Significant at 1 percent (***), 5 percent (**), and 10 percent (*) levels.

targets of unsuccessful takeovers between 1982 and 1991. Saffieddine and Titman find significant increases in leverage after the takeover attempts, as well as a positive relation between the change in leverage and subsequent operating performance and stock returns.

Alternatively, the heavy repurchases of stock after unsuccessful tender offers could represent greenmail payments or attempts by managers to increase their own voting power, consistent with Stulz (1988). One could also view higher leverage after unsuccessful tender offers as a type of "scorched earth" tactic in which managers lever the firm as a defensive measure to buy time and credibly commit to a restructuring plan. Saffieddine and Titman's results are not necessarily inconsistent with this theory, since they observe increases in firm performance when leverage is increased after failed takeover attempts and cannot observe how well their sample firms would have performed had the takeovers attempts succeeded. However, direct empirical evidence for the effectiveness of leverage as an entrenchment device is mixed. Dann and DeAngelo (1988) conclude that a broad class of defensive adjustments entrenches target management, but Denis (1990) finds that defensive payouts prevent neither high management turnover following the control contest, nor the frequent adoption by the target of restructuring programs tied directly to the control battle and the defensive payout. Moreover, even if defensive recapitalizations do increase the security of managers, they serve a beneficial purpose by forcing the disgorgement of resources to shareholders.

We examine news stories about companies in our sample to gather more information about the timing and motive for leverage changes that occur in the same year as failed tender offers. We first seek to verify that the leverage increases usually occur after and not before the takeover bids. We base this assessment on the dollar amounts revealed in news stories of public issuances and redemptions of debt and equity for the 21 of 35 targets of unsuccessful takeovers that increased leverage by more than 2 percent in the event year.[6] We find, based on an equally-weighted average across the 21 firms, that 98.6 percent of the publicly disclosed dollar value of leverage increase during the fiscal year of the unsuccessful takeover occurs after the date of the offer.

We also seek to assess whether a direct link exists between the takeover offer and the leverage increase, and, if so, to identify the purpose(s) of the leverage increase. For 17 of the 21 firms (81 percent) we find news stories expressing a direct link between the leverage increase and the takeover offer. The increase in net debt in these 17 firms is generally used to finance large special dividends, equity repurchase tender offers, or restructuring of operations. These uses of funds suggest that the leverage increase generally helps firms remain independent by committing them to undertake the improvements that the potential acquirer would make.

For five firms, however, the net debt increase is used for general corporate purposes, to pay greenmail that exceeds the amount of any repurchase tender offers, or to engage in the "Pac-Man" defense of purchasing the prospective acquirer. The uses of funds from the leverage increase in this minority of target firms are consistent with levering up being a defensive response that increases entrenchment and keeps managers in command of the same resources as before.

We do not find a systematic pattern in the use of proceeds by firms that issue significant amounts of new equity.

Returning to our regression analysis in Table IV, we find that another episode representing a threat to managerial security, the replacement of a company's CEO, also leads to greater ex post leverage. The coefficient on the CEO replacement variable in the second column of Table IV is positive at 0.7 percent of total assets, though not significant. Redefining this variable to narrow the CEO turnover episodes to those cases likely to have been forced or involuntary—when the exiting CEO is age 62 or less, does not remain on the company's board, and is not described in news stories as leaving to take a similar position at another firm—dramatically increases the magnitude and significance of the coefficient estimate. As shown by the third column of Table

---

[6] Note that eight of these 35 firms drop out of our regression analysis due to missing values for one or more explanatory variables, accounting for the sample size of 27 reported in Figure 1. Similar patterns of missing values affect the sample size for our measures of involuntary CEO turnover and the presence of large blockholders on the board of directors.

*Managerial Entrenchment and Capital Structure Decisions*     1431

IV, leverage rises by 8.8 percent of total assets in years following the forced departure of a CEO. Table V suggests that new debt issues account for the majority of this total, with some funds devoted to stock repurchases as well.

We read news stories published around the time of these CEO turnover events in an attempt to narrow further our sample of forced turnover events. Of the 34 episodes that we originally classify as involuntary turnover, 11 are accompanied by news reports whose language clearly indicates that the CEO was forced out by the board.[7] When the analysis in Table IV is repeated using only this group of observations, the coefficient on the involuntary turnover variable rises substantially, to approximately 0.30, and remains significant at better than the 1 percent level.

We also use these news stories to assess the timing of any leverage increases exceeding 2 percent of assets that occur in the fiscal year of the CEO replacement, and to assess the use of funds in these cases. An equally-weighted average across the 17 forced CEO replacements accompanied by leverage increases exceeding 2 percent reveals that 73.3 percent of the publicly disclosed dollar value of the leverage increase during the fiscal year of the replacement occurs after the date that the new CEO is appointed. Only six (35 percent) of these 17 firms have news stories that clearly indicate a direct link between the replacement and the leverage increase. In all but one of these six cases the use of the debt increase is to pay special dividends or to restructure operationally, with the remaining firm stating it was using the funds for general corporate purposes.

Our third variable indicating a threat to managerial entrenchment, an increase in the number of 5 percent stockholder-directors, is also associated with greater leverage. Estimates in the fourth column of Table IV suggest that leverage rises by 6.9 percent in the year following the addition of a blockholder to the board. Table V indicates that this effect is largely due to new issues of debt. We do not pursue an examination of news stories related to the arrival of new blockholder-directors, because we are generally unable to date precisely when these events occur.

Our three events indicating threats to managerial security— unsuccessful tender offers, involuntary CEO replacements, and the arrival of major stockholder-directors— coincide for some observations, as discussed previously. To increase our confidence that each of these events, by itself, carries sufficient importance to cause CEOs to increase leverage, we estimate a final regression model and include all three indicator variables. As shown in the right column of Table IV, the coefficient on each variable remains strongly positive and significant. Two of the three coefficients decline slightly in magnitude compared to the models in which they appear alone, a pattern that should be expected due to the existence of some overlap events in our sample.

---

[7] This language includes such information as the former CEO suing the firm and/or board members over his dismissal, the former CEO having no part in the decision to replace him, the replacement being the result of a board power struggle or a takeover, and the direct phrasing that the board "forced out" the former CEO.

A further result, consistent across every specification in Table IV, is that leverage increases when CEOs' holdings of exercisable stock options increase. This finding implies that when CEOs are subject to greater performance incentives tied to the value of the firm, they are more likely to take on higher debt levels. The effect appears to have economic as well as statistical significance: for a one standard deviation change in the independent variable, the estimated change in leverage is plus or minus 1.9 percent of debt over total assets. Interestingly, this result remains positive but has less magnitude and no statistical significance if the variable is specified as the number of new options awarded divided by shares outstanding, rather than the change in options held. This suggests that measuring CEO incentives simply by counting the number of new options awarded ignores the diminution in incentives that occurs due to the exercise or expiration of previously held options.

Finally, one result among our control variables in Table IV is somewhat puzzling: we find that firms become more levered when their market-to-book ratios are high, although many prior studies have found that firms are especially likely to issue equity under these conditions. Further analysis of the data shows that high market-to-book firms are more likely to issue both new equity *and* new debt. These results suggest that firms with high market values have many investment opportunities that motivate them to raise funds from all types of sources. We further find that firms with a high market-to-book ratio are also more likely to repurchase their own stock, and this effect accounts for the overall change in leverage being positively associated with a high market-to-book ratio.

Prior studies such as Opler and Titman (1996) have found that firms with high market-to-book ratios are more likely to choose equity over debt, given that they decide to raise external funds. Our results are not necessarily inconsistent, since our models use continuous instead of binary dependent variables, our analysis includes stock repurchases as part of the leverage change, and our sample does not exclude those firms that issue both securities as well as the large majority of firm-year observations in which a company does not issue substantial amounts of either security. To check our results for sample selection bias, we replicate the analysis of Opler and Titman (1996) using our data, and we obtain estimates with similar magnitude and significance for most variables, especially the market-to-book ratio. We also check whether our market-to-book coefficient is driven by multicollinearity, reestimating our model after dropping the variables measuring the collateral value of assets, R&D over sales, and SGA over sales (we drop each variable separately and then drop all three from the model). No coefficients exhibit a meaningful change in magnitude or significance in any of these reestimations, and the estimates also prove robust to dropping the market-to-book variable itself.

## C. Leverage Changes in Low- and High-Leverage Firms

Our main results in Table IV indicate that managers increase leverage in response to shocks that reduce their entrenchment. However, we note in our discussion above that more leverage may not always represent a value-increas-

## Managerial Entrenchment and Capital Structure Decisions          1433

ing strategy, and it is possible that CEOs overlever their firms beyond the value-maximizing level as a defensive measure when their security is threatened.

We explore this issue further by analyzing how leverage changes as a function of a firm's apparent leverage deficit or surplus at the start of the year. We use our model of leverage levels, introduced earlier in this article, to estimate predicted values of leverage for all our observations. The specification of the model used for this purpose is identical to that in the first column of Table II, except that we exclude the corporate governance variables appearing in the first seven rows of the table. Next, we regress firms' annual changes in leverage, using our COMPUSTAT flow-of-funds variables, against the control variables used in Table IV and the leverage surplus at the start of the year, with the surplus defined as the difference between actual and predicted leverage. Table VI shows the results, with the top half of the table displaying estimates for all firms, and the lower half showing estimates over the subsample of firms with less leverage than predicted. The coefficient of $-0.166$ in the first cell of the table indicates that absent unusual shocks to managerial security, firms generally adjust leverage toward its expected level, closing approximately one-sixth of the surplus or deficit in a given year. The coefficient estimate for underlevered firms on the bottom of the table is a very similar $-0.139$.

To study the effect of entrenchment shocks, we add to the model interaction terms between the leverage deficit and the indicator variables we use for shocks to managerial security. The next four columns of Table VI show negative estimates on each of the interaction terms, implying that entrenchment shocks increase the speed at which firms move toward the expected level of leverage (Figure 1 illustrates that firms whose CEOs become subject to entrenchment shocks do not have abnormally low leverage compared to the rest of the sample before shocks occur). Moreover, estimates in the lower half of the table indicate that the effect is pronounced for underlevered firms, with most of the entrenchment shocks causing firms to add leverage that takes them beyond their expected levels. For example, underlevered firms experiencing an unsuccessful tender offer tend to close approximately 150 percent of the gap between actual and expected leverage, according to the sum of the estimates for the intercept and interaction terms. Underlevered firms close about 227 percent of this gap in the year after the involuntary departure of a CEO, and about 192 percent of the gap after a major stockholder joins the board. In contrast, estimates for these interaction terms for firms with more leverage than predicted (not shown) are generally positive rather than negative and are not statistically significant, suggesting that leverage also increases or stays unchanged for overlevered firms. The very large effects observed for underlevered firms appear to cause the negative estimates for the overall sample.

We check our results by reestimating our regression models of leverage changes, introduced in Table IV, over subsamples of firms that appear to be underlevered. The top half of Table VII shows models estimated over the subsample of firms with less leverage than predicted by a regression model, as described above. As expected, when compared to the Table IV results for the full sample, the tendency of CEOs to add leverage in response to diminished

### Table VI

## OLS Regression Estimates: Changes in Leverage as a Function of Prior Leverage and Shocks to CEO Entrenchment

Ordinary least squares (OLS) regression coefficients for models of changes in leverage. The change in leverage during the year is regressed against the leverage surplus at the start of the year. The leverage surplus is assumed to equal the residual from an OLS model of leverage levels. In addition, each model includes an interaction term between the leverage surplus and one of the variables used as a proxy for shocks to CEO entrenchment. The top half of the table shows estimates for the entire sample, while the lower half shows estimates for the subset of observations with actual leverage below predicted leverage. All models include the full range of control variables used in other models of leverage changes. The absolute values of $t$-statistics appear in parentheses below each coefficient.

| Dependent Variable: (Net Debt Issued − Net Equity Issued) ÷ Total Assets | | | | | |
|---|---|---|---|---|---|
| **Panel A: All Observations** | | | | | |
| Leverage surplus | −0.166*** | −0.163*** | −0.130*** | −0.132*** | −0.124*** |
| | (7.81) | (7.66) | (5.81) | (5.82) | (5.15) |
| Leverage surplus $x$ indicator for unsuccessful tender offer events | | −0.213 (1.05) | | | |
| Leverage surplus $x$ indicator for first year of new CEO | | | −0.219*** (3.96) | | |
| Leverage surplus $x$ indicator for new CEO (involuntary replacement) | | | | −0.816*** (5.99) | |
| Leverage surplus $x$ indicator for addition of 5% blockholder to board | | | | | −0.886*** (6.58) |
| Number of observations | 2,196 | 2,196 | 2,191 | 2,008 | 1,854 |
| **Panel B: Firms with (Total Debt ÷ Total Assets) Below Predicted Level** | | | | | |
| Leverage surplus | −0.139** | −0.123** | −0.085 | −0.071 | −0.081* |
| | (2.42) | (2.15) | (1.54) | (1.28) | (1.28) |
| Leverage surplus $x$ indicator for unsuccessful tender for offer events | | −1.372*** (4.14) | | | |
| Leverage surplus $x$ indicator for CEO replacement | | | −0.588*** (5.64) | | |
| Leverage surplus $x$ indicator for new CEO (involuntary replacement) | | | | −2.195*** (11.20) | |
| Leverage surplus $x$ indicator for addition of 5% blockholder to board | | | | | −1.842*** (9.83) |
| Number of observations | 1,225 | 1,225 | 1,223 | 1,120 | 1,024 |

Significant at 1 percent (***), 5 percent (**), and 10 percent (*) levels.

entrenchment has uniformly stronger magnitude for all of our main explanatory variables. The magnitude of the key coefficient estimates is roughly 50 percent to 100 percent higher over the sample of low-leverage firms as compared to the coefficient estimates for all firms. In the lower half of Table VII, we show estimates based on partitioning the sample according to whether the book value of debt over total assets is below 0.35, chosen arbitrarily to represent a moderate threshold of leverage. For this subsample, which includes about four-fifths of our observations, we again find uniformly stronger in-

**Table VII**

## Determinants of Capital Structure Changes in Low-Leverage Firms

Ordinary least squares (OLS) regression coefficients for models of capital structure changes, with the analysis confined to firm-year observations with low levels of leverage. Coefficients are shown for variables used to indicate changes in managerial entrenchment, although the regressions are estimated using all control variables from other models of leverage changes. The absolute values of *t*-statistics appear below each estimate in parentheses.

Estimates in the top half of the table are produced by analyzing observations with book value leverage below a predicted value, based upon fitted values from a regression model of leverage levels. Estimates in the lower half of the table are produced by analyzing observations with book value leverage below a cutoff value of 0.35. The entire sample includes 2,196 observations for 409 firms in the 1984 to 1991 period.

| Dependent Variable: (Net Debt Issued − Net Equity Issued) ÷ Total Assets | | | |
|---|---|---|---|
| **Panel A: Firms with (Total Debt ÷ Total Assets) Below Predicted Level** | | | |
| Year following unsuccessful tender offer | 0.210*** (5.61) | | |
| First year of new CEO | | 0.021 (1.63) | |
| First year of new CEO following involuntary departure of predecessor | | 0.154*** (4.48) | |
| Year following addition of 5% blockholder to board of directors | | | 0.127*** (4.36) |
| Number of observations | 1,225 | 1,223 | 1,120 | 1,024 |
| **Panel B: Firms with (Total Debt ÷ Total Assets) Below 0.35** | | | |
| Year following unsuccessful tender offer | 0.184*** (5.73) | | |
| First year of new CEO | | 0.019* (1.65) | |
| First year of new CEO following involuntary departure of predecessor | | 0.120*** (4.23) | |
| Year following addition of 5% blockholder to board of directors | | | 0.081*** (3.14) |
| Number of observations | 1,734 | 1,730 | 1,592 | 1,477 |

Significant at 1 percent (***), 5 percent (**), and 10 percent (*) levels.

creases in leverage in response to events that threaten managerial entrenchment, compared to the leverage increases observed for the entire sample.[8]

We conclude that when firms have pursued a low-debt capital structure in the past, an outside event that threatens managerial security is an especially strong predictor of increased leverage. This leverage generally takes firms beyond the expected debt to equity ratio for our sample, although we cannot observe directly whether these firms move to a level of leverage in excess of the value-maximizing point. We do not observe a converse effect for firms that

---

[8] However, leverage changes are not significant for those firms that have a debt ratio below 0.35 but an estimated leverage surplus as defined just above, consistent with our findings for all firms that have leverage surpluses.

have pursued a high-debt capital structure, as these companies exhibit no significant change in leverage—and, in particular, do not reduce leverage in the direction of the expected level—in the aftermath of shocks to managerial entrenchment. This asymmetric pattern of leverage changes indirectly suggests that most firms have less leverage than optimal in their capital structures. However, it is also possible that a firm's optimal leverage level increases at least temporarily during a period of restructuring or managerial turnover.

## IV. Conclusions

Theories based on Jensen's (1986) argument that leverage reduces managerial discretion imply that managers will not issue the optimal amount of debt without pressure from a disciplining force. Our results support predictions of this type. We find evidence that firm leverage is affected by the degree of managerial entrenchment, and most of our results indicate that entrenched managers seek to avoid debt.

We examine cross-sectional relations between leverage levels and corporate governance variables. We find that leverage is lower when the CEO has a long tenure in office, has weak stock and compensation incentives, and does not face strong monitoring from the board of directors or major stockholders. These results are consistent with CEOs who are entrenched pursuing less levered capital structures but are also open to other interpretations; for example, the positive association we observe between leverage and fractional CEO stock ownership is consistent with Stulz's (1988) theory that managers use leverage to inflate the voting power of their equity.

Since our cross-sectional results do not clarify whether the associations between leverage and corporate governance variables are causal ones, we conduct further analysis into whether leverage changes significantly in the aftermath of events that represent entrenchment-reducing shocks to companies' governance structures. We find that book value leverage increases by an average of about 13 percent of assets when firms are targets of unsuccessful tender offers. The targets that increase leverage generally use the funds from new debt to finance large special dividends, equity repurchase offers, or operational restructuring. These uses of proceeds are consistent with theories that entrenched managers use leverage as a defensive commitment device, to buy time for the implementation of their own restructuring program instead of the outside raider's. However, the apparent persistence of higher leverage for two years after unsuccessful takeovers, as shown in Figure 1, seems to argue against this interpretation. Instead, the higher leverage observed after takeovers may simply represent efforts by managers to move toward a more optimal mix of debt and equity, which they would have preferred to have avoided if they had been able to remain highly entrenched.

The replacement of a company's CEO leads to significantly greater leverage when the turnover appears "forced" because the exiting CEO is under age 62 and does not remain on the board of directors; leverage rises by about 9 percent of total assets in these cases. These events are consistent with decreases in

*Managerial Entrenchment and Capital Structure Decisions*    1437

managerial entrenchment leading to increases in leverage, and our examination of news stories following the turnover generally supports this interpretation. Similarly, we find that leverage rises by about 7 percent of total assets in the year after a major stockholder joins the board of directors.

To refine our understanding of entrenchment and leverage, we examine how leverage changes as a function of a firm's apparent leverage deficit or surplus at the start of the year. We find that firms with leverage deficits react to threats to entrenchment by levering themselves beyond the predicted level, whereas firms with leverage surpluses respond to these shocks by either not changing or increasing their leverage. In addition, we find that the leverage increases that follow entrenchment-reducing events are much larger for underlevered firms than for all firms. These results are consistent with the average level of leverage for firms in our sample lying below the optimal level, although we cannot observe the value-maximizing leverage point in order to test this conjecture directly.

## REFERENCES

Amihud, Yakov, and Baruch Lev, 1981, Risk reduction as a managerial motive for conglomerate mergers, *Bell Journal of Economics* 12, 605–617.
Dann, Larry Y., and Harry DeAngelo, 1988, Corporate financial policy and corporate control: A study of defensive adjustments in asset and ownership structure, *Journal of Financial Economics* 20, 87–128.
DeFusco, Richard A., Robert R. Johnson, and Thomas S. Zorn, 1990, The effect of executive stock option plans on stockholders and bondholders, *Journal of Finance* 45, 617–627.
Denis, David J., 1990, Defensive changes in corporate payout policy: Share repurchases and special dividends, *Journal of Finance* 45, 1433–1456.
Fama, Eugene F., 1980, Agency problems and the theory of the firm, *Journal of Political Economy* 88, 288–307.
Friend, Irwin, and Larry H. P. Lang, 1988, An empirical test of the impact of managerial self-interest on corporate capital structure, *Journal of Finance* 47, 271–281.
Grossman, Sanford J., and Oliver D. Hart, 1982, Corporate financial structure and managerial incentives, in J. McCall, Ed.: *The Economics of Information and Uncertainty* (University of Chicago Press, Chicago, Ill.).
Harris, Milton, and Artur Raviv, 1988, Corporate control contests and capital structure, *Journal of Financial Economics* 20, 55–86.
Harris, Milton, and Artur Raviv, 1990, Capital structure and the informational role of debt, *Journal of Finance* 45, 321–349.
Harris, Milton, and Artur Raviv, 1991, The theory of capital structure, *Journal of Finance* 46, 297–355.
Hart, Oliver D., 1993, Theories of optimal capital structure: A managerial discretion perspective, in Margaret M. Blair, Ed.: *The Deal Decade: What Takeovers and Leveraged Buyouts Mean for Corporate Governance* (Brookings Institution, Washington, D.C.).
Hart, Oliver D., and John Moore, 1990, A theory of corporate financial structure based on the seniority of claims, Working paper No. 560, Massachusetts Institute of Technology.
Haugen, R., and Lemma Senbet, 1981, Resolving the agency problems of external capital through options, *Journal of Finance* 36, 629–648.
Jensen, Michael C., 1986, Agency costs of free cash flow, corporate finance, and takeovers, *American Economic Review* 76, 323–339.
Jensen, Michael C., 1993, The modern industrial revolution, exit, and the failure of internal control systems, *Journal of Finance* 48, 831–880.

Jensen, Michael C., and William H. Meckling, 1976, Theory of the firm: Managerial behavior, agency costs, and capital structure, *Journal of Financial Economics* 3, 305–360.

Jensen, Michael C., and Kevin J. Murphy, 1990, Performance pay and top-management incentives, *Journal of Political Economy* 98, 225–264.

Jung, Kooyul, Yong-Cheol Kim, and René Stulz, 1996, Timing, investment opportunities, managerial discretion, and the security issue decision, *Journal of Financial Economics* 42, 159–186.

Lipton, Martin, and Jay W. Lorsch, 1992, A modest proposal for improved corporate governance, *Business Lawyer* 48, 59–77.

MacKie-Mason, Jeffrey K., 1990, Do taxes affect corporate financing decisions? *Journal of Finance* 45, 1471–1493.

Mehran, Hamid, 1992, Executive incentive plans, corporate control, and capital structure, *Journal of Financial and Quantitative Analysis* 27, 539–560.

Mørck, Randall, Andrei Shleifer, and Robert Vishny, 1988, Management ownership and market valuation: An empirical analysis, *Journal of Financial Economics* 20, 293–315.

Novaes, Walter, and Luigi Zingales, 1995, Capital structure choice when managers are in control: Entrenchment versus efficiency, Working paper, Graduate School of Business, University of Chicago.

Ofek, Eli, 1994, Efficiency gains in unsuccessful management buyouts, *Journal of Finance* 49, 637–654.

Opler, Tim, and Sheridan Titman, 1996, The debt-equity choice: An analysis of issuing firms, Working paper, Ohio State University.

Saffieddine, Assem, and Sheridan Titman, 1996, Debt and corporate performance: Evidence from unsuccessful takeovers, Working paper, Broad Graduate School of Management, Michigan State University.

Smith, Clifford W., and Ross L. Watts, 1982, Incentive and tax effects of U.S. executive compensation plans, *Australian Management Journal* 7, 139–157.

Smith, Clifford W., and Ross L. Watts, 1992, The investment opportunity set and corporate financing, dividend, and compensation policies, *Journal of Financial Economics* 32, 263–292.

Stulz, René, 1988, Managerial control of voting rights: Financing policies and the market for corporate control, *Journal of Financial Economics* 20, 25–54.

Stulz, René, 1990, Managerial discretion and optimal financing policies, *Journal of Financial Economics* 26, 3–27.

Titman, Sheridan, and Roberto Wessels, 1988, The determinants of capital structure choice, *Journal of Finance* 43, 1–19.

Weisbach, Michael, 1988, Outside directors and CEO turnover, *Journal of Financial Economics* 20, 431–460.

Williamson, Oliver, 1988, Corporate finance and corporate governance, *Journal of Finance* 43, 567–591.

Yermack, David, 1995, Do Corporations award CEO stock options effectively? *Journal of Financial Economics* 39, 237–270.

Yermack, David, 1996, Higher market valuation of companies with a small board of directors, *Journal of Financial Economics* 40, 185–211.

Zwiebel, Jeffrey, 1994, Dynamic capital structure under managerial entrenchment, Working paper, Graduate School of Business, Stanford University.

# D
# Debt as Precommitment

THE JOURNAL OF FINANCE • VOL. LIV, NO. 2 • APRIL 1999

# Leverage and Corporate Performance: Evidence from Unsuccessful Takeovers

ASSEM SAFIEDDINE and SHERIDAN TITMAN*

## ABSTRACT

This paper finds that, on average, targets that terminate takeover offers significantly increase their leverage ratios. Targets that increase their leverage ratios the most reduce capital expenditures, sell assets, reduce employment, increase focus, and realize cash flows and share prices that outperform their benchmarks in the five years following the failed takeover. Our evidence suggests that leverage-increasing targets act in the interests of shareholders when they terminate takeover offers and that higher leverage helps firms remain independent not because it entrenches managers, but because it commits managers to making the improvements that would be made by potential raiders.

THE MARKET FOR CORPORATE CONTROL was quite active and controversial in the 1980s. Although there were many successful takeovers, there were also many takeover attempts that failed. Consequently, an analysis of the behavior of firms that successfully resist takeover attempts is needed to fully understand the economic effects of corporate control activity. In this paper, we investigate this issue by examining a sample of 573 unsuccessful takeover attempts during the 1982 to 1991 period.

In many of the failed takeovers, the target's management expressed the opinion that the acquirer's offer was insufficient and that the firm would be worth more if it remained independent. For example, 47 targets in our sample explicitly announced that they were rejecting offers because "the price is too low or inadequate." In response to these 47 announcements, target stock prices declined 3.42 percent on average. Whatever the stated reason, it is clear that investors are generally skeptical when target managers terminate a takeover attempt. In our entire sample, target stock prices decline 5.14 percent, on average, around the date of the termination announcement.

* Safieddine is at the Eli Broad Graduate School of Management, Michigan State University, and Titman is from the University of Texas at Austin. We thank participants of seminars at Boston College, Michigan State University, Iowa State University, University of Colorado at Denver, University of Texas at Dallas, Rutgers University, the New York Fed, and the NBER, along with Scott Gibson, Charles Hadlock, Cliff Holderness, Ed Kane, Robyn McLaughlin, Tim Mech, Tim Opler, Anil Shivdasani, René Stulz, Nick Travlos, Gopala Vasudevan, Karen Wruck, Yanfang Yan, and an anonymous referee for helpful suggestions on earlier drafts. We are particularly indebted to Edith Hotchkiss and William Wilhelm for insightful comments and suggestions. Earlier drafts of the paper were circulated under the title "Debt and Corporate Performance: Evidence from Unsuccessful Takeovers."

It is often said that "talk is cheap" and that "actions speak louder than words." However, in many cases, target managers combine their cheap talk with meaningful actions. In particular, many of the targets of failed takeovers substantially increased their leverage ratios, which can be viewed as either a signal (e.g., Ross (1977)) or a commitment (e.g., Grossman and Hart (1982) or Jensen (1986)) that the promised improvements would in fact take place. In our sample of 328 targets of failed takeovers with adequate data, 207 increased their leverage ratios. The median level of total debt scaled by the book value of assets of these firms increased from 59.8 percent one year before the unsuccessful takeover attempt to 71.5 percent one year afterward.[1]

These leverage increases appear to be part of the targets' defensive strategies. Targets of hostile takeover attempts increase leverage ratios three times as much as their friendly counterparts. This indicates that leverage increases may reduce the probability that a firm will be taken over in the future. Indeed, we find that only 38 percent of the target firms that increased their leverage ratio more than the median between years $-1$ and $+1$ are taken over in the five years following the initial failed takeover attempt. In contrast, 57 percent of the target firms that increased their leverage ratios less than the median are taken over within five years.

The existing literature suggests two possible explanations for this observed relation between leverage changes and subsequent takeover activity. First, as mentioned above, an increase in leverage can increase the credibility of a target manager's promises, which in turn increases the target's stock price, thereby increasing the cost of the takeover.[2] Second, leverage can increase the cost of the target without improving its value by improving the target's bargaining power.[3] In contrast to the first explanation, the second explanation does not imply that increased debt, following failed takeovers, should lead to increased performance.

Our empirical evidence supports the view that higher leverage ratios deter takeovers because they are associated with performance improvements. In particular, we find that the operating performance of former targets following failed takeover attempts is positively related to the change in the target's leverage ratio. This finding continues to hold after controlling for

---

[1] Berger, Ofek, and Yermack (1996) report similar evidence for a much smaller sample of Fortune 500 firms. Denis (1990), using a sample of 37 firms that announced a defensive plan of either a large dividend or a stock repurchase, reports that long-term debt of firms that remain independent after a takeover contest increases from 21.0 percent in the precontest period to 42.6 percent in the postcontest period.

[2] Zweibel (1996) presents a model along these lines which is based on the overinvestment models of Jensen (1986) and Stulz (1990). See also Stein (1988) who discusses how the possibility of a takeover increases a firm's incentive to signal its value.

[3] Harris and Raviv (1988) and Stulz (1988) find that leverage increase makes the target firm more costly to take over because it increases the percentage ownership of the target's management. In Israel (1991), increased debt deters takeovers that result in wealth transfers to the target's existing debtholders. These explanations are not necessarily mutually exclusive. Firms might, for example, repurchase shares to increase the cost of a takeover and, in doing so, inadvertently commit to a higher output level and lower investment level because of the increased leverage.

management turnover (documented by Denis and Serrano (1996)), and several other characteristics of unsuccessful takeovers that may explain performance. We also document that failed targets that increase leverage the most decrease investment, sell off assets, reduce employment, and increase the focus of their firms, which supports the views expressed by Jensen (1986).

An analysis of the targets' stock prices reveals that investors partially anticipate the positive effects of higher leverage on the firms' future performance when the takeover attempts are terminated. For example, the cumulative prediction errors (CPEs) between five days before the announcement date of a takeover attempt to five days after the termination date are higher for those targets that increase leverage the most. Furthermore, the termination period returns are less negative for those targets that increase leverage the most.

The fact that target returns were negative around the termination date suggests that target managers were not acting in the interests of their shareholders. However, our analysis of the long-term performance of targets that terminate takeover offers suggests that the market underestimated the effect of higher leverage on future performance, which in turn implies that target managers who increased leverage may have beeen acting in the interest of shareholders when they terminated these takeovers. In particular, target firms that increased leverage more than the median have higher stock returns in the years following the termination date than a matched sample of firms of similar size, book-to-market, and momentum. In contrast, targets that increased their leverage less than the median significantly underperformed their matching benchmarks during this time period, suggesting that, on average, the shareholders of these firms would have been better off if the takeover had not been terminated.

This paper is organized as follows: Section I describes the sample and examines the use of leverage as a defense against unwanted takeovers. Section II examines the investment decisions of firms that increased their debt ratios. Section III reports the frequency of asset sales, changes in employment, and the focusing of operations. Section IV examines the relation between leverage and operating performance following failed takeover attempts. Section V analyzes stock returns around the termination announcements. Section VI investigates the relationship between the long-run stock price performance and leverage. Section VII summarizes and concludes the paper.

## I. Sample Description

### A. Sample Selection

The sample of unsuccessful takeovers is obtained from *W.T. Grimm Mergerstat Review*, which provides a listing of 721 terminated takeover attempts during the 1982 to 1991 period. Of these firms, 573 have data available on COMPUSTAT data files.[4] The W.T. Grimm data set makes no restriction on

---

[4] The 573 target firms have valid data on book value of assets in the year prior to the failed takeover attempt in both research and primary COMPUSTAT data files. Of these, 532 targets have valid debt data in the year prior to the failed takeover attempt year.

**Table I**

## Characteristics of Sample Firms

The number and percentage of transactions terminated by bidders and others is reported for a sample of 573 unsuccessful takeovers for the period 1982 to 1991 obtained from *Mergerstat Review*, published annually by *W.T. Grimm*. Panel B includes the frequency of targets receiving subsequent offer(s) within one year through five years. Panel C reports the number of targets delisted from CRSP by year for each of the major criteria for delisting. The number of months denotes time from the termination of the takeover attempt.

| Panel A: Distribution by Identity of Terminator | | |
|---|---|---|
| | No. of Firms | Percentage |
| Higher bid | 75 | 13% |
| Mutually rejected | 63 | 11% |
| No reason given | 86 | 15% |
| Rejected by target | 183 | 32% |
| Terminated by bidder | 154 | 27% |
| Miscellaneous | 12 | 2% |
| Total | 573 | 100% |

Panel B: Distribution of Targets Receiving Subsequent Offer(s)
and Number of Successful Offers

| Time of Subsequent Offer(s) | No. of Firms | Percentage | No. of Successful Offers | Percentage |
|---|---|---|---|---|
| One year | 187 | 33% | 156 | 27% |
| Two years | 241 | 42% | 208 | 36% |
| Three years | 265 | 46% | 232 | 40% |
| Four years | 297 | 52% | 261 | 45% |
| Five years | 316 | 55% | 278 | 48% |

Panel C: Distribution of Targets Delisted from CRSP within $j$ Months

| | CRSP Criteria for Delisting | | | | |
|---|---|---|---|---|---|
| Number of Months | Takeover | Liquidation | Bankruptcy | Insufficient Capital | Other Delisting |
| 1–12 | 156 | 3 | 1 | 4 | 24 |
| 13–24 | 208 | 7 | 5 | 8 | 32 |
| 25–36 | 232 | 9 | 5 | 14 | 38 |
| 37–48 | 261 | 9 | 6 | 16 | 40 |
| 49–60 | 278 | 10 | 8 | 17 | 47 |

the fraction of shares sought by bidders. The data set includes the announcement of the transaction, the termination date, the offered price, the premium offered, the means of payment, the names of the target and the bidder, and the reason for the cancellation when available.

The sample of 573 firms consists of 274 (48 percent) Nasdaq-listed targets and 299 (52 percent) targets listed on NYSE/AMEX. Panel A of Table I reports the distribution by terminator of the transaction. The table reveals that 27 percent of the transactions were terminated by bidders and the remaining 73 percent failed for other reasons. "Other reasons" includes 32 percent of takeover attempts rejected by targets, 11 percent mutually rejected, 15 percent with no reason given in either *Mergerstat Review* or *The Wall Street Journal Index*, 13 percent due to a higher bid, and 2 percent for miscellaneous reasons. In 1988, W.T. Grimm did not report the reason for termination. For these cases, the *Wall Street Journal Index* is used instead. Panel B of Table I shows the number of target firms that received subsequent offer(s) after the termination of the original takeover attempt. Within the first year, 187 firms received a second offer (156 of which were successful). By the end of the fifth year more than half the sample received another offer and 278 (48 percent) of the sample firms were successfully taken over. Panel C reports the frequency of delisting of sample firms using CRSP criteria for delisting. These criteria include takeovers, liquidations, bankruptcy filings, insufficient capital, and other infrequent criteria, which are grouped into the Other Delisting category. The total number of Other Delisting is 47. The reasons for Other Delisting are as follows: no reason available (10), insufficient number of market makers (10), insufficient number of shareholders (2), the price fell below an acceptable level (3), upon company's request with no specific reason given (7), firms went private (4), delinquent in filing (5), and firms did not meet the exchange's financial guidelines for continued listing (6).[5]

## B. Summary Statistics

Table II reports summary statistics for sample firms. The median leverage ratio, measured as the book value of total debt scaled by the book value of assets, increases from 0.598 in year $-1$ to 0.715 in year $+1$, after staying virtually constant for the five years prior to year $-1$. Target leverage ratios are about the same as the leverage ratios of other firms in their industries in the five years before the takeover attempt. The increase in their leverage ratios in year $+1$ thus puts the target firms at leverage ratios substantially above their industry counterparts and they stay above their industry counterparts for at least five years after the termination of the takeover attempt.[6,7]

---

[5] According to CRSP, there are only eight cases in which targets filed for bankruptcy. Using Hotchkiss's (1995) sample, we find 21 cases.

[6] It may be difficult to interpret the changes in debt and cash flows (later) in event time because the sample is changing (532 in year $-1$, 396 in year 0, and 328 in year $+1$). For example, leverage ratios increase from year 0 to year $+1$. Two possibilities arise: (1) firms increase their leverage by an additional amount, or (2) firms that drop out between years 0 and $+1$ are those that have lower leverage ratios. Our findings support the second conjecture. Of the 68 firms that drop out between years 0 and $+1$ we find that 60 have a leverage ratio that is lower than the median leverage ratio in year 0. Given that the composition of our sample is changing from year to year, we compute the change in leverage after restricting our sample to the surviving targets as of year 5. We find that the median changes in leverage from year $-1$ to years $+1$, $+2$, $+3$ are 15.1 percent, 20.6 percent, and 16.7 percent, respectively. This com-

The observed increase in leverage ratios is due to a combination of factors. Some firms issued special dividends, a larger number repurchased shares, and a number of firms issued new debt. Table III shows that targets that increase their leverage above the median change generally return capital to their shareholders, reducing the book value of their equity by 37.54 percent on average. In Panel C, we report mean values for special dividends and share repurchases for the same group of targets. Over years 0 and +1, targets that increase leverage the most pay out about 5 percent of the market value of equity to their shareholders in the form of special dividends and they repurchase more than 11 percent of their shares. On the other hand, targets that increase their leverage the least show an economically insignificant change in special dividend and repurchases activities over the same period.

For each firm, annual industry-adjusted performance measures are calculated by subtracting from the target firm's change in performance the change in performance over the same period for the target firm's industry (which is defined by the company's two-digit SIC code). Industry data are collected from the COMPUSTAT Industrial, Tertiary, and Research data files.

Targets in the year prior to the failed takeover attempt have a median (mean) industry-adjusted cash flow to book value of $-0.0015$ ($-0.0096$). Industry-adjusted cash flow to sales has a median (mean) of $-0.0034$ ($-0.0018$). Both industry-adjusted cash flow to book value of assets and cash flow to sales, though negative, are not significantly different from zero. The median (mean) market-to-book ratio is 1.21 (1.61) in the year prior to the takeover attempt. Target firms have poor stock price performance in the year prior to the takeover attempt, starting 300 trading days and ending 21 trading days (one month) before the announcement of the takeover attempt. Over this period, the median (mean) of the target firms' holding period returns minus the holding period returns of the value-weighted index is a significant $-4.76$ percent ($-4.08$ percent). This evidence is consistent with prior studies that show that target firms are poor performers prior to the takeover attempt.

## C. Management Turnover Following Failed Takeovers

Because we are interested in understanding how operating changes following unsuccessful takeover attempts relate to leverage changes, it is important to first examine whether leverage affects the probability of a

---

pares to a median change of 3.2 percent, 3.09 percent, and 4.48 percent, respectively, if we impose no restriction on sample firms.

[7] To get further information about the timing of the leverage increase, we use the *Securities Data Corporation (SDC) Corporate Securities Offerings* database, which includes a listing of publicly and privately placed debt offerings. However, we were able to identify only 74 debt offerings out of 207 leverage increases by target firms. Of the 74 offerings, 14 occurred within six months before the initial announcement of the takeover attempt and 20 occurred between the announcement and the termination date. (The average time from announcement date to termination date is 76 days.) An additional 32 offerings occurred within the first six months after the termination of the takeover attempt. The remaining 8 were offered in the second six months after the termination date.

*Leverage and Corporate Performance after Takeover Attempts*    553

### Table II
## Summary Statistics for Sample Firms

Summary statistics are presented for targets of unsuccessful takeover attempts and transaction characteristics. The sample of unsuccessful takeovers during the 1982 to 1991 period is obtained from *Mergerstat Review*, published annually by *W.T. Grimm*. Reported are median, mean, standard deviation, and the number of observations of total debt scaled by the book value of assets, industry-adjusted cash flow to book value, industry-adjusted cash flow to sales, market-to-book, and holding period returns of targets minus the holding period returns of the CRSP value-weighted index over the year prior to the announcement of the takeover attempt. The year of the variable is indicated by a subscript: $-1$ is the year before the termination, 0 is the termination year, and $+1$ is the year following the termination. Panel B reports top management turnover following unsuccessful takeover attempts. The top manager is defined as the CEO if there is one and the president otherwise. Management changes are identified through comparisons in *Standard and Poor's Register of Corporations, Directors, and Executives*. Firms are classified based on whether the change ($\Delta$) in leverage is higher or lower than the median change, and on whether the takeover attempt is hostile or friendly. The percentage of management changes is presented and a difference in means test is also reported.

| Panel A: Summary Statistics | | | | |
|---|---|---|---|---|
| Variable | Median | Mean | Std. Dev. | N |
| Total debt to book value of assets$_{-1}$ | 0.598 | 0.600 | 0.248 | 532 |
| Total debt to book value of assets$_0$ | 0.643 | 0.678 | 0.383 | 396 |
| Total debt to book value of assets$_{+1}$ | 0.715 | 0.756 | 0.473 | 328 |
| Total debt to market value of equity$_{-1}$ | 0.287 | 0.394 | 0.289 | 530 |
| Total debt to market value of equity$_0$ | 0.305 | 0.442 | 0.446 | 394 |
| Total debt to market value of equity$_{+1}$ | 0.352 | 0.503 | 0.515 | 327 |
| Cash flow to book value$_{-1}$ | 0.119 | 0.109 | 0.130 | 557 |
| Cash flow to sales$_{-1}$ | 0.123 | 0.126 | 0.141 | 555 |
| Industry-adjusted cash flow to book value$_{-1}$ | $-0.0015$ | $-0.0096$ | 0.093 | 557 |
| Industry-adjusted cash flow to sales$_{-1}$ | $-0.0034$ | $-0.0018$ | 0.072 | 555 |
| Market-to-book$_{-1}$ | 1.21 | 1.61 | 2.43 | 507 |
| Target $-$ CRSP value weighted index | $-0.0476$ | $-0.0408$ | 0.3108 | 443 |
|  | (0.00) | (0.00) | | |

| Panel B: Management Turnover | | | |
|---|---|---|---|
| Classification | Mean (%) | $p$-value | N |
| All sample firms | 32.42 | | 524 |
| Bidder terminated | 37.56 | | 134 |
| Rejected by nonbidder | 30.65 | 0.134 | 390 |
| $\Delta$ in total debt $<$ median $\Delta$ | 30.00 | | 152 |
| $\Delta$ in total debt $>$ median $\Delta$ | 36.78 | 0.154 | 146 |
| Hostile takeover attempt | 44.10 | | 114 |
| Friendly takeover attempt | 29.17 | 0.028 | 410 |

management change. Panel B of Table II reports statistics on management turnover for our sample of companies that remain independent for at least one year. These statistics are based on data from *Standard and Poor's Register of Corporations, Directors, and Executives*. Management turnover reflects the change in the top executive of the firm, defined as the CEO if there is one and the president otherwise. We compare the CEO in year $+1$ to

## Table III
## Changes in Common Equity, Special Dividends, and Share Repurchases

This table reports changes in common equity, special dividends, and share repurchase of targets with an increase in leverage (measured as total debt scaled by the book value of assets) higher (lower) than the median change. Our sample consists of 573 targets of unsuccessful takeovers for the 1982–1991 period obtained from *Mergerstat Review*, published annually by *W.T. Grimm*. Panel A reports the frequency of percentage changes in common equity for targets with leverage changes higher (lower) than the median change. For example, the frequency reported in the table for the interval of (−95% < Δ ≤ −85%) refers to the number of targets with percentage reduction in common equity greater than 95 percent and less than or equal to 85 percent. Panel B reports summary statistics for changes in total debt and percentage changes in common equity. Panel C reports mean values for special dividends and share repurchases for targets with leverage changes higher (lower) than the median change (Δ).

### Panel A: Frequency of Percentage Changes in Common Equity

| | Percentage Changes in Book Value of Common Equity from Year −1 to Year +1 | |
|---|---|---|
| | Δ in Leverage > Median Δ | Δ in Leverage < Median Δ |
| −95% < Δ ≤ −85% | 15 | 0 |
| −85% < Δ ≤ −75% | 21 | 0 |
| −75% < Δ ≤ −65% | 13 | 1 |
| −65% < Δ ≤ −55% | 11 | 1 |
| −55% < Δ ≤ −45% | 10 | 3 |
| −45% < Δ ≤ −35% | 10 | 5 |
| −35% < Δ ≤ −25% | 10 | 5 |
| −25% < Δ ≤ −15% | 8 | 8 |
| −15% < Δ ≤ −5% | 10 | 11 |
| −5% < Δ < 0% | 8 | 2 |
| Δ = 0 | 3 | 4 |
| 0 < Δ ≤ 10 % | 6 | 19 |
| 10% < Δ ≤ 20% | 4 | 22 |
| 20% < Δ ≤ 40% | 6 | 24 |
| 40% < Δ ≤ 60% | 3 | 6 |
| 60% < Δ ≤ 80% | 2 | 9 |
| 80% < Δ < 100% | 2 | 5 |
| Δ ≥ 100% | 0 | 14 |
| Total | 142 | 141 |

Panel B: Summary Statistics for Changes in Common Equity and Total Debt Ratio

| | Changes in Total Debt Ratio from Year −1 to Year +1 | | Percentage Changes in Book Value of Common Equity from Year −1 to Year +1 | |
|---|---|---|---|---|
| | Δ in Debt > Median Δ | Δ in Debt < Median Δ | Δ in Debt > Median Δ | Δ in Debt < Median Δ |
| Mean | 0.3299 | −0.0969 | −37.54% | 29.06% |
| Median | 0.1910 | −0.0311 | −43.71% | 14.87% |
| Min | 0.0362 | −1.6596 | −94.68% | −68.43% |
| Max | 3.4531 | 0.0349 | 95.77% | 296.20% |

Panel C: Mean Values for Special Dividends and Share Repurchases

| | Subsample: Δ in Debt > Median Δ | | Subsample: Δ in Debt < Median Δ | |
|---|---|---|---|---|
| | Levels in Year(s) $i$ | | Levels in Year(s) $i$ | |
| | −1 | 0 and +1 | −1 | 0 and +1 |
| Special dividend | 0.0207[a] | 0.0508[a] | 0.0223[a] | 0.0245[a] |
| Share repurchase | 0.0137[a] | 0.1129[a] | 0.0362[a] | 0.0327[a] |

[a]Estimates are statistically different from zero at the 1 percent significance level.

the CEO in year $-1$, where year 0 is the year of the unsuccessful takeover attempt. If the top executive's name is different then we assume that the firm has experienced turnover in the top management.

We document in Panel B of Table II a 32 percent turnover rate for the entire sample, which is much higher than the 17 percent average turnover rate reported by Denis and Denis (1995) in their study of 1,689 firms covered by the Value Line Investment Survey. In comparison, Denis and Serrano (1996) document a 34 percent management turnover rate for their sample of failed takeovers, and Agrawal and Walkling (1994) document a 44 percent rate of turnover in the two years following a failed takeover bid in their study.

Management turnover rates are reported separately for failed targets that increase their leverage ratios either less or more than the median amount. For the first subsample (change ($\Delta$) in leverage < median $\Delta$), 30 percent of the top managers were removed, compared to 36.78 percent for the second subsample. However, because the difference in these percentages is not statistically significant, we cannot conclude that leverage has an appreciable affect on management turnover. We also examine management turnover in the hostile and friendly subsamples. If the takeover attempt is hostile, 44.10 percent of top managers are replaced, whereas if the takeover attempt is friendly, only 29.17 percent are replaced. The difference in these percentages is significant at the 5 percent level.

## D. Leverage as a Takeover Defense

As mentioned in the introduction, we believe that failed targets increased leverage to defend against unwanted takeover attempts. The observed difference in the change in leverage ratios between friendly and hostile takeovers is consistent with this belief. Table IV reports the percentage change in total debt scaled by the book value of assets for the two subsamples consisting of friendly and hostile takeovers. For the friendly takeover group the median percentage changes in the leverage ratio from one year prior, to one, two, and three years following the failed takeover attempt are 2.07, 2.45, and 4.09 percent, respectively. For the hostile group, the median total debt increases amount to 12.24, 8.97, and 7.59 percent over the same period.[8] We

---

[8] The total number of observations in the analysis differs from year to year because of data availability. For example, Table II reports that there are 532 targets with valid debt data in year $-1$. Over the first 12 months following the termination of the failed takeover attempt 188 (156 + 3 + 1 + 4 + 24) firms were delisted as reported in Table I. Table IV reports 90 and 238 debt observations for the hostile and friendly group respectively. The difference between 532 and 188 is 344, and the sum of 90 and 238 is 328. In Table IV, year +1 denotes the end of the first fiscal year after the termination of the takeover attempt; it does not necessarily mean 12 months after the termination. For example, a takeover attempt was terminated in March, and the target firm has a December fiscal year end. We are measuring whether it was delisted on CRSP from March through February of the following year (12-months period; Panel C of Table I). In the analysis using COMPUSTAT data, year +1 means the end of the following fiscal year—that is, December, not February, of the following year.

**Table IV**
## Changes in Total Debt Scaled by the Book Value of Assets

Summary statistics are presented for changes in total debt scaled by the book value of assets for hostile and the friendly takeover attempts five years following the termination year for the sample of 573 targets of unsuccessful takeovers for the 1982–1991 period, obtained from *Mergerstat Review*, published annually by *W.T. Grimm*. The median and mean percentage changes in book value of debt scaled by the book value of total assets are reported, as well as the number of firms with valid observations. Nonparametric significance levels for tests in difference in medians are based on the Mann–Whitney–Wilcoxon test.

| | From Year $i$ to Year $j$ | | | | |
|---|---|---|---|---|---|
| | −1 to +1 | −1 to +2 | −1 to +3 | −1 to +4 | −1 to +5 |
| Hostile group | | | | | |
| Median | 12.24% | 8.97% | 7.59% | 7.23% | 10.99% |
| Mean | 19.84 | 18.91 | 16.12 | 18.64 | 20.60 |
| $N$ | 90 | 81 | 73 | 66 | 56 |
| Friendly group | | | | | |
| Median | 2.07%[a] | 2.45%[a] | 4.09%[a] | 4.33%[a] | 4.41%[a] |
| Mean | 11.15 | 11.74 | 11.64 | 12.31 | 11.98 |
| $N$ | 238 | 219 | 185 | 156 | 116 |

[a]Median figures for the hostile and friendly groups are statistically different at the 1 percent significance level.

find that the difference between these percentage changes in each of the three years following the failed takeover attempt is statistically significant at the 1 percent level using the Mann–Whitney–Wilcoxon test.

Consistent with prior studies, it appears that the higher leverage does reduce the likelihood of targets getting taken over. For example, 38 percent of the target firms that increased their leverage ratio more than the median between years −1 and +1 were taken over in the five years following the initial failed takeover attempt. In contrast, 57 percent of those target firms that increased their leverage ratios less than the median were taken over within five years. The percentage of firms that remained independent after failed takeovers is substantially higher in our sample than it is in the sample examined by Bradley, Desai, and Kim (1983), which is for an earlier time period. Bradley et al. report that 77 percent (86 out of 112) of their sample were taken over after five years of the initial failed takeover attempt. In contrast, in our later sample only about 48 percent (278 out of 573) of the failed targets get taken over within five years. The increased percentage of firms that remain independent in the later period is probably due to the increased use of poison pills and other antitakeover defenses, antitakeover legislation, and, perhaps, the deterrent effect of higher leverage.

We expect that some target managers chose not to increase leverage because they were able to use other defensive mechanisms to deter acquisitions. To investigate this possibility we examined a wide variety of defensive tactics, which include stock lockup, white knight, white squire, greenmail, pacman, scorched earth, and targeted repurchases. We compute the frequency of cases where targets have used a defensive tactic in the two groups: targets that increased leverage and targets that did not.

Our sample includes 121 cases where targets did not increase their leverage. About half (61) of these firms adopted a defensive tactic other than debt. In contrast, only 33 of the 207 firms that increased their leverage adopted a defensive tactic. A plausible interpretation is that financial restructuring and other defensive tactics are substitutes. For some firms, financial restructuring is the optimal defense, while others prefer different options.

## II. Changes in Leverage and Investment Choices

Our main goal is to test the hypothesis that higher leverage commits failed targets to make changes that improve their operating performance and as a result increase their stock prices. To examine this we first look explicitly at the kinds of changes made by failed targets and then examine the extent to which these changes lead to operating improvements and higher stock prices.

As discussed in Myers (1977), higher leverage can have the effect of decreasing a firm's investment expenditures.[9] Thus, as Jensen (1986) explains, if managers have a tendency to overinvest, higher leverage can have the effect of reducing their level of investment to what might approximate the value-maximizing level.

Although we are unable to determine whether target firms are overinvesting or underinvesting, we can document whether investment expenditures increase or decrease after the takeover attempts and can compare how these changes relate to changes in leverage. To investigate this issue we examine capital expenditures and research and development expenses for the seven years around the failed takeover attempts. Panel B of Table V indicates that the median (mean) level of capital expenditures scaled by the book value of assets of target firms that increase their leverage more than the median in year $-1$ is 0.067 (0.086),[10] and is 0.048 (0.050) in year $+2$. The median (mean) percentage reduction of this ratio is a statistically significant 35.36 percent (12.16 percent) from one year prior to two years after the takeover attempt. Research and development expenditures show a similar decline for the leverage increasing targets, though the decline is not significant at conventional levels. Target firms that increase their leverage less than the median have an insignificant change in their capital and research and development expenditures.

The negative relation between the change in investment expenditures and the change in leverage is consistent with the Myers (1977) and Jensen (1986) models. The results, however, do not support the Ross (1977) signaling model, which suggests that managers who are the most optimistic about future

[9] Lang, Ofek, and Stulz (1996) provide evidence suggesting that increased debt does induce firms to invest less, at least for firms with low Tobin's q ratio.

[10] Results are qualitatively identical when we scale capital expenditures and research and development expense by sales rather than book value of assets.

productivity increase leverage. We would expect, holding all else equal, that those managers who are the most optimistic about future prospects will increase investment expenditures as well as increase leverage, but that is not what we observe.

## III. Corporate Restructuring

The evidence presented above indicates that increases in leverage following failed takeovers are correlated with decreases in investment. This section examines whether leverage is related to other restructuring activities that are typically associated with takeovers. For example, Bhagat, Shleifer, and Vishny (1990) and Berger and Ofek (1998) document that successfully acquired firms usually undergo an extensive restructuring involving asset sales and layoffs. Berger and Ofek (1998), and Denis, Denis and Sarin (1997) argue that firms that implement corporate refocusing programs often do so in the presence of external control pressures such as takeover threats.

To examine whether leverage is related to these restructuring activities, we report in Panel E of Table V summary statistics for restructuring activity in our sample. The table shows that 45.4 percent of those targets that increase leverage more than the median have asset sales reported in the *Wall Street Journal* in the two years following the failed takeover. In contrast, only 16.5 percent of those targets that increase leverage less than the median have asset sales reported. Additionally, failed targets that increase leverage the most reduce their labor force by more than 5 percent, but those targets that increase leverage the least do not change employment significantly. Failed targets that increase leverage the most also increase their focus, as indicated by the change in the number of SIC codes that Dun and Bradstreet report the firm doing business in. On average, targets that increase leverage the least report that they do business in 0.156 *more* SIC codes following a failed takeover. In contrast, failed targets that increase leverage the most do business in 0.645 *fewer* SIC codes. These differences between the restructuring activities of firms that increase leverage more and less than the median amount are all statistically significant.

## IV. Changes in Leverage and Operating Performance

*A. Univariate Analysis of Firm Level Data*

The previous section documented that failed targets that increase their leverage the most make a number of changes that can potentially improve their productivity. In this section we attempt to estimate these productivity changes by examining changes in the firms' pretax operating cash flows.[11]

---

[11] This measure of operating performance is used in previous studies by Ravenscraft and Scherer (1987), Kaplan (1989), and Smith (1990). Pretax operating cash flow is measured as net sales, less cost of goods sold, less selling and administrative expenses, before deducting depreciation and amortization expense. We focus on pretax operating cash flows that are unaffected by changes in tax status or capital structure.

## Table V
## Corporate Restructuring for Targets with a Change in Leverage that is Lower (Higher) than the Median Change

Summary statistics are given for capital expenditures scaled by the book value of assets, and research and development expense scaled by the book value of assets for seven years around the failed takeover attempt year, changes in the number of employees scaled by the book value of assets from one year before to one year after the failed takeover attempt year, changes in the number of SIC codes from one year before to five years after the failed takeover attempt year, and the frequency of assets sales in the two years after the failed takeover attempt year. Our sample includes 573 targets of unsuccessful takeovers during the 1982–1991 period obtained from *Mergerstat Review*, published by *W.T. Grimm*. Panel A reports the median, mean, and standard deviation of capital expenditures, and research and development expense for targets with a change (Δ) in total debt that is less than the median change (Δ). Panel B reports the same statistics for targets with a change in total debt that is greater than the median change (Δ). Percentage changes in capital expenditures scaled by the book value of assets and in research and development expense scaled by the book value of assets for various intervals are reported in Panels C and D. Panel E reports the mean values and the *p*-values for the difference in means *t*-test.

| | Year −3 | Year −2 | Year −1 | Year 0 | Year +1 | Year +2 | Year +3 |
|---|---|---|---|---|---|---|---|
| Panel A: Change in Leverage Lower than the Median Change | | | | | | | |
| Capital expenditures scaled by the book value of assets | | | | | | | |
| Median | 0.066 | 0.064 | 0.063 | 0.056 | 0.056 | 0.052 | 0.057 |
| Mean | 0.117 | 0.106 | 0.092 | 0.077 | 0.080 | 0.079 | 0.086 |
| Std. dev. | 0.143 | 0.116 | 0.084 | 0.075 | 0.080 | 0.092 | 0.097 |
| N | 148 | 153 | 152 | 164 | 145 | 122 | 100 |
| Research and development expense scaled by the book value of assets | | | | | | | |
| Median | 0.039 | 0.044 | 0.044 | 0.050 | 0.054 | 0.056 | 0.047 |
| Mean | 0.018 | 0.024 | 0.024 | 0.023 | 0.024 | 0.025 | 0.019 |
| Std. dev. | 0.044 | 0.056 | 0.052 | 0.073 | 0.093 | 0.077 | 0.090 |
| N | 59 | 58 | 57 | 58 | 54 | 44 | 38 |
| Panel B: Change in Leverage Higher than the Median Change | | | | | | | |
| Capital expenditures scaled by the book value of assets | | | | | | | |
| Median | 0.064 | 0.067 | 0.067 | 0.058 | 0.052 | 0.048 | 0.049 |
| Mean | 0.086 | 0.085 | 0.086 | 0.081 | 0.078 | 0.050 | 0.056 |
| Std. dev. | 0.083 | 0.066 | 0.077 | 0.080 | 0.073 | 0.051 | 0.043 |
| N | 156 | 164 | 169 | 171 | 168 | 159 | 133 |
| Research and development expense scaled by the book value of assets | | | | | | | |
| Median | 0.010 | 0.011 | 0.011 | 0.008 | 0.007 | 0.007 | 0.010 |
| Mean | 0.029 | 0.032 | 0.027 | 0.026 | 0.022 | 0.028 | 0.032 |
| Std. dev. | 0.047 | 0.083 | 0.055 | 0.034 | 0.031 | 0.048 | 0.058 |
| N | 77 | 82 | 82 | 76 | 79 | 73 | 62 |

## Leverage and Corporate Performance after Takeover Attempts     561

|  | Δ in Debt < Median Δ | | | Δ in Debt > Median Δ | | |
|---|---|---|---|---|---|---|
|  | −1 to +1 | −1 to +2 | −1 to +3 | −1 to +1 | −1 to +2 | −1 to +3 |
| **Panel C: Percentage Change in Capital Expenditures from Year $i$ to Year $j$** | | | | | | |
| Median | −7.93% | −9.22% | −10.11% | −17.62%[b] | −35.36%*** | −27.93%*** |
| Mean | 6.91 | 29.62 | 14.52 | −13.23* | −12.16 | −2.87 |
| Percent positive | 44 | 44 | 43 | 39 | 30 | 33 |
| Std. errors | 0.77 | 2.71 | 1.04 | 0.58 | 0.93 | 0.87 |
| N | 143 | 119 | 97 | 166 | 158 | 132 |
| **Panel D: Percentage Change in Research and Development from Year $i$ to Year $j$** | | | | | | |
| Median | −1.39% | 9.38% | 11.51% | −8.88%* | −11.84% | −8.82% |
| Mean | 19.04* | 54.52** | 91.84 | −9.50* | 9.09 | 13.79 |
| Percent positive | 48 | 57 | 63 | 38 | 39 | 45 |
| Std. errors | 0.67 | 1.33 | 3.04 | 0.42 | 0.98 | 1.14 |
| N | 44 | 35 | 27 | 61 | 56 | 47 |

**Panel E: Various Characteristics Scaled by the Book Value of Assets (reported values are means)**

| Characteristic | Δ in Debt < Median Δ | Δ in Debt > Median Δ | t-test (p-values) |
|---|---|---|---|
| Asset sales in the two years following the initial failed takeover attempt | 16.5%*** | 45.4%*** | 0.000 |
| Δ in the number of SIC codes from year −1 to +5 | 0.156 | −0.645*** | 0.002 |
| Percentage Δ in the number of employees from year −1 to +1 | −1.09% | −5.67%** | 0.026 |

*, **, *** Statistically different from zero at the 10, 5, and 1 percent significance levels, respectively.

Cash flow is scaled by book value of assets, as well as sales and the market value of the firm in year $-1$, to allow comparison across firms and through time.

Target firm operating performance is measured relative to the performance of equally weighted portfolios of control firms constructed for each target firm using a procedure based on the methodology suggested by Barber and Lyon (1996). These control firms are selected from firms listed on COMPUSTAT which have not been subject to a takeover attempt (whether successful or not) during the prior five years. The control portfolio is constructed with the following three-step algorithm:

1. Each target firm is matched to all nontargets in the same two-digit SIC code.
2. To match on size, potential control firms with book values that are not within 70 to 130 percent of the target's book value of assets in the year prior to the takeover attempt are eliminated.
3. To match on prior performance, potential control firms that are not within 90 to 110 percent of the target firm's ratio of cash flow to book value of assets in the year prior to the takeover attempt are eliminated.

If no firm matches on SIC code, size, and prior performance, the firm with the best prior performance with the same SIC code and size is selected as the control portfolio. If this algorithm results in either no matching firms or missing data, an alternative rule is followed. First, we repeat the original algorithm using a one-digit SIC code screen. If we still have no match we eliminate the SIC code screen.

All sample firms are matched using either the original algorithm or the alternative rules. Target abnormal operating performance is then estimated by subtracting from its operating performance the performance of the control portfolio (henceforth, matched-adjusted performance). We report the matched-adjusted percentage change in these cash flows which is calculated as follows:

$$\text{CFBV}_j - \text{CFBV}_i | \text{CFBV}_i |] - \left[ \frac{\text{AVG}(\text{CFBV})_j - \text{AVG}(\text{CFBV})_i}{|\text{AVG}(\text{CFBV})_i|} \right], \tag{1}$$

where $\text{CFBV}_j$ is the cash flow to book value in year $j$, and $\text{AVG}(\text{CFBV})_i$ is the equally weighted average of the cash flow to book value of assets of the matching firms in year $i$. Raw changes rather than percentage changes give qualitatively identical results.

We use this methodology to choose the control portfolio and measure abnormal operating performance for several reasons. First, a matching portfolio controls for economy-wide and industry-wide effects on target performance. Second, matching on operating performance controls for potential mean reversion in earnings and other operating ratios that have been documented in prior studies (Fama and French (1995) or Penman (1991)). Barber and Lyon (1996) conclude that tests using control firms not matched on performance are misspecified when the event firms have particularly good or poor prior operating performance.

By looking at cash flows over a five-year period, we can capture both long- and short-run effects of the debt changes. It is important to examine cash flows over a long time period because increased debt can make firms more shortsighted in their operating and investment decisions, making immediate cash flows higher at the expense of later cash flows. For example, Maksimovic and Titman (1991) argue that debt may distort a firm's incentive to offer high quality products, boosting short-run profits by cutting costs at the expense of its long-term reputation and profits. Further, managers may have incentives to manipulate their earnings following a failed takeover attempt and these incentives may differ depending on the firm's leverage ratio. If reported operating income increases because of either shortsighted incentives or manipulated accounting numbers, reported operating income should initially increase but later decline.

Since cash flow measures are skewed, we present results for medians rather than means and report significance levels based on a two-tailed sign test. The null hypothesis is that post-termination cash flows equal pre-termination cash flows. In order to examine the relation between leverage and performance, we split the sample into two groups based on the median change in leverage between year $-1$ and year $+1$.

Table VI documents that those target firms that increase their leverage the least realize reductions in their adjusted operating cash flows and those that increase their leverage the most realize increases in their adjusted cash flows. Specifically, Panel A shows that for those targets that increase debt less than the median change, cash flows significantly decline relative to the year prior to the termination of the takeover attempt. The adjusted percentage change in cash flow/book value of assets relative to year $-1$ has a median of $-10.25$, $-23.04$, and $-19.18$ percent in each of years 3, 4, and 5 following the failed attempt. When cash flows are scaled by sales or by market value in year $-1$, the results are qualitatively similar. Panel B reports the same operating performance measures for targets where the change in total debt is higher than the median change. The adjusted percentage change in cash flow scaled by market value in year $-1$ increases by 20.16, 19.79, and 18.23 percent in the years 3, 4, and 5 following the failed takeover attempt.

A potential bias in the results reported in Panels A and B would arise if firms with the poorest performance were subsequently taken over and were dropped from our sample. If this were the case, aggregate cash flows would show improvement even if individual firms did not improve. To examine whether the improvements in operating profits reported in Table VI are due to poorly performing targets dropping out of the sample (about 40 percent drop out after five years), we separately examine the performance of those firms that survived through year 5. These results are reported in Panels C,

**Table VI**

## Changes in Operating Performance

Median matched-adjusted percentage changes are reported for cash flow to book value and cash flow to sales around the failed takeover attempt year for the sample of 573 targets of unsuccessful takeovers over the 1982 to 1991 period, obtained from *Mergerstat Review*, published by *W.T. Grimm*. The cash flow to book value and cash flow to sales in year $-1$ is taken as the benchmark year. Matched-adjusted percentage change is calculated as follows:

$$CFBV_j - CFBV_i|CFBV_i| - \left[ \frac{AVG(CFBV)_j - AVG(CFBV)_i}{|AVG(CFBV)_i|} \right],$$

where $CFBV_i$ is the cash flow to book value in year $j$, and $AVG(CFBV)_i$ is the equally weighted average of the cash flow to book value of assets of the matching firms in year $i$. Also reported are the percentage change in cash flow scaled by the market value of the firm in year $-1$. Significance levels are based on a two-tailed sign test, reported in parentheses. Panel A reports the median matched-adjusted percentage change in cash flow to book value, cash flow to sales, and cash flow to market value for targets with a change in total debt that is less than the median change. Panel B reports the same statistics for targets with a change in total debt that is greater than the median change. Panel C reports the same statistics for the overall sample that survived through year 5. Panels D and E report the same statistics for targets that survived through year 5 with changes in leverage lower (higher) than the median change respectively.

| | From Year $i$ to Year $j$ | | | | |
| --- | --- | --- | --- | --- | --- |
| | $-1$ to $+1$ | $-1$ to $+2$ | $-1$ to $+3$ | $-1$ to $+4$ | $-1$ to $+5$ |
| **Panel A: Change in Leverage Less than the Median Change** | | | | | |
| Matched-adjusted percentage change in cash flow to book value | -6.09% | -8.22% | -10.25% | -23.04% | -19.18% |
| | (0.234) | (0.126) | (0.109) | (0.033) | (0.028) |
| Matched-adjusted percentage change in cash flow to sales | -4.78% | -11.24% | -12.05% | -18.69% | -21.70% |
| | (0.313) | (0.117) | (0.097) | (0.041) | (0.015) |
| Percentage change in cash flow scaled by the market value in year $-1$ | -9.19% | -14.77% | -20.65% | -16.56% | -22.58% |
| | (0.147) | (0.071) | (0.052) | (0.039) | (0.026) |
| $N$ | 144 | 139 | 120 | 96 | 70 |
| **Panel B: Change in Leverage Greater than the Median Change** | | | | | |
| Matched-adjusted percentage change in cash flow to book value | 5.81% | 9.83% | 12.19% | 14.56% | 13.56% |
| | (0.554) | (0.188) | (0.095) | (0.077) | (0.061) |
| Matched-adjusted percentage change in cash flow to sales | 9.61% | 11.58% | 19.12% | 16.42% | 18.99% |
| | (0.180) | (0.126) | (0.029) | (0.040) | (0.028) |
| Percentage change in cash flow scaled by the market value in year $-1$ | 6.29% | 12.57% | 20.16% | 19.79% | 18.23% |
| | (0.310) | (0.101) | (0.012) | (0.024) | (0.031) |
| $N$ | 160 | 152 | 129 | 112 | 100 |

### Panel C. Overall Sample that Survived through Year 5

| | | | | | |
|---|---|---|---|---|---|
| Matched-adjusted percentage change in cash flow to book value | 1.12% (0.542) | 6.11% (0.294) | 0.52% (0.879) | 1.87% (0.759) | 3.13% (0.432) |
| Matched-adjusted percentage change in cash flow to sales | 4.16% (0.341) | 2.15% (0.429) | 3.92% (0.246) | 7.76% (0.421) | 3.51% (0.319) |
| Percentage change in cash flow scaled by the market value in year −1 | 1.33% (0.634) | 3.99% (0.312) | 1.78% (0.546) | 5.11% (0.308) | 7.61% (0.193) |
| $N$ | 170 | 170 | 170 | 170 | 170 |

### Panel D: Change (Δ) in Leverage Less than Median Δ Conditional on Surviving through Year 5

| | | | | | |
|---|---|---|---|---|---|
| Matched-adjusted percentage change in cash flow to book value | −4.36% (0.233) | −7.17% (0.325) | −15.71% (0.051) | −25.19% (0.024) | −19.18% (0.028) |
| Matched-adjusted percentage change in cash flow to sales | −5.16% (0.239) | −10.56% (0.191) | −12.52% (0.068) | −17.18% (0.032) | −21.70% (0.015) |
| Percentage change in cash flow scaled by the market value in year −1 | −6.77% (0.294) | −9.96% (0.373) | −19.98% (0.015) | −20.15% (0.034) | −22.58% (0.026) |
| $N$ | 70 | 70 | 70 | 70 | 70 |

### Panel E: Change (Δ) in Leverage Greater than Median Δ Conditional on Surviving through Year 5

| | | | | | |
|---|---|---|---|---|---|
| Matched-adjusted percentage change in cash flow to book value | 5.08% (0.172) | 12.26% (0.106) | 13.78% (0.086) | 16.13% (0.040) | 13.56% (0.061) |
| Matched-adjusted percentage change in cash flow to sales | 8.15% (0.179) | 14.59% (0.088) | 19.98% (0.024) | 20.41% (0.011) | 18.99% (0.028) |
| Percentage change in cash flow scaled by the market value in year −1 | 4.19% (0.356) | 12.11% (0.074) | 19.55% (0.031) | 23.65% (0.009) | 18.23% (0.031) |
| $N$ | 100 | 100 | 100 | 100 | 100 |

D, and E. Consistent with Panel B, leverage-increasing firms that survive through year 5 experience significant improvements in operating cash flows. The similarity between the cash flow improvements in the samples with and without the survival requirement suggests that the cash flow improvements for firms that were and were not subsequently taken over were not significantly different.

### B. Univariate Analysis of the Targets' Largest Segments

The evidence in the preceding subsection is consistent with the idea that leverage induces managers to expend additional effort that improves their firms' cash flows. The evidence, however, is also consistent with the possibility that the more highly levered firms sell off underperforming assets, perhaps in an attempt to focus on their more profitable lines of business. To investigate whether the improvement in cash flow is solely due to the elimination of unprofitable lines of business we replicate the tests reported in the last subsection on the cash flows of the firms' largest segments as reported in the COMPUSTAT segment data. This analysis assumes that it is much less likely that firms benefit from selling off underperforming assets within their core segments, so improvements in cash flows within these segments is likely to be due to the elimination of unproductive activities.

Our analysis of the individual segments indicates that there are operating improvements that are independent of the asset sales. In particular, targets that increase their leverage ratio more than the median amount experience an improvement in the operating cash flows of their largest segment. The industry-adjusted percentage change in cash flow/book value of assets relative to year $-1$, reported in Panel B of Table VII, has a median of 11.01, 15.34, and 16.57 percent in each of years 3, 4, and 5 following the failed attempt. Unadjusted cash flows scaled by the book value of the segment have a similar pattern. On the other hand, targets that increase their leverage ratios less than the median have an insignificant median change in the operating cash flows of their largest segments.

### C. Multivariate Analysis

Up to this point we have established that leverage increases are associated with asset sales, reductions in capital expenditures, increased focus, and reductions in employment. We have also established that leverage increases are associated with improvements in cash flows. It is likely that some of the observed increase in cash flows is due to cuts in unprofitable investment, sales of underperforming assets, and reductions in employment. However, our analysis of the cash flows of the firms' largest segments indicates that there are improvements in cash flows that come about because of unobserved incentive improvements that are also associated with increased leverage. To investigate this possibility further, we estimate multivariate regressions that examine the effect of leverage changes on cash flow changes after controlling for these and other factors.

## Table VII
## Changes in Operating Performance for Largest Segment of Targets with a Change in Leverage that is Lower (Higher) than the Median Change

This table reports median change, median industry-adjusted change, and median industry-adjusted percentage change for the biggest segment (in assets as of year −1) in cash flow to book value around the failed takeover attempt year for the sample of 573 targets of unsuccessful takeovers over the 1982–1991 period, obtained from *Mergerstat Review*, published by *W.T. Grimm*. The cash flow to book value in year −1 is taken as the benchmark year. Industry-adjusted cash flow to book value measures are calculated by subtracting from the target's largest segment change in cash flow to book value the change in cash flow to book value over the same period for the target largest segment's industry (defined by the segment's two-digit SIC code). Industry data are collected from the COMPUSTAT Industrial, Tertiary, and Research data files. Significance levels are based on a two-tailed sign test, reported in parentheses. Panel A reports the median change, median percentage change, and industry-adjusted percentage change in cash flow to book value for targets with a change in total debt that is less than the median change. Panel B reports the same statistics for targets with a change in total debt that is greater than the median change.

|  | From year $i$ to year $j$ | | | | |
|---|---|---|---|---|---|
|  | −1 to +1 | −1 to +2 | −1 to +3 | −1 to +4 | −1 to +5 |
| Panel A: Change in Leverage Less than the Median Change | | | | | |
| Change in cash flow to book value | −0.0017 | −0.0094 | −0.0169 | −0.0203 | −0.0206 |
|  | (0.936) | (0.165) | (0.179) | (0.047) | (0.033) |
| Industry-adjusted change in cash flow to book value | 0.0012 | −0.0039 | −0.0101 | −0.0200 | −0.0233 |
|  | (0.921) | (0.862) | (0.566) | (0.034) | (0.059) |
| Industry-adjusted percentage change in cash flow to book value | 7.91% | −2.99% | −0.36% | −12.77% | −14.60% |
|  | (0.298) | (0.972) | (0.741) | (0.151) | (0.103) |
| $N$ | 142 | 133 | 109 | 92 | 64 |
| Panel B: Change in Leverage Greater than the Median Change | | | | | |
| Change in cash flow to book value | 0.0022 | 0.0071 | 0.0115 | 0.0195 | 0.0161 |
|  | (0.665) | (0.372) | (0.072) | (0.003) | (0.006) |
| Industry-adjusted change in cash flow to book value | 0.0131 | 0.0215 | 0.0248 | 0.0240 | 0.0377 |
|  | (0.054) | (0.021) | (0.001) | (0.002) | (0.001) |
| Industry-adjusted percentage change in cash flow to book value | 1.19% | 4.81% | 11.01% | 15.34% | 16.57% |
|  | (0.938) | (0.233) | (0.029) | (0.014) | (0.011) |
| $N$ | 158 | 153 | 128 | 110 | 96 |

In addition to the leverage change, the independent variables in these regressions include the following:

- a dummy variable for CEO turnover, taking the value of 1 if the CEO in year +1 is different from the CEO in year −1, and 0 otherwise
- a dummy variable taking the value of 1 if the company reports the sale of an asset in the year of or the year after the failed takeover attempt and 0 otherwise
- the change in the number of SIC codes from one year before to five years following the takeover attempt
- the percentage change in the level of employment
- a dummy variable for whether the takeover attempt was terminated by the bidder or the target
- a dummy variable for whether or not the takeover attempt was hostile
- the level of insider ownership scaled by the number of shares outstanding. Insider ownership is defined as the total direct ownership obtained from *Spectrum 6 Insider Holdings*.[12]

We expect that performance is likely to improve the most for those targets with new managers and for those offers that were hostile. Furthermore, following Dodd (1980), we hypothesize that bidder-terminated takeover offers reveal more negative information about the target firm than other terminated offers.[13]

The results of these cross-sectional regressions, reported in Tables VIII and IX, indicate that the change in leverage has a significant effect on cash flows even after accounting for the other variables. This is especially true when we examine long-run changes in cash flow (e.g., from year −1 to year +5), where the effect of the leverage change on cash flows is quite strong. With the exception of CEO turnover, consistent with Denis and Serrano's (1996) observation that cash flows improve more for firms that get new CEOs, the control variables have virtually no marginal explanatory power in the long-term regressions. Perhaps this is because changes in employment, asset sales, and the scaling back in employment is a mixed signal;

---

[12] All results are robust to alternative specifications of the ownership variable. One alternative specification that we examine is the piecewise regression by Morck, Shleifer, and Vishny (1988).

[13] Asquith (1983) analyzes the abnormal stock price performance of firms that engage in merger bids He documents a −6.40 percent return for unsuccessful target firms on the termination date and interprets this finding to indicate that termination of the merger attempt conveys negative information. We measure the cumulative prediction errors (CPEs) for the termination period using the market model over a seven-day window (−5,1). We estimate the beta of the firm using 100 trading days of data (day −199 to −99 relative to the announcement of the transaction) and use the CRSP value-weighted index as the market index. When the bidder terminates the transaction, the CPEs are −8.42 percent compared to −3.14 percent for other-rejected transactions (not reported). The difference in the means is statistically significant using parametric and nonparametric tests at the 1 percent level.

Leverage and Corporate Performance after Takeover Attempts 569

### Table VIII
## Multivariate Analysis for Matched Adjusted Ratio of Cash Flows to Sales

Estimates are given of cross-sectional ordinary least squares regressions relating changes in operating performance to firm variables for 573 target firms in unsuccessful takeovers for the 1982–1991 period. The dependent variables are the change from year $i$ to year $j$ in matched adjusted ratio of cash flow to sales. Leverage is measured as the book value of total debt scaled by the book value of total assets. $\Delta$ in leverage is measured between one year prior to the failed takeover attempt and one year afterward. Asset sales is a dummy variable taking the value of 1 if an asset sale occurred in the year of or the year after the failed takeover attempt and 0 otherwise. Change in the number of SIC codes is measured from one year before to five years following the takeover attempt. CEO turnover is a dummy variable taking the value of 1 for a change in the top management from year $-1$ to $+1$ and 0 otherwise. The percentage change in the number of employees and in capital expenditures is measured from one year before to two years after the failed takeover attempt. Hostile bid is a dummy variable taking the value of 1 for hostile takeovers and 0 otherwise. Insider ownership represents the level of insider ownership scaled by the number of shares outstanding. Bidder terminated is a dummy variable taking the value of 1 for non-bidder terminated takeover attempts and 0 for bidder terminated transactions. ($t$-statistics are in parentheses).

| | Dependent Variable: Change from Year $i$ to Year $j$ in Matched Adjusted Ratio of Cash Flow to Sales | | | |
|---|---|---|---|---|
| | $-1$ to $+2$ | $-1$ to $+3$ | $-1$ to $+4$ | $-1$ to $+5$ |
| Intercept | $-0.0784$ | $-0.0967$ | $-0.1498$ | $-0.1738$ |
| | $(-3.26)$*** | $(-3.59)$*** | $(-4.16)$*** | $(-4.08)$*** |
| $\Delta$ in leverage | 0.0786 | 0.0897 | 0.1432 | 0.1838 |
| | $(1.88)$* | $(1.91)$* | $(2.31)$** | $(2.61)$** |
| Asset sales | 0.0581 | 0.0440 | 0.0075 | 0.0280 |
| | $(3.04)$*** | $(2.04)$** | $(0.25)$ | $(0.82)$ |
| $\Delta$ in number of SIC codes | 0.0003 | $-0.0005$ | $-0.0023$ | $-0.0012$ |
| | $(0.06)$ | $(-0.09)$ | $(-0.29)$ | $(-0.13)$ |
| CEO turnover | 0.0145 | 0.0463 | 0.0884 | 0.0952 |
| | $(0.80)$ | $(2.25)$** | $(3.24)$*** | $(3.12)$*** |
| %$\Delta$ in number of employees | 0.0418 | 0.0118 | $-0.0129$ | 0.0074 |
| | $(1.54)$ | $(0.38)$ | $(-0.31)$ | $(0.16)$ |
| %$\Delta$ in capital expenditures | $-0.0159$ | $-0.0220$ | $-0.0466$ | $-0.0441$ |
| | $(-0.87)$ | $(-1.06)$ | $(-1.79)$* | $(-1.46)$ |
| Hostile bid | 0.0412 | 0.0391 | 0.0451 | 0.0508 |
| | $(1.80)$* | $(1.52)$ | $(1.44)$ | $(1.48)$ |
| Insider ownership | $-0.0285$ | $-0.0623$ | $-0.0368$ | 0.0090 |
| | $(-0.82)$ | $(-1.59)$ | $(-0.70)$ | $(0.15)$ |
| Bidder terminated | 0.0068 | 0.0083 | 0.0137 | 0.0135 |
| | $(1.11)$ | $(1.21)$ | $(1.52)$ | $(1.23)$ |
| $N$ | 123 | 121 | 103 | 84 |
| Adjusted $R^2$ | 0.1466 | 0.1451 | 0.1638 | 0.1808 |
| $F$ | 3.39*** | 3.32*** | 3.29*** | 3.11*** |

*, **, *** Statistically different from zero at the 10, 5, and 1 percent significance levels, respectively.

### Table IX
## Multivariate Analysis for Matched Adjusted Ratio of Cash Flow to Book Value of Assets

Estimates are given of cross-sectional regressions relating changes in operating performance to firm variables for 573 target firms in unsuccessful takeovers for the 1982–1991 period. The dependent variables are the change from year $i$ to year $j$ in the matched adjusted ratio of cash flow to book value of assets. Leverage is measured as the book value of total debt scaled by the book value of total assets. $\Delta$ in leverage is measured between one year prior to the failed takeover attempt and one year afterward. Asset sales is a dummy variable taking the value of 1 if an asset sale occurred in the year of or the year after the failed takeover attempt and 0 otherwise. $\Delta$ in number of SIC codes is measured from one year before to five years following the takeover attempt. CEO turnover is a dummy variable taking the value of 1 for a change in the top management from year $-1$ to $+1$ and 0 otherwise. The $\%\Delta$ in the number of employees and in capital expenditures is measured from one year before to two years after the failed takeover attempt. Hostile bid is a dummy variable taking the value of 1 for hostile takeovers and 0 otherwise. Insider-ownership represents the level of insider ownership scaled by the number shares outstanding. Bidder terminated is a dummy variable taking the value of 1 for non-bidder terminated takeover attempts and 0 for bidder-terminated transactions. ($t$-statistics are in parentheses).

| | Dependent Variable: Change from Year $i$ to Year $j$ in Matched Adjusted Cash Flow to Book Value of Assets | | | |
| --- | --- | --- | --- | --- |
| | $-1$ to $+2$ | $-1$ to $+3$ | $-1$ to $+4$ | $-1$ to $+5$ |
| Intercept | −0.0668 | −0.0741 | −0.1079 | −0.1173 |
| | (−3.05)*** | (−3.03)*** | (−3.53)*** | (−3.29)*** |
| $\Delta$ in leverage | 0.0701 | 0.0861 | 0.1298 | 0.1541 |
| | (1.69)* | (2.02)** | (2.49)** | (2.69)*** |
| Asset sales | 0.0576 | 0.0385 | 0.0026 | 0.0231 |
| | (3.35)*** | (1.99)** | (0.11) | (0.83) |
| $\Delta$ in number of SIC codes | 0.0012 | −0.0057 | −0.0124 | −0.0144 |
| | (0.25) | (−1.11) | (−1.81)* | (−1.85)* |
| CEO turnover | 0.0124 | 0.0417 | 0.0706 | 0.0698 |
| | (0.76) | (2.27)** | (3.07)*** | (2.76)*** |
| $\%\Delta$ in number of employees | 0.0291 | 0.0179 | 0.0071 | 0.0295 |
| | (1.15) | (0.63) | (0.19) | (0.75) |
| $\%\Delta$ in capital expenditures | −0.0076 | −0.0224 | −0.0445 | −0.0401 |
| | (−0.46) | (−1.21) | (−2.04)** | (−1.62) |
| Hostile bid | 0.0283 | 0.0219 | 0.0230 | 0.0224 |
| | (1.80)* | (0.95) | (0.88) | (0.79) |
| Insider ownership | −0.0347 | −0.0615 | −0.0365 | −0.0001 |
| | (−1.11) | (−1.76)* | (0.83) | (−0.01) |
| Bidder terminated | 0.0043 | 0.0040 | 0.0075 | 0.0058 |
| | (0.78) | (0.65) | (1.01) | (0.64) |
| $N$ | 124 | 122 | 104 | 85 |
| Adjusted $R^2$ | 0.1484 | 0.1527 | 0.1910 | 0.2231 |
| $F$ | 3.40*** | 3.44*** | 3.74*** | 3.71*** |

*, **, *** Statistically different from zero at the 10, 5, and 1 percent significance levels, respectively.

firms benefit from cutting back waste, but they are less likely to take these actions if they believe that their businesses are improving. Leverage increases, on the other hand, simultaneously signal that managers have the intention of cutting waste and are optimistic about the firm's prospects.[14]

## V. Are the Positive Effects of Leverage Anticipated?

To examine whether investors anticipate the effect of leverage on performance we examine the stock returns of the failed targets in the period around the termination date as well as the longer period between the initial announcement of the proposed takeover and the termination date. As mentioned in the introduction, target stock prices drop on the termination announcement. However, consistent with earlier studies by Bradley (1980) and Dodd (1980), the target stock prices do not fall to the levels observed prior to the initial takeover announcement.

Our evidence indicates that target stock prices fall significantly less on the termination announcement for those firms that increase leverage more than the median, suggesting that investors at least partially anticipate the leverage increase as well as the positive effects of leverage on performance.[15] Specifically, targets that increase leverage more than the median have mean cumulative prediction errors of $-2.7$ percent from 5 days before the termination announcement until 1 day after the termination day. This compares to $-7.8$ percent for targets that increase leverage less than the median. The difference between the two means is significant at conventional levels. Furthermore, target firms that increase leverage more than the median have a mean (median) CPE during the announcement-termination period of 13.2 percent (11.5 percent), which is significantly higher than the 6.1 percent (5.6 percent) return of target firms that increase leverage less than the median.

To test whether other factors that are correlated with the leverage change also influence stock returns over this time period, we run a series of multivariate regressions, which are reported in Table X. In the univariate regression, Model 1, the coefficient of the change in leverage is positive and significant. In Models 2 through 5, which control for whether there was a change in the top management, whether or not the offer was terminated by the bidder, whether the takeover attempt was hostile or not, and whether a subsequent offer was made, the coefficient of the leverage change is still significantly positive.

---

[14] We replicate Tables VIII and IX with the difference in buy-and-hold returns between the targets and their matching benchmarks from the termination month to the earlier of five years or the delisting date as the dependent variable. Consistent with Tables VIII and IX, we find leverage and management turnover to be the only variables with significant coefficients.

[15] Most of the large debt offerings take place following the termination announcement. However, targets sometimes make statements like "negotiating with our bank to extend a credit line" or the new restructuring plan includes "raising a certain amount of short-term debt prior to the termination."

**Table X**

## Relation between Cumulative Prediction Errors during the Announcement-Termination Period and Change in Leverage

The relation between cumulative prediction errors during the announcement-termination period and change in leverage is examined. The dependent variable is the cumulative prediction errors during the announcement-termination period. It is calculated over five days before the announcement and five days after termination of the takeover attempt. Tests are conducted for a sample of 300 different firms with valid leverage data on COMPUSTAT. Leverage is measured as the book value of total debt scaled by the book value of total assets. Δ in leverage is measured between one year prior to the failed takeover attempt and one year afterward. CEO turnover is a dummy variable taking the value of 1 for a change in the top management and 0 otherwise. Bidder terminated is a dummy variable taking the value of 1 for non-bidder terminated takeover attempts and 0 for bidder terminated transactions. Hostile bid is a dummy variable taking the value of 1 for hostile takeovers and 0 otherwise. Subsequent is a dummy variable taking the value of 1 if the target firm receives a subsequent offer in the following five years, and 0 otherwise. The $t$-statistics in parentheses are based on the White adjusted standard errors.

| | Dependent Variable: Cumulative Prediction Errors during the Announcement-Termination Period | | | | |
| --- | --- | --- | --- | --- | --- |
| | (1) | (2) | (3) | (4) | (5) |
| Intercept | 0.0129 | −0.0053 | 0.0913 | −0.0060 | 0.0822 |
| | (0.62) | (−0.22) | (2.35)** | (−0.25) | (1.34) |
| Δ in leverage | 0.2036 | 0.2106 | 0.2207 | 0.1977 | 0.2156 |
| | (2.13)** | (2.07)** | (2.39)** | (2.01)** | (2.09)** |
| CEO turnover | | 0.0419 | | | −0.0216 |
| | | (0.92) | | | (−0.57) |
| Bidder terminated | | | −0.0330 | | −0.0395 |
| | | | (−2.47)** | | (−2.53)** |
| Hostile bid | | | | | 0.0166 |
| | | | | | (1.71)* |
| Subsequent | | | | 0.0774 | 0.1012 |
| | | | | (1.65)* | (1.62)* |
| $F$ | 4.547** | 2.844* | 5.556*** | 3.878** | 3.942** |
| $N$ | 300 | 265 | 296 | 300 | 265 |
| Adjusted $R^2$ | 0.0117 | 0.0137 | 0.0299 | 0.0212 | 0.0425 |

*, **, *** Statistically different from zero at the 10, 5, and 1 percent significance levels, respectively.

## VI. Leverage and Post-Termination Stock Price Performance

This section examines the long-run stock price performance of firms following the termination of takeover offers. We have two motivations for examining these long-run returns. First, we are interested in looking in more detail at whether the improvements described in previous sections translate into gains to shareholders. Our event study evidence suggests that at the time of the termination announcement, the terminated targets that increase leverage the most suffer lower losses. However, there have been a number of studies that suggest that stock prices often underreact when new information is announced.[16] Moreover, since the differences in stock returns between the two samples are small relative to the improvements subsequently realized by the firms that increase leverage the most, we have reasons to suspect that the stock price reaction on the termination announcement does not fully anticipate these improvements.

Our second motivation has to do with the question raised in the introduction regarding whether a target's management is acting in the shareholders' interests by turning down a takeover offer. In most cases, the immediate stock price reaction to the termination suggests that investors do not believe that the managers of terminated targets are acting in the shareholders' interests. However, a complete evaluation of the managers' choices requires an analysis of the long-term consequences of their decisions.

## A. Long-Run Performance

In order to examine the long-run stock price performance of target firms we follow each firm from the termination month until the earliest of the delisting month, the termination's fifth anniversary month, or December 1994. For every target, the buy-and-hold return is calculated over 60 months, starting from the termination month of the takeover attempt to the closing price five years afterward. If a target firm is delisted prior to its anniversary month, we truncate its total return on that month. Thus the percentage buy-and-hold return for firm $i$ is

$$R_{iT} = \left[ \prod_{t=+1}^{\min[T, delist]} (1 + r_{it}) + 1 \right] \times 100\%, \tag{2}$$

where $+1$ stands for one month after the termination month of the takeover attempt; $\min[T, delist]$ is the earliest of the last month of CRSP-listed trading, the end of the five-year window, or December 1994; and $r_{it}$ is the return for firm $i$ on month $t$.

For the purpose of comparison, each target firm is matched with a benchmark portfolio consisting of stocks in the same size quintile, the same book-to-market quintile, and the same momentum quintile as the target in the year before the event.[17] The composition of this portfolio is updated yearly to reflect changes in the target's characteristics. However, because we are simply rolling over the returns from this strategy without adding or subtracting money from the benchmark, over time the values of the benchmark and the target will diverge as their cumulative returns diverge.

---

[16] See for example, Loughran and Ritter (1995), Lakonishok and Vermaelen (1990), Ikenberry, Lakonishok, and Vermaelen (1995), and Michaely, Thaler, and Womack (1995).

[17] These are the benchmark portfolios used by Daniel et al. (1997) to evaluate mutual funds.

**Table XI**

**Holding Period Returns for Targets and their Matching Firms
during the Five Years Following Termination
of the Failed Takeover Attempt**

Holding-period returns (HPRs) are reported for 437 target firms in unsuccessful takeover attempts for the 1982–1991 period, obtained from *Mergerstat Review*, published by *W.T. Grimm.* HPRs are computed using the CRSP-listed closing price as the purchase price. The difference in holding period returns is calculated as $\Sigma_i(1 + R_{it}) - \Sigma_j(1 + R_{jt})$, where $R_{it}$ is the holding period return starting the month after the termination month of the takeover attempt until the earlier of the delisting date or the five-year anniversary of the takeover attempt, $R_{jt}$ is the holding period return on a matching firm. Each target firm is matched with a characteristic benchmarks portfolio of the same size quintile, the same book-to-market quintile, and the same momentum quintile in the year prior to the event. Percent negative is the percentage of negative returns.

|  | First Quartile | Median | Mean | Third Quartile | Percent Negative |
|---|---|---|---|---|---|
| *Panel A: All Target Firms (N = 437)* | | | | | |
| Target firms | −5.83% | 22.82% | 38.18% | 73.87% | |
| Matching firms | 6.94 | 29.05 | 35.85 | 54.26 | |
| Target matching | −35.96 | 0.64 | 2.33 | 37.89 | 49% |
| *Panel B: Target Firms with a Change in Debt Less than the Median Change (N = 121)* | | | | | |
| Target firms | 36.13% | 4.31% | 21.94% | 71.08% | |
| Matching firms | 6.82 | 29.09 | 36.11 | 51.87 | |
| Target-matching | −69.15 | −24.07 | −14.16 | 38.36 | 64% |
| *Panel C: Target Firms with a Change in Debt Greater than the Median Change (N = 119)* | | | | | |
| Target firms | 13.95% | 44.06% | 54.69% | 73.90% | |
| Matching firms | 7.07 | 31.04 | 35.58 | 55.47 | |
| Target-matching | −8.42 | 13.72 | 19.10 | 37.69 | 34% |

Panel A of Table XI reports the post-termination buy-and-hold long-run returns for the sample of target firms. For the entire sample these buy-and-hold returns have a mean (median) of 38.18 percent (22.82 percent), which should be compared to the long-run buy-and-hold returns for their matching benchmarks, which have a mean (median) of 35.85 percent (29.05 percent). In order to examine the effect of leverage on the long-run stock-price performance, we separately examine the long-term post-termination performance of targets with leverage changes above and below the median change. In Panel B, the mean (median) benchmark-adjusted buy-and-hold return for targets with a change in leverage less than the median change is −14.16 percent (−24.07 percent). Panel C reports the long-run post-termination performance of targets that increase leverage more than the median change. For this group the mean (median) benchmark-adjusted buy-and-hold return is 19.10 percent (13.72 percent).

*Leverage and Corporate Performance after Takeover Attempts*     575

One might conjecture that the higher long-run returns of the more levered targets are due to their higher betas (see Hamada (1972)). However, this does not appear to be the case. We measure beta for both groups over the five-year period under analysis. The mean (median) beta for targets that increase leverage more than the median change is 1.019 (1.023), which compares to 1.005 (1.003) for targets that increase leverage less than the median change. Perhaps the reduction in investment by the leverage-increasing firms reduces risk and thereby offsets the effect of leverage on their stocks' betas. In any event, we do not believe that it is differences in systematic risk that drive these differences in return.

One might also question whether we should conclude that investors underreacted to the leverage increase, when in many cases investors did not know about the leverage increase until many months after the takeover was terminated. To address this issue, we examine buy-and-hold returns of terminated targets from one year after the termination date, when the leverage change was definitely known, until five years after the termination date. We again find that the targets that increase their leverage the most outperform their benchmarks, in this case by 18.26 percent on average. In contrast, those terminated targets that increase leverage the least underperform their benchmarks by 12.25 percent on average. These results suggest that most of the excess returns associated with the leverage change following the termination date occurred subsequent to when the leverage change became known.

## B. Was the Termination Decision in the Target Shareholders' Interests?

In order to determine whether the termination decision was in the interests of the leverage-increasing target shareholders, we must ask whether the positive stock price performance following the failed takeover offsets the loss of the premium that investors would have received had these takeovers succeeded. To address this question we compute the returns realized by the shareholders of these firms with a hypothetical return they would have realized had they sold their shares to the acquirer at the stated offer price and invested the proceeds in the benchmarks described earlier.[18]

Our analysis indicates that one dollar invested just after the termination in the shares of targets with leverage increases that are above the median is worth, on average, \$1.5469 when the firm is either delisted (e.g., because of a takeover) or after five years. In contrast, this initial dollar would have

---

[18] Because the targets were offered the acquiring firm's stock in many of these takeover attempts it might make sense to consider the possibility that the target shareholders invest the proceeds of the takeover in the acquiring firm's stock rather than the benchmark portfolios. Loughran and Vijh (1997) examine the gains to receiving the acquiring firm's stock in successful offers and find that target shareholders who hold the acquiring firm's stock for five years following the takeover realize negative adjusted returns even after accounting for the takeover premium. Their results suggest that, had the takeover been successful, target shareholders may have realized returns that were considerably worse than is indicated by our benchmark portfolios.

been worth, on average, $1.12 if the firm had been taken over at the offer price, and this $1.12 would have subsequently grown, on average, to $1.5185 if it were invested in the target's benchmark and held either until the sooner of the target's delisting date or five years. This evidence indicates that these target managers realize approximately the same level of wealth keeping their firms independent as they would have realized by accepting the takeover offer. On the other hand, shareholders of targets with leverage increases below the median are clearly made worse off, on average from the termination of the takeover.

## C. Time-Series Analysis

The evidence presented in the previous subsection indicates that terminated targets that increase leverage more than the median perform considerably better than their characteristic-matched benchmarks. However, because of the difficulties associated with evaluating the statistical significance of long-term performance, we do not attempt to estimate whether the benchmark-adjusted long-term returns are statistically significant.[19]

To examine whether the excess returns of the leverage-increasing targets are statistically significant we perform a time-series analysis of an "investment portfolio" trading strategy. The trading strategy consists of forming separate portfolios of target firms and their matched counterparts over the entire period of the sample (January 1982 through December 1994). Each target firm is added to the target portfolio in the month following the termination of the failed takeover attempt and is kept in the portfolio for 60 months or until the firm ceases trading.

Similar to the last subsection, a characteristic-matched benchmark portfolio is formed for each target firm and these portfolios are then combined into a larger portfolio that mimics the characteristics of the target portfolio described above. The average monthly returns of this benchmark portfolio are then compared to the average monthly target portfolio returns. Assuming that the time-series of returns are independently and identically distributed allows us to test whether these monthly averages are reliably different.

Panel A of Table XII reports the mean monthly returns for portfolios of targets that change their leverage more than the median change. The results confirm the earlier finding that target firms that increase their leverage more than the median change outperform their matching counterparts. The monthly average difference between these target firms and their matching counterparts is 0.516 percent, which is significant at the 10 percent level. Panel B shows that target firms with changes in leverage that are below the median change have slightly lower returns than their matching counterparts.

---

[19] See for example, Barber and Lyon (1997), Kothari and Warner (1996), and Brav (1997).

**Table XII**

## Times-Series Analysis of Percentage Monthly Portfolio Returns Post Failed Takeover Attempt for Targets and Their Matched Firms from February 1982 to December 1994

Average monthly portfolio returns are reported for 437 target firms in unsuccessful takeover attempts and monthly returns for the portfolio of their matching firms from the period February 1982 to December 1994. Portfolio monthly returns are equally weighted averages of firm monthly returns. Target firms are added to their portfolio in the month following the termination of the takeover attempt and kept in the portfolio for 60 months or when the firm ceases trading. The matching firm is added to and removed from the matching-firm portfolio when its target firm is added or removed. Sample firms in unsuccessful takeover attempts for the 1982–1991 period are obtained from *Mergerstat Review*, published by *W.T. Grimm*. Returns are computed for calendar months using CRSP daily returns. Significance levels are based on *t*-tests.

| | Mean Monthly Returns (%) |
|---|---|
| **Panel A: Above-Median Change** | |
| Portfolio of target firms with above-median change | 1.652%*** |
| Portfolio of matching firms for target firms | 1.136%*** |
| Portfolio return to target firms minus the portfolio return to their matching firms | +0.516%* |
| **Panel B: Below-Median Change** | |
| Portfolio of target firms with below-median change | 0.949%*** |
| Portfolio of matching firms for target firms | 1.140%*** |
| Portfolio return to target firms minus the portfolio return to their matching firms | −0.191% |

*, **, *** Statistically different from zero at the 10, 5, and 1 percent significance levels, respectively.

## D. *Bradley, Desai, and Kim (1983) Revisited*

In an earlier study of rejected takeovers, Bradley et al. (1983) report that targets that reject takeover offers and are not subsequently taken over lose all of the initial announcement period gains. Their evidence suggests that there are no long-run performance improvements in firms that remain independent. This should be contrasted with the significant performance improvements observed for the firms in our sample that increase leverage.

Our sample is different from the Bradley et al. sample in two important respects. First, as we mentioned in the introduction, a larger percentage of our failed targets remain independent and this is especially true in the sample of firms that increase leverage the most. Second, we do not find that failed targets that remain independent perform poorly on average. In fact, those target firms that increase their leverage outperform their matching counterparts by 41.16 percent (median = 29.73 percent) over the following five years. For targets that do not increase their leverage, the mean difference is $-24.62$ percent (median $= -19.4$ percent), suggesting that these failed targets perform very much like the failed targets in the Bradley, Desai, and Kim sample.

## VII. Summary and Conclusions

Firms that increase leverage following an unsuccessful takeover attempt are subsequently taken over less often than those targets that do not increase leverage. Our results suggest that higher leverage decreases the probability of a firm being taken over because it commits the target's manager to make the improvements that would have been made by a potential raider. Specifically, those firms with the largest increase in leverage following a failed takeover reduce their levels of capital expenditures, sell off assets, reduce employment, increase focus, and increase their operating cash flows. These results are consistent with earlier evidence showing that the operating performance of firms improves following leverage-increasing recapitalizations (Kaplan (1989), Smith (1990), and Denis and Denis (1993)), and suggesting that leverage increases are associated with a change in incentives.[20] In contrast, failed targets that increase their leverage the least show insignificant changes in investment expenditures, assets sales, employment, and focus and show no improvements in their operating cash flows.

Our evidence suggests that investors anticipate the positive effects associated with higher leverage. During the period between the initial takeover announcement and the termination announcement the stock price performance is significantly less negative for those failed targets that increase leverage the most. However, stock prices of the leverage-increasing targets outperform their benchmarks for five years following the termination, which implies that investors initially underestimated the extent to which the values of these firms were improved. This evidence of long-term abnormal stock price performance indicates that, despite the initial drop at the time of the termination announcement, target managers may have been acting in the interests of shareholders when they turned down the takeover offer.

This evidence of underreaction is consistent with a growing body of research that suggests that investors underreact to both leverage-increasing and leverage-decreasing announcements (see, e.g., the articles cited in footnote 16). Daniel, Hirshleifer, and Subramanyam (1998) provide a behavioral

---

[20] However, Lowenstein (1985) suggests that the improvements following LBOs are due to the fact that managers choose to instigate LBOs only when they have favorable information about future productivity. Kaplan (1989) and Smith (1990) recognize this potential information bias and provide indirect evidence suggesting that superior management information is unlikely to account for the observed gains from management buyouts. First, Kaplan compares the prebuyout financial projections managers give to shareholders with the actual postbuyout realizations. He finds no evidence that the projections are low. He also finds that management turnover at the time of the buyout is unusually high. He concludes that none of these findings support the "managers' private information" hypothesis. Smith finds that operating returns do not increase after the failed management buyout attempts. She also finds that whether management initiated the MBO or not is not a factor in the postbuyout performance.

*Leverage and Corporate Performance after Takeover Attempts* 579

explanation for this underreaction. They argue that investors are overconfident about their abilities to value the stocks prior to the announcements and thus place too little weight on the information conveyed by the leverage changes. Although our results are consistent with the Daniel, Hirshleifer, and Subramanyam theory, they also suggest an alternative explanation: perhaps investors simply failed to anticipate the productivity improvements that tend to be associated with leverage increases.

## REFERENCES

Agrawal, Anup, and Ralph Walkling, 1994, Executive careers and compensation surrounding takeover bids, *Journal of Finance* 49, 985–1014.

Asquith Paul, 1983, Merger bids, uncertainty, and stockholder returns, *Journal of Financial Economics* 11, 51–83.

Barber, Brad, and John Lyon, 1996, Detecting abnormal operating performance: The empirical power and specification of test-statistics, *Journal of Financial Economics* 41, 359–400.

Barber, Brad, and John Lyon, 1997, Detecting long-run abnormal stock returns: The empirical power and specification of test-statistics, *Journal of Financial Economics* 43, 341–372.

Berger, Phillip, and Eli Ofek, 1998, Causes and consequences of corporate refocusing programs, *Review of Financial Studies*, forthcoming.

Berger, Phillip, Eli Ofek, and David Yermack, 1996, Managerial entrenchment and capital structure, *Journal of Finance* 52, 1411–1438.

Bhagat, Sanjai, Andrei Shleifer, and Robert Vishny, 1990, Hostile takeovers in the 1980s: The return to corporate specialization, Brookings papers on economic activity: Microeconomics, 1–72.

Bradley, Michael, 1980, Interfirm tender offers and the market for corporate control, *Journal of Business* 53, 345–376.

Bradley, Michael, Anand Desai, and E. Han Kim, 1983, The rationale behind interfirm tender offers: Information or synergy?, *Journal of Financial Economics* 11, 183–206.

Brav, Alon, 1997, Inference in long-horizon event studies: A parametric-bootstrap approach, Working paper, University of Chicago.

Daniel, Kent, Mark Grinblatt, Sheridan Titman, and Russ Wermers, 1997, Measuring fund performance with characteristic based benchmarks, *Journal of Finance* 52, 1035–1058.

Daniel, Kent, David Hirshleifer, and Avanidhar Subramanyam, 1998, Investor psychology and security market under- and overreactions, *Journal of Finance* 53, 1839–1885.

Denis, David, 1990, Defensive changes in corporate payout policy: Share repurchases and special dividends, *Journal of Finance* 45, 1433–1456.

Denis, David J., and Diane K. Denis, 1993, Managerial discretion, organizational structure, and corporate performance: A study of leveraged recapitalization, *Journal of Accounting and Economics* 16, 209–236.

Denis, David J., and Diane K. Denis, 1995, Performance changes following top management dismissals, *Journal of Finance* 50, 1029–1057.

Denis, David J., Diane K. Denis, and Atulya Sarin, 1997, Agency problems, equity ownership, and corporate diversification, *Journal of Finance* 52, 135–160.

Denis, David, and J. Serrano, 1996, Active investors and management turnover following unsuccessful control contests, *Journal of Financial Economics* 40, 239–266.

Dodd, Peter, 1980, Mergers proposals, management discretion, and stockholder wealth, *Journal of Financial Economics* 8, 105–138.

Fama, Eugene F., and Kenneth French, 1995, Size and book-to-market factors in earnings and returns, *Journal of Finance* 50, 131–155.

Grossman, Sanford, and Oliver Hart, 1982, Corporate financial structure and managerial incentives; in J. McCall, ed.: *The Economics of Information and Uncertainty* (University of Chicago Press, Chicago, Ill.).

Hamada, Robert S., 1972, The effect of the firm's capital structure on the systematic risk of common stocks, *Journal of Finance* 27, 435–452.

Harris, Milton, and Artur Raviv, 1988, Corporate control contests and capital structure, *Journal of Financial Economics* 20, 55–86.

Hotchkiss, Edith, 1995, Postbankruptcy performance and management turnover, *Journal of Finance* 50, 3–21.

Ikenberry, David, Josef Lakonishok, and Theo Vermaelen, 1995, Market underreaction to open market share repurchases, *Journal of Financial Economics* 39, 181–208.

Israel, Ronen, 1991, Capital structure and the market for corporate control: The defensive role of debt financing, *Journal of Finance* 46, 1391–1410.

Jensen, Michael, 1986, Agency costs of free cash flow, corporate finance and takeovers, *American Economic Review* 76, 323–329.

Kaplan, Steven, 1989, The effects of management buyouts on operating performance and value, *Journal of Financial Economics* 24, 217–254.

Kothari, S. P., and Jerold Warner, 1997, Measuring long-horizon security price performance, *Journal of Financial Economics* 43, 301–340.

Lakonishok, Josef, and Theo Vermaelen, 1990, Anomalous price behavior around repurchase tender offers, *Journal of Finance* 45, 455–478.

Lang, Larry, Eli Ofek, and René Stulz, 1996, Leverage, investment, and firm growth, *Journal of Financial Economics* 40, 3–29.

Loughran, Tim, and Jay R. Ritter, 1995, The new issues puzzle, *Journal of Finance* 50, 23–51.

Loughran, Tim, and Anand Vijh, 1997, Do long-term shareholders benefit from corporate acquisitions?, *Journal of Finance,* 52, 1765–1790.

Lowenstein, Louis, 1985, Management buyouts, *Columbia Law Review* 85, 730–784.

Maksimovic, Vojislav, and Sheridan Titman, 1991, Financial policy and reputation for product quality, *Review of Financial Studies* 4, 175–199.

Michaely, Roni, Richard Thaler, and Kent Womack, 1995, Price reactions to dividend initiations and omissions: Overreaction or drift?, *Journal of Finance* 50, 573–608.

Morck, Randall, Andrei Shleifer, and Robert Vishny, 1988, Management ownership and market valuation: An empirical analysis, *Journal of Financial Economics* 20, 293–316.

Myers, Stewart, 1977, Determinants of corporate borrowing, *Journal of Financial Economics* 5, 147–175.

Penman, Stephen, 1991, An evaluation of accounting rate of return, *Journal of Accounting, Auditing and Finance* 6, 233–255.

Ravenscraft, David, and F. M. Scherer, 1987, Mergers, selloffs and economic efficiency (The Brookings Institution, Washington, D.C.).

Ross, Stephen, 1977, The determination of financial structure: The incentive-signaling approach, *Bell Journal of Economics* 8, 23–40.

Smith, Abbie, 1990, Corporate ownership structure and performance: The case of management buyouts, *Journal of Financial Economics* 27, 143–164.

Stein, Jeremy C., 1988, Takeover threats and managerial myopia, *Journal of Political Economy* 96, 61–80.

Stulz, René, 1988, Managerial control of voting rights: Financing policies and the market of corporate control, *Journal of Financial Economics* 20, 25–54.

Stulz, René, 1990, Managerial discretion and optimal financing policies, *Journal of Financial Economics* 26, 3–28.

Zweibel, Jeffrey, 1996, Dynamic capital structure under management entrenchment, *American Economic Review* 86, 1197–1215.

# E
# Consequences for Valuation, Product Markets and Firm Survival

# [8]

Journal of Financial Economics 39 (1995) 131–157

# Equity ownership and the two faces of debt

John J. McConnell*,[a], Henri Servaes[b]

[a] *Krannert Graduate School of Management, Purdue University, West Lafayette, IN 47907, USA*
[b] *Kenan-Flagler Business School, University of North Carolina at Chapel Hill, Chapel Hill, NC 27599, USA*

(Received November 1992; final version received December 1994)

## Abstract

We empirically investigate the relation between corporate value, leverage, and equity ownership. For 'high-growth' firms corporate value is negatively correlated with leverage, whereas for 'low-growth' firms corporate value is positively correlated with leverage. The results also hint that the allocation of equity ownership among insiders, institutions, blockholders, and atomistic outside shareholders is of marginally greater significance in low-growth than in high-growth firms. The overall interpretation of the results is that debt policy and equity ownership structure 'matter' and that the way in which they matter differs between firms with many and firms with few positive net present value projects.

*Key words*: Capital structure; Equity ownership; Growth opportunities
*JEL classification*: G32

## 1. Introduction

The positive and negative attributes of debt as a corporate financing instrument, as perceived both by financial scholars and perhaps to a lesser extent by practitioners, have evolved over the past several decades. In the aftermath of the

*Corresponding author.

We thank Jennifer Conrad, Werner De Bondt, David Denis, Michael Jensen, Wayne Marr, William Parke, Gordon Phillips, Jerry Thursby, Cynthia Van Hulle, Marc Zenner, an anonymous referee, and seminar participants at Clemson University, the Katholieke Universiteit Leuven, and the University of North Carolina at Chapel Hill for helpful comments. Carl Ackermann has provided excellent research assistance. Some of the work on this paper was completed when the second author was visiting the University of Chicago and the Katholieke Universiteit Leuven, Belgium.

132     *J.J. McConnell, H. Servaes/Journal of Financial Economics 39 (1995) 131–157*

Great Depression and throughout the 1930s and 1940s, debt was predominantly viewed as a clearly evil, but occasionally necessary, ingredient of a well-managed corporation's capital structure, but even then only if used in careful moderation.[1] With the publication of the famous Modigliani and Miller (M&M) irrelevance proposition in 1958, academics' attitudes toward debt began to soften. This softening of attitude turned to a warm embrace in 1963, when M&M published their 'tax correction' paper. The embrace derived from, and was solely dependent on, the tax advantages of debt financing. Furthermore, the warmth of the embrace for debt financing was limited by the costs, especially bankruptcy costs, associated with it. If the deductibility of interest payments for tax purposes were ever to be rescinded, then presumably debt would once again assume its posture of an inferior financing instrument.

More recently, however, scholars have broadened their perspectives on debt financing, and have identified other virtues and vices associated with it as a corporate financing instrument.[2] Much of this attention has focused on the role of debt in influencing corporate investment decisions. On one side of the coin, Myers (1977) demonstrates that 'too much' debt induces managers acting in shareholders' interests to forego positive net present value projects. This phenomenon has been labeled the 'underinvestment' problem of debt financing. That is, for firms with 'growth opportunities' debt has a negative effect on the value of the firm. On the other side of the coin, Jensen (1986) argues that when firms have more internally generated funds than positive net present value investment opportunities, the presence of debt in the firm's capital structure forces managers to pay out funds that might otherwise have been invested in negative net present value projects. This argument requires an additional ingredient, however, and that is that managers are rewarded for expanding the scale of the firm, and therefore have an incentive to do so, even if it is detrimental to shareholders' interests. In this framework, managers have both the incentive and the opportunity (i.e., excess cash flow) to undertake wasteful investment projects. This phenomenon has been labeled the 'overinvestment problem'. The overinvestment problem can, however, be curtailed if managers are forced to pay out excess funds to service debt. That is, for firms with more internally generated funds than investment opportunities, debt financing has a positive effect on the value of the firm.

Fundamentally, the overinvestment problem arises because of a separation between corporate equity ownership and management. In Jensen's analysis, managers have an incentive to increase the size of the firm at shareholders' expense. They will do so, of course, unless their interests coincide with those of shareholders for some other reason. One way in which managers' and

---

[1] See, for example, Donaldson (1963).

[2] For a comprehensive review of the recent literature, see Harris and Raviv (1991).

*J.J. McConnell, H. Servaes/Journal of Financial Economics 39 (1995) 131–157* 133

shareholders' interests coincide is if they are one and the same. Equity ownership on the part of managers can align shareholders' and managers' interests, and thereby reduce the overinvestment problem.

Concern about the misallocation of resources that follows from the separation of ownership and management is, of course, not new. It can be traced, at least, to Berle and Means (1932). There are numerous, more recent contributors to the debate regarding the way in which the allocation of equity ownership between outsiders (i.e., atomistic shareholders) and insiders (i.e., managers) influences corporate value. They include, for example, Morck, Shleifer, and Vishny (MSV, 1988). As with debt, MSV argue that the managers' ownership of equity can have both a positive and a negative effect on the value of the firm. To put it simply, at low levels of management equity ownership, an increase in their shareholdings more closely aligns managers' and outside shareholders' interests. As insider ownership increases beyond some point, however, further increases effectively insulate managers from outside shareholder demands. At this point, managers can allocate corporate resources in their own self-interest regardless of the effects on outside shareholders.

Recent empirical contributions by Holderness and Sheehan (1988), MSV (1988), McConnell and Servaes (1990), Hermalin and Weisbach (1991), Phelps (1991), and Kole (1994) have explored the relation between corporate value and the allocation of shares among corporate insiders and other shareholders. While the results differ across the various studies, a consensus interpretation is that the allocation of equity ownership matters.

Despite the apparent theoretical connection between the roles of equity ownership and debt in determining the allocation of corporate resources, the empirical studies cited above have given only peripheral attention to the relation between corporate value, debt, and equity ownership. This paper seeks to fill that void. For the years 1976, 1986, and 1988, we separate large samples of firms into two categories, those with low growth opportunities and those with high growth opportunities. For each sample, we then investigate the relation between Tobin's $Q$, debt, and equity ownership. We find that for firms with few growth opportunities, $Q$ is positively correlated with the level of debt financing. For firms with high growth opportunities, $Q$ is negatively correlated with the level of debt financing. These results are consistent with the hypothesis that debt can have either a positive or negative effect on the value of the firm, depending upon the availability of positive net present value projects to the firm. As regards equity ownership, when $Q$ is regressed against the fractions of shares owned by corporate insiders, institutional investors, and large-block shareholders, we find that the coefficients of these ownership variables are typically, but not always, larger for low-growth firms than for high-growth firms. We interpret these results as weakly supporting the conjecture that the allocation of equity ownership among corporate insiders and other investors is of greater importance in firms with fewer profitable investment opportunities.

134     *J.J. McConnell, H. Servaes/Journal of Financial Economics 39 (1995) 131–157*

Section 2 discusses in more detail related theoretical and empirical work, and develops the hypotheses to be tested. Section 3 describes the data employed in the analysis. Section 4 presents the results, Section 5 comments on the results, and Section 6 concludes.

## 2. Hypotheses

### 2.1. Growth and debt

Building on Myers (1977) and Jensen (1986), Stulz (1990) argues that debt can have both a positive and negative effect on the value of the firm (even in the absence of corporate taxes and bankruptcy costs). He develops a model in which debt financing can both alleviate the overinvestment problem and exacerbate the underinvestment problem. In Stulz's model, however, the origin of the underinvestment problem is fundamentally different from Myers'. Stulz assumes that managers have no equity ownership in the firm and that they receive utility from managing a larger firm, and, as a consequence, have an incentive to increase the size of the firm. This incentive leads managers to undertake negative net present value projects. Shareholders recognize this incentive.

The solution to the problem is twofold: First, shareholders force managers to issue debt. Second, shareholders, recognizing that managers have an incentive to overstate investment opportunities, are unwilling to contribute equity funds in the future. It turns out that the seeds of the underinvestment problem lie in the solution to the overinvestment problem. Because the firm has issued debt, managers are forced to pay out funds in the future. The net result is that financial resources available to management are limited, and that there are some occasions on which managers are forced to forego positive net present value investment opportunities. The tradeoff between the positive and negative effects of debt financing leads to an optimal level of debt that maximizes the value of the firm.

The element that Myers, Jensen, and Stulz have in common is that each focuses on a connection between the firm's investment opportunity set and the effect of debt on the value of the firm. Presumably, both the positive and negative effects of debt are present for all firms. However, a reasonable conjecture is that for firms with plentiful growth opportunities, the negative effect will predominate because, in at least some circumstances, debt forces managers to pass up positive net present value projects. That is, for firms with many positive net present value projects, the effect of debt on the value of the firm is negative. Similarly, a reasonable conjecture is that for firms with few growth opportunities, the positive effect will predominate because, in at least some circumstances, debt prevents managers from taking on negative net present value projects.

*J.J. McConnell, H. Servaes/Journal of Financial Economics 39 (1995) 131–157* 135

That is, for firms with few positive net present value projects, the effect of debt on the value of the firm is positive.

Recently, Lang, Ofek, and Stulz (1994) have explored the relation between leverage and future growth for all *Compustat* firms over the period 1970–89. They find a strong negative relation between leverage (book value of debt over total assets) and subsequent growth in number of employees and capital expenditures, but only for firms with poor investment opportunities (i.e., Tobin's $Q < 1$). Consistent with Jensen (1986) and Stulz (1990), these results suggest that leverage prevents firms with poor investment opportunities from overinvesting.

## 2.2. Growth and inside equity ownership

Morck, Shleifer, and Vishny (1988) begin with the presumption that managers respond to two opposing forces, and that the relation between ownership and corporate value depends upon which force dominates over any particular range of managerial equity ownership. Their analysis leads them to the conclusion that the relation between the value of the firm and inside equity ownership is nonlinear, but that the precise form of the relation cannot be predicted a priori. Furthermore, it is possible that the relation differs across different types of firms. They urge that the data be the judge.

Stulz (1988) also predicts that the relation between corporate value and the fraction of shares held by managers is nonlinear. He arrives at this conclusion by a different route, however. In Stulz's model, because managers receive utility from holding their positions with the firm, they resist any outside takeover attempt that would dislodge them from their managerial positions. The most powerful deterrent to an outside takeover is managers' ownership of shares. To be successful, the premium that a bidder must pay to acquire the firm increases as the fraction of shares held by managers increases. Concurrently, of course, as the fraction of shares held by managers increases, the probability that the takeover attempt will be successful declines. The value of the firm is a function of the premium that a bidder must pay to be successful and of the probability of the bidder's success. Because the first of these terms is a positive function of managerial equity ownership and the second is a negative function of managerial equity ownership, the value of the firm first increases, and then decreases as the fraction of shares held by managers increases.

MSV (1988) estimate the relation between corporate value and insider ownership. For the year 1980, using a sample of 371 *Fortune 500* firms; they estimate a piecewise linear regression in which Tobin's $Q$ is the dependent variable and the fraction of shares held by corporate insiders (plus other control variables) is the independent variable. Their regressions indicate that $Q$ increases as inside equity ownership rises up to 5 percent, then decreases as inside ownership increases to 25 percent. Finally, $Q$ increases slightly again for inside ownership levels above 25 percent. McConnell and Servaes (1990) provide further evidence

136        *J.J. McConnell, H. Servaes/Journal of Financial Economics 39 (1995) 131–157*

on the relation between $Q$ and the allocation of share ownership between corporate insiders and atomistic outside shareholders. In doing so, they recognize two other potentially important identifiable categories of corporate investors, large-block shareholders, and institutional investors.

Based upon Stulz (1988), McConnell and Servaes estimate a quadratic regression in which Tobin's $Q$ is the dependent variable. Four independent variables are employed to represent the allocation of shares among the four constituent categories of investors (along with four control variables): (1) the fraction of shares owned by corporate insiders (i.e., officers and members of the board), (2) the fraction of shares owned by corporate insiders, squared, (3) a dummy variable to indicate the presence of a large-block shareholder,[3] and (4) the fraction of shares held by institutional investors. The regression is estimated for a sample of 1,173 firms for 1976 and a sample of 1,093 firms for 1986. In these regressions, the coefficient of the fraction of shares held by insiders is positive, and the coefficient of this variable squared is negative. Further, the coefficient of the fraction of shares held by institutional investors is positive and significant, but the coefficient of block ownership is never significantly different from zero. In short, McConnell and Servaes report a significant curvilinear relation between $Q$ and the fraction of shares held by corporate insiders. Thus, their results are consistent with the empirical predictions of MSV and Stulz.

Note, however, that in neither the MSV nor the Stulz analyses do growth opportunities play a role. Thus, their analyses make no direct predictions as to whether the relation between corporate value and equity ownership differs between those firms with many investment growth opportunities and those with few. In that regard, our empirical analysis can be viewed as an exploration to determine whether the specific form of the relation between $Q$ and equity ownership differs between firms with few and those with many growth opportunities.

Before doing so, however, we can make some predictions about the relative importance of equity ownership in high- and low-growth firms. Consider the following: The allocation of share ownership between insiders and other shareholders matters when the interests of the two groups are not aligned. If we assume, as suggested by Jensen (1986) and Stulz (1990), that managers receive utility from increasing the size of the firm, even if it is contrary to shareholders' interests, then the potential for divergence of interests is greatest in firms with fewer profitable growth opportunities. That is, managers prefer to manage a larger firm. If the firm has few profitable growth opportunities, the only way to increase its size is to undertake negative net present value projects. Thus, regardless of the specific form of the empirical relation between corporate value

---

[3]When the fraction of shares held by the largest single blockholder and the fraction of shares held by the blockholders in aggregate were used, there was no difference in results.

and the fraction of shares held by insiders, it is reasonable to predict that if the allocation of equity ownership matters, it will be more important in firms with fewer growth opportunities. The empirical prediction, then, is that the relation between $Q$ and the fraction of shares held by insiders is stronger for firms with relatively fewer growth opportunities.

## 2.3. Growth, blockholders, and institutional investors

Of course, atomistic shareholders, managers, and members of the board of directors are not the only identifiable categories of equity owners. Two other investor categories have been identified as having a potentially important role in determining the allocation of corporate resources, institutional investors and large-block shareholders. Pound (1988) proposes that institutional investors may have either a positive or negative effect on the value of the firm. The positive effect occurs because institutional investors may be more efficient monitors of managers than are atomistic shareholders. The negative effect happens because institutional investors may collude with corporate managers against the best interests of atomistic shareholders, either because it is in the institutional investor's interest to do so, or because they are coerced into doing so by corporate managers. McConnell and Servaes (1990) report that the relation between $Q$ and the fraction of shares held by institutional investors is positive and statistically significant across their full sample of firms for both 1976 and 1986. They interpret this result as being consistent with the efficient monitoring hypothesis. Pound makes no prediction as to whether the role of institutional investors differs between high- and low-growth firms. As with equity ownership by insiders, if managers' and outside shareholders' interests are more likely to diverge in firms with few growth opportunities, and if the efficient monitoring hypothesis is the appropriate interpretation of the positive relation between $Q$ and the fraction of shares held by institutional investors, then presumably this relation is stronger for firms with fewer growth opportunities.

Shleifer and Vishny (1986) develop a model of the relation between the value of the firm and the presence of a large-block shareholder. In their model, the block shareholder takes an active role in the activities of the firm and, if the need arises, takes control of the firm and replaces poorly performing managers. McConnell and Servaes (1990) analyze the relation between $Q$ and large-block shareholders, employing several different measures of block ownership. In none of their specifications, for either 1976 or 1986, is the relation between $Q$ and block ownership statistically significant. They do not find evidence to support the hypothesis that blockholders are important monitors of corporate managers. They do not, however, separate their sample into firms with many and those with few profitable growth opportunities. If the blockholder monitoring hypothesis is correct, it is more likely to show up in firms with fewer profitable

138        *J.J. McConnell, H. Servaes/Journal of Financial Economics 39 (1995) 131–157*

growth opportunities. The prediction is that if blockholders perform an important monitoring function, the empirical relation between $Q$ and the fraction of shares held by blockholders is stronger for firms with fewer growth opportunities.

## 3. Data

In constructing our database, we begin with the data employed by McConnell and Servaes (1990). Their 1976 sample includes 1,173 firms and their 1986 sample includes 1,093 firms listed on the New York Stock Exchange (NYSE) or the American Stock Exchange (AMEX). For each firm, data on insider, institutional, and block equity ownership are taken from the *Value Line Investment Survey*. Data employed to estimate $Q$ are taken from *Compustat* and Hall (1990). The procedure used to construct these samples is described in McConnell and Servaes. For this paper, these samples are supplemented with a sample of firms from 1988. The starting point for assembly of the 1988 sample is all nonfinancial firms listed on the NYSE or the AMEX that are contained in the *Compustat* database for 1988. To be included in the sample for further analysis, we require that sufficient data be available to compute the firm's Tobin's $Q$. This yields a sample of 1,943 firms. For each of these firms, Tobin's $Q$ is computed as the market value of common stock, preferred stock, and debt divided by the replacement value of assets. Leverage is estimated as the market value of long-term debt divided by the replacement value of assets $(DEBT/RV)$.[4] Data on equity ownership are taken from *Disclosure, Inc.* These data include the number of shares held at year-end 1988 by corporate officers and members of the board of directors, the number of shares held by blockholders (where a blockholder is any shareholder who owns at least 5 percent of the outstanding stock and who is not an officer or director), and the number of shares held by institutional investors (where institutional investors include insurance companies, commercial banks, investment companies, pension funds, educational foundations, and trust funds). Firms are eliminated in this process if they are not listed on the *Disclosure* database, if the number of shares reported in the individual categories of equity ownership sums to a total greater than the reported number of shares outstanding, or if the *Disclosure* data are incomplete This requirement reduces the sample to 830 firms. Consistent with McConnell and Servaes (1990), to obviate problems with outlier observations, firms were further deleted if their $Q$ ratios exceeded 6.0 or were less than 0.16. This screen reduced the sample to 826 firms.

---

[4]A variation of the Lindenberg and Ross (1981) algorithm is used to compute the market value of the firm and the replacement value of its assets. A description of the procedure used to compute these values is available from the authors.

*J.J. McConnell, H. Servaes/Journal of Financial Economics 39 (1995) 131–157* 139

We analyze the difference in the relation between $Q$, debt, and equity ownership for firms with many and those with few profitable growth opportunities. To distinguish between these two types of firms, we use the firm's price-to-operating-earnings $(P/E)$ ratio. This ratio is calculated by dividing the stock price at the end of 1976, 1986, and 1988 by operating earnings per share for these years, as reported on the *Compustat* database. Because operating earnings are calculated before interest payments, the earnings number is unaffected by leverage. Firms with negative operating earnings are discarded from the sample; 20 firms are deleted for 1976, 46 are deleted for 1986, and 48 are deleted for 1988.

For each year, firms are ranked according to their end-of-year $P/E$ ratio. The one-third of the firms with the highest $P/E$ ratio are placed into a high-growth sample and the one-third with the lowest $P/E$ ratio into a low-growth sample.[5] Thus, there is a high-growth sample and a low-growth sample for 1976, 1986, and 1988. Descriptive statistics for each category of firms are displayed in Table 1.

By construction, the differences in the $P/E$ ratios between the high- and low-growth samples are dramatic. For example, for the 1988 low-growth sample, the average $P/E$ ratio is 2.70; for the high-growth sample it is 11.02. Similarly, for each year, the average $Q$ ratios are dramatically different for the high- and low-growth samples; $Q$'s for the high-growth samples are always much greater than those for the low-growth samples. The next four rows of the table give data on leverage and equity ownership. In each year, leverage is significantly greater for the low-growth sample than it is for the high-growth sample. These data evidence a negative relation between growth opportunities and leverage. However, these data are also consistent with the joint conjecture that for firms with many positive net present value projects (i.e., the high $P/E$ sample), the negative effects of debt on their investment opportunities are more consequential than are the positive effects. For firms with few positive net present value projects (i.e., the low $P/E$ sample), the positive effects of debt are greater than the negative effects. This joint conjecture would predict a relatively higher use of debt for low-growth firms than for high-growth firms, and it is this effect that gives rise to the apparent negative relation between growth and debt for the overall sample. To distinguish between these possibilities, we estimate separate cross-sectional regressions for the high- and low-growth samples. If our conjecture is correct, the correlation between $Q$ and leverage will be negative for the high-growth sample and positive for the low-growth sample.

The rest of our story has to do with the role of equity ownership in high- and low-growth firms. The three equity ownership variables are the percent of shares

---

[5]We repeated all our analyses using the top and bottom quartiles of the growth classification. In general, these results are more supportive of our hypotheses than the results based on the classification into three equal groups presented in this paper. These results are available from the authors upon request.

140    J.J. McConnell, H. Servaes/Journal of Financial Economics 39 (1995) 131–157

Table 1

Summary statistics for 1976, 1986, and 1988 for samples of firms classified into high- and low-growth samples according to their *P/E* ratio. Sample means are on the first line of each row and medians are in parentheses below. *P*-values are reported for tests of equality of the means and medians of the high- and low-growth samples. All firms are listed on the NYSE or the AMEX. Balance sheet data are obtained from *Compustat*; ownership data are obtained from *Value Line* for the 1976 and 1986 samples and from *Disclosure* for the 1988 sample.

| Variable | 1976 Low-growth | 1976 High-growth | 1976 P-value diff. | 1986 Low-growth | 1986 High-growth | 1986 P-value diff. | 1988 Low-growth | 1988 High-growth | 1988 P-value diff. |
|---|---|---|---|---|---|---|---|---|---|
| Sample size | 330 | 331 | | 292 | 292 | | 259 | 260 | |
| P/E | 1.94 | 6.62 | 0.00 | 3.14 | 10.84 | 0.00 | 2.70 | 11.02 | 0.00 |
| | (1.99) | (5.41) | (0.00) | (3.28) | (9.24) | (0.00) | (2.83) | (7.99) | (0.00) |
| Q | 0.674 | 1.309 | 0.00 | 0.905 | 1.781 | 0.00 | 0.913 | 1.58 | 0.00 |
| | (0.817) | (1.155) | (0.00) | (0.897) | (1.547) | (0.00) | (0.904) | (1.35) | (0.00) |
| DEBT/RV (%) | 20.98 | 11.19 | 0.00 | 29.41 | 15.39 | 0.00 | 30.69 | 15.95 | 0.00 |
| | (20.20) | (10.38) | (0.00) | (27.99) | (10.70) | (0.00) | (29.88) | (12.37) | (0.00) |
| INOWN (%) | 12.88 | 14.90 | 0.14 | 8.54 | 13.97 | 0.00 | 6.37 | 11.10 | 0.00 |
| | (5.00) | (7.00) | (0.17) | (1.50) | (9.05) | (0.00) | (0.75) | (4.30) | (0.00) |
| LB (%) | 3.23 | 3.36 | 0.89 | 6.27 | 5.99 | 0.81 | 11.64 | 12.62 | 0.52 |
| | (0.00) | (0.00) | (0.75) | (0.00) | (0.00) | (0.97) | (5.56) | (6.20) | (0.58) |
| INSTO (%) | 3.56 | 6.36 | 0.00 | 33.65 | 40.97 | 0.00 | 34.95 | 37.48 | 0.16 |
| | (1.74) | (4.97) | (0.00) | (32.22) | (41.32) | (0.00) | (32.63) | (37.90) | (0.15) |
| RV ($million) | 1116 | 1272 | 0.45 | 5891 | 1458 | 0.00 | 5327 | 1120 | 0.00 |
| | (294) | (426) | (0.01) | (1678) | (485) | (0.00) | (1373) | (265) | (0.00) |

P/E:      end-of-year price divided by operating earnings per share during the year.
Q:      market value of common stock, preferred stock, and debt divided by the estimated replacement value of assets.
DEBT/RV:   estimated market value of debt divided by the estimated replacement value of assets.
INOWN:   fraction of common stock (in percent) owned by corporate officers and members of the board of directors.
LB:      fraction of common stock (in percent) owned by all outside shareholders who own more than 5% of the common stock.
INSTO:   fraction of common stock (in percent) owned by institutional investors.
RV:      estimated replacement value of assets.

owned by corporate insiders (*INOWN*), the percent of shares held by all blockholders (*LB*), and the percent of shares held by institutional investors (*INSTO*). In each year, the mean (median) percentage of shares owned by corporate insiders and institutional investors is greater in the high-growth than in the low-growth sample. The difference is statistically significant in two of the three years. The percentage of shares held by blockholders is not noticeably different between the high- and low-growth samples. Contrary to our conjecture, these data could suggest that equity ownership is more important in high-growth than in low-growth firms. However, these univariate tests do not control for other factors that may influence concentration of equity ownership, such as the size of the firm. Table 1 shows that in two of the three years high-growth firms are significantly smaller in their replacement value of assets, and that these are the two years for which insider ownership is significantly lower in the low-growth sample. If capital constraints inhibit managers in larger firms from acquiring a large fraction of the stock, our univariate results might emerge, even though insider ownership is more important in low-growth firms. To investigate this possibility, we estimate cross-sectional regressions between firm value and insider ownership. If our story is correct, we expect insider ownership to be more highly correlated with firm value for low-growth firms than for high-growth firms. The same is true for the percentage of shares held by institutional investors and by blockholders.

## 4. Regression results

### 4.1. Value and leverage

The functional form of the regressions that we estimate follows McConnell and Servaes (1990). Specifically, the dependent variable in the regressions is Tobin's $Q$. The independent variables are *DEBT/RV*, *INOWN*, *INOWN*-squared, *LB*, *INSTO*, *R&D/RV*, *ADV/RV*, and *RV*. The variables *R&D/RV*, *ADV/RV*, and *RV* are included as control variables because they have been shown elsewhere to be statistically significant in explaining $Q$. As a preliminary step in the analysis, the quadratic regression estimated in McConnell and Servaes (1990) for 1976 and 1986 is estimated with the full 1988 sample. The results are remarkably similar to those reported for 1976 and 1986. The coefficient of *INOWN* is positive and significant ($t = 3.24$), and the coefficient of *INOWN*-squared is negative and significant ($t = -2.53$). These results are consistent with MSV (1988), who predict a nonlinear relation between corporate value and ownership of equity by insiders, and with Stulz's (1988) more specific prediction of a curvilinear relation between corporate value and inside equity ownership. Additionally, as it is for 1976 and 1986, the 1988 coefficient of *INSTO* is positive and significant ($t = 3.16$). Different from 1976 and 1986, the

1988 regressions show a significant positive relation between $Q$ and the fraction of shares controlled by large blockholders ($t = 2.61$). Overall, the results indicate that the distribution of equity ownership is related to the value of the firm; the consistency of the relation between $Q$ and equity ownership across years is, at a minimum, reassuring.[6]

The more important question for this paper, though, is whether the relation between corporate value and debt differs between those firms with few and those with many growth opportunities. In the regressions, corporate value is standardized by the replacement value of assets (i.e., market value of assets/replacement value of assets $= Q$) as is debt (i.e., market value of debt/replacement value of assets $= DEBT/RV$). The results of the regressions are reported in Table 2.

For each year in the low-growth (i.e., low $P/E$) sample, the coefficient of debt is positive and significant ($p$-values are 0.00 for all years). For each year in the high-growth sample, the coefficient of debt is negative and significant ($p$-values are 0.00, 0.00, and 0.07, respectively). Additionally, for each year, the coefficients of the leverage variable for the high- and low-growth samples are different from each other at the 0.001 level of significance. These results are consistent with our conjecture and suggest that debt plays a fundamentally different role in firms with many and in those with few positive net present value investment opportunities. The magnitude of the coefficients indicates that the leverage effect is also economically consequential. For example, in the 1988 low-growth sample, the 25th percentile of the leverage ratio is 19.80 percent and the 75th percentile is 39.03 percent. According to our regression, an increase in leverage from the 25th to the 75th percentile is associated with an *increase* in $Q$ of 0.11. For the high-growth sample, the 25th percentile of the leverage ratio is 4.11 percent and the 75th percentile is 24.60 percent. According to our regression, an increase in leverage from the 25th to the 75th percentile is associated with a *decrease* in $Q$ of 0.14.

The empirical results may, of course, depend on the specific classification scheme and variable definitions employed. A particular concern here is whether the $P/E$ ratio comprises a reasonable proxy for the firm's future investment growth opportunities. As an alternative measure of growth opportunities, we collected sales growth forecasts from the *Value Line Investment Survey*. For 1988, not all of the companies are listed in *Value Line*, and *Value Line* does not provide sales growth forecasts for every firm that is listed. As a result, our 1988 sample declines to 530 observations. For 1976 and 1986, all firms are listed in *Value Line*, but, as with 1988, sales growth forecasts are not available for every firm. The result is a sample of 924 observations in 1976 and 899 observations in

---

[6]One reason these results are reassuring is that for 1976 and 1986, the ownership data are taken from *Value Line Investment Survey*, whereas the ownership data for 1988 are taken from *Disclosure, Inc.* Occasionally, debates have arisen as to which of these two data sources is the more reliable. This analysis suggest that the results are robust to alternative sources of equity ownership data.

*J.J. McConnell, H. Servaes/Journal of Financial Economics 39 (1995) 131–157*      143

1986. Again, we subdivide our sample into three groups of equal size according to their *Value Line* sales growth forecasts. The middle third of the sample is discarded, and our regression models are estimated separately for the high-and low-growth firms. The results displayed in Table 3 confirm our previous findings. For low-growth firms, the relation between firm value and leverage is positive and significant; for high-growth firms, the relation is negative and significant. Further, the sizes of the debt coefficients are comparable to those in Table 2 for both the high- and low-growth samples.

A shortcoming of the *Value Line* sales growth forecast is that it is not available for all firms in our sample, especially for 1988. To remedy this deficiency, we employ the firm's five-year historical growth rate in sales as a proxy for future growth opportunities. One possible concern with this measure of future growth opportunities is that it relies upon historical growth, and presumes that historical growth is a reasonable proxy for future growth opportunities. A second problem is that the observed growth in sales may represent an increase in sales due to an acquisition rather than to positive net present value investment opportunities. For both of these deficiencies, we note that the results we generate with this classification scheme may be weakened by misclassification of high- and low-growth firms.

Further, there is an alternative interpretation for the results based on this classification scheme. If the lowest-quality firms increased growth the most through debt-financed acquisitions, we would find a negative relation between leverage and firm value for high-growth firms. But this finding is unrelated to our story that debt 'crowds out' investment by high-growth firms.

With the above caveats in mind and with the classification scheme based on five-year historical average growth rates in sales, the regressions are estimated for the high- and low-growth samples for 1976, 1986, and 1988. The results are reported in Table 4. As before, for each year in the low-growth sample, the coefficient of $DEBT/RV$ is positive and significant; for each year in the high-growth sample, the coefficient of $DEBT/RV$ is negative and significant; and the magnitudes of the debt coefficients continue to be comparable to those in Table 2. Again, these results suggest that debt plays a fundamentally different role in high- and low-growth firms. For low-growth firms an increase in leverage is associated with an increase in value, whereas for high-growth firms an increase in leverage is associated with a decrease in value.

We also estimate our regressions after excluding all firms that made acquisitions over the six-year period during which the historical sales growth rate is estimated. Firms that made acquisitions during this period are identified via the footnotes in the *Compustat* database. The footnotes indicate whether individual data items have been affected by acquisitions. This procedure excludes 348 firms in 1976, 458 firms in 1986, and 411 firms in 1988, thereby reducing our sample size by about half in each year. Our results (not reported) remain essentially unchanged for 1976 and 1988. That is, the relation between corporate value and

Table 2

Cross-sectional regression analysis of Tobin's $Q$ on debt, equity ownership, and control variables for samples of firms from 1976, 1986, and 1988 classified into high- and low-growth categories according to their $P/E$ ratios. $P$-values are in parentheses below the coefficients. All firms are listed on the NYSE or the AMEX. Balance sheet data are obtained from *Compustat*; ownership data are obtained from *Value Line* for the 1976 and 1986 samples and from *Disclosure* for the 1988 sample.

| Variable | 1976 | | 1986 | | 1988 | |
|---|---|---|---|---|---|---|
|  | Low-growth | High-growth | Low-growth | High-growth | Low-growth | High-growth |
| $N$ | 330 | 331 | 292 | 292 | 259 | 260 |
| Intercept | 0.55 | 1.12 | 0.51 | 1.53 | 0.59 | 1.46 |
|  | (0.00) | (0.00) | (0.00) | (0.00) | (0.00) | (0.00) |
| DEBT/RV | 0.25 | −1.13 | 0.56 | −1.11 | 0.58 | −0.70 |
|  | (0.00) | (0.00) | (0.00) | (0.00) | (0.00) | (0.07) |
| INOWN | 0.48 | 0.81 | 1.09 | 2.34 | 1.62 | 0.31 |
|  | (0.00) | (0.14) | (0.00) | (0.04) | (0.00) | (0.74) |
| $INOWN^2$ | −0.79 | −0.08 | −1.36 | −4.19 | −2.48 | −1.13 |
|  | (0.00) | (0.92) | (0.00) | (0.06) | (0.01) | (0.46) |
| LB | 0.07 | −0.08 | 0.34 | −0.17 | 0.31 | 0.39 |
|  | (0.34) | (0.81) | (0.00) | (0.64) | (0.01) | (0.20) |

|          |         |         |         |         |         |         |
|----------|---------|---------|---------|---------|---------|---------|
| INSTO    | 0.31    | 1.43    | 0.31    | 0.29    | 0.21    | 0.01    |
|          | (0.06)  | (0.01)  | (0.00)  | (0.31)  | (0.03)  | (0.97)  |
| R&D/RV   | 2.35    | 3.05    | 1.21    | −0.15   | −0.78   | 0.51    |
|          | (0.00)  | (0.07)  | (0.12)  | (0.93)  | (0.43)  | (0.64)  |
| ADV/RV   | 0.21    | 1.58    | 0.64    | 4.47    | 0.25    | 3.85    |
|          | (0.50)  | (0.08)  | (0.11)  | (0.00)  | (0.71)  | (0.00)  |
| RV       | −0.000006 | −0.000003 | −0.00 | −0.00001 | −0.000002 | −0.000004 |
|          | (0.04)  | (0.83)  | (0.63)  | (0.47)  | (0.12)  | (0.89)  |
| Adj. $R^2$ | 0.11  | 0.11    | 0.28    | 0.07    | 0.20    | 0.06    |

$Q$:        market value of common stock, preferred stock, and debt divided by the estimated replacement value of assets.
$DEBT/RV$:  estimated market value of debt divided by the estimated replacement value of assets.
$INOWN$:    fraction of common stock (in percent) owned by corporate officers and members of the board of directors.
$LB$:       fraction of common stock (in percent) owned by all outside shareholders who own more than 5% of the common stock.
$INSTO$:    fraction of common stock (in percent) owned by institutional investors.
$R&D/RV$:   research and development expenditures for the year divided by the replacement value of assets.
$ADV/RV$:   advertising expenditures for the year divided by the replacement value of assets.
$RV$:       estimated replacement value of assets.

146        *J.J. McConnell, H. Servaes/Journal of Financial Economics 39 (1995) 131–157*

Table 3

Cross-sectional regression analysis of Tobin's $Q$ on debt, equity ownership, and control variables for samples of firms from 1976, 1986, and 1988 classified into high- and low-growth categories according to the *Value Line* sales growth forecasts. *P*-values are in parentheses below the coefficients. All firms are listed on the NYSE or the AMEX. Balance sheet data are obtained from *Compustat*; ownership data are obtained from *Value Line* for the 1976 and 1986 samples and from *Disclosure* for the 1988 sample.

| Variable | 1976 | | 1986 | | 1988 | |
|---|---|---|---|---|---|---|
| | Low-growth | High-growth | Low-growth | High-growth | Low-growth | High-growth |
| $N$ | 287 | 296 | 285 | 310 | 188 | 194 |
| Intercept | 0.57 | 1.18 | 0.54 | 1.89 | 0.45 | 1.74 |
| | (0.00) | (0.00) | (0.00) | (0.00) | (0.00) | (0.00) |
| DEBT/RV | 0.42 | −2.02 | 0.28 | −1.91 | 0.60 | −0.88 |
| | (0.04) | (0.00) | (0.01) | (0.00) | (0.00) | (0.00) |
| INOWN | 0.34 | 0.49 | 1.80 | 1.47 | 0.99 | 0.40 |
| | (0.31) | (0.32) | (0.00) | (0.05) | (0.07) | (0.73) |
| $INOWN^2$ | 0.27 | −0.09 | −2.69 | −2.40 | −0.66 | −1.05 |
| | (0.65) | (0.91) | (0.00) | (0.06) | (0.52) | (0.73) |

*J.J. McConnell, H. Servaes/Journal of Financial Economics 39 (1995) 131–157*   147

|        |         |         |         |         |         |         |
|--------|---------|---------|---------|---------|---------|---------|
| LB     | 0.17    | 0.38    | 0.26    | -0.37   | 0.68    | -0.40   |
|        | (0.38)  | (0.24)  | (0.01)  | (0.20)  | (0.00)  | (0.21)  |
| INSTO  | 0.46    | 1.54    | 0.19    | 0.25    | 0.33    | -0.63   |
|        | (0.36)  | (0.00)  | (0.02)  | (0.31)  | (0.01)  | (0.04)  |
| R&D/RV | -0.24   | 3.54    | 2.50    | -1.80   | 1.07    | 1.43    |
|        | (0.88)  | (0.02)  | (0.00)  | (0.19)  | (0.24)  | (0.25)  |
| ADV/RV | -0.13   | 2.46    | 1.26    | 3.79    | 0.65    | 3.32    |
|        | (0.85)  | (0.01)  | (0.01)  | (0.00)  | (0.37)  | (0.00)  |
| RV     | -0.000002 | -0.000007 | -0.000001 | -0.00002 | -0.000001 | -0.000006 |
|        | (0.56)  | (0.41)  | (0.64)  | (0.08)  | (0.75)  | (0.09)  |
| Adj. $R^2$ | 0.04 | 0.25 | 0.16 | 0.17 | 0.18 | 0.14 |

$Q$:      market value of common stock, preferred stock, and debt divided by the estimated replacement value of assets.
$DEBT/RV$: estimated market value of debt divided by the estimated replacement value of assets.
$INOWN$:  fraction of common stock (in percent) owned by corporate officers and members of the board of directors.
$LB$:     fraction of common stock (in percent) owned by all outside shareholders who own more than 5% of the common stock.
$INSTO$:  fraction of common stock (in percent) owned by institutional investors.
$R&D/RV$: research and development expenditures for the year divided by the replacement value of assets.
$ADV/RV$: advertising expenditures for the year divided by the replacement value of assets.
$RV$:     estimated replacement value of assets.

Table 4

Cross-sectional regression analysis of Tobin's $Q$ on debt, equity ownership, and control variables for samples of firms from 1976, 1986, and 1988 classified into high- and low-growth categories according to their five-year historical sales growth. *P*-values are in parentheses below the coefficients. All firms are listed on the NYSE or the AMEX. Balance sheet data are obtained from *Compustat*; ownership data are obtained from *Compustat*; ownership data are obtained from *Value Line* for the 1976 and 1986 samples and from *Disclosure* for the 1988 sample.

| Variable | 1976 | | 1986 | | 1988 | |
|---|---|---|---|---|---|---|
| | Low-growth | High-growth | Low-growth | High-growth | Low-growth | High-growth |
| $N$ | 321 | 324 | 293 | 293 | 246 | 247 |
| Intercept | 0.50 | 1.32 | 0.48 | 2.05 | 0.43 | 1.60 |
| | (0.00) | (0.00) | (0.00) | (0.00) | (0.00) | (0.00) |
| DEBT/RV | 0.44 | −2.63 | 0.29 | −1.66 | 0.67 | −1.42 |
| | (0.01) | (0.00) | (0.08) | (0.00) | (0.00) | (0.00) |
| INOWN | 0.72 | 0.41 | 2.15 | 1.04 | 2.19 | 1.65 |
| | (0.01) | (0.43) | (0.00) | (0.23) | (0.00) | (0.03) |
| $INOWN^2$ | −0.79 | 0.54 | −3.35 | −1.97 | −3.70 | −2.58 |
| | (0.10) | (0.56) | (0.00) | (0.24) | (0.00) | (0.09) |

J.J. McConnell, H. Servaes/Journal of Financial Economics 39 (1995) 131–157      149

|        |           |           |           |           |           |            |
| ------ | --------- | --------- | --------- | --------- | --------- | ---------- |
| LB     | 0.02 (0.88)   | −0.20 (0.50)  | 0.33 (0.05)   | −0.42 (0.18)  | 0.23 (0.16)   | −0.14 (0.54)    |
| INSTO  | 1.04 (0.02)   | 1.69 (0.00)   | 0.27 (0.03)   | 0.12 (0.65)   | 0.46 (0.00)   | −0.06 (0.76)    |
| R&D/RV | 2.16 (0.06)   | 1.38 (0.38)   | 2.27 (0.06)   | −3.01 (0.03)  | 0.81 (0.07)   | −0.23 (0.76)    |
| ADV/RV | 1.95 (0.04)   | 1.78 (0.06)   | 3.71 (0.00)   | 1.19 (0.34)   | 2.52 (0.00)   | −0.11 (0.85)    |
| RV     | 0.0001 (0.11) | −0.00002 (0.01) | 0.000001 (0.84) | −0.00002 (0.00) | −0.000008 (0.09) | −0.000007 (0.02) |
| Adj. $R^2$ | 0.09      | 0.32      | 0.18      | 0.17      | 0.11      | 0.12       |

*Q*:       market value of common stock, preferred stock, and debt divided by the estimated replacement value of assets.
*DEBT/RV*: estimated market value of debt divided by the estimated replacement value of assets.
*INOWN*:   fraction of common stock (in percent) owned by corporate officers and members of the board of directors.
*LB*:      fraction of common stock (in percent) owned by all outside shareholders who own more than 5% of the common stock.
*INSTO*:   fraction of common stock (in percent) owned by institutional investors.
*R&D/RV*:  research and development expenditures for the year divided by the replacement value of assets.
*ADV/RV*:  advertising expenditures for the year divided by the replacement value of assets.
*RV*:      estimated replacement value of assets.

leverage is positive and statistically significant for low-growth firms and negative and statistically significant for high-growth firms. For 1986, the relation between corporate value and leverage for high-growth firms is negative and significant. For low-growth firms, the relation between corporate value and leverage is also negative, albeit not significant.

We perform one additional sensitivity test on our growth measure. We subdivide the sample into three groups according to the firms' $Q$ ratios. ($Q$ can be thought of as a measure of future growth opportunities, since $Q$ can be defined as the capitalized value of income from assets in place plus the capitalized value of future investment opportunities divided by the replacement value of the assets.) The results based on this classification procedure are consistent with the results based upon other classification schemes. For low-growth (i.e., low $Q$) firms, the relation between $Q$ and debt is positive and significant. For high-growth (i.e., high $Q$) firms, the relation between $Q$ and debt is negative and significant.[7] Thus, our results appear to be robust to the choice of a growth measure.

In each of the regressions so far, corporate value and debt are standardized by the replacement value of assets. An alternative measure by which these variables can be standardized is the book value of assets. In this regression, the dependent variable is the market value of the firm divided by the book value of assets. The independent variables are the market value of debt divided by the book value of assets, $INOWN$, $INOWN$-squared, $INSTO$, $LB$, advertising expenditures for the year divided by the book value of assets, research and development expenditures for the year divided by the book value of assets, and the book value of assets. The regressions are then re-estimated for each year for both the high- and low-growth samples, where the firms are classified as high- or low-growth according to their $P/E$ ratios. The coefficients of the leverage variable from these regressions are reported in panel A of Table 5. For the low-growth samples, each of the coefficients is positive and significantly different from zero; for the high-growth samples, each of the coefficients is negative and statistically significant, and the sizes of the coefficients are again comparable to those in Table 2. These results indicate that our findings do not depend on the use of the replacement value of assets to standardize the variables employed in our regression analysis.

In each of the regressions to this point, the dependent and independent variables have been scaled by either the replacement value of assets or the book value of assets. A third candidate with which the variables could be scaled is the

---

[7]The problem with this classification procedure, however, is that we sample on $Q$ before estimating the regression, which is not appropriate since it violates the assumptions of OLS regressions. As an alternative measure, we employ the firm's industry $Q$ ratio as our growth measure and the firm's individual $Q$ ratio as the dependent variable. The results based on this procedure are again similar to those reported in Tables 2, 3, 4, and 5.

Table 5

Coefficients on leverage variable using different standardization variables. This table presents the coefficient of the measure of leverage in cross-sectional regressions of firm value on leverage, ownership structure, and control variables, where firm value and leverage are standardized by the book value of assets and the market value of the firm. The $P/E$ ratio is used to subdivide the sample into low- and high-growth firms. $P$-values are in parentheses below the coefficients.

| Variable | 1976 | | 1986 | | 1988 | |
|---|---|---|---|---|---|---|
| | Low-growth | High-growth | Low-growth | High-growth | Low-growth | High-growth |
| *Panel A* | | | | | | |
| Standardization measure: | | | | | | |
| Book value of assets | 0.17 | − 1.91 | 0.28 | − 1.30 | 0.35 | − 0.91 |
| | (0.00) | (0.00) | (0.00) | (0.00) | (0.00) | (0.00) |
| *Panel B* | | | | | | |
| Standardization measure: | | | | | | |
| Market value of firm | − 0.37 | − 3.01 | − 0.17 | − 3.32 | − 0.14 | − 2.56 |
| | (0.00) | (0.00) | (0.08) | (0.00) | (0.13) | (0.00) |

All the differences in coefficients between the low-growth and high-growth samples are significant at the 0.1% level.

market value of the firm. The virtue of this variable is that the debt ratio would be specified in terms of market values – the market value of debt divided by the market value of the firm. It could be argued that the market value leverage ratio is the appropriate ratio to use in investigating the questions here. Of course, the deficiency of normalizing by the market value of the firm is that the left-hand side of the regressions becomes market value of the firm divided by the market value of the firm. A way to circumvent this problem is to continue to use market value of the firm divided by the replacement value as the dependent variable, and to scale debt, advertising expenditures, and R&D expenditures by the market value of the firm. This procedure solves one problem, but introduces another. In particular, the market value of the firm enters as the numerator of the left-hand-side variable and the denominator of the right-hand-side variable. Therefore, the coefficient on the independent variables, and especially the leverage variable, will have a negative bias. This bias can be strong enough to change the sign on the leverage variable from positive to negative in the low-growth regressions. Lang, Ofek, and Stulz (1994) also point out this problem. They note that since firms do not adjust leverage continuously, but instead make large discrete adjustments, an increase in the value of the firm increases its $Q$ ratio and decreases its leverage ratio. This induces a negative relation between $Q$ and leverage. Nevertheless, the market value of debt standardized by the market value of the firm can still lead to useful insights on the relation between leverage and firm value. Whereas, because of the downward bias, the coefficient of the leverage variable may be negative for both the low- and high-growth sample, our story predicts that the coefficient of debt for the low-growth sample will be significantly greater than the coefficient of the high-growth sample.

Panel B of Table 5 presents the results, using the replacement value of assets to standardize the market value of the firm, and the market value of the firm to standardize the market value of debt, R&D expenditures, and advertising expenditures. Several comments are in order: First, the coefficients of the debt variable are negative in both the high- and low-growth samples in each year. However, consistent with the possibility that this specification of the regression induces a negative bias in the coefficients, the coefficients of the debt variable in the high-growth sample are much larger in absolute value than the coefficients of the debt variable in any of the other regressions for the high-growth sample. Second, the negative coefficients of the debt variable in the high-growth sample are significantly different from zero at the 0.001 level in each year, whereas the coefficient of the debt variable in the low-growth sample is significantly different from zero at the 0.05 level only in 1976 (although the $p$-values are 0.08 and 0.13 in 1986 and 1988). Third, the coefficients of the debt variable in the high-growth sample range from 10 to 20 times the magnitude of the coefficients of the debt variable in the low-growth sample. For example, for 1988, the coefficient of the debt variable is $-0.14$ ($t = -1.53$) in the low-growth sample, compared with the coefficient of $-2.56$ ($t = -7.01$) in the high-growth sample.

J.J. McConnell, H. Servaes/Journal of Financial Economics 39 (1995) 131–157      153

Further robustness tests could be conducted using other definitions of growth and other measures of corporate leverage, and undoubtedly some of the results would not be consistent with the tests conducted so far. Overall, though, the estimated regressions indicate that the relation between corporate value and leverage is fundamentally different between firms with few, and those with many positive net present value investment opportunities. Moreover, the results are consistent with the proposition that debt has both a positive and a negative effect on the value of the firm. The negative effect is more pronounced for firms with many positive net present value investment opportunities, whereas the positive effect is more pronounced for firms with few positive net present value investment opportunities.

### 4.2. Value and equity ownership

We now turn to the question of whether the relation between $Q$ and equity ownership differs between low- and high-growth firms. Here the predictions are somewhat softer. The prediction is not that the relation between corporate value and the fraction of shares owned by insiders, institutional investors, or block stockholders is positive for low-growth firms and negative for high-growth firms, it is only that ownership by these groups is likely to be more important for low-growth than for high-growth firms. Visual inspection of Tables 2, 3, and 4 provides some (albeit weak) support for that contention. For each year, and for both measures of growth opportunities, the coefficient of insider ownership $(INOWN)$ is positive; eight times out of nine it is significantly greater than zero for the low-growth sample. For each regression of the high-growth sample, the coefficient of $INOWN$ is positive, but significantly different from zero in only two of the nine regressions. These results hint that the fraction of shares held by insiders is more closely tied to corporate value for low-growth than for high-growth firms. There is, however, a fly in the ointment: In three of the nine pairs of regressions, the coefficient of $INOWN$ is larger in the high-growth than in the low-growth sample. In two of those three cases, the coefficient is also significantly different from zero. The insignificance of the coefficient of $INOWN$ in the high-growth sample in the other cases could be due to the greater dispersion in the $Q$ ratios for the high-growth firms. For example, in 1988, when the $P/E$ ratio is used to classify firms, the standard deviation of the $Q$ ratio in the low-growth sample is 0.31, whereas the standard deviation of the $Q$ ratio in the high-growth sample is 0.82.

The coefficients of institutional ownership $(INSTO)$ and block ownership $(LB)$ are also mixed. For $LB$ the coefficient of the low-growth sample is larger than the coefficient of the high-growth sample in seven of the nine regressions. For $INSTO$ the coefficient of the low-growth sample is larger than the coefficient of the high-growth sample in only five of the nine regressions. Interestingly, the coefficient of block ownership is positive in all nine low-growth regressions and positive and significant in five of the nine low-growth regressions. These results indicate that block equity ownership is more likely to be related to firm value in those firms that have few positive net present value investment opportunities.

Overall, the regressions give only modest support to the proposition that the distribution of equity ownership among insiders, blockholders, institutional investors, and atomistic shareholders is more consequential in low- than in high-growth firms. There is, however, another intriguing relation in the data: The regressions for both the low- and high-growth samples show evidence of a curvilinear relation between $Q$ and inside ownership in which $Q$ first increases, and then decreases, as the fraction of shares owned by insiders increases. This result holds in eight of the nine regressions. Thus, the fundamental relation between $Q$ and inside ownership documented by McConnell and Servaes (1990) appears to prevail for both low- and high-growth firms. Along these lines a caveat is appropriate, however: While the curvilinear relation exists in eight of the nine regressions, the coefficients are not significant in every case.

## 5. Commentary

Results from the types of regressions that we present here are, of course, subject to multiple interpretations. In describing the empirical results, we have trodden carefully around the question of causality. In the story that we propose to explain the results, the direction of causality clearly runs from leverage to value. The story also attributes a different role to debt for firms with many and those with few positive net present value projects. In describing the empirical results, however, we have been careful to use causality-free terms such as 'association' or 'relation' between the dependent and independent variables. A reversal of causality means that value determines leverage, and that more valuable high-growth firms choose to have less leverage than less valuable high-growth firms. Conversely, more valuable low-growth firms choose to have more leverage than less valuable low-growth firms. The data cannot reject that interpretation. Indeed, we could envision a story that leads to that prediction.

The 'pecking order' theory proposed by Myers (1984) does suggest a negative relation between firm value and leverage, where leverage is determined by firm value. According to the pecking order theory, firms first use internally generated funds to finance their projects. When internally generated funds are exhausted, the firm turns to debt financing. Only as a last resort is additional equity issued. Thus, our results for high-growth firms are consistent with the pecking order theory. For low-growth firms, however, we find a positive relation between firm value and leverage, while the pecking order theory predicts a negative correlation. Here too, it is possible to make a reverse causality argument; that is, for low-growth firms, firms with higher $Q$ ratios choose to have more leverage.

If our tests fail to control for growth opportunities within the high-growth and low-growth samples, it is possible that our measure of firm value (i.e., $Q$) also proxies for growth opportunities. A firm with better growth opportunities will generate higher cash flows in the future, and consequently it can issue more debt currently. This might lead to a positive relation between $Q$ and the ratio of the market value of debt to the replacement value of the firm's assets. But this argument assumes that differences in $Q$ are due to differences in growth opportunities. To investigate this assumption, we add both the $P/E$ ratio and our measure of past sales growth to the estimated regression models. In several of the models, we find a significant positive relation between $Q$ and our measures of growth, but our other results remain unchanged. In particular, we always find a strong positive relation between leverage and firm value for low-growth firms, and a strong negative relation between leverage and firm value for high-growth firms. If anything, the statistical significance of our results increases.

The equity ownership results are also subject to the same criticism. As with debt, the direction of causality in our story runs from equity ownership to $Q$, but care must be taken in that interpretation. McConnell and Servaes (1990) note that the direction of causality could run in the opposite direction. They do point out, however, that it is difficult to reconcile the reverse causality argument (where managers who perform well are compensated with additional stock) with the negative relation between ownership and $Q$ that occurs at high levels of insider ownership. Concerning the positive association between block equity ownership and corporate value in some low-growth specifications, it is possible that blocks are formed after superior firm performance. Thus, it is possible that causality is reversed. What is less clear, however, is why this would occur only for firms with few growth opportunities. This issue perhaps deserves further exploration if reverse causality is the explanation for these results.

## 6. Summary and conclusions

This paper explores empirically the cross-sectional relation between Tobin's $Q$, debt, and equity ownership for high- and low-growth firms. The analysis is conducted with large samples of U.S. firms for the years 1976, 1986, and 1988. The investigation is motivated by the theoretical work of Myers (1977), Jensen (1986), Shleifer and Vishny (1986), Stulz (1988, 1990), and Morck, Shleifer, and Vishny (MSV) (1988), and by the empirical work of MSV (1988) and McConnell and Servaes (1990). Prior theoretical work posits that debt has both a positive and negative effect on the value of the firm because of its influence on corporate investment decisions. Based on this prior theoretical work, we conjecture that the negative effect of debt will dominate the positive effect for firms with many positive net present value projects (i.e., high-growth firms) and that the positive effect will dominate the negative effect for firms with few positive net present

156     *J.J. McConnell, H. Servaes/Journal of Financial Economics 39 (1995) 131–157*

value projects (i.e., low-growth firms). The empirical prediction of this conjecture is that for high-growth firms the relation between corporate value and leverage is negative, and that for low-growth firms the relation between corporate value and leverage is positive.

Prior theoretical work also predicts that the value of the firm is a nonlinear function of the allocation of equity ownership between managers and outside shareholders, and a positive function of the presence of a large-block shareholder and of the fraction of shares held by institutional investors.

Prior empirical work supports the hypothesis that the relation between corporate value and the fraction of shares held by corporate insiders is nonlinear. In particular, with large samples of firms for 1976 and 1986, McConnell and Servaes (1990) document a significant curvilinear relation between Tobin's $Q$ and the fraction of shares owned by corporate insiders: $Q$ first increases as the fraction of shares held by corporate insiders increases, and then declines as insider ownership increases beyond some critical level. They also find that the relation between $Q$ and the fraction of shares held by institutional investors is positive and significant. In sum, their results support the hypothesis that the allocation of equity ownership matters.

This paper extends the work of McConnell and Servaes in three ways. First, we find that the significant quadratic relation between $Q$ and the fraction of shares held by corporate insiders is also present in 1988 data, as is the significant positive relation between $Q$ and the fraction of shares held by institutional investors, thus providing further evidence that the allocation of equity ownership matters.

Second, when the sample is divided into high- and low-growth firms, we find that the relation between $Q$ and debt is negative for high-growth firms and positive for the low-growth firms. These results indicate that debt also matters, and that the way in which it matters depends upon the investment opportunity set confronted by the firm.

Third, there is some (albeit weak) evidence that the allocation of equity ownership between corporate insiders and other types of investors is more important in low-growth than in high-growth firms. This evidence, although modest, is sufficiently intriguing to call for further exploration of whether the way in which equity ownership matters differs between firms, according to their investment opportunities and other characteristics.

## References

Berle, Adolf A., Jr. and Gardner C. Means, 1932, The modern corporation and private property (Macmillan, New York, NY).
Donaldson, Gordon, 1963, Financial goals: Management vs. stockholders, Harvard Business Review 41, 116–129.
Hall, Bronwyn, 1990, The manufacturing sector, master file: 1959–1987, NBER working paper 3366.

Harris, Milton and Artur Raviv, 1991, The theory of capital structure, Journal of Finance 46, 297–355.

Hermalin, Benjamin E. and Michael S. Weisbach, 1991, The effects of board composition and direct incentives on firm performance, Financial Management 20, 101–112.

Holderness, Clifford G. and Dennis P. Sheehan, 1988, The role of majority shareholders in publicly held corporations, Journal of Financial Economics 20, 317–346.

Jensen, Michael C., 1986, Agency costs of free cash flow, corporate finance and takeovers, American Economic Review 76, 323–339.

Kole, Stacey R., 1994, Managerial ownership and firm performance: Incentives or rewards?, Working paper (University of Rochester, Rochester, NY).

Lang, Larry, Eli Ofek, and René Stulz, 1994, Leverage, investment, and firm growth, Working paper (New York University, New York, NY; Ohio State University, Columbus, OH).

Lindenberg, Eric and Stephen Ross, 1981, Tobin's $q$ ratio and industrial organization, Journal of Business 54, 1–32.

McConnell, John J. and Henri Servaes, 1990, Additional evidence on equity ownership and corporate value, Journal of Financial Economics 27, 595–612.

Modigliani, Franco and Merton H. Miller, 1958, The cost of capital, corporation finance, and the theory of investment, American Economic Review 48, 261–297.

Modigliani, Franco and Merton H. Miller, 1963, Corporate income taxes and the cost of capital: A correction, American Economic Review 53, 433–443.

Morck, Randall, Andrei Shleifer, and Robert W. Vishny, 1988, Management ownership and market valuation: An empirical analysis, Journal of Financial Economics 20, 293–315.

Myers, Stewart C., 1977, Determinants of corporate borrowing, Journal of Financial Economics 5, 147–175.

Myers, Stewart C., 1984, The capital structure puzzle, Journal of Finance 39, 575–592.

Phelps, Shawn, 1991, Managerial ownership and firm value: Inside vs. outside incentives, Unpublished Ph.D. dissertation (University of North Carolina at Chapel Hill, Chapel Hill, NC).

Pound, John, 1988, Proxy contests and the efficiency of shareholder oversight, Journal of Financial Economics 20, 237–265.

Shleifer, Andrei and Robert W. Vishny, 1986, Large shareholders and corporate control, Journal of Political Economy 94, 461–488.

Stulz, René, 1988, Managerial control of voting rights: Financing policies and the market for corporate control, Journal of Financial Economics 20, 25–54.

Stulz, René, 1990, Managerial discretion and optimal financing policies, Journal of Financial Economics 26, 3–27.

# [9]

# Capital Structure and Product-Market Competition: Empirical Evidence from the Supermarket Industry

*By* Judith A. Chevalier*

*This paper establishes an empirical link between firm capital structure and product-market competition using data from local supermarket competition. First, an event-study analysis of supermarket leveraged buyouts (LBO's) suggests that an LBO announcement increases the market value of the LBO chain's local rivals. Second, I show that supermarket chains were more likely to enter and expand in a local market if a large share of the incumbent firms in the local market undertook LBO's. The study suggests that leverage increases in the late 1980's led to softer product-market competition in this industry. (JEL D43, G14, G32, G34, L13, L81)*

During the late 1980's corporate debt rose dramatically, due in large part to an unprecedented wave of leveraged buyouts (LBO's). This large-scale experiment with firm capital structure refocused both popular and academic attention on the issue of how a firm's financing choices might affect its performance and behavior. Numerous recent theoretical works have examined one component of this issue—the question of how a firm's capital structure affects competition in the market for the firm's products. However, very little work has been done to determine empirically whether a real linkage exists between capital markets and product markets.[1]

In this paper, I test between two classes of theoretical models by examining the share price response of supermarket chains to the announcement of a rival chain's leveraged buyout and by examining the entry, exit, and expansion behavior of supermarket chains. The first class of models predicts that increases in firm leverage tend to "soften" product-market competition. The second class of models predicts that increases in firm leverage tend to "toughen" product-market competition.[2] A finding that *either* of these two hypotheses is true would be important in that it would suggest that financing decisions can have real product-market effects.

I examine the effect of debt on product-market competition by studying supermarket chains in local markets. The supermarket industry is a natural laboratory for testing these theoretical models for two reasons. First, many large supermarket chains undertook leveraged buyout transactions in the late 1980's. This allows examination of how product-market competition "shakes out" after competitors undertake sudden,

*Graduate School of Business, University of Chicago, 1101 East 58th Street, Chicago, IL 60637, and National Bureau of Economic Research. This paper is a revised version of Chapters 1 and 2 of my M.I.T. dissertation. My advisors, Paul Joskow and David Scharfstein, provided invaluable guidance and advice. Christopher Avery, Tasneem Chipty, Glenn Ellison, Franklin Fisher, Ruth Judson, Steven Kaplan, Brigitte Madrian, Christopher Mayer, Wallace Mullin, James Poterba, Nancy Rose, Julio Rotemberg, Fiona Scott Morton, Jeremy Stein, and two anonymous referees provided helpful comments. Charles Hadlock provided invaluable data guidance. Financial assistance from the National Science Foundation at the beginning of this project is gratefully acknowledged. All errors and omissions remain my own.

[1] The only empirical work of which I am aware is A. Michael Spence (1985), José C. Guedes and Tim C. Opler (1992), and Gordon M. Phillips (1992).

[2] The terms "tough" and "soft" price competition are used in the sense of John Sutton (1991). The "toughness" of price competition differs in two markets if, holding the concentration in the two markets constant, price–cost margins in the two markets differ.

dramatic increases in debt. Second, super-market competition takes place at the local level. This allows a comparison of super-market competition across markets.

The findings in this paper are consistent with the group of theoretical models of capital structure and product-market com-petition that suggest that product-market competition becomes "softer" when lever-age increases. These models include work by Drew Fudenberg and Jean Tirole (1986), Patrick Bolton and David S. Scharfstein (1990), and Phillips (1991). The results are inconsistent with other models, including James A. Brander and Tracy R. Lewis (1986), Vojislav Maksimovic (1988), and Julio J. Rotemberg and Scharfstein (1990), which predict that leverage changes man-agerial and shareholder incentives in a way that makes product-market competition "tougher."

The organization of the rest of the paper is as follows. Section I describes LBO activ-ity in the supermarket industry. Section II presents an event study examining the an-nouncement effects of supermarket lever-aged buyouts on rival supermarket chains. Section III describes the empirical predic-tions of the hypotheses of capital structure and product-market competition for entry, exit, and expansion. Section IV describes the data for the study of entry, exit, and expansion. Section V presents the results. Section VI examines an alternative explana-tion for the empirical results in Section V, and my conlcusions are presented in Sec-tion VII.

## I. LBO Activity in the Supermarket Industry

A supermarket is defined by the publica-tion *Progressive Grocer* (1989) as a retail food store that has annual sales of more than $2 million and has greater than 9,000 square feet of selling space. Supermarkets account for 70 percent of retail food store sales but only 10 percent of retail food establishments. According to *Progressive Grocer* (1989), there were approximately 30,754 supermarkets in the United States in 1988, 55 percent of which belonged to chains of 11 or more stores.

At the national level, the supermarket industry appears to be relatively unconcen-trated. The four largest supermarket chains accounted for only 16 percent of U.S. gro-cery store sales in 1982 (Phillip K. Kaufman and Charles R. Handy, 1989). However, no supermarket chain in the United States is truly national. For example, the largest chain in the United States, American Stores, op-erated in only 18 states in 1990. Thus, while the industry is relatively unconcentrated on a national level, local markets can be highly concentrated. The average metropolitan statistical area in the United States had a four-firm supermarket concentration ratio of 58 percent in 1982.

Supermarket LBO's occurred primarily between 1985 and 1988.[3] The largest trans-actions were the $5.3 billion Safeway LBO, the $4.1 billion Kroger leveraged recapital-ization, the $1.8 billion Supermarkets Gen-eral LBO, and the $1.2 billion Stop & Shop LBO. These four companies alone owned nearly 4,000 U.S. supermarkets at the time of their LBO's. During this period, it was also common for smaller regional chains and divisions of larger chains to undertake LBO's. Altogether, 19 of the 50 biggest su-permarket chains in the United States have undertaken LBO's. They accounted for ap-proximately $72 billion of the $297 billion in supermarket sales in 1991.

LBO activity has not been concentrated in any single geographic region. In the sam-ple used in this study, LBO firms accounted for 16 percent of the stores in Midwestern markets, 17 percent of the stores in South-ern markets, 21 percent of the stores in Northeastern markets, and 42 percent of the stores in Western markets. Part of the large LBO concentration in the West is due to the enormous importance of Safeway on

---

[3]There is also one instance of a leveraged recapital-ization in this industry, which was undertaken by Kroger. A leveraged recap is a transaction in which a firm borrows in order to pay a large dividend to share-holders of at least 50 percent of the former equity value of the firm. Because this recap resulted in debt levels for Kroger similar to typical LBO debt levels, it is included in this analysis as an LBO.

*Empirical Corporate Finance III*

the West Coast. Safeway's 1985 market share in cities in the sample in the West totaled nearly 25 percent.

The vast majority of the leveraged buyouts were not the result of unconstrained decisions by management and shareholders. Instead, most of them were undertaken in response to unwanted takeover attempts. In fact, all four of the biggest deals (and many of the smaller ones) were undertaken to thwart the unwanted takeover attempts of the Haft family, which controls the Dart drugstore chain.

This description of LBO activity in the supermarket industry leaves unanswered the question of what caused the LBO's in this industry.[4] It has been suggested by Peter Magowan (1989), the CEO of Safeway stores, which undertook an LBO in 1986, that the main effect of the Safeway LBO was to force Safeway to sell or spin off divisions which were not profitable. Magowan suggests that Safeway excised the divisions in which it was not as strong a competitor as its rivals (see Magowan, 1989). This suggestion by Magowan is practically a restatement of the basic "empire-building" rationale for LBO's suggested by Michael C. Jensen (1989). If a good firm has a few bad divisions, then value can be gained by buying the firm and turning over the bad divisions to higher-valued users. These post-LBO asset sales were common among LBO chains. If this model of LBO's is correct, then, in the study of entry, exit, and expansion, by examining the local markets in which Safeway chose to remain an active

competitor, one examines those local markets where competition was not an important cause of the LBO.[5] The local-market nature of supermarket competition helps to "clean out" the endogeneity of the LBO in the study of entry, exit, and expansion. The issue of how the endogeneity of LBO's affects the results will be taken up in Section VI.

## II. An Event Study of Supermarket LBO's

In this section, I examine the stock-return response of supermarket chains to the announcement that a rival chain is undertaking a leveraged buyout.[6] This approach of looking at the event responses of rival firms was pioneered by B. Espen Eckbo (1983) and Robert S. Stillman (1983) in the merger literature. If leveraged buyouts are expected to make product-market competition softer, rival supermarket chains should exhibit positive abnormal returns around the time of LBO announcements; if LBO's are expected to lead to tougher product-market competition, rival supermarket chains should exhibit negative abnormal returns around the time of LBO announcements.

### A. *Methodology and Data*

I focus my analysis on a single industry in order to separate the hypothesis that the LBO leads to a change in product-market

---

[4] Perhaps, given the importance of the Haft family in initiating takeover attempts in this industry, the better question to ask is: what factors contributed to the Haft family's choices of takeover targets? An examination of newspaper and magazine accounts of these takeovers reveals no statements by the Haft family indicating why it chose particular targets. One might hope to analyze the family's plan by examining the reforms that the family instituted at the supermarket chains that were actually taken over. However, the only supermarket chain that the Haft family actually took over was Shoppers Food Warehouse. It is difficult to try to infer what the Haft family would have done with Safeway or Kroger by examining what changes they effected at a chain with only 30 stores.

[5] The explanation suggested here for LBO's—that they serve to force firms to excise bad divisions, and to leave them only with divisions in which they are relatively efficient producers—is supported by the evidence. LBO firms are not statistically significantly more likely to be closing stores in unclosed divisions than non-LBO firms. At least in this regard, their behavior in the divisions not sold off seems unaffected by the LBO.

[6] I do not focus on the stock-return response of the leveraging firm itself. A leveraged buyout transaction occurs when the managers of the firm (or others) offer to pay a premium over the prevailing market price of the firm. The stock price rises to reflect this premium. The managers of the firm would not undertake a leveraged buyout if they did not believe that they could improve firm value.

competition from the alternative hypothesis that abnormal event returns are due to increased speculation that more LBO's will occur in the industry. I use information about local-market competition to separate firms in the industry that are directly competing with the leveraging firms from firms that are not directly competing with the leveraging firms.[7] If an LBO greatly improves the financial outlook of the firm undertaking the LBO and the LBO announcement increases speculation that other supermarket chains will also undertake an LBO, then one would expect all firms in the industry to experience a positive stock-return response to the LBO announcement. However, if the LBO is expected to soften product-market competition, then one would expect supermarket chains operating in the same local markets as the leveraging chain to exhibit a positive stock-return response to the LBO announcement. Supermarkets that do not compete directly with the leveraging chain should have no return response to the LBO announcement. Finally, if LBO's are expected to make product-market competition tougher, then direct competitors should experience a negative share price response, while noncompetitors should experience no significant share price response.

I examine the leveraged buyouts of Safeway, Supermarkets General, and Stop & Shop and the leveraged recapitalization of Kroger, the largest leveraged transactions undertaken in the industry. The event window begins 30 days prior to the first announcement suggestive that an LBO or leveraged recapitalization might occur and ends on the day of the firm's final announcement that it was undertaking an LBO or leveraged recapitalization.[8] Announce-

ments and announcement dates were obtained from the *Wall Street Journal Index*. Since all four of the transactions studied here were undertaken in response to takeover attempts, the event window begins prior to the first public announcement suggesting that a takeover might occur. Because the event window extends until the announcement of the LBO, it can be interpreted as reflecting the market's expectation of the change in the value of the rival firm due to the LBO, as long as no confounding information was released within the event window.

The first announcement leading up to each leverage transaction under study and its date are listed in Table 1. Table 1 also lists the date of the announcement that the leverage transaction would definitely occur. The daily stock returns of 13 supermarket rivals are studied. The rivals are listed in Table 2. These rivals represent all firms that derived at least 80 percent of their revenues from supermarket sales and traded continuously from January 1, 1985, through October 10, 1988, the date of the announcement of the Kroger leveraged recapitalization.

The event study was conducted using daily data on the stock-market returns of the supermarket chains. The equation to be estimated, a variant of the basic market model has the form following form:[9]

$$R_{it} = \alpha_i + \beta_i R_{mt} + \sum_j \delta_{ij} D_{jt} + e_{it}$$

where $R_{it}$ = firm $i$'s return at date $t$, $R_{mt}$ = the return on the value-weighted NYSE/AMEX index at date $t$, $j$ indexes the four events, $\alpha_i$, $\beta_i$, and $\delta_{ij}$ are parameters to be estimated, $e_{it}$ is an error term, and $D_{jt}$ is a dummy variable which equals 1 during the event window for event $j$ and 0 otherwise.

The stock return data used for estimation start on the first trading day of 1985 and extend through Kroger's announcement of

---

[7]Michael D. Whinston and Scott C. Collins (1992) separate competing airlines from noncompeting airlines in their event study of the entry of People Express.

[8]This wide event window was chosen because convicted insider-trader Ivan Boesky was investigated by the Securities Exchange Commission for insider-trading in at least one of these transactions.

[9]For a discussion of the market model, see Eugene F. Fama (1976).

TABLE 1—EVENTS INCLUDED IN THE EVENT ANALYSIS

| Event | First announcement | Date | Date final transaction announced |
|---|---|---|---|
| Safeway LBO | Dart Group announces that it has acquired a 6-percent stake in Safeway | 6/13/86 | 7/29/86 |
| Supermarkets General LBO | Dart Group proposes to buy Supermarkets General | 3/10/87 | 4/23/87 |
| Stop & Shop LBO | Dart Group announces that it seeks a major stake in Stop & Shop | 1/15/88 | 3/1/88 |
| Kroger leveraged recap | The Haft family (who control Dart Group) reveals that it has a major stake in Kroger | 9/13/88 | 10/10/88 |

*Note:* The event window is from 30 days prior to the first announcement, through the announcement of the final transaction.

TABLE 2–RIVAL SUPERMARKET CHAINS INCLUDED IN THE EVENT STUDY

Albertsons
American Stores
Brunos
Delchamps
Food Lion
Foodarama
Giant Food Stores
Great Atlantic and Pacific Tea Company
Hannaford Brothers
Marsh Supermarkets
Ruddick
Weis Markets
Winn-Dixie

its leveraged recapitalization in October 1988. These data are obtained from the Center for Research in Security Prices.

The event response parameters are estimated using seemingly unrelated regressions (SUR). This methodology is employed because the error terms from the market-model equation for a supermarket chain should be contemporaneously correlated with the error terms for other supermarket chains. For each debt event, I calculate the average event coefficient of firms that compete directly with the leveraging firm, and I calculate the average event coefficient of firms that do not compete directly with the leveraging firm. The firms directly competing with the leveraging firm are constrained

to have a single event response, and the firms not directly competing with the leveraging firm are constrained to have a single event response for each event. These constraints cannot be rejected at conventional significance levels.

For each event, volumes of the *Supermarket News*'s annual *Distribution Study of Grocery Store Sales* were used to determine which chains competed with the chain undertaking the LBO. This book lists the names of stores operating in each of the Metropolitan Statistical Areas (MSA's) in the United States. The *Supermarket News* guide lists store names, not parent firms. Information from annual 10K filings with the Securities and Exchange Commission and the 1988 *Retail Tenants Directory* were used to link store names to parent firms. Two supermarket chains were considered to be in direct competition with one another if there was any MSA in which both owned stores listed in the *Supermarket News* guide.

### B. *Results*

Table 3 shows the results of an SUR estimation of return responses to the four events. The return responses for the competing firms are shown in column 1; the return responses for noncompeting firms are shown in column 2. The table shows that the return responses of the competing firms

TABLE 3—EVENT COEFFICIENTS

| Event | Event coefficient for other supermarket chains | |
| | (1) Competing | (2) Not competing |
| --- | --- | --- |
| Safeway LBO | 0.003168** (0.000966) | 0.001614 (0.001044) |
| Supermarkets General LBO | 0.001782 (0.001141) | −0.000175 (0.000817) |
| Stop & Shop LBO | 0.001573 (0.001381) | −0.000082 (0.000793) |
| Kroger leveraged recapitalization | 0.001857* (0.000930) | 0.000991 (0.001229) |

*Notes:* Column 1 reports event coefficients for firms competing in some of the same MSA's as the "event" firm; column 2 reports event coefficients for firms competing in none of the same MSA's as the "event" firm. The coefficients were estimated using seemingly unrelated regressions. Standard errors are given in parentheses.

*Statistically different from zero at the 5-percent level.

**Statistically different from zero at the 1-percent level.

are positive for all four events, consistent with the hypothesis that competition is expected to become softer following the LBO. The return responses are statistically significant at the 5-percent level for the Safeway and Kroger events but statistically significant at only the 12-percent level for the Supermarkets General event and at the 25-percent level for the Stop & Shop event. The joint hypothesis that the event coefficients for all four events equal zero is rejected at the 1-percent significance level.

The return responses for the noncompeting firms are positive for two of the four events, but are not statistically different from zero at standard significance levels. The Safeway event is statistically different from zero at the 12-percent level. It is not surprising that this event is the one in which there is some response of the noncompeting firms since the Safeway LBO was the first large LBO in this industry, and thus, the speculation effect might have been important for this LBO. However, the joint hypothesis that the event coefficients for all four events equal zero cannot be rejected at even the 55-percent significance level.

The measured return responses for the competing firms, while statistically significant as a group, appear to be quite small. The Safeway event, for example, is estimated to lead to an abnormal increase in value for the competing firms of only 0.32 percent, and the other event coefficients are even smaller. However, this small event response may be due to the small amount that even the "direct competitors" compete with the firm undertaking the LBO. For example, at the time of the Kroger leveraged recapitalization, American Stores owned approximately 1,500 stores in 29 states; Kroger owned approximately 1,400 stores in 25 states. However, I could find records of the two firms competing in the same MSA in only seven states. Thus, the magnitudes of the coefficients estimated do not reflect the changes in the expected profitability of those operations of each supermarket rival that actually competes with the leveraging chain.[10]

The event-study results suggest that the present discounted value of the expected future profits of a supermarket chain rises when a rival supermarket chain announces that it is undertaking an LBO or leveraged recapitalization. These results are consistent with the hypothesis that product-market competition following the LBO is expected to become softer. In the next section, this hypothesis is tested further using data on the entry and exit of supermarket chains.

### III. Empirical Predictions for Entry and Expansion

The theories of capital structure and product-market competition posit that changes in capital structure change the toughness of product-market competition. If an LBO changes the toughness of product-market competition, then, following the

---

[10]R. Preston McAfee and Michael A. Williams (1988) make a similar point about the estimated magnitudes of the effects of mergers on rival firms.

LBO of a supermarket market chain in a local market, one should observe a change in the structure of the local market.[11] Specifically, if an LBO leads to an *increase* in the "toughness" of product-market competition, then rival firms would want to exit the local market or close stores in the local market. On the other hand, if a leverage increase leads to a *decrease* in the toughness of product-market competition, firms competing in the local market would want to add stores there, and firms not competing in the local market would want to enter.

In the analysis which follows, I will examine whether, controlling for local market conditions, supermarket chains tend to be adding or subtracting stores in markets dominated by LBO firms. I measure the percentage change in total supermarkets across cities in which LBO's were of differential importance. The analysis is complicated by the fact that the LBO episode is very recent. The empirical strategy undertaken here assumes that one should observe gradual movement toward a market structure with more firms and stores if competition is "softened" by LBO's; one should observe gradual movement toward a market structure with fewer firms and stores if competition is "toughened" by LBO's.

To address the problem that all post-LBO adjustments may not have occurred by the time the data were constructed, two additional tests are undertaken. I examine the decision by large supermarket chains to add or subtract stores in cities in which they were incumbents. I separately study whether local markets experience de novo entry by nonincumbent supermarket chains. This is done because one would expect that a chain operating in a local market is familiar with local real estate and conditions and has

established supply channels and, therefore, can begin to respond quickly to a change in the competitive situation in the local market. Supermarket trade sources confirm that de novo entry into a city requires more time and planning.

Obviously, this empirical strategy assumes that the LBO changes capital structure and that these changes in capital structure impact subsequent product-market competition. If, on the other hand, the LBO were in some way endogenously determined by product-market competition, then any inference about the effect of LBO's on product-market competition would be spurious. This issue will be taken up in Section IV and Section VI.

### IV. Data

The data consist of information on supermarket chains in 85 Metropolitan Statistical Areas (MSA's) in 1985 and 1991. The data are drawn from *Progressive Grocer*'s (1986, 1992) publication *Market Scope*.[12] This publication lists the supermarket chains and the number of stores operated by each chain in the most-populated 100 MSA's in the United States.[13] The book also lists the total number of supermarkets owned by independent firms in the MSA. The 85 MSA's studied consist of those MSA's which were among the largest 100 in both 1985 and 1991 and for which the official Census definition of the MSA borders remained un-

---

[11]Sutton (1991) refers to the "toughness" of price competition as determining market structure. Here, I will refer to the "toughness" of product-market competition. I use this term because the competition takes place on both the price and quality dimensions. The methodology in this paper cannot separate changes in price competition from changes in quality competition.

[12]This is a different data source than the one used to determine supermarket locations for the event study. The *Progressive Grocer* data provide high-quality counts of the number of stores owned by each supermarket chain in an MSA. The *Supermarket News* data include counts, but they are obtained by surveying the local newspapers and are of lesser quality. For the event study, the *Supermarket News* data were used to determine whether firms competed in any of the same MSA's. For this reason, a source was needed which, unlike the *Progressive Grocer* data source, included all MSA's.

[13]Some of the *Progressive Grocer* data were checked against microfilm copies of old telephone books to confirm the quality of the data source.

changed between the two years.[14] The use of MSA-level data may be of concern, since there is no reason to assume that an MSA is the correct measure of the relevant market when considering supermarket competition. However, my examination of the *Progressive Grocer* data shows that the MSA's correspond closely to divisions of large supermarket chains. In general, all of the supermarkets that one chain has in a division are overseen by a single divisional manager and are served by a single division warehouse. Furthermore, one important way in which supermarkets compete is by distributing weekly circulars in the local newspapers that describe the sales in the supermarkets that week. A single flyer is generally issued for all of the supermarkets in a division or, approximately, all of the supermarkets in an MSA.

All of the firms in the 85 MSA's are classified by whether or not they have undertaken an LBO. I use this mechanism to divide firms into low-debt and high-debt firms because actual leverage ratios are unavailable for privately owned firms. The power of the test is weakened by the fact that many of the "low-leverage" firms may have reasonably high levels of debt although they did not undertake an LBO.[15]

The information on LBO's was obtained in two ways. First, quarterly editions of *Mergers and Acquisitions* contain all ownership transactions (including LBO's) of greater than $1 million. Second, all references to transactions involving the supermarket parent companies in the sample were searched using *Predicasts Funk and Scott Index, United States*, which indexes *Supermarket News*, *Supermarket Business*, and *Progressive Grocer*, the major industry trade

publications. From these sources, a definitive list of LBO's was assembled. A leveraged or LBO firm is defined as a firm that underwent an LBO (or leveraged recapitalization) any time between 1981 and 1990.

LBO firms typically exit several local markets following the LBO, usually by selling the local division to another chain or spinning it off to the division's managers soon after the LBO. In total, 633 of the 13,512 supermarkets in the study were sold in a post-LBO asset sale. Of these 633 supermarkets, 187 were sold to the division's management in a second LBO of the division.

My approach is to treat the assets as if they were always owned by the eventual purchaser.[16] I take this conservative approach because, otherwise, one would see increased entry into LBO markets simply because of these asset transfers, not because of a change in post-LBO product-market competition.

For example, Safeway sold its Southern California division to Vons shortly after the Safeway LBO in 1986. Here, I add the stores in my sample that were part of Safeway's Southern California division to Vons's store total for 1985. Thus, for a Southern California city, the change in stores for Vons equals the net total of Safeway and Vons stores opened or closed in that city between 1985 and 1991. The change in the number of Safeway stores in any Southern California city equals zero. In constructing independent variables such as the LBO share of a market, the same convention is used.

Mergers among non-LBO firms were handled in a similar way. The stores of two firms which merged were treated as if they were always owned by the same firm. The one exception to this rule is that information about the acquisitions of very small independent chains was not generally available. Purchases of small independent chains by chains in the sample are thus counted as entry or expansion.

---

[14] Unfortunately, because the MSA's were redefined for most of New England, the Bridgeport, Connecticut, MSA is the only New England MSA appearing in the sample. This removes from consideration most of one LBO chain which was very successful (Stop & Shop) and most of another which was very unsuccessful (Supermarkets General).

[15] I have confirmed that the debt ratios of non-LBO firms with publicly traded debt or equity are in fact, much lower than the debt levels of LBO firms.

[16] This treatment is undertaken in constructing both the dependent and the independent variables that will be described later.

Information about asset sales was obtained by checking the *Wall Street Journal Index*, *Mergers and Acquisitions*, *Supermarket News*, *Supermarket Business*, and *Progressive Grocer*. Demographic data are obtained from Donnelly Marketing Information Services, a market research firm which provided the demographic data for the *Progressive Grocer* volume.

## V. Methodology and Results

### A. *Full-Market Regressions*

I first test the hypothesis that LBO's changed product-market competition by determining whether LBO's lead to more or fewer stores "fitting" in the local market. If a market can support more stores following an LBO than it could before (adjusting for other changes in the market), this supports the hypothesis that LBO's "soften" product-market competition. If fewer stores fit, this supports the hypothesis that LBO's "toughen" product-market competition.

The strategy employed here is to measure the percentage change in the number of stores in each MSA between 1985 and 1991 and to check whether this measure is related to the share of stores in each market in 1985 owned by chains that eventually undertook LBO's. This allows measurement of how market structure changed over the period in which the LBO's took place.

The specifications in this section control for several factors that might be expected to contribute to the growth of the number of supermarkets in a local market over this period: the growth in the number of households in the MSA and household growth adjusted for MSA area, the growth in median income and its square, and the change in the share of households that have an income of less than $10,000 were included. These variables are described in Table 4.

The use of these five market characteristics implicitly assumes that each market was in an equilibrium state in 1985: changes in the market structure between 1985 and 1991 should be due to changes in the market characteristics between 1985 and 1991. To adjust for the possibility that an MSA was

in an "over-stored" or "under-stored" equilibrium in 1985, I also include two characteristics of the market in 1985: a measurement of a city's deviation from the expected number of stores per household in 1985, and a measure of market concentration in 1985. These variables are also described in Table 4. The variable of interest, the share of LBO firms in the MSA, is the share of stores in the market in 1985 owned by a supermarket chain that would undertake an LBO by 1990.

Table 4 provides summary statistics for all of the variables used in this and subsequent specifications. Results for an ordinary least-squares (OLS) regression of the percentage change in the number of stores in a city between 1985 and 1991 on the LBO share of the market and the controls for market conditions described above are shown in column 1 of Table 5.

Table 5 shows that the LBO share of the market has a positive coefficient, but the coefficient is only statistically significant at the 22-percent level. The magnitude of the coefficient implies that, if a firm in an MSA owning 10 percent of the stores undertakes an LBO, the number of stores in the market is expected to grow by 1-percent more than it would otherwise. This insignificant effect may be due to there being, in fact, no effect of LBO's on the toughness of product-market competition or may be due to the fact that there simply may not have been enough time for market conditions to respond fully to the LBO's.

The second column of Table 5 makes a preliminary attempt to ascertain whether an effect might have been observed had more time elapsed since the LBO's. It repeats the regression specification of the first column but separates the LBO share of total stores into two groups: the share of stores that undertook LBO's prior to 1988 and the share of stores that undertook LBO's during or after 1988. This is done because, if it takes time for the market to adjust to changes in competition, one might not expect to see much response to the later LBO's. Indeed, Table 5 shows that the coefficient for the store share of LBO firms which took place prior to 1988 is positive

TABLE 4—SUMMARY STATISTICS

| Variable | Description | Mean | Standard deviation |
|---|---|---|---|
| A. *Variables:* | | | |
| Change in households (10,000's) [percentage change households] | Change in the number of households in the MSA between 1985 and 1991 | 5.50 [12.0] | 5.93 [10.1] |
| Change in households per square mile [percentage change households per square mile] | Change in households per square mile in the MSA between 1985 and 1991. This is included because the change in households may have a different impact if spread over a very large or very small area. | 49.7 [0.01] | 157 [0.03] |
| Change in median income ($10,000's) [percentage change in median income] | Change in median income in the MSA between 1985 and 1991 | 1.53 [64.2] | 4.73 [16.5] |
| Change in median income squared (in $1 × 10^8) [percentage change in squared income] | Change in squared median income in the MSA between 1985 and 1991 | 9.95 [172] | 4.66 [53.7] |
| Change in the share households with income less than $10,000 | Change in the share of households with annual incomes of less than $10,000 in the MSA between 1985 and 1991 | −0.0534 | −0.0227 |
| Deviation in mean stores per household [percentage deviation in mean stores per household] | MSA's deviation in 1985 from the number of stores that it would be predicted to have given the number of households in the MSA in 1985. I estimate that MSA's in 1985 have 40 stores plus $2.3 \times 10^{-4}$ stores per household. | 0.00 [−7.11] | 30.0 [24.8] |
| Share of LBO firms | Share of stores in the MSA in 1985 owned by firms that would undertake LBO's by 1991 | 0.220 | 0.191 |
| Share of early-LBO firms | Share of stores in the MSA in 1985 owned by firms that would undertake LBO's prior to 1988 | 0.108 | 0.156 |
| Share of late-LBO firms | Share of stores in the MSA in 1985 owned by firms that would undertake LBO's in 1988 or later | 0.111 | 0.128 |
| Herfindahl index | Sum of the squared market shares of the five firms with the largest market shares in the MSA, where a firm's market share is defined as its share of total stores in a market | 0.120 | 0.020 |
| B. *Incumbent Firm Variables:* | | | |
| Store share, non-LBO incumbents | Incumbent firm's share of the total stores in the MSA in 1985 | 0.116 | 0.098 |
| Store share, LBO incumbents | Incumbent firm's share of the total stores in the MSA in 1985 | 0.143 | 0.108 |
| Total stores in chain, non-LBO incumbents | Total stores in the sample of 100 MSA's owned by the incumbent in 1985 | 307 | 284 |
| Total stores in chain, LBO incumbents | Total stores in the sample of 100 MSA's owned by the incumbent in 1985 | 283 | 227 |

TABLE 4—*Continued.*

**B.** *Incumbent Firm Variables: (Continued)*

| | |
|---|---|
| Number of firm-MSA observations in which non-LBO incumbents add stores: | 79 |
| Number of firm-MSA observations in which non-LBO incumbents neither add nor subtract stores: | 20 |
| Number of firm-MSA observations in which non-LBO incumbents subtract stores: | 85 |
| Number of firm-MSA observations in which LBO incumbents add stores: | 47 |
| Number of firm-MSA observations in which LBO incumbents neither add nor subtract stores: | 19 |
| Number of firm-MSA observations in which LBO incumbents subtract stores: | 47 |
| Number of MSA's in which de novo entry occurs: | 39 |

TABLE 5—OLS SPECIFICATIONS

| Variable | Coefficients | | |
|---|---|---|---|
| | (1) | (2) | (3) |
| Constant | −0.0070 | 0.0075 | −0.0006 |
| | (0.1386) | (0.1380) | (0.1572) |
| Percentage change in households | 0.6347** | 0.5952** | 0.5377** |
| | (0.1569) | (0.1581) | (0.1651) |
| Percentage change in income | −0.6731 | −0.7661 | −0.5778 |
| | (1.1708) | (1.6374) | (1.1935) |
| Percentage change in income squared | 0.1974 | 0.2282 | 0.1918 |
| | (0.3558) | (0.3537) | (0.3630) |
| Change in share with income less than $10,000 | −0.0071 | −0.0076 | −0.0044 |
| | (0.0084) | (0.0084) | (0.0088) |
| Percentage change in households per square mile | 58.7209 | 60.0863 | 52.8402 |
| | (54.0745) | (53.6788) | (54.2677) |
| Percentage deviation from mean stores per household | −0.0866 | −0.0831 | −0.1194 |
| | (0.0575) | (0.0571) | (0.0620) |
| Herfindahl index | −0.1079 | −0.1171 | −0.2920 |
| | (0.2818) | (0.2798) | (0.3036) |
| Share LBO | 0.0966 | — | — |
| | (0.0775) | | |
| Share early LBO | — | 0.1736* | 0.1438 |
| | | (0.0931) | (0.1369) |
| Share late LBO | — | −0.0175 | 0.0280 |
| | | (0.1094) | (0.1141) |
| Regional dummies included? | no | no | yes |
| $R^2$ | 0.30 | 0.32 | 0.34 |
| $N$ | 85 | 85 | 85 |

*Notes:* The dependent variable is the percentage change in the total number of stores in the MSA between 1985 and 1991. Standard errors are in parentheses.

   *Significantly different from zero at the 5-percent level.

  **Significantly different from zero at the 1-percent level.

and significant at the 7-percent significance level. The coefficient for the share of later LBO's is insignificant at standard levels.

It has been suggested that regional dummy variables should be included in this regression to control for unmodeled city heterogeneity. The regression was reestimated using dummy variables for the Northeast, Midwest, and South (with the West as a base case). None of the dummy variables was statistically significant at even the 30-percent level. The inclusion of the dummies shrank the estimated coefficient of the share of early LBO's slightly, to 0.144 from 0.174, and decreased the statistical significance level of the coefficient to 30 percent. The coefficient for late LBO's became positive, but remained insignificant.

These results offer a preliminary suggestion that the presence of leveraged firms in the market does lead to a change in market structure. However, many hypotheses other than a change in the "toughness" of product-market competition could be put forth to explain these results. For example, if undertaking an LBO greatly decreased a firm's total costs, then LBO firms might find it profitable to expand. Markets populated by these firms might experience faster total store growth than other markets. In the following section, I introduce tests which will avoid these alternative hypotheses and which attempt to measure separately those changes in market structure which would be expected to occur relatively quickly following the LBO from those which might be expected to take more time to occur.

## B. *Expansion by Incumbent Firms*

In this section, I examine the question of why large supermarket chains that are actively competing in a market might choose to add or subtract stores in that market on net. To do this, I identify the 50 chains with the largest number of stores in 1985 in the sample.[17] After adjusting for mergers and

acquisitions as described in Section III, 48 chains are left for study. It is the expansion decisions of these firms in each of the 85 markets in which they are incumbents that will be studied. These firms account for 6,068 of the 13,512 supermarkets in the MSA's in the study. There are a total of 297 firm-city pairs in which the firm is an incumbent in the city in 1985.

Because of the small, integer number of stores added or subtracted by a chain in a local market, one should not ignore the discreteness of the data when analyzing these decisions; in 36 percent of the observations for incumbent firms the incumbent adds or subtracts no more than one store. Thus, I adopt an ordered-probit methodology, estimating whether each large supermarket chain adds stores in a market, neither adds nor subtracts stores in a market, or subtracts stores in a market.[18] Because the determinants of these decisions may be very different for LBO and non-LBO incumbent firms, the specifications are estimated separately for the two sets of firms.

I measure the relationship between a firm's decision to add or subtract stores and the share of rival stores in the market in 1985 owned by firms that would eventually undertake LBO's. I control for demographic changes in the market and control for the possibility that the market was under- or over-stored in 1985. These control variables are described in Table 4.

---

[17]One set of firms is left out of the sample of top firms. These firms are those involved in the only major

antitrust challenge to a supermarket merger during the period. After the federal antitrust supervisory bodies decided not to challenge the purchase of Lucky Stores by American Stores, the California Attorney General's Office decided to pursue a challenge of the merger under the California antitrust statutes. The case was tied up in the courts for over a year, during which time American Stores was not allowed to merge the operations of the two firms and was restricted from opening and closing new stores in California. The parties to this merger are left out of the specifications here, though results including them were checked and are extremely similar.

[18]The ordered-probit methodology was used in the context of measuring the determinants of how many firms compete in a city in Timothy F. Bresnahan and Peter C. Reiss (1987, 1990).

TABLE 6—MAXIMUM-LIKELIHOOD ESTIMATION RESULTS FOR INCUMBENT FIRMS

| Variables | A. Non-LBO incumbents | | | B. LBO incumbents | | |
|---|---|---|---|---|---|---|
| | | Marginal effects | | | Marginal effects | |
| | Coefficient | $d \Pr[y=-1]$ $dx$ | $d \Pr[y=1]$ $dx$ | Coefficient | $d \Pr[y=-1]$ $dx$ | $d \Pr[y=1]$ $dx$ |
| Change in households | 0.0339[a] (0.0198) | −0.0134 | 0.0129 | −0.0262 (0.0262) | 0.0102 | −0.0054 |
| Change in income | −2.7210 (2.0230) | 1.0788 | −1.0358 | 3.9310 (2.6440) | −1.5337 | 0.8153 |
| Change in income squared | 0.2590 (0.1850) | −0.1027 | 0.0986 | −0.3690 (0.2400) | 0.1440 | −0.0765 |
| Change in share with income less than $10,000 | −0.2128 (0.1435) | 0.0844 | −0.0810 | 0.2154 (0.1764) | −0.0840 | 0.0447 |
| Change in households per square mile | −0.0008 (0.0006) | 0.0003 | −0.0003 | 0.0005 (0.0063) | −0.0002 | 0.0001 |
| Deviation from mean stores per household | 0.0010 (0.0038) | −0.0004 | 0.0004 | 0.0032 (0.0046) | −0.0012 | 0.0007 |
| Total stores | −0.0012** (0.0004) | 0.0005 | −0.0004 | 0.0007 (0.0006) | −0.0003 | 0.0001 |
| Market share | 2.1970* (1.0566) | −0.8711 | 0.8363 | −2.7866[a] (1.5580) | 1.0872 | −0.5780 |
| Herfindahl index | 2.1396 (1.7995) | −0.8483 | 0.8145 | 0.1315 (3.6680) | −0.0513 | 0.0273 |
| Share LBO | 1.7016* (0.7557) | −0.6746 | 0.6477 | 1.7620 (1.1292) | −0.6875 | 0.3655 |
| Exit threshold | 0.0996 (0.6693) | | | 0.8998 (0.9534) | | |
| Entry threshold | 0.4173 (0.6697) | | | 1.3547 (0.9561) | | |
| Number of observations | 184 | | | 113 | | |

*Notes:* The dependent variable has the following values: $Y_{ij} = +1$ if firm $i$ withdraws at least one store from market $j$, $Y_{ij} = 0$ if firm $i$ neither adds nor withdraws stores from market $j$, and $Y_{ij} = +1$ if firm $i$ adds stores in market $j$. Standard errors are reported in parentheses.
[a]Significantly different from zero at the 10-percent level.
*Significantly different from zero at the 5-percent level.
**Significantly different from zero at the 1-percent level.

I also include variables to describe the rivalry faced by firm $i$ in market $j$. These are a measure of concentration in the local market and firm $i$'s share of total stores in market $j$. To control for chain size, I include a variable measuring the total number of stores that firm $i$ has in the entire sample in 1985. These are described in Table 4 as well. The variable of most interest, Share LBO$_{ij}$, is the share of LBO firms among firm $i$'s rivals in market $j$. Firm $i$'s own stores are not counted when constructing either the numerator or the denominator of this share. Thus, the variable characterizes the rivalry facing firm $i$ in market $j$.

Part A of Table 6 shows the results of this specification for non-LBO incumbents (a total of 184 firm-market pairs). The coeffi-

cients for the demographic variables, with the exception of the change in households per square mile, have the same sign as the corresponding variables in Table 5. Only the coefficient for the change in households is statistically significant. The coefficient for the firm's market share is positive and significant. This suggests that firms with large market shares in a market are the most likely to expand. The results also suggest that large chains are less likely to expand than smaller chains. This result should be interpreted with caution because the coefficients are only estimated for a sample of fairly large chains.

The coefficient for the share of firm $i$'s rivals in market $j$ which have undertaken LBO's is positive and significant at the 3-

percent level. The "marginal effects" show that, in a city in which all market characteristics are held at their mean, adding the LBO of a firm with a 10-percent market share would increase the probability that a given non-LBO firm will add stores in the market by approximately 6.5 percent. This result supports the results in Section I which suggest that LBO's lead to a decrease in the toughness of competition in the market; when a firm undertakes an LBO, rival non-LBO firms in the market find expansion attractive.

Part B of Table 6 repeats the specification of Part A, except the expansion decisions of LBO firms are used as the dependent variables. The coefficients for all of the demographic variables are statistically insignificant, and many have the opposite signs from the previous specifications. In contrast to the specification for non-LBO stores, the coefficient for total stores is positive, and the coefficient for the firm's own market share is negative.

The coefficient for the share of firm $i$'s rivals in market $j$ which are LBO firms is positive, as in the previous specification, but significant only at the 12-percent level. This result provides some evidence for the hypothesis that LBO's decrease the "toughness" of product-market competition, although the results are clearly weaker than for non-LBO firms.

As mentioned before, one reason for examining expansion by incumbent firms separately from new entry into local markets is that one would expect that incumbent firms would be able to begin to respond relatively quickly to local market conditions. Thus, one would expect that a firm adding stores in response to an LBO would have added at least one store by 1991, since the last LBO took place in early 1990. In Table 7, I divide LBO's into those that took place prior to 1988 (early LBO's) and those that took place during or after 1988 (late LBO's) and repeat the specifications of Tables 6. In both columns, the coefficient for the early-LBO share is only slightly larger than the coefficient for the late-LBO share. The hypothesis that the coefficient for early LBO's is

larger than the coefficient for late LBO's is not rejected at standard significance levels. This is consistent with the view that expansion by rival incumbents in response to LBO's should begin quickly.

Several tests were undertaken to test the robustness of the results. First, because these specifications use firm-level data, the concern arises that unmodeled firm heterogeneity may affect the basic results. These results were reestimated including firm dummy variables. Because of the number of firm dummy variables relative to the number of observations, it was necessary to pare down the specification in order to estimate this relationship. The basic specification was thus reestimated pooling data from LBO and non-LBO firms and including firm dummy variables. The coefficient for the LBO share of the market remains positive and is statistically significant at the 6-percent level.

Unfortunately, the results could not be reestimated with city or even state dummy variables because there are not enough observations per geographic area. However, the results for both LBO and non-LBO firms are robust to the inclusion of dummy variables for the Midwest, West, South, and East Coast. The coefficient for share LBO in the non-LBO firm regressions remains positive and significant at the 3-percent level; the coefficient for share LBO in the LBO firm regressions remains positive and significant at the 6-percent level.

Cross-firm within-city correlation of the error term might lead to the estimation of inflated significance levels. The regression results were checked for robustness to this possibility. Table 7 was reestimated using one observation per MSA. The dependent variable took the value of 1 if the supermarket chains in the sample in the MSA added stores on net; it took the value of 0 if they neither added nor subtracted stores, and it took the value of −1 if they subtracted stores on net. The right-hand-side variables took their mean value for the MSA. The specification was done separately for LBO firms and non-LBO firms, as before. In the specification for non-LBO firms, there were

TABLE 7—MAXIMUM-LIKELIHOOD ESTIMATION RESULTS FOR INCUMBENT FIRMS

| | A. Non-LBO incumbents | | | B. LBO incumbents | | |
|---|---|---|---|---|---|---|
| | | Marginal effects | | | Marginal effects | |
| Variables | Coefficient | $\frac{d\Pr[y=-1]}{dx}$ | $\frac{d\Pr[y=1]}{dx}$ | Coefficient | $\frac{d\Pr[y=-1]}{dx}$ | $\frac{d\Pr[y=1]}{dx}$ |
| Change in households | 0.0330[a] (0.0202) | −0.0131 | 0.0126 | −0.0283 (0.0265) | 0.0110 | −0.0057 |
| Change in income | −2.6630 (2.0190) | 1.0553 | −1.0152 | 4.2400 (2.6840) | −1.6511 | 0.8565 |
| Change in income squared | 0.2550 (0.1850) | −0.1010 | 0.0972 | −0.3950 (0.2430) | 0.1538 | −0.0798 |
| Change in share with income less than $10,000 | −0.2125 (0.1438) | 0.0842 | −0.0810 | 0.2358 (0.1793) | −0.0918 | 0.0476 |
| Change in households per square mile | −0.0008 (0.0006) | 0.0003 | −0.0003 | 0.0008 (0.0064) | −0.0003 | 0.0002 |
| Deviation from mean stores per household | 0.0012 (0.0038) | −0.0005 | 0.0004 | 0.0032 (0.0046) | −0.0013 | 0.0007 |
| Total stores | −0.0012** (0.0004) | 0.0005 | −0.0004 | 0.0006 (0.0006) | −0.0002 | 0.0001 |
| Market share | 2.1043* (1.0503) | −0.8339 | 0.8022 | −2.7507[a] (1.5434) | 1.0712 | −0.5557 |
| Herfindahl index | 2.0584 (1.8184) | −0.8157 | 0.7847 | −0.2282 (3.6914) | 0.0889 | −0.0461 |
| Share early LBO | 1.7032[a] (0.9073) | −0.6749 | 0.6493 | 1.9126 (1.1192) | −0.7448 | 0.3864 |
| Share late LBO | 1.4087 (0.8865) | −0.5582 | 0.5370 | 1.13798 (1.3221) | −0.5373 | 0.2787 |
| Exit threshold | 0.0996 (0.6693) | | | 0.9035 (0.9542) | | |
| Entry threshold | 0.4173 (0.6697) | | | 1.3866 (0.9569) | | |
| Number of observations | 184 | | | 113 | | |

*Notes:* The dependent variable has the following values: $Y_{ij} = -1$ if firm $i$ withdraws at least one store from market $j$, $Y_{ij} = 0$ if firm $i$ neither adds nor withdraws stores from market $j$, and $Y_{ij} = +1$ if firm $i$ adds stores in market $j$. Standard errors are reported in parentheses.
[a]Significantly different from zero at the 10-percent level.
*Significantly different from zero at the 5-percent level.
**Significantly different from zero at the 1-percent level.

79 observations, and the coefficient for the average share of LBO rivals remained positive and was statistically significant at the 5-percent level. In the specification for LBO firms, the coefficient for the average share of LBO rivals remained positive but was statistically significant at only the 25-percent confidence level. The results for this LBO incumbent specification should be treated with extreme caution, however, as only 28 observations were available.

Finally, the importance of the use of the ordered-probit specification was investigated. Table 8 reestimates Table 7 using the actual change in the number of stores for each incumbent firm as the dependent vari-

able. Because the left-hand-side variable varies so much in scale, heteroscedasticity-robust standard errors are used, following the method of Halbert White (1980). The coefficient for the share of early-LBO firms remains positive and statistically significant at the 6-percent level in the regression for non-LBO incumbents. The coefficients for the share of late-LBO firms is approximately zero. This is not surprising. The ordered-probit methodology examines whether any response to the LBO has occurred, while this specification measures the magnitude of the response. It is not surprising that, by 1991, very few stores have been built "responding" to the later LBO's. The

TABLE 8—OLS ESTIMATION RESULTS
FOR INCUMBENT FIRMS

| | Coefficients | |
| --- | --- | --- |
| | (1) | (2) |
| | Non-LBO | LBO |
| Variables | incumbents | incumbents |
| Change in households | −0.0660 | −0.2690 |
| | (0.1170) | (0.2350) |
| Change in income | 0.2860 | 14.0750 |
| | (6.2420) | (14.1650) |
| Change in income squared | 0.0900 | −1.3100 |
| | (0.5750) | (1.2500) |
| Change in share with income | −0.4167 | 0.5441 |
| less than $10,000 | (0.4084) | (0.9351) |
| Change in households per | −0.0033 | 0.0003 |
| square mile | (0.0039) | (0.0352) |
| Deviation from mean stores | 0.0575* | 0.0268 |
| per household | (0.0250) | (0.0435) |
| Total stores | −0.0055* | −0.0005 |
| | (0.0022) | (0.0042) |
| Market share | 7.0556 | −28.1176** |
| | (5.4637) | (10.2838) |
| Herfindahl index | 29.6984 | 30.6566 |
| | (11.9950) | (27.0131) |
| Share, early LBO | 7.9665ᵃ | 0.7648 |
| | (4.1466) | (5.7235) |
| Share, late LBO | −1.0105 | −5.8049 |
| | (3.9945) | (9.0537) |
| Constant | −6.4550* | −3.2238 |
| | (3.1960) | (6.7199) |
| $R^2$ | 0.12 | 0.14 |
| Number of observations | 184 | 113 |

*Notes:* The dependent variable is the number of stores that firm $i$ has added to market $j$. It is negative if the firm has subtracted stores from market $j$. White (1980) robust standard errors are in parentheses.

ᵃSignificantly different from zero at the 10-percent level.

*Significantly different from zero at the 5-percent level.

**Significantly different from zero at the 1-percent level.

cumbent firms would be the first detectable response to a change in conditions in a local market.

## C. *Entry*

In this subsection, I examine de novo entry by a large supermarket chain into a local market.[19] I extended the data set to 1993 by searching the Nexis data base for announcements of new entry. This is done for the entry specifications and not for the expansion specifications above for two reasons. First, because one expects entry to lag changes in market conditions more than expansion, it is more important to have as recent data as possible for new entry. Second, the supermarket trade press does not, in general, announce that a supermarket chain is opening new stores in a city in which it already has stores, though it does report that a large supermarket chain is entering a new local market.

The specification for the entry model in column 1 of Table 9 is a simple probit. The dependent variable takes the value of 0 if no entry occurs in the city between 1985 and 1993. The dependent variable takes the value of 1 if entry occurs in that period. Entry is defined to occur when a large supermarket chain of more than 25 stores opens at least one store in an MSA in which it was not an incumbent in 1985. Also included as entry is the opening of a hypermarket by K Mart or WalMart.[20]

The variables included in the entry regressions are a subset of those included in

results in column 2 of Table 8 offer no support for the hypothesis that LBO firms respond to the LBO's of their rivals.

The results in this subsection suggest that non-LBO firms find expansion attractive in markets dominated by LBO firms. As expected, the results in this subsection are stronger than those which pool the store additions of incumbent firms and new entrants. This is consistent with the expectation that expansion or contraction by in-

[19] This is not the first paper to study de novo entry into local markets in the supermarket industry. Ronald W. Cotterill and Lawrence E. Haller (1992) study de novo entry into cities by supermarket chains. They do not consider the leverage characteristics of incumbent firms. They consider entry over a different time period using a different data set and methodology.

[20] A hypermarket is a full supermarket combined with a general merchandise store. While neither K Mart nor WalMart owned 25 supermarkets at the time that they opened hypermarkets, they are obviously large retailing chains and were thus included.

TABLE 9—RESULTS FOR NEW ENTRY

| Variable | (1)<br>Coefficient | (2)<br>Marginal effects<br>$\dfrac{d \Pr[y=1]}{dx}$ | (3)<br>Coefficient |
|---|---|---|---|
| Change in households | 0.0841*<br>(0.0395) | 0.0126 | $2.23 \times 10^{-6}$*<br>$(1.13 \times 10^{-6})$ |
| Change in income | 4.6880<br>(2.9970) | 0.7038 | $1.15 \times 10^{-4}$<br>$(7.0 \times 10^{-5})$ |
| Change in income squared | $-0.4950^{a}$<br>(0.2910) | $-0.0743$ | $1.22 \times 10^{-9a}$<br>$(6.75 \times 10^{-10})$ |
| Change in share with income<br>less than \$10,000 | 0.2859<br>(0.1806) | 0.0429 | 0.0702<br>(0.0388) |
| Change in households per<br>square mile | $-0.0025$<br>(0.0032) | $-0.0004$ | $4.19 \times 10^{-4}$<br>$(3.97 \times 10^{-4})$ |
| Deviation mean stores per<br>household | 0.0012<br>(0.0064) | 0.0002 | $6.95 \times 10^{-4}$<br>(0.0021) |
| Herfindahl index | 0.0887<br>(2.9218) | 0.0133 | 0.0147<br>(1.0290) |
| Share, early LBO's | $2.4183^{a}$<br>(1.1330) | 0.3630 | $0.7904^{a}$<br>(0.3835) |
| Share, late LBO's | 0.6756<br>(1.2177) | | 0.2960<br>(0.4317) |
| Constant | $-1.518$<br>(1.0364) | | 0.0758<br>(0.3248) |
| $R^2$ | | | 0.2010 |

*Notes:* The first column shows probit results. The dependent variable has the following values: $Y_j = 0$ if no entry occurs in market $j$; $Y_j = 1$ if entry occurs. The second column shows the marginal effects implied by the coefficients in column 1. The third column shows the results of the linear probability specification. Entry occurs in 39 of the 85 markets. Standard errors are reported in parentheses.

$^a$Significantly different from zero at the 10-percent level.

*Significantly different from zero at the 5-percent level.

the expansion regressions above. Since these regressions examine entry at the market level rather than the firm level, firm-specific characteristics must be excluded.

Table 9 shows that the coefficient for the early-LBO share is of a larger magnitude than the coefficient for the share of late-LBO firms. However, the hypothesis that the coefficient for the share of early LBO's is different from the coefficient for the share of late LBO's is rejected at only the 24-percent significance level. As expected, the share of early-LBO firms in the local market has a positive coefficient, statistically significant at the 3-percent level. The coefficient for the share of late-LBO firms is positive, but statistically significant at only the 58-percent level. This table thus sug-

gests that large supermarket chains find entry into local markets dominated by firms that undertook LBO's prior to 1988 attractive. There is only very limited evidence, however, that entry has responded to LBO's that took place during or after 1988.[21] The results of a linear probability model, shown in column 3 of Table 9 are substantially the same as the probit results.

[21] Once again, the results are robust to the inclusion of regional dummy variables. The coefficient for the share of early LBO's is positive and statistically significant at the 10-percent level; the coefficient for the share of late LBO's is positive and significant at the 42-percent level.

TABLE 10—COMPARISON OF 1985 ACCOUNTING VALUES FOR FIRMS THAT WOULD
EVENTUALLY UNDERTAKE AN LBO AND FIRMS THAT WOULD NOT
EVENTUALLY UNDERTAKE AN LBO

| | Mean | | |
| --- | --- | --- | --- |
| Accounting ratio | LBO firm | Non-LBO firm | $t$ statistic of difference |
| Operating income/sales | 0.0363 | 0.0395 | 0.48 |
| Net income/sales | 0.0040 | 0.0043 | 0.14 |
| Market value/book value of assets | 0.8316 | 0.8194 | 0.10 |
| Capital expenditures/assets | 0.1461 | 0.1300 | 0.80 |
| Retained earnings/net income | 0.3703 | 0.3266 | 0.76 |
| Dividends/net income | 0.2375 | 0.1896 | 0.39 |

## VI. An Alternative Hypothesis

The results of Section V suggest that supermarket firms find entry and expansion
attractive in markets dominated by firms
that undertook LBO's. I have suggested that
entry and expansion are attractive because
competition becomes less "tough" following
an LBO. In this section, I briefly explore the
alternative hypothesis that LBO's did not
change the toughness of product-market
competition, but rather, that firms that undertook LBO's were weak firms. If weak
firms undertook LBO's, then one might expect to see entry and expansion occur in
those markets dominated by LBO firms.

### A. Asset Sales

Even if LBO firms were underperformers
on average prior to their LBO's, this would
not necessarily affect the results of Section V if LBO firms sold off all underperforming divisions to non-LBO firms in post-
LBO asset sales. As discussed in Section IV,
the methodology used in Section V assigns
assets sold after LBO's to their eventual
owners. The sale of the division is not
counted as a loss of stores for the LBO firm,
nor is it counted as entry or expansion for
the purchaser. More importantly, the presence in a city of supermarkets that were
sold in a post-LBO asset sale is not counted
in calculating the store share of LBO firms
in the city. The asset-assignment procedure

helps to diminish the effect of these underperforming divisions on the results.

### B. Accounting Evidence

If the LBO event selects for firms that
were underperformers, then one might expect accounting data to reflect that LBO
firms were underperformers on average
prior to their LBO's. Table 10 contains accounting data for all of the supermarket
chains that were publicly traded in 1985.[22]
Eleven of these firms undertook an LBO
after 1985, and 20 did not.

The table shows that, on average, LBO
and non-LBO firms do not differ significantly. In particular, LBO firms do not generate significantly less operating income as a
share of sales or less net income as a share
of sales. Furthermore, the ratio of market
to book value of assets, a proxy for the
market's estimation of a firm's future
prospects, is slightly higher for LBO firms.
The ratio of capital expenditures to assets
and the ratio of retained earnings to net
income are somewhat higher for LBO firms,
although the difference is not statistically
significant.[23]

---

[22] These data are from Compustat.
[23] Firms which undertook LBO's early do not differ
significantly from firms which undertook them later,
except that firms which undertook LBO's early have
higher ratios of capital expenditures to assets than do
firms that undertook LBO's later.

## C. *Event-Study Evidence*

The event-study evidence presented in Section II does not support the alternative hypothesis. If it was common knowledge that LBO firms were underperformers and their behavior was unchanged by the LBO, then the LBO announcements would not contain positive information for rival firms, and there would be no share price response. On the other hand, if LBO's were expected to increase the toughness of product-market competition, then rivals would be expected to experience a negative share price response to the LBO announcement. Thus, the event-study finding of a positive share price response of firms to rivals' LBO's is consistent with the findings here that LBO's decrease the toughness of product-market competition. The event-study evidence is inconsistent with the hypothesis that LBO's were undertaken by firms that were known underperformers and that product-market competition did not change much following the LBO's.

## D. *Evidence from Early versus Late LBO's*

If LBO's select for firms that were chronic underperformers, and the LBO did not change the LBO firm's behavior, then one would expect to find that the LBO firm attracted entry and expansion even prior to its LBO. The pattern of coefficients for early and late LBO's in Tables 7 and 9 do not lend support to this suggestion.

In particular, if LBO's select for firms that were chronic weak underperformers, then one would expect that new entry into a city (in Table 9) would have responded to late LBO's. It seems unlikely that these firms were chronically weak and yet did not attract entry. It might be suggested that this is because early-LBO firms were very poor firms, while late-LBO firms were good firms. The results in Table 7, however, run counter to this suggestion. These results show that non-LBO incumbents are almost as likely to have *expanded* in the presence of late LBO's as in the presence of early LBO's.

The grocery trade press and firm 10K's and prospectuses indicate that the time elapsed between the decision to build a new store in a city and the actual building of the store is much longer for firms that are not incumbents in the city. Thus, if the LBO's that took place during or after 1988 actually changed product-market competition, one would expect to see that expansion by incumbent firms had responded by 1992, but one would not necessarily expect to see much evidence that new entry had responded by 1993. However, if nothing changed at the time of the LBO, then one would expect to see either that *neither* entry nor expansion is correlated with these LBO's or that *both* entry and expansion are correlated with these LBO's. The findings in Tables 7 and 9 are consistent with the hypothesis that competition did *change* at the time of the LBO's.

## VII. Summary and Conclusion

The principal results of this paper are that the announcement of an LBO increases the expected future profits of a firm's product-market rivals and that the presence of LBO firms encourages local entry and expansion by rivals. Both sets of results are suggestive that leverage makes product-market competition less "tough." The results lend empirical support to the theoretical models of Fudenberg and Tirole (1986), Bolton and Scharfstein (1990), and Phillips (1991).

The basic finding, that markets in which LBO's have occurred attract entry and expansion, is consistent with the alternative hypothesis that LBO firms were simply underperformers prior to their LBO's. Evidence against this hypothesis was presented.

The results of this paper strongly suggest that product-market competition changes when firms radically increase their leverage. However, it would be interesting to determine the dimensions on which competition in the product market changes. For example, neither the event-study evidence nor the evidence on entry, exit, and expansion can distinguish the hypothesis that price competition becomes less vigorous following an LBO from the hypothesis that quality competition becomes less vigorous following an LBO. For example, it has been suggested in the trade literature that LBO firms compete less fiercely in the area of store quality, placing their stores on slower renovation and repair schedules. It has also been suggested that LBO firms refuse to become embroiled in price wars with rivals. This study cannot identify which, if any, of these mechanisms brings about the change in product-market competition. An examination of price competition by leveraged and unleveraged supermarket chains is the subject of future research.

Finally, while this paper does suggest that the nature of competition changes when firm leverage changes, the results do not necessarily make any contribution to the debate concerning whether or not leveraged buyouts were value-maximizing. Clearly, LBO firms would rather their rivals did not expand and enter their markets. However, it is impossible to know whether the amount that firms deterred this entry and expansion prior to LBO's was efficient or inefficient. Thus, while these results cannot prescribe an optimal capital structure based on product-market outcomes, the results make clear that product-market effects of capital-market decisions must be considered a component of the choice of optimal capital structure.

## REFERENCES

Bolton, Patrick and Scharfstein, David S. "A Theory of Predation Based on Agency Problems in Financial Contracting." *American Economic Review*, March 1990, *80*(1), pp. 93–106.

Brander, James A. and Lewis, Tracy R. "Oligopoly and Financial Structure." *American Economic Review*, December 1986, *76*(5), pp. 956–70.

Bresnahan, Timothy F. and Reiss, Peter C. "Do Entry Conditions Vary Across Markets?" *Brookings Papers on Economic Activity*, 1987, (3), pp. 833–71.

_____. "Entry in Monopoly Markets." *Re-view of Economic Studies*, October 1990, *57*(4), pp. 531–53.

Cotterill, Ronald W. and Haller, Lawrence E. "Barrier and Queue Effects: A Study of Leading U.S. Supermarket Chain Entry Patterns." *Journal of Industrial Economics*, December 1992, *40*(4), pp. 427–40.

Eckbo, B. Espen. "Horizontal Mergers, Collusion, and Stockholder Wealth." *Journal of Financial Economics*, April 1983, *11*(1–4), pp. 241–73.

Fama, Eugene F. *Foundations of finance*. New York: Basic Books, 1976.

Fudenberg, Drew and Tirole, Jean. "A 'Signal-Jamming' Theory of Predation." *Rand Journal of Economics*, Autumn 1986, *17*(3), pp. 366–76.

Guedes, José C. and Opler, Tim C. "The Strategic Value of Leverage: An Exploratory Study." Mimeo, Cox School of Business, Southern Methodist University, 1992.

Jensen, Michael C. "The Eclipse of the Public Corporation." *Harvard Business Review*, September–October 1989, *67*(5), pp. 61–74.

Kaufman, Phillip R. and Handy, Charles R. *Supermarket prices and price differences: City, firm, and store-level determinants*, Economic Research Service Publication TB-1776. Washington, DC: U.S. Department of Agriculture, December 1989.

Magowan, Peter. "The Case for LBOs: The Safeway Experience." *California Management Review*, Fall 1989, *32*(1), pp. 9–18.

Maksimovic, Vojislav. "Capital Structure in Repeated Oligopolies." *Rand Journal of Economics*, Autumn 1988, *19*(3), pp. 389–407.

McAfee, R. Preston and Williams, Michael A. "Can Event Studies Detect Anticompetitive Mergers?" *Economics Letters*, 1988, *28*(2), pp. 199–203.

*Mergers and Aquisitions*. Philadelphia, PA: MLR, bimonthly, 1985–1992.

Phillips, Gordon M. "Financial Slack, Refinancing Decisions, and Firm Interaction." Working paper, Krannert School of Management, Purdue University, 1991.

_____. "Increased Debt and Product Market Competition: An Empirical Analysis."

Working paper, Krannert School of Management, Purdue University, 1992.

**Predicasts Funk and Scott index, United States.** Cleveland, OH: Predicasts, annual, 1985–1991.

**Progressive Grocer.** "Annual Report of the Supermarket Industry." April 1989, *68*(4).
_____. *Market scope.* White Plains, NY: MacLean Hunter Media, 1986, 1992.

**Retail tenants directory.** Clearwater, FL: National Mall Monitor, 1988.

**Rotemberg, Julio J. and Scharfstein, David S.** "Shareholder-Value Maximization and Product Market Competition." *Review of Financial Studies*, 1990, *3*(3), pp. 367–91.

**Spence, A. Michael.** "Capital Structure and the Corporation's Product Market Environment," in Benjamin Friedman, ed., *Corporate capital structures in the United States.* Chicago: University of Chicago Press, 1985, pp. 353–82.

**Supermarket News.** *Distribution study of gro-cery store sales.* New York: Fairchild, annual, 1987–1990.

**Stillman, Robert S.** "Antitrust Horizontal Merger Policy." *Journal of Financial Economics*, April 1983, *11*(1–4), pp. 225–40.

**Sutton, John.** *Sunk costs and market structure: Price competition, advertising, and the evolution of concentration.* Cambridge, MA: MIT Press, 1991.

**Wall Street Journal Index.** New York: Dow Jones, 1985–1991.

**Whinston, Michael D. and Collins, Scott C.** "Entry and Competitive Structure in Deregulated Airline Markets: An Event Study Analysis of People Express." *Rand Journal of Economics*, Winter 1992, *23*(4), pp. 445–62.

**White, Halbert.** "A Heteroskedasticity-Consistent Covariance Matrix Estimator and a Direct Test for Heteroskedasticity." *Econometrica*, May 1980, *48*(4), pp. 817–38.

# [10]

# Capital Structure and Product Market Behavior: An Examination of Plant Exit and Investment Decisions

**Dan Kovenock**
Purdue University and the Tinbergen Institute

**Gordon M. Phillips**
University of Maryland

*We examine whether sharp debt increases through leveraged buyouts and recapitalizations interact with market structure to influence plant closing and investment decisions of recapitalizing firms and their rivals. We take into account the fact that recapitalizations and investment decisions are both endogenous and may be simultaneously influenced by the same exogenous events. Following their recapitalizations, firms in industries with high concentration are more likely to close plants and less likely to invest. Rival firms are less likely to close plants and more likely to invest when the market share of leveraged firms is higher.*

We are grateful to David Denis, Owen Lamont, Peter MacKay, Vojislav Maksimovic, Steve Michael, Tim Opler, David Scharfstein, Dennis Sheehan, Jerry Thursby, Kathleen Weiss Hanley, and the referee and the editor, David Hirshleifer, for helpful discussions and comments, and to researchers at the Center for Economic Studies, where this research was conducted. We are also grateful to seminar participants at the Department of Justice, Indiana University, the University of Florida, Penn State University, Tilburg University, and Virginia Polytechnic Institute, as well as participants at the European Economic Association 1994 meetings, the Econometric Society's European meetings, the 5th Annual Conference in Finance and Accounting at the University of Michigan and the Western Finance Association. D. Kovenock would like to acknowledge comments from seminar participants and financial support from Erasmus University, the Center for Economic Studies at the University of Munich, and the Institut d'Analisi Economica CSIC at the Universitat Autonoma de Barcelona. Both authors would like to acknowledge financial support from the Center for the Management of Manufacturing Enterprises at the Krannert School of Management. This article was completed while Phillips was an ASA/NSF Research Fellow at the Center for Economic Studies. Any interpretations of the results as well as any errors or omissions are the authors'. Address correspondence to Gordon Phillips, College of Business, University of Maryland, College Park, MD, 20742.

*The Review of Financial Studies* Fall 1997 Vol. 10, No. 3, pp. 767–803
© 1997 The Review of Financial Studies 0893-9454/97/$1.50

*The Review of Financial Studies / v 10 n 3 1997*

Corporate finance has traditionally examined the influence of capital structure on investment and exit decisions without explicitly considering the nature of competition within an industry.[1] Recently there has been a growing interest in both finance and economics on the interaction between capital structure and product market behavior.[2] This article adds to the literature by examining whether capital structure decisions interact with plant closing and investment decisions after controlling for product market characteristics. We use plant-level data from the Longitudinal Research Database at the Bureau of the Census to examine whether factors predicted to be important in the finance and industrial organization literatures affect the plant closing and investment behavior of leverage increasing firms and their rivals. In addition to capital structure, factors we examine include industry variables, such as capacity utilization, demand and demand variability, and market concentration, and firm variables, such as market share and direct measures of plant-level productivity.

We examine 10 industries in which at least one of the top four firms recapitalizes using a large discrete change in capital structure through a leveraged buyout or financial recapitalization. Our results show that industry concentration, capacity utilization, and relative plant productivity are significant determinants of the recapitalizations and subsequent plant (dis)investment decisions. As might be expected, high capacity utilization is positively associated with firm investment and negatively associated with plant closings. We also find a significant negative association between total factor productivity and plant closings, providing evidence that firms closed relatively less efficient plants. Total factor productivity is also positively associated with firm investment. This provides evidence that firms increase their investment in their most productive plants. The high significance of these variables in explaining closing and investment decisions underscores the importance of controlling for productivity and capacity utilization when examining the effects of capital structure changes.

Market structure has important implications for the effect of debt. High debt by itself, when controlling for productivity and market structure, is not significantly related to closure and investment. The effect of high leverage on investment and plant closing is significant when the industry is highly concentrated. Following its recapitalization, a firm in an industry with high concentration is more likely to close

---

[1] Jensen (1993) has recently drawn attention to the importance of financial factors, productivity, and capacity utilization to the exit decision in his 1993 AFA presidential address.

[2] Theoretical articles include Brander and Lewis (1986, 1988), Maksimovic (1988), Poitevin (1989), and Bolton and Scharfstein (1990). Empirical articles include Chevalier (1995) and Phillips (1995). Kovenock and Phillips (1995) examine how to reconcile theory and evidence.

plants and less likely to invest. In addition, rival firms are less likely to close plants and more likely to invest when the market share of leveraged firms is higher. We find that a recapitalization, insofar as it increases the market share of high-debt firms, has a significant impact on rival firms' plant closing and investment decisions. Our results are consistent with the view that recapitalization is a strategic commitment that has an independent effect on rival firm investment.

Given that recapitalizations and investment decisions may be simultaneously influenced by contemporaneous shocks, and thus recapitalization may be endogenous, we also use predicted recapitalization as a measure of capital structure change in our regressions.[3] We estimate a first-stage regression using lagged values of plant-level productivity, industry capacity utilization, and market concentration to predict whether or not a firm recapitalizes and replace the recapitalization variable in our original regressions with its predicted value. The results with the predicted recapitalization variable are similar to those in the original regression, which shows that the debt change is indeed endogenous and is significantly associated with lagged values of productivity, industry demand, capacity utilization, and market concentration. The significance of the lagged values of capacity utilization, concentration, and demand in predicting the recapitalization shows that the capital structure change is a response to longer-run changes in industry demand and supply conditions. Single-period models and empirical analyses of changes in capital structure do not fully capture this adjustment.

These results augment previous findings for leveraged buyout firms by Kaplan (1989), Lichtenberg and Siegel (1990), and for firms in an industry setting by Chevalier (1995) and Phillips (1995).[4] Previous large sample analyses of leveraged buyouts did not examine whether recapitalization influences rival firms' decisions. Kaplan shows that firms that undergo management leveraged buyouts experience higher operating cash flows and decrease capital expenditures relative to their competitors. Our results add to Kaplan's by linking the closure decision to both leverage and market structure. Also, while Kaplan focuses on firm-level capital expenditures, we are able to look at more detailed investment decisions and control for confounding factors such as plant-level productivity and industry capacity utilization. Lichten-

---

[3] Note that this approach does not solve all potential endogeneity problems. Lagged shocks to the marginal product of capital that are not captured by the exogenous variables predicting (dis)investment may influence both contemporaneous investment and closure decisions along with predicted capital structure.

[4] The distinction between capital structure decisions made in a single-firm setting and in an industry equilibrium setting is the focus of the recent survey article by Maksimovic (1995).

*The Review of Financial Studies / v 10 n 3 1997*

berg and Siegel (1990) use census data to examine plant-level productivity. They examine a balanced sample of manufacturing plants without considering industry structure and decisions such as exit and investment and the interaction of capital structure with product market behavior. This study adds to Lichtenberg and Siegel by examining exit and investment decisions controlling for productivity, industry demand, and market structure.

Chevalier (1995) examines the exit decisions of firms in an intraindustry setting in the supermarket industry. This work extends Chevalier by examining 10 different manufacturing industries and by considering the influence of capacity utilization, market structure, and plant-level efficiency on investment and closing decisions. In her study of the supermarket industry, Chevalier finds that unleveraged firms are more likely to open stores and less likely to exit in markets where competitors have recently experienced a leveraged buyout. Chevalier controls for demand differences in multiple markets but does not consider differential efficiency or capacity utilization as factors that influence the closure decision.[5] We construct two different measures of plant-level efficiency: total factor productivity and relative plant scale. We also calculate market concentration variables and include direct measures of capacity utilization by industry.

This work augments Phillips (1995) by considering individual firm investment and plant closing decisions. Phillips examines price and quantity at the industry level subsequent to increases in leverage in four manufacturing industries. Finally, these results on how financing decisions interact with product market decisions add to the evidence in industrial organization which has analyzed exit decisions without considering financial structure.[6,7]

Our results shed light on the accuracy of several theoretical predictions appearing in the literature on the direct and strategic effects of capital structure changes on firm behavior. Capital structure affects a firm's behavior directly because it can influence contracting and alter the distribution of cash flows between claimants, as well as convey information about future investment. One prominent theory, most

---

[5] A recent article by Zingales (1995) examines firm exit in the trucking industry after deregulation. He finds that exit is more likely by financially constrained firms in the industry. Zingales' analysis does not include industry factors such as capacity utilization, and does not distinguish between capacity that changes ownership and capacity that leaves the industry. He does not find as strong an effect of productivity on exit with trucking data.

[6] Theoretical articles which examine plant exit in industrial organization include Ghemawat and Nalebuff (1985, 1990), Reynolds (1988), and Whinston (1988). Empirical articles on exit in industrial organization include Lieberman (1990) and Hayes (1992).

[7] Other related nonstrategic papers from the finance literature include Kim and Maksimovic (1990), Schary (1991), Long and Ravenscraft (1993), and DeAngelo and DeAngelo (1991).

commonly associated with Jensen (1986, 1993), argues that reducing retained earnings and free cash flow by increasing debt payments forces firms to raise money from external capital markets and helps to alleviate the agency problem associated with the allocation of internal funds. According to Jensen, in the 1980s leveraged acquisitions and buyouts were instrumental in helping to eliminate excess capacity caused by negative demand shocks and changes in productivity. Debt facilitated disinvestment.

The industrial organization literature has focused on the interaction between recapitalizing firms' and rival firms' decisions. This strategic product market effect of leverage is examined in Brander and Lewis (1986, 1988), Maksimovic (1986, 1988), Poitevin (1989), and Bolton and Scharfstein (1990). While the predictions of these models vary with the particular underlying assumptions chosen, one prominent model in this genre is the limited liability model of Brander and Lewis (1986). In the most popular version of this model, increased debt causes a firm to behave aggressively, increasing output, and its rivals to behave passively.

We find that increasing the share of debt in a firm's capital structure is consistent with more passive investment behavior (increased probability of closure and decreased investment) by recapitalizing firms and more aggressive behavior by rival firms. The significance of the concentration-debt interaction term on own investment and plant closing and the effect of high debt on rival investment and plant closing indicates the importance of strategic considerations. These strategic reactions need to be incorporated in any cost-benefit calculation for increasing debt. At the same time it is clear that most models addressing the strategic effects of debt are not capturing the salient features of increased leverage. In particular, our findings are not consistent with the prediction of more aggressive behavior of leveraged firms as in the Brander and Lewis limited liability model.[8]

This evidence does appear to provide some evidence that increased debt is associated with reduced investment. However, the capital structure change variables are only significant when interacted with market concentration. The importance of this interaction between concentration and increased debt suggests that the agency problems are more prevalent in concentrated industries, where the discipline of the market does not weed out nonoptimizing firms [see Leibenstein (1966)].

---

[8] Brander and Lewis explicitly consider quantity choice. We claim that the primary interest in the Brander–Lewis model derives from its investment interpretations and the resulting implications. The relationship between the Brander–Lewis quantity variable and investment is discussed in Section 2.1.

*The Review of Financial Studies / v 10 n 3 1997*

This article is organized as follows: Section 1 presents the factors, including capital structure, considered in empirical work to be potential determinants of plant investment and exit, and summarizes the theory describing their effects. Section 2 describes the data and the industries in this study. Section 3 presents the empirical results and discusses their implications. Section 4 concludes.

## 1. Models of Investment and Exit

### 1.1 Theoretical models

This section reviews the models that predict the important factors influencing a firm's investment decision and the decision to close down a plant. We focus on how industry factors interact with capital structure to influence firms' decisions. We classify theoretical models into three categories. First, we consider the direct and strategic effects of capital structure. Second, we consider plant productivity and capacity utilization. Third, we consider models of how market structure, demand, and demand changes influence investment and plant closing.

**1.1.1 Capital structure and investment: Direct effect of capital structure.** As noted by Harris and Raviv (1991) and many other authors, capital structure can affect investment because it changes the allocation of cash flows among claimants and conveys information about investment opportunities. Given a set of investment opportunities, capital structure is chosen to align incentives to maximize firm value. Early analyses of capital structure have noted the significance of industry conditions to the amount of debt financing by firms. Myers' (1977) analysis of the affect of debt on firms in industries with growth options is relevant to our analysis in that we examine the decision to invest as well as disinvest (close). In Myers' analysis, debt decreases investment because of "debt overhang." New investment cannot be financed because of existing senior debt claims. Jensen (1986, 1993) focuses explicitly on the disinvestment decision in the face of declining demand or technological change and argues that information and contracting problems between implicit or explicit claimants to the firm can make the disinvestment decision difficult for managers. Debt and debtlike instruments reduce free cash flow that may otherwise be allocated to inefficient investments and help align managerial incentives with those of stockholders.

This disinvestment hypothesis is one of the hypotheses addressed with our evidence. Its empirical implications are that increases in debt are associated with a reduction in own investment and an increase in the incidence of own plant closings. However, this disinvestment hypothesis does not consider how rival firm behavior might be related to a firm's debt choice.

**Strategic effect of capital structure.**   Models of strategic effects of capital structure begin with capital structure representing a credible commitment to alter plant closing or investment behavior. Given this commitment to change investment or closing decisions, rival firms may also change their closing or investment decisions. We identify and explore two different classes of models of strategic interaction. The first emphasizes the limited liability effect of debt, while the second deals with strategic investment effects of debt finance.[9]

The limited liability effect of debt financing was developed by Brander and Lewis (1986) and Maksimovic (1986). Brander and Lewis consider a two-stage game with two firms in which debt levels are chosen in the first stage to maximize firm value and output is chosen simultaneously in the second stage to maximize the return to equity. Due to the limited liability enjoyed by equity, a unilateral increase in debt leads to an output strategy that raises returns in good states and lowers returns in bad states. Under the assumptions of the "normal case" of the model, this will lead to an increase in the leveraged firm's output for each level of output of the rival firm.[10] This leads to a reduction in the equilibrium output chosen by the rival. As a result of this strategic effect, each firm would like to precommit to a high debt level, leading to a prisoners' dilemma in which positive debt levels arise in equilibrium and output is greater and profits lower than in the absence of debt.

The empirical implications of the Brander–Lewis limited liability model depend on the interpretation that is given to investment. The most common interpretation of quantity setting models is as a reduced form for a choice of scale of capacity that determines the firms' cost functions and the conditions of price competition [see, for instance Tirole (1988, p. 217), Shapiro (1989), Allen et al. (1994)]. Using this interpretation, quantity adjustment in the Brander–Lewis model may be equated with scale or capital adjustment, that is, investment. Hence, a firm's unilateral increase in debt would have a positive effect on its own investment and profits and a negative effect on its rival's investment and profits. These effects are also predicted when an increase in

---

[9] In Kovenock and Phillips (1995) we also examine the implications of a set of models known as strategic bankruptcy models. We do not examine the implications of these models in this article.

[10] In the alternative case considered by Brander and Lewis, where marginal profits are lower in better states of the world, neither firm will want to have a positive level of debt.

*The Review of Financial Studies / v 10 n 3 1997*

debt is an equilibrating response to previous adjustments in leverage on the part of rivals.[11]

The "strategic investment effect" is based on the pecking-order model of finance as in Myers (1984), in which internally generated funds are less costly, or are viewed by the firm's managers as less costly, than externally generated funds. Kovenock and Phillips (1995) detail how this effect might work in a model with profit-maximizing firms that engage in price competition with goods that are imperfect substitutes. In this model, debt causes own investment to decrease and rival investment to increase. The same result would occur with quantity setting firms, but own-firm profit would be lower than in the absence of debt. Hence we would not expect firms to issue debt unless other effects, such as the direct agency costs, are present. In Kovenock and Phillips, increasing debt payments in low demand states increases the cost of investment and helps alleviate an agency induced over-production problem. The empirical predictions are higher profits for both firms, higher investment for the rival firm, and lower investment for the high-debt firm.

### 1.1.2 Plant-level productivity and capacity utilization.

Several authors have predicted that productivity and capacity utilization are the primary exogenous factors that effect plant closing and investment. Jensen (1993, p. 833) argues that "Technological and other developments that began in the mid-twentieth century have culminated in the past two decades in ... rapidly improving productivity, the creation of excess capacity and, consequently, the requirement for exit." Other authors have also examined the influence of capacity utilization and productivity on exit. A recent study by Bresnahan and Raff (1993) shows that technological heterogeneity in the auto industry in the 1930s was important in determining survival probabilities. Those plants that adopted production line techniques and had larger sunk fixed capital had higher survival probabilities when faced with the strong decline in demand during the Depression. In addition to examining capital structure, we thus examine the influence of plant-level productivity, plant size, and industry capacity utilization, on investment and exit decisions. We calculate several different measures of plant-level productivity to examine whether low-productivity plants were indeed more likely to be closed in these industries.

---

[11] Capacity or scale adjustment is not the only interpretation that is consistent with the use of the Brander–Lewis model. Other models of investment share the same implications within the Brander and Lewis framework. For instance, reasonable specifications of standard models of cost-reducing investment [see, for instance, the case of no spillovers in d'Aspremont and Jacquemin (1988)] also have the property that increases in debt would lead to more aggressive own-firm behavior and passive rival-firm behavior.

### 1.1.3 Industry market structure, demand and demand uncertainty.

Several studies have examined plant-level exit from a strategic management and an industrial organization perspective. Harrigan (1980, 1988) and Harrigan and Porter (1983) examine the exit decision from a strategic management perspective. They propose that conditions of competition, uncertainty, demand changes, durable and specialized assets, and managerial resistance are important factors in the exit decision.

Ghemawat and Nalebuff (1985, 1990), Reynolds (1988), and Whinston (1988) offer more formal models of the exit decision. Ghemawat and Nalebuff (1985) examine who exits first in a declining demand industry in which a firm's production equals its total capacity or zero. They show that smaller firms will be the last to exit when faced with declining demand. Using a simulation, they conclude that large firms may require substantial scale economies in order to reverse this finding.[12] Whinston shows that with the existence of multiplant firms no strong prediction emerges. Who exits first depends on a number of market structure factors, including the size of the firms and the number of plants per firm. In our analysis, we include both these variables as control variables.

The finance literature has emphasized the role of demand uncertainty in investment and exit decisions. Brennan and Schwartz (1985), McDonald and Siegel (1986), Pindyck (1988), and Dixit (1989) examine the importance of output price uncertainty and the irreversibility of investment decisions. We examine both investment and closing decisions. We take the view that this option to close is not costless and there is a cost of investment similar to that in Brennan and Schwartz's analysis of the option to close a copper mine. They show that when firms are faced with stochastic output prices, initial investment decisions and plant closing decisions will be different from the decisions under perfect certainty. An increase in output price uncertainty will cause the optimal investment time and the optimal plant closing time to be at a later date. Irreversibility of investment will cause the optimal stock of capital to be lower. Our article does not attempt to directly estimate real option models, but rather tests whether demand and the variance of output prices in these industries influence investment and plant closing decisions.

### 1.2 The econometric specification

We estimate logistic and random effects probit regressions to identify factors that influence plant closings. The dependent variable equals

---

[12] Other models include Reynolds (1988), Ghemawat and Nalebuff (1990), and Hunsaker and Kovenock (1994). Lieberman (1990) and Hayes (1992) empirically examine plant closure in declining industries.

*The Review of Financial Studies / v 10 n 3 1997*

one if the firm closed a plant in a given year. The independent variables capture the firm and market conditions for each of the years for the firm and the industry. The equations are estimated using 12 years of data from 1979 to 1990, allowing varying observations per firm. As discussed in the theory section, in addition to variables capturing the capital structure changes, we include variables that capture plant-level efficiency, capacity utilization, and market structure. After estimating the probit specifications, we estimate the equations using a random effects panel probit model. This model, presented in Equation (1), allows for a random firm effect and equicorrelated errors within panel units [see Butler and Moffitt (1982) and Chamberlain (1984)]. In Equation (1) $y_{it}^*$ is the unobserved value of closing a plant, $y_{it}$ is the realized closure decision, $X_{it}$ is the matrix of $K$ independent variables which influence this decision each period, and $u_i$ is the random firm effect:

$$
\begin{aligned}
&y_{it}^* = \beta' X_{it} + u_i + v_{it}; \ i = 1, \ldots, N; \ t = 1, \ldots, T; \\
&y_{it} = 1 \text{ if } y_{it}^* > 0 \text{ and } 0 \text{ otherwise}; \\
&\text{var}[u_i + v_{it}] = \text{var}[\varepsilon_{it}] = \sigma_u^2 + \sigma_v^2; \\
&\text{corr}[\varepsilon_{it}, \varepsilon_{is}] = \rho = \sigma_u^2 / (\sigma_u^2 + \sigma_v^2).
\end{aligned}
\tag{1}
$$

This model also allows varying observations per firm [an unbalanced panel as in Hsiao (1986)]. The random effects probit model has an advantage over the logit model in that it allows for residual serial correlation within panel units as shown above. A disadvantage of the probit model is its specific distributional assumption based on the normal distribution [see the discussion in Chamberlain (1984), pp. 1270–1282].

A recapitalization variable and interaction variables are included as independent variables in the above specification. To attempt to control for the fact that debt choice is endogenous, we estimate a two-stage regression model replacing the recapitalization variable in the second-stage regression with its predicted value. We use a first-stage regression, given in Equation (2), to predict whether or not a firm recapitalizes.

$$
\begin{aligned}
z_{it}^* = \sum_{k=1}^{2} [&\beta_{1k}' \text{ (Market concentration)}_{i,t-k} \\
&+ \beta_{2k}' \text{ (Capacity utilization)}_{i,t-k} \\
&+ \beta_{3k}' \text{ (Output price variance)}_{i,t-k} \\
&+ \beta_{4k}' \text{ (Change in Demand)}_{i,t-k}] \\
&+ \beta_5' \text{ (Plant productivity)}_{i,t-1} \\
&+ \beta_6' \text{ (Firm size)}_{i,t} + \varepsilon_{it}; \\
z_{it} = 1 &\text{ if } z_{it}^* > 0 \text{ and } 0 \text{ otherwise};
\end{aligned}
\tag{2}
$$

In this first-stage recapitalization logistic regression, $z_{it}^*$ is the unobserved value of recapitalizing and $z_{it}$ is the realized recapitalization decision. This equation is estimated using an unbalanced panel logistic regression. In this regression our independent variables capture existing industry and firm conditions, following the specification of Kovenock and Phillips (1995). We include two lags ($k = 2$) of market concentration, capacity utilization, output price variance and industry demand, and one lag of relative plant productivity, along with contemporaneous firm size. Our measure of plant productivity is described below. The rest of the variables are described in detail in the next section.

We replace the debt change variable with the predicted probability of recapitalization in the second-stage regressions [Equation (1) above]. This predicted value is taken to be the measure of capital structure change in these equations. Comparing the results of the estimation using the predicted recapitalization with those using a contemporaneous capital structure change variable allows us to determine whether we are capturing a contemporaneous shock that might cause a firm to recapitalize and alter investment and plant closing decisions.

This two-stage procedure removes the influence of contemporaneous shocks that may influence both the capital structure change and the closure decision and thus impart a spurious causality to the capital structure change. This method does not solve all simultaneity problems. Lagged shocks may also influence predicted capital structure and contemporaneous investment decisions. Accordingly, we estimated other lag structures predicting capital structure change using data from two to four periods prior to the recapitalization (omitting $t - 1$ variables) and found qualitatively similar results.

Central in the above specification is a measure of plant productivity. We follow the procedure used by Caves and Barton (1990) and Lichtenberg and Siegel (1990), with several adjustments, to construct a measure of productivity called total factor productivity (TFP). Our calculations of TFP are described in the data appendix to this article. Unlike Lichtenberg and Siegel we do not require a balanced sample of either firms or plants for our analysis. Using a balanced sample, requiring that a plant is present for all years, potentially introduces a severe source of sample selection bias. New plants or old plants that close are thus not excluded from our sample.

To calculate TFP we have to make an assumption about the production function of the firm. We assume that the production function is Cobb–Douglas. The Cobb–Douglas form's advantage over merely calculating the factor share of each of the inputs is that it does not impose constant returns to scale. It is a fairly flexible form of the production function, but does assume that there is constant elasticity of

*The Review of Financial Studies / v 10 n 3 1997*

substitution. We also calculated TFP using a translog production function which relaxes the restriction of constant elasticity of substitution. The Cobb–Douglas form is given in Equation (3):

$$Q_{it} = A^* L_{1it}^{a_{1i}} L_{2it}^{a_{2i}} \ldots L_{Nit}^{a_{Ni}}; \tag{3}$$

where $Q_{it}$ represents output of plant $i$, in year $t$, the quantity $L_{jit}^{a_{ji}}$ ($j = 1, \ldots, N$) denotes the quantity of input $j$ used in production for plant $i$, in period $t$, $A$ represents a technology shift parameter, assumed to be constant by industry, and $a_i = \sum_{j=1}^{N} a_{ji}$ indexes returns to scale. Under constant returns to scale, $a_i = 1$; under increasing returns to scale, $a_i$ is greater than one.

We take the log of this production function and run a regression of log (total value of production) on log (inputs).[13] The difference between actual shipments and predicted shipments is our measure of TFP. It is a relative measure of productivity, thus average TFP for an industry will be zero. The census data that we use, described in the next section, has detailed information on inputs that the firm uses to produce its output. These variables used in the calculations, both outputs and inputs, and how we account for inflation and depreciation are described in detail in the Appendix.

We also estimate limited dependent variable and Tobit censored regression models to examine the factors that influence a firm's investment decisions. For the logistic regressions we code the dependent variable as one if the firm increases its capital expenditures by 5% or more in a given year. We estimate the regressions using a limited dependent variable for two reasons. First, observed investment is truncated at zero, as we do not observe disinvestment except for plant closure. Second, given that we scale the investment by net book value of the plant's assets, large investments by firms that begin the year with a small capital stock make this variable have very skewed positive values. Coding all values greater than a given cutoff as equal to one reduces the extent of this problem. We also used 10% as a cutoff value and found the results to be similar to those using a 5% cutoff. We also estimate the investment equations using a Tobit censored regression model. The dependent variable is defined as investment in machinery and buildings divided by beginning of period book value of assets.

---

[13] Ideally we would use the actual quantity produced. This data is, however, not available. We do control for changes in prices at the four-digit SIC code level to control for price movements of output produced. We describe the calculations and source of the data used to deflate output and some inputs in the Appendix. Actual input data in quantities is used for labor.

## 2. Data and Sample Selection

### 2.1 Plant closing and investment data

We examine exit and investment decisions using data from the Longitudinal Research Database (LRD),[14] located at the Center for Economic Studies at the Bureau of the Census. The LRD database contains detailed plant-level data on the value of shipments produced by each plant, the number of employees, and investment broken down by equipment and buildings. Plant-level data is aggregated to the firm level to examine investment decisions. In addition to the detailed plant-level data, there are several other advantages to this data. First, the database covers both public and private firms in manufacturing. Second, coverage is at the plant level and the output is assigned by plants at the four-digit industry SIC code. Thus, firms that produce in multiple SIC codes are not assigned to just one industry. Third, coverage at the plant level allows us to track plants as they change owners. Fourth, the database identifies when plants are closed and not merely changing ownership.

The LRD covers approximately 50,000 manufacturing plants every year in the Annual Survey of Manufactures (ASM), the database we utilize. In the ASM, plants are covered with certainty if they have more than 250 employees, smaller plants are randomly selected every fifth year to complete a rotating 5-year panel.[15] We confine our analysis to 1979–1990. We use 1979 as the starting year of our analysis because it is the first year of one of the 5-year panels and, second, because it allows us to include several years before the first of our capital structure changes; 1990 is the last year of data available at the time the analysis was undertaken.

We also examined whether plant openings are significant relative to closures for the industries examined in this study. There were 23 explicitly identified openings in the ASM versus 512 plant closures. We also examined the full quinennial 1982 Census of Manufactures to check the relative magnitude of plant closures versus openings in the full population of plants for the United States. In the 1982 Census of Manufactures there were 28 plant openings and 132 closures for the 10 industries in this study. Of these plants, 6 of the openings and 75 of

---

[14] See McGuckin and Pascoe (1988). The Longitudinal Research Database is unique in that it contains the underlying plant-level microdata that is released in aggregate form in the Annual Survey of Manufacturers and the Census of Manufacturers. All work must be done on site at the Census Bureau in Washington, D.C., because the individual plant data used in this study is confidential.

[15] For the industries in this study, the 1982 Annual Survey of Manufactures comprised a total of 1879 plants, with a total value of shipments of $73.879 billion. The 1982 Census of Manufactures (CM) comprised 4099 plants with a total value of shipments of $82.958 billion. Thus, the ASM represents 89% of the total value of shipments in the CM. Both the annual survey and the census cover public and private firms.

*The Review of Financial Studies / v 10 n 3 1997*

the closures were in the 1982 Annual Survey of Manufactures. Given this finding of a much smaller number of openings versus closures in the data, both in the LRD and in the 1982 census, only closures are analyzed. We did not count as a closure or opening cases in which a firm both closed and opened a plant in the same or subsequent years.

### 2.2 Industry selection

We identified 10 industries for this study: broadwoven fabrics, mattresses, paper products, polyethylene, flat glass, fiberglass, gypsum, car and consumer batteries, and tractor trailers. We identified increases in debt that have occurred because of discrete events, including leveraged buyouts, management leveraged buyouts, and public leveraged recapitalizations.

The 10 industries selected for this study satisfied the following three criteria: First, the industry has to have had significant financial recapitalizations either through leveraged buyouts or public leveraged recapitalizations. An industry is defined as having a firm with a major recapitalization if at least one of the top four firms (in market share) in the industry has had an increase in debt of at least 25 percentage points through either a leveraged buyout or a leveraged recapitalization. Second, the industry has to produce commodity products. An industry is defined as a commodity industry if the products are easily compared across producers.[16] This criterion reduces the problems of defining the scope of the market in which the firms interact and reduces issues of product differentiation. Third, the industry has to be a manufacturing industry (SIC code between 2000 and 3999). The LRD plant-level data that we are using for this study are only available for manufacturing.

Before proceeding it should be emphasized that, in relating our evidence to theory, the choice of industries examined is based on the primary criterion that at least one of the four largest (by market share) firms experienced a discrete increase in debt through a leveraged buyout or public recapitalization—further emphasizing that capital structure is a choice variable by firms. Thus we do *not* select industries that are necessarily characterized by having firms in economic or financial distress.[17] We do not select firms that have high leverage and decreased equity values because of poor product market performance.

The industries and firms involved in recapitalizations were identified by first finding firms that were involved in leveraged buyouts,

---

[16] This criterion was applied using the authors' judgment at the start of the analysis. No industry was dropped subsequent to the start of the study.

[17] See Ofek (1993) and Opler and Titman (1994) for analysis that specifically examine firms in financial distress.

management buyouts, or leveraged recapitalizations. To identify the leveraged buyout (LBO) and management buyout (MBO) firms we examined the *Wall Street Journal* index and also used two lists of LBO firms used in Opler (1993) and Rodin (1992). The public recapitalizations were identified using COMPUSTAT, Securities Data Corp. (SDC), and the *Wall Street Journal* index to find firms that paid out large cash dividends by increasing the debt in their capital structure. We identified 40 firms that recapitalized using LBOs and public recapitalizations in the industries examined in this study. The choice of relatively homogeneous product industries enables us to examine plant- and firm-level investment for specific products and match price and demand data from other sources such as the Federal Reserve Board and the Bureau of Labor Statistics.

### 2.3 Empirical specification

We include three broad classes of independent variables. First, we include variables that capture the capital structure changes. We identify the changes in financial structure and the market share of leveraged firms. The financial structure variables include the market share of highly leveraged rival firms (the sum of the value of shipments of all highly leveraged firms divided by the total industry value of shipments less the firm's own market share if the firm itself is highly leveraged), and a dummy variable that indicates whether the firm is highly leveraged as a result of a leveraged buyout or public recapitalization. We also include a variable that interacts the own high leverage variable with the four-firm market share index.

The second class of independent variables that we examine captures average plant-level efficiency for each firm. We calculate relative plant scale for each firm and two measures of plant-level productivity. A related question that this data allows us to address is whether inefficient plants close and whether the firms with relatively efficient plants increase investment in the face of changes in industry demand conditions and capital structure changes. The plant scale variable is calculated as plant capital stock divided by average industry capital stock. The two measures of plant-level productivity we investigated are relative labor productivity and total factor productivity (TFP). Relative labor productivity is calculated as output per worker divided by average industry output per worker at the plant level.

Our third class of independent variables captures market structure, demand, and demand changes. We include variables that measure the market structure of the industry, the size of firms, and the number of plants per firm. For market structure, we include the market share of the top four producers and the firm's market share. We lag the market share variable to capture the beginning period concentration faced by

*The Review of Financial Studies / v 10 n 3 1997*

a firm. Including end-of-period market structure would incorporate the result of closing and production decisions.

The market structure variables allow us to test the hypothesis that capital structure is a strategic choice variable that affects competition among firms in an industry. The market share variables combined with the efficiency variables allow us to examine whether plant closings result in the survival of more efficient firms and whether market shares change in the same direction as average efficiency changes in the industry.

For demand variables we include capacity utilization, the change in demand, and the variance of the output prices. This class of variables allows us to examine the conjecture, advanced recently by Jensen (1993), that there has been a failure of firms to adjust to broad structural shifts in demand and technology, causing excess capacity to exist in many industries. To provide some evidence on this hypothesis, we include capacity utilization at the four-digit SIC code. The capacity utilization number is obtained from *The Annual Survey of Capacity Utilization*, a publication of the Bureau of the Census. The capacity utilization measure we use from this survey represents output as a percentage of normal full production.[18] The external demand variables are from the Survey of Current Business and represent demand indices for the user of the industry's product. These demand indices vary by industry and were selected to correspond as closely as possible to a demand proxy for that industry. For example, for the gypsum industry we use the level of new residential and commercial construction, for the tractor-trailer industry we use shipments of new manufactures, and for chemicals used in plastics we use auto production.

We include the variance of output prices to capture the stochastic nature of demand prices that is predicted to affect investment and plant closing by Brennan and Schwartz (1985), McDonald and Siegel (1986), Pindyck (1988), and Dixit (1989). Output price data by industry is obtained from the Bureau of Labor Statistics. We use the data at the disaggregated seven-digit SIC code product level. These are available monthly over the period of time we consider. To get a measure of the product price variance we use 24 months of data—12 months of lagged data and 12 months of leading data. It is therefore calculated using a time series of data for each product, and thus does not represent a true cross-sectional variance. Assuming that prices are from

---

[18] The procedure the census uses to calculate capacity utilization changed in 1989. We did not attempt to adjust the pre-1989 numbers but assume that the relative differences across industries are not affected greatly. See the *Annual Survey of Capacity Utilization*, Bureau of the Census, 1989.

a stationary distribution, it should provide a good proxy for output price uncertainty.

## 3. Results

In this section we present our results on plant closing and firm-level investment decisions of both recapitalizing firms and their rivals following sharp increases in debt financing. Table 1 provides statistics for the firms and plants examined in our analysis, including the number of plants and firms in the year before the recapitalizations. We also present average TFP measures for closures. Our calculation of TFP using a translog production function revealed that for nearly every industry the coefficients on the additional second-order cross-product terms were not significantly different from zero—thus we maintain the Cobb–Douglas specification.

Table 1 shows that average TFP of all the plants was not significantly different in the two samples. For each of the sets of closures, average TFP was significantly lower than the average industry plant's TFP. Average TFP for closures of the nonrecapitalizing firms was −.2061, with a standard error of the mean of .0284. The average TFP for closures of the recapitalizing firms was −.260, with a standard error of the mean of .0655. Thus, the unconditional average TFP of plants closed by recapitalizing and nonrecapitalizing firms is not statistically different.

### 3.1 Plant closure decisions

Table 2 presents summary statistics by individual industries. We present both the number of firms and the number of plants they operated in 1979. The number of plant closures over the period 1979 to 1990 and their total factor productivity are also presented for each industry.[19]

The summary statistics by industry reveal several interesting patterns. First, plant closures represent a fairly large fraction, 25.6%, of the total number of plants operating in 1979. Second, the productivity measure for all plants closed is significantly negative. These numbers are relative to the unclosed plants in the same industry and year. Finally, the plants closed by high-debt firms were of lower average productivity than the industry plants, and in all but two of the industries, were of lower average productivity (though not significantly so) than the plants closed by nonrecapitalizing firms.

Table 3 estimates a logistic dependent variable regression to examine plant closing decisions. We aggregate all plant-level variables

---

[19] In compliance with government disclosure restrictions, we are prohibited from presenting any individual firm statistics from the LRD. This prevents us from presenting TFP statistics by industry for the plant closures of the recapitalizing firms.

*The Review of Financial Studies / v 10 n 3 1997*

**Table 1**
**Sample characteristics by recapitalization**

| | Sample of firms | |
| --- | --- | --- |
| | Nonrecapitalizing firms | Public recapitalization and LBO firms |
| Number of firms at time of recapitalization[a] | 827 | 40 |
| Average firm size | 220.68 | 569.77 |
| (value of shipments in $ millions) | | |
| Average industry concentration index | 0.420 | 0.552 |
| Standard deviation | (0.150) | (0.224) |
| Number of plants[a] | 1482 | 405 |
| Average plant age (years)[b] | 9.04 | 13.39 |
| Standard error of mean | (0.104) | (0.197) |
| Total factor productivity | | |
| Average TFP | 0.0084 | −0.0125 |
| Standard error of mean | (0.0073) | (0.0141) |
| Number of plant closures (1979–1990) | 452 | 60 |
| Total factor productivity of closures | | |
| Average TFP | −0.2061 | −0.2602 |
| Standard error of mean | (0.0284) | (0.0655) |
| Number of plant openings (1979–1990)[c] | 23 | 0 |

Plant-level data is obtained from the Annual Survey of Manufactures (ASM) from the Bureau of the Census, U.S. Department of Commerce. Total factor productivity statistics are given for the year prior to the recapitalization for each of the recapitalizing firms. Plant-level data for the nonrecapitalizing industry firms is for the year of the first recapitalization in the same four-digit SIC code. The data appendix contains the procedure used to calculate TFP. It is a relative measure of productivity calculated such that the average industry TFP equals zero. The industry concentration index is the total value of shipments of the largest four firms divided by the industry total shipments.
[a]Mergers and plant closures between 1979 and the recapitalizations prevent these numbers from adding up to the totals for 1979 reported in Table 2. In addition, a new five-year panel of firms begins in 1984.
[b]Average plant age is calculated as the recapitalizing year less the first time the plant appeared in the database. We checked back as far as the 1972 Census of Manufactures for plant births.
[c]There were 23 explicitly indentified openings in the Annual Survey of Manufactures (ASM). However, the ASM does not cover with certainty plants of less than 250 employees. Given the much smaller number of openings versus closures in the data, only closures are analyzed. In the full quintennial Census of Manufactures for 1982 there were 28 plant openings and 132 closures for the 10 industries in this study. Of these plants, 6 of the openings and 75 of the closures were in the ASM.

to the firm level. For productivity, however, we use the productivity level for the firm's least productive plant. Logistic limited dependent variable regressions are estimated to examine the factors which are associated with plant closing decisions for both recapitalizing and non-recapitalizing firms. The results are estimated using an unbalanced panel. This approach does not throw out firms which do not have an observation for each of the 12 years, thus avoiding a survivorship bias—especially important for the investment analysis.[20] In the plant closure analysis, the dependent variable equals one for a firm that closed at least one plant in that year. In the second logit specification

---

[20] In Table 5 we present the estimation results from a random effects panel dataset model, allowing for firm-specific random effects.

*Capital Structure and Product Market Behavior*

**Table 2**
**Productivity and plant closures: summary statistics**

| Industry | Number of firms (in 1979) | Number of plants (in 1979) | Number of plant closures (1979–1990) | Average productivity (TFP) of closed plants | High-debt firms (number of plants)[a] |
|---|---|---|---|---|---|
| Fabric mills (2211, 2221, 2231) | 235 | 505 | 138 | −0.288*** (0.048) | 106 |
| Mattresses (2515) | 92 | 110 | 42 | −0.234*** (0.081) | 24 |
| Paper mills (2611, 2621, 2631) | 157 | 417 | 47 | −0.256*** (0.065) | 59 |
| Oil-based chemicals (2821) | 117 | 209 | 61 | −0.027 (0.090) | 35 |
| Glass products (3211, 3221, 3231) | 163 | 316 | 104 | −0.248*** (0.063) | 31 |
| Gypsum (3275) | 16 | 74 | 9 | −0.273 (0.270) | 61 |
| Roofing and insulation (3296) | 23 | 53 | 14 | −0.147 (0.103) | 36 |
| Batteries: car (3691) | 67 | 145 | 39 | −0.181* (0.105) | 23 |
| Batteries: consumer (3692) | 13 | 28 | 5 | −0.071 (0.188) | 13 |
| Tractor trailers (3715) | 117 | 139 | 53 | −0.149* (0.082) | 17 |
| All industries | 1000 | 1996 | 512 | −0.212*** (0.026) | 405[a] |

Total factor productivity is a relative measure of productivity calculated using a Cobb–Douglas production function at the four-digit SIC code level. Given that TFP is the residual of this production function, the average TFP in an industry equals 0. Thus the TFP numbers for the closed plants show the relative productivity versus all plants in the industry. Standard errors of the mean are in parentheses. *, **, *** average significantly different from zero at the 10%, 5%, and 1% level of significance, respectively, using a two-tailed $t$-test.
[a] There were 60 plant closures by high-debt firms across the 10 industries. Average TFP for these closures was −0.260 with a standard error of 0.066. Average TFP for the 452 plants closed by nonrecapitalizing firms was −0.206 with a standard error of the mean of 0.028. Individual industry data on closures for these high-debt firms cannot be disclosed because of government restrictions regarding the disclosure of confidential data.

*The Review of Financial Studies / v 10 n 3 1997*

we lag the TFP productivity variable, in order to control for the potential problem of low contemporaneous productivity caused by the decision not to upgrade a plant that the firm plans to close. The third logit specification in Table 3 includes the predicted capital structure change variable, which is calculated using two lags of capacity utilization, industry price variance, industry concentration, and the change in industry demand, one lag of productivity, and firm size.

Results from the analysis of plant closings presented in Table 3 indicate that industry capacity utilization and plant productivity are negatively associated with plant closings. The demand growth variable shows that plants are less likely to be closed when industry growth is high. The coefficient on the four-firm market share is negative and significant. Plants are less likely to be closed in industries with high market share by the top four firms. The coefficients on the variables capturing firm size and plant scale show that large plants are less likely to be closed, because the plant scale variable is negative and highly significant. The coefficient estimate on the number of plants is positive and significant, a finding that might not be surprising given the firm may have several older or more inefficient plants and chooses to close one given demand or efficiency considerations. This finding also supports the theoretical prediction by Ghemawat and Nalebuff (1990) that a firm with multiple plants will be more likely to close a plant down first.

The negative significant association between total factor productivity and plant closing decisions provides support for the claim that the relatively more inefficient plants were the ones being closed down by firms. Jensen claims that increased debt taken on by high-debt firms is important in facilitating industry adjustment to new demand conditions. We find that debt is significantly related to closure decisions only in highly concentrated industries. Both of the dummy variables for the debt change and the predicted capital structure change are insignificant by themselves, but positive and significant when interacted with the industry concentration index. These results indicate that the probability of a plant closing is higher in a concentrated industry when the firm has high financial leverage.

In logit specification C we replaced the recapitalization variable with the predicted recapitalization variable from our first-stage regression. We do not report the results from the first-stage regression in this article, but discuss the results of that estimation here.[21] We found that our explanatory variables are significant in predicting firm recapital-

---

[21] Specific results from this regression run in cross section at the time of recapitalization are reported in Kovenock and Phillips (1995).

*Capital Structure and Product Market Behavior*

**Table 3**
**Plant closing decisions, productivity, and capital structure**

| Variable | Dependent variable: plant closing | | |
|---|---|---|---|
| | Logit A | Logit B | Logit C |
| Industry demand and price variables | | | |
| Capacity utilization | −0.023 | −0.014 | −0.033 |
| | (−3.589)*** | (−2.793)*** | (−2.70)*** |
| Output price variance | −0.002 | −0.004 | −0.002 |
| | (−1.092) | (−1.805)* | (−0.899) |
| Change in output demand | −1.517 | −1.233 | −0.719 |
| | (−1.659)* | (−1.544) | (−.889) |
| Market-structure variables | | | |
| Lagged industry concentration | −3.405 | −3.469 | −1.193 |
| | (−5.262)*** | (−5.52)*** | (−2.794)*** |
| Number of plants owned by firm | 0.254 | 0.261 | 0.241 |
| | (12.007)*** | (14.055)*** | (12.757)*** |
| Value of firm shipments | −0.001 | −0.001 | −0.001 |
| | (−3.857)*** | (−3.991)*** | (−3.420)*** |
| Productivity variables | | | |
| Total factor productivity | | | |
| Firm's lowest productivity plant | −0.575 | | |
| | (−3.906)*** | | |
| Lagged TFP | | −0.932 | −0.299 |
| | | (−5.270)*** | (−1.802)* |
| Relative plant scale | −3.671 | −3.141 | −3.082 |
| | (−5.008)*** | (−5.134)*** | (−5.209)*** |
| Maximum plant age | 0.058 | 0.026 | 0.005 |
| | (4.015)*** | (2.061)** | (0.404) |
| Capital-structure variables | | | |
| High-debt dummy variable | 0.741 | 0.412 | |
| | (1.136) | (0.641) | |
| Predicted capital–structure change | | | 1.497 |
| | | | (.851) |
| Capital-structure variable * concentration | 0.668 | 0.319 | 1.338 |
| | (1.827)* | (1.806)* | (1.910)* |
| Rival high-debt market share | −0.502 | −0.571 | −0.556 |
| | (−1.716)* | (−2.057)** | (−1.783)* |
| Total firm years | 10395 | 8214 | 8214 |
| Plant closings | 476 | 424 | 424 |
| Chi-square statistic | 557.83 | 550.34 | 288.94 |
| Significance level (*p*-value) | < 1% | < 1% | < 1% |

Regressions test the effects productivity and increases in debt on plant closing decisions of recapitalizing firms and other nonrecapitalizing industry firms. Regressions are estimated using a logistic limited dependent variable model. The dependent variable equals one if a firm has closed a plant in that year. Lagged industry concentration is the proportion of industry sales by the top four firms. Total factor productivity is calculated assuming a Cobb–Douglas production function. Plant scale is the average for the firm of its plants asset size divided by the average assets for plants in each industry. Predicted capital structure change is calculated using a first-stage regression with two lags of capacity utilization, output price variance, plant productivity, and firm size. Data are yearly from 1979 to 1990. *t*-statistics are in parentheses. *, **, *** significantly different from zero at the 10%, 5%, and 1% level of significance, respectively, using a two-tailed *t*-test.

ization, demonstrating that capital structure changes are a response to productivity and market conditions. We found that firms are more likely to recapitalize when they have individual plants of low productivity, when they operate in an industry that is highly concentrated, or when industry capacity utilization is low. The lagged values of productivity, market concentration, capacity utilization, and demand that

*The Review of Financial Studies / v 10 n 3 1997*

are included in this regression are highly significant. The significance of the multiple lagged values, up to three years prior to the recapitalization, that are not included in the main regression show that capital structure changes are a result of an adjustment to longer-run changes to supply and demand conditions.

The results of logit specification C with the predicted recapitalization variable are similar to those in the original regression. These results show that the debt change is indeed endogenous and is significantly associated with lagged values of productivity, industry demand, and market structure. Since the results of the estimation using the predicted recapitalization are similar to those using the capital structure variables, we conclude that we not capturing a contemporaneous shock.

We also find that the market share of recapitalizing firms has a significant impact on rival firms' plant closing decisions. The total market share of highly leveraged rival firms has a negative coefficient in all regressions in Table 3. This variable excludes the firm's market share when it is also highly leveraged. This result is consistent with the conjecture that firms are less likely to close plants when large rival firms have sharply increased the debt in their capital structure. Furthermore, the effect of recapitalizations on rival firms' decisions remains significant when including the predicted recapitalization variable as an independent regressor in place of the actual recapitalization in the two-stage procedure described in the methodology section. While we do not control for all possible endogeneity problems, the fact that the market share of highly leveraged rival firms remains significant is consistent with the view that recapitalization is a strategic commitment that has an independent effect on rival firm behavior.

Table 4 indicates the economic significance of the logistic regression results.[22] We compute probabilities of closing a plant holding all other variables besides TFP and debt interaction terms at their sample means. For the nonrecapitalizing firms and the LBO and recapitalizing firms probabilities are computed with the dummy variable equal to zero and one, respectively. For the public recapitalization and LBO sample, the debt interaction term with concentration is evaluated at the mean of the concentration variable for this subsample. All other variables are evaluated at their overall sample means.

Table 4 shows that the probability of closure increases by 1% for logit specification A and approximately 2% for specification B, as productivity goes from the 90th percentile to the 10th percentile for the

---

[22] We do not present the economic significance of the regressions with the predicted recapitalization variable because we wanted to focus on actual realizations in this table.

*Capital Structure and Product Market Behavior*

**Table 4**
**Plant closure and productivity: estimated closure probabilities**

| Total factor productivity | | Sample of firms | |
|---|---|---|---|
| | All firms | Nonrecapitalizing firms | LBO and recapitalizing firms[a] |
| Probabilities estimated from Table 3, logit regression A, with lowest productivity plant | | | |
| Probability at TFP 10th percentile | 3.77% | 2.86% | 6.42% |
| at TFP 25th percentile | 3.45% | 2.61% | 5.88% |
| at TFP 50th percentile | 3.15% | 2.38% | 5.39% |
| at TFP 90th percentile | 2.61% | 1.97% | 4.48% |
| Probabilities estimated from Table 3, logit regression B, with lagged TFP | | | |
| Probability at TFP 10th percentile | 5.00% | 4.59% | 7.52% |
| at TFP 25th percentile | 4.38% | 4.02% | 6.61% |
| at TFP 50th percentile | 3.82% | 3.50% | 5.76% |
| at TFP 90th percentile | 2.90% | 2.66% | 4.42% |

Estimated probabilities of plant closure for firms at the 10th, 25th, 50th, and 90th percentiles of TFP for the full sample of firms and by whether firm recapitalized increasing its debt. The time period covered is 1979–1990. Probabilities are computed holding all other variables besides TFP and debt interaction terms at their sample means. For the non-recap firms and the LBO and recapitalization firms probabilities are computed with the dummy variable equal to zero and one respectively. Estimated probabilities are from logit regressions predicting plant closure, controlling for market structure and industry demand.
[a]For the recap and LBO sample, the debt interaction term with concentration is evaluated at the mean of the concentration variable for this subsample. All other variables are evaluated at their overall sample mean.

nonrecapitalizing firms. For the recapitalizing firms the probability of closing increases from 4.48% to 6.42% as TFP decreases from the 90th to the 10th percentile. The probability of closing at the 10th percentile of TFP goes from 2.86% for the nonrecapitalizing firms to 6.42% for the recapitalizing firms. Both of these results use the coefficients from the first logit regression. The second panel of Table 4 uses the coefficients from the second logit regression. These probabilities incorporate both the debt variable and the debt variable interacted with concentration. These results show that the estimated effects in Table 3 have a significant economic impact in addition to their statistical significance. Both productivity and concentration interacted with debt have a significant economic effect on plant closing.

We reestimate the regressions in Table 3 to control for unbalanced panels and correlation within years for a given firm. Table 5 presents the results estimated using a random effects probit panel dataset model. This specification explicitly captures possible firm-specific random effects. It also allows for residual serial correlation which may be possible if firms make current decisions based on earlier period "errors." The firm size variable is excluded from these two specifications because the likelihood function did not converge with both a firm size variable and a firm random effect. Probit specification A includes the actual recapitalization indicator variable, while specification B replaces the realized recapitalization variable with its predicted value.

*The Review of Financial Studies / v 10 n 3 1997*

**Table 5**
**Plant closing decisions: panel probit estimation**

| Variable | Dependent variable: plant closing | |
|---|---|---|
| | Random effects panel probit model | |
| | Panel Probit: A | Panel Probit: B |
| Industry demand and price variables | | |
| Capacity utilization | −0.019 | −0.019 |
| | (−13.049)*** | (−13.139)*** |
| Output price variance | −0.002 | −0.001 |
| | (−1.310) | (−1.302) |
| Change in output demand | −0.286 | −0.276 |
| | (−.719) | (−.687) |
| Market-structure variables | | |
| Lagged industry concentration | −0.699 | −0.730 |
| | (−3.043)*** | (−3.296)*** |
| Number of plants owned by firm | 0.111 | 0.110 |
| | (14.061)*** | (14.122)*** |
| Productivity variables | | |
| Total factor productivity | −0.137 | −0.139 |
| Lowest productive plant: lagged TFP | (−1.936)* | (−1.944)* |
| Relative plant scale | −1.924 | −1.927 |
| | (−8.344)*** | (−8.418)*** |
| Maximum plant age | 0.029 | 0.027 |
| | (.445) | (.414) |
| Capital-structure variables | | |
| High-debt dummy variable | 0.192 | |
| | (.509) | |
| Predicted capital-structure change | | 0.566 |
| | | (.530) |
| Capital-structure variable * concentration | 0.766 | 0.781 |
| | (1.987)** | (2.028)** |
| Rival high-debt market share | −0.302 | −0.317 |
| | (−1.766)* | (−1.888)** |
| Joint significance test of capical structure variables (chi-square statistic) | 9.662** | 14.0*** |
| Total firm years | 8214 | 8214 |
| Plant closings | 424 | 424 |
| Chi-square statistic (full model) | 271.34*** | 272.98*** |
| Chi-square random effects vs. full | 12.9*** | 12.49*** |

Regressions test the effects of productivity and increases in debt on plant closing decisions of recapitalizing firms and other nonrecapitalizing firms. Regressions are estimated using random effects probit panel data model. This model allows for a random firm effect and different number of observations per firm (an unbalanced panel). The dependent variable equals one if a firm has closed a plant in that year. Lagged industry concentration is the proportion of industry sales by the top four firms. Total factor productivity is calculated assuming a Cobb–Douglas production function. Plant scale is the average for the firm of its plants asset size divided by the average assets for plants in each industry. Predicted capital structure change is calculated using a first-stage regression with lagged independent variables. Data are yearly from 1979 to 1990. *t*-statistics are in parentheses. *, **, * * * significantly different from zero at the 10%, 5%, and 1% level of significance, respectively, using a two-tailed *t*-test.

The results of this model show that the signs and significance of the coefficients are very similar to those presented in Table 3. The capital structure change variables remain insignificant by themselves and are only significant when interacted with the concentration index, again indicating the importance of market structure.

790

## 3.2 Firm-level investment decisions

This section examines the investment decisions of firms in the 10 industries. Table 6 presents summary statistics for investment aggregated up to the firm level. The table shows the average investment rates for each of the five TFP quintiles. Quintile 1 is thus the average investment rate for the least productive 20% of plants. Investment is measured as the expenditures on building and equipment divided by the average of beginning and ending plant assets. The standard error of the mean investment rate is in parentheses. Several facts stand out in this table. Without considering capital structure it is clear that total factor productivity is important in influencing investment. Investment rates are almost monotonically increasing in productivity. The last column shows that investment by firms in the highest productivity quintile is significantly higher than investment by firms in the lowest productivity quintile. These findings remain when total factor productivity is lagged. Firms that are more productive invest more.

Table 7 presents logistic regressions and a Tobit censored regression that test whether productivity of the firm's plants and increases in debt affect the investment of the recapitalizing firms and other nonrecapitalizing industry firms. As in Table 6, firms that have more productive plants invest more. The market structure variables are also highly significant. The number of the firm's plants and the firm market share are both highly significant. Firm market share has a negative coefficient indicating that larger firms are investing less (implicitly disinvesting). Productivity remains highly significant and positively related to investment throughout all specifications.

Consistent throughout, both in the logit and Tobit models, is a negative association between the firm's investment and the interaction between debt and market concentration. On the debt change variable by itself the evidence is mixed. For the first two logit specifications the coefficient on the variables identifying whether the firm recapitalized through an LBO or public recapitalization is significant and negative, indicating that high debt firms reduced their investment rate. However, in the third logit specification, predicted capital structure is insignificantly related to investment. Also, in the Tobit specification the capital structure change variable is insignificantly related to investment. These results indicate that the distinction between predicted and realized recapitalization is important. The actual recapitalization variable may capture a contemporaneous shock. The significance of the capital structure variable interacted with market concentration and the significance of the market share of rival leveraged firms, even when including the predicted capital structure, is consistent with the recapitalization having an effect on behavior in concentrated industries.

*The Review of Financial Studies / v 10 n 3 1997*

**Table 6**
**Investment across productivity quintiles**

| Industry | TFP Quintile 1 | TFP Quintile 2 | TFP Quintile 3 | TFP Quintile 4 | TFP Quintile 5 | Quintile 5-Quintile 1 Difference |
|---|---|---|---|---|---|---|
| Fabric mills (2211, 2221, 2231) | −0.055 (0.018) | 0.041 (0.11) | 0.061 (0.009) | 0.072 (0.010) | 0.040 (0.013) | 0.094** (0.022) |
| Mattresses (2515) | 0.019 (0.035) | 0.062 (0.036) | 0.111 (0.029) | 0.100 (0.032) | 0.139 (0.047) | 0.120* (0.058) |
| Paper mills (2611, 2621, 2631) | 0.062 (0.017) | 0.074 (0.009) | 0.083 (0.007) | 0.075 (0.007) | 0.103 (0.008) | 0.041* (0.019) |
| Oil-based chemicals (2821) | 0.023 (0.021) | 0.041 (0.015) | 0.072 (0.013) | 0.120 (0.018) | 0.148 (0.024) | 0.125** (0.032) |
| Glass products (3211, 3221, 3231) | 0.026 (0.022) | 0.101 (0.017) | 0.099 (0.018) | 0.127 (0.016) | 0.125 (0.021) | 0.099** (0.031) |
| Gypsum (3275) | 0.088 (0.044) | 0.117 (0.021) | 0.079 (0.023) | 0.067 (0.025) | 0.064 (0.020) | −0.024 (0.049) |
| Roofing and insulation (3296) | −0.026 (0.045) | 0.056 (0.028) | 0.076 (0.012) | 0.089 (0.029) | 0.041 (0.033) | 0.067 (0.056) |
| Batteries: car (3691) | −0.025 (0.036) | 0.061 (0.023) | 0.094 (0.022) | 0.093 (0.021) | 0.083 (0.030) | 0.108* (0.046) |
| Batteries: consumer (3692) | 0.009 (0.069) | .084 (.040) | .092 (0.018) | .090 (0.054) | .146 (0.056) | .136 (0.088) |
| Tractor trailers (3715) | −0.105 (0.034) | −0.004 (0.036) | 0.091 (0.033) | 0.170 (0.037) | 0.166 (0.036) | 0.271** (0.050) |
| All industries | 0.005 (0.008) | 0.062 (0.006) | 0.082 (0.005) | 0.096 (0.006) | 0.100 (0.007) | 0.094** (0.011) |

This table shows the average investment rates for each five TFP quintiles. Quintile 1 thus represents the average investment rate for the 20% least productive plants. Investment is measured as the expenditures on building and equipment divided by the average of beginning and ending plant assets. The standard error of the mean investment rate is in parentheses. *, **, difference between Quintiles 5 and 1 are significantly different from zero at the 5% and 1% level of significance, respectively, using a two-tailed *t*-test.

*Capital Structure and Product Market Behavior*

**Table 7**
**Investment decisions, productivity, and capital structure**

| Variable | Dependent variable: investment > 5% beginning assets | | | |
|---|---|---|---|---|
| | Logit A | Logit B | Logit C | Tobit |
| **Industry demand and price variables** | | | | |
| Capacity utilization | 0.003 | 0.004 | 0.002 | 0.007 |
| | (1.316) | (1.845)* | (0.474) | (2.104)* |
| Output price variance | −0.002 | −0.002 | −0.007 | −0.002 |
| | (−1.902)* | (−2.361)** | (−3.639)** | (−1.997)** |
| Change in output demand | −0.093 | −0.197 | −0.083 | −0.034 |
| | (−0.259) | (−0.513) | (−0.977) | (−0.675) |
| **Market-structure variables** | | | | |
| Lagged industry concentration | 0.381 | 0.226 | 0.050 | 0.163 |
| | (1.503) | (0.808) | (1.062) | (4.279)*** |
| Number of plants owned by firm | 0.099 | 0.092 | 0.024 | 0.059 |
| | (7.292)*** | (6.568)*** | (6.744)*** | (3.931)*** |
| Firm market share | −1.829 | −1.775 | −0.544 | −0.253 |
| | (−2.473)** | (−2.273)** | (−2.950)*** | (−2.688)*** |
| Total firm shipments | 0.0001 | 0.0001 | 0.0001 | −0.00005 |
| | (0.847) | (0.698) | (1.406) | (−2.799)*** |
| **Productivity variables** | | | | |
| Total factor productivity | 0.211 | | | |
| Firm's lowest productivity plant | (3.049)*** | | | |
| Lagged TFP | | 0.269 | 0.050 | 0.024 |
| | | (3.168)*** | (2.750)*** | (2.105)** |
| Relative plant scale | 1.599 | 1.719 | 0.371 | 0.129 |
| | (8.529)*** | (8.294)*** | (7.998)*** | (5.251)*** |
| Maximum plant age | −0.014 | −0.003 | 0.001 | −0.080 |
| | (−3.032)*** | (−0.645) | (1.077) | (−10.451)*** |
| **Capital-structure variables** | | | | |
| High-debt dummy variable | −0.641 | −0.596 | | 0.003 |
| | (−1.863)* | (−1.709)* | | (−0.071) |
| Predicted capital–structure change | | | −0.120 | |
| | | | (−0.427) | |
| Capital–structure variable * concentration | −0.492 | −0.309 | −0.231 | −0.103 |
| | (−3.932)*** | (−2.182)** | (−3.049)*** | (−4.708)*** |
| Rival high-debt market share | 0.650 | 0.464 | 0.062 | 0.081 |
| | (2.496)** | (1.654)* | (1.677)* | (2.118)** |
| Total firm years | 10395 | 8220 | 8220 | 8220 |
| Years investment > 5% assets | 5961 | 4604 | 4604 | |
| Chi-square statistic | 432.85 | 368.08 | 278.60 | na |
| Significance level (*p*-value) | < 1% | < 1% | < 1% | |

Regressions test the effects of productivity and increases in debt on investment decisions of recapitalizing firms and other nonrecapitalizing firms. Regressions are estimated using logistic limited dependent variable and censored regression (Tobit) models. For the Logit models the dependent variable equals one if the firm invested 5% of ending period assets in that year. For the Tobit model the dependent variable equals capital expenditures divided by beginning period assets. Industry concentration is the proportion of industry sales by the top four firms. Total factor productivity is calculated assuming a Cobb–Douglas production function. Plant scale is the average for the firm of its plants asset size divided by the average assets for plants in each industry. Predicted capital structure change is calculated using a first-stage regression with two lags of capacity utilization, output price variance, plant productivity, and firm size. Data are yearly from 1979–1990. *t*-statistics are in parentheses. *, **, *** significantly different from zero at the 10%, 5%, and 1% level of significance, respectively, using a two-tailed *t*-test. Note that a joint significance test for the coefficients in the Tobit model is not possible.

Kaplan (1989) finds that LBO firms decrease their investment subsequent to the debt increase. Our results add evidence on where this decreased investment is present. We find that the negative association between investment and the recapitalization is significant in highly concentrated industries. We also examine whether firms that com-

*The Review of Financial Studies / v 10 n 3 1997*

pete against LBO firms increase their investment subsequent to the
increased debt of LBO firms. To investigate this issue we include a
variable that measures the share of output of highly leveraged firms.
We find a positive association between debt and rival firms' investment. Investment is higher as the market share of highly leveraged
rival firms increases. This result is consistent and very strong across
all specifications investigated. Unleveraged firms invest more when
faced with a high-debt rival.

These results are consistent with several different but not mutually exclusive theories. The results are consistent with decreased investment following the recapitalizations. In Myers (1977), debt has a
negative effect on investment in industries with growth options. In industries where these growth options have decreased, increased debt
may be associated with decreased investment. As noted by Jensen
(1986), agency costs may affect investment and the size of the firm,
as well as operating efficiency. Managers may have incentives to expand investment and sales beyond the optimal level. If the increase
in financial leverage increases incentives for managers to maximize
shareholder wealth or forces managers to pay out free cash flow to
make interest payments, managers may change investment and sales.

However, we do not find unqualified support for a decreased investment and high debt association independent of market structure.
We find that the negative association between investment and the recapitalization is present in concentrated industries. The importance
of this interaction between concentration and increased debt points
to an effect working through market structure. The evidence in this
article suggests that the agency problems are more prevalent in concentrated industries, where the discipline of the market does not weed
out nonoptimizing firms. A firm recapitalizing in a concentrated industry exhibits more passive investment behavior. A rival firm's incentive
to expand will depend on the efficiency of its plants and the incentives of its managers. However, rival firms are more likely to invest
when faced with high-debt firms.

Table 8 presents the economic significance of the logistic regression
results. We compute probabilities of investing more than the 5% cutoff, holding all other variables besides TFP and debt interaction terms
at their sample means. For the nonrecapitalizing firms and the LBO
and recapitalizing firms probabilities are computed with the dummy
variable equal to zero and one, respectively. For the public recapitalization and LBO sample, the debt interaction term with concentration
is evaluated at the mean of the concentration variable for this subsample. All other variables are evaluated at their overall sample mean.

Table 8 shows that the probability of investing for the recapitalizing firms increases from 37.8% to 40.6% as TFP increases from the

*Capital Structure and Product Market Behavior*

**Table 8**
**Investment and productivity: estimated probabilities**

| | Sample of Firms | | |
|---|---|---|---|
| Total factor productivity | All firms | Nonrecapitalizing firms | LBO and Recapitalizing firms[a] |
| Probabilities estimated from Table 6, logit regression A, with lowest productivity plant | | | |
| Probability at TFP 10th percentile | 56.48% | 59.47% | 37.79% |
| at TFP 25th percentile | 57.20% | 60.17% | 38.48% |
| at TFP 50th percentile | 57.45% | 60.86% | 39.16% |
| at TFP 90th percentile | 59.23% | 62.29% | 40.62% |
| Probabilities estimated from Table 6, logit regression B, with lagged TFP | | | |
| Probability at TFP 10th percentile | 55.15% | 57.41% | 38.96% |
| at TFP 25th percentile | 56.14% | 58.39% | 39.91% |
| at TFP 50th percentile | 57.16% | 59.39% | 40.91% |
| at TFP 90th percentile | 59.15% | 61.35% | 42.90% |

Estimated probabilities of investing a minimum of 5% of assets for firms at the 10th, 25th, 50th, and 90th percentiles of TFP for the full sample of firms and by whether the firm recapitalized, increasing its debt. The time period covered is 1979 to 1990. Probabilities are computed holding all other variables besides TFP and debt interaction terms at their sample means. For the nonrecapitalizing firms and the LBO and recapitalizing firms probabilities are computed with the dummy variable equal to zero and one, respectively. Estimated probabilities are from logit regressions predicting investment, controlling for industry demand and market structure.
[a]For the recapitalizing and LBO sample the debt interaction term with concentration is evaluated at the mean of the concentration variable for this subsample. All other variables are evaluated at their overall sample mean.

10th to the 90th percentile. The probability of investing at the 10th percentile of TFP is 59.5% for the nonrecapitalizing firms and 37.8% for the recapitalizing firms. The estimated recapitalization effect is to decrease the probability of investing by 21.7%. Both of these results use the coefficients from the first logit regression. The second panel of Table 8 uses the coefficients from the second logit regression. These probabilities incorporate both the debt variable and the debt variable interacted with concentration. These results show that the factors detailed in Table 6 have a significant economic impact in addition to their statistical significance. Both productivity and concentration interacted with debt have a significant economic effect on investment.

Table 9 presents the results estimated using a random effects probit panel dataset model. This explicitly captures firm-specific random components. Again, this specification allows for residual serial correlation which may be possible if firms make decisions based on earlier period "errors." Probit specification A includes the actual recapitalization indicator variable, while specification B replaces the realized recapitalization variable with its predicted value. The results of this model show that the signs and significance of the coefficients are very similar to the nonrandom effects models. However, the capital structure change variables are insignificant for both the actual and predicted specifications. The variable capturing the interaction between

*The Review of Financial Studies / v 10 n 3 1997*

capital structure and market concentration is significant and negative, signifying decreased investment by recapitalizing firms in highly concentrated industries. Finally the variable "market share of leveraged rivals," which captures the effect on rival firms, is significant and positive, again emphasizing a strategic effect on rival firms. Rival firms expand investment when faced with highly leveraged firms.

## 4. Conclusions

This article provides an analysis of how capital structure choices and product market characteristics relate to investment and plant closing decisions. Our analysis takes explicit account of changes in industry demand, plant-level efficiency, market structure, and actual and predicted capital structure changes. We investigate product market behavior following financial recapitalizations by firms that have had substantial increases in debt through leveraged buyouts and leveraged recapitalizations. The results show that single-period models and empirical analyses of changes in capital structure do not capture the adjustment process to new demand and supply conditions without controlling for market structure. The empirical evidence adds to the evidence presented by Kaplan (1989) on capital structure changes and to the evidence from Chevalier (1995) and Phillips (1995) on product market interactions with capital structure. It extends previous work by including both market structure and plant-level efficiency as determinants of investment and plant closing decisions.

We have several significant empirical findings that relate capital structure to plant closure and investment decisions. The association between high debt and plant closing is positive and significant when we interact the debt variables with market concentration variables. The significance of this interaction effect emphasizes the importance of considering market structure in explaining the effects of changes in capital structure. We also find that competitors are less likely to close down plants when leveraged firms have high market share. Two similar results are found when examining plant investment decisions. First, recapitalization and investment are negatively associated in highly concentrated industries. Second, there is a significant positive association between rival firms' investment and a recapitalizing firm's increase in leverage. Firms are more likely to increase their investment when rival firms have high debt. Our results are consistent with strategic models of capital structure in which debt commits leveraged firms to behave less aggressively in product markets. These strategic effects of debt financing emphasize the point that firms do not operate in isolation. Firms' decisions, both real and financial, are taken into consideration by competing firms.

*Capital Structure and Product Market Behavior*

**Table 9**
**Investment decisions: panel probit estimation**

| Variable | Dependent Variable: Investment > 5% Beginning Assets | |
| --- | --- | --- |
| | Random effects panel probit model | |
| | Panel probit A | Panel probit B |
| Industry demand and price variables | | |
| Capacity utilization | 0.010 | 0.001 |
| | (0.906) | (0.899) |
| Output price variance | −0.002 | −0.002 |
| | (−2.818)*** | (−2.846)*** |
| Change in output demand | −0.292 | −0.300 |
| | (−1.162) | (−1.191) |
| Market-structure variables | | |
| Lagged industry concentration | −0.111 | −0.104 |
| | (−0.643) | (−0.610) |
| Number of plants owned by firm | 0.084 | 0.084 |
| | (8.331)*** | (8.276)*** |
| Firm market share | −1.848 | −1.772 |
| | (−2.738)*** | (−2.613)*** |
| Productivity variables | | |
| Total factor productivity | 0.138 | 0.138 |
| Lowest productive plant: lagged TFP | (2.398)** | (−2.399)** |
| Relative plant scale | 1.469 | 1.464 |
| | (9.119)*** | (9.085)*** |
| Maximum plant age | −0.006 | −0.006 |
| | (−1.236) | (−1.256) |
| Capital-structure variables | | |
| High-debt dummy variable | −0.059 | |
| | (−0.212) | |
| Predicted capital-structure change | | −0.654 |
| | | (−0.504) |
| Capital-structure variable * concentration | −0.373 | −0.466 |
| | (−0.647) | (−1.890)* |
| Rival high-debt market share | 0.390 | 0.381 |
| | (1.892)* | (1.855)** |
| Joint significance test of capital-structure variables (chi-square statistic) | 9.6** | 14.0*** |
| Total firm years | 8220 | 8220 |
| Years investment > 5% assets | 4604 | 4604 |
| Chi-square statistic (full model) | 277.18*** | 275.95*** |
| Chi-square random effects vs. full | 686.14*** | 687.68*** |

Regressions test the effects of productivity and increases in debt on investment decisions of recapitalizing firms and other nonrecapitalizing industry firms. Regressions are estimated using random effects probit panel data model [Chamberlain (1984)]. This model allows for a random firm effect and different number of observations per firm (unbalanced panel). The dependent variable equals one if a firm has invested 5% of beginning period assets in that year. Lagged industry concentration is the proportion of industry sales by the top four firms. Total factor productivity is calculated assuming a Cobb–Douglas production function. Plant scale is the average for the firms of its plants asset size divided by the average assets for plants in each industry. Predicted capital structure change is calculated using a first-stage regression with lagged independent variables. Data are yearly from 1979 to 1990. *t*-statistics are in parentheses. *, **, *** significantly different from zero at the 10%, 5%, and 1% level of significance, respectively, using a two-tailed *t*-test.

The final result we wish to emphasize is that plant-level productivity and industry capacity utilization are highly significant variables in explaining investment and plant closings. These variables seem to be more important for closing and investment decisions than capital structure, by itself, as it is measured. This article shows the importance of taking into account underlying exogenous industry conditions. The

_The Review of Financial Studies / v 10 n 3 1997_

negative significant association between total factor productivity and plant closing provides support for the claim that the relatively more inefficient plants were the ones being closed down by firms. In addition, high capacity utilization is positively associated with firm investment and negatively associated with plant closing.

Our results give qualified support to the predictions of Myers (1977) about the effect of debt on investment varying with industry characteristics. We also find qualified support for Jensen's (1993) predictions about the importance of technological productivity, capacity utilization, and capital structure in explaining industry adjustment to new demand conditions. The evidence in this article suggests that capital structure may have more of a role in influencing investment and closure in concentrated industries, where the discipline of the market may not weed out nonoptimizing firms. The effect on rival firms' investment and closing decisions is supportive of the conclusion that capital structure signals new behavior to the firms' rivals. The results are consistent with models in which debt commits the leveraged firms to behave less aggressively and decrease investment.

We explicitly recognize that capital structure is chosen in response to industry and firm characteristics and estimate our regressions with a predicted capital structure change variable to help control for some of the endogeneity problems that arise because capital structure is a choice variable. We include lags of both industry- and firm-specific variables to obtain a predicted capital structure change variable. We find that these lagged values are significantly associated with the recapitalization decision, showing that capital structure and investment decisions are the result of an adjustment to long-run supply and demand conditions. To the extent that we appropriately control for plant productivity, demand, capacity utilization, and other exogenous industry variables, we reduce the problem that capital structure change captures contemporaneous shocks to industry demand and supply conditions. Our main conclusions, the negative association between recapitalization and own-firm investment in concentrated industries, and the positive association between recapitalization and rival firms' investment, remain significant. Rival firms invest more and are less likely to close plants subsequent to recapitalizations in highly concentrated industries.

We wish to emphasize that the effects and results in this article are sensitive to industry-specific market structures, cost and size asymmetries, as well as the dynamics of costly industry adjustment. An estimation of a dynamic model that explicitly takes into account the adjustment to industry demand and supply shocks is the next step in understanding the role of capital structure. By directing attention to plant-level and industry-specific factors we hope to provide a clearer picture of how industry structure and industry supply and demand conditions influence the extent and nature of the role that capital structure plays in investment and product market decisions.

## Appendix: Total Factor Productivity Calculations

We calculate TFP using a regression-based approach assuming a Cobb–Douglas production function. This approach compares the amount of output produced for a given amount of inputs with coefficients derived given the regression-based approach. In other words, the TFP measure is the estimated residual from the regression model. We calculate TFP for each industry and also include year dummy variables. Average TFP is thus zero for each industry. Given the data available, we include three different types of inputs: capital, labor, and materials. All of these data exist at the plant level. Adjustments for price-level changes and depreciation are made using industry-level data. Price deflators at the four-digit industry level were obtained from the Bartelsman and Gray (1994) database at the National Bureau of Economic Analysis.

Some adjustments to each of the inputs had to be made in order to run the regressions. The LRD does not contain the actual amount of output produced but rather contains plant-level value of output, which is equal to price times quantity. For labor, we also make an adjustment. Data on total number of employees, the number of production workers, and hours worked by production workers exist at the plant level. Given that non-production worker hours are not reported in the LRD, we make the following adjustment to production worker hours. Labor input is defined as production worker hours times the ratio of total wages to production wages. This adjustment assumes that relative production and salary wages are equal to the ratio of their marginal products. Material input used is the value of materials used in producing the product. We included energy used in the production process in the materials numbers. Ideally we would want an estimate of the quantity of each input used in producing the product. However, we only have the reported total value of materials consumed. As noted by Lichtenberg and Siegel (1990), using the available data on the value of materials will not cause any distortions as long as the markets for materials are perfectly competitive. There is some reported evidence [Baker and Wruck (1989)] that high-debt firms were able to negotiate better terms from their suppliers. Thus, we might expect TFP to increase for the highly leveraged firms. This would bias our results against finding an influence of debt on closing decisions because high-debt firms would be less likely to close plants for a fixed TFP cutoff.

*The Review of Financial Studies / v 10 n 3 1997*

To construct measures of real capital stock, we followed a procedure similar to Lichtenberg and Siegel (1990). In the initial year of the time series for any plant, we deflated the gross book value (GBV) of equipment and structures separately using two-digit deflators for each type of capital from the Bureau of Economic Analysis. Deflators were given by the ratio of industry net capital stock in constant dollars divided by the industry gross capital stock in historical dollars. The initial year for capital stock is thus

$$K_{ijt} = GBV_{ijt} * \frac{NSTK_{jt}}{GSK_{jt}}$$

This measure allows a constant amount of depreciation depending on the amount of capital and differences in the price level for plants that begin in different years that have already depreciated over time. We use this procedure for plants that appear in the database for the first time but are not new plants. Plants will appear for the first time in the database, in cases other than newly opened plants, at either the beginning of the database (1972) or for smaller plants when they become part of the annual survey. For new plants we adjust for differences in the price level and make no adjustment for depreciation. To come up with a value of capital stock for subsequent years we use the following recursive formula:

$$K_{ijt} = K_{ijt-1} * (1 - \delta_{jt}) + CAPEXP_{ijt}/IDEF_{jt}$$

For subsequent years we use a recursive formula to come up with the net values of capital stock, adjusting for depreciation at the industry level. We used depreciation rates, $\delta_{jt}$, from the BEA at the two-digit industry for each form of capital. $IDEF_{jt}$ is the price deflator for industry $j$ for period $t$. Since separate data exist for both plant and equipment, we calculate the capital stock for each and add them together to get our final measure of capital stock.

**References**

Allen, B., R. Deneckere, T. Faith, and D. Kovenock, 1994, "Capacity Precommitment as a Barrier to Entry: A Bertrand-Edgeworth Approach," Tinbergen Institute Discussion Paper no. 94-125.

Baker, G. P., and K. H. Wruck, 1989, "Organizational Changes and Value Creation in Leveraged Buyouts: The Case of the O. M. Scott & Sons Company," *Journal of Financial Economics*, 25, 163–190.

Bartelsman, E. J., and W. Gray, 1994, "NBER Manufacturing Productivity Database," mimeo.

Bolton, P., and D. Scharfstein, 1990, "A Theory of Predation Based on Agency Problems in Financial Contracting," *American Economic Review*, 80, 93–106.

Brander, J., and T. Lewis, 1986, "Oligopoly and Financial Structure," *American Economic Review*, 76, 956–970.

*Capital Structure and Product Market Behavior*

Brander, J., and T. Lewis, 1988, "Bankruptcy Costs and the Theory of Oligopoly," *Canadian Journal of Economics*, 21, 221–243.

Brennan, M. J., and E. S. Schwartz, 1985, "Evaluating Natural Resource Investments," *Journal of Business*, 58, 135–157.

Bresnahan, T. F., and D. M. G. Raff, 1993, "Technological Heterogeneity, Adjustment Costs, and the Dynamics of Plant Shutdown Behavior: The American Motor Vehicle Industry in the Time of the Great Depression," working paper, Stanford University.

Butler, J. S., and R. Moffitt, 1982, "A Computationally Efficient Quadrature Procedure for the One-Factor Multinomial Probit Model," *Econometrica*, 50, 761–764.

Caves, R. E., and D. R. Barton, 1990, *Efficiency in U.S. Manufacturing*. MIT Press, Cambridge, Mass.

Chamberlain, G., 1984, "Panel Data," in Z. Griliches and M. D. Intriligator (eds.), *Handbook of Econometrics* (vol. 2), Elsevier Science, New York, 1247–1318.

Chevalier, J., 1995, "Debt and Product Market Competition: Local Market Entry, Exit, and Expansion Decisions of Supermarket Chains," *American Economic Review*, 85, 415–435.

d'Aspremont, C., and A. Jacquemin, 1988, "Cooperative and Noncooperative R&D in Duopoly with Spillovers," *American Economic Review*, 78, 1133–1137.

DeAngelo, H., and L. DeAngelo, 1991, "Union Negotiations and Corporate Policy: A Study of Labor Concessions in the Domestic Steel Industry During the 1980s," *Journal of Financial Economics*, 26, 3–43.

Dixit, A., 1989, "Entry and Exit Decisions under Uncertainty," *Journal of Political Economy*, 97, 620–638.

Ghemawat, P., and B. Nalebuff, 1985, "Exit," *Rand Journal of Economics*, 16, 184–194.

Ghemawat, P., and B. Nalebuff, 1990, "The Devolution of Declining Industries," *Quarterly Journal of Economics*, 105, 184–186.

Harrigan, K. R., 1980, "The Effect of Exit Barriers upon Strategic Flexibility," *Strategic Management Journal*, 1, 165–176.

Harrigan, K. R., 1988, *Strategies for Declining Businesses*, Lexington Books, Lexington, Mass.

Harrigan, K. R., and M. E. Porter, 1983, "End-Game Strategies for Declining Industries," *Harvard Business Review*, 61, 112–120.

Harris, M., and A. Raviv, 1991, "The Theory of Capital Structure," *Journal of Finance*, 46, 297–355.

Hayes, J., 1992, "Do Firms Play Exit Games? Some Evidence on Exit Games and the Strategic Role of Size," working paper, University of Wisconsin.

Hsiao, C., 1986, *Analysis of Panel Data*. Cambridge University Press, Cambridge.

Hunsaker, J., and D. Kovenock, 1994, "The Pattern of Exit from Declining Industries," mimeo, Purdue University.

Jensen, M. C., 1986, "Agency Costs of Free Cash Flow, Corporate Finance, and Takeovers," *American Economic Review*, 76, 323–329.

Jensen, M. C., 1993, "The Modern Industrial Revolution and the Challenge to Internal Control Systems," *Journal of Finance*, 48, 831–880.

*The Review of Financial Studies / v 10 n 3 1997*

Kaplan, S. N., 1989, "The Effects of Management Buyouts on Operating Performance and Value," *Journal of Financial Economics*, 24, 217–254.

Kim, M., and V. Maksimovic, 1990, "Debt and Input Misallocation," *Journal of Finance*, 45, 795–816.

Kovenock, D., and G. Phillips, 1995, "Increased Debt and Product-Market Rivalry: How Do We Reconcile Theory and Evidence," *American Economic Review*, 85, 403–408.

Leibenstein, H., 1966, "Allocative Efficiency vs. 'X-Efficiency'," *American Economic Review*, 56, 392–415.

Lichtenberg, F. R., and D. Siegel, 1990, "The Effects of Leveraged Buyouts on Productivity and Related Aspects of Firm Behavior," *Journal of Financial Economics*, 27, 165–194.

Lieberman, M., 1990, "Exit from Declining Industries: "Shakeout" or "Stakeout"?," *Rand Journal of Economics*, 21, 538–554.

Long, W. F., and D. J. Ravenscraft, 1993, "Decade of Debt: Lessons from LBOs in the 1980s," in M. Blair (ed.), *The Deal Decade: What Takeovers and Leveraged Buyouts Mean for Corporate Governance*, Brookings Press, Washington, D.C., pp. 205–238.

McDonald, R., and D. Siegel, 1986, "The Value of Waiting to Invest," *Quarterly Journal of Economics*, November, 707–727.

Maksimovic, V., 1986, "Capital Structure in a Stochastic Oligopoly," Ph.D. dissertation, Harvard University.

Maksimovic, V., 1988, "Capital Structure in Repeated Oligopolies," *Rand Journal of Economics*, 19, 389–407.

Maksimovic, V., 1995, "Financial Structure and Product Market Competition," in R. Jarrow, V. Maksimovic, and W. Ziemba (eds.), *Handbook of Finance*, North-Holland, Amsterdam.

McGuckin, R. H, and G. Pascoe, 1988, "The Longitudinal Research Database: Status and Research Possibilities," *Survey of Current Business*.

Myers, S., 1977, "Determinants of Corporate Borrowing," *Journal of Financial Economics*, 5, 147–175.

Myers, S., 1984, "The Capital Structure Puzzle," *Journal of Finance*, 39, 575–592.

Ofek, E., 1993, "Capital Structure and Firm Response to Poor Performance: An Empirical Analysis," *Journal of Financial Economics*, 34, 3–30.

Opler, T., 1993, "Controlling Financial Distress Costs in Leveraged Buyouts with Financial Innovation," *Financial Management*, 22, 79–90.

Opler, T., and S. Titman, 1994, "Financial Distress and Corporate Performance," *Journal of Finance*, 49, 1015–1040.

Phillips, G. M., 1995, "Increased Debt and Industry Product Markets: An Empirical Analysis," *Journal of Financial Economics*, 37, 189–238

Pindyck, R. S., 1988, "Irreversible Investment, Capacity Choice, and the Value of the Firm," *American Economic Review*, 78, 969–985.

Poitevin, M., 1989, "Financial Signaling and the "Deep-Pocket" Argument," *Rand Journal of Economics*, 20, 26–40.

*Capital Structure and Product Market Behavior*

Reynolds, S., 1988, "Plant Closings and Exit Behavior in Declining Industries," *Economica*, 55, 493–503.

Rodin, D., 1992, "The Effects of Leveraged Buyouts on Firm Investment," Ph.D. dissertation, Purdue University.

Schary, M. A., 1991, "The Probability of Exit," *Rand Journal of Economics*, 22, 339–353.

Shapiro, C., 1989, "Theories of Oligopoly Behavior," in R. Schmalensee and R. D. Willig (eds.), *Handbook of Industrial Organization*, North-Holland, Amsterdam, pp. 329–410.

Tirole, J., 1988, *The Theory of Industrial Organization*, MIT Press, Cambridge, Mass.

Whinston, M. D., 1988, "Exit with Multiplant Firms," *Rand Journal of Economics*, 19, 568–588.

Zingales, L., 1995, "Survival of the Fittest or the Fattest? Exit and Financing in the Trucking Industry," mimeo, University of Chicago.

# [11]

THE JOURNAL OF FINANCE • VOL LIII, NO. 3 • JUNE 1998

# Survival of the Fittest or the Fattest? Exit and Financing in the Trucking Industry

LUIGI ZINGALES*

## ABSTRACT

This paper studies the impact that capital market imperfections have on the natural selection of the most efficient firms by estimating the effect of the prederegulation level of leverage on the survival of trucking firms after the Carter deregulation. Highly leveraged carriers are less likely to survive the deregulation shock, even after controlling for various measures of efficiency. This effect is stronger in the imperfectly competitive segment of the motor carrier industry. High debt seems to affect survival by curtailing investments and reducing the price per ton-mile that a carrier can afford to charge after deregulation.

MOST ECONOMIC THEORIES ARE either implicitly or explicitly based on an evolutionary argument: Competition and exit assure that only the most efficient firms survive. This argument implicitly relies on the existence of perfect capital markets. In the presence of capital market imperfections, efficient firms may be forced to exit due to lack of funds. Although this argument is well understood in theory (Telser (1966) and Bolton and Scharfstein (1990)), its empirical relevance is much less clear.

The crucial issue in trying to assess the effects of financing choices on the survival of firms and, thus, on the product market competition is the endogeneity of capital structure choices to the industry structure. If leverage affects a firm's competitive position, then the firm's financing decisions will take this into account. As a result, in the absence of a structural model we cannot determine whether it is the product market competition that affects capital structure choices or a firm's capital structure that affects its competitive position and its survival.

This paper attempts to address the endogeneity problem by looking at the effects of leverage on the survival of trucking firms after the Carter dereg-

* Graduate School of Business, University of Chicago. I wish to thank Abhay Pande for interesting me in the trucking industry, and Judy Chevalier, Kent Daniel, Colin Mayer, Antonio Merlo, Marzio Galeotti, Austan Goolsbee, Charlie Himmelberg, Vojislav Maksimovic, Steve Kaplan, Anil Kashyap, Sam Peltzman, Raghu Rajan, Fabio Schiantarelli, Per Stromberg, Sheridan Titman, Rob Vishny, an anonymous referee, René Stulz (the editor), and participants at seminars at a CEPR conference on "International Perspectives on the Macroeconomic and Microeconomic Implications of Financing Constraints," in Bergamo, the University of Chicago, the London Business School, the NBER, the WFA meetings, and the AEA meetings for useful comments. Andy Pruitt provided excellent research assistance. Research expenses have been supported by the Center for the Study of the Economy and the State. The author also acknowledges financial support from the Center for Research in Security Prices and NSF grant #SBR-9423645.

ulation. Deregulation was an exogenous shock that unexpectedly changed both the competitive environment in which firms operate and the leverage of firms, driving the effective leverage far away from the desired one. By decreasing the value of firms' operating certificates, a sort of monopoly license, deregulation sharply increased leverage above the desired level. Also, because deregulation increased the risk in the industry and made predation possible, it is likely that the target leverage decreased at the same time that firms' real leverage increased dramatically.

I study the survival of trucking companies during the eight years following the beginning of deregulation as a function of their economic efficiency (fitness) and their financial resources (fatness). I find evidence that more efficient firms are more likely to survive after deregulation, but I also find evidence that their leverage at the beginning of the deregulation period has an impact on the probability of survival eight years later. Therefore, not only the "fittest" but also the "fattest" firms survive.

This result might appear obvious. It is well known that firms in a weak financial position are more likely to go bankrupt; this may be true independent of any effects of financing on a firm's competitive position. To address this issue, I try to control for the ex ante risk of default by using Altman's (1973) Z-score method. Even after controlling for the ex ante probability of default, leverage still has a negative and statistically significant impact on survival. I also show that this effect is not present in the early years after deregulation, but is concentrated in the 1980 to 1985 period, when the industry shakeout was more dramatic. Interestingly, this effect is not homogeneous across different segments of the industry. It is most pronounced in the segment that remains imperfectly competitive even after deregulation, and it is zero in the segment that becomes fully competitive.

I also try to probe deeper into the reasons why debt may jeopardize survival. In particular, I look at the investments undertaken by motor carriers after deregulation and their pricing policy as a function of their initial level of leverage.

I find that the initial level of leverage has a negative impact on the ability of a motor carrier to invest in the years following deregulation. The effect is particularly pronounced in those companies that are eventually forced to exit, suggesting that the underinvestment problem caused by the high debt level might have forced these firms out of the market.

I also find evidence that the preregulation level of leverage negatively impacts the price per ton-mile that a carrier charged during the price war that followed deregulation. This effect is entirely concentrated in the less competitive segment of the industry.

This paper is part of a growing literature on the interaction between capital structure and product market competition. Besides a very early article by Spence (1985), the pioneer works in this area are Phillips (1995) and Chevalier (1995a, 1995b). They study the effects of leverage on price competition and exit in industries that experienced a large number of leveraged buyouts (LBOs). Both find significant effects of the LBOs on the competitive environment, under the form of increased prices and increased exit. Similarly, Kovenock and Phillips (1997) use plant-level data to analyze the impact of a company's leverage on its plant closing decisions in industries where at least one of the major players undertook an LBO. They find that debt affects plant closing and investment decisions only in highly concentrated industries.

The interpretation of all these results, however, is made controversial by the fact that the decision to undertake an LBO is not necessarily exogenous with respect to the competitive environment in which a prospective LBO firm operates. If the managers of LBO firms anticipated the ultimate outcome of their actions, it would be impossible to distinguish whether these outcomes are the desired effects that LBOs tried to achieve in the first place or their unwanted side effects.

A step forward in addressing the endogeneity problem is represented by Chevalier and Scharfstein (1996). They look at supermarkets' profit margins during recessions in regional markets differentially affected by LBOs. To the extent that some major recessions (like the Texas oil shock) are unexpected or very unlikely ex ante and that these recessions change the very nature of the competitive environment, it is possible to interpret the results in a causal sense. A related paper by Holtz-Eakin, Jouflaian, and Rosen (1994) studies the effects of liquidity constraint on survival by using an exogenous shock. They study the impact of inheritance on the probability of survival of small entrepreneurial firms.

The rest of the paper proceeds as follows. Section I provides some background information on the characteristics of the trucking industry before and after deregulation. Section II describes the competing hypotheses on the effects of financial variables on the survival of firms and explains why the natural experiment represented by trucking deregulation helps identify these effects. Section III introduces the reader to the new dataset used in this paper. Section IV presents the results on the determinants of survival and Section V discusses the possible sources of this effect. Finally, Section VI concludes.

## I. The Trucking Industry

Interstate motor carriers were brought under federal regulation by the Motor Carrier Act of 1935, designed "to protect the public interest by maintaining an orderly and reliable transportation system, by minimizing duplications of services, and by reducing financial instability." The act exempted the trucking industry from the antitrust law and required all interstate motor carriers to file their rates with the Interstate Commerce Commission (ICC), which had the authority to set minimum rates and suspend rate cuts. Similarly, the ICC had the power to regulate entry into the industry through the concession of operating certificates. The ICC followed a policy of not granting authority to serve a route already being served if the existing carriers provided adequate service.

As a result of this regulation, rates were above marginal costs, as shown by the fact that the operating certificates were priced at 15 to 20 percent of carrier annual revenue (Breen (1977)). Besides the holders of the operating certificates, the other big beneficiaries of regulation were the unionized employees (International Brotherhood of Teamsters) who, according to Moore (1978), earned 30 percent more than similar workers in unregulated carriers.

The deregulation process began as a change in policy at the ICC level and was sanctioned by the passage of the Motor Carrier Act of 1980. The appointment of Daniel O'Neal as a chairman of the ICC in 1977 was instrumental in this change. A detailed chronology of the events and their impacts on the stock prices of publicly traded carriers is contained in Rose (1985) and Schipper, Thompson, and Weil (1987). In sum, between 1978 and 1979 the ICC reversed its policy toward entry, accepting well over 90 percent of new service applications and beginning to liberalize rate settings. The effect was a substantial drop in the stock market value of trucking companies and a reduction in the premium of unionized workers in the trucking industry (Rose (1987)).

The deregulation effects on the entire industry were devastating. Carriers started to compete on price. As the president of a Teamsters local viewed it, "the rate cutting is horrible. The shippers are pitting one trucking company against the other. I heard that one cut the rate 47 percent."[1] As a result of this new intense price competition, between 1980 and 1985 a total of 4,589 trucking companies across the nation shut down, compared to 1,050 that closed between 1975 and 1980.[2] At the same time the industry experienced a huge wave of new entries. The number of carriers at the end of 1983 was about 40 percent higher than the number that existed when the Motor Carrier Act went into effect.[3] In many cases unionized trucking companies were closing to leave room for new, nonunionized companies.

There is no question, then, that the regulatory reform of the late 1970s changed the competitive environment of the trucking industry (see also Winston (1993)). However, there might be some question about how expected this event was when it took place. Had this event been perfectly anticipated, its effects would have already been reflected in the financing policy of trucking firms. Rose (1985) mentions that some initial steps for industry reform were taken by the ICC as early as 1975, with the main activity taking place in the 1978 to 1979 period. In a subsequent paper, Rose (1987) adopts the convention of dating deregulation from 1979. From an analysis of the S&P Industry Outlook of those years, I conclude that it is probably safe to take 1977 as the watershed. In that year, the industry report stated: "The industry will continue to be faced with the threat of regulatory reform. . . . However, given the strong opposition of the Teamsters' union, the successful lobbying campaign by the industry, and the opposition of the ICC, the ma-

---

[1] United Press International, January 19, 1986.
[2] Ibid.
[3] *The New York Times*, December 13, 1983.

terialization of any serious threat over the near term remains unlikely." The large decline in stock prices during the 1978 to 1980 period (see Rose (1985) and Schipper et al. (1987)) confirms that deregulation was largely unanticipated, and that deregulation hit the industry during that period.

In studying the trucking industry, it is important to keep in mind its division into two fairly different segments: the truckload (TL), with shipments of 10,000 pounds or more, and the less-than-truckload (LTL), with shipments of less than 10,000 pounds. The TL segment is characterized by easy-to-finance capital investment and facility of market entry (in the absence of regulation). The LTL segment requires large capital investments to create hubs and generate a network able to distribute loads across different trucks, minimizing empty backhaul mileage.[4]

The competitive pressure was experienced differently in the two segments. According to Moore (1986), rates in the TL sector fell 25 percent from 1977 to 1982. During the same period the LTL rates fell only 12 percent. The source of competition was also different. The TL segment suffered from both the entry of new carriers and the expansion of private carriers (businesses that haul their own products). By contrast, the LTL segment quickly became crowded with existing carriers that expanded in the LTL market as a way to refocus their operating strategy in the face of entry by nonunionized carriers in the TL market.

## II. The Competing Hypotheses

### A. The Theoretical Predictions

This paper addresses two related questions. First, how does leverage affect a firm's ability to respond to unexpected changes in the competitive environment? Second, what are the sources of these effects? In this section, I briefly summarize what theory has to say about these two questions and how my "natural experiment" helps test these predictions.

If a firm's financial structure is irrelevant, then I should find no effects of the initial leverage on a firm's ability to survive, provided I can properly control for a firm's efficiency level. Otherwise, there are three main reasons why the preregulation level of leverage may negatively impact a motor carrier's survival during deregulation.

First, the initial level of debt may negatively affect survival because highly indebted firms may be unable to finance large new investments (Myers (1977)).

---

[4] As Glaskowsky (1986) points out, while the TL segment of the industry is fairly close to the textbook definition of a competitive market, with no significant economies of scale, very low barriers to entry and many atomistic players, "the LTL carrier segment is *not* atomistic in any sense of the word. A small and still shrinking group of increasingly large firms dominates this traffic nationally. LTL operations *do* have significant economies of scale. The established large national LTL carriers are beneficiaries of an almost insurmountable financial barrier to entry: their large and widespread terminal networks." The emphasis is in the original text.

This debt overhang might force leveraged firms to pass up profitable growth opportunities and, in the most extreme cases, even force them out of the market. As Myers (1977) points out, this problem is more likely to arise when investments cannot be collateralized easily. Therefore, debt overhang should not in general be a very serious problem for TL trucking companies, which have easy-to-collateralize assets. LTL carriers, however, might suffer more, because a larger fraction of their assets is intangible.

Second, the initial level of debt may negatively affect survival because it directly affects a firm's ability to compete. For example, in Bolton and Scharfstein (1990), shallow-pocket firms are prone to predation by deep-pocket competitors. This predation may force highly leveraged firms to lose their market share or even exit the industry. This effect should be present only in less competitive industries, because only in the presence of some barriers to entry can the predator recover the short-run costs of preying in the long run. Alternatively, a high level of leverage may affect a firm's competitiveness because customers avoid dealing with a company that is likely to go bankrupt (Titman (1984)), or because the leverage affects a firm's incentive to maintain its reputation for producing a high-quality product (Maksimovic and Titman (1991)). All of these effects should be unimportant for TL carriers, which provide a standardized service, but they may be relevant for LTL companies.

Finally, the initial level of debt may negatively affect survival, because it forces inefficient firms to liquidate (Harris and Raviv (1990) and Stulz (1990)). Note that here, unlike in the two previous examples, a negative correlation between survival and leverage is not evidence of a cost, but of a benefit of debt. The costs of liquidating a TL versus an LTL carrier are likely to be very different. Most of TL carriers' assets are represented by trucks, which can be liquidated at no significant cost. By contrast, part of the value of an LTL carrier comes from its terminal network and its sales organization, which are more costly to liquidate. As a result, it is plausible that the reduction in profitability produced by deregulation makes it optimal to liquidate more TL carriers than LTL ones. It follows, then, that debt should have a stronger negative impact on survival of TL carriers, rather than LTL ones.

On the other hand, there are two main reasons why the prederegulation level of leverage may positively impact a motor carrier's survival during deregulation.

First, debt might force firms into restructuring sooner (Jensen (1989)), maximizing their chances of survival. This might be particularly true in the trucking industry, where one of the biggest problems of existing firms was to convince unionized workers to accept wage cuts. For example, Perotti and Spier (1993) have modeled the benefits of debt in extracting wage concessions from unions. If this is the case, then highly indebted carriers should be able to address their wage bargaining problems sooner and more effectively and, by so doing, should be more likely to survive. Because the TL market is more likely to be nonunion and to pay competitive wages (through purchased transportation agreements), this effect is likely to be more pronounced in the LTL sector.

Second, a highly leveraged firm may compete more aggressively because of the option-like payoff of leveraged equity (Brander and Lewis (1986)). If ex post an aggressive expansion turned out to be the winning strategy, then I should find that more highly leveraged firms are more likely to survive in the post deregulation period. This argument should apply mainly to the LTL segment of the industry because of its less competitive structure.

## B. The Nature of the Experiment

As it is well known, any attempt to investigate the effects of financial variables on real variables is affected by two econometrics problems. First, capital structure choices are endogenous and, in the absence of an accepted structural model, we cannot determine whether, for instance, it is the product market competition that affects capital structure choices or rather the firms' capital structure that affects their competitive position and, eventually, their survival. Second, an econometrician can only observe imperfect proxies of the firm's characteristics that determine its capital structure and its performance. As a result, a correlation between the initial financial position and the probability of exit may arise even if there is no causal relationship between the two, simply because both a company's debt level and its survival are affected by the same company's characteristics that are unobservable to the econometrician.

The "natural experiment" provided by trucking deregulation helps address the first problem in several ways. First, motor carrier deregulation brought a major and unexpected change in the competitive structure of the trucking industry. During the regulated period firms had been barred from price competition and isolated from new entry, but beginning in 1979 they suddenly faced intense price competition and massive new entry. This change in the competitive environment is exogenous with respect to trucking firms' leverage and their performance.[5] Because this exogenous change in the competitive environment was largely unexpected, it is difficult to argue that the capital structure was optimally chosen beforehand to deal with it. As a result, I can try to separate the undesired effects of debt from the desired ones by estimating the effect of debt on exit after controlling for the expected defaults under the preexisting conditions.

Second, not only did deregulation change the product market environment, but it directly affected firms' capital structure. In fact, a significant portion of a motor carrier's assets was represented by the value of the operating certificates. In many cases, these were also used as a collateral for bank loans. I have estimated that in the 1977 to 1980 period the market-to-book value ratio of assets of publicly traded trucking firms dropped by 20 percent. This translates into a sudden and unwanted increase in the

---

[5] One could claim that regulatory actions are not independent of the economic performance. Although this argument is generally valid, it does not seem to fit well the trucking deregulation. For instance, Rothenberg, as cited in Rose (1987), argues that motor carrier deregulation was largely independent of interest lobbying activity. In fact, both the American Trucking Association and the Teamsters Union aggressively opposed deregulation.

effective level of leverage. As a result, it is likely that motor carriers found themselves excessively leveraged. This is especially true if one considers the increased uncertainty that followed deregulation.

Third, the nature of the sample makes it very unlikely that companies could promptly adjust their capital structure to the deregulation shock. In fact, most of the firms in my sample are small, privately held firms with little or no access to the public equity or bond markets. This makes it harder for them to quickly readjust the leverage after a negative shock such as the loss of the operating rights value and the change in the competitive environment.

The natural experiment of deregulation, though, does not resolve by itself the second problem: the possibility of spurious correlation due to unobservable characteristics. I address this problem in three ways. First, I address it directly, by using a wide variety of control variables that should help capture all firms' characteristics. Second, I look for evidence of the mechanism by which an excessive amount of debt forces exit. In particular, I focus on its effect on investment and on pricing. Third, I divide the sample according to a carrier's percentage of LTL revenues and estimate the impact of debt across different groups. Because the theories discussed above suggest that debt has different impacts for high and low LTL carriers, in a linear probability model I can use this splitting as an instrumental variable.[6] In this way, my estimate of the differential effect of debt on survival across groups is consistent even if there are unobservable firm characteristics correlated with leverage.

## III. The Data

As a consequence of the Motor Carrier Act of 1935, each regulated motor carrier holding interstate operating authority is required to file a calendar year report. In this report, trucking companies have to disclose not only

---

[6] Assume that, after partialing out the observable measures of qualities, the true relationship between survival and leverage is given by $y = x\beta + z\gamma + \epsilon$, where $x$ is leverage and $z$ is an unobservable measure of quality. The concern is that $\text{cov}(z,x) \neq 0$ so that $\hat{\beta}$ is inconsistent. In particular, I am concerned that $\text{cov}(z,x) < 0$; that is, worse quality firms are more highly leveraged. This is the case in a pecking order theory à la Myers (1984), where firms become highly leveraged because they are unprofitable. In this case, however, $\text{cov}(z,x)$ will be the same across different market segments. I can, then, divide the sample in high LTL carriers and high TL carriers. In a linear probability model the estimate of the impact of leverage on survival in the two groups is given by

$$\hat{\beta}_{\text{LTL}} = \beta_{\text{LTL}} + \frac{\text{cov}(z,x)}{\text{var}(x)}\, \gamma_{\text{LTL}} + \frac{\text{cov}(z,x)}{\text{var}(x)}\, \epsilon_{\text{LTL}}$$

and

$$\hat{\beta}_{\text{TL}} = \beta_{\text{TL}} + \frac{\text{cov}(z,x)}{\text{var}(x)}\, \gamma_{\text{TL}} + \frac{\text{cov}(z,x)}{\text{var}(x)}\, \epsilon_{\text{TL}}.$$

If the impact of quality on survival is similar between the two groups (i.e., $\gamma_{\text{TL}} = \gamma_{\text{LTL}}$), then it is easy to see that the difference between the two estimated coefficients is a consistent estimate of the true difference between the two coefficients.

financial variables but also operating statistics, like the number of shipments made, the total number of ton-miles hauled, etc. The level of disclosure depends on the size of the carrier. Before 1980, carriers with gross revenue above $500,000 (Class I and Class II) filed comprehensive reports, including operating statistics. Carriers with gross annual revenues above $100,000 but below $500,000 (Class III) had to file brief statements. In 1980, the minimum threshold for class II carriers was increased to $1,000,000 and Class III carriers were released from filing. The data used for this paper come from the American Trucking Association, which has been collecting and reclassifying ICC filings since 1976.

To determine the survival after deregulation, I have to establish when the deregulation shock hit the industry, and when the transition to a more competitive industry can be considered to be accomplished. On the basis of the stock price evidence and of the industry report I identify three periods: the pre-1978 years can be considered a fully regulated period, 1978 to 1980 represents a transition period, and the post-1980 years represent the deregulation period. By reviewing the S&P Industry Outlooks for every year since 1977, I decided that the industry transition was complete by 1985. The 1982 to 1983 recession hit the trucking industry particularly hard and caused enormous exits. However, by 1984 to 1985 profits and rates in the industry became more stable. This can be considered as the first period in which the industry returned to normal.

Thus, my dataset consists of all ICC filings collected by the ATA for the period 1976 to 1985. As a result of the higher threshold for disclosure and the reduction in Class I and Class II carriers following deregulation, the number of carriers in the dataset drops from 2,897 in 1976 to 1,922 in 1985.

The ICC divides carriers into 13 categories as a function of the goods hauled: from general freight to household goods, from package (courier) to bulk commodities, etc. These categories can be thought of as different market segments. Specialized commodity carriers, for example, use different trucks, which cannot be easily adapted to carry general freight. As Table I shows, general freight carriers are by far the largest group (41 percent of the carriers). They are required to disclose more detailed information than specialized carriers. For both of these reasons, I restrict my analysis to this segment of the market. This guarantees greater homogeneity within the sample used and greater availability of data.

## A. Definition of Exit

For the purpose of this study it is important to understand how I measure exit. I consider that a firm exits when it disappears from the ATA dataset. Trucking firms keep reporting to the ICC even if they are acquired, as long as they are separately operated. Each one has its own identification number, so name changes should have no impact. As a result, firms disappear from the dataset if they are liquidated (both voluntary liquidation and bankruptcy) or if they are acquired and merged with the acquiring firm. There-

**Table I**

**Industry Segments in 1977**

This table reports the distribution by main activity (types of goods hauled) of the 3,150 carriers reporting to the Interstate Commerce Commission (ICC) in 1977. These categories can be thought of as different market segments. The data used come from the American Trucking Association, which has been collecting and reclassifying ICC filings since 1976. In the rest of the paper, I focus only on general freight carriers.

| Commodity | Frequency | Percent |
|---|---|---|
| General freight | 1,300 | 41.27 |
| Household goods | 248 | 7.87 |
| Heavy machinery | 80 | 2.54 |
| Petroleum products | 162 | 5.14 |
| Refrigerated liquids | 12 | 0.38 |
| Refrigerated solids | 143 | 4.54 |
| Dump trucking | 84 | 2.67 |
| Agricultural commodity | 97 | 3.08 |
| Motor vehicles | 49 | 1.56 |
| Armored truck service | 2 | 0.06 |
| Building materials | 135 | 4.29 |
| Films & Associated commodities | 5 | 0.16 |
| Forest products | 22 | 0.70 |
| Mine ores not including coal | 5 | 0.16 |
| Retail store delivery service | 26 | 0.83 |
| Dangerous and hazardous materials | 7 | 0.22 |
| Other commodities not elsewhere classified | 773 | 24.54 |
| Total | 3,150 | 100.00 |

fore, by using the disappearance from the ATA dataset as an indication of exit, I measure the survival of a trucking company as a separate organization.

During the postderegulation period exit took place not only through bankruptcy, but also through voluntary liquidation. ICC reports show that, during the 1979 to 1985 period, 1,328 Class I, II, and III interstate motor carriers ceased operations for "legal, personal, economic or labor reasons," not involving bankruptcy.[7] Although the different ways in which firms exit from a market are also an interesting subject, the objective of this paper is to test whether the most efficient organizations survived, regardless of the way they were financed. The measure I obtained seems appropriate for this scope.

Firms exit from my dataset also because they fall below the minimum level of revenues that mandates disclosure ($500,000 up to 1979, $1 million afterward). Although a significant drop in revenues can be regarded as an indication of failure in the marketplace, I do not want to consider as exited those firms that have a temporary drop in sales. For this reason, I classify a carrier as exited in year $t$ only if it is not present in the dataset in that year and does not appear in any subsequent year, up to and including 1985.

[7] Cited in Glaskowsky (1986).

Furthermore, to reduce this problem and to try to eliminate the bias induced by the change in disclosure requirements during the sample period, I restrict my analysis to companies having at least $1 million in revenues in 1977. Note that, given the high level of inflation in those years, a carrier with $1 million in revenues in 1977 will easily qualify as a Class II carrier in 1980 even with a significant drop in real revenues.[8]

### B. Summary Statistics

Table II presents summary statistics for Class I and II general freight carriers with more than $1 million in revenues in 1977. In that year there were 941 firms satisfying these criteria.

A particularly detailed level of disclosure is requested of the so-called Instruction 27 carriers. These are carriers that derive on average 75 percent or more of their revenues from the intercity transportation of general commodities (approximately 60 percent of general freight carriers). Information for total ton-miles hauled, number of shipments made, and percentage of shipments of more or less than 10,000 pounds tends to be present only for these carriers. Therefore, whenever I use this information, I lose 20 to 30 percent of the observations.

As the preregulation level of all the variables I use the average of the 1976 and 1977 values. The extremely high return on assets (ROA), equal to 18 percent, can be viewed as a sign of the rents enjoyed by trucking companies during the regulation era. Similarly, return on sales (ROS) is 8 percent. Another effect of regulation is the high value of intangibles as a fraction of assets (6 percent). Operating certificates bought from other carriers are included under this category. This is simply a rough estimate of the true value of operating certificates, because only the certificates recently acquired (through a direct purchase or a merger) are valued fully.

Leverage measured as total debt divided by total debt plus book equity is 40 percent (median 35 percent). By subtracting cash reserves from the total debt, the mean leverage becomes 22 percent (median 20 percent). It is difficult to judge whether these are high or low levels of leverage, because very little is known about the capital structure of privately held companies (as most of these are). What makes the comparison even harder is that firms are required to file with the ICC on a nonconsolidated basis. As a benchmark, I collected data for the 66 trucking firms present in COMPUSTAT in 1977 (SIC codes 4210 to 4213). For these firms the ratio of debt to capital is 44 percent, not very different from the ICC sample.

The book value of leverage probably overestimates the actual leverage before deregulation, because the book value of equity does not include the market value of monopoly profits (except for the recently traded operating certificates). A more appropriate measure of actual leverage before deregu-

---

[8] The results are not sensitive to the level of this cutoff. In fact, the pre-1980 exits appear to be uncorrelated with leverage.

### Table II
### Summary Statistics

Data are presented for the population of 941 general freight carriers with more than $1 million in operating revenues in 1977. Variables are defined in Panel A and are averages of the 1976 and 1977 values. Advance payables include any notes payable. Negative book values of equity are set equal to zero. Coverage is set equal to zero when earnings before interest, taxes, and depreciation (EBITDA) are less than or equal to zero and is set equal to 100 when coverage is greater than or equal to 100. Observations with a return on assets larger than 1 or smaller than −1 are set equal to missing. The difference column (Diff.) reports the difference in means between carriers that were still alive in 1985 and carriers that were not alive at that date. The p-values refer to the null hypothesis that the difference between the two means is equal to zero.

#### Panel A: Variable Definitions

| Variable | Definition |
|---|---|
| Average load | Ton-miles/Total miles |
| Average haul | Ton-miles hauled/Tons of revenue freight |
| Cost per ton-mile | Operating expenses/Ton-miles hauled |
| Coverage | EBITDA/Interest expenses |
| Debt | Short term + Long term debt + Advances payables |
| Debt-to-capital | Debt/(Debt + Equity) |
| Intangibles | Intangibles/Total assets |
| Labor cost | (Wages + Benefits)/Operating costs |
| Net debt-to-capital | (Debt − Cash reserves)/(Debt + Equity) |
| Market share | Operating revenues/Total operating revenues of carriers in the same state |
| Proportion LTL revenues | Freight revenues up to 10,000 pounds/Freight revenues |
| Return on assets | EBITDA/Total assets |
| Return on sales | EBITDA/Operating revenues |
| Revenue per ton-mile | Operating revenues/Ton-miles hauled |

#### Panel B: Summary Statistics

| Variable | Mean | Median | Std. Dev. | Min. | Max. | Diff. | p-value | Obs. |
|---|---|---|---|---|---|---|---|---|
| Revenues ($ million) | 15.0 | 3.25 | 47.52 | 0.90 | 684 | 6.33 | 0.041 | 941 |
| Assets ($ million) | 6.88 | 1.22 | 2.41 | 0.05 | 355 | 4.08 | 0.009 | 941 |
| Debt-to-capital | 0.40 | 0.35 | 0.30 | 0.00 | 1.00 | −0.10 | 0.000 | 940 |
| Net debt-to-capital | 0.22 | 0.20 | 0.38 | −0.97 | 1.00 | −0.13 | 0.000 | 910 |
| Coverage | 27.33 | 9.78 | 33.42 | 0.00 | 100 | 10.96 | 0.000 | 923 |
| Return on assets | 0.18 | 0.18 | 0.13 | −0.45 | 0.88 | 0.07 | 0.000 | 939 |
| Return on sales | 0.08 | 0.07 | 0.06 | −0.43 | 0.52 | 0.04 | 0.000 | 941 |
| Intangibles | 0.06 | 0.03 | 0.08 | 0.00 | 0.64 | −0.01 | 0.005 | 930 |
| Labor cost | 0.48 | 0.54 | 0.18 | 0.01 | 0.88 | −0.03 | 0.005 | 939 |
| Revenue per ton-mile | 0.32 | 0.21 | 0.42 | 0.02 | 6.9 | −0.03 | 0.405 | 773 |
| Cost per ton-mile | 0.41 | 0.21 | 0.70 | 0.00 | 6.87 | −0.09 | 0.059 | 768 |
| Proportion LTL revenues | 0.58 | 0.66 | 0.27 | 0.00 | 1.00 | 0.00 | 0.949 | 649 |
| Average load | 10.32 | 10.04 | 5.33 | 0.47 | 36.54 | 0.26 | 0.502 | 772 |
| Average haul | 227.15 | 169.40 | 209.92 | 6.93 | 1713 | −27.70 | 0.105 | 606 |
| Market share | 0.05 | 0.01 | 0.12 | 0.00 | 1.00 | 0.02 | 0.016 | 941 |
| Number of employees | 418.46 | 86.25 | 1405.37 | 2.00 | 26,035 | 184.36 | 0.048 | 906 |

lation is provided by the level of coverage (earnings before interest, taxes, and depreciation over interest expenses).[9] A median coverage of 9.8 gives a sense of the rather healthy financial conditions of the trucking industry before deregulation. The book leverage, however, is probably a good estimate of the market leverage after deregulation, when operating certificates became worthless.

During the 1977 to 1985 period 57 percent of general freight carriers with more than $1 million in revenues exited the industry. Of those, 22 percent exited in the 1977 to 1980 period, and 35 percent exited between 1980 and 1985.

Although the trucking industry did not grow very much during the period, surviving trucking companies experienced substantial growth during both subperiods. For carriers surviving up to 1980 the average rate of nominal growth in revenues during the 1977 to 1980 period is 40 percent. The same rate during the 1980 to 1985 period for carriers surviving up to 1985 is 92 percent.

## C. *The TL versus LTL Distinction*

In the following analysis, an important role is played by the distinction between TL carriers and LTL carriers. Ideally, we would like to compare "pure" TL carriers with "pure" LTL carriers. As the summary statistics indicate, however, there is no such clear-cut distinction. In 1977, most carriers hauled both truck loads and less-than-truck loads, and on average 58 percent of general-freight carrier revenues came from LTL shipments.

To try to disentangle the differential effects of leverage in these two different segments of the market, I create three groups: carriers with less than 30 percent of their revenues in LTL, carriers with 30 to 70 percent in LTL, and carriers with more than 70 percent in LTL. In 1977, among those carriers that reported information about their revenues per class of weight, there are 113 carriers in the first group, 266 in the second, and 270 in the third. The attrition rate is identical in the two extreme groups (59 percent), it is slightly higher in the middle one (67 percent).

## D. *Ex Ante Differences between Survivors and Non-Survivors*

Before turning to a multivariate analysis, it is interesting to analyze the ex ante differences in financial and operating characteristics of carriers as a function of their fate in 1985. This is done in the sixth and seventh columns of Table II, Panel B.

Survivors tend to be larger firms, with higher profitability and lower leverage. In particular, the 1977 return on sales of future survivors is 4 percentage points higher, while ROA is 7 percentage points higher. This result suggests that deregulation did, on average, select more efficient firms. This

---

[9] Whenever EBITDA is negative I put the value of coverage to zero. If coverage exceeds 100 or the interest expenses are zero I artificially equate coverage to 100.

finding is confirmed by cost per mile (9 cents per ton-mile lower for survivors), although this difference is not statistically significant at conventional levels. Quite surprisingly, survivors tend to have lower revenues (3 cents) per ton-mile. This might be an effect of the fact that carriers who used to enjoy large monopoly rents are less likely to survive. The same effect is observed in the fraction of intangibles: survivors have on average 1 percent fewer assets represented by intangibles. If the value of operating certificates reflected in intangibles is an indication of the degree of monopoly enjoyed by a certain carrier in its routes, this fact suggests that survivors are firms that enjoyed lower monopoly rents during the regulation era. It is remarkable how much lower was the 1977 level of leverage of firms that survived. The median ratio of debt over debt plus equity for survivors is 0.30, while for nonsurvivors it is 0.41. The difference is similar when I subtract cash reserves: 0.13 versus 0.27.[10]

Motor carriers can differ substantially in their cost structures. Some carriers rely mostly on employees for their shipments, others contract out a significant amount of transportation services. Contracting out transportation services was often used to prevent the unionization of the workforce.

The proportion of wage and benefits over total operating expenses captures these differences in cost and degree of unionization, because transportation services contracted out are recorded as purchased transportation and, thus, they reduce the fraction of reported labor cost over operating expenses. Interestingly, survivors have a significantly smaller percentage of their operating costs accounted for by wages.

By contrast, there is no statistically significant difference between the average haul and the average load of survivors versus nonsurvivors. Similarly, the percentage of LTL revenue is not significantly different for survivors.

## IV. The Effect of Leverage on Survival

The first question I want to answer empirically is whether initial leverage has any effect on a firm's probability of surviving, beyond what efficiency considerations would suggest. In a perfect capital market world the survival and the growth of a firm should be entirely determined by its efficiency characteristics. Therefore, the null hypothesis is

$$Pr\{\text{survival in 1985}\}_i = f(X_i^{1985}) + v_i, \tag{1}$$

where $X_i$ is a measure of firm $i$'s efficiency. Unfortunately, $X_i^{1985}$ is not observable for the firms that exited. Even if it was, I would not necessarily

---

[10] One might wonder whether these differences in leverage simply reflect differences in the investment opportunities across firms (for example, see Smith and Watts (1992)). However, Rajan and Zingales (1995) show that the negative relation between investment opportunities (measured as Tobin's $q$) and leverage appears to be mainly driven by equity issuers. Because almost all the firms in this sample are privately held (and thus cannot issue equity at wish), this negative correlation is not likely to be a major source of concern.

want to use it because the observed level of efficiency might be affected by the preexisting level of leverage. However, I can use some ex ante efficiency measures as a proxy for a motor carrier level of expected efficiency in the absence of any real impact of financial variables. In other words, I use $X_i^{1977}$ as a proxy for $X_i^{1985}$.

This substitution corresponds to the assumption that the prederegulation level of efficiency is linked to the postderegulation one. As long as surviving companies are concerned, this assumption is supported by the data (for instance, the level of return on sales (ROS) in 1985 is statistically and economically significantly related to the level of ROS in 1977). Nevertheless, one potential concern is that the preexisting level of leverage is correlated to some unobservable characteristics that determine future efficiency. In what follows, I present a series of proxies designed to address this concern.

In sum, the basic regression relates a firm's status in 1985 to financial and operating variables in 1977, or

$$Pr\{\text{survival in 1985}\}_i = f(X_i^{1977}, Lev_i^{1977}) + \epsilon_i, \tag{2}$$

where $Lev_i$ is a measure of financial leverage.

Table III presents the results of estimating equation (2) through a probit model. For ease of interpretation, I report the coefficients as the derivative of the probability of survival with respect to the corresponding right-hand-side variable computed at the mean of the dependent variable. This represents the marginal impact of a change in the explanatory variable.

In the basic specification the explanatory variables, besides leverage, are: return on sales, a company's size (logarithm of the level of the average sales in 1976 and 1977), the level of intangibles (as a fraction of total assets), the proportion of wages over total costs, and nine regional dummies.

Return on sales is chosen as a main measure of efficiency for two reasons. It is directly related to the operating ratio (operating expenses over operating revenues), which is the leading efficiency index used in the trucking industry. Second, it is less sensitive than return on assets to misvaluation of assets or to the extent to which some transportation is done with "for hire" trucks.

A measure of size is inserted for various reasons. Size might be a proxy for efficiency, because only efficient firms become big.[11] Larger firms may also have more bargaining power on the product market and/or have easier access to financing. Finally, size may matter for spurious reasons, because small firms are more likely to fall below the threshold that requires them to file with the ICC. All these explanations predict a positive impact of size on the chances of survival.

---

[11] This argument, although standard, is not necessarily appropriate to this case because the industry was regulated until 1977, and thus the size of a firm may be influenced more by regulation than by efficiency.

920                          *The Journal of Finance*

**Table III**

**Effect of Initial Leverage on the Probability of Survival**

The dependent variable is the probability that a general freight motor carrier with more than $1 million in revenues in 1977 survives until 1985. The reported coefficients are probit estimates of the effect of a marginal change in the corresponding regressor on the probability of survival, computed at the average of the dependent variable. All the independent variables are measured as of 1977 (average of the 1976 and 1977 values). Net debt-to-capital is total debt minus cash reserves divided by total debt plus equity. Intangibles is the ratio of intangible assets to total assets. Labor cost is the ratio of the wages and benefits to operating costs. Among the independent variables there are also nine regional dummies (not reported). Standard errors are reported in parentheses.

| Independent Variables | I | II | III |
|---|---|---|---|
| Net debt-to-capital | −0.180*** | −0.180*** | |
| | (0.049) | (0.048) | |
| log(1 + Coverage) | | | 0.042*** |
| | | | (0.016) |
| Return on sales | 2.878*** | | 2.584*** |
| | (0.347) | | (0.363) |
| Return on assets | | 0.925*** | |
| | | (0.134) | |
| log(Revenues) | 0.048*** | 0.044*** | 0.043*** |
| | (0.014) | (0.014) | (0.014) |
| Intangibles | −0.299 | −0.583** | −0.355 |
| | (0.249) | (0.245) | (0.245) |
| Labor cost | −0.324*** | −0.233** | −0.319*** |
| | (0.103) | (0.103) | (0.102) |
| Pseudo-$R^2$ | 0.12 | 0.09 | 0.11 |
| $N$ | 889 | 887 | 902 |

***, **, * Significantly different from zero at the 1 percent level or less, at the 5 percent level, or at the 10 percent level, respectively.

I insert the level of intangible assets as a proxy for the extent to which a carrier enjoyed monopoly rents before deregulation. This is admittedly a poor proxy, because only recently acquired operating certificates appear in the balance sheet.[12] It is important, though, to attempt to control for monopoly rents before deregulation because the measure of efficiency used (ROS) is distorted by the presence of monopoly rents. For a given level of profitability, a higher degree of monopoly indicates that a firm is less efficient. The level of intangibles, then, is expected to have a negative effect on survival.

A high proportion of wage and benefits over total operating expenses reflects a limited role of purchased transportation and/or a more expensive labor force. Because both these phenomena are generally associated with unionization, a high proportion of wage and benefits can also be interpreted as a proxy for unionization. All these factors are likely to have a negative impact on a firm's ability to survive in a deregulated environment.

---

[12] These intangibles might also appear in the balance sheet in case of a merger, if the acquiring company used the purchased method of accounting. In such case, the potential impact of intangibles is ambiguous.

Finally, regional dummies are inserted to control for possible heterogeneity across different areas. Carriers are attributed to one of the nine geographical groups established by the ICC on the basis of a carrier's main location.

As expected, more profitable firms are more likely to survive, and so are larger firms. By contrast, firms with a higher proportion of labor cost over total cost are less likely to survive. All these effects are statistically significant at the 5 percent level or less. Even after controlling for these variables the initial level of debt seems to jeopardize a firm's chances of survival. The effect is statistically significant at the 1 percent level and is also economically relevant, although not huge. An increase in leverage of one standard deviation reduces the probability of survival by 8 percent.

An alternative way to measure the economic importance of this effect is by answering the following question: How much more efficient (i.e., profitable) must a company be to offset the negative impact on survival produced by an increase in leverage from 0.2 (the average) to 0.3? By using the probit estimates, I obtain that a trucking company needs to have a return on sales 0.7 percentage points higher (i.e., 10 percent higher with respect to the median ROS of 7 percent) in order to offset 10 percent more capital financed by debt. The effect, thus, is small but not trivial.

The impact of leverage remains unchanged when I use return on assets (ROA) rather than return on sales as a measure of a firm's efficiency (see column II). Similarly, results are not substantially changed if other measures of leverage are used. For example, specification III uses coverage instead of net debt-to-capital, with similar results.

## A. *Alternative Measures of Efficiency*

Using return on sales (or on assets) as a measure of efficiency can pose some problems. First, given that in 1977 the trucking industry was regulated, a high return on sales may just indicate the presence of large monopoly rents, not a high degree of efficiency. Second, high return on sales is also associated with a greater availability of cash flow from operations, and ROS may also capture this additional effect.

In order to test the robustness of my findings, I try some alternative measures of efficiency. The first is an estimate of the distance of each motor carrier from the production possibility frontier. This is a measure of technical inefficiency, which does not rely on any assumption on the market in which a firm operates. As described in the Appendix, I estimate this by following the technique suggested by Schmidt and Sickles (1984).

The results are reported in the first column of Table IV. The degree of inefficiency has a *positive* (and not negative) effect on the probability of survival, and this effect is borderline statistically significant.[13] However, it is

---

[13] In their original article Schmidt and Sickles (1984) apply their technique to the airline industry and find that there is no link between estimated inefficiency and survival of airline carriers.

### Table IV
## Robustness to Different Measures of Efficiency

The dependent variable is the probability that a general freight motor carrier with more than $1 million in revenues in 1977 survives until 1985. The reported coefficients are probit estimates of the effect of a marginal change in the corresponding regressor on the probability of survival, computed at the average of the dependent variable. Net debt-to-capital is total debt minus cash reserves divided by total debt plus equity. Intangibles is the ratio of intangible assets to total assets. Labor cost is the ratio of the wages and benefits to operating costs. All the independent variables are measured as of 1977 (average of the 1976 and 1977 values) except the 1980 return on sales in the last column. Column I uses the estimated inefficiency of a carrier as additional proxy for a carrier's efficiency. This is computed as the distance of its output from the production frontier, estimated using a translog function (see the Appendix). Column II uses as additional proxy for efficiency the cost per ton-mile. Cost per ton-mile is the ratio of operating expenses to ton-miles hauled. Column III uses the ex post value of efficiency as of 1980 as a proxy for efficiency. In such case the dependent variable is the probability of survival after 1980. All regressions contain nine regional dummies (not reported). Standard errors are reported in parentheses.

| Independent Variables | I | II | III |
|---|---|---|---|
| Net debt-to-capital | −0.245*** | −0.226*** | −0.277*** |
|  | (0.066) | (0.057) | (0.058) |
| Return on sales | 3.142*** | 3.101*** | 1.131** |
|  | (0.481) | (0.410) | (0.512) |
| log(Revenues) | 0.030* | 0.029* | 0.022 |
|  | (0.017) | (0.016) | (0.015) |
| Intangibles | −0.045 | −0.234 | −0.066 |
|  | (0.303) | (0.274) | (0.280) |
| Labor cost | −0.332** | −0.436*** | −0.187 |
|  | (0.152) | (0.124) | (0.119) |
| Estimated inefficiency | 0.504* |  |  |
|  | (0.266) |  |  |
| Cost per ton-mile |  | −0.019 |  |
|  |  | (0.032) |  |
| Return on sales in 1980 |  |  | 2.450*** |
|  |  |  | (0.452) |
| Pseudo-$R^2$ | 0.13 | 0.14 | 0.14 |
| N | 574 | 723 | 670 |

***, **, * Significantly different from zero at the 1 percent level or less, at the 5 percent level, or at the 10 percent level, respectively.

interesting to notice that the impact of leverage on the probability of survival remains unchanged after this additional measure of efficiency is introduced.

Another measure of efficiency is the cost of operations. For the carriers that disclose the number of ton-miles hauled, I can obtain a measure of the cost per ton-mile. This measure has the advantage of being independent of the market structure in which a carrier operates. Regardless of the size of monopoly rents, a trucking company should always minimize costs. This measure has the drawback that it improperly accounts for a firm's cost of capital. In fact, operating expenses include depreciation (accounting, not economic, depreciation) and do not include the opportunity cost of capital. Another disadvantage is the fact that cost per ton-miles does not control for differences in the traffic mix (i.e., different average hauls and different average length of hauls).

The second column of Table IV reports the results of the previous probit model, when cost per ton-mile is inserted as an additional measure of efficiency. Notice that, because of data limitation, the number of observations available drops by 25 percent with respect to Table III. Higher-cost carriers are not at all less likely to survive after deregulation than low-cost carriers. Again, the impact of leverage is still present and statistically significant.

Finally, a last attempt to control for the expected efficiency of motor carriers after deregulation is done in column III, by using the return on sales in 1980. I use 1980 because it is a watershed year. The major changes in the trucking industry took place in the 1980 to 1985 period, following the ICC deregulation started in 1978. Therefore, the 1980 ROS should at least partially capture the after-deregulation efficiency level, while leaving enough observations of exit.

Column III in Table IV shows that the results are not substantially changed when I disregard 1978 to 1980 exits and insert the 1980 ROS as an additional explanatory variable. This suggests that 1977 leverage is not simply a proxy for an unobserved efficiency factor.[14]

## B. Controlling for the Ex Ante Risk of Default

It is possible that the most highly leveraged firms in 1977 were also the most inefficient and, thus, the most likely to exit the industry independent of any negative effect of debt. In the event that my measures of efficiency do not fully capture a firm's quality, the observed effect of leverage may simply be a spurious one.

To address this problem I try to control for the ex ante probability of default. I do that by using Altman's Z-score method. Altman (1968) is the first to develop a discriminant analysis method to forecast the probability of a firm's default using accounting information. One of the many applications of Altman's method is to the railroad industry (Altman (1973)). Given the similarities of the regulatory environment and of the accounting disclosure between the railroad and trucking industries, I choose to use the estimates of the Z-score model derived in this context.[15] Each firm is assigned a score according to the following formula in Altman (1973):

$$Z = 0.2003X_1 - 0.2070X_2 + 0.0059X_3 + 0.1040X_4 + 0.0885X_6 + 0.0688X_7,$$

$$(3)$$

[14] It also implies that the 1977 level of leverage has some predictive power on the probability of a firm's survival between three and eight years after. This rejects the hypothesis that the impact of leverage on survival is simply driven by firms on the verge of bankruptcy in 1977.

[15] A preferable alternative would be to estimate the Z-score model with trucking data. Unfortunately, the ATA dataset starts in 1976, making it impossible to estimate the Z-score model for trucking firms in the prederegulation period.

### Table V
### Effect of Leverage Controlling for the Ex Ante Risk of Default

The dependent variable is the probability that a general freight motor carrier with more than $1 million in revenues in 1977 survives until 1985. The reported coefficients are probit estimates of the effect of a marginal change in the corresponding regressor on the probability of survival, computed at the average of the dependent variable. Net debt-to-capital is total debt minus cash reserves divided by total debt plus equity. Intangibles is the ratio of intangible assets to total assets. Labor cost is the ratio of the wages and benefits to operating costs. The first column reports the results of the basic regression of the probability of survival when the Altman Z-score is used as an additional explanatory variable. The Altman Z-score is an index, based on accounting information, of the risk of default. The higher the Z-score, the lower the probability of default is. The second regression reports results of the basic regression of the probability of survival conditioned on the fact the Z-score model predicted survival. The third regression reports the results of the basic regression of the probability of survival conditioned on the fact the Z-score model predicted default. All regressions contain nine regional dummies (not reported). Standard errors are reported in parentheses.

| Independent Variables | | Predicted Survivors | Predicted Defaults |
|---|---|---|---|
| Net debt-to-capital | −0.150** | −0.199** | −0.183** |
| | (0.064) | (0.078) | (0.083) |
| Return on sales | 2.344*** | 2.930*** | 2.138*** |
| | (0.397) | (0.563) | (0.526) |
| Log-revenues | 0.039*** | 0.078*** | 0.017 |
| | (0.015) | (0.023) | (0.019) |
| Intangibles | −0.372 | −0.639* | 0.107 |
| | (0.262) | (0.350) | (0.371) |
| Labor cost | −0.149 | −0.331** | −0.298 |
| | (0.150) | (0.163) | (0.320) |
| Z-score | 0.012** | | |
| | (0.005) | | |
| Pseudo-$R^2$ | 0.12 | 0.15 | 0.07 |
| $N$ | 778 | 369 | 409 |

***, **, * Significantly different from zero at the 1 percent level or less, at the 5 percent level, or at the 10 percent level, respectively.

where $X_1$ is cash flow over fixed charges, $X_2$ is transportation expenses over operating revenues, $X_3$ is earned surplus over total assets, $X_4$ is the 1-year growth rate in operating revenues,[16] $X_5$ is earnings after taxes over operating revenues, $X_6$ is operating expenses over operating revenues, and $X_7$ is income before interest and taxes over total assets. The higher the Z-score, the lower the probability of default is.

Table V, column I, reports the estimates of the basic regression after having inserted a carrier Z-score as a proxy for the ex ante probability of exit. As expected, companies with a higher Z-score are more likely to survive. Nevertheless, the initial leverage still has a negative and statistically significant impact on the chances of survival, and its magnitude is substantially unchanged.

---

[16] Altman (1973) uses a three-year growth rate, but I use the one-year growth because I have just one year of accounting data for the pre-1977 period.

I can also use the Z-score to separate the desired effect of debt on exit from the undesired one. Suppose that the predegulation level of leverage was chosen to induce the optimal liquidation policy of motor carriers in the predegulation environment. Then, the predegulation Z-score should capture the desired effect of debt on exit and any residual effect can be interpreted as the undesired effect. Therefore, I want to estimate the effect of debt conditioned on the fact that the Z-score method predicted survival.

To transform the Z-score into a prediction on a firm's default I need to choose a cutoff point. If I use Altman's cutoff point, I obtain very few defaults and the results are substantially identical to that reported in Table III. Therefore, I choose the cutoff point so that the number of predicted defaults corresponds to the number of actual exits from my sample. Note that by doing so I bias the results against finding any effect of debt. In fact, ex ante people did not expect such a large exit from the trucking industry.

Table V, column II, reports the estimates of the basic regression restricted to the firms that the Z-score method predicts would survive. The initial level of leverage still has a negative impact on survival, and this impact is statistically significant at the 1 percent level. Profitability and size have coefficients similar to the basic estimates and are both statistically significant at the 1 percent level. This negative effect of debt can be interpreted as the undesired effect of debt on survival.

For completeness, I also report the estimates conditioned on the Z-score model predicting a default (column III). Again leverage has a negative impact on the probability of survival, statistically significant at the 5 percent. All the other variables have the same sign, and all except the ratio of intangible assets are significant at the 10 percent level or better.

## C. Comparison of Leverage and Its Effects in the TL and LTL Segment

Table VI, Panels A, B, and C, report summary statistics for carriers in the different segments of the market. LTL carriers tend to be larger, in terms both of sales and of assets, and to be less highly levered. Interestingly, there is no difference in the initial level of debt between survivors and nonsurvivors among TL carriers, but this difference is large and statistically significant for carriers with at least 30 percent of revenues in LTL and for carriers with more than 70 percent of revenues in LTL (see the last two columns of Table VI).

This differential impact of leverage, however, does not control for the different characteristics of the carriers in the three segments. This is done in Table VII, which reports the estimates of equation (2) for the three segments. Interestingly, the initial level of debt has no impact on the probability of survival of motor carriers with less than 30 percent of their revenues in LTL. The point estimate is actually positive (0.02), albeit not statistically significant. By contrast, the initial level of debt has a strong and statistically significant negative effect on survival in the other two groups, more heavily involved in LTL. In particular, the impact of debt on survival of the

**Table VI**

## Summary Statistics Split According to the Industry Segment

General freight carriers with more than $1 million in operating revenues in 1977 are divided in three groups according to the fraction of their revenues coming from less-than-truckload (LTL) shipments as of 1977. Net debt-to-capital is total debt minus cash reserves divided by total debt plus equity. Intangibles is the ratio of intangible assets to total assets. Labor cost is the ratio of the wages and benefits to operating costs. Revenues per ton-mile is the ratio of operating revenues to ton-miles hauled. Average load is the ratio of ton-miles hauled to total miles traveled. Average haul is the ratio of ton-miles hauled to tons of revenues freight. Market share is the ratio between carriers' operating revenues and the sum of the operating revenues of all the carriers located in the same state. The Diff. column reports the difference in means between carriers that still existed in 1985 and carriers that did not exist at that date. The $p$-values refer to the null that the difference is equal to zero.

| Variable | Mean | Median | Std. Dev. | Min. | Max. | Diff. | $p$-value | Obs |
|---|---|---|---|---|---|---|---|---|
| Panel A: Carriers with Less than 30 percent of revenues from LTL | | | | | | | | |
| Revenues ($ millions) | 5.35 | 2.45 | 7.85 | 0.92 | 46.60 | 3.61 | 0.014 | 113 |
| Assets ($ millions) | 2.06 | 0.90 | 3.32 | 0.16 | 23.70 | 1.86 | 0.003 | 113 |
| Debt-to-capital | 0.45 | 0.38 | 0.32 | 0.00 | 1.00 | −0.03 | 0.575 | 113 |
| Net debt-to-capital | 0.27 | 0.25 | 0.43 | −0.88 | 0.99 | 0.00 | 0.984 | 109 |
| Coverage | 22.27 | 7.52 | 30.10 | 0.00 | 100.00 | 3.52 | 0.538 | 112 |
| Return on assets | 0.19 | 0.19 | 0.13 | −0.19 | 0.73 | 0.05 | 0.033 | 113 |
| Return on sales | 0.08 | 0.07 | 0.07 | −0.03 | 0.42 | 0.02 | 0.059 | 113 |
| Intangibles | 0.07 | 0.03 | 0.08 | 0.00 | 0.44 | −0.01 | 0.740 | 111 |
| Labor cost | 0.28 | 0.30 | 0.18 | 0.02 | 0.64 | −0.04 | 0.198 | 112 |
| Revenues per ton-mile | 0.11 | 0.07 | 0.10 | 0.03 | 0.62 | −0.01 | 0.625 | 90 |
| Cost per ton-mile | 0.19 | 0.07 | 0.41 | 0.03 | 3.68 | −0.12 | 0.170 | 90 |
| Average load | 13.55 | 13.45 | 5.75 | 1.00 | 31.10 | 0.96 | 0.432 | 90 |
| Average haul | 252.51 | 217.64 | 196.32 | 6.93 | 1164.46 | 74.62 | 0.077 | 87 |
| Market share | 0.05 | 0.01 | 0.13 | 0.00 | 1.00 | 0.03 | 0.156 | 113 |
| Number of employees | 88.89 | 47.25 | 114.28 | 2.00 | 596.50 | 23.60 | 0.290 | 106 |
| Panel B: Carriers with 30 to 70 percent of Revenues from LTL | | | | | | | | |
| Revenues ($ millions) | 28.80 | 6.79 | 56.60 | 0.95 | 508.00 | 4.42 | 0.530 | 266 |
| Assets ($ millions) | 13.80 | 2.48 | 32.00 | 0.05 | 309.00 | 5.06 | 0.203 | 266 |
| Debt-to-capital | 0.42 | 0.36 | 0.29 | 0.00 | 1.00 | −0.13 | 0.000 | 265 |
| Net debt-to-capital | 0.25 | 0.26 | 0.36 | −0.86 | 1.00 | −0.20 | 0.000 | 257 |
| Coverage | 24.55 | 8.67 | 31.66 | 0.00 | 100.00 | 12.72 | 0.001 | 261 |
| Return on assets | 0.17 | 0.17 | 0.14 | −0.30 | 0.88 | 0.08 | 0.000 | 264 |
| Return on sales | 0.07 | 0.07 | 0.07 | −0.43 | 0.52 | 0.05 | 0.000 | 266 |
| Intangibles | 0.07 | 0.04 | 0.09 | 0.00 | 0.64 | −0.01 | 0.293 | 265 |
| Labor cost | 0.52 | 0.55 | 0.13 | 0.01 | 0.76 | −0.00 | 0.942 | 266 |
| Revenues per ton-mile | 0.24 | 0.18 | 0.21 | 0.06 | 1.86 | 0.03 | 0.230 | 259 |
| Cost per ton-mile | 0.26 | 0.18 | 0.32 | 0.06 | 2.46 | 0.04 | 0.286 | 259 |
| Average load | 10.90 | 11.45 | 4.21 | 0.80 | 29.54 | 0.35 | 0.504 | 259 |
| Average haul | 278.45 | 207.31 | 261.05 | 12.52 | 1713 | −61.39 | 0.062 | 258 |
| Market share | 0.08 | 0.02 | 0.14 | 0.00 | 0.94 | 0.02 | 0.273 | 261 |
| Number of employees | 760.90 | 199.25 | 1421.08 | 2.00 | 13157 | 148.26 | 0.401 | 266 |

**Table VI—***Continued*

| Variable | Mean | Median | Std. Dev. | Min. | Max. | Diff. | *p*-value | Obs |
|---|---|---|---|---|---|---|---|---|
| | | | | | | | | |

*Panel C: Carriers with More than 70 percent of Revenues from LTL*

| Variable | Mean | Median | Std. Dev. | Min. | Max. | Diff. | *p*-value | Obs |
|---|---|---|---|---|---|---|---|---|
| Revenues ($ millions) | 14.70 | 3.70 | 55.70 | 0.93 | 684.00 | 11.70 | 0.083 | 270 |
| Assets ($ millions) | 6.73 | 1.45 | 28.50 | 0.23 | 355.00 | 6.83 | 0.048 | 270 |
| Debt-to-capital | 0.34 | 0.29 | 0.28 | 0.00 | 1.00 | −0.15 | 0.000 | 270 |
| Net debt-to-capital | 0.14 | 0.09 | 0.37 | −0.97 | 1.00 | −0.20 | 0.000 | 261 |
| Coverage | 33.10 | 13.35 | 36.05 | 0.00 | 100.00 | 19.66 | 0.000 | 264 |
| Return on assets | 0.19 | 0.18 | 0.12 | −0.33 | 0.56 | 0.06 | 0.000 | 270 |
| Return on sales | 0.08 | 0.07 | 0.05 | −0.07 | 0.30 | 0.04 | 0.000 | 270 |
| Intangibles | 0.06 | 0.04 | 0.07 | 0.00 | 0.47 | −0.02 | 0.007 | 268 |
| Labor cost | 0.56 | 0.59 | 0.11 | 0.02 | 0.78 | 0.00 | 0.923 | 269 |
| Revenues per ton-mile | 0.44 | 0.32 | 0.37 | 0.12 | 3.46 | 0.04 | 0.402 | 261 |
| Cost per ton-mile | 0.44 | 0.31 | 0.39 | 0.11 | 3.20 | 0.01 | 0.861 | 261 |
| Average load | 8.25 | 8.47 | 3.99 | 0.81 | 24.06 | −0.35 | 0.477 | 261 |
| Average haul | 167.98 | 134.76 | 126.86 | 17.45 | 788.00 | −11.60 | 0.461 | 261 |
| Market share | 0.05 | 0.01 | 0.12 | 0.00 | 0.90 | 0.02 | 0.204 | 270 |
| Number of employees | 426.64 | 114.25 | 1398.94 | 6.00 | 18015 | 310.07 | 0.072 | 264 |

carriers most concentrated in LTL is statistically different (at the 10 percent level) from the impact of debt on survival of the carriers least concentrated in LTL.

In an unreported regression, I also estimate the effect of debt on survival across the three groups using a linear probability model. As discussed in Section II.B, in a linear framework the estimated difference in the impact of debt in the high LTL carriers and in the low LTL carriers is a consistent estimate of the true difference. The estimated difference is −0.26, which is statistically different from zero at the 10 percent level. Thus, consistent with the theories predicting a negative effect of debt, this effect is larger (in absolute value) for predominantly LTL carriers. This finding also supports the view that the impact of debt on survival is not simply an effect of unobserved quality differences.

It is important to notice that these results arise in spite of the fact that the percentage of exits in the two extreme groups is the same. This fact makes implausible the assumption that these results are driven by a difference in an unobserved firm characteristic that affects both leverage and exit.

## V. Why Does Debt Affect Survival?

The findings thus far suggest that the initial level of debt might have some consequences on the ability of a motor carrier to survive during deregulation. In this section, I try to uncover the sources of this observed relationship.

## Table VII
## Differential Impact of the Initial Leverage on Survival in Different Segments of the Trucking Industry

The dependent variable is the probability that a general freight motor carrier with more than $1 million in revenues in 1977 survives until 1985. The reported coefficients are probit estimates of the effect of a marginal change in the corresponding regressor on the probability of survival, computed at the average of the dependent variable. Net debt-to-capital is total debt minus cash reserves divided by total debt plus equity. Intangibles is the ratio of intangible assets to total assets. Labor cost is the ratio of the wages and benefits to operating costs. All the independent variables are measured as of 1977 (average of the 1976 and 1977 values). Among the independent variables there are also nine regional dummies (not reported). General freight carriers are divided into three groups according to the fraction of their revenues coming from less-than-truckload shipments as of 1977. The first column reports the estimates for motor carriers with less than 30 percent of revenues from less than truckload (LTL) shipments. Estimates in the second column are for motor carriers with more than 30 percent but less than 70 percent of their revenues in LTL shipments. Estimates in the third column are for motor carriers with more than 70 percent of their revenues in LTL shipments. Standard errors are reported in parentheses.

| Independent Variables | LTL < 0.3 | 0.3 < LTL < 0.7 | LTL > 0.7 |
|---|---|---|---|
| Net debt-to-capital | 0.021 | −0.224** | −0.277*** |
|  | (0.127) | (0.102) | (0.101) |
| Return on sales | 1.481* | 3.520*** | 3.247*** |
|  | (0.829) | (0.730) | (0.821) |
| log(Revenues) | 0.125* | -0.010 | 0.063** |
|  | (0.064) | (0.025) | (0.031) |
| Intangibles | 0.151 | 0.089 | −0.591 |
|  | (0.687) | (0.464) | (0.512) |
| Labor cost | −0.417 | 0.086 | −0.320 |
|  | (0.341) | (0.300) | (0.341) |
| Pseudo-$R^2$ | 0.09 | 0.17 | 0.15 |
| N | 100 | 249 | 259 |

***, **, * Significantly different from zero at the 1 percent level or less, at the 5 percent level, or at the 10 percent level, respectively.

### A. Investment

If highly leveraged motor carriers are weeded out because they cannot successfully finance new investment, then I should be able to find some effects of initial leverage on the amount of investment undertaken by each firm during the postderegulation period.

Because the ATA data set does not contain flow of funds data, I measure the total amount of capital expenditures in the postderegulation period as the difference in gross operating property over the period 1977 to 1985 divided by the 1977 level of net operating property. I then estimate a reduced form equation in which investments are a function of a company's profitability, its size, the level of intangibles, and the proportion of labor cost.

Table VIII reports the OLS estimates of this equation. After controlling for the likely determinants of investments, the initial level of leverage seems to

*Survival of the Fittest or the Fattest?*                          929

### Table VIII
### Investments

This table reports the OLS estimates obtained by regressing capital investments of general freight motor carriers with more than $1 million in revenues in 1977 on some predetermined explanatory variables. Investments are computed as differences in carriers' gross operating properties over the period divided by the 1977 level of net operating properties. Net debt-to-capital is total debt minus cash reserves divided by total debt plus equity. Intangibles is the ratio of intangible assets to total assets. Labor cost is the ratio of the wages and benefits to operating costs. All the independent variables are measured as of 1977 (average of the 1976 and 1977 values). The period 1977–1980 is also considered with the sample restricted to the motor carriers that survived until 1985 and with the sample restricted to motor carriers that exited between 1980 and 1985. All the regressions also contain nine regional dummies (not reported). Standard errors are reported in parentheses.

| | Investment Period | | | |
|---|---|---|---|---|
| Independent Variables | 1977–1985 | 1977–1980 | 1977–1980 of survivors | 1977–1980 of nonsurvivors |
| Net debt-to-capital | −0.092 | −0.224** | −0.068 | −0.379** |
| | (0.203) | (0.106) | (0.131) | (0.180) |
| Return on sales | 2.249* | 2.208*** | 1.840*** | 1.619 |
| | (1.173) | (0.693) | (0.796) | (1.493) |
| log(Revenues) | −0.125** | −0.063*** | −0.057*** | −0.034 |
| | (0.052) | (0.028) | (0.033) | (0.053) |
| Intangibles | −0.697 | 0.645 | 0.504 | 0.556 |
| | (1.137) | (0.518) | (0.733) | (0.761) |
| Labor cost | −1.081*** | −0.087 | −0.005 | −1.438*** |
| | (0.393) | (0.084) | (0.082) | (0.400) |
| $R^2$ | 0.09 | 0.05 | 0.05 | 0.11 |
| $N$ | 420 | 669 | 412 | 257 |

***, **, * Significantly different from zero at the 1 percent level or less, at the 5 percent level, or at the 10 percent level, respectively.

have no impact on the amount of investment actually made during the post-deregulation period.

One caveat, however, is warranted. If debt affects a firm's investment policy, the negative efficiency consequences of this underinvestment are likely to jeopardize a firm's ability to survive. We can observe the investment over a certain period only for the firms that survived until the end of the period; therefore, by estimating the investment over the entire postderegulation period I may miss the most important effect. To overcome this problem, I estimate the same investment equation considering only the investments that took place up to 1980. By that time the deregulation shock on leverage has already occurred, but the large exodus from the industry has not.

The results are reported in the second column of Table VIII. In this case we do observe a negative effect of leverage on investment. An increase of one standard deviation in the initial level of leverage decreases the total investment in the three years following deregulation by 10 percent, and this effect is statistically significant at the 5 percent level.

If the proposed explanation is indeed the source of these ambivalent results, then I should find that the effect of debt on investments is mostly concentrated among firms that eventually exit the industry. The last two columns of Table VIII show that this is indeed the case. The investment policy of firms that eventually survive is not very much affected by debt. By contrast, this effect is very strong (both economically and statistically) among firms that exit the industry.

Why is the effect of debt mostly limited to firms that eventually exited? One possible explanation is that the market had different perceptions of the long-term viability of highly leveraged carriers. Some were perceived as viable, obtained financing, invested as much as the low leveraged carriers, and survived. Others, which were not perceived as viable, were forced to curtail their investments and eventually left the industry. This explanation is consistent with Lang, Ofek, and Stulz (1996), who find that debt reduces the growth of firms with a low Tobin's q, but not of firms with a high Tobin's q. In fact, if one interprets survival ex post as a proxy for the ex ante Tobin's q (which I cannot observe because the firms are privately held), my results are analogous to Lang et al. (1996). This interpretation is consistent with some unobserved heterogeneity, but it does not necessarily imply that the nonsurviving carriers were of inferior quality. As Lang et al. (1996) point out, it might just be that they were perceived by the market as such.

Another (related) possibility, which does not rely on the surviving carriers being of a higher quality, is that highly leveraged firms differ in the resources available to their owners. Some firms may be owned by deep-pocket investors, ready to support the necessary financing. These highly leveraged carriers, then, invest as the low leveraged ones and survive. By contrast, highly leveraged carriers without a deep-pocket investor cannot keep up the investment level and, as a result, are forced to exit eventually.

In sum, the evidence suggests that the firms that exited the industry have suffered from an underinvestment problem linked to their initial level of debt. Yet, I cannot rule out the possibility that this effect is caused by unobserved heterogeneity in carriers' quality.

## B. Pricing

Leverage may affect survival also by weakening a firm's competitive position. As reviewed in Section II, several models suggest that a high leverage may force firms into cutting their prices. These models, however, differ substantially in the nature of their predictions. Bolton and Scharfstein's (1990) model of predation makes predictions on the equilibrium price prevailing in a certain market as a function of the incentive of deep-pocket firms to prey on their shallow-pocket competitors. By contrast, Titman (1984) and Maksimovic and Titman (1991) do not make any prediction on the market equilibrium price but only on the price differential between a firm and its competitors.

### B.1. Price Data

General freight carriers are required to disclose the amount of ton-miles transported in a calendar year. By dividing a carrier's operating revenues by the number of ton-miles reported, I obtain a proxy of the actual price per ton-mile charged by each carrier. This measure is noisy because the price changes not only as a function of the segment of the market a carrier is in (TL versus LTL), but also as a function of the average haul of a carrier because there is a fixed cost for loading and unloading each shipment.

However, if the composition of shipments of each individual carrier is fairly stable over time (a nontrivial assumption during deregulation), I can eliminate some of the noise by considering the changes in the prices charged by the same carriers over a certain period. Therefore, I will use these estimated price changes over different time intervals to analyze the effects of the initial level of leverage on a carrier's pricing policy.

### B.2. Estimates of the Impact of Leverage on Prices

To test the predation hypothesis I would need to identify many separate markets. Unfortunately, I lack a clear way to do that. If I use the nine geographical regions identified by the ICC, I will have too few observations to estimate a cross-market regression. Using state boundaries would give me more observations, but it is highly unsatisfactory from an economic point of view as there is no reason why the effective market in which a carrier competes is limited to the state in which its headquarters is located. To make things worse, the results would be very sensitive to the way a market is defined (and, thus, to who the main competitors in this market are). Therefore, I cannot test the predation hypothesis with the available data.

By contrast, I am better positioned to test the effect of leverage on the prices of individual carriers. Although it would certainly be better to be able to control for factors that affect prices at a local-market level, the lack of a precise definition of market only weakens the power of the test.

For this reason, I try to explain changes in the prices charged by individual carriers as a function of some real variables and the initial level of leverage. The control variables are: first, state dummies, which absorb any regional effect; second, the proportion of labor cost over total cost at the beginning of the period, as a proxy of the cost structure of each carrier and, indirectly, of its degree of unionization; third, the size of the carrier vis-à-vis its state competitors in 1977 (which I improperly refer to as market share), fourth, the percentage of revenues obtained through LTL shipments.

Table IX reports OLS estimates obtained from regressing the changes in the price charged by each carrier on these controlling variables and the initial leverage. I estimate separate equations for every year from 1980 to 1985. The rate setting was liberalized in 1980, so that year marks the beginning of price competition. On the other hand, 1985 can be considered the year when the postderegulation industry equilibrium was reached. In between, 1982

**Table IX**

**Firm-Level Prices and Leverage**

This table reports OLS coefficient estimates for a sample of general freight motor carriers with more than \$1 million in revenues in 1977 that disclose data on the volume of their shipments (Instruction 27 carriers). The dependent variable is the difference between the price per ton-mile charged by a carrier in the year of reference and the price charged in 1977. Net debt-to-capital in 1977 is debt minus cash reserves divided by debt plus equity. Labor cost in 1977 equals wages plus benefits over operating costs. A carrier market share in 1977 is the ratio between carriers' operating revenues and the sum of the operating revenues of all the carriers located in the same state. Medium less-than-truckload (LTL) carriers are carriers with more than 30 percent but less than 70 percent of their revenues in LTL shipments. High LTL carriers are carriers with more than 70 percent of their revenues in LTL shipments. All the regressions contain state fixed effects (not reported). Standard errors are reported in parentheses.

| Independent Variables | 1980 | 1981 | 1982 | 1983 | 1984 | 1985 |
|---|---|---|---|---|---|---|
| Net debt-to-capital in 1977 | 0.046 | −0.037 | −0.138*** | −0.126** | −0.120** | −0.103 |
| | (0.031) | (0.040) | (0.051) | (0.050) | (0.058) | (0.073) |
| Labor cost in 1977 | 0.092 | 0.088 | 0.087 | 0.249 | 0.328* | 0.201 |
| | (0.090) | (0.124) | (0.159) | (0.157) | (0.193) | (0.240) |
| Market share in 1977 | 0.063 | 0.121 | 0.058 | 0.138 | 0.101 | 0.102 |
| | (0.100) | (0.122) | (0.157) | (0.164) | (0.184) | (0.216) |
| Medium LTL revenues in 1977 | 0.054 | 0.089* | 0.063 | −0.008 | −0.015 | −0.023 |
| | (0.039) | (0.052) | (0.064) | (0.065) | (0.080) | (0.101) |
| High LTL revenues in 1977 | 0.107** | 0.141** | 0.119* | 0.080 | 0.034 | 0.066 |
| | (0.042) | (0.055) | (0.068) | (0.069) | (0.082) | (0.106) |
| $R^2$ | 0.14 | 0.17 | 0.16 | 0.20 | 0.22 | 0.22 |
| $N$ | 428 | 376 | 354 | 333 | 302 | 264 |

\*\*\*, \*\*, \* Significantly different from zero at the 1 percent level or less, at the 5 percent level, or at the 10 percent level, respectively.

represents the trough of a recession when, according to industry sources, price cuts were most aggressive.

Interestingly, in 1980 the price changes are unaffected by the initial level of debt; the coefficient is actually positive, but is economically and statistically indistinguishable from zero. It is only beginning in 1982 that carriers entering the deregulation period with more leverage start to charge significantly lower prices than their direct competitors. This effect is both economically and statistically significant. One standard deviation increase in the initial level of leverage decreases a carrier's prices by 7 cents per ton-mile. This represents approximately a 22 percent discount with respect to the average price per ton-mile. This effect persists in 1983 and 1984, then in 1985 it is economically weaker and not statistically significant.

These results seem to support the idea that more highly leveraged firms are forced to discount their products, especially during recessions. It is less clear, though, what the ultimate reason for this discount is. It might be the fact that highly leveraged carriers are desperate for cash, or that consumers require compensation for the risk of dealing with a company that might go bankrupt (Titman (1984)). The first effect should hold indifferently across

TL and LTL carriers, but the second one is more likely to be important in LTL carriers that deliver a nonstandardized product, where service is more important. It is worth noting that at the time there was much discussion in the press about the potential cost a less-than-truckload shipper might incur if its carrier defaulted in the middle of an important shipment.

For this reason, I explore the differences in the impact of debt across industry segments. To present these results in a concise form, I pool the price changes over the six-year period and estimate a separate coefficient of the initial level of debt for every year (the results are substantially identical if I estimate six separate regressions). Year dummies (not reported) are also inserted. Table X reports the results. Interestingly, the initial level of debt has no effect in the price changes of "pure" TL carriers. By contrast, the effect is very pronounced for the "pure" LTL carriers. It starts to manifest itself in 1981 and is particularly pronounced in 1982 and 1983. This finding is consistent with the hypothesis that leveraged carriers discount their services to compensate consumers for the risk associated with the probability of default of the carrier.

These results seem to contrast with Phillips (1995) and Chevalier (1995b), who find a positive relation between the increase in leverage caused by LBOs and increases in prices. The contrast, however, is more apparent than real. In fact, the industries studied by Phillips (gypsum, polyethylene, fiberglass insulation, and tractor trailer) and Chevalier (supermarkets) do not involve much specific investment by the customers. Thus, the need to discount the goods in order to compensate the customers from the risk of bankruptcy, which is present for LTL carriers, is not likely to arise for their firms.

Moreover, neither paper finds that prices always increase. Phillips (1995) finds that, in one of the four industries he analyzes, prices drop after the LBOs. Similarly, Chevalier (1995b) finds that, in some local markets, supermarket prices drop after the LBO wave. In both cases, the authors point out that this phenomenon occurs in markets where there are some competitors with deep pockets. This is certainly the case in the trucking industry, if I consider that carriers are competing throughout the nation. In sum, the relation between prices and leverage seems to be very dependent on the nature of the goods and the financial position of competitors.

## VI. Conclusions

This paper studies the impact of capital market imperfections on the survival of firms. In general, the feasibility of such a study is seriously impaired by an endogeneity problem. It is impossible to determine whether firms perform poorly and exit because they are highly leveraged, or vice versa, that they are highly leveraged because they perform poorly and should be induced to leave. Deregulation in the trucking industry provides a unique natural experiment that may overcome this problem.

I study the effect of the prederegulation level of leverage on the subsequent survival of trucking firms during deregulation. I find that firms that

934                    The Journal of Finance

### Table X

## Prices and Leverage in Different Segments of the Trucking Industry

This table reports OLS coefficient estimates for a sample of general freight motor carriers with more than $1 million in revenues in 1977 that disclose data on the volume of their shipments (Instruction 27 carriers). The dependent variable is the vector of the differences between the price per ton-mile charged by a carrier in any year from 1980 to 1985 and the price charged in 1977. Net debt-to-capital in 1977 is debt minus cash reserves divided by debt plus equity. Labor cost in 1977 equals wages plus benefits over operating costs. A carrier market share in 1977 is the ratio between carriers' operating revenues and the sum of the operating revenues of all the carriers located in the same state. The first column reports the estimates for motor carriers with less than 30 percent of revenues from less than truckload (LTL) shipments. Estimates in the second column are for motor carriers with more than 30 percent but less than 70 percent of their revenues in LTL shipments. Estimates in the third column are for motor carriers with more than 70 percent of their revenues in LTL shipments. All the regressions contain state fixed effects and yearly dummies (not reported). Standard errors are reported in parentheses.

| Independent Variables | LTL < 0.3 | 0.3 < LTL < 0.7 | LTL > 0.7 |
|---|---|---|---|
| Net debt-to-capital in 1977 | 0.087 | 0.027 | 0.017 |
| *1980 dummy | (0.056) | (0.054) | (0.069) |
| Net debt-to-capital in 1977 | 0.108 | −0.053 | −0.080 |
| *1981 dummy | (0.063) | (0.056) | (0.079) |
| Net debt-to-capital in 1977 | 0.080 | −0.090 | −0.239*** |
| *1982 dummy | (0.062) | (0.058) | (0.079) |
| Net debt-to-capital in 1977 | 0.037 | −0.064 | −0.222*** |
| *1983 dummy | (0.066) | (0.061) | (0.084) |
| Net debt-to-capital in 1977 | 0.002 | −0.054 | −0.212** |
| *1984 dummy | (0.076) | (0.062) | (0.083)* |
| Net debt-to-capital in 1977 | 0.074 | −0.130** | −0.091 |
| *1985 dummy | (0.079) | (0.066) | (0.091) |
| Labor cost | 0.086 | 0.281*** | 0.185 |
|  | (0.083) | (0.083) | (0.144) |
| Market share | −0.078 | 0.189** | −0.112 |
|  | (0.514) | (0.076) | (0.134) |
| $R^2$ | 0.19 | 0.24 | 0.12 |
| $N$ | 300 | 831 | 927 |

***, **, * Significantly different from zero at the 1 percent level or less, at the 5 percent level, or at the 10 percent level, respectively.

happened to be highly leveraged at the beginning of deregulation are less likely to survive afterward, even when controlling for some measures of efficiency and for the ex ante probability of default.

I find that the initial level of leverage has a negative impact on the ability of a motor carrier to invest in the years following deregulation. The effect is particularly pronounced in those companies that are eventually forced to exit, suggesting that the underinvestment problem caused by the high debt level might have forced these firms out of the market.

I also find evidence that the prederegulation level of leverage negatively impacts the price that a carrier charges during the price war which follows deregulation. This effect is entirely concentrated in the LTL segment of the industry.

In general, my findings raise the possibility that sometimes natural selection leads to the survival of relatively inefficient firms, which happen (or choose) to have deep pockets. In industries with high barriers to entry (like LTL shipments), relatively inefficient firms that survive are not likely to be challenged by new entrants. Thus, in these industries, the selection "mistakes" may have long-lasting effects. In other words, my findings challenge the commonly held assumption that competition will necessarily lead to the survival of the fittest. Only future research will be able to answer how generalizable these findings are.

## Appendix: Technical Measure of Efficiency

The first step consists of estimating a production function with a panel of firms. The firm-specific effect represents the difference between a firm's output and the predicted level of output given the observed inputs. This difference can be used to assess the relative degree of inefficiency of each firm with respect to the most productive firm in the sample.

I use the period 1976 to 1978 to estimate the degree of relative inefficiency before deregulation started.[17] Following the literature on the subject, and especially its application to the trucking industry (see Friedlaender and Spady (1981)), I estimate a translog production function of the form

$$\ln Y_{it} = \alpha_i + \sum_z^K \beta_z \ln X_{zit} + \sum_z^K \gamma_z \frac{\ln^2 X_{zit}}{2}$$

$$+ \sum_z^K \sum_j^K \delta_{zj} \ln X_{zit} \ln X_{jit} + \sum_l^L F_{lit} + \epsilon_{it}, \qquad (A1)$$

where $\ln Y_{it}$ is the logarithm of firm $i$'s output at time $t$, $X_z$ are the $K$ factors used in the production process, and $F_l$ are $L$ controlling factors to account for possible heterogeneity of the principal input categories.

In this context, the firm's specific factor $\alpha_i$ is the algebraic sum of a common intercept $\alpha$ and a firm specific level of inefficiency $u_i$:

$$\alpha_i = \alpha - u_i. \qquad (A2)$$

The output $Y$ is the number of ton-miles transported by carrier $i$ in year $t$. The factors used are capital (net carrier operating properties), labor (number

---

[17] The estimator of a firm's inefficiency is consistent for $T$ (number of periods) going to infinity. Therefore, I decide to include 1978 as a prederegulation year to increase the precision of the estimates. I also try to estimate a model using data up to 1980 without significant changes in the results.

936                          *The Journal of Finance*

### Table AI
### Production Function Estimate

This table reports a fixed effect estimate of a translog production function where capital (K), labor (L), and intermediate goods (M) are the three factors. The sample is an unbalanced panel of firms present for at least two years in the period 1976 to 1978. The dependent variable is the logarithm of ton-miles hauled each year. Capital is the book value of net carrier operating properties. Labor is the number of workers employed. Intermediate goods are deflated expenses in fuel and supplies. As a factor controlling for possible heterogeneity of the principal input categories, the average haul and the average load plus two yearly dummies are used. The average load is the ratio of ton-miles hauled to total miles traveled. The average haul is the ratio of ton-miles hauled to tons of revenues freight. Standard errors are reported in parentheses.

| | |
|---|---|
| $\log K$ | $-0.432^{***}$ |
| | $(0.078)$ |
| $\log L$ | $0.832^{***}$ |
| | $(0.112)$ |
| $\log M$ | $-0.334^{**}$ |
| | $(0.147)$ |
| $\dfrac{(\log K)^2}{2}$ | $0.040^{***}$ |
| | $(0.007)$ |
| $\dfrac{(\log L)^2}{2}$ | $0.110^{***}$ |
| | $(0.016)$ |
| $\dfrac{(\log M)^2}{2}$ | $0.052^{***}$ |
| | $(0.017)$ |
| $\log K \log L$ | $-0.043^{***}$ |
| | $(0.008)$ |
| $\log K \log M$ | $0.015^{**}$ |
| | $(0.007)$ |
| $\log L \log M$ | $-0.045^{***}$ |
| | $(0.012)$ |
| Average load | $0.049^{***}$ |
| | $(0.002)$ |
| Average haul | $0.002^{***}$ |
| | $(0.000)$ |
| 1977 dummy | $0.014^{**}$ |
| | $(0.006)$ |
| 1978 dummy | $0.000$ |
| | $(0.007)$ |
| $R^2$ | $0.60$ |
| $N$ | $1683$ |

$^{***}, ^{**}, ^{*}$ Significantly different from zero at the 1 percent level or less, at the 5 percent level, or at the 10 percent level, respectively.

of workers), and intermediate goods (deflated expenses in fuel and supplies). As controlling factor I use the size of the average haul and the average load, plus two yearly dummies. The within estimates of equation (3) are presented in Table AI.

The estimates look reasonable. The estimated elasticity of output with respect to capital is 0.09, with respect to labor 0.20, and the elasticity with respect to fuel and supplies is 0.32. The within regression can explain 60 percent of the variability.

Schmidt and Sickles's (1984) intuition is that the estimated firm-specific effect $\hat{\alpha}_i$ can be used to obtain an estimate of the production inefficiency of firm $i$ ($\hat{u}_i$). This is obtained as

$$\hat{u}_i = \max\{\hat{\alpha}_i\} - \hat{\alpha}_i. \tag{A3}$$

I estimate the $\hat{u}_i$ by using regression (A1) and then use the estimated value as a measure of inefficiency in regression (2).

## REFERENCES

Altman, Edward, 1968, Financial ratios, discriminant analysis, and the prediction of corporate bankruptcy, *Journal of Finance* 23, 589–609.

Altman, Edward, 1973, Predicting railroad bankruptcies in America, *Bell Journal of Economics and Management* 4, 184–211.

Bolton, Patrick, and David Scharfstein, 1990, A theory of predation based on agency problems in financial contracting, *American Economic Review* 80, 93-106.

Brander, James, and Tracy Lewis, 1986, Oligopoly and financial structure, *American Economic Review* 76, 956–970.

Breen, Dennis A., 1977, The monopoly value of household-goods carrier operating certificates, *The Journal of Law and Economics* 20, 153–185.

Chevalier, Judith, 1995a, Capital structure and product market competition: Empirical evidence from the supermarket industry, *American Economic Review* 85, 206–256.

Chevalier, Judith, 1995b, Do LBO supermarkets charge more: An empirical analysis of the effects of LBOs on supermarket pricing, *Journal of Finance* 50, 1095–1113.

Chevalier, Judith, and David Scharfstein, 1996, Capital-market imperfections and countercyclical markups: Theory and evidence, *American Economic Review* 86, 703–725.

Friedlaender, Ann, and Richard H. Spady, 1981. *Freight Transport Regulation. Equity Efficiency, and Competition in the Rail and Trucking Industries* (The MIT Press, Cambridge, Mass.).

Glaskowsky, Nicholas A., 1986. *Effects of Deregulation on Motor Carriers* (Eno Foundation for Transportation Inc., Westport, Conn.).

Harris, Milton, and Artur Raviv, 1990, Capital structure and the informational role of debt, *Journal of Finance* 45, 321–350.

Holtz-Eakin, Douglas, David Jouflaian, and Harvey Rosen, 1994, Sticking it out: Entrepreneurial survival and liquidity constraint, *Journal of Political Economy* 102, 53–75.

Jensen, Michael C., 1986, Agency costs of free cash flow, corporate finance and takeovers, *American Economic Review* 76, 323–329.

Jensen, Michael C., 1989, The eclipse of the public corporation, *Harvard Business Review* 67, 61–74.

Kovenock, Dan, and Gordon M. Phillips, 1997, Capital structure and product market behavior: An examination of plant exit and investment decisions, *Review of Financial Studies*, forthcoming.

Lang, Larry, Eli Ofek, and René Stulz, 1996, The leverage, investment, and firm growth, *Journal of Financial Economics* 40, 3–31.

Maksimovic, Vojislav, and Sheridan Titman, 1991, Financial policy and reputation for product quality, *Review of Financial Studies* 4, 175–200.

Moore, Thomas G., 1978, The beneficiaries of trucking regulation, *The Journal of Law and Economics* 21, 327–344.

Moore, Thomas G., 1986, Rail and trucking deregulation, in Leonard W. Weiss and Michael W. Klass, eds.: *Regulatory Reform. What Actually Happened* (Little Brown and Company, Boston, Mass.).

Myers, Stewart C., 1977, The determinants of corporate borrowing, *Journal of Financial Economics* 5, 146–175.

Myers, Stewart C., 1984, The capital structure puzzle, *Journal of Finance* 89, 575–592.

Perotti, Enrico, and Kathryn Spier, 1993, Capital structure as a bargaining tool: The role of leverage in contract renegotiation, *American Economic Review* 83, 1131–1141.

Phillips, Gordon, 1995, Increased debt and product-market competition, *Journal of Financial Economics* 37, 189–238.

Rajan, Raghuram, and Luigi Zingales, 1995, What do we know about capital structure? Some evidence from international data, *Journal of Finance* 50, 1421–1460.

Rose, Nancy, 1985, The incidence of regulatory rents in the motor carrier industry, *Rand Journal of Economics* 16, 299–318.

Rose, Nancy, 1987, Labor rent sharing and regulation: Evidence from the trucking industry, *Journal of Political Economy* 95, 1146–1178.

Schipper, Katherine, Rex Thompson, and Roman L. Weil, 1987, Disentangling interrelated effects of regulatory changes on shareholder wealth: The case of motor carrier deregulation, *Journal of Law and Economics* 30, 67–100.

Schmidt, Peter, and Robin C. Sickles, 1984, Production frontiers and panel data, *Journal of Business and Economic Statistics* 2, 367–374.

Smith, Clifford W. Jr., and Ross L. Watts, 1992, The investment opportunity set and corporate financing, dividend, and compensation policies, *Journal of Financial Economics* 32, 263–292.

Spence, Michael, 1985, Capital structure and the corporation's product market environment, in Benjamin M. Friedman, ed.: *Corporate Capital Structures in the United States* (The University of Chicago Press, Chicago, Ill.).

Standard & Poors, various years, S&P Industry Outlook.

Stulz, René, 1990, Managerial discretion and optimal financing policies, *Journal of Financial Economics* 26, 3–28.

Telser, Lester G., 1966, Cutthroat competition and the long purse, *Journal of Law and Economics* 9, 259–277.

Titman, Sheridan, 1984, The effect of capital structure on a firm's liquidation decision, *Journal of Financial Economics* 13, 137–151.

Winston, Clifford, 1993, Economic deregulation: Days of reckoning for microeconomists, *Journal of Economic Literature* 31, 1263–1289.

# Part II
# Capital Market Financing: Timing and Source of Funds

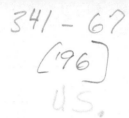

**[12]**

Journal of Financial Economics 42 (1996) 159–185

# Timing, investment opportunities, managerial discretion, and the security issue decision

Kooyul Jung[a], Yong-Cheol Kim[b], René M. Stulz[*,c,d]

[a]*M.J. Neeley School of Business, Texas Christian University, Fort Worth, TX 76129, USA*
[b]*College of Commerce and Industry, Clemson University, Clemson, SC 29634, USA*
[c]*Max M. Fisher College of Business, Ohio State University, Columbus, OH 43210, USA*
[d]*National Bureau of Economic Research, Cambridge, MA 02831, USA*

(Received January 1995; final version received November 1995)

## Abstract

This paper investigates the ability of the pecking-order model, the agency model, and the timing model to explain firms' decisions whether to issue debt or equity, the stock price reaction to their decisions, and their actions afterward. We find strong support for the agency model. Firms often depart from the pecking order because of agency considerations. We fail to find support for the timing model.

*Key words*: Security issue; Managerial discretion; Equity; Debt; Investment opportunities
*JEL classification*: G32

## 1. Introduction

Why is it that some firms raise new funds by issuing equity and others issue debt? There are three important explanations for this choice in the literature:

---

* Corresponding author.

We are grateful for useful comments to Steve Buser, K.C. Chan, David Denis, Harry DeAngelo, Thomas George, David Mayers, Kathy Kahle, Steve Kaplan, Tim Opler, John Persons, Patricia Reagan, Jay Ritter, David Scharfstein, Clifford Smith (the editor), Rick Smith, Chester Spatt, Robert Vishny, an anonymous referee, and to the participants in the 1993 NBER Summer Institute, the 1995 American Finance Association meetings, and at finance seminars at Arizona State University, Hong Kong Institute of Science and Technology, University of British Columbia, Ohio State University and University of St. Gallen. The first author acknowledges financial support from the Charles Tandy American Enterprise Center at Texas Christian University.

(1) the pecking-order model, (2) the agency model, and (3) the timing model. The pecking-order model is based on the view that information asymmetries between new investors and managers who maximize the wealth of existing shareholders make equity issues more costly than debt issues and therefore imply a financing hierarchy.[1] Firms therefore prefer issuing debt to issuing equity, and experience a negative stock price reaction if forced to issue equity. The agency model relies on the argument that managers sometimes pursue their own objectives, such as firm growth, at the expense of shareholders. If management pursues growth objectives, equity issues are valuable for shareholders when undertaken by firms that have good investment opportunities, but not otherwise. The timing model has evolved from the striking finding of Loughran and Ritter (1995) and Spiess and Affleck-Graves (1995) that firms experience long-term underperformance after they issue equity. As argued by Stein (1995), if equity is overpriced and the market underreacts to equity issues, then management maximizes the wealth of existing shareholders by issuing equity.

A theory of the corporate security issue choice should explain (1) why firms choose to issue a particular security, (2) how the market reacts to that choice, and (3) the actions of the firm after the issue. The pecking-order model is well-articulated and addresses each one of these questions. The agency model is much better developed as an explanation of the cross-sectional variation in capital structures (see Harris and Raviv, 1991; Smith and Watts, 1992) than as a model of security issue choice. The timing model addresses the three questions, but it relies on the assumption that the market fails to incorporate all the information communicated by a security issue. In this paper, we develop a unified analysis of the implications of the agency model to address the three questions that have to be answered to provide a satisfactory model of security issue choice. We then proceed to investigate how well the pecking-order model, the agency model, and the timing model explain the data.

Our results strongly support the agency model. We find that firms issuing equity are of two types: (i) firms with valuable investment opportunities that seek financing to grow profitably and (ii) firms that do not have valuable investment opportunities and have debt capacity. Without agency costs of managerial discretion, one would not expect the latter firms to issue equity. The agency model predicts that equity issues by such firms are bad news for shareholders, since they enhance managerial discretion when managers' objectives differ from shareholders' objectives. We find that, controlling for other firm and issue characteristics, firms without valuable investment opportunities have a more negative stock price reaction to equity issues than firms with better

---

[1]See Myers (1984). Information asymmetries between management and outside investors do not necessarily imply a financing hierarchy. Examples of models which emphasize informational asymmetries but do not obtain a pecking-order result are Brennan and Kraus (1987) and Noe (1988).

investment opportunities. We provide other evidence supporting the view that some firms issue equity to benefit management rather than shareholders. In particular, we show that firms without valuable investment opportunities issuing equity invest more than similar firms issuing debt, that firms with low managerial ownership have worse stock price reactions, and that the worst stock price reactions occur for firms without valuable investment opportunities issuing equity to finance capital expenditures.

Even though firms issuing equity perform more poorly than firms issuing debt on average, our cross-sectional regressions show that the subsequent evolution of the stock price does not explain the firms' security issue choice. The reason for this is that the cross-sectional standard deviation of post-issue cumulative abnormal performance is extremely large, so that extremely large samples are required to obtain statistically significant results. One interpretation of this result is that our sample of 192 primary equity issues and 276 bond issues is too small to obtain a powerful test of the timing model. Alternatively, one might argue that there is too much variation in long-term performance following equity issues for it to be an important determinant of management's decision. We provide evidence that the second interpretation should be taken seriously using a sample that is similar in size to the samples used in long-term performance studies.

We proceed as follows. In Section 2, we provide a more detailed analysis of the agency argument and its implications for the interpretation of the stock price reaction to equity issues. In Section 3, we introduce our sample and discuss the characteristics of firms issuing debt and equity. Section 4 provides estimates of an issue choice model. In Section 5, we investigate how the stock price reaction relates to firm characteristics. Section 6 shows that debt- and equity-issuing firms have distinct investment patterns following the new issue. Concluding remarks are presented in Section 7.

## 2. Models of the security issue decision

In this section, we analyze the role of agency costs in the security issue decision and compare the predictions of the agency cost model to the predictions of other models in the literature. To understand the role of agency costs in the security issue decision, it is best to investigate a special case of Myers and Majluf (1984). In their model, management has better information than investors about assets in place and about the firm's investment opportunities. If management can issue securities at a higher price than they are truly worth given its information, it chooses to do so to maximize the wealth of the existing shareholders. Riskless debt cannot be sold for more than it is worth, but risky debt and equity can. When the firm announces issues of risky securities, therefore, outsiders adjust their valuation of the firm to reflect the new information. This adjustment is trivial if the securities issued are not very sensitive to firm value, but is significant in the case of equity. The valuation impact of equity issues increases their cost and induces firms to issue equity only as a way of raising funds when debt financing would be extremely costly because the firm has exhausted its ability to sell low-risk debt. For these results to hold, though, it is crucial for outsiders to be less well-informed than management about the components of firm value.

Suppose now that outsiders know the value of assets in place in the Myers and Majluf model. Then, as recognized by Myers and Majluf, the model collapses: the firm always invests if it has a positive NPV project and, in their set-up, always issues equity to finance it. With agency costs, this special case remains interesting. To see why, consider an all-equity firm that is highly unlikely to have profitable investment opportunities. If the management of that firm always maximizes shareholder wealth, an equity issue undertaken to fund a project is good news. It means that the firm has unexpectedly obtained a positive NPV investment project. In the presence of agency costs of managerial discretion, however, an equity issue that enables management to invest is not necessarily good news and can be bad news altogether. A management investing in negative NPV projects would rather finance that investment with equity; debt financing for a negative NPV project eventually reduces resources under management's control since the present value of the debt payouts exceeds the present value of the project's payoffs.

Jensen (1986) and Stulz (1990) show that leverage limits management's discretion and hence reduces the agency costs of managerial discretion. First, management has less control over the firm's cash flows since these cash flows have to be used to repay creditors. Second, management is monitored by creditors who want to make sure that they will be repaid. However, leverage also has adverse effects on firm value. A firm with good projects but high leverage is less able to take full advantage of these projects. For instance, the impact on investment of an adverse liquidity shock increases with the amount of leverage. Consequently, firms with good projects want to limit their leverage and, if levered, are more likely to choose equity financing. Bernanke, Gertler, and Gilchrist (1993) review the literature on the relation between liquidity shocks and investment, and Lang, Ofek, and Stulz (1996) show that investment is negatively related to leverage for low-$q$ firms. The agency costs that arise because a levered firm may be unable to pursue the investment policy that would maximize the value of an all-equity firm are called here the agency costs of debt (see Jensen and Meckling, 1976; Myers, 1977). Smith and Watts (1992) provide extensive cross-sectional evidence of such agency costs, showing a negative relation between investment opportunities and leverage, and Titman and Wessels (1988) document a negative relation between R&D and leverage.

In Fig. 1, we show the optimal amount of leverage for given investment opportunities. The optimal amount of leverage is the amount at which the

K. Jung et al. / Journal of Financial Economics 42 (1996) 159–185          163

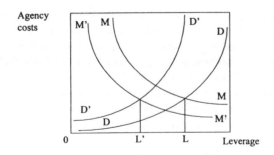

Fig. 1. Optimal leverage and agency costs of debt and managerial discretion.

This figure shows optimal leverage as a function of the marginal agency costs of debt ($DD$) and the marginal agency costs of managerial discretion ($MM$) for a given investment opportunity set. An improvement in investment opportunities shifts the marginal agency costs of debt curve to $D'D'$ and the marginal agency costs of managerial discretion curve to $M'M'$, so that optimal leverage falls from $L$ to $L'$.

marginal agency costs of debt equal the marginal agency costs of managerial discretion. Based on our previous discussion, the marginal agency costs of debt should increase with leverage and the marginal agency costs of managerial discretion should fall with leverage. We show how a shift in investment opportunities leads to a decrease in the optimal amount of leverage: for each level of leverage, an increase in investment opportunities (1) increases the marginal agency costs of debt because the firm has more to lose from financial distress and (2) decreases the marginal agency costs of managerial discretion because the objectives of management and shareholders become more congruent when investment opportunities become better.

Since equity provides unrestricted funds, why is it that management ever chooses to issue debt? Issuing equity has both direct and indirect consequences for management. The direct effect is an increase in managerial discretion, which management values. However, the indirect effect can be quite adverse for management depending on the firm's situation. If the firm does not have valuable investment opportunities, an equity issue means that the agency costs of managerial discretion increase, providing greater incentives for outsiders to try to affect management's actions. In particular, control activities, such as takeovers, active monitoring by large shareholders, monitoring by board members, and proxy fights, all become more advantageous for shareholders and outside investors. Issuing equity inappropriately can therefore increase the probability that management will lose control through corporate control actions unless it is well protected from such actions. Zwiebel (1994) presents a model in which management issues debt because of a threat from the market for corporate control. Hoshi, Kashyap, and Scharfstein (1993) have a related model in which the better firms choose financing with low monitoring, intermediate-quality firms choose financing with high monitoring, and the worst firms choose financing with low monitoring. (In their paper, financing with low monitoring is public debt and financing with high monitoring is bank financing; here, financing with low monitoring is equity and financing with high monitoring is public debt.) In addition, equity financing reduces the fraction of votes controlled by management and its allies unless they increase their investment in the firm (see Stulz, 1988). Consequently, equity financing both increases the benefits from outside intervention and makes outside intervention easier.

Taking into account the agency costs of managerial discretion makes the information content of new security issues more complicated. To understand this information content, it is best to focus on the cross-sectional relation between stock price reactions and a firm's investment opportunities, since the agency costs of managerial discretion are inversely related to the quality of the firm's investment opportunities. If there is no uncertainty about the value of a firm's investment opportunities, the issuing decision is straightforward in the pecking-order model. If a firm has sufficiently good investment opportunities, it issues equity if it cannot issue debt and the issue is not very informative about the value of assets in place. In contrast, if the firm has no valuable investment opportunities, it never issues equity. For firms with sufficiently good investment opportunities, the interests of management and shareholders should coincide so that they will follow the pecking-order model. Firms that can finance with low-risk debt do so; otherwise they either issue equity or do not invest at all if equity is too underpriced. For firms that have no valuable investment opportunities, however, there are good reasons to expect departures from the pecking-order model if management pursues objectives of its own. In particular, management may issue equity to keep the firm growing even though the firm has no positive NPV investment opportunities. For such firms, an equity issue reveals to outsiders that management has to raise funds to finance its plans, that it has decided to proceed with poor investments, and, finally, that it views the risks to its position from doing all this to be worth taking. If the equity issues are equally unanticipated, the news for outsiders is worse for the firm with no valuable investment opportunities.

At this point, it is useful to summarize the view that agency costs matter for security issues by showing how these costs affect the firm's decision regarding which security to issue (the issue decision), how stock price reactions are consistent with the existence of such costs (the information content), and how the firm's behavior after the issue is affected by these costs (the ex post actions): If the threat of outside intervention is held constant, agency considerations imply that managers favor equity over debt, so that firms for which the agency costs of managerial discretion are important issue equity even though shareholders would be better off with a debt issue or no issue at all. However, an

*K. Jung et al./Journal of Financial Economics 42 (1996) 159–185*          165

equity issue that is not in the interests of shareholders will have a negative impact on shareholder wealth to the extent that it is not anticipated, because the funds are likely to be invested poorly and because management is not as constrained by monitoring from outside investors as was expected. Finally, whether they have good investment opportunities or not, the firms that issue equity do so to have the flexibility to grow and should therefore grow more than debt-issuing firms. This should be true even for firms that have debt capacity but no valuable investment opportunities, since in these firms management chooses to issue equity to have more freedom to invest in poor projects.

It is important to note that the implications of agency costs do not make the considerations emphasized in the pecking-order model irrelevant. Irrespective of the importance of the agency costs of managerial discretion, there will always be some level of undervaluation of the existing shares at which management chooses not to issue. For firms whose agency costs of managerial discretion are small enough, it may be that the pecking-order model applies exactly. The pecking-order model based on information asymmetries assumes that management maximizes shareholder wealth whereas the agency cost view assumes that management pursues objectives of its own. As emphasized by Dybvig and Zender (1991) and others, the pecking-order model makes an ad hoc assumption about management's objectives that would not be appropriate if shareholders could choose a compensation policy for management such that the ex ante value of the firm is maximized. Since both the pecking-order model and the agency model rely on ad hoc assumptions about managerial objectives, only empirical evidence can allow us to evaluate the economic relevance of each model for the security issue decision.

Models with information asymmetries that assume away the agency costs of managerial discretion are most successful at explaining the negative stock price reaction to equity issues. As modified by Cooney and Kalay (1993), the Myers and Majluf model can explain that high-growth firms issuing equity would have a more positive stock price reaction than low-growth firms. Hence, relating the stock price reaction to investment opportunities is not sufficient to make the case for the agency model of security issues. This is why it is also important to consider the choice decision and the post-issue actions of the firm.

With the timing model, managers issue equity when they know that it is overvalued. Since the market underreacts to equity issues, firms issuing equity perform poorly in the long run as the market corrects the overvaluation that exists at the time of issue. A market underreaction to equity issues could play a role both in the agency model and in the pecking-order model. The question we therefore want to address is whether timing is a first-order consideration in the security issue choice decision. Importantly, none of the models explain the long-run post-issue abnormal returns.

## 3. The sample

To obtain our sample of new bond issues and primary stock offerings, we use the Registered Offerings Statistics File from 1977 to 1984. For the stock offerings, we use the Corporate Financing Directory published by the Investment Dealer's Digest to exclude all issues that involve secondary stock offerings and all shelf offerings. We restrict the sample to firms whose stock returns are available on the Center for Research in Security Prices (CRSP) tape for the whole calendar year before the announcement date. The announcement dates come from the Wall Street Journal Index. We use as our event date the first mention of a security issue before the offering date and exclude security issues for which such announcements are not available. We exclude utilities and banking firms to conform to the earlier literature. We also eliminate firms that have confounding announcements, such as dividend or earnings announcements.

We compute abnormal returns using a method similar to the one used by Asquith and Mullins (1986). For each calendar year in the sample we rank securities in the CRSP daily file according to their beta estimated using the market model. We then divide the securities into ten portfolios based on estimated betas. For each firm issuing a security, we compute the abnormal return over a two-day period that includes the day of the Wall Street Journal announcement and the day preceding the announcement. The abnormal return is defined to be the return of the issuing firm minus the return of the portfolio to which the firm belongs, although all of our results hold if we compute abnormal returns as market model residuals.

Table 1 provides a summary of the abnormal return data for the stock and bond issues. The results are similar to those reported in earlier papers in that equity announcements have a significant negative stock price reaction and debt announcements have an insignificant stock price reaction.[2] Table 1 also reports various characteristics of firms issuing debt and equity. The median debt-issuing firm has a stock market capitalization about four times larger than the median equity-issuing firm and raises about four times more funds through the issue. The equity-issuing firms are riskier than the debt-issuing firms in that they have both a higher beta and greater stock return volatility. The leverage measure that uses the market value of common stock in the denominator does not differ between firms issuing debt and those issuing stock, whereas the leverage

---

[2]For instance, Mikkelson and Partch (1986) find an average abnormal return for stock issues of − 3.56% and straight debt of − 0.23%. Eckbo (1986) finds a similar result for debt issues. Asquith and Mullins (1986) find an abnormal return for primary stock issues for industrial firms of − 3.0% whereas Masulis and Korwar (1986) find a stock price reaction of − 3.25%. Barclay and Litzenberger (1988) find an abnormal return of − 2.44% for the three hours surrounding the announcement on the Broad Tape.

Table 1
Abnormal returns and firm characteristics for 192 equity and 276 bond issues from 1977 to 1984

The abnormal returns are computed for the day of the WSJ announcement and the previous day. Amount equals the gross proceeds of the issue in millions of dollars. *LTD* is the book value of the firm's long-term debt. Cash flow is operating income before depreciation minus total taxes adjusted for changes in deferred taxes, minus gross interest expense and minus dividends paid on common and preferred stock, divided by total assets (*TA*). Market-to-book is the ratio of firm market value (market value of equity plus *TA* minus book value of equity) to *TA*. All accounting data are for the end of the fiscal year before the issue. The leading indicators are the six-month leading indicators. The volatility of the firm's stock return and the firm's beta are obtained using the CRSP daily data file for the period ( − 240, − 40). Difference is the mean of a variable for stock issues minus the mean of the same variable for bond issues; the $p$-value is for the null hypothesis that the difference is zero assuming unequal variances for the two subsamples.

| | Stock issues | | Bond issues | | |
| --- | --- | --- | --- | --- | --- |
| | Mean | Median | Mean | Median | Difference |
| *Abnormal return* | − 2.70% | − 2.63% | − 0.09% | − 0.15% | − 2.62* |
| *Amount* | 47.98 | 28.25 | 140.00 | 100.00 | − 92.01* |
| *Market value of equity* (*MVCS*) | 682.74 | 186.02 | 2941.70 | 883.62 | − 2258.97* |
| *Proceeds/MVCS* | 0.15 | 0.13 | 0.24 | 0.13 | − 0.09* |
| *Dividend yield* | 2.06 | 1.43 | 3.96 | 3.69 | − 1.90* |
| *LTD/MVCS* | 0.65 | 0.42 | 0.72 | 0.41 | − 0.07 |
| *LTD/TA* | 0.29 | 0.28 | 0.23 | 0.21 | 0.06* |
| *Cash flow* | 0.09 | 0.09 | 0.10 | 0.09 | − 0.01 |
| *Cash + Liquid assets/TA* | 0.06 | 0.04 | 0.06 | 0.04 | 0.00 |
| *Market-to-book* | 1.48 | 1.25 | 1.13 | 1.02 | 0.35* |
| *Leading indicators* | 0.03 | 0.03 | 0.00 | 0.00 | 0.03* |
| *11-month prior cumulative excess return* | 13.95% | 15.07% | − 1.63% | − 3.26% | 15.58* |
| *Beta* | 1.39 | 1.35 | 1.15 | 1.06 | 0.24* |
| *Volatility* | 7.27% | 6.28% | 4.67% | 3.20% | 2.60* |
| *3-year raw returns* | 59.47% | 37.86% | 76.20% | 52.49% | − 16.73 |
| *5-year raw returns* | 98.88% | 57.12% | 146.75% | 98.56% | − 47.87** |
| *Size-matched 3-year cumulative returns* | − 7.89% | − 13.90% | − 5.16% | − 3.64% | − 2.74 |
| *Size-matched 5-year cumulative returns* | − 32.69% | − 46.81% | 2.03% | − 18.60% | − 34.72 |

* (**) denotes significance at the 0.01 (0.05) level.

measure that uses the book value of total assets in the denominator is higher for firms that issue equity. Therefore, book leverage is more supportive of the pecking-order story than a market measure of leverage.

The pecking-order model predicts that firms are more likely to issue equity when the stock price experiences positive abnormal returns before the issue. Measuring the cumulative excess return of the issuing firm's common stock as in

Asquith and Mullins (1986), we find that firms that issue common stock have experienced significant positive abnormal returns for the 11 months before the stock issue, whereas firms that issue bonds experience insignificant negative cumulative abnormal returns on average. Mikkelson and Partch (1986) obtain a similar result on a smaller sample of bond offerings. The result for debt is inconsistent with the conjecture of Lucas and McDonald (1990) that firms issuing risky debt should have positive cumulative abnormal returns on average if debt is viewed as equity with less risk. The firms issuing equity and those issuing debt have similar cash flows before the issue. We also investigate, but do not report here, earnings to total assets, earnings before interest and taxes (*EBIT*) to total assets, and net operating income to total assets. In all cases, the mean for equity-issuing firms is larger, but the difference in means is significant only for net operating income. Finally, the firms issuing debt have a substantially higher dividend yield than the firms issuing equity.

Using the ratio of firm market value (defined as the market value of equity plus the book value of total assets minus the book value of equity) to the book value of assets (market-to-book) as a proxy for investment opportunities as in Smith and Watts (1992), firms issuing equity have better investment opportunities than firms issuing debt at the time of the announcement. In addition, firms issuing equity (but not those issuing debt) are more likely to do so when the leading indicators suggest good economic conditions and therefore good investment opportunities; Choe, Masulis, and Nanda (1993) observe the same result. Finally, the cumulative abnormal returns before the issue (discussed in the previous paragraph) are consistent with an improvement in the investment opportunities of firms issuing equity before the issue.

The timing model relies on the observation that equity-issuing firms perform poorly following the issue. Since this long-term performance is poor on average, it is consistent with the view that firms time their issues to coincide with periods when their equity is overvalued. Cheng (1994) provides further support for this view by showing that debt-issuing firms do not have poor long-term abnormal returns and that firms issuing equity that do not invest the proceeds have the worst abnormal returns. In Table 1, we provide evidence on the long-term performance of the firms in our sample. The cumulative returns are buy-and-hold returns. We show both raw returns and excess returns obtained by subtracting from the return of the issuing firm the return of a matching firm of similar size that has not issued equity in previous sample years. We also compute net-of-market returns but do not report them here since they lead to the same conclusions as the results we report. Our procedures are the same as the ones used by Loughran and Ritter (1995).

The raw returns are significantly positive both for bond- and equity-issuing firms. The difference between the raw returns of bond-issuing firms and equity-issuing firms is significant at the five-year horizon with a *t*-statistic of 2.06, but is not significant at the three-year horizon. The substantial worsening of the

*K. Jung et al./Journal of Financial Economics 42 (1996) 159-185* 169

performance of equity-issuing firms over the last two years of the five-year horizon is surprising. Turning to excess returns, we find that equity-issuing firms have significant negative excess returns on a five-year horizon at the 0.10 level. The excess returns are negative but not significant at the three-year horizon. Irrespective of the horizon, though, the mean excess return is large in absolute value for equity-issuing firms and consistent with previous evidence on the underperformance of equity-issuing firms. Bond-issuing firms have positive, although not significant, average excess returns at the five-year horizon. Using nonparametric statistics (rank and sign tests), excess returns are significantly negative for equity-issuing firms but not for debt-issuing firms. There is no significant difference in the means of excess returns between bond- and equity-issuing firms, but the medians are significantly different. That such large differences in means are not significant is consistent with the view articulated in Kothari and Warner (1995) that long-term returns have considerable cross-sectional variation so that statistical tests using such returns have low power. The limited significance of our results using long-term returns is no doubt partly explained by the fact that the number of equity issues used here is less than one-tenth of the number used in Loughran and Ritter (1995). In addition, however, our sample contains larger and more established firms since it only has Compustat firms. Brav, Géczy, and Gompers (1994) argue that underperformance is more pronounced for small issuing firms.

## 4. An empirical analysis of the security issue choice

In this section, we investigate an empirical model of security issue choice for our sample firms. This model uses standard variables from the literature to predict the security issue choice plus a proxy for investment opportunities and measures of long-term post-issue abnormal returns. Since the agency costs of debt are higher for firms with better investment opportunities, one expects the probability that a firm will issue equity to increase with investment opportunities if management maximizes shareholder wealth. Firms with high agency costs of managerial discretion will issue equity when they have poor investment opportunities, but such firms are expected to be a subset of the sample so that in a logistic regression model they will be firms that are not expected to issue equity and hence issue against type. If our proxy for investment opportunities simply proxies for firm overvaluation, as partisans of the timing model might argue, then inclusion of long-term abnormal returns should account for overvaluation. Further, if the timing model plays an important role in the issuing firm's decision, long-term cumulative excess returns should significantly affect the firm's issuing decision because the timing model relies on the argument that management knows when future performance will be poor and issues accordingly. Using actual long-term returns as a proxy for management's expectations

170                  *K. Jung et al. / Journal of Financial Economics 42 (1996) 159–185*

of long-term returns amounts to assuming that management has perfect foresight.

The literature on the determinants of firms' capital structures is extensive, but some variables are pervasive in the existing empirical work. Masulis (1988) and Harris and Raviv (1991) contain references to empirical studies that use these variables as well as references to theoretical papers that motivate their use. In this paper, we focus on a small number of determinants of leverage that are commonly considered by empiricists and reflect certain key ideas:

*1. Taxation.* Because of the deductibility of interest payments, a number of papers argue that the gain from debt financing relative to equity financing increases with the firm's tax rate. The literature has shown that the firm's tax status affects the issue decision (see MacKie-Mason, 1990). As a proxy for these benefits, we use tax payments divided by the book value of total assets for the year preceding the issue.

*2. Costs of financial distress.* As debt and firm risk increase, financial distress and bankruptcy become more likely. As a risk proxy, we use stock return volatility measured over the 200 days preceding the issue. Profitability is measured as cash flow divided by total assets, and leverage is measured as long-term debt divided by total assets. We use other proxies for risk (beta instead of volatility), profitability (earnings measures), and leverage (market value of equity instead of total assets) but do not report the results because our conclusions are insensitive to the choice of proxies for bankruptcy risks and costs.

*3. Asymmetric information.* Following Myers and Majluf (1984), it is well-established that issuing equity is more expensive when there is asymmetric information between firm insiders and outsiders. Therefore, firms for which this information asymmetry is large should issue debt if they can or abstain from raising funds altogether. As emphasized by Korajczyk, Lucas, and McDonald (1991), firms should time equity issues for periods when the information asymmetry is smaller. Following Lucas and McDonald (1990), firms are more likely to have good projects and hence raise funds if their returns before the issue are high (measured here by net-of-market returns over the 200 days before the issue) and leading indicators of economic activity are favorable. Firms that issue when they have slack are also more likely to do so because of low information asymmetries. We measure slack by cash and liquid assets normalized by total assets.

In some of our regressions, we also control for the amount raised through the security issue since net proceeds have been found to affect the stock price reaction in some studies. Presumably, the amount raised by the firm and the type of security issued are jointly endogenous variables. This suggests that logistic regressions that do not include the amount raised as an explanatory variable have the interpretation of reduced-form equations, whereas equations that include the amount raised suffer from a simultaneous equation bias. A more important reason to consider regressions without the amount raised as an explanatory variable is that such regressions can be used by investors to forecast whether a firm will issue equity or debt, whereas regressions that incorporate the size of the issue cannot (since they incorporate information not available before announcement of the type of security issued).

Regression (1) in Table 2 shows that investment opportunities play a substantial role in the new issue decision. With our logistic model, an equity issue takes the value one and a debt issue takes the value zero. Therefore, a positive coefficient indicates that a firm is more likely to issue equity. Market-to-book has a positive coefficient that is highly significant. Further, market-to-book has substantial explanatory power in that, if it is omitted, the pseudo-$R^2$ falls by almost one-third. Other variables indicative of good investment opportunities are significant also. Past cumulative excess returns and leading indicators have positive coefficients with $p$-values of less than 0.01. Cash flow is not significant, but some variables emphasized by other capital structure theories are significant. The coefficient on tax payments divided by total assets is negative as expected and highly significant. Leverage, as measured by long-term debt to total assets, is insignificant. This result holds when we use alternate leverage measures and is not surprising considering the earlier literature. For instance, Baxter and Cragg (1970) do not find a significant leverage coefficient either, although Marsh (1982) uses deviations from target leverage in his regressions and finds that firms with high leverage relative to a target are more likely to issue equity. Since leverage and volatility are correlated, we omit volatility in a regression not reproduced here; doing so does not make the coefficient on leverage significant. Finally, we would expect slack to have a positive coefficient, but instead it has an insignificant negative coefficient. In regression (2), we add total assets as an explanatory variable. Total assets could be a proxy for the degree of information asymmetry, since large firms are followed more closely by analysts and have more stringent reporting requirements. The coefficient on total assets is significantly negative, indicating that large firms are less likely to issue equity. All our other inferences remain unchanged by the addition of total assets, except that stock return volatility ceases to have a significant effect on the probability of issuing equity.

In regression (3), we add post-issue cumulative excess returns as an explanatory variable. The timing model suggests that the coefficient on post-issue cumulative excess returns should be significantly negative, so that firms expecting poor performance would be more likely to issue equity. We report only the regression with the five-year size-adjusted excess returns. We estimate the same regression using three-year size-adjusted excess returns, three-year and five-year raw returns, and three-year and five-year net-of-market returns, but the coefficient on long-term returns is never significant. This finding has two possible interpretations, however. First, it could mean that timing considerations are not important in firms' decisions. Second, there could be so much variation in the

Table 2
Determinants of firm type

Logistic regressions in which the dependent variable takes the value one for equity issues and zero otherwise. The sample has 276 debt issues and 192 equity issues from 1977 to 1984. Market-to-book is the ratio of firm market value to total assets ($TA$). Cash flow is operating income before depreciation minus total taxes adjusted for changes in deferred taxes, minus gross interest expense and dividends paid on common and preferred stock, divided by $TA$. All book values are obtained from Compustat for the year prior to the issue announcement. The volatility of the stock return is for the period ( $-240$, $-40$). $MVCS$ is the market value of equity. The post-issue cumulative abnormal return is the excess return of issuing firms over firms with similar size before the issue. The pseudo-$R^2$ equals $1 - $ (log-likelihood at convergence/log-likelihood at zero); $p$-values for the chi-square statistic are in parentheses.

| Regression | (1) | (2) | (3) | (4) | (5) |
|---|---|---|---|---|---|
| *Intercept* | $-3.27$ | $-2.57$ | $-3.23$ | $-2.50$ | 3.16 |
| | (0.01) | (0.01) | (0.01) | (0.01) | (0.01) |
| *Tax payments/TA* | $-11.99$ | $-12.97$ | $-9.31$ | $-9.09$ | $-20.37$ |
| | (0.01) | (0.01) | (0.02) | (0.03) | (0.01) |
| *Long-term debt/TA* | 0.81 | 0.25 | 0.97 | 1.83 | $-1.02$ |
| | (0.36) | (0.78) | (0.31) | (0.06) | (0.32) |
| *Market-to-book* | 2.13 | 1.96 | 2.06 | 1.68 | 2.20 |
| | (0.01) | (0.01) | (0.00) | (0.00) | (0.00) |
| *Cash flow* | 0.11 | 0.23 | $-0.58$ | $-2.07$ | 0.96 |
| | (0.96) | (0.93) | (0.83) | (0.47) | (0.75) |
| *Stock return volatility* | 5.40 | 2.99 | 5.98 | 13.24 | $-5.86$ |
| | (0.08) | (0.35) | (0.07) | (0.01) | (0.12) |
| *6-month leading indicators* | 12.42 | 12.23 | 12.20 | 13.64 | 13.72 |
| | (0.01) | (0.01) | (0.01) | (0.01) | (0.01) |
| *Past 11-month cumulative excess return* | 2.33 | 2.29 | 2.10 | 2.74 | 1.53 |
| | (0.01) | (0.01) | (0.01) | (0.01) | (0.01) |
| *Cash and liquid assets/TA* | $-2.65$ | $-2.10$ | $-2.94$ | $-1.26$ | $-1.30$ |
| | (0.18) | (0.29) | (0.17) | (0.60) | (0.57) |
| *Total assets* | | $-0.01$ | | | |
| | | (0.01) | | | |
| *Gross proceeds/MVCS* | | | | $-5.04$ | |
| | | | | (0.00) | |
| *Log of (Amount/MVCS)* | | | | | $-1.32$ |
| | | | | | (0.0) |
| *Post-issue 5-year excess returns* | | | $-0.01$ | | |
| | | | (0.75) | | |
| *Pseudo-$R^2$* | 0.26 | 0.28 | 0.26 | 0.33 | 0.41 |
| *% correct* | 75.4% | 75.8% | 74.6% | 79.5% | 80.8% |

cross-sectional post-issue performance of firms that timing considerations are only identifiable in large samples.

To investigate whether our lack of support for the timing model is due to our sample size, we estimate a logistic regression using a sample more comparable in size to the samples used in other long-run performance studies. Our expanded sample includes 2,272 equity issues and 2,617 bond issues from 1970 to 1991 and is constructed from the Registered Offerings Tapes and the Investment Dealer's Digest. This sample includes non-Compustat firms as well as Compustat firms. We compute five-year post-issue buy-and-hold raw returns and size-adjusted excess returns as we did for our original sample. The average return measures are similar to those obtained in the long-run performance studies in that long-run returns following equity issues are significantly negative and large in absolute value and long-run returns following debt issues are insignificantly different from zero. In a logistic regression with the post-issue cumulative returns as the only dependent variable in addition to the constant, the post-issue cumulative returns have a significant negative coefficient irrespective of how they are computed, so that firms with poor post-issue returns are more likely to issue equity. However, post-issue returns seem to explain very little: the pseudo-$R^2$ is on the order of 0.01 irrespective of how the post-issue returns are computed. The regression with raw returns classifies 63.2% of the observations correctly. The percentage of correct classifications falls to 54.3% for size-matched excess returns. Even with a very large sample, therefore, it still turns out that the timing model is not very helpful in understanding new issue decisions. Interestingly, however, when we add to these regressions the cumulative abnormal return for the year before the issue, this variable has an extremely significant positive coefficient and the pseudo-$R^2$ increases strongly. In the regression using raw returns, the pseudo-$R^2$ increases to 0.21 and the fraction of issues predicted correctly increases to 72.8%; in the regression using size-adjusted returns, the pseudo-$R^2$ increases to 0.09 and the fraction predicted correctly increases to 70.5%.

In regressions (4) and (5), we add measures of the size of the security issue normalized by the market value of the firm's equity as an explanatory variable. These measures of the relative size of the security issue have no impact on the effect of investment opportunities on the new issue decision. Not surprisingly, given the statistics of Table 1, the relative size of the issue is negatively related to the probability of issuing equity. Two firm characteristics seem to have effects that depend on the relative size variable: leverage becomes significant for one relative size measure and volatility ceases to be significant for the other. The size measures have a substantial impact on the explanatory power of the regressions. In regressions not reproduced here, we add total assets and the market value of equity as separate explanatory variables. The addition of these variables does not affect the conclusions drawn from Table 2, but their coefficients are significantly negative. We re-estimate regressions (4) and (5) adding long-term post-issue abnormal returns as explanatory variables but do not report the results in the table. In the regression with the ratio of proceeds to pre-issue market value of equity, long-term post-issue performance has a positive insignificant coefficient. In the regression with the log of the amount of the issue, the coefficient on long-term performance is negative and significant at the 0.10 level. The coefficient on market-to-book is 2.11 instead of 2.20 and its significance level is unchanged. In this case, the percentage of correct predictions is 81.5% instead of 82.1%. There is therefore no convincing evidence that expectations of long-term cumulative excess returns play an important role in the firm's issue decision.

Although our regressions are parsimonious, they correctly classify a fraction of the decisions similar to the fraction correctly classified in earlier papers. For instance, the frequently cited paper by Marsh (1982) correctly classifies 75% of the decisions, whereas our regressions in Table 2 correctly classify from 74% to 81% of the decisions.

With this logistic model, we have firms that issue equity even though they resemble firms that issue debt. One way to see this is to compare these firms to the firms that issue debt and the firms that issue equity when predicted to do so. To classify firms, we use regression (1) of Table 2. For that equation, the threshold that minimizes the sum of the probability of a type I and the probability of a type II error is 0.42. We find that 46 firms issue equity against type using that threshold. In all characteristics except the ratio of proceeds to the market value of equity, the firms that issue equity when predicted to issue debt are indistinguishable from debt-issuing firms. In contrast, these equity-issuing firms have many characteristics that are significantly different from firms that issue equity and are predicted to do so. The firms issuing equity against type pay more taxes relative to assets than other equity-issuing firms, so that one would expect the tax deductibility of interest to be valuable for them. These firms have less leverage than firms predicted to issue equity, although not significantly so. They issue at times when leading indicators are neutral. Their past abnormal returns are insignificantly different from zero. Their volatility is closer to the volatility of firms issuing debt. Finally, these firms have much poorer investment opportunities than firms predicted to issue equity. Their mean and median market-to-book ratio is only trivially different from the mean and median market-to-book ratio of firms issuing debt. There are no significant cash flow differences among the three sets of firms. Given the characteristics of these firms, it is difficult to argue that they would benefit from the flexibility resulting from issuing equity instead of debt.

Why do these firms issue equity against type? With the pecking-order model, these firms should issue debt if information asymmetries are significant. Hence, these firms might be issuing equity because they happen to have low information asymmetries. Viswanathan (1993) models such deviations from the pecking-order model. In this case, one would expect the information content of equity issues to be low as well because it must be public knowledge that information asymmetries are low since otherwise firms will face high costs of issuing equity anyway. This would suggest that firms that issue equity against type would have a small stock price reaction. It would not make sense for firms to issue against type if information asymmetries are high because these firms have similar characteristics to debt-issuing firms and therefore could issue debt. The pecking-order model cannot explain why firms for which information asymmetries are high would issue equity when they could issue debt. Equity issues by such firms are consistent with the managerial discretion model, however. Investigating the stock price reaction to equity issues should therefore help us distinguish between the two models.

## 5. The stock price reactions to security issues and investment opportunities

Among firms issuing equity, there are firms with good investment opportunities and limited debt capacity (provided that we can interpret firms with high leverage to be firms with low debt capacity). One would expect these firms to issue equity if they raise funds and that this action would be in the interest of shareholders. Other firms have poor investment opportunities and look like they could issue debt. The pecking-order model explanation for this behavior is that information asymmetries for these firms are not important, suggesting that the stock price reaction should be small. The agency model, in contrast, predicts large stock price reactions if these issues are unexpected because the shareholders of these firms would be better off having the firm either issue debt or not raise funds. Since firms form a continuum across types, the agency cost model would expect the firms for which issuing equity is the least likely to benefit shareholders to have the largest fall in stock price at the announcement of an equity issue, assuming that all issues are equally unanticipated. Earlier work by Bayless and Chaplinsky (1991) demonstrates, using a different logistic model, that firms issuing unexpectedly according to the logistic model have a greater abnormal return in absolute value. This result holds for our logistic model also. Table 3 provides estimates of the correlation between a firm's type, defined by the probability that a firm will issue equity based on the logistic model of the previous section, and the firm's abnormal return for each type of issue. The correlation estimates for the equity issues are positive and significant; the estimates for debt issues are negative but insignificant. These results are consistent with the agency cost model but cannot be explained with the pecking-order model.

We now turn to the relation between abnormal returns and a firm's investment opportunities. With the managerial discretion model, equity issues are not in the interest of shareholders for firms with poor investment opportunities. The Pearson correlation between the stock price reaction to equity issues and the

Table 3
Correlations between firms' types and abnormal returns

Firm type is obtained from regression (1) of Table 2. Abnormal returns (*AR*s) are cumulative abnormal returns for days ( − 1, 0), with day 0 the day of the Wall Street Journal announcement of the security issue.

| Correlation measures | Correlation between firm type and *AR*s for bond issues (*p*-values) | Correlation between firm type and *AR*s for equity issues (*p*-values) |
|---|---|---|
| Correlation coefficient between firm type and abnormal returns | − 0.03 (0.65) | 0.17 (0.02) |
| Spearman rank-sum correlation between firm type and abnormal returns | − 0.07 (0.25) | 0.17 (0.02) |

market-to-book ratio is 0.22 (*p*-value of less than 0.01) and the Spearman rank-sum correlation is 0.18 (*p*-value of 0.01). When we divide the sample into market-to-book deciles, we find that the highest market-to-book decile has a mean abnormal return of − 0.22% whereas the lowest market-to-book decile has a mean abnormal return of − 4.60%. Therefore, there is a robust relation between stock price reactions to equity issues and market-to-book. For debt issues, the correlation measures are respectively 0.11 (*p*-value of 0.07) and 0.10 (*p*-value of 0.10). The relation between stock price reactions and market-to-book is much weaker for debt issues. In a regression of abnormal returns on a constant and market-to-book, the coefficient on market-to-book is 0.97 with a *t*-statistic of 2.63 for equity issues and it is 0.51 with a *t*-statistic of 1.39 for debt issues. These results are stronger than the results from earlier research which either uses the market-to-book ratio or Tobin's *q*. Barclay and Litzenberger (1988) and Pilotte (1992) find insignificant results using conventional levels of significance, but they have fewer issues than we do. Denis (1994) has a large sample yet finds a weaker relation than here. However, our sample stops in 1984, so that it is not affected by the subsequent change in reporting practices of the Wall Street Journal.[3]

Market-to-book is positively correlated with a variable emphasized in models that focus on adverse selection, namely the runup in the firm's stock

---

[3]Before 1985, the WSJ reports on equity issues as a regular news item. From 1985, most of the information on new issues is reported in the 'new securities issues column' which contains mostly offering information. Hence, the event dates since 1985 reflect issues that are more likely to be anticipated because the announcement of an equity issue is typically made earlier (by days or weeks) via news-wire services than the WSJ listing. This biases the abnormal return estimate.

price before the issue. Market-to-book is also likely to be correlated with other variables emphasized in the literature. Therefore, it is important to investigate whether the relation between abnormal returns and market-to-book can be attributed to its role as a proxy for other variables that may have nothing to do with managerial discretion. We investigate this in Table 4 for stock issues. It is immediately apparent that the coefficient on market-to-book is not affected by the inclusion of the additional variables emphasized by the earlier literature. In these regressions, though, the stock runup is not significant and the leading indicators are not significant either. It seems therefore that market-to-book dominates the variables emphasized in papers that focus on adverse selection. When we regress the abnormal return on market-to-book and past cumulative abnormal returns alone, the coefficient on past cumulative abnormal returns is 1.62 with a $t$-statistic of 1.52, while market-to-book has a coefficient of 0.93 with a $t$-statistic of 2.52. The inclusion of market-to-book results in a substantial weakening of the variables emphasized in papers that focus on adverse selection.

Is market-to-book successful because it proxies for the firm overvaluation that underlies the timing model? In regression (8) of Table 4, we include the long-term cumulative excess return as an explanatory variable. Presumably, firms that are more overvalued have more negative cumulative excess returns. The coefficient on long-term cumulative excess return is insignificant. More importantly, though, the coefficients on the other variables, especially our proxy for investment opportunities, are not significantly altered. We also estimate regressions (9) and (10) with the same long-term cumulative excess return as a dependent variable. The cumulative excess return is never significant. Finally, we estimate regression (7) using three-year and five-year raw returns, three-year and five-year net-of-market returns, and three-year size-adjusted returns. Only one coefficient is significant, but it has the opposite sign from the prediction of the timing model that investors underreact to the announcement. The coefficient on five-year raw returns is negative with a $t$-statistic of $-1.72$. If taken seriously, this estimate implies that the stock price reaction is closer to zero for firms that underperform more after the issue. None of this evidence is supportive of the view that the stock price reaction to an equity issue is a fraction of the long-run cumulative excess returns.

We estimate similar regressions for debt issues, but do not report them here. The only variable that is ever significant in these regressions is the amount of the issue divided by the value of common stock, which has a coefficient of $-1.57$ and a $t$-statistic of $-1.97$. The adjusted $R^2$ for these regressions is never greater than zero.

Table 5 shows the abnormal returns for equity issues divided according to the purpose of the issue. The results provided are consistent with the role of agency costs in the new issue decision. An equity issue allows firms with poor investment opportunities to invest in poor projects and/or to reduce the disciplinary

178              K. Jung et al. / Journal of Financial Economics 42 (1996) 159–185

Table 4

Cross-sectional regressions of equity issue abnormal returns on firm characteristics

Abnormal returns ($ARs$) are cumulative abnormal returns for days ($-1, 0$), with day 0 the day of the Wall Street Journal announcement of the security issue. The regression models are estimated using weighted least squares with the weight for each issue being the inverse of the variance of the market model residual for the firm issuing the security. The sample includes 189 equity issues from 1977 to 1984. The proceeds of an issue correspond to the gross proceeds in millions of dollars. Market-to-book is the ratio of firm market value (market value of equity plus book value of total assets minus book value of equity) to total assets ($TA$). Cash flow is operating income before depreciation minus total taxes adjusted for changes in deferred taxes, minus gross interest expense and minus dividends paid on common and preferred stock. All book values are obtained from Compustat for the year before the announcement. The leading indicators are the six-month leading indicators. The volatility of the stock return is computed for the period ($-240, -40$). The post-issue cumulative excess returns are five-year size-adjusted returns. $T$-statistics are given in parentheses.

| Regression | (6) | (7) | (8) | (9) | (10) |
|---|---|---|---|---|---|
| *Intercept* | − 3.72 | − 3.86 | − 4.15 | − 4.061 | − 3.94 |
| | ( − 3.64) | ( − 3.75) | ( − 3.82) | ( − 3.77) | ( − 2.83) |
| *Market-to-book* | 0.97 | 1.01 | 0.96 | 0.95 | 0.97 |
| | (2.11) | (2.20) | (2.00) | (2.08) | (2.11) |
| *Cash/TA* | − 6.78 | − 6.29 | − 8.27 | − 7.82 | − 6.73 |
| | ( − 1.63) | ( − 1.50) | ( − 1.85) | ( − 1.82) | ( − 1.61) |
| *Tax payments/TA* | − 6.09 | − 4.65 | − 1.94 | − 5.41 | − 5.68 |
| | ( − 0.73) | ( − 0.55) | ( − 0.22) | ( − 0.65) | ( − 0.67) |
| *Long-term debt/TA* | − 1.14 | − 1.51 | − 1.54 | − 1.09 | − 1.13 |
| | ( − 0.61) | ( − 0.80) | ( − 0.73) | ( − 0.59) | ( − 0.60) |
| *Cash flow* | 5.09 | 3.72 | 5.03 | 6.17 | 4.87 |
| | (0.89) | (0.64) | (0.83) | (1.06) | (0.84) |
| *Stock return volatility* | − 3.49 | − 0.55 | 3.23 | − 4.76 | − 2.74 |
| | ( − 0.49) | ( − 0.07) | ( − 0.39) | ( − 0.66) | ( − 0.35) |
| *Leading indicators* | 1.64 | 1.31 | 1.18 | 2.20 | 1.48 |
| | (0.32) | (0.25) | (0.22) | (0.42) | (0.28) |
| *Past cumulative excess return* | 1.68 | 1.79 | 1.31 | 1.59 | 1.71 |
| | (1.53) | (1.62) | (1.09) | (1.44) | (1.54) |
| *Total assets* | | 0.00 | | | |
| | | (1.07) | | | |
| *Post-issue cumulative excess return* | | | − 0.08 | | |
| | | | ( − 0.70) | | |
| *Proceeds/Market value of common stock* | | | | 2.47 | |
| | | | | (1.00) | |
| *Log of proceeds* | | | | | 0.05 |
| | | | | | (0.24) |
| *Adjusted $R^2$* | 0.04 | 0.04 | 0.04 | 0.04 | 0.03 |

K. Jung et al./Journal of Financial Economics 42 (1996) 159–185 179

Table 5
Abnormal returns of equity issues by purpose of issue

Abnormal returns (*AR*s) are cumulative abnormal returns for days ( − 1, 0), with day 0 the day of the Wall Street Journal announcement of the security issue. The purpose of the issue is obtained from the Wall Street Journal announcement. We do not reproduce results for cells smaller than 10 or when the purpose could not be determined unambiguously.

| Purpose | Number of issues | Abnormal return | *t*-statistic |
|---|---|---|---|
| To repay bank debt | 26 | − 2.93 | − 4.54 |
| Capital expenditures | 40 | − 3.04 | − 5.16 |
| To repay long-term debt | 20 | − 4.15 | − 6.16 |
| To repay short-term debt | 15 | − 1.16 | − 1.15 |
| Working capital | 51 | − 2.34 | − 4.43 |

role of debt. The stock price reactions for firms that plan to use the proceeds for capital expenditures, firms that plan to replace long-term debt, and firms that plan to replace bank debt are above the average stock price reaction of the whole sample. At the 0.10 level, firms that plan to replace long-term debt have significantly lower abnormal returns than firms that plan to use the proceeds to replace short-term debt or to invest in working capital; further, at the 0.11 level, firms that plan to use the proceeds for capital expenditures have significantly lower abnormal returns than firms that plan to replace short-term debt. The *p*-values for the other differences are much higher. We investigate whether there is a relation between firm type and the abnormal return for a given issuing purpose. The problem with this investigation is that the cell sizes become small. Nevertheless, it is interesting that the 11 firms that are not of the equity-issuing type and plan to use the proceeds for capital expenditures have an average abnormal return of − 4.43% with a *t*-statistic of − 5.52, whereas the 29 firms of the equity-issuing type that plan to use the proceeds for capital expenditures have an average abnormal return of − 2.52% with a *t*-statistic of − 3.41. The difference between these two abnormal returns has a *t*-statistic of 1.75. This evidence should be treated with caution given the cell sizes, but it nevertheless provides support for the argument that outsiders view a firm that invests the proceeds when it is not of the equity-issuing type negatively.

It is often argued that agency costs of managerial discretion are lower for firms with high managerial ownership because management bears more of the monetary consequences from pursuing its own objectives. We have managerial ownership data available from Value Line for 100 equity-issuing firms. For this smaller sample, we find that when we split the sample into high and low ownership, the low-ownership sample has a mean abnormal return of − 3.71% and the high-ownership sample has a mean abnormal return of − 2.56%. The difference between the two groups is 1.16% with a *t*-statistic of 1.72. This

180                    *K. Jung et al. / Journal of Financial Economics 42 (1996) 159–185*

difference could be size-related since ownership is inversely related to size, but when we split the sample according to firm size, there is no difference in abnormal returns.

## 6. Ex post characteristics of firms issuing debt and equity

So far, we have shown that the typical equity-issuing firm has good investment opportunities compared with the typical debt-issuing firm, and that the market reaction to an equity issue is positively related to the issuing firm's investment opportunities. It could be that firms issuing equity with poor investment opportunities do so because they believe that they are worth less than the market's valuation since they are low market-to-book firms. If this were the case, these firms should invest less than the other equity-issuing firms. In contrast, agency considerations predict that these firms issue equity for investment purposes even though they have poor investment opportunities.

In this section, we investigate whether the post-issue characteristics of firms issuing equity against type resemble those of debt-issuing firms of similar type or those of equity-issuing firms of different type. We provide this information for all firms issuing a type of security and for subsamples of firms that issue as expected and those that do not. To distinguish between firms that are expected to issue a security and those that are not, we proceed in the same way as discussed at the end of Section 4 by defining firms predicted to issue equity as all those firms that have a probability of issuing equity greater than 0.42 using regression (1) of Table 2. For each variable, we compute the change in the variable from the fiscal year before the issue to the fiscal year after the issue, expressed as a percentage of the variable in the fiscal year before the issue. We reproduce the change in cash flow and leverage, even though the type of security issued affects these variables directly, reducing cash flow and increasing leverage for debt-issuing firms compared with equity-issuing firms.

The results of Table 6 are striking. Firms predicted to issue debt that actually issue equity invest more than the comparable debt-issuing firms: their plant, property, and equipment (*PP&E*), total assets, and capital expenditures all grow at a significantly higher rate. The differences in growth are economically large: a firm issuing equity against type has 20% more *PP&E* at the end of the year following the security issue than a firm expected to issue debt. Since both categories of firms have similar market-to-book ratios, these results are fully consistent with the view that firms that issue equity against the pecking order do so to pursue a more aggressive investment policy that is not in the interest of their shareholders. Compared to the firms expected to issue equity, the firms that issue equity when expected to issue debt have total assets that grow at a significantly lower rate, but their *PP&E* and capital expenditures have insignificantly different growth rates than firms that issue equity as expected. *EBIT*

K. Jung et al./Journal of Financial Economics 42 (1996) 159–185          181

Table 6
Percentage changes in firm characteristics according to firm type and security type for the three-year period overlapping the security issue

The sample includes 283 debt issues and 189 equity issues from 1977 to 1984. Cash flow is operating income before depreciation minus total taxes adjusted for changes in deferred taxes, minus gross interest expense and minus dividends paid on common and preferred stock. $TA$ denotes the book value of assets. For each characteristic, we use Compustat to compute the percentage increase from the year before the issue to the year after the issue. High-type firms are those expected to issue equity based on regression (1) of Table 2.

| | Bond issues (Number of firms) | Equity issues (Number of firms) | Difference ($t$-statistic) |
|---|---|---|---|
| *PP&E* | 41.83% (267) | 68.19% (178) | − 26.36% ( − 4.42) |
| *PP&E*, low type | 38.48% (210) | 58.98% (46) | − 20.50% ( − 1.77) |
| *PP&E*, high type | 54.16% (57) | 71.39% (132) | − 17.24% ( − 1.73) |
| *Total assets* | 37.83% (269) | 65.60% (180) | − 27.77% ( − 5.79) |
| *Total assets*, low type | 32.70% (211) | 45.82% (46) | − 13.13% ( − 2.11) |
| *Total assets*, high type | 56.50% (58) | 72.39% (134) | − 15.88% ( − 1.70) |
| *Net capital expenditures* | 51.57% (210) | 107.50% (177) | − 55.93% ( − 3.57) |
| *Net capital expenditures,* low type | 43.12% (206) | 93.92% (46) | − 50.80% ( − 1.70) |
| *Net capital expenditures,* high type | 82.67% (56) | 112.27% (131) | − 29.60% ( − 1.20) |
| *Long-term debt/TA* | 36.55% (268) | − 8.18% (181) | 44.73% ( − 4.52) |
| *Long-term debt/TA,* low-type firms | 40.67% (210) | − 5.45% (46) | 46.13% (3.20) |
| *Long-term debt/TA,* high-type firms | 21.65% (58) | − 9.11% (135) | 30.76% (2.33) |
| *Cash flow* | − 17.50% (265) | 2.08% (178) | − 19.58% ( − 1.90) |
| *Cash flow*, low-type firms | − 21.85% (209) | 0.96% (45) | − 22.81% ( − 2.71) |
| *Cash flow*, high-type firms | − 1.25% (45) | 2.46% (133) | − 3.71% ( − 0.19) |
| *EBIT* | 15.45% (266) | 53.15% (181) | − 37.70% ( − 2.28) |

182 *K. Jung et al./Journal of Financial Economics 42 (1996) 159–185*

Table 6 (continued)

|  | Bond issues (Number of firms) | Equity issues (Number of firms) | Difference (*t*-statistic) |
|---|---|---|---|
| *EBIT*, low type | 6.84% (210) | 10.60% (46) | – 3.76% (– 0.11) |
| *EBIT*, high type | 47.72% (56) | 67.65% (135) | – 19.92% (– 1.01%) |
| *Change in dividend yield* | 0.18 (269) | – 0.10 (183) | 0.28 (1.78) |
| *Change in dividend yield,* low type | – 0.02 (209) | – 0.21 (48) | 0.19 (0.77) |
| *Change in dividend yield,* high type | 0.84 (60) | – 0.07 (135) | 0.91 (3.98) |
| *Five-year size-matched excess return* | 2.03 (242) | – 32.69% (178) | 34.72 (1.33) |
| *Five-year size-matched excess return,* high type | 11.04% (56) | – 39.20% (135) | 50.24% (0.88) |
| *Five-year size-matched excess return,* low type | – 0.69% (186) | – 12.26% (43) | 11.58% (0.31) |

increases substantially for the firms expected to issue equity but not for the firms that issue equity when expected to issue debt. We also report some evidence on dividend policy. Firms issuing equity have a drop in dividend yield in contrast to firms issuing debt. Though firms issuing equity against type form the subsample with the largest drop in dividend yield, the difference between the change in dividend yield for that subsample and for the subsample of firms issuing debt according to type is not significant.

We explore the long-term stock performance of the issuing firms according to their type and find that for all subsamples, equity-issuing firms have mean cumulative excess returns that are much lower than debt issuing firms, although the mean differences are not significant. The firm characteristics that proxy for agency costs are not helpful in explaining the cross-sectional variation in post-issue cumulative abnormal returns. Such a result is not surprising for those who believe that markets are efficient. It points towards a risk-based explanation of long-term abnormal returns.

## 7. Conclusions

In this paper, we investigate the empirical relevance of three explanations of the security issue decision: the pecking-order model, the agency model, and the timing model. Our results support the agency model. We show that the typical firm issuing equity has valuable investment opportunities and experiences considerable asset growth from the year before the equity issue to the end of the year following the issue. Firms with the most valuable investment opportunities do not experience adverse stock returns when they issue equity. We find that some firms with poor investment opportunities issue equity even though the pecking-order model suggests that they should issue debt to raise funds. These firms, otherwise similar to debt-issuing firms, experience substantially higher asset growth than debt-issuing firms. However, they register an extremely significant drop in their share price when they issue. Though it is true that these firms reveal that they are overvalued when they issue, an explanation consistent with this excessive valuation is that, given their investment opportunities, the market did not expect these firms to issue equity and does not expect the investments undertaken with the proceeds to increase shareholder wealth. The behavior of the firms issuing equity against type is inconsistent with the pecking-order model or asymmetric information models which assume that managers maximize shareholder wealth. If the firms that issue against type have valuable investment opportunities that are not recognized by the financial markets, they should not be issuing equity since their equity is underpriced and they could issue debt. The evidence we present in this paper is also inconsistent with the view that firms time equity issues to take advantage of equity overvaluation when they know that the firm's equity will underperform in future years.

An agency approach that emphasizes the costs of managerial discretion provides a consistent framework in which evidence on the issue decision, the stock price reaction, and the post-issue investment policy of the issuing firm can be understood. In contrast to the agency model, models based on information asymmetries alone are at best consistent only with our evidence on the stock price reaction, and the timing model receives almost no support in our sample.

## References

Asquith, Paul and David W. Mullins, Jr., 1986, Equity issues and offering dilution, Journal of Financial Economics 15, 31–60.

Barclay, Michael J. and Robert H. Litzenberger, 1988, Announcement effects of new equity issues and the use of intraday price data, Journal of Financial Economics 21, 71–99.

Baxter, Nevins D. and John G. Cragg, 1970, Corporate choice among long-term financing instruments, Review of Economics and Statistics 52, 225–235.

Bayless, Mark and Suzanne Chaplinsky, 1991, Expectations of security type and the information content of debt and equity offers, Journal of Financial Intermediation 3, 195–214.

Bernanke, Ben, Mark Gertler, and Simon Gilchrist, 1993, The financial accelerator and the flight to quality, Working paper (Princeton University, Princeton, NJ).

Brav, Alon, Christopher Géczy, and Paul A. Gompers, 1994, The long-run underperformance of seasoned equity offerings revisited, Working paper (University of Chicago, Chicago, IL).

Brennan, Michael and Alan Kraus, 1987, Efficient financing under asymmetric information, Journal of Finance 42, 1225–1243.

184                        *K. Jung et al./Journal of Financial Economics 42 (1996) 159–185*

Cheng, Li-Lan, 1994, Equity issue under-performance and the timing of security issues, Working paper (Massachusetts Institute of Technology, Cambridge, MA).

Choe, Hyuk, Ronald Masulis, and Vik Nanda, 1993, Common stock offerings across the business cycle: Theory and evidence, Journal of Empirical Finance 1, 3–31.

Cooney, John W., Jr. and Avner Kalay, 1993, Positive information from equity issue announcements, Journal of Financial Economics 33, 149–172.

Denis, David J., 1994, Investment opportunities and the market reaction to equity offerings, Journal of Financial and Quantitative Analysis 29, 159–177.

Dybvig, Philip H. and Jaime F. Zender, 1991, Capital structure and dividend irrelevance with asymmetric information, Review of Financial Studies 4, 201–220.

Eckbo, Bjorn E.,1986, Valuation effects of corporate debt offerings, Journal of Financial Economics 15, 119–151.

Harris, Milton and Artur Raviv, 1991, The theory of capital structure, Journal of Finance 46, 297–356.

Hoshi, Takeo, Anyl Kashyap, and David Scharfstein, 1993, The choice between public and private debt: An analysis of post-deregulation corporate financing in Japan, Working paper (Massachusetts Institute of Technology, Cambridge, MA).

Jensen, Michael C., 1986, Agency costs of free cash flow, corporate finance and takeovers, American Economic Review 76, 323–329.

Jensen, Michael C. and William H. Meckling, 1976, Theory of the firm: Managerial behavior, agency costs and ownership structure, Journal of Financial Economics 3, 305–360.

Korajczyk, Robert, Debbie J. Lucas, and Robert L. McDonald, 1991, The effect of information releases on the pricing and timing of security issues, Review of Financial Studies 4, 685–708.

Kothari, S.P. and Jerrold B. Warner, 1995, Measuring long-horizon security price performance, Working paper (University of Rochester, Rochester, NY).

Lang, Larry, Eli Ofek, and René M. Stulz, 1996, Leverage, investment, and firm growth, Journal of Financial Economics 40, 3–30.

Loughran, Timothy and Jay R. Ritter, 1995, The new issue puzzle, Journal of Finance 50, 23–52.

Lucas, Debbie J. and Robert L. McDonald, 1990, Equity issues and stock price dynamics, Journal of Finance 45, 1019–1043.

MacKie-Mason, Jeffrey K., 1990, Do taxes affect corporate financing decisions?, Journal of Finance 45,1471–1495.

Marsh, Paul, 1982, The choice between equity and debt, Journal of Finance 37, 121–144.

Masulis, Ronald, 1988, The debt/equity choice (Ballinger Publishing Company, Lexington, MA).

Masulis, Ronald W. and A.N. Korwar, 1986, Seasoned equity offerings: An empirical investigation, Journal of Financial Economics 15, 91–118.

Mikkelson, Wayne and Megan Partch, 1986, Valuation effects of security offerings and the issuance process, Journal of Financial Economics 15, 31–60.

Myers, Stewart, 1977, Determinants of corporate borrowing, Journal of Financial Economics 5, 147–175.

Myers, Stewart, 1984, The capital structure puzzle, Journal of Finance 39, 575–592.

Myers, Stewart and Nicholas Majluf, 1984, Corporate financing and investment decisions when firms have information that investors do not have, Journal of Financial Economics 13, 187–221.

Noe, Thomas, 1988, Capital structure and signaling equilibria, Review of Financial Studies 1, 331–356.

Pilotte, Eugene, 1992, Growth opportunities and the stock price response to new financing, Journal of Business 65, 371–395.

Smith, Clifford W. and Ross L. Watts, 1992, The investment opportunity set and corporate financing, dividend, and compensation policies, Journal of Financial Economics 32, 263–292.

Spiess, D. Katherine and John Affleck-Graves, 1995, Underperformance in long-run stock returns following seasoned equity offerings, Journal of Financial Economics 38, 243–267.

Stein, Jeremy C., 1995, Rational capital budgeting in an irrational world, Working paper (Massachusetts Institute of Technology, Cambridge, MA).

Stulz, René M., 1988, Managerial control of voting rights: Financing policies and the market for corporate control, Journal of Financial Economics 20, 25–54.

Stulz, René M., 1990, Managerial discretion and optimal financing policies, Journal of Financial Economics 26, 3–27.

Titman, Sheridan and Roberto Wessels, 1988, The determinants of capital structure choice, Journal of Finance 43, 1–20.

Viswanathan, P.V., 1993, Strategic considerations, the pecking order hypothesis, and market reactions to equity financing, Journal of Financial and Quantitative Analysis 28, 213–234.

Zwiebel, Jeffrey, 1994, Dynamic capital structure under managerial entrenchment, Working paper (Stanford University, Palo Alto, CA).

# [13]

THE JOURNAL OF FINANCE • VOL. L, NO. 1 • MARCH 1995

# The New Issues Puzzle

## TIM LOUGHRAN and JAY R. RITTER*

### ABSTRACT

Companies issuing stock during 1970 to 1990, whether an initial public offering or a seasoned equity offering, have been poor long-run investments for investors. During the five years after the issue, investors have received average returns of only 5 percent per year for companies going public and only 7 percent per year for companies conducting a seasoned equity offer. Book-to-market effects account for only a modest portion of the low returns. An investor would have had to invest 44 percent more money in the issuers than in nonissuers of the same size to have the same wealth five years after the offering date.

IN THIS ARTICLE, WE show that companies issuing stock during 1970 to 1990, whether an initial public offering (IPO) or a seasoned equity offering (SEO), significantly underperform relative to nonissuing firms for five years after the offering date. The average annual return during the five years after issuing is only 5 percent for firms conducting IPOs, and only 7 percent for firms conducting SEOs. While evidence that firms going public subsequently underperform has been documented previously, our evidence that the same pattern holds for firms conducting SEOs is new.

The magnitude of this underperformance is economically important: based upon the realized returns, an investor would have had to invest 44 percent more money in the issuers than in nonissuers of the same size to have the same wealth five years after the offering date. Surprisingly, this number is the same for both IPOs and SEOs. While the difference in returns between issuers and nonissuers on which the 44 percent number is based only holds

*Loughran is from the University of Iowa. Ritter is from the University of Illinois at Urbana-Champaign. We would like to thank Laurie Simon Bagwell, Christopher Barry, Randolph Beatty, Louis Chan, Robert Chirinko, Kent Daniel, Harry DeAngelo, Eugene Fama, Wayne Ferson, Kathleen Weiss Hanley, Robert S. Hansen, David Ikenberry, Sherry Jarrell, Josef Lakonishok, Inmoo Lee, Roni Michaely, Wayne Mikkelson, Stewart Myers, Dennis Sheehan, René Stulz, Michael Vetsuypens, Jerold Warner, Ivo Welch, Karen Wruck, Luigi Zingales, an anonymous referee, and seminar participants at the following institutions: Boston College, the University of California-Irvine, UCLA, Chicago, Colorado, Georgia Tech, Harvard, Illinois, Indiana, Iowa, London Business School, MIT, McMaster, Missouri, the National Bureau of Economic Research, Notre Dame, Ohio State, Oklahoma, Penn State, Pittsburgh, Purdue, Rice, Texas A & M, Texas Christian, Tulane, the University of Washington, the May 1993 CRSP Seminar, and the June 1994 Western Finance Association meetings for useful suggestions. Some of the data on SEOs have been supplied by Robert S. Hansen and Dennis Sheehan. Eugene Fama has supplied us with a time series of factor realizations. We would like to thank James Davis, Inmoo Lee, and Quan Shui Zhao for excellent research assistance. An earlier version of this article was circulated under the title of "The Timing and Subsequent Performance of New Issues."

size constant, we also calculate abnormal performance after adjusting for book-to-market effects. Only a modest portion of the underperformance of issuing firms can be explained as a manifestation of book-to-market effects.

Since most SEOs occur after a period of high returns, we address whether the poor subsequent performance is merely a manifestation of long-term return reversals. We find that extreme winners that do not issue equity dramatically outperform extreme winners that do issue. We also document that the degree to which issuing firms underperform varies over time: firms issuing during years when there is little issuing activity do not underperform much at all, whereas firms selling stock during high-volume periods severely underperform.

We calculate the statistical significance of the underperformance using three different procedures. The first procedure calculates $t$-statistics using annual holding-period returns on issuing firms relative to nonissuing firms. The second procedure calculates $t$-statistics using a time series of cross-sectional regressions on monthly individual firm returns. The third procedure calculates $t$-statistics using 3-factor time-series regressions of monthly returns for portfolios of issuing and nonissuing firms. All three procedures result in rejection of the null hypothesis of no underperformance at high degrees of statistical significance.

The low returns on issuing firms demand an explanation. We show that the traditional measure of risk, beta, is slightly higher for issuing firms than nonissuers, implying that issuers should have higher, not lower, returns. As mentioned above, the poor performance of issuers is not merely proxying for long-term return reversals, and book-to-market effects can explain only a modest portion of the low returns. We are left with a puzzle: why do firms issuing equity produce such low returns for investors over the next five years?

The organization of the rest of this article is as follows. Section I describes the data. Section II presents evidence on the long-run performance of firms issuing stock during 1970 to 1990 and addresses some potential explanations. Section III presents statistical tests controlling for size and book-to-market effects. Section IV summarizes the findings and hypothesizes why the patterns exist and persist.

## I. Data on New Issues

### A. Initial Public Offerings

We use a sample of 4,753 operating companies going public in the United States during 1970 to 1990 and listed within the next three years on the University of Chicago Center for Research in Security Prices (CRSP) Nasdaq or American Stock Exchange (Amex) and New York Stock Exchange (NYSE) daily tapes. Closed-end funds, real estate investment trusts, and American Depository Receipts are excluded from our sample. Data on firms going public during 1970 to 1990 come from several sources. For 1970 to 1974, the "New

Market Names" section of *Investment Dealer's Digest* is used. For 1975 to 1984, *Going Public: The IPO Reporter* is used. For 1985 to 1990, we purchased listings of IPOs from IDD Information Services, Inc. and Securities Data Company. After the February 1971 introduction of Nasdaq, most firms going public have listed on Nasdaq, although CRSP does not start reporting Nasdaq returns until December 14, 1972. Prior to the introduction of Nasdaq, many newly public firms listed on the Amex, although typically with a delay of six months or more from the offering date.

### B. Seasoned Equity Offerings

We use a sample of 3,702 seasoned equity offerings during 1970 to 1990, all of which involve at least some newly issued (primary) shares. Because utility offerings tend to be different from those of other operating companies, we exclude all utility offerings (standard industrial classification (SIC) codes 491 to 494) from our sample.[1] The data come from several sources: for 1970 to 1973, the Securities and Exchange Commission's registered offering statistics tape; for 1980 to 1984, the Loderer, Sheehan, and Kadlec (1991) sample; and for other years, data purchased from Securities Data Co. Our sample includes companies listed on the Amex, the NYSE, and Nasdaq, including offerings from the years before December 1972, when CRSP started recording Nasdaq prices. The 3,702 SEOs were conducted by 2,680 different companies, with only 15 firms conducting more than five SEOs during the 1970 to 1990 sample period. Thus, our sample of seasoned equity offerings is far more comprehensive than that used in all but one previous study of seasoned equity offerings. The exception is Choe, Masulis, and Nanda (1993), where a sample of 5,694 SEOs (many of which are by utilities) from 1971 to 1991 is used. Choe, Masulis, and Nanda (1993) focus on announcement period returns, unlike this article.

In Figure 1, we present the annual volume of IPOs and SEOs in our samples for each year during 1970 to 1990. As can be seen, there are large variations in the volume of equity issues, with the variations more extreme for IPOs than for SEOs.

### C. Stock Returns

Using the CRSP Nasdaq and Amex-NYSE daily tapes, we follow each issuing firm from its offer date until the earlier of its delisting date, the offering's fifth anniversary, or December 31, 1992. We define a year as twelve 21-trading day intervals (252 days). Since most years actually have 253 trading days, our five-year anniversary date is typically a week before the actual five-year anniversary. The choice of an interval over which to measure the long-run performance of new issues involves a tradeoff: the longer the interval, the greater is the total underperformance, but the greater is the

---

[1] See Eckbo and Masulis (1995) for reasons why utility equity offerings are different from the equity offerings of other operating companies.

Number of issues

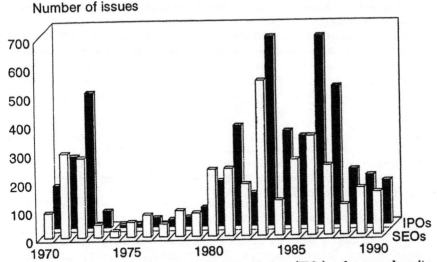

**Figure 1. The annual volume of initial public offerings (IPOs) and seasoned equity offerings (SEOs), 1970–1990.** The SEO volume excludes issues by utilities. The numbers graphed above are reported in Tables I (IPOs) and II (SEOs).

variability of returns. Balancing these two features, we have chosen two intervals: a three-year (756 trading days) window, to facilitate comparisons with other studies, and a five-year (1,260 trading days) window, which captures almost the entire period of underperformance. We choose a five-year interval based upon the evidence in Loughran (1993), who reports that IPOs underperform for approximately five years.[2]

To avoid problems caused by frequent transactions, we calculate the buy-and-hold return from the first CRSP-listed postissue closing price to the appropriate anniversary date of the offering. We do not include the issue-day return for several reasons. First, for offers from the early 1970s, there is frequently a multimonth or even multiyear period before the firm is listed on the CRSP tapes, primarily because the CRSP Nasdaq tape does not report returns before December 14, 1972. Second, for unit offerings, which typically involve shares and warrants, we only have the unit offering price and the market price of the stock (CRSP does not report unit prices; all of our returns are for common stock only). Third, and most importantly, it is frequently difficult for an investor to purchase shares at the offering price, whereas the

[2] Loughran (1993, Figure 2) reports underperformance for the five calendar years following the year of the IPO for 3,656 Nasdaq-listed IPOs from 1967 to 1988. Seyhun (1992) also reports underperformance for about six years after going public for a sample of 2,298 U.S. IPOs from 1975 to 1987. Levis (1993a) reports that British IPOs underperform beyond a three-year period as well.

market price represents a price that is available for an implementable portfolio strategy.

If an issuing firm is delisted prior to its anniversary date, we truncate its total return on that date. Thus, the percentage buy-and-hold return for firm $i$ is

$$R_{iT} = \left[ \prod_{t=start}^{\min[T,delist]} (1 + r_{it}) - 1 \right] \times 100\%, \qquad (1)$$

where *start* is the date of the first postissue CRSP-listed closing price, $\min[T, delist]$ is the earlier of the last day of CRSP-listed trading or the end of the three- or five-year window, and $r_{it}$ is the return for firm $i$ on date $t$. For firms that went public near the end of our sample period, the delisting date is no later than December 31, 1992, since we are using the version of the CRSP tapes ending on this date.

### D. Matching Firms

For each issuing firm, we choose a nonissuing matching firm. To choose a matching firm, on each December 31 all common stocks listed on the CRSP Amex-NYSE and Nasdaq tapes that have not issued stock within the last five years are ranked by their market capitalization.[3] The firm with the market capitalization closest to but higher than that of the issuing firm is then chosen as its matching firm. If a matching firm is delisted before the ending date for its corresponding issuing firm, a second (and, if necessary, third, fourth, etc.) matching firm is spliced in after the delisting date of the first matching firm. The replacement firm is the nonissuing company with the market capitalization on the original ranking date immediately higher than the original matching firm. If a chosen matching firm subsequently issues stock, we treat it as if it is delisted on its offering date (although the announcement date is still in our returns).[4] As a result of these procedures, buy-and-hold returns over identical intervals, with companies matched by size, are created for both the issuing and nonissuing firms. These procedures introduce no survivorship or look-ahead biases and minimize the number of transactions implicit in the computations.

Matching by industry is not done for several reasons. First, if firms in an industry time their offers to take advantage of industry-wide misvaluations, controlling for industry effects will reduce the ability to identify abnormal performance. Second, there are frequently only a few publicly traded companies in an industry with approximately the same market capitalization as the

---

[3]This excludes all companies for their first five years after going public. Note that a newly listed company becomes eligible to be a matching firm after any five-year period during which it has not issued equity. Because the CRSP Nasdaq tape does not begin until December 1972, no Nasdaq-listed firms are included in our matching firms until the ranking on December 31, 1977.

[4]For example, if a firm issues equity on December 2, 1986 and its first matching firm's last CRSP-listed return is on July 7, 1987, a second matching firm is added starting on July 8, 1987. If this second matching firm issues equity on February 27, 1989, a third matching firm is added starting on February 28, 1989.

issuing firms, resulting in the same nonissuing firm being matched with numerous issuers. For empirical studies of the long-run performance of IPOs that control for industry effects, see Ritter (1991) and Rajan and Servaes (1993). Spiess and Affleck-Graves (1995) control for both size and industry effects in measuring the long-run performance of SEOs. They report that approximately one-third of the long-run underperformance of SEOs is associated with industry effects.

## II. Time-Series Evidence on IPOs and SEOs

For IPOs and SEOs separately, we compute the average equally weighted holding-period returns for both the firms issuing in calendar year $\tau$ (which we refer to as the year $\tau$ cohort) and for their size-matched nonissuing firms, with the average $T$-year buy-and-hold return measured as

$$R_{\tau,T} = \frac{1}{n} \sum_{i=1}^{n} R_{iT} \qquad (2)$$

where $R_{iT}$ is the percentage buy-and-hold return on firm $i$ for holding period $T$. To be precise, the $T$-year holding period for firm $i$ is the maximum of either $T$ years or the portion of this time during which it is listed on the CRSP tapes. We also calculate wealth relatives for each cohort year, where a wealth relative is defined as the ratio of the end-of-period wealth from holding a portfolio of issuers (IPOs or SEOs) to the end-of-period wealth from holding a portfolio of matching firms with the same starting market capitalization. The wealth relatives are ratios of average gross returns and are not averages of ratios.

### A. *Equally Weighted Buy-and-Hold Returns on IPOs*

In Table I we report buy-and-hold returns and wealth relatives for the 4,753 sample firms going public between 1970 and 1990. Focusing first on the three-year returns, the overall three-year wealth relative is 0.80, close to the 0.83 reported in Ritter (1991) for 1,526 IPOs from 1975 to 1984.[5] Thus, it appears that the patterns existing in 1975 to 1984 are representative of a longer stretch of capital markets history.

We also report total returns and wealth relatives based upon five-year holding periods. The continued poor performance of IPOs in years 4 and 5 of the aftermarket shows up, with the mean wealth relative falling to 0.70. The average holding-period raw return is only 16 percent for the five years after going public. While not reported in the table, the median five-year raw return is $-39$ percent for the 4,753 IPOs and 16 percent for their matching firms, reflecting the skewness in the distributions of five-year buy-and-hold returns.

---

[5] Because we allow the stock portion of unit offerings into our sample, unlike Ritter (1991), during the first three years of seasoning our 1975 to 1984 sample size is 1,806 IPOs. The inclusion of firms conducting unit offerings has little impact on any of our conclusions.

*The New Issues Puzzle*      29

Table I

## The Long-Run Performance of IPOs by Cohort Year, 1970 to 1990

The sample consists of 4,753 IPOs by firms subsequently listed on Nasdaq, the American Stock Exchange (Amex), or the New York Stock Exchange (NYSE). Buy-and-hold returns for the companies going public in cohort year $\tau$ are computed using the first CRSP-listed closing price as the purchase price. Wealth relatives are computed as $[(\Sigma(1 + R_{iT}))/(\Sigma(1 + R_{mT}))]$, where $R_{iT}$ is the holding-period return from the first CRSP-listed closing price until the earlier of the delisting date or the three-year (or five-year) anniversary of the IPO, $R_{mT}$ is the holding-period return on a matching firm over the same holding period, and the summations are over the $N$ observations in a cohort year. For example, 1970's five-year wealth relative of 0.67 is computed as 0.537/0.800, with 0.537 being the terminal wealth per dollar invested after having lost 46.3 percent on the IPO portfolio. The average holding period for firms held up to five years is 47 months.

| | | 3 Years | | | 5 Years | | |
|---|---|---|---|---|---|---|---|
| | | Mean Buy-and-Hold Returns (%) | | | Mean Buy-and-Hold Returns (%) | | |
| Cohort Year | Number of IPOs | IPOs | Matching Firms[b] | Wealth Relative | IPOs | Matching Firms[b] | Wealth Relative |
| 1970[a] | 151 | −20.9 | −12.9 | 0.91 | −46.3 | −20.0 | 0.67 |
| 1971[a] | 252 | −55.6 | −27.3 | 0.65 | −31.6 | 6.1 | 0.64 |
| 1972[a] | 473 | −47.2 | −10.8 | 0.59 | −18.2 | 33.4 | 0.61 |
| 1973 | 60 | −33.6 | 29.5 | 0.51 | 0.8 | 104.4 | 0.49 |
| 1974 | 8 | 73.2 | 87.5 | 0.92 | 234.4 | 173.0 | 1.22 |
| 1975 | 12 | 59.3 | 106.5 | 0.77 | 117.9 | 127.3 | 0.96 |
| 1976 | 33 | 135.3 | 81.3 | 1.30 | 259.4 | 205.0 | 1.18 |
| 1977 | 26 | 151.3 | 126.2 | 1.11 | 173.8 | 234.0 | 0.82 |
| 1978 | 34 | 131.0 | 87.5 | 1.23 | 217.9 | 227.0 | 0.97 |
| 1979 | 68 | 63.0 | 80.6 | 0.90 | 52.6 | 193.1 | 0.52 |
| 1980 | 162 | 80.1 | 123.4 | 0.81 | −2.1 | 188.0 | 0.34 |
| 1981 | 354 | 6.3 | 90.5 | 0.56 | 14.9 | 194.7 | 0.39 |
| 1982 | 118 | 21.4 | 83.9 | 0.66 | 76.7 | 137.6 | 0.74 |
| 1983 | 665 | 21.4 | 55.4 | 0.78 | 3.8 | 67.2 | 0.62 |
| 1984 | 334 | 48.1 | 60.0 | 0.93 | 44.0 | 82.2 | 0.79 |
| 1985 | 316 | 5.7 | 28.9 | 0.82 | 9.5 | 58.6 | 0.69 |
| 1986 | 666 | 5.3 | 29.9 | 0.81 | 9.3 | 33.4 | 0.82 |
| 1987 | 489 | −10.4 | 0.3 | 0.89 | 6.2 | 14.0 | 0.93 |
| 1988[c] | 198 | 17.5 | 26.1 | 0.93 | 80.8 | 60.3 | 1.13 |
| 1989[c] | 177 | 44.3 | 20.6 | 1.20 | 44.4 | 25.3 | 1.15 |
| 1990[c] | 157 | 22.7 | 42.7 | 0.86 | 22.7 | 42.7 | 0.86 |
| 1970–90 | 4,753 | 8.4 | 35.3 | 0.80 | 15.7 | 66.4 | 0.70 |

[a]Prior to December 14, 1972, only returns from firms listed on the Amex and NYSE are included. After December 14, 1972, returns on Nasdaq-listed firms are included.

[b]At the time of going public, each IPO is matched with the seasoned firm (CRSP-listed for at least five years, without having issued equity during the prior five years) having the closest, but higher, market capitalization on the prior December 31. If this matching firm is delisted or issues equity prior to the end of the IPO aftermarket return interval, the next highest seasoned market cap firm that has not issued equity is spliced in on the delisting date. The same procedure is used if this firm is subsequently removed. For 1970 to 1977, all matching firms are Amex-NYSE listed. After 1977, the universe of firms from which matching firms are picked includes all operating companies listed on the Amex-NYSE and Nasdaq tapes which have not conducted an equity issue during the prior five years.

[c]The return window for these cohorts is truncated at December 31, 1992.

## B. Equally Weighted Buy-and-Hold Returns on SEOs

If private firms are successful at selling stock at prices such that investors subsequently realize low returns, one would expect that publicly traded firms should have some ability to do the same. While numerous authors have documented that SEOs occur on average after substantial price runups and that there is a 3 percent price drop on average when an SEO is announced, there has been little focus on long-term postissue performance.[6] Here, we present evidence that there are low postissue returns on seasoned issuers.

In Table II, we report the average buy-and-hold return for firms conducting SEOs for windows of three and five years after the offerings. Also reported is the average buy-and-hold return during the year prior to the offerings, and the postissue returns on matching firms chosen using the same procedure as in Table I. The wealth relatives for three- and five-year holding periods are also reported.

Table II reports that in the year prior to the offering, the average issuer has experienced a total return of 72 percent. Not reported in the table is that approximately half of this return is due to market runups, and half is due to the issuers outperforming the market. In the (up to) five years after an SEO, the average buy-and-hold return on issuing firms is 33 percent, while the average buy-and-hold return on their matching firms is 93 percent, with a wealth relative of 0.69. The wealth relative is virtually identical to that for IPOs reported in Table I. *Firms conducting seasoned equity offerings underperform just as severely as firms going public.* Although not reported in the table, the median five-year buy-and-hold return on the issuing firms is $-8$ percent, whereas the median five-year buy-and-hold return on their matching firms is 50 percent.

## C. The Required Investments to Achieve the Same Terminal Wealth Levels

The five-year buy-and-hold return numbers in Tables I and II can be used to measure the investment in issuing firms that is required in order to have the same wealth five years later as would be produced by an investment in nonissuers. To illustrate, assume that a representative nonissuer sold for

---

[6] The announcement-period price drop has been documented by numerous authors, including Asquith and Mullins (1986), Masulis and Korwar (1986), Mikkelson and Partch (1986), Kalay and Shimrat (1987), Korajczyk, Lucas, and McDonald (1990), Loderer, Sheehan, and Kadlec (1991), Choe, Masulis, and Nanda (1993), Jegadeesh, Weinstein, and Welch (1993), Manuel, Brooks, and Schadler (1993), and Bayless and Chaplinsky (1993). Asquith and Mullins (1986) report postannouncement cumulative average returns (CARs) for 480 postannouncement trading days for their sample of 189 SEOs of industrial firms during 1963 to 1981, all of which were announced in the *Wall Street Journal*. They report a downward drift of about 6 percent in cumulative excess returns. Korajczyk, Lucas, and McDonald (1990) report postannouncement CARs for 100 trading days for their sample of 1,480 seasoned equity offerings from 1974 to 1983. They report postannouncement CARs of 0 percent using an equally weighted market index. Spiess and Affleck-Graves (1994) report long-run underperformance for the five years after the SEO for a sample of 1,247 nonutility offerings from 1975 to 1989. Their sample is restricted to firms selling primary shares only.

## Table II

## The Long-Run Performance of SEOs by Cohort Year, 1970 to 1990

The sample consists of 3,702 seasoned equity offers (SEOs) involving at least some newly issued shares (primary or combined primary and secondary shares) by firms listed on Nasdaq, the American Stock Exchange (Amex), or New York Stock Exchange (NYSE). Offerings by utilities (SIC codes 491–494) are excluded. The prior return is the raw buy-and-hold return for the 252 trading days ending on the issue date. If less than 252 trading days are available, the shorter holding period is used. For firms that went public less than one year before the SEO, the prior return is measured from the first CRSP-listed closing price. Wealth relatives are computed as $[(\Sigma(1 + R_{iT}))/(\Sigma(1 + R_{mT}))]$, where $R_{iT}$ is the holding-period return from the closing price on the issue date until the earlier of the delisting date or the three-year (or five-year) anniversary of the SEO, $R_{mT}$ is the holding-period return on a matching firm over the same holding period, and the summations are over the $N$ observations in a cohort year. The average holding period for firms held up to five years is 52 months.

| Cohort Year | Number of SEOs | Prior Return (%) | 3 Years Mean Buy-and-Hold Returns (%) | | | 5 Years Mean Buy-and-Hold Returns (%) | | |
|---|---|---|---|---|---|---|---|---|
| | | | SEOs | Matching Firms[b] | Wealth Relative | SEOs | Matching Firms[b] | Wealth Relative |
| 1970[a] | 88 | −6.2 | −11.1 | −4.2 | 0.93 | −29.2 | −4.7 | 0.74 |
| 1971[a] | 296 | 59.2 | −50.7 | −29.9 | 0.70 | −35.0 | 16.3 | 0.56 |
| 1972[a] | 280 | 43.1 | −49.3 | −19.5 | 0.63 | −22.0 | 25.9 | 0.62 |
| 1973 | 45 | −1.4 | −34.6 | 3.2 | 0.63 | −15.7 | 37.9 | 0.61 |
| 1974 | 22 | −1.0 | 50.1 | 74.0 | 0.86 | 91.0 | 155.0 | 0.75 |
| 1975 | 53 | 70.3 | 50.9 | 81.1 | 0.83 | 107.6 | 162.4 | 0.79 |
| 1976 | 78 | 80.8 | 35.8 | 45.6 | 0.93 | 135.5 | 136.4 | 1.00 |
| 1977 | 45 | 40.3 | 147.8 | 103.2 | 1.22 | 181.2 | 178.3 | 1.01 |
| 1978 | 92 | 65.2 | 83.5 | 101.5 | 0.91 | 126.1 | 266.5 | 0.62 |
| 1979 | 83 | 59.0 | 54.9 | 70.8 | 0.91 | 90.0 | 193.5 | 0.65 |
| 1980 | 236 | 99.0 | 69.4 | 140.7 | 0.70 | 43.7 | 214.2 | 0.46 |
| 1981 | 239 | 92.0 | 9.6 | 77.8 | 0.62 | 36.9 | 178.2 | 0.49 |
| 1982 | 184 | 53.3 | 51.3 | 113.2 | 0.71 | 90.6 | 207.9 | 0.62 |
| 1983 | 545 | 138.8 | 17.4 | 70.5 | 0.69 | 20.3 | 95.9 | 0.61 |
| 1984 | 125 | 16.6 | 49.3 | 80.2 | 0.83 | 73.4 | 105.4 | 0.84 |
| 1985 | 268 | 57.7 | 11.9 | 60.3 | 0.70 | 24.2 | 84.0 | 0.68 |
| 1986 | 350 | 68.7 | 11.3 | 30.8 | 0.85 | 23.2 | 32.4 | 0.93 |
| 1987 | 247 | 51.7 | 1.4 | 13.7 | 0.89 | 37.5 | 40.2 | 0.98 |
| 1988[c] | 107 | 18.2 | 16.5 | 23.1 | 0.95 | 65.2 | 63.4 | 1.01 |
| 1989[c] | 167 | 65.8 | 17.6 | 16.3 | 1.00 | 31.0 | 31.1 | 1.00 |
| 1990[c] | 152 | 45.1 | 37.2 | 42.5 | 0.96 | 37.2 | 42.5 | 0.96 |
| 1970–90 | 3,702 | 72.3 | 15.0 | 48.0 | 0.78 | 33.4 | 92.8 | 0.69 |

[a]Prior to December 14, 1972, only returns from firms listed on the Amex and NYSE are included. After December 14, 1972, returns on Nasdaq-listed firms are included. Because CRSP Nasdaq returns are unavailable prior to December 14, 1972, the prior returns are available for only 283 of the 664 SEOs during 1970 to 1972.

[b]At the time of the new issue, each firm conducting an SEO is matched with the seasoned firm (CRSP-listed for at least five years, without having issued equity during the prior five years) having the closest, but higher, market capitalization on the prior December 31. If this matching firm conducts an SEO or is delisted prior to the end of the three- or five-year postissue holding period, the next highest seasoned market cap firm that has not issued equity is spliced in on the removal date. The same procedure is used if this firm is subsequently removed. For 1970 to 1977, all matching firms are Amex–NYSE listed. After 1977, the universe of firms from which matching firms are picked includes all operating companies listed on the Amex-NYSE and Nasdaq tapes which have not conducted an equity issue during the prior five years.

[c]The return window for these cohorts is truncated at December 31, 1992.

32                          *The Journal of Finance*

$10.00 at the close of the day on which another company with the same postissue market capitalization issued stock. The average five-year buy-and-hold return of 66.4 percent on IPO matching firms implies that $10.00 invested in size-matched nonissuers grows to $16.64 after five years. Because the average five-year buy-and-hold return on IPOs is only 15.7 percent, an investment of $14.38 is required to receive the same $16.64 at the end of the holding period (1.157 × $14.38 = $16.64). Thus, an investor buying IPOs at the first closing market price would have to invest 43.8 percent more money than if nonissuers of the same size were purchased at the same time, in order to achieve the same terminal wealth level five years later.[7]

For SEOs, the Table II returns imply that $10.00 invested in size-matched nonissuers at the first postissue closing price will grow to $19.28 five years later, whereas an investment of $14.45 in issuers would be required to grow to this same $19.28, since the average total return for these issuers is only 33.4 percent (1.334 × $14.45 = $19.28). Thus, the required investment in SEOs at the first postissue closing market price is 44.5 percent higher than that required for nonissuing firms of the same size in order to achieve the same terminal wealth level. Hence, for both IPOs and SEOs, 44 percent more money must be invested in issuers than in nonissuers of the same size to achieve the same wealth level five years later.

## D. Annualized Returns on New Issues

While the average equally weighted five-year holding-period return on IPOs is 16 percent and that on SEOs is 33 percent, it is conventional to report annual returns. In Table III and Figure 2, we present the annual returns on issuers and their matching firms during the five years after the offerings. In Table III, we also divide the first year into two six-month periods.

For both unseasoned and seasoned stock issuers, returns are lower during each of the five years after issuing than on their size-matched nonissuing firms. For both groups of issuers, there is no underperformance during the six months after the offering. There is severe underperformance during the next 18 months. By the fifth year, the underperformance is narrowing noticeably. While we do not report it in Table III, the underperformance in years six and seven is only about 1 percent per year. In the last column, we report the geometric average annual return during the first five postissuing years for the issuing firms and for nonissuing firms with the same market capitalizations. The average return on firms going public is 5 percent per year, compared to 12 percent for their matching firms, an underperformance effect of 7 percent per year. For firms conducting SEOs, the average return is 7 percent per year, compared to 15 percent for their matching firms, an

---

[7]For those lucky enough to buy each IPO at the offering price, the required investment in issuers is only 30 percent higher than in nonissuers, since the 10 percent average initial return moves the price from $13.00 to a $14.38 market price immediately after issuing. This $13.00 offering price is still 30 percent higher than the $10.00 investment in nonissuing firms that produces $16.64 in terminal wealth.

**Table III**

## Average Annual Percentage Returns during the Five Years after Issuing for Firms Conducting Initial Public Offerings (IPOs) and Seasoned Equity Offerings (SEOs) during 1970 to 1990, and Their Matching Firms

Using the first closing postissue market price, the equally weighted average buy-and-hold return for the year after the issue is calculated for the issuing firms and for their matching firms (firms with the same market capitalization that have not issued equity during the prior five years). On each anniversary of the issue date, the portfolios are rebalanced to equal weights and the average buy-and-hold return during the next year for all of the surviving issuers and their matching firms is calculated. The first two columns report returns per six months (or shorter, if less than six months of returns are available). For matching firms that get delisted (or issue equity) while the issuer is still trading, the proceeds from the sale on the delisting date are reinvested in a new matching firm for the remainder of that year (or until the issuer is delisted). For each of the five years, the average holding period is about seven or eight days shorter than 252 trading days because about six percent of the firms are subject to either a late listing (especially for years 1 and 2) or a midyear delisting (especially for years 4 and 5). Returns are calculated until December 31, 1992. The $t$-statistics for the difference in returns are calculated using the difference in returns for each issuer and its matching firm, and assume independence of the observations.

| | First 6 Months | Second 6 Months | First Year | Second Year | Third Year | Fourth Year | Fifth Year | Geometric Mean, Years 1–5 |
|---|---|---|---|---|---|---|---|---|
| *Panel A. Firms Going Public* | | | | | | | | |
| (1) IPO firms (%) | 3.1 | −1.1 | 1.6 | 3.6 | 5.0 | 4.0 | 11.6 | 5.1 |
| (2) Matching firms (%) | 3.0 | 3.4 | 6.1 | 14.1 | 13.3 | 11.3 | 14.3 | 11.8 |
| (3) $t$-Statistic for difference | 0.13 | −5.50 | −3.51 | −8.01 | −6.45 | −5.61 | −1.67 | −11.37 |
| (4) Sample size | 4,082 | 4,351 | 4,363 | 4,526 | 4,277 | 3,717 | 3,215 | 4,753 |
| *Panel B. Firms Conducting SEOs* | | | | | | | | |
| (5) SEO firms (%) | 5.6 | 0.5 | 6.6 | 0.1 | 7.5 | 9.1 | 11.8 | 7.0 |
| (6) Matching firms (%) | 5.7 | 6.8 | 12.9 | 12.3 | 16.2 | 17.7 | 17.4 | 15.3 |
| (7) $t$-Statistic for difference | −0.22 | −9.00 | −5.59 | −12.24 | −8.08 | −7.35 | −4.50 | −16.80 |
| (8) Sample size | 3,469 | 3,550 | 3,561 | 3,614 | 3,496 | 3,154 | 2,805 | 3,702 |

underperformance effect of 8 percent per year. It is also worth noting that the average annual returns on issuing firms are no higher than T-bill returns, which have averaged 7 percent per year during our sample period.

In rows 3 and 7 of Table III, we report $t$-statistics for the null hypothesis that the difference in annual returns between the issuing firms and their matching firms is zero. Except for IPOs in their fifth year of seasoning, the null hypothesis can be rejected at high levels of statistical significance, with $t$-statistics in the second year of seasoning as large as −8.01 for IPOs and −12.24 for SEOs. The $t$-statistics are calculated using the standard deviation of the mean of $r_{it} - r_{mt}$, where $r_{it}$ is the return on issuing firm $i$ during year $t$ of seasoning, and $r_{mt}$ is the return on its matching firm during the identical time period. Because the $t$-statistics are calculated assuming independence of

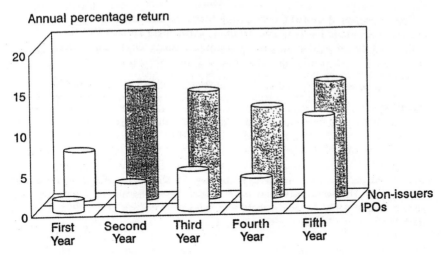

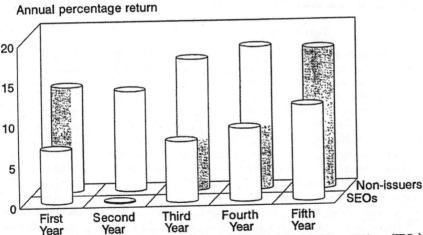

**Figure 2. The average annual raw returns for 4,753 initial public offerings (IPOs), and their matching nonissuing firms (top), and the average annual raw returns for 3,702 seasoned equity offerings (SEOs), and their matching nonissuing firms (bottom), during the five years after the issue.** The equity issues are from 1970 to 1990. Using the first closing postissue market price, the equally weighted average buy-and-hold return for the year after the issue is calculated for the issuing firms and for their matching firms (firms with the same market capitalization that have not issued equity during the prior five years). On each anniversary of the issue date, the equally weighted average buy-and-hold return during the next year for all of the surviving issuers and their matching firms is calculated. For matching firms that get delisted (or issue equity) while the issuer is still trading, the proceeds from the sale on the delisting date are reinvested in a new matching firm for the remainder of that year (or until the issuer is delisted). The numbers graphed above are reported in Table III.

the observations, they should be viewed as only suggestive.[8] Further statistical tests (reported in Tables VIII and IX) explicitly adjust for the correlation of contemporaneous returns that is ignored in Table III.

In Table III, we rebalance the portfolios on each anniversary date, so that the annual returns weight each firm equally. This differs from our use of three- and five-year buy-and-hold returns, where a firm that has already appreciated 1000 percent during its first four years would receive 20 times as much weight in the fifth year as a firm that has declined in value by 50 percent during its first four years. We should note, however, that the annualized returns are not very sensitive to whether we rebalance the portfolios annually or not. We should also note that the sample sizes with which we compute the annual returns are always less than the total sample sizes because of three effects: (i) delayed listings in the early 1970s; (ii) delistings before the fifth-year anniversaries; and (iii) the truncation of the return data at the end of 1992, which affects the cohorts from the late 1980s. The fact that the average holding period is less than five years also explains why the average buy-and-hold return numbers from Tables I and II are less than those implied by compounding the five annual numbers in Table III. For IPOs, the average five-year holding period is 47 months, and for SEOs, the average is 52 months.[9]

### E. Alternative Benchmarks

The measurement of long-term abnormal performance is sensitive to the benchmark used. Although in Tables I and II we only report the returns on issuing firms relative to the returns on companies of the same size that have not issued equity within the previous five years, we have also computed wealth relatives using common indices. In Table IV, we calculate wealth relatives using, in addition to our matching firms, five common indices as benchmarks. As can be seen, while the exact magnitude of the underperformance of issuing firms is dependent upon the benchmark used, both IPOs (Panel A) and SEOs (Panel B) have underperformed all of the commonly used benchmarks: the CRSP equally weighted and value-weighted Amex-NYSE and Nasdaq indices, and the S&P 500. The underperformance relative to the S&P 500 Index is particularly noteworthy, for it does not include dividend income. When using the equally weighted CRSP indices as the benchmark, we do not compound the daily index to get the buy-and-hold return. Instead,

---

[8]The *t*-statistics assume normality and independence of the observations. While three- and five-year buy-and-hold returns are highly skewed, the distribution of *differences* in annual returns closely approximates a normal distribution. The *t*-statistics are overstated because the cross-sectional dependence existing in contemporaneous returns is not accounted for, but they are understated by using matching firm returns, rather than using an index return as the benchmark, due to the firm-specific risk that could be diversified away by using an index. Also, high *t*-statistics might be expected due to the relatively large sample size.
[9]There is a second reason why the average buy-and-hold returns in Tables I and II are not equal to the compounded annual returns in Table III. This is due to the covariance of returns and the length of the holding period: on average, losers are delisted earlier than winners.

**Table IV**

## Average Five-Year Returns and Wealth Relatives for New Issues from 1970 to 1990 Computed Using Alternative Benchmarks

The average five-year buy-and-hold returns from Table I for initial public offerings (IPOs) and Table II for seasoned equity offerings (SEOs) are compared with alternative benchmarks, including the matching firms used in Tables I and II. For each issuing firm, the benchmark return is calculated by compounding the daily returns on the index for the identical days that the issuing firm is held. (For equally weighted index returns, we compound the CRSP monthly index returns for all full calendar months in order to minimize bid-ask spread bias.) Wealth relatives are calculated by dividing the average terminal value from investing $1 in each issuing firm with the average terminal value from investing $1 in the relevant index. The S&P 500 Index returns do not include dividends. The CRSP Nasdaq index returns do not start until December 14, 1972. In calculating the wealth relatives using the Nasdaq indices, we use samples of IPOs and SEOs that issued equity after December 14, 1972. EW signifies equally weighted, and VW signifies value-weighted.

| | Average 5-Year Return (%) | | |
| --- | --- | --- | --- |
| Benchmark | Issuers | Benchmark | 5-Year Wealth Relative |
| Panel A. Initial Public Offerings | | | |
| Size-matched firms | 15.7 | 66.4 | 0.70 |
| CRSP Amex-NYSE EW index | 15.7 | 48.8 | 0.78 |
| CRSP Amex-NYSE VW index | 15.7 | 57.3 | 0.74 |
| Standard & Poor's 500 | 15.7 | 38.3 | 0.84 |
| CRSP Nasdaq EW index (3,886 firms) | 25.2 | 47.5 | 0.85 |
| CRSP Nasdaq VW index (3,886 firms) | 25.2 | 54.2 | 0.81 |
| Panel B. Seasoned Equity Offerings | | | |
| Size-matched firms | 33.4 | 92.8 | 0.69 |
| CRSP Amex-NYSE EW index | 33.4 | 67.7 | 0.79 |
| CRSP Amex-NYSE VW index | 33.4 | 66.3 | 0.80 |
| Standard & Poor's 500 | 33.4 | 43.0 | 0.93 |
| CRSP Nasdaq EW index (3,042 firms) | 46.9 | 75.2 | 0.84 |
| CRSP Nasdaq VW index (3,042 firms) | 46.9 | 66.4 | 0.88 |

to minimize the substantial bid-ask spread bias that exists in the daily equally weighted indices, we compound the monthly index returns except for the partial months at the beginning and ending of each five-year period.[10]

### F. Value-Weighted Buy-and-Hold Returns on New Issues

The equally weighted five-year wealth relatives reported in Tables I and II reflect the results of a portfolio strategy of investing an equal dollar amount in every issuing firm versus investing an equal dollar amount in every

---

[10] The upward bias in the daily equally weighted index returns is substantial. For example, compounding the 60 monthly returns of the CRSP Amex-NYSE equally weighted index from January 1974 to December 1978 gives a total return of 154.0 percent, whereas compounding the daily returns for the identical time period gives a total return of 243.4 percent.

**Table V**

## The Aggregate Total Dollar Returns on New Issues in 1970 to 1990 During the Five Years after Issuing

The Panel A sample consists of 4,753 initial public offerings (IPOs) during 1970 to 1990 subsequently listed by CRSP. All numbers are exclusive of initial returns. The Panel B sample consists of 3,702 nonutility CRSP-listed seasoned equity offerings (SEOs) during 1970 to 1990. Dollar values are computed after converting all nominal proceeds into dollars of 1991 purchasing power using the U.S. consumers price index. For example, all of the issues in 1970 have their proceeds multiplied by 3.49. The dollar value of the return is computed as the number of shares issued multiplied by the first CRSP-reported postissue price per share (using 1991 purchasing power) multiplied by the return. Most issuing firms from prior to 1973 and after 1987 have less than five years of returns included due to either delays in being listed by CRSP or the truncation of returns at December 31, 1992. In 1991 dollars, the average SEO postissue market value of the newly issued shares is $48 million, twice the size of the IPO average of $25 million. The average postissue market value of the seasoned issuers is $374 million, six times as large as the $61 million for firms going public.

| Panel A. Initial Public Offerings | |
|---|---|
| (1) Dollar value (1991 purchasing power) of IPOs valued at first CRSP-listed price | $117.6 billion |
| (2) Dollar value (1991 purchasing power) of returns on IPOs | $39.8 billion |
| (3) Dollar value (1991 purchasing power) of returns on matched seasoned firms | $78.8 billion |
| (4) Value-weighted percentage return [(2) ÷ (1)] × 100% | 33.8% |
| (5) Value-weighted wealth relative [(1) + (2)] ÷ [(1) + (3)] | 0.80 |
| Panel B. Seasoned Equity Offerings | |
| (6) Dollar value (1991 purchasing power) of SEOs valued at first CRSP-listed price | $176.8 billion |
| (7) Dollar value (1991 purchasing power) of returns on SEOs | $67.9 billion |
| (8) Dollar value (1991 purchasing power) of returns on matched seasoned firms | $145.6 billion |
| (9) Value-weighted percentage return [(7) ÷ (6)] × 100% | 38.4% |
| (10) Value-weighted wealth relative [(6) + (7)] ÷ [(6) + (8)] | 0.76 |

size-matched nonissuing firm. One might argue that a more relevant portfolio strategy would involve investing an amount in every issuing firm (and matching firm) that is proportional to the size of the offering.

Table V reports the dollar value of five-year returns that investors received in the aggregate from the 4,753 CRSP-listed firms going public (Panel A) and the 3,702 CRSP-listed seasoned equity issuers (Panel B) in 1970 to 1990. Since there was substantial inflation during this 21-year period, we have converted all nominal amounts into dollars of 1991 purchasing power. Valued at the first CRSP-listed market price, the aggregate dollar value of investment (in 1991 dollars) is $118 billion for the IPOs, as reported in row 1 of

Panel A. The aggregate dollar value of returns (capital gains plus dividends) from this investment is $40 billion, resulting in a value-weighted five-year buy-and-hold return of 34 percent. This is higher than the equally weighted 16 percent average five-year return for the 4,753 IPOs going public in 1970 to 1990, reflecting the pattern that smaller offerings (frequently more speculative firms) underperform by more than larger offerings. For matching firms, the aggregate dollar value of returns from a nearly identical investment is $79 billion, resulting in a value-weighted five-year return of 67 percent, virtually the same as the equally weighted five-year return of 66 percent reported in Table I.

As reported in row 5 of Table V, the value-weighted five-year wealth relative on IPOs is 0.80, higher than the 0.70 equally weighted number reported in Table I, but still substantially below 1.00. More striking is the value of the foregone returns from investing in IPOs: $39 billion was foregone by investors relative to what others earned by investing the same amount of money in nonissuing firms of the same size. Now, it should be noted that our IPO returns do not include the initial returns earned by investors lucky enough to be allocated shares at the offering price. If the value-weighted average initial return is 10 percent, aggregate aftermarket returns would increase by $12 billion, reducing the opportunity loss from $39 billion to about $27 billion.

The value-weighted five-year wealth relative for the firms conducting SEOs is 0.76, indicating that small issues are not driving the equally weighted results. The value-weighted five-year buy-and-hold return is 38 percent, only slightly above the equally weighted return of 33 percent reported in Table II.

## G. SEOs Categorized by Years of Seasoning

Because many of the firms conducting SEOs had gone public within the prior five years, the wealth relatives for SEOs are not independent of the wealth relatives for IPOs. Consequently, in Table VI, we divide the SEO sample into those firms conducting SEOs more than five years after going public (2,561 issues) and those firms issuing within five years of the IPO date (1,141 issues).[11]

Inspection of Table VI discloses that firms conducting SEOs more than five years after going public underperform by slightly more than young firms: the five-year wealth relative is 0.68, slightly less than the five-year wealth relative of 0.72 for firms conducting SEOs within five years of going public.

---

[11] It is also worth noting that the number of SEOs implies a probability of issuing of about 3 percent per year, although this number fluctuates considerably from year to year. This probability is only slightly higher for young firms. This number is calculated by taking the average number of SEOs per year and dividing by the average number of CRSP-listed firms per year. The frequency of SEOs by young firms in our sample is consistent with the numbers reported in Table 1 of Jegadeesh, Weinstein, and Welch (1993).

## Table VI

### The Long-Run Performance of Seasoned Equity Offerings Categorized by Whether the Issuing Firm Went Public within the Prior Five Years

The Table II sample of 3,702 seasoned equity offerings (SEOs) by nonutilities during 1970 to 1990 is categorized by whether the issuer went public within the previous five years. Wealth relatives are computed as $[(\Sigma(1 + R_{iT}))/(\Sigma(1 + R_{mT}))]$, where $R_{iT}$ is the holding-period return from the first postissue closing price until the earlier of the delisting date or the three-year (or five-year) anniversary of the SEO, $R_{mT}$ is the holding-period return on a matching firm over the same holding period, and the summations are over the $N$ observations in a category. At the time of the new issue, each firm conducting an SEO is matched with the seasoned firm (CRSP-listed for at least five years, without having issued equity during the prior five years) having the closest, but higher, market capitalization on the prior December 31. If this seasoned firm conducts an SEO or is delisted prior to the end of the three- or five-year aftermarket-return window, the next highest seasoned market cap firm that has not issued equity is spliced in on the removal date. The same procedure is used if this firm is subsequently removed. For 1970 to 1977, all matching firms are Amex-NYSE listed; after 1977, Nasdaq firms are also included.

| | | 3 Years | | | 5 Years | | |
|---|---|---|---|---|---|---|---|
| | | Mean Buy-and-Hold Returns (%) | | | Mean Buy-and-Hold Returns (%) | | |
| Length of Time Since IPO at Date of SEO | Number of SEOs | SEOs | Matching Firms | Wealth Relative | SEOs | Matching Firms | Wealth Relative |
| 5 or fewer years | 1,141 | 2.3 | 34.4 | 0.76 | 19.5 | 66.9 | 0.72 |
| More than 5 years | 2,561 | 20.7 | 54.1 | 0.78 | 39.5 | 104.4 | 0.68 |
| Total | 3,702 | 15.0 | 48.0 | 0.78 | 33.4 | 92.8 | 0.69 |

Thus, the poor long-run performance of seasoned equity issuers is not merely another manifestation of the low returns on IPOs.

### H. Returns on Extreme Winners

The pronounced underperformance of seasoned issuers, following a substantial runup (72 percent, on average) in the year prior to issuing, raises a question as to whether the low returns are merely a manifestation of long-term mean reversion, as documented in De Bondt and Thaler (1987). In Table VII, we compare the subsequent returns on firms that have large price runups, categorized by whether they subsequently issue or not. In this table, we delete stocks with a price below $10 because of the large number of low-priced stocks that would otherwise be present among the nonissuing firms. Unlike previous tables where we calculate five-year returns starting on the issue date, here we calculate five-year returns beginning six months after the calendar year of the runup. Among these winners, the average issuer has a five-year return of 26 percent, compared with 98 percent for the nonissuers. In summary, what matters for future returns is not the previous year's return, but whether or not a firm has issued stock.

**Table VII**

**The Long-Run Performance of Extreme Winners from 1969 to 1989 Categorized by Whether or Not They Issued Equity**

The average buy-and-hold returns and wealth relatives are calculated for the companies with a market-adjusted return of at least 50 percent more than the CRSP American Stock Exchange (Amex)-New York Stock Exchange (NYSE) value-weighted index in a calendar year. The sample includes Nasdaq, Amex, and NYSE domestic operating companies, exclusive of utilities. A firm is classified as an issuer if it conducted an SEO during the 18-month interval ending on the June 30 after the calendar year in which it outperformed the market. Thus, the 21 cohorts have long-run returns measured starting on June 30, 1970 through June 30, 1990. Firms must have a price of at least $10 on this June 30, which is when the five-year buy-and-hold return period begins. For firms that are delisted before the end of this interval, buy-and-hold returns are calculated until the delisting date, and the index return is truncated on this date as well. If a nonissuer issues equity during the five-year period, it is retained in the sample, rather than having its buy-and-hold return truncated at this date.

| | Sample Size | Mean 5-Year Buy-and-Hold Return (%) | | Wealth Relative |
| | | Firms | Index | |
|---|---|---|---|---|
| Issuers | 896 | 26.4 | 74.6 | 0.72 |
| Nonissuers | 5,219 | 98.3 | 71.9 | 1.15 |

## III. Statistical Tests Controlling for Size and Book-to-Market Effects

Many firms going public are growth stocks, and most firms conducting SEOs have had a substantial increase in share price during the prior year. As a result, most issuing firms have relatively low (postissue) book-to-market ratios, and firms with low book-to-market ratios have had low returns in recent decades, as documented by, among others, Rosenberg, Reid, and Lanstein (1985), De Bondt and Thaler (1987), Fama and French (1992), and Hawawini and Keim (1993). While the average raw return on new issues is very low and firms selling equity underperform nonissuing firms of the same market capitalization, one might ask whether the appropriate benchmark for measuring abnormal performance is size-matched firms. We address this by presenting (i) cross-sectional and (ii) time-series multiple regression results, using monthly returns controlling for both size and book-to-market effects.

### A. The Cross-section of Realized Returns

To test whether there is an independent "new issue effect" above and beyond other determinants of the cross-sectional variation of returns during 1973 to 1992, we run cross-sectional regressions on the universe of all CRSP-listed Amex, NYSE, and Nasdaq firms for which we have the book value of equity.

We calculate the book-to-market ratio annually on June 30, using the book value of equity for the most recent fiscal year ending on or before January 31, and the market value of equity on June 30. COMPUSTAT (including the historical and research files) is the primary source of information for book values (COMPUSTAT annual data item 60). We augment the COMPUSTAT book value of equity numbers, without introducing a survivorship bias, by using the 1973 and 1974 *Moody's OTC Industrial Manual* for pre-1975 IPOs, the prospectuses for IPOs in 1975 to 1984, and the IDD and SDC databases for firms going public after 1984. For firms that conducted SEOs between the end of their fiscal year and June 30, we compute the June 30 book values by adding the gross proceeds raised by the firm (exclusive of any overallotment option) in the offering to the preissue book value.[12]

In Table VIII, we report the average coefficients from 240 cross-sectional regressions with a dependent variable of monthly returns on individual stocks:

$$r_{it} = a_o + a_1 \ln MV_{it} + a_2 \ln(BV/MV)_{it} + a_3 ISSUE_{it} + e_{it} \qquad (3)$$

As explanatory variables, we use three variables: the natural logarithm of the market value of equity, the natural logarithm of the book-to-market ratio, and a dummy variable taking on the value of 1 if a firm conducted one or more public equity issues within the previous five years.[13] (While we do not report the results in order to conserve space, when we use separate IPO and SEO dummy variables, the coefficients are virtually identical.) The two explanatory variables in addition to the new issue dummy are motivated by prior empirical studies of the determinants of stock returns, including work by Banz (1981), Chan, Hamao, and Lakonishok (1991), Fama and French (1992), Davis (1994), and Lakonishok, Shleifer, and Vishny (1994). When we include a cross-product term to allow for more severe underperformance of firms conducting SEOs within five years of their IPOs, the cross-product term is economically and statistically insignificant. We compute $t$-statistics using the standard deviation of the 240 coefficient estimates, an approach introduced by Fama and MacBeth (1973). We also report the proportion of the coefficients that are positive.

In row 1 of Table VIII, using all months, the average coefficient of $-0.05$ on size (ln $MV$) is not statistically significant at conventional levels. This parameter implies that a \$50 million firm would have a monthly return 23 basis points higher than a \$5 billion firm. The coefficient of 0.30 on ln $BV/MV$ is reliably different from zero and implies that, ceteris paribus, a firm with a book-to-market ratio of 1 would have a monthly return 27 basis points higher than a firm with a ratio of 0.4. On an annual basis, this amounts to about 3

---

[12] In practice, the net proceeds are boosted by the exercise of overallotment options (after 1983, typically 15 percent of the base issue amount), and lowered by commissions and other issuing costs. Hanley (1993) reports that 66 percent of firm commitment IPOs in 1983 to 1987 exercise overallotment options. Muscarella, Peavy, and Vetsuypens (1992) report similar numbers.

[13] For companies with book values of less than \$100,000, including negative book values, we assign a book value of \$100,000. We do this to avoid problems with outliers and the logarithm of negative numbers. The results are robust to an alternative procedure of excluding companies with negative book values.

### Table VIII
## Average Parameter Values from Monthly Cross-sectional Regressions of Percentage Stock Returns on Size, Book-to-Market, and a New Issues Dummy Variable, 1973 to 1992

The universe is New York Stock Exchange (NYSE), American Stock Exchange (Amex), and Nasdaq firms for which the book value of equity is available from COMPUSTAT or our new issues data. $t$-Statistics, computed from the time-series standard deviation of the parameter values, and the percentage of the coefficient estimates that are positive, are listed in brackets. $r_{it}$ is the percentage return on stock $i$ in calendar month $t$. $MV_{it}$ is the market value of equity (in millions) on the most recent June 30. $BV/MV_{it}$ is the ratio of the book value of equity to the market value of equity, where the book value is the book value of equity for the most recent fiscal year ending on or before the January 31 preceding June 30. For recent IPOs where the offering was after the end of the fiscal year, the postoffering book value is used. For companies conducting SEOs after the end of their fiscal year, we add the proceeds to the prior book value. Companies with book values below \$100,000, including negative book values, are assigned book values of \$100,000. $ISSUE_{it}$ is a [0, 1] dummy variable taking on the value of 1 if a company conducted at least one public equity offering within the 60 months preceding a given June 30. The sample includes issues through June 30, 1992. Utility stocks (SIC = 491–494) are excluded from the universe of firms. Logs are natural logarithms. Firms are excluded from the following 12 months if they have a market value on June 30 of less than \$1,000,000 during 1973 to 1979, \$2,000,000 during 1980 to 1989, and \$3,000,000 during 1990 to 1992. Periods following light and heavy volume are based upon the fraction of our sample stocks that have the $ISSUE$ dummy variable equal to 1. The periods following heavy volume during our 20-year sample period are January 1973 to June 1974 and July 1983 to December 1991.

$$r_{it} = a_o + a_1 \ln MV_{it} + a_2 \ln BV/MV_{it} + a_3 ISSUE_{it} + e_{it}$$

| Model | Average Parameter Values | | | | Avg. $R^2$ | No. of Months |
|---|---|---|---|---|---|---|
| | Intercept | ln $MV$ | ln $BV/MV$ | $ISSUE$ | | |
| All months (1) | 1.70 [3.46, 59%] | −0.05 [−0.91, 50%] | 0.30 [4.57, 65%] | −0.38 [−3.68, 40%] | 0.019 | 240 |
| January only (2) | 12.94 [5.88, 95%] | −1.46 [−6.12, 5%] | 0.55 [1.47, 60%] | 0.00 [0.01, 45%] | 0.039 | 20 |
| Feb.–Dec. only (3) | 0.68 [1.55, 55%] | 0.08 [1.45, 55%] | 0.27 [4.40, 66%] | −0.42 [−4.03, 39%] | 0.017 | 220 |
| All months (4) | 1.42 [3.67, 63%] | | | −0.49 [−3.98, 37%] | 0.004 | 240 |
| All months (5) | 1.58 [3.10, 59%] | −0.05 [−0.84, 51%] | 0.33 [4.82, 66%] | | 0.016 | 240 |
| Periods following light volume (6) | 3.45 [4.63, 71%] | −0.26 [−3.12, 42%] | 0.20 [1.80, 59%] | −0.17 [−1.19, 44%] | 0.021 | 120 |
| Periods following heavy volume (7) | −0.05 [−0.08, 47%] | 0.16 [2.11, 59%] | 0.39 [6.30, 72%] | −0.60 [−3.98, 35%] | 0.016 | 120 |

percent per year. The coefficient of $-0.38$ on the issuing firm dummy variable implies that, ceteris paribus, issuing firms underperform by 38 basis points per month, or over 4 percent per year, during the next five years.

In rows 2 and 3, we report the average coefficients for January and non-January months. Consistent with other studies, the size effect is purely a January phenomenon. Unlike almost all other anomalies, the new issue effect is not concentrated in January.

Since most issuing firms have relatively low book-to-market ratios, it is worthwhile to examine how much of the low returns on issuing firms can be attributed to book-to-market effects. In row 4, we report the average coefficients from monthly regressions where the sole explanatory variable is the new issue dummy variable. The mean parameter value of $-0.49$ indicates that firms conducting new issues subsequently underperform by 49 basis points per month, or about 6 percent per year. Comparing the *ISSUE* coefficients of $-0.38$ in row 1 and $-0.49$ in row 4 indicates that less than 25 percent of the underperformance of new issues can be attributed to size and book-to-market effects. Thus, the underperformance of issuing firms is partly, but only partly, a manifestation of the more general tendency for firms with low book-to-market ratios (growth firms) to have low returns.

In Table III, we reported size-adjusted underperformance of 7 percent per year for IPOs and 8 percent per year for SEOs. These numbers are larger than those implied by the coefficients in rows 1 to 4 of Table VIII. Why is there a difference?

The answer is simple: in Table III, we are weighting each *issuer* equally, whereas in Table VIII, we are weighting each *month* equally, so we do not pick up the tendency of more severe underperformance following heavy new issue activity that is apparent in Tables I and II. In rows 6 and 7, we divide the sample period into months following light issuance activity and months following heavy issuance activity.[14] Following light issuance activity, issuing firms underperform by only 17 basis points per month, whereas after heavy issuance activity, issuing firms underperform by 60 basis points per month. Thus, weighting each month equally understates the extent of underperformance.

Our interpretation of Table VIII is that there are economically and statistically significant book-to-market and new issue effects. Neither subsumes the other. Since they are correlated, any study of return patterns that uses Nasdaq stocks should take these effects into account. Indeed, Loughran (1993) finds that much of the return difference between NYSE and Nasdaq stocks, documented by Reinganum (1990), is due to the fact that Nasdaq has been intensive in recent IPOs.

Of course, it is possible that we have mismeasured the abnormal returns on firms that issued equity. It should be noted, however, that we have controlled

---

[14] Months are categorized as following light or heavy issuance activity on the basis of the fraction of the sample firms in a month that have issued equity during the prior five years, as listed in Table VIII.

for both size and book-to-market in our Table VIII regressions, and these two variables have been demonstrated by Fama and French (1992) to be the most important determinants of cross-sectional return patterns during our sample period. As an alternative check on the robustness of our underperformance findings, we also perform time-series regressions.

## B. *Three-Factor Time-Series Regressions*

In Table IX, we report the results of time-series regressions of monthly portfolio returns on three factors, as used in Fama *et al.* (1993). A desirable feature of these tests is that by forming portfolios, the cross-sectional dependence problem that exists in Table III is eliminated. One disadvantage of these tests is that by forming portfolios, power is sacrificed. Another disadvantage is that to the degree that the portfolios are correlated with omitted factors, the intercepts can embody factors other than what is explicitly being controlled for.

Our regressions use as the dependent variable either the portfolio excess return ($R_{pt} - R_{ft}$) or the difference in returns between portfolios of issuing and nonissuing firms:

$$R_{pt} - R_{ft} = a + b[R_{mt} - R_{ft}] + sSMB_t + hHML_t + e_t \qquad (4)$$

where $R_{mt}$ is the return on the value-weighted index in month $t$; $R_{ft}$ is the three-month T-bill rate in month $t$; $SMB_t$ is the return on small firms minus the return on large firms in month $t$; and $HML_t$ is the return on high book-to-market stocks minus the return on low book-to-market stocks in month $t$.[15] In Table IX, we report results after dividing the sample into large and small firms; large firms are those whose market capitalization is above the size of the median Amex and NYSE firm in our sample. Panel A reports results using value-weighted portfolios, whereas Panel B reports results weighting each firm in a portfolio equally. To save space, we do not report results for all firms; the value-weighted numbers are similar to the value-weighted large firm results, whereas the equally weighted numbers are similar to the equally weighted small firm results.

If the poor performance of issuing firms is merely a manifestation of confounding effects (differences in beta, differences in size, and differences in book-to-market ratios), then the intercepts in the regressions should be economically and statistically indistinguishable from zero. Inspection of the Table IX coefficients shows that this is not the case: in regressions (3), (6), (9), and (12), issuing firms underperform by, respectively, 24, 26, 36, and 47 basis points per month. The $t$-statistics range from $-2.0$, to $-5.0$ on these coefficients. These numbers are of the same order of magnitude as the point estimates on the new issue dummy variable in the Table VIII regressions, suggesting that the underperformance of new issues is robust to alternative

---

[15] The construction of the explanatory variables that we use in the three-factor equation is explained in Table II of Fama *et al.* (1993). They measure size relative to the median NYSE firm.

### Table IX
## Time-series Regressions of Equally Weighted and Value-Weighted Monthly Percentage Returns on Fama and French's Market, Size, and Book-to-Market Return Realizations, for Portfolios of Large and Small Firms, Categorized by Whether the Firm Issued Equity during the Prior Five Years, January 1973 to December 1992

The universe is CRSP-listed New York Stock Exchange (NYSE), American Stock Exchange (Amex), and Nasdaq firms for which the book value of equity is available from COMPUSTAT or our new issues data. Large firms are those whose market cap on June 30 of year $t$ is greater than the market cap of the median NYSE and Amex operating company in our sample; while small firms are those whose market cap is below this median. $R_{mt}$ is the return on the value-weighted index of NYSE, Amex, and Nasdaq stocks in month $t$; $R_{ft}$ is the beginning-of-month three-month T-bill yield in month $t$; $SMB_t$ is the return on small firms minus the return on large firms in month $t$; and $HML_t$ is the return on high book-to-market stocks minus the return on low book-to-market stocks in month $t$. The factor definitions are described in Fama *et al.* (1993). The dependent variable in regressions (3), (6), (9), and (12) is the difference in returns between the issuing and nonissuing portfolios. $t$-Statistics are in parentheses. Each regression uses 240 monthly observations.

$$R_{pt} - R_{ft} = a + b[R_{mt} - R_{ft}] + sSMB_t + hHML_t + e_t$$

| | Coefficient Estimates | | | | |
|---|---|---|---|---|---|
| | $a$ | $b$ | $s$ | $h$ | $R^2_{adj}$ |
| Panel A. Value-Weighted Portfolio Returns | | | | | |
| (1) Large nonissuers | 0.03 | 1.02 | −0.05 | 0.00 | 0.99 |
| | (1.0) | (159.9) | (−5.0) | (0.1) | |
| (2) Large issuers | −0.21 | 1.03 | 0.19 | −0.19 | 0.92 |
| | (−1.9) | (40.0) | (5.0) | (−4.2) | |
| (3) Return difference | −0.24 | 0.01 | 0.24 | −0.19 | 0.19 |
| (2) − (1) | (−2.0) | (0.2) | (5.7) | (−3.9) | |
| (4) Small nonissuers | −0.08 | 0.97 | 1.19 | 0.31 | 0.98 |
| | (−1.3) | (63.9) | (51.9) | (11.8) | |
| (5) Small issuers | −0.34 | 1.12 | 1.36 | −0.01 | 0.95 |
| | (−3.0) | (41.0) | (33.0) | (−0.3) | |
| (6) Return difference | −0.26 | 0.15 | 0.17 | −0.32 | 0.51 |
| (5) − (4) | (−2.6) | (6.4) | (4.9) | (−8.0) | |
| Panel B. Equally Weighted Portfolio Returns | | | | | |
| (7) Large nonissuers | 0.08 | 1.07 | 0.52 | 0.18 | 0.99 |
| | (1.8) | (101.5) | (32.5) | (10.1) | |
| (8) Large issuers | −0.27 | 1.16 | 0.80 | −0.21 | 0.96 |
| | (−2.8) | (50.8) | (23.0) | (−5.3) | |
| (9) Return difference | −0.36 | 0.10 | 0.28 | −0.39 | 0.62 |
| (8) − (7) | (−4.2) | (4.9) | (9.3) | (−11.3) | |
| (10) Small nonissuers | 0.02 | 0.91 | 1.34 | 0.36 | 0.94 |
| | (0.2) | (35.1) | (34.2) | (8.2) | |
| (11) Small issuers | −0.45 | 1.05 | 1.50 | 0.09 | 0.92 |
| | (−3.1) | (31.0) | (29.2) | (1.6) | |
| (12) Return difference | −0.47 | 0.14 | 0.16 | −0.27 | 0.48 |
| (11) − (10) | (−5.0) | (6.4) | (4.7) | (−7.1) | |

46                           *The Journal of Finance*

specifications. As with Table VIII, weighting each month equally understates the extent of underperformance.

Note also that the $b$ coefficients in the regressions indicate that issuers have betas slightly above nonissuers, and slightly above 1.0. Thus, to the degree that beta risk is priced, issuers should have *higher* returns than nonissuers.

## IV. Summary and Conclusions

Investing in firms issuing stock is hazardous to your wealth. Firms issuing stock during 1970 to 1990, whether an IPO or an SEO, have been poor long-run investments for investors. The average annual return during the five years after issuing is only 5 percent for firms conducting IPOs, and only 7 percent for firms conducting SEOs. Investing an equal amount at the same time in a nonissuing firm with approximately the same market capitalization, and holding it for an identical period, would have produced an average compound return of 12 percent per year for IPOs and 15 percent for SEOs. The magnitude of the underperformance is large: it implies that 44 percent more money would need to be invested in the issuers than in the nonissuers to be left with the same wealth five years later.

We have entertained a number of possible explanations for the poor subsequent performance of issuing firms. Holding both size and the book-to-market ratio constant, issuing firms have lower subsequent returns than nonissuers. In addition, the poor performance of firms conducting SEOs is not a manifestation of long-term return reversals, nor is it attributable to differences in betas. While it is possible that some as yet unidentified risk factor or factors can explain some or all of the low returns, there is another possible explanation.

Our evidence is consistent with a market where firms take advantage of transitory windows of opportunity by issuing equity when, on average, they are substantially overvalued. We now explore related evidence and implications of this hypothesis.

### A. The Misvaluation of IPOs

For IPOs, the prior rapid growth of many of the young companies makes it easy to justify high valuations by investors who want to believe that they have identified the next Microsoft. Consistent with the hypothesis that IPOs have poor subsequent returns due to misvaluations at the time of going public, Jain and Kini (1994) report that for 682 firms going public during the 1976 to 1988 period, the median operating cash flow-to-assets ratio fell dramatically between the year prior to going public and three years later. Mikkelson and Shah (1994) report similar findings for IPOs from 1980 to 1983: while sales grew, total cash flows did not grow sufficiently to justify high valuations at the time of the offerings.

Evidence that cycles in IPO volume are due to issuers taking advantage of windows of opportunity is contained in Lerner (1994). Lerner tracks all of the financing of the biotechnology industry in the United States during January 1978 to September 1992, using information on both private and public sources of capital. Lerner finds that IPO activity is highly related to the inflation-adjusted price that public investors are willing to pay, with much of the IPO activity substituting for additional venture capital financing.

The finding that IPOs are poor long-run investments has been publicized for years. *Forbes* has periodically run stories along these lines since December 1985 (see Stern and Bornstein (1985)). Working with typical academic speed, it took until March 1991 for Ritter to confirm this in the academic literature. Yet 1992 was characterized by numerous biotechnology and restaurant chain companies going public at high multiples, and 1993 saw golf club manufacturers and riverboat casinos rushing to market.

A possible reason for why these patterns persist is that investors are betting on longshots. If the true probability that a given IPO will be the next Microsoft is 3 percent, but investors have instead estimated that it is 4 percent (resulting in a 33 percent overvaluation), it takes a very large sample over a long period of time before Bayesian investors would adequately revise their estimates. In other words, investors seem to be systematically misestimating the probability of finding a big winner. It is the triumph of hope over experience.

## B. The Misvaluation of SEOs

The finding that SEOs are poor long-run investments is largely new. In some of the academic literature from the 1960s, e.g., Stigler (1964) and Friend and Longstreet (1967), there is evidence using small samples that issuing firms do poorly in the long run, but this early literature largely has been forgotten.

This poor postissuing performance is not predicted by asymmetric information models for the timing of seasoned equity issues, such as that of Lucas and McDonald (1990). In their model, firms that are undervalued postpone their equity offerings. An equity issue announcement is associated with the market revaluing the firm so that, on average, it is no longer overvalued or undervalued. Our evidence is consistent with a market in which companies announce stock issues when their stock is grossly overvalued, the market does not revalue the stock appropriately, and the stock is still substantially overvalued when the issue occurs.

The ability to sell grossly overvalued equity, where the degree of misvaluation varies through time, is also consistent with the large swings in SEO volume graphed in Figure 1. Existing articles, such as Korajczyk, Lucas, and McDonald (1990), Choe, Masulis, and Nanda (1993), and Bayless and Chaplinsky (1993), explain the cycles in volume on the basis of firms choosing to issue equity when the announcement price drop is 2.8 percent rather than 3.2 percent. But does it make sense that a firm would wait years to issue equity just to save 10 cents on a $25 issue? Our focus is on whether the company can sell at an offer price of $28.80 rather than $20.00, not whether it will save 10 cents.

Our numbers can be used to back out what the announcement effect should be when companies announce seasoned equity offerings, if investors are to receive the same returns on issuers as on nonissuers of the same size. If firms conducting SEOs are overpriced by 44.5 percent at the time of the new issue, after having already fallen by 3 percent at the time of the announcement, they were at a price 49 percent too high (1.445/0.97) beforehand. A 33 percent drop would be required to eliminate this 49 percent overvaluation. Thus, our numbers imply that if the market fully reacted to the information implied by an equity issue announcement, the average announcement effect would be $-33$ percent, not $-3$ percent.

Healy and Palepu (1990), Hansen and Crutchley (1990), and Loughran and Ritter (1994) investigate the operating performance of SEOs. Loughran and Ritter find that the median issuer reports substantial improvements in operating measures (profit margins, return on assets, etc.) in the year of the issue. If the operating performance improvement persists, the 72 percent stock price runup in the year prior to the offering that we document in Table II can be justified. However, Loughran and Ritter (1994) show that this improvement is largely transitory, with operating performance deteriorating to levels below the preissue years.

Are issuers knowingly selling overvalued equity? One way of addressing this is to look at the insider trading behavior around SEOs. Lee (1994) finds that insiders seem to be subject to the same misperceptions that the market has: while there is some increase in insider selling (as normally occurs after price increases, whether or not there is an equity issue), firms in which insiders are net buyers underperform just as severely as those where insiders are net sellers.

## C. Related Evidence and Implications

The patterns documented here do not appear to be unique to the United States. Levis (1993a) reports that companies going public in the United Kingdom during 1980 to 1988 subsequently underperform, and Levis (1993b) reports that firms conducting SEOs in the United Kingdom subsequently underperform. Marsh (1979) reports that firms conducting SEOs in the United Kingdom during 1962 to 1972 outperform the market during the following year and then underperform in the second year after the offering. Loughran, Ritter, and Rydqvist (1994) document that during the last 20 to 30 years, in 14 of 15 countries, including the United States, there is a positive correlation between the annual volume of IPOs and the level of the stock market. In 10 of 14 countries, including the United States, annual IPO volume is negatively related to the market return during the following year.

Ikenberry, Lakonishok, and Vermaelen (1994) document that firms repurchasing shares in the open market subsequently overperform. Nelson (1994) shows that since 1926, NYSE firms that increase the number of (split-adjusted) shares outstanding subsequently underperform relative to those that reduce the number of shares outstanding. These studies, in conjunction with the evidence of this article, raise serious questions about the validity of using announcement-period returns as unbiased estimates of the impact of corporate decisions on stockholder welfare.

More generally, issuing firms typically have had recent improvements in their operating performance. The market appears to overweight this recent improvement and underweight long-term, mean-reverting tendencies in operating performance measures. The market is systematically misestimating the autocorrelation of earnings growth. Consequently, at the time of issue, market prices reflect the capitalization of transitory operating improvements. When the transitory nature of the operating performance becomes apparent, the stocks underperform. But this underperformance does not start immediately after issuing. In Table III, we report that there is no underperformance during the first six months after issuing for either IPOs or SEOs. Because the underperformance is delayed, the connection with issuing firms is less obvious to the market.

If issuing firms are successful at selling stock when the firm is substantially overvalued, is the market catching on? An inspection of Tables I and II discloses that our last three cohort years, 1988 to 1990, have wealth relatives close to 1.0 for both IPOs and SEOs, possibly suggesting that a prior inefficiency is disappearing. There are two reasons that we doubt that this is the case, however. First, there is no evidence that the first-day returns on IPOs and the announcement effects for SEOs have changed. Second, the period between the October 1987 market crash and the February 1991 Gulf War victory was a period of low issuing volume, and previous periods of low issuing volume produced wealth relatives close to 1.0 as well. An out-of-sample test of the windows of opportunity hypothesis is whether the issuing companies from the high-volume period of 1992 to 1993 will underperform in the long run. This hypothesis predicts that these stocks will be a disaster for investors.

## REFERENCES

Asquith, Paul, and David W. Mullins, 1986, Equity issues and offering dilution, *Journal of Financial Economics* 15, 61–89.

Banz, Rolf W., 1981, The relationship between return and market value of common stocks, *Journal of Financial Economics* 9, 3–18.

Bayless, Mark, and Susan Chaplinsky, 1993, Favorable pricing and seasoned equity issuance in hot and cold markets, Working paper, Northwestern University.

Chan, Louis K. C., Yasushi Hamao, and Josef Lakonishok, 1991, Fundamentals and stock returns in Japan, *Journal of Finance* 46, 1739–1764.

Choe, Hyuk, Ronald W. Masulis, and Vikram Nanda, 1993, Common stock offerings across the business cycle: Theory and evidence, *Journal of Empirical Finance* 1, 3–31.

Davis, James, 1994, The cross-section of realized returns: The pre-COMPUSTAT evidence, *Journal of Finance* 49, 1579–1593.

De Bondt, Werner F. M., and Richard H. Thaler, 1987, Further evidence on investor overreaction and stock market seasonality, *Journal of Finance* 42, 557–581.

Eckbo, B. Espen, and Ronald W. Masulis, 1995, Seasoned equity offerings: A survey, in R. A. Jarrow, V. Maksimovic, and W. T. Ziemba, Eds.: *North-Holland Handbooks of Operation Research and Management Science: Finance* (North-Holland Publishing Co., Amsterdam).

Fama, Eugene, F., and Kenneth R. French, 1992, The cross-section of expected stock returns, *Journal of Finance* 47, 427–465.

———, David Booth, and Rex Sinquefield, 1993, Differences in the risks and returns of NYSE and NASD stocks, *Financial Analysts Journal* 49, 37–41.

Fama, Eugene F., and James MacBeth, 1973, Risk, return and equilibrium: Empirical tests, *Journal of Political Economy* 81, 607–636.

Friend, Irwin, and J. R. Longstreet, 1967, Price experience and return on new stock issues, in I. Friend, J. Longstreet, M. Mendelson, E. Miller, and A. Hess, Eds.: *Investment Banking and the New Issues Market* (World Publishing Co., Cleveland).

*Going Public: The IPO Reporter*, 1975–1984 (Howard and Co., Philadelphia).

Hanley, Kathleen Weiss, 1993, The underpricing of initial public offerings and the partial adjustment phenomena, *Journal of Financial Economics* 34, 177–197.

Hansen, Robert S., and Claire Crutchley, 1990, Corporate earnings and financing: An empirical analysis, *Journal of Business* 63, 347–371.

Hawawini, Gabriel, and Donald Keim, 1995, On the predictability of common stock returns: World-wide evidence, in R. A. Jarrow, V. Maksimovic, and W. T. Ziemba Eds.: *North-Holland Handbooks of Operation Research and Management Science: Finance* (North-Holland Publishing Co., Amsterdam).

Healy, Paul M., and Krishna G. Palepu, 1990, Earnings and risk changes surrounding primary stock offers, *Journal of Accounting Research* 28, 25–48.

Ikenberry, David, Josef Lakonishok, and Theo Vermaelen, 1994, Market underreaction to open market share repurchases, Working paper, University of Illinois.

*Investment Dealers Digest*, 1970–1974 (New York).

Jain, Bharat A., and Omesh Kini, 1994, The post-issue operating performance of IPO firms, *Journal of Finance* 49, 1699–1726.

Jegadeesh, N., Mark Weinstein, and Ivo Welch, 1993, Initial public offerings and subsequent equity offerings, *Journal of Financial Economics* 34, 153–175.

Kalay, Avner, and Adam Shimrat, 1987, Firm value and seasoned equity issues: Price pressure, wealth redistribution, or negative information, *Journal of Financial Economics* 19, 109–126.

Korajczyk, Robert A., Deborah Lucas, and Robert McDonald, 1990, Understanding stock price behavior around the time of equity issues, in R. Glenn Hubbard, Ed.: *Asymmetric Information, Corporate Finance, and Investment* (University of Chicago Press, Chicago).

Lakonishok, Josef, Andrei Shleifer, and Robert W. Vishny, 1994, Contrarian investment, extrapolation, and risk, *Journal of Finance* 49, 1541–1578.

Lee, Inmoo, 1994, Do firms knowingly sell overvalued equity?, Working paper, University of Illinois.

Lerner, Joshua, 1994, Venture capitalists and the decision to go public, *Journal of Financial Economics* 35, 293–316.

Levis, Mario, 1993a, The long-run performance of initial public offerings: The U.K. experience 1980–88, *Financial Management* 22, 28–41.

———, 1993b, Initial public offerings, subsequent rights issues and long-run performance, Working paper, City University, London.

Loderer, Claudio, Dennis Sheehan, and Gregory Kadlec, 1991, The pricing of equity offerings, *Journal of Financial Economics* 29, 35–57.

Loughran, Tim, 1993, NYSE vs. NASDAQ returns: Market microstructure or the poor performance of Initial Public Offerings?, *Journal of Financial Economics* 33, 241–260.

———, and Jay R. Ritter, 1994, The operating performance of firms conducting seasoned equity offerings, Working paper, University of Iowa.

———, and Kristian Rydqvist, 1994, Initial public offerings: International insights, *Pacific-Basin Finance Journal* 2, 165–199.

Lucas, Deborah, and Robert McDonald, 1990, Equity issues and stock price dynamics, *Journal of Finance* 45, 1019–1043.

Manuel, Timothy A., LeRoy D. Brooks, and Frederick P. Schadler, 1993, Common stock price effects of security issues conditioned by current earnings and dividend announcements, *Journal of Business* 66, 571–593.

Marsh, Paul, 1979, Equity rights issues and the efficiency of the U.K. stock market, *Journal of Finance* 34, 839–862.

Masulis, Ronald W., and Ashok N. Korwar, 1986, Seasoned equity offerings: An empirical investigation, *Journal of Financial Economics* 15, 91–118.

Mikkelson, Wayne H., and H. Megan Partch, 1986, Valuation effects of security offerings and the issuance process, *Journal of Financial Economics* 15, 31–60.

Mikkelson, Wayne H., and Ken Shah, 1994, Performance of companies around initial public offerings, Working paper, University of Oregon.

*Moody's OTC Industrial Manual*, 1973 and 1974 (Moody's, New York).

Muscarella, Chris J., John W. Peavy, and Michael R. Vetsuypens, 1992, Optimal exercise of over-allotment options in IPOs, *Financial Analysts Journal* 48, 76–81.

Nelson, William R., 1994, Do firms buy low and sell high? Working paper, Federal Reserve Board.

Rajan, Raghuram G., and Henri Servaes, 1993, The effect of market conditions on initial public offerings, Working paper, University of Chicago.

Reinganum, Marc R., 1990, Market microstructure and asset pricing: An empirical investigation of NYSE and Nasdaq securities, *Journal of Financial Economics* 28, 127–147.

Ritter, Jay R., 1991, The long-run performance of initial public offerings, *Journal of Finance* 46, 3–27.

Rosenberg, Barr, Kenneth Reid, and Ronald Lanstein, 1985, Persuasive evidence of market inefficiency, *Journal of Portfolio Management* 11, 9–16.

Seyhun, H. Nejat, 1992, Information asymmetry and price performance of IPOs, Working paper, University of Michigan.

Spiess, D. Katherine, and John Affleck-Graves, 1995, The long-run performance following seasoned equity offerings, *Journal of Financial Economics,* Forthcoming.

Stern, Richard L., and Paul Bornstein, 1985, Why new issues are lousy investments, *Forbes* 136, 152–190.

Stigler, George J., 1964, Public regulation of the security market, *Journal of Business* 37, 117–142.

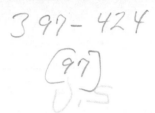

**[14]**

THE JOURNAL OF FINANCE • VOL. LII, NO. 5 • DECEMBER 1997

# The Operating Performance of Firms Conducting Seasoned Equity Offerings

TIM LOUGHRAN and JAY R. RITTER*

**ABSTRACT**

Recent studies have documented that firms conducting seasoned equity offerings have inordinately low stock returns during the five years after the offering, following a sharp run-up in the year prior to the offering. This article documents that the operating performance of issuing firms shows substantial improvement prior to the offering, but then deteriorates. The multiples at the time of the offering, however, do not reflect an expectation of deteriorating performance. Issuing firms are disproportionately high-growth firms, but issuers have much lower subsequent stock returns than nonissuers with the same growth rate.

SEVERAL RECENT EMPIRICAL STUDIES have documented the poor stock market performance of firms conducting seasoned equity offerings (SEOs) in the United States and other countries.[1] Loughran and Ritter (1995) report that the average raw return for issuing firms is only 7 percent per year during the five years after the offering, compared to 15 percent per year for nonissuing firms of the same market capitalization. These low postissue returns follow extremely high returns in the year prior to the offering: 72 percent on average.[2]

This article links the stock price performance of these issuing firms to their operating performance, and in so doing, addresses four questions: 1) Does the postissue operating performance of issuers deteriorate relative to comparable nonissuing firms? 2) Are the patterns for large issuers different from those for small issuers? 3) Do the capital expenditure decisions of issuers suggest that the managers are just as overoptimistic as investors are? 4) Given that issuing firms tend to be rapidly growing, and rapidly growing firms display strong

---

* Loughran is from the University of Iowa, Ritter is from the University of Florida. We thank Brad Barber, David P. Brown, Tom Carroll, Hsuan-chi Chen, Dan Collins, Harry DeAngelo, Linda DeAngelo, Amy Dunbar, Paul Gompers, Charles Hadlock, Robert S. Hansen, Paul Healy, David Ikenberry, Josef Lakonishok, Inmoo Lee, Ronald Masulis, Stewart Myers, John Phillips, Mort Pincus, Kevin Rock, Theodore Sougiannis, Jeremy Stein, René Stulz, Mohan Venkatachalam, Anand Vijh, Xuemin Yan, two anonymous referees, and seminar participants at the NBER, the Milken Institute, the 1995 Illinois-Indiana-Purdue finance conference, the 1996 WFA meetings, Dartmouth, Massachusetts Institute of Technology, Northwestern, Yale, and the Universities of Florida and Iowa for useful comments.

[1] For the US, see Loughran and Ritter (1995) and Spiess and Affleck-Graves (1995), for the United Kingdom, see Levis (1995), and for Japan, see Cai (1996) and Kang, Kim, and Stulz (1996).

[2] Asquith and Mullin (1986), Korajczyk, Lucas, and McDonald (1990), and others also report high returns preceding the seasoned equity offering.

mean reversion in both growth rates and stock returns, is there an independent new issues effect once growth is controlled for?

Our empirical findings are as follows: the operating performance of issuing firms, as measured by numerous accounting measures, peaks at approximately the time of the offering. Using a sample of 1,338 SEOs from 1979–1989, we show that the median profit margin for our issuing firms decreases from 5.4 percent in the fiscal year of the offering to 2.5 percent four years later. The median return on assets (ROA) falls from 6.3 percent to 3.2 percent. The median operating income to assets ratio falls from 15.8 percent to 12.1 percent. These declines are much larger, in both an economic and a statistical sense, than the corresponding declines for nonissuing firms matched by asset size, industry, and operating performance. While these patterns are present for both large and small issuers, the postissue deterioration is more severe for smaller issuers.

We find that many of the issuing firms have improvements in profitability before the offering and declines in profitability after the offering. In and of itself, a pattern where firms issue following a transitory improvement in operations is fully consistent with a semi-strong form efficient market, as Stein's (1989) signal-jamming model demonstrates. The high market-to-book ratios for issuing firms, however, are consistent with the hypothesis that the market expects the recent improvement to be permanent.

Since the market is in general too optimistic about the prospects of issuing firms, we examine whether there are identifiable characteristics that can be used to forecast which groups of issuers will have the worst subsequent operating and investment (stock market) performance. In particular, we test whether the stock market underperformance of issuers is merely a manifestation of the correlation of prior growth rates and subsequent returns.

We find that firms which rapidly increase either sales or capital expenditures have lower subsequent stock returns than other firms. But while issuers are disproportionately fast-growing firms, we find that holding the growth rate constant, issuing firms substantially underperform nonissuers. One interpretation of this is that the firms are investing in what the market views as positive net present value (NPV) projects, but in fact the projects all too often have negative NPVs. We find that issuers continue to invest heavily even while their performance deteriorates. This suggests that the managers are just as overoptimistic about the issuing firms' future profitability as are investors. It is also consistent with Jensen's (1993) hypothesis that corporate culture is excessively focused on growth.

This is not the first article to examine the operating performance of companies conducting SEOs. Healy and Palepu (1990) report that seasoned offering announcements convey no new information about subsequent earnings by the firm. Their issuing sample consists of 93 industrial firms listed on the New York (NYSE) and American (AMEX) Stock Exchanges during 1966–1981. Healy and Palepu find no earnings decline relative to the prior year's earnings either before or after adjusting earnings to an industry median. Hansen and Crutchley (1990), however, find a statistically significant postissue decline in return on assets for their sample of 109 issuing firms during 1975–1982. Even if these findings were not in conflict, however, it is an open question as to whether their findings would generalize to the young Nasdaq-listed growth firms that have predominated among equity issuers in the 1980s and 1990s.

A number of concurrent studies have incorporated Nasdaq-listed issuers in their samples. McLaughlin, Safieddine, and Vasudevan (1996), using a sample similar to ours, document median operating performance patterns consistent with ours. They interpret their findings as consistent with agency and information models of the decision to issue equity. Another contemporaneous study, Cheng (1995), uses 618 SEOs from 1977–1988 to examine the motives of issuers. His cross-sectional results, which are generally inconsistent with ours, will be discussed in Section III.

Two other studies examine the quality of earnings and subsequent stock returns for issuing firms. Teoh, Welch, and Wong (1997), using a sample similar to ours, test an earnings management hypothesis. They find that firms that are more aggressive in the use of discretionary accruals have the worst subsequent investment performance. Rangan (1997), using a sample of 331 SEOs from 1986–1990, also reports that companies making more aggressive use of accruals subsequently underperform.

The organization of the remainder of this article is as follows. Section I describes the seasoned equity data and our matching firm algorithm. Section II presents the empirical findings concerning the time-series of operating performance. Section III presents evidence concerning growth rates, equity issuance, and subsequent stock returns. The last section offers a summary and interpretation of the findings.

## I. Data

The sample consists of all seasoned equity offerings (with at least some primary shares in the offering) of operating companies during 1979 through 1989 on the NYSE, AMEX, and Nasdaq stock exchanges meeting certain criteria.[3] In common with many other studies, we exclude financial institution and regulated utility offerings.[4] The sample of issuing data are purchased from Securities Data Company.

Several data restrictions are present in this study. The issuing firms must be present on the COMPUSTAT (primary industrial, supplementary industrial, tertiary, full coverage, and industrial research) tapes for the fiscal year of the

---

[3] Most of the 1970s are excluded for two reasons: i) because of the survivorship bias in firms for which COMPUSTAT has comprehensive accounting information, and ii) due to the low number of equity issues in the mid to late 1970s. Issues from the 1990s are not included in the sample because of data truncation problems.

[4] See Eckbo and Masulis (1995) for a discussion on the reasons why utility offerings are different from other equity offerings. See Cornett and Tehranian (1994) for a discussion of the market reaction to involuntary bank equity offerings. An additional reason for our exclusion of financial institutions is that their extremely high leverage ratios distort many of our accounting ratios.

offering, and they must be on the University of Chicago Center for Research in Security Prices (CRSP) tapes on the issue date to be included in the sample. The offer must be a cash offer of common stock. Because we examine the multiyear operating performance of issuers, we follow Healy and Palepu's (1990) procedure and exclude SEOs by the same firm during the five years after an SEO that is in our sample. We exclude these offerings in order to reduce dependence for the statistical tests. Thus, once a firm has a seasoned equity offering, that firm cannot reenter the SEO sample until five years from the issue date have passed. This restriction results in the exclusion of 390 SEOs, with more SEOs excluded in the later years of the sample than in the earlier years.[5] Note that because whether or not a firm had previously issued is observable at the time of an issue, we do not introduce an ex post sample selection bias. *We include offers* if the issuing firm has not conducted an SEO within the previous five years, *whether or not this firm subsequently issues again*.

We also require that the book value of assets at the end of the fiscal year of issuing be at least $20 million, measured in terms of dollars of 1993 purchasing power. This requirement deletes an additional 206 SEOs. The only other restriction is that COMPUSTAT data on sales, net income, and operating income are available in the fiscal year of the offering, which deletes 21 additional SEOs. No restriction is made on the length of time the COMPUSTAT numbers must be available before or after the offering.

Panel A of Table I reports the number of SEOs, all of which involve at least some shares issued by the firm, by calendar year. This study contains 1,338 offerings, roughly thirteen times the size of the Healy and Palepu (1990) or Hansen and Crutchley (1990) samples. Twenty-four percent of the sample is in 1983, corresponding to the heavy issuance activity associated with the bull market that commenced in August 1982. Panel B reports the industry classification (using 2-digit Standard Industrial Classification (SIC) codes) for the SEO sample.

As we will document, the median issuer experiences a substantial operating performance decline in the years following the offering. This decline must be compared to a proper benchmark to ensure that the decline is not simply a manifestation of the mean reversion in operating ratios that has been widely documented in the accounting literature. Thus, each issuing firm is matched with a COMPUSTAT-listed nonissuer chosen on the basis of i) industry, ii) asset size, and iii) operating performance. The specific algorithm for choosing a matching firm, suggested by the work of Barber and Lyon (1996), is as follows: Candidate matching firms are those listed on the AMEX, NYSE, or

---

[5] In unreported results, we have analyzed the operating patterns of the 390 issues that we exclude because the firm had conducted an SEO during the prior five years. The qualitative postissue patterns are the same for these issuers as for those that we include: their operating performance deteriorates substantially by year +4. For example, between fiscal years 0 and +4 the median operating income before depreciation and amortization (OIBD)/assets falls from 14.2 percent to 11.4 percent, the median profit margin falls from 5.1 percent to 2.4 percent, and the median market/book falls from 1.98 to 1.42.

### Table I

## Number of Seasoned Equity Offerings (SEOs) by Year and Industry

The sample includes Center for Research in Security Prices (CRSP)-listed Nasdaq, American Stock Exchange (AMEX), and New York Stock Exchange (NYSE) firms that have assets (expressed in dollars of 1993 purchasing power) of at least $20 million at the end of the fiscal year of issuing (year 0). SEOs must have at least some shares issued by the company to be included in the sample. An SEO is excluded if the issue date is within five years after an SEO by the same firm that is in our sample. Regulated utilities (SIC = 481 and 491–494) and financial institutions and their holding companies (SIC = 600–699) are excluded. The industries (defined by CRSP 2-digit Standard Industrial Classification (SIC) codes) listed in Panel B have 45 or more SEOs.

| Panel A: Number of SEOs by Calendar Year | | |
|---|---|---|
| Year | Number of Sample SEOs | Percentage of Sample |
| 1979 | 58 | 4.3% |
| 1980 | 170 | 12.7% |
| 1981 | 126 | 9.4% |
| 1982 | 104 | 7.8% |
| 1983 | 318 | 23.8% |
| 1984 | 55 | 4.1% |
| 1985 | 106 | 7.9% |
| 1986 | 135 | 10.1% |
| 1987 | 120 | 9.0% |
| 1988 | 55 | 4.1% |
| 1989 | 91 | 6.8% |
| Total | 1338 | 100.0% |

| Panel B: Number of SEOs by Industrial Classification | | |
|---|---|---|
| Industry | SIC code | Number of Offerings |
| Office and computer equipment | 35 | 157 |
| Communication and electronic equipment | 36 | 151 |
| Computer and data processing services | 73 | 97 |
| Engineering and scientific instruments | 38 | 73 |
| Oil and gas | 13 | 72 |
| Chemicals, pharmaceuticals, and biotechnology | 28 | 71 |
| Restaurants | 58 | 46 |
| Other | — | 671 |

Nasdaq that have not issued equity during the five years prior to the offering date.[6] From this universe, firms in the same industry (using 2-digit SIC codes)

---

[6] Nonissuers are defined as COMPUSTAT-listed operating companies that have not issued equity (either an initial public offering or SEO) during the prior five years, which report sales (COMPUSTAT data item 12), operating income (item 13), and net income (item 172) in a given calendar year, with at least $20 million in assets (item 6), measured in terms of 1993 purchasing power. Nonissuers must have been listed by CRSP for at least five years. If a nonissuer subsequently issues equity, we do not replace it. If a nonissuer gets delisted, we replace it, on a point-forward basis, with another firm in the same industry with the closest, but higher, OIBD/assets ratio, as of the original ranking date. In choosing a replacement firm, we exclude firms which have issued equity between the original offer date and the replacement date. Twenty-five

with asset size as of the end of year 0 between 25 percent and 200 percent of the issuer are ranked by their year 0 operating income before depreciation and amortization (OIBD) relative to assets. The firm with the closest OIBD/assets ratio from among these nonissuing firms is picked as the matching firm.

If there are no nonissuers in the appropriate industry meeting the above asset-size requirement, a matching firm is then chosen without regard to industry. All nonissuers with asset-size within 90 percent to 110 percent of the issuer are ranked by OIBD/assets, and the firm with the closest, but higher, ratio is chosen as the matching firm.

## II. Time-series Patterns

### A. Performance Measures for Issuers and Nonissuers

Due to the skewness of accounting ratios, it is typical to report median values in studies examining operating performance.[7] In Table II, we report the median operating income to assets ratio, profit margin, return on assets, operating income relative to sales, capital expenditures plus research and development (R&D) expenses relative to assets, and market value of equity relative to book value of equity for the sample of issuing firms.[8] We define operating income (OIBD) as operating income before depreciation, amortization, and taxes, plus interest income. The reason that we include interest income in operating income is that many issuers temporarily "park" some of the proceeds in interest-earning instruments prior to investing it in operating assets. These interest-earning instruments are included in measured assets. OIBD is commonly referred to as EBITDA (earnings before interest, taxes, depreciation, and amortization).

A clear trend is observable for all of the ratios reported in Panel A of Table II. For the median issuer, operating income relative to assets falls to 12.1 percent four years after the offering compared to 15.8 percent in the year of the offering. The median profit margin for issuing firms is 5.4 percent in the fiscal year of the offering, but only 2.5 percent four years after the offering. Return on assets for the median SEO is also halved within four years of the offering. The median market-to-book ratio peaks at 2.40 at the end of the fiscal year

---

percent (335 of 1338) of our matching firms need one or more replacements. When an issuing firm gets delisted we remove its matching firm at the same time. Thus, for both our operating performance and investment performance numbers, we are always comparing issuing firms with an identical number of matched firms, event-year by event-year. For an issuing firm that is present on COMPUSTAT starting in event year $-t$, we choose a matching firm in year 0 that is present on COMPUSTAT in event year $-t$.

[7] DeAngelo (1988), Kaplan (1989), Healy and Palepu (1990), Degeorge and Zeckhauser (1993), Jain and Kini (1994), Mikkelson, Partch, and Shah (1997), and McLaughlin, Safieddine, and Vasudevan (1996), among others, all report median values.

[8] The COMPUSTAT data items for the variables are reported in Table II. If R&D expense is missing for a firm in year $t$, we assume that the value is zero. This assumption is motivated by the fact that firms with no R&D expenses do not list R&D = 0; instead, they omit this line from their income statements. To check the validity of our procedure, we note that almost no biotech firms have missing R&D information, whereas almost all retailers do.

## Table II

## Median Operating Performance Measures and Market-to-Book Ratios for the Issuers and Matching Nonissuers, 1979–1989

Panel A reports median ratios for the 1,338 issuing firms, all of which are present on COMPUSTAT for their issuing year. Matching nonissuing firms are chosen by matching each issuing firm with a firm that has not issued equity during the prior five years using the following algorithm: i) If there is at least one nonissuer in the same two-digit industry with end-of-year 0 assets within 25 percent to 200 percent of the issuing firm, the nonissuer with the closest operating income before depreciation, amortization, and taxes, plus interest income (OIBD)/assets is used; ii) if no nonissuer meets this criteria, then all nonissuers with year 0 assets of 90 percent to 110 percent of the issuer are ranked, and the firm with the closest, but higher, OIBD/assets is used. Panel B reports the median ratios for these nonissuers. If a nonissuer is delisted from COMPUSTAT while the issuer is still trading, a replacement nonissuing firm is spliced in on a point-forward basis. The COMPUSTAT data items for the variables are operating income before depreciation/assets (OIBD + interest income (items 13 + 62)/assets (item 6)), profit margin (net income including extraordinary items (item 172)/sales (item 12)), return on assets (net income (item 172)/assets (item 6)), OIBD/sales (OIBD + interest income (items 13 + 62)/sales (item 12)), CE + RD/assets (capital expenditures (item 128) + research and development expense (item 46)/assets (item 6)), market value/book value (shares (item 54) times price (item 199)/book value of equity (item 60)).

| Fiscal Year Relative to Offering | OIBD/ Assets | Profit Margin | ROA | OIBD/ Sales | CE + RD/ Assets | Market/ Book | Number of Firms |
|---|---|---|---|---|---|---|---|
| | | | Panel A: Issuer Medians | | | | |
| −4 | 16.1% | 4.0% | 5.8% | 11.3% | 8.2% | 1.20 | 920 |
| −3 | 16.6% | 4.2% | 6.0% | 11.5% | 8.5% | 1.42 | 1,051 |
| −2 | 16.4% | 4.4% | 6.0% | 12.3% | 9.9% | 1.59 | 1,242 |
| −1 | 17.0% | 4.8% | 6.4% | 13.1% | 10.2% | 2.40 | 1,327 |
| 0 | 15.8% | 5.4% | 6.3% | 13.8% | 10.0% | 1.96 | 1,338 |
| +1 | 14.2% | 4.3% | 5.3% | 12.3% | 10.6% | 1.68 | 1,298 |
| +2 | 12.7% | 3.3% | 3.9% | 11.2% | 9.3% | 1.65 | 1,227 |
| +3 | 12.1% | 2.7% | 3.3% | 11.3% | 8.7% | 1.58 | 1,158 |
| +4 | 12.1% | 2.5% | 3.2% | 10.7% | 8.1% | 1.43 | 1,084 |
| | | | Panel B: Nonissuer Medians | | | | |
| −4 | 16.4% | 4.3% | 6.1% | 11.4% | 5.0% | 1.04 | 920 |
| −3 | 15.6% | 3.9% | 5.8% | 11.1% | 5.4% | 1.12 | 1,051 |
| −2 | 15.4% | 3.7% | 5.3% | 10.8% | 5.6% | 1.19 | 1,242 |
| −1 | 15.1% | 3.7% | 5.5% | 10.7% | 5.7% | 1.30 | 1,327 |
| 0 | 15.8% | 3.9% | 5.7% | 11.2% | 5.9% | 1.45 | 1,338 |
| +1 | 15.2% | 3.8% | 5.3% | 10.9% | 6.5% | 1.41 | 1,298 |
| +2 | 14.1% | 3.7% | 4.8% | 10.7% | 6.5% | 1.43 | 1,227 |
| +3 | 13.8% | 3.4% | 4.6% | 10.4% | 6.6% | 1.48 | 1,158 |
| +4 | 13.5% | 3.3% | 4.2% | 10.4% | 6.6% | 1.44 | 1,084 |

Panel C: Z-Statistics Testing the Yearly Equality of Distributions Between the SEOs and Matching Nonissuers Using the Wilcoxon Matched-Pairs Signed-Ranks Test

| | OIBD/ Assets | Profit Margin | ROA | OIBD/ Sales | CE + RD/ Assets | Market/ Book | Number of Firms |
|---|---|---|---|---|---|---|---|
| −4 | −0.92 | −1.97 | −2.10 | −0.51 | 12.00 | 3.65 | 920 |
| −3 | 2.87 | 0.51 | 1.12 | 1.81 | 13.69 | 5.64 | 1,051 |
| −2 | 4.73 | 2.77 | 3.42 | 4.21 | 16.16 | 8.87 | 1,242 |
| −1 | 7.68 | 6.98 | 6.58 | 8.07 | 17.10 | 16.98 | 1,327 |
| 0 | −1.06 | 9.06 | 6.50 | 8.64 | 15.46 | 10.36 | 1,338 |
| +1 | −3.02 | 3.15 | 0.35 | 3.71 | 14.55 | 7.52 | 1,298 |
| +2 | −5.29 | −2.77 | −5.26 | 0.60 | 11.24 | 4.11 | 1,227 |
| +3 | −5.40 | −5.07 | −6.58 | 0.18 | 8.64 | 1.74 | 1,158 |
| +4 | −4.43 | −4.89 | −5.76 | 0.68 | 7.91 | −0.51 | 1,084 |

Panel D: Z-Statistics Testing the Equality of Distributions Between the Change in the Ratios from Year 0 to Year +4 Using the Wilcoxon Matched-Pairs Signed-Ranks Test

| Time Period | OIBD/ Assets | Profit Margin | ROA | OIBD/ Sales | CE + RD/ Assets | Market/ Book | Number of Changes |
|---|---|---|---|---|---|---|---|
| Year 0 to +4 | −4.59 | −6.30 | −5.57 | −5.46 | −5.96 | −8.52 | 1,084 |

before the offering, and falls to 1.43 four years after the offering. All six of the ratios peak at about the time of the offering, only to rapidly decline in the following years. Note that the postissue decline in the market-to-book ratio is in spite of the substantial increase in this ratio for the market as a whole during the 1980s and 1990s.

Panel B of Table II reports the median values for nonissuers. Since we are matching partly on the basis of OIBD/assets, it is not surprising that both the issuers and nonissuers have the same year 0 median value of 15.8 percent for OIBD/assets. For nonissuing firms, the median operating income relative to assets, profit margin, return on assets, and operating income relative to sales ratios decline in the four years after the fiscal year of the offering. Barber and Lyon (1996) report a downtrend in these ratios for COMPUSTAT-listed, AMEX and NYSE firms during our sample period.

Figure 1 plots the issuer and nonissuer median values, as reported in Panels A and B of Table II, for operating income relative to assets, profit margin, and capital expenditures plus R&D expense relative to assets, during the four years before and after the offering. Several years prior to issuing, issuers and nonissuers have the same level of profitability, although issuers are investing more. In the year before the offering, the median issuer's operating performance substantially improves relative to the median nonissuer. In the years after the offering, however, the median issuer's performance rapidly deteriorates relative to the nonissuers. The falloff in OIBD relative to assets is especially noteworthy, given the heavy investment (capital expenditures plus R&D expense) before and after the offering.

To measure statistical significance, we compute $Z$-statistics to conduct Wilcoxon matched-pairs signed-rank tests of the hypothesis that the distribution of issuer and nonissuer ratios are identical. Letting the difference in the accounting measure (for example, OIBD/assets) between issuer $i$ and its matching firm be denoted by $d_i = \text{Measure}(\text{SEO}_i) - \text{Measure}(\text{matching}_i)$, we rank the absolute values of the $d_i$ values from 1 to $n$ (for year 0, $n = 1,338$). We then sum the ranks of the positive values of $d_i$, with this sum denoted as $D$. The $Z$-statistics are computed as

$$Z = \frac{D - E(D)}{\sigma_D} \tag{1}$$

$$E(D) = \frac{n(n+1)}{4} \tag{2}$$

$$\sigma_D^2 = \frac{n(n+1)(2n+1)}{24} \tag{3}$$

Under the null hypothesis that the issuer and nonissuer accounting measures are drawn from the same distribution, $Z$ follows a unit normal distribution.

In Panel C of Table II, we report year-by-year $Z$-statistics. The year 0 ratios for issuers dominate those for nonissuers, except for OIBD/assets. (Since our

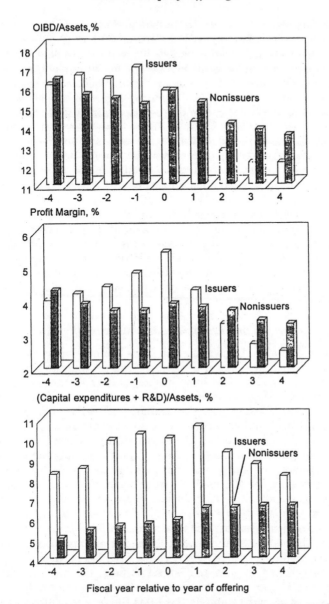

**Figure 1. Operating income before depreciation, amortization, and taxes, plus interest income (OIBD)/assets (top), profit margins (middle), and (capital expenditures + research & development expenses (R&D))/assets (bottom) for the median issuer and nonissuer.** The numbers plotted are reported in Table II for the nine fiscal years centered on the fiscal year of the offering for 1,338 firms conducting seasoned equity offerings during 1979–1989 with at least $20 million in assets, measured in terms of 1993 purchasing power, at the end of the fiscal year of the offering. Nonissuing firms are matched by asset size, OIBD/assets, and industry.

matching-firm algorithm uses OIBD/assets to choose nonissuers, the lack of a difference in the distributions is to be expected.) For all six ratios, Panel D reports statistically significant deterioration in the ratios between years 0 and +4 for the issuers relative to the nonissuers. For example, the $Z$-statistic on the change in OIBD/assets for issuers relative to nonissuers between years 0 and +4 is −4.59.[9]

To provide further information on the dispersion of profit margins among issuers and their matching firms, in Figure 2 we present histograms of the profit margins of issuers and nonissuers in year 0, and, for the surviving firms, in year +4. Inspection of Figure 2 shows that at the time of issuing, relatively few issuers have substantially negative profit margins. By year +4, however, issuers are overrepresented among firms reporting large losses per dollar of sales.

While we report median ratios in this article, in unreported results we find that the patterns hold in the aggregate as well. In particular, the combined sales and assets for our issuing firms increase in the four years after issuing, while the combined profits decrease. In addition to examining median ratios, we have also analyzed the patterns using mean ratios (after winsorizing the top and bottom 1 percent of the observations), with qualitatively similar patterns.

## B. *Operating Performance Categorized by Asset-Size Quartiles*

To examine whether large and small firms exhibit similar declines in operating performance, we categorize issuing firms by their year 0 assets (measured in terms of dollars of 1993 purchasing power). Four categories are used, with the cutoffs being assets of $55.4 million, $120.8 million, and $351 million.[10] In Table III we report the median OIBD/assets (Panel A) and the median profit margin (Panel B) for issuers and nonissuers by size quartile for the nine fiscal years centered on the year of the offering. In Figure 3, we illustrate the patterns for each of the size quartiles using the median OIBD/assets of issuers and nonissuers. In general, there is a deterioration in operating performance for the median issuer relative to the median nonissuer during the years after the offer, for both large and small firms. The deterioration from year 0 to year +4 is usually, but not always, statistically significant at conventional levels. As is true in almost all studies, the changes tend to be somewhat larger for the smaller firms. For example, among the smallest issuers the median profit margin declines from 5.8 percent in year 0 to 1.3 percent in year +4. Among the largest issuers, the median profit margin declines from 4.2 percent to 2.9 percent. If we delete the smallest quartile of firms (i.e., restrict our sample to the 1,003 SEOs with postissue assets of at least $55 million), the median OIBD/assets for issuing firms is 15.9 percent in

---

[9] When the sample is split into two subperiods, deterioration of the issuer ratios relative to the nonissuer ratios is present in both subperiods.

[10] Although the median value of assets is $121 million, the average is $730 million.

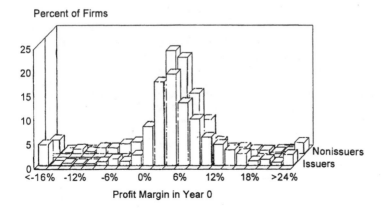

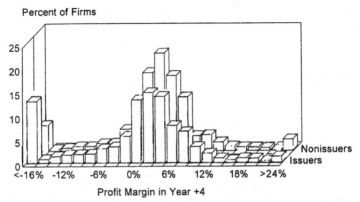

**Figure 2. Profit margins in year 0 (top) and in year +4 (bottom) for issuers and nonissuers.** The fiscal year 0 histogram is for 1,338 issuing firms and their size-, operating income before depreciation, amortization, and taxes, plus interest income (OIBD)/assets-, and industry-matched nonissuing firms for the fiscal year in which the seasoned equity offering was conducted. The fiscal year +4 histogram is for the 1,084 COMPUSTAT-listed surviving issuing firms and their matching firms. For each firm, the profit margin is defined as the net income, including extraordinary items, divided by annual sales. The profit margin categories are defined in terms of their lower bound: the 0 percent category represents firms with profit margins of 0.1 percent to 2.0 percent.

year 0 and 12.7 percent in year +4. The median profit margin for issuing firms is 5.2 percent in year 0 and 2.9 percent year +4.

Although we have followed the convention in the operating performance literature and reported median operating performance ratios in Tables II and III, there are serious conceptual problems with the use of median ratios to evaluate performance. In particular, for both investors and for the general economy, it matters a great deal whether there is a positive covariance between operating performance ratios and changes in scale. To be specific, a highly profitable firm that expands in size can more than offset several less-

### Table III

## Median Operating Ratios for Issuer and Matching Nonissuer Firms Categorized by Asset Size Quartiles, for 1,338 Seasoned Equity Offerings (SEOs) from 1979–1989

Assets are measured (in dollars of 1993 purchasing power) at the end of the fiscal year (year 0) during which the offering occurred, and after pooling all 1,338 issuing firms together, companies are then ranked and assigned to quartiles. Matching (nonissuer) firms are chosen on the basis of industry, size, and OIBD/assets. In Panel A, OIBD/assets is defined as operating income before depreciation and amortization, plus interest income, divided by end-of-year assets. In Panel B, profit margin is defined as net income including extraordinary items divided by sales. The Z-statistics test the equality of distributions for matched pairs of observations using the Wilcoxon signed-ranks test.

| | | | | Fiscal Year Relative to the Year of Issuing | | | | | | |
|---|---|---|---|---|---|---|---|---|---|---|
| | −4 | −3 | −2 | −1 | 0 | +1 | +2 | +3 | +4 | 0 to +4 |
| Panel A: Median OIBD/Assets for the Nine Fiscal Years Centered on the Year of Issuing | | | | | | | | | | |
| First Quartile (Postissue Assets Between $20 Million and $55 Million) | | | | | | | | | | |
| Issuers | 15.3% | 16.2% | 17.8% | 18.6% | 15.2% | 12.8% | 9.0% | 9.2% | 10.2% | |
| Nonissuers | 14.5% | 14.5% | 14.4% | 14.3% | 14.9% | 14.2% | 13.2% | 12.6% | 12.0% | |
| Z-statistic | −0.18 | 0.95 | 3.24 | 5.44 | −1.03 | −3.61 | −4.49 | −4.37 | −3.22 | −3.64 |
| Second Quartile (Postissue Assets Between $55 Million and $121 Million) | | | | | | | | | | |
| Issuers | 16.6% | 17.8% | 17.7% | 18.8% | 16.7% | 15.6% | 13.3% | 12.0% | 12.3% | |
| Nonissuers | 16.4% | 14.6% | 14.9% | 16.0% | 16.7% | 15.1% | 14.6% | 13.6% | 14.1% | |
| Z-statistic | 1.47 | 4.33 | 4.30 | 5.55 | 0.84 | −0.76 | −1.97 | −1.78 | −1.94 | −2.16 |
| Third Quartile (Postissue Assets Between $121 Million and $351 Million) | | | | | | | | | | |
| Issuers | 16.3% | 17.1% | 16.3% | 16.7% | 16.0% | 14.3% | 12.9% | 12.6% | 12.5% | |
| Nonissuers | 16.8% | 16.4% | 16.0% | 15.7% | 16.2% | 15.9% | 14.2% | 13.2% | 13.1% | |
| Z-statistic | −0.53 | 1.02 | 1.69 | 3.55 | −0.85 | −1.15 | −2.10 | −1.93 | −0.67 | −0.41 |
| Fourth Quartile (Postissue Assets Between $351 Million and $86 Million) | | | | | | | | | | |
| Issuers | 15.8% | 15.8% | 15.1% | 14.7% | 14.9% | 14.4% | 13.7% | 13.3% | 13.0% | |
| Nonissuers | 16.7% | 16.1% | 16.1% | 15.1% | 14.9% | 15.4% | 15.1% | 14.9% | 14.6% | |
| Z-statistic | −2.80 | −0.89 | −0.58 | −0.70 | −0.96 | −0.25 | −1.82 | −2.82 | −2.86 | −2.99 |
| Panel B: Median Profit Margins for the Nine Fiscal Years Centered on the Year of Issuing | | | | | | | | | | |
| First Quartile (Postissue Assets Between $20 Million and $55 Million) | | | | | | | | | | |
| Issuers | 3.5% | 3.9% | 4.7% | 5.0% | 5.8% | 4.0% | 2.3% | 1.9% | 1.3% | |
| Nonissuers | 3.6% | 3.6% | 3.3% | 3.4% | 3.7% | 3.5% | 3.1% | 3.0% | 2.5% | |
| Z-statistic | −1.42 | 0.25 | 1.72 | 4.20 | 4.91 | 1.23 | −2.82 | −3.23 | −3.27 | −3.20 |
| Second Quartile (Postissue Assets Between $55 Million and $121 Million) | | | | | | | | | | |
| Issuers | 4.3% | 4.2% | 4.5% | 6.0% | 6.3% | 5.2% | 4.0% | 3.3% | 3.3% | |
| Nonissuers | 3.6% | 3.4% | 3.3% | 3.9% | 4.2% | 4.0% | 4.0% | 3.4% | 3.0% | |
| Z-statistic | 1.21 | 1.95 | 2.77 | 5.44 | 5.94 | 2.97 | −0.40 | −0.63 | 0.55 | −1.43 |
| Third Quartile (Postissue Assets Between $121 Million and $351 Million) | | | | | | | | | | |
| Issuers | 3.8% | 4.2% | 4.1% | 4.8% | 5.3% | 4.3% | 2.9% | 2.3% | 2.5% | |
| Nonissuers | 4.3% | 4.2% | 3.8% | 3.4% | 4.0% | 3.7% | 3.6% | 3.0% | 3.4% | |
| Z-statistic | −2.27 | −0.05 | 1.04 | 3.25 | 4.26 | 0.90 | −1.44 | −3.27 | −2.26 | −3.07 |
| Fourth Quartile (Postissue Assets Between $351 Million and $86 Billion) | | | | | | | | | | |
| Issuers | 4.4% | 4.3% | 4.0% | 3.7% | 4.2% | 4.2% | 3.7% | 3.2% | 2.9% | |
| Nonissuers | 4.7% | 4.5% | 4.4% | 4.1% | 3.9% | 4.2% | 3.9% | 3.8% | 3.8% | |
| Z-statistic | −1.46 | −1.36 | −0.63 | 0.23 | 2.23 | 0.83 | −1.04 | −3.26 | −3.94 | −4.87 |

profitable firms that shrink. The use of medians does not capture the extent of this covariation.

One approach that will capture the covariation of profitability and scale changes is to calculate a portfolio ratio, using the aggregate numerator divided by the aggregate denominator. The two disadvantages of doing this are that a few large firms can dominate the ratio, and significance levels are difficult to calculate. To reduce this first problem, in Table IV we calculate portfolio profitability measures after categorizing firms by asset-size quartile. We do not calculate significance levels.

As an example, for the smallest quartile, we calculate the portfolio profit margin of 4.1 percent in event year 0 by adding up the profits of all 335 issuers, and dividing by the aggregate sales of these 335 firms. For each of the other eight fiscal years, we do the same, with the restriction that we can only use the firms listed on COMPUSTAT. In Panel B of Table IV, we report the portfolio ratios for nonissuing firms.

Inspection of Table IV shows that, at the portfolio level, issuers underperform relative to nonissuers in all size quartiles. There is one noteworthy difference, however, between the largest issuers and other issuers. Whereas the issuing firms in the smallest three quartiles tend to issue after a period of improving operating performance, the largest issuers sell stock after years of undistinguished performance. The qualitative conclusions are similar to those obtained from the medians reported in Table III.

Tables III and IV show that issuing firms have high levels of capital expenditures plus R&D both before and after issuing, in spite of a postissue deterioration in operating margins. This suggests that managers are just as optimistic as investors are about the existence of positive NPV investment opportunities.

## C. Operating Performance Categorized by Pure Primary versus Combination Offerings

Healy and Palepu (1990) report no postissue operating performance decline for the median issuer using a sample of 93 SEOs in which all of the shares offered were newly-issued by the firm (pure primary offerings). This is in contrast to our Tables II–IV findings of underperformance for issuing firms. One of the dimensions on which our sample differs from that of Healy and Palepu is that 40 percent of our sample is comprised of combination offerings, in which some of the shares being issued are coming from existing shareholders.

In Table V, we address whether the operating performance patterns differ between pure primary and combination SEOs. In Panels A and B, we report the median OIBD/assets ratios for, respectively, pure primary and combination offerings. Inspection of Panels A and B shows similar qualitative patterns. In Panels C and D, we report the median profit margins for, respectively, pure primary and combination offerings. Once again, the qualitative patterns are

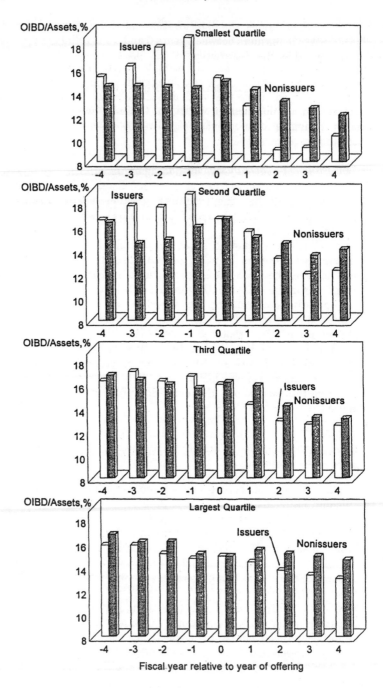

Fiscal year relative to year of offering

similar.[11] In all four panels, the deterioration in the operating performance of issuers relative to nonissuers between years 0 and +4 is reliably different from zero, as measured by the $Z$-statistics.

## III. Operating Performance Changes and Stock Returns

In this section, we document a variety of cross-sectional relations between the prior operating performance of issuing firms and their subsequent market-adjusted stock returns.

### A. The Investment Performance of Issuing Firms

In general, we measure the subsequent stock return on a portfolio by computing the average annual return on the issuing firms during the five years after issuing. We compute the average annual arithmetic return on portfolio $p$ as

$$r_p = \frac{1}{n} \sum_{t=1}^{5} \sum_{i=1}^{n_t} r_{it} \qquad (4)$$

where $r_{it}$ is the annual return on firm $i$ in event-year $t$, $n_t$ is the number of surviving firms in event-year $t$, and $n$ is the total number of firm-year observations. Thus, a firm that is CRSP-listed in the five years after the issue date will have five annual returns counted, whereas a firm that is delisted after 2.5 years will have three annual returns counted. For firms that are delisted during a year, we compute the annual return by splicing in the CRSP value-weighted NYSE-AMEX index return (inclusive of dividends) for the remainder of the year. In computing returns, we measure time relative to the date of the offering (event-time). Thus, in general the stock returns are computed over periods that do not correspond directly to the fiscal years that we use for all of the operating performance measures. For our tests of the relation between growth, issuing activity, and stock returns, we compute portfolio returns using the five years starting on the June 30 after the fiscal year of issuing, in order

---

[11] Primary offerings tend to be from larger firms than combination offerings. When we control for size, the lack of a distinction between primary and combination offerings continues to hold.

---

**Figure 3. Median OIBD/assets for issuers and nonissuers for the 4 years before and after the fiscal year of issuing, by asset-size quartiles.** OIBD/assets, as reported in Panel A of Table III, is calculated as operating income before depreciation and amortization, with interest income added, divided by the end-of-year assets. Issuers have end of fiscal year 0 assets of $20 million to $55.4 million in the smallest quartile, $55.4 million to $120.8 million in the second quartile, $120.8 million to $351 million in the third quartile, and $351 million to $86 billion in the largest quartile. All of the assets are measured in terms of 1993 purchasing power. The issuing sample is comprised of 1,338 seasoned equity offerings during 1979–1989. The nonissuing sample is constructed by matching each issuer with a COMPUSTAT-listed firm chosen on the basis of industry, year 0 assets, and OIBD/assets, that has not issued equity during the prior five years.

### Table IV

## Operating Performance Measures for Issuers and Their Matching Firms Categorized by Asset Size Quartiles, with Performance Measures Calculated as the Portfolio Aggregate Numerator Divided by the Portfolio Aggregate Denominator, for 1,338 Seasoned Equity Offerings from 1979–1989

Assets are measured (in dollars of 1993 purchasing power) at the end of the fiscal year (year 0) during which the seasoned equity offering occurred, and after pooling all 1,338 issuing firms together, companies are then ranked and assigned to quartiles. The COMPUSTAT data items for the variables are profit margin (net income (item 172)/sales (item 121)), return on assets (net income (item 172)/assets (item 6)), operating income before depreciation/assets (OIBD + interest income (items 13 + 62)/assets (item 6)), CE + RD/assets (capital expenditures (item 128) + research and development expense (item 46)/assets (item 6)), market value/book value (shares (item 54) times price (item 199)/book value of equity (item 60)). Panel A reports the portfolio ratios for issuing firms, and Panel B reports the portfolio ratios for asset size-, year 0 OIBD/assets-, and industry-matched nonissuing firms.

| Fiscal Year Relative to Offering | N | Panel A: Issuing Firms | | | | | Panel B: Matching Firms | | | | |
|---|---|---|---|---|---|---|---|---|---|---|---|
| | | Profit Margin | ROA | OIBD/ Assets | CE + RD/ Assets | Market/ Book | Profit Margin | ROA | OIBD/ Assets | CE + RD/ Assets | Market/ Book |
| First Quartile (Postissue Assets Between $20 Million to $55 Million) | | | | | | | | | | | |
| −4 | 197 | 0.4 | 0.6 | 11.5 | 9.6 | 1.71 | 2.2 | 3.1 | 12.8 | 5.7 | 1.37 |
| −3 | 248 | 2.4 | 3.4 | 13.7 | 10.0 | 2.23 | 3.2 | 4.6 | 13.3 | 6.2 | 1.46 |
| −2 | 304 | 2.9 | 4.1 | 15.5 | 12.1 | 2.51 | 1.4 | 2.2 | 12.9 | 7.0 | 1.51 |
| −1 | 331 | 4.0 | 5.5 | 17.1 | 13.9 | 3.81 | 1.8 | 2.7 | 13.2 | 7.2 | 1.65 |
| 0 | 335 | 4.1 | 4.6 | 14.1 | 13.2 | 2.81 | 2.7 | 4.0 | 14.4 | 7.3 | 1.80 |
| 1 | 324 | 1.8 | 2.0 | 11.4 | 13.9 | 2.55 | 2.4 | 3.4 | 13.8 | 7.9 | 1.81 |
| 2 | 303 | 0.2 | 0.3 | 9.7 | 12.4 | 2.35 | 2.2 | 3.1 | 12.8 | 8.5 | 1.79 |
| 3 | 287 | 0.6 | 0.7 | 10.5 | 11.8 | 2.49 | 2.5 | 3.5 | 12.9 | 8.1 | 1.94 |
| 4 | 266 | 0.0 | −0.1 | 10.2 | 10.8 | 2.37 | 1.9 | 2.7 | 12.5 | 7.6 | 1.97 |
| Second Quartile (Postissue Assets Between $55 Million to $121 Million) | | | | | | | | | | | |
| −4 | 181 | 2.5 | 3.9 | 15.1 | 9.8 | 1.78 | 3.2 | 4.5 | 14.8 | 5.5 | 1.27 |
| −3 | 221 | 2.7 | 4.2 | 16.7 | 10.1 | 2.09 | 2.0 | 2.9 | 13.6 | 6.4 | 1.41 |
| −2 | 300 | 3.1 | 4.8 | 16.5 | 12.0 | 2.20 | 2.0 | 3.0 | 14.3 | 6.8 | 1.56 |
| −1 | 332 | 4.8 | 7.1 | 18.4 | 13.4 | 3.36 | 2.7 | 4.2 | 15.8 | 7.0 | 1.80 |
| 0 | 334 | 5.6 | 7.1 | 16.9 | 13.0 | 2.69 | 3.8 | 5.8 | 17.2 | 7.6 | 1.94 |
| 1 | 322 | 4.0 | 4.9 | 15.0 | 14.3 | 2.70 | 3.7 | 5.4 | 16.1 | 8.3 | 1.95 |
| 2 | 301 | 2.7 | 3.1 | 14.1 | 12.9 | 2.70 | 3.4 | 4.6 | 14.9 | 8.7 | 2.08 |
| 3 | 279 | 2.6 | 2.9 | 13.0 | 12.3 | 2.59 | 2.3 | 3.1 | 14.1 | 9.1 | 2.08 |
| 4 | 258 | 2.6 | 2.7 | 11.8 | 10.2 | 2.47 | 2.2 | 2.9 | 14.2 | 8.0 | 2.18 |
| Third Quartile (Postissue Assets Between $121 Million to $351 Million) | | | | | | | | | | | |
| −4 | 241 | 2.8 | 5.0 | 16.3 | 8.7 | 1.50 | 4.0 | 6.1 | 17.2 | 6.3 | 1.33 |
| −3 | 269 | 3.0 | 5.2 | 16.4 | 9.6 | 1.68 | 3.8 | 5.5 | 16.5 | 6.5 | 1.50 |
| −2 | 312 | 3.0 | 4.9 | 15.9 | 11.3 | 1.98 | 3.2 | 4.7 | 15.8 | 7.1 | 1.58 |
| −1 | 333 | 3.8 | 5.7 | 16.4 | 12.2 | 2.64 | 3.0 | 4.4 | 15.2 | 7.1 | 1.73 |
| 0 | 335 | 4.5 | 6.1 | 15.9 | 12.1 | 2.54 | 3.7 | 5.4 | 16.0 | 7.4 | 1.99 |
| 1 | 325 | 3.2 | 4.2 | 14.5 | 13.1 | 2.41 | 3.1 | 4.4 | 15.1 | 8.3 | 1.94 |
| 2 | 308 | 2.1 | 2.6 | 13.0 | 12.0 | 2.31 | 3.1 | 4.3 | 15.0 | 8.5 | 2.08 |
| 3 | 295 | 1.1 | 1.4 | 13.0 | 11.8 | 2.47 | 3.2 | 4.3 | 14.5 | 8.1 | 2.06 |
| 4 | 275 | 1.2 | 1.5 | 13.2 | 10.9 | 2.55 | 3.1 | 4.1 | 13.6 | 8.0 | 1.91 |
| Fourth Quartile (Postissue Assets Between $351 Million to $86 Billion) | | | | | | | | | | | |
| −4 | 301 | 3.3 | 4.2 | 14.0 | 11.2 | 1.12 | 3.5 | 5.0 | 15.3 | 7.6 | 1.11 |
| −3 | 313 | 2.9 | 3.6 | 13.4 | 10.1 | 1.23 | 3.7 | 5.1 | 15.3 | 7.6 | 1.19 |
| −2 | 326 | 3.3 | 4.1 | 14.3 | 9.8 | 1.21 | 4.1 | 5.7 | 15.7 | 7.6 | 1.27 |
| −1 | 331 | 2.6 | 3.1 | 13.2 | 9.8 | 1.36 | 3.4 | 4.5 | 15.1 | 7.8 | 1.35 |
| 0 | 334 | 3.5 | 3.9 | 13.4 | 9.9 | 1.44 | 3.6 | 4.6 | 14.4 | 7.3 | 1.54 |
| 1 | 327 | 3.1 | 3.4 | 13.3 | 10.2 | 1.44 | 3.7 | 4.8 | 14.7 | 8.0 | 1.54 |
| 2 | 315 | 3.0 | 3.3 | 12.2 | 9.2 | 1.48 | 4.0 | 5.0 | 15.4 | 8.0 | 1.72 |
| 3 | 297 | 2.8 | 2.8 | 11.8 | 8.0 | 1.54 | 3.7 | 4.1 | 14.3 | 7.3 | 1.86 |
| 4 | 285 | 2.2 | 2.1 | 11.8 | 8.2 | 1.56 | 3.8 | 4.1 | 13.9 | 7.4 | 1.89 |

Table V

## Median OIBD/Assets and Profit Margin for Issuers and Matching Nonissuing Firms Categorized by Pure Primary versus Combination Offerings, for 1,338 SEOs from 1979–1989

Pure primary offerings are those where all of the shares sold in a seasoned equity offering (SEO) are newly-issued by the firm. Combination offerings are those where some of the shares are newly-issued, and some are being sold by existing shareholders. In Panels A and B, OIBD/assets is defined as operating income before depreciation and amortization, plus interest income, divided by end-of-year assets. In Panels C and D, profit margin is defined as net income including extraordinary items divided by sales. The Z-statistic tests the equality of distributions for matched pairs of observations using the Wilcoxon matched-pairs signed-ranks test.

| | \multicolumn{9}{c}{Fiscal Year Relative to the Year of Issuing} | |
| | −4 | −3 | −2 | −1 | 0 | +1 | +2 | +3 | +4 | 0 to +4 |
|---|---|---|---|---|---|---|---|---|---|---|
| \multicolumn{11}{l}{Panel A: Median OIBD/Assets for Pure Primary Offerings ($N = 806$)} |
| SEOs | 15.6 | 15.6 | 15.0 | 15.4 | 14.8 | 13.9 | 12.4 | 12.0 | 11.8 | |
| Matching | 16.5 | 15.7 | 15.1 | 14.7 | 14.9 | 14.8 | 14.2 | 13.8 | 13.1 | |
| Z-statistic | −1.28 | 0.65 | 0.68 | 3.22 | −1.66 | −1.76 | −4.41 | −5.19 | −3.04 | −2.88 |
| \multicolumn{11}{l}{Panel B: Median OIBD/Assets for Combination Offerings ($N = 532$)} |
| SEOs | 16.6 | 18.5 | 18.5 | 19.6 | 16.7 | 14.7 | 13.3 | 12.7 | 12.6 | |
| Matching | 16.1 | 15.1 | 15.9 | 15.9 | 16.8 | 15.5 | 14.0 | 13.7 | 14.2 | |
| Z-statistic | 0.25 | 3.79 | 6.41 | 7.98 | 0.39 | −2.56 | −3.06 | −2.37 | −3.31 | −3.74 |
| \multicolumn{11}{l}{Panel C: Median Profit Margin for Pure Primary Offerings ($N = 806$)} |
| SEOs | 4.2 | 4.2 | 4.0 | 4.2 | 5.0 | 4.3 | 3.3 | 2.4 | 2.4 | |
| Matching | 4.4 | 4.1 | 3.9 | 3.7 | 3.9 | 3.8 | 3.8 | 3.7 | 3.3 | |
| Z-statistic | −1.53 | −0.17 | −0.10 | 1.96 | 4.94 | 1.91 | −1.85 | −5.31 | −4.29 | −5.54 |
| \multicolumn{11}{l}{Panel D: Median Profit Margin for Combination Offerings ($N = 532$)} |
| SEOs | 3.8 | 4.2 | 4.8 | 5.7 | 6.0 | 4.3 | 3.5 | 2.9 | 2.7 | |
| Matching | 3.8 | 3.7 | 3.4 | 3.7 | 4.0 | 3.8 | 3.5 | 3.0 | 3.3 | |
| Z-statistic | −1.23 | 1.07 | 4.56 | 8.65 | 8.37 | 2.66 | −2.16 | −1.34 | −2.46 | −3.20 |

to permit investors, prior to forming portfolios, to observe the operating performance numbers used in computing growth rates.

In Table VI, we present evidence on the degree to which the market is surprised by the poor postissue operating performance of issuing firms. In Panel A we report the average stock price runup in the year before the offer date, and the average annual return during the subsequent five years, for the same asset-size quartiles as used in Tables III and IV. We also report the average annual return on the CRSP value-weighted NYSE-AMEX index, and the average annual return on our nonissuing firms purchased at the same time as the issuing firms.

## Table VI

### Average Annual Returns of Issuers, Matching Nonissuing Firms, and the Market, during the Five Years after Issuing

In Panel A, the average annual returns are calculated for the 1,338 companies conducting seasoned equity offerings (SEOs) in 1979–1989 meeting the criteria used in this article. Matching (nonissuer) firms are chosen on the basis of industry, asset size, and OIBD/assets where OIBD is operating income before depreciation, amortization, and taxes, plus interest income. 1-year and 5-year return periods are measured from the issue date, rather than using fiscal years. The average CRSP value-weighted (VW) NYSE-AMEX market return during the prior year is 27.4 percent. Index returns are calculated by compounding the daily CRSP value-weighted NYSE-AMEX index over the same trading days. In Panel A, the number of firm-years is calculated by summing, over the number of firms in a portfolio, the number of post-issue event-years for which the firm is listed on the CRSP tapes for at least part of a year. For the majority of firms, this is 5 years. For a firm that is delisted early, it may be less than 5 years. Firms in the smallest quartile have postissue assets (in 1993 dollars) of $20 to $55.4 million, those in quartile 2 have assets of $55.4 to $120.8 million, those in quartile 3 have assets of $120.8 to $351 million, and those in the largest quartile have assets of $351 million to $86 billion. In Panel B, average annual returns are computed for the 5 post-issue event years. Each year, the average is computed only for those issuers that are still CRSP-listed during the year. If a firm is delisted during the year, the CRSP VW NYSE-AMEX index is spliced in for the remainder of the year. The *t*-statistics are calculated assuming independence and normality.

Panel A: Average Annual Returns during the Pre- and Postissue Periods

| Asset Portfolio | Number of Firms | Mean Prior Annual Return on Issuers | Mean Postissue Annual Returns | | | Number of Firm-Years |
|---|---|---|---|---|---|---|
| | | | Issuing Firms | VW Index | Matching Firms | |
| Smallest | 335 | 115.2% | 1.6% | 15.5% | 15.2% | 1570 |
| 2 | 334 | 95.7% | 10.9% | 15.4% | 15.7% | 1539 |
| 3 | 335 | 97.1% | 10.0% | 15.2% | 16.1% | 1556 |
| Largest | 334 | 64.1% | 13.6% | 15.3% | 18.6% | 1573 |
| Total | 1338 | 93.1% | 9.0% | 15.4% | 16.4% | 6238 |

Panel B: Annual Returns by Event-Year for Issuers and the CRSP Value-Weighted Index

| Portfolio | Postissue Event Year | | | | |
|---|---|---|---|---|---|
| | Year 1 | Year 2 | Year 3 | Year 4 | Year 5 |
| SEOs | 12.6% | 6.4% | 15.0% | 6.8% | 3.2% |
| VW-Index | 11.5% | 16.3% | 20.4% | 17.8% | 10.4% |
| Matching firms | 16.3% | 18.0% | 21.9% | 15.3% | 9.5% |
| Market-adjusted | 1.1% | −9.9% | −5.4% | −11.0% | −7.2% |
| *t*-statistic | (0.68) | (−7.68) | (−3.52) | (−6.93) | (−4.56) |
| Matching-firm adjusted | −3.7% | −11.6% | −6.9% | −8.5% | −6.3% |
| *t*-statistic | (−1.92) | (−6.63) | (−3.39) | (−4.24) | (−2.91) |

The patterns are striking: the average annual return on issuers is 9.0 percent per year during the five years after issuing, whereas the average annual return is 15.4 percent on the CRSP value-weighted NYSE-AMEX index and 16.4 percent on nonissuing firms. Whether we use the CRSP index or matching firm returns, issuing firms underperform by about 7 percent per year. While the smallest firms have the largest preissue runup, and the greatest postissue underperformance, even the largest issuers underperform by 5 percent per year relative to nonissuers.[12]

In Panel B of Table VI, we report the average annual return for each of the five postissue event-years. During the first postissue year, there is no reliable underperformance relative to either the CRSP value-weighted NYSE-AMEX index or matching firms (possibly due to momentum effects benefiting the issuers). During years 2 through 5, there is substantial underperformance, suggesting that the deteriorating operating performance was unanticipated. For measuring abnormal investment performance in subsequent empirical tests, we use market-adjusted returns, which have the advantage of diversifying away the idiosyncratic portion of matching-firm returns.

## B. Is the Poor Performance of Issuing Firms Due to Confounding Effects?

Dreman (1982) and De Bondt and Thaler (1985) motivate their empirical work on stock market overreaction by describing work by psychologists including Kahneman and Tversky (1982) documenting widespread tendencies for humans to overweight recent experience at the expense of long-term averages. Whether or not there are tendencies for the stock market to overextrapolate recent growth is controversial (e.g., Lakonishok, Shleifer, and Vishny (1994) and Dechow and Sloan (1997)). Since issuing firms tend to i) be high-growth firms, and ii) have low postissue stock returns, we test whether the low postissue stock returns on issuing firms are merely a manifestation of the fact that most issuers are rapidly growing. We call this the confounding effect hypothesis.

To test the confounding effect hypothesis, we need to specify what measure of growth investors are focusing on. One potential class of items are measures of company growth, such as sales or assets, and items that are obviously endogenous, such as capital expenditures and research and development expenditures. Unlike earnings, these items are relatively noise-free and not easily subject to accounting manipulations.

For our cross-sectional tests of the relation between firm growth and subsequent stock returns, we need a measure of subsequent stock returns. Because of the lack of consensus regarding the measurement of abnormal long-term returns, we use several measures of market-adjusted returns. In particular, we use i) the one-year market-adjusted return, ii) the average annual geometric (compounded) market-adjusted return, iii) the average annual arithmetic mar-

---

[12] Brav, Géczy, and Gompers (1995) emphasize that SEOs classified as small growth.firms underperform the most in Fama-French three-factor model time-series regressions during 1975–1995. The three-factor model regressions treat each calendar month as an observation. In Table VI, we are equally weighting each issuer, rather than each month. Because the underperformance is worst following heavy issue volume, the magnitude of the measured underperformance differs depending upon the weighting scheme, as discussed by Loughran and Ritter (1995) on pp. 43 and 46.

## Table VII

## Mean Market-adjusted Abnormal Returns for COMPUSTAT-listed Issuers and Nonissuers, Segmented by Sales Growth Rates (Panel A) and Capital Expenditure plus Research and Development Expense (R&D) Changes (Panel B)

All CRSP and COMPUSTAT-listed domestic operating companies with positive fiscal year −1 and year 0 sales, with at least $20 million in year 0 assets, and meeting certain other criteria are used. On June 30 of the year following the calendar year in which fiscal year 0 ends, firms are classified as to whether they issued equity during the prior 12 months or did not. All firms that issued equity during years −4 to −1 are discarded, as are all firms with a June 30 stock price below $10.00 at the time of the initial portfolio formation. Market is the value-weighted CRSP NYSE-AMEX index. For firms that are delisted before the end of a holding period, the market-adjusted returns are calculated until the delisting date. The annual geometric and annual arithmetic mean returns for a firm are calculated over the maximum of either 5 years or, in the case of early delistings, the number of years through which it is delisted. The sample period for issuing is 1979–1989, with returns going through June 30, 1995. In Panel A, the percentage sales growth rate is calculated as fiscal year 0 sales minus fiscal year −1 sales, divided by fiscal year −1 sales (and then multiplied by 100). In Panel B, the change in R&D plus capital expenditures/total assets is measured as the fiscal year 0 numerator minus the fiscal year −1 numerator, divided by fiscal year −1 total assets (and then multiplied by 100).

### Panel A: Issuers and Nonissuers Categorized by Sales Growth Rates (SG)

| | | | | | Average Percentage Market-Adjusted Returns | | | | | |
| | Proportion | | 1-year | | Annual Geometric | | Annual Arithmetic | | 5-year Buy & Hold | |
| Sales Group | Issuers | Nonissuers | Issuers | Nonissuers | Issuers | Nonissuers | Issuers | Nonissuers | Issuers | Nonissuers |
|---|---|---|---|---|---|---|---|---|---|---|
| SG ≤ −20% | 5.0% | 6.4% | −13.36 | 0.09 | −12.40 | −4.55 | −8.46 | 0.30 | −62.42 | −7.03 |
| −20% < SG ≤ −10% | 6.0% | 10.5% | −3.02 | 5.72 | −8.14 | 1.20 | −2.45 | 6.08 | 20.53 | 31.08 |
| −10% < SG ≤ 0% | 13.9% | 24.0% | −5.06 | 6.17 | −4.19 | 2.37 | 1.12 | 6.53 | −17.23 | 35.81 |
| 0% < SG ≤ 10% | 20.3% | 32.0% | −6.58 | 4.49 | −8.84 | 1.50 | −3.44 | 5.37 | −30.22 | 22.62 |
| 10% < SG ≤ 20% | 17.7% | 15.3% | 1.72 | 4.81 | −9.39 | 0.42 | −3.27 | 5.43 | −41.87 | 17.81 |
| 20% < SG ≤ 30% | 10.1% | 5.8% | −2.16 | 5.33 | −9.40 | −1.54 | −1.10 | 4.18 | −36.60 | 5.09 |
| 30% < SG ≤ 40% | 5.9% | 2.5% | 5.11 | 1.34 | −13.99 | −4.27 | −5.12 | 1.80 | −66.34 | −7.75 |
| 40% < SG ≤ 50% | 4.9% | 1.2% | 13.94 | 1.38 | −19.03 | −7.20 | −10.11 | 0.07 | −77.21 | −26.00 |
| 50% < SG | 16.2% | 2.3% | −12.32 | 0.24 | −21.31 | −7.92 | −9.48 | 0.19 | −59.75 | −11.17 |
| All | 100% | 100% | −3.81 | 4.62 | −11.31 | 0.48 | −4.14 | 5.06 | −38.91 | 20.88 |

**Table VII—Continued**

Panel B: Issuers and Nonissuers Categorized by the Change in R&D plus Capital Expenditures/Total Assets (CE)

| Cap. Expend. Group | Proportion | | 1-year | | Average Percentage Market-Adjusted Returns | | | | | |
| | | | | | Annual Geometric | | Annual Arithmetic | | 5-year Buy & Hold | |
| | Issuers | Nonissuers | Issuers | Nonissuers | Issuers | Nonissuers | Issuers | Nonissuers | Issuers | Nonissuers |
|---|---|---|---|---|---|---|---|---|---|---|
| CE ≤ −6% | 8.8% | 5.9% | 1.81 | 3.63 | −12.34 | −2.32 | −3.93 | 2.97 | −44.72 | 13.48 |
| −6% < CE ≤ −4% | 2.8% | 4.8% | −7.44 | 3.69 | −12.31 | −0.10 | −6.42 | 4.90 | −33.39 | 13.96 |
| −4% < CE ≤ −2% | 8.5% | 10.2% | −4.26 | 5.64 | −7.67 | 1.42 | −1.83 | 6.06 | −1.21 | 34.22 |
| −2% < CE ≤ 0% | 16.7% | 24.2% | −3.25 | 4.88 | −3.53 | 1.40 | 0.91 | 5.48 | −19.83 | 24.59 |
| 0% < CE ≤ 2% | 15.0% | 27.0% | −7.30 | 5.24 | −9.46 | 1.23 | −3.94 | 5.32 | −34.63 | 21.79 |
| 2% < CE ≤ 4% | 11.0% | 12.6% | −2.08 | 4.64 | −12.08 | 1.02 | −4.94 | 5.40 | −53.21 | 22.59 |
| 4% < CE ≤ 6% | 8.1% | 6.1% | −6.70 | 6.57 | −14.06 | 0.37 | −6.54 | 5.68 | −34.60 | 21.34 |
| 6% < CE ≤ 8% | 5.1% | 3.2% | −15.76 | 1.16 | −13.60 | −2.36 | −6.42 | 3.57 | −57.31 | 15.59 |
| 8% < CE | 24.1% | 6.1% | 0.16 | 0.99 | −16.72 | −3.86 | −6.84 | 2.67 | −57.50 | −4.93 |
| All | 100% | 100% | −3.57 | 4.64 | −11.27 | 0.52 | −4.17 | 5.09 | −38.88 | 21.12 |

ket-adjusted return, and iv) the five-year buy-and-hold market-adjusted return.

We define the average annual geometric market-adjusted return on issuing firm $i$ as

$$\bar{r}_i = \sqrt[T]{\prod_{t=1}^{T}(1 + r_{it})} - \sqrt[T]{\prod_{t=1}^{T}(1 + r_{mt})} \tag{5}$$

where $r_{it}$ is the annual return in event-year $t$ on firm $i$, $r_{mt}$ is the market return for that year, and $T = \min$(event-year in which delisting occurs, 5). For a firm that is delisted early, the CRSP value-weighted NYSE-AMEX index is spliced in for the remainder of the year in which it is delisted. In both Tables VII and VIII, for all four return metrics, we calculate returns starting on the June 30 after the 12-month period during which a firm has issued. We wait until June 30 because our cross-sectional evidence uses accounting information from the fiscal year ending at least six months prior to then.

To examine the relation between issuing activity, growth, and subsequent stock returns, we use two measures of growth: i) the sales growth rate, and ii) the change in the rate at which the firm is investing. Sales growth is measured as the year-over-year percentage increase in sales. The change in the rate of investing is measured as the year-over-year change in R&D plus capital expenditures, divided by total assets, expressed as a percent.

In Table VII, we classify firms by their sales growth (Panel A) or the change in their capital expenditures (Panel B). As the "Proportions" columns show, a higher proportion of issuing firms are in the fast growth categories. We find that, using either measure of growth, the rapidly growing firms tend to have worse subsequent market-adjusted stock returns than the slower-growing firms. On average, when segmenting firms by sales growth, the fast-growing firms underperform the slow-growing firms by several percent per year using any of our return metrics.[13] When firms are segmented by capital expenditures growth, the results are qualitatively similar, although not as pronounced.[14]

All four return metrics show that issuers have lower market-adjusted returns than nonissuers, on average. Of the 72 differences in returns, only two show issuers outperforming nonissuers. While the high-growth firms tend to have lower market-adjusted returns within a category, issuers almost always

---

[13] Lakonishok, Shleifer, and Vishny (1994, Table I) test whether sales growth has predictive power for the cross-section of stock returns among NYSE and AMEX firms (issuers and nonissuers). As their measure of sales growth, they use a five-year growth rate, with declining weights on the more distant past (5/15 for year $-1$, 4/15 for $-2$, 3/15 for $-3$, 2/15 for $-4$ and 1/15 for $-5$). We use a one-year growth rate in order to retain more firms in our sample. They report a difference in average annual returns of about 3 percent in the year after portfolio formation for the top half of firms relative to the bottom half of firms, as segmented by sales growth.

[14] Cheng (1995) finds that issuing firms that do not rapidly increase their capital expenditures have the worst subsequent market-adjusted returns. Cheng uses two measures of capital expenditures growth: an ex post measure, which suffers from the problem that the least successful firms will not invest as much, and an ex ante measure, which doesn't suffer from this problem. His ex ante measure relies on the volume of equity issues in the calendar year of issuing, however, and thus is correlated with future returns.

do worse than nonissuers. These conclusions are not very sensitive to the return metric employed. Furthermore, the return differences are economically important, with issuers underperforming nonissuers by 8–12 percent per year, depending upon the return metric. These numbers are consistent with those reported in Loughran and Ritter (1995) and Spiess and Affleck-Graves (1995).

In Table VIII, we report the results of panel dataset regressions with cohort year fixed effects using the four measures of market-adjusted returns. The advantage of the regression approach is that significance levels can be calculated. Inspection of Table VIII shows that, with the exception of sales growth and one-year returns, both growth measures are significantly related to subsequent market-adjusted returns. For all return metrics, there is a significant new issues effect. Thus, Tables VII and VIII show that, while issuing firms tend to be high growth firms, there is an independent new issues effect.

## IV. Summary and Interpretation

### A. Summary

This article documents the poor postissue operating performance of firms conducting 1,338 seasoned equity offerings during 1979–1989. Consistent with the findings of Hansen and Crutchley (1990), new equity offerings can be used to forecast poor subsequent operating performance.[15] The profit margin and return on assets for the median issuer are cut approximately in half within four years of the offering. This deterioration is much larger than for nonissuers matched by asset size, industry, and operating performance. For example, the median issuer's profit margin falls from 5.4 percent in year 0 to 2.5 percent in year +4, whereas the median nonissuer's profit margin falls from 3.9 percent to 3.3 percent.

At the time of issuing, these patterns are not impounded into market prices, for financial markets assign market-to-book multiples reflecting expectations of above-average operating performance. The subsequent deterioration in the operating performance is reflected in low postissue stock returns. While the subsequent stock returns are lowest for the smallest issuers, both large and small issuers display deteriorating postissue operating performance relative to nonissuing firms.

We show that issuers are disproportionately fast-growing firms, a result that shouldn't be too surprising. Given that fast-growing firms historically have had lower subsequent stock returns than slow-growing firms, we examine whether the low returns on issuing firms are merely due to the confounding of growth rates and issuing activity. Our evidence shows that there is a strong, independent issuing effect: issuers have much lower subsequent stock returns than nonissuers with the same growth rate.

---

[15] Our results are not consistent with those of Healy and Palepu (1990). It is possible that their large AMEX-NYSE issuers from the 1966–1981 period have different patterns than the primarily smaller Nasdaq-listed firms that dominate our 1979–1989 sample.

### Table VIII

## Panel Dataset Regressions with Cohort Year Fixed Effects, with Firm Growth and an SEO Dummy Variable as Explanatory Variables and Four Measures of Market-Adjusted Returns as Dependent Variables

The sample period for issuing is 1979–1989, with returns going through June 30, 1995. On June 30 of each year, firms are classified as to whether or not they conducted a seasoned equity offering (SEO) during the prior 12 months. All Center for Research in Security Prices (CRSP) and COMPUSTAT-listed domestic operating companies with positive fiscal year −1 and year 0 sales, with at least $20 million in year 0 assets, and meeting certain other criteria are used. All firms that issued equity during year −4 to −1 are discarded, as are firms with a June 30 stock price below $10.00 at the time of the initial portfolio formation. Fiscal year 0 is deemed to be the most recent fiscal year ending at least six months prior to the June 30 classifications. In Panel A, the percentage sales growth rates are calculated as fiscal year 0 sales minus fiscal year −1 sales, divided by fiscal year −1 sales (and then multiplied by 100). In Panel B, the change in research and development expense (R&D) plus capital expenditures/total assets is measured as the fiscal year 0 numerator minus the fiscal year −1 numerator, divided by fiscal year −1 total assets (and then multiplied by 100). Sales and R&D plus capital expenditures growth rates are winsorized at the 1 percent and 99 percent levels. The SEO dummy variable takes on a value of 1 if a firm conducted an SEO during the prior 12 months, and 0 otherwise. In each regression, there are 11 cohort year dummy variables. No dummy variable is present for cohort year 1990 (comprised of offerings from the last six months of 1989). The sample size is 14,460 observations. For firms that are delisted before the end of a holding period, the market-adjusted (using the value-weighted CRSP NYSE-AMEX index) returns are calculated until the delisting date. The annual geometric and annual arithmetic mean returns for a firm are calculated over the maximum of either five years or, in the case of early delistings, the number of years through which it is delisted. White's heteroskedasticity-adjusted $t$-statistics are in parentheses.

$$r_i - r_m = \alpha_o + \alpha_1 \text{Growth Measure}_i + \alpha_2 \text{SEO Dummy}_i + \sum_{j=1979}^{1989} \alpha_j \text{Dummy}_j + e_i$$

Panel A: Regression Results Using Market-adjusted Returns as the Dependent Variable and Sales Growth, SEO Dummy and Cohort Year Fixed Effects as Explanatory Variables

| Dependent Variable | Parameter Estimates | | |
| --- | --- | --- | --- |
| | Intercept | Sales Growth | SEO Dummy |
| 1-Year | −1.94 | −0.022 | −6.00 |
| | (−1.80) | (−0.97) | (−3.73) |
| Annual geometric | −1.10 | −0.080 | −9.39 |
| | (−1.98) | (−7.46) | (−10.95) |
| Annual arithmetic | 2.76 | −0.045 | −7.19 |
| | (4.37) | (−3.84) | (−7.92) |
| 5-Year buy-and-hold | 16.92 | −0.369 | −46.63 |
| | (3.36) | (−4.17) | (−7.43) |

Panel B: Regression Results Using Market-adjusted Returns as the Dependent Variable and the Change in R&D plus Capital Expenditures/Total Assets, SEO Dummy and Cohort Year Fixed Effects as Explanatory Variables

| Dependent Variable | Parameter Estimates | | |
| --- | --- | --- | --- |
| | Intercept | Change in R&D + Capex | SEO Dummy |
| 1-Year | −1.88 | −0.175 | −5.68 |
| | (−1.73) | (−2.40) | (−3.60) |
| Annual geometric | −1.44 | −0.222 | −10.29 |
| | (−2.62) | (−5.84) | (−11.29) |
| Annual arithmetic | 2.64 | −0.156 | −7.65 |
| | (4.18) | (−3.80) | (−8.50) |
| 5-Year buy-and-hold | 15.88 | −1.257 | −50.22 |
| | (3.15) | (−4.41) | (−8.29) |

## B. Interpretation and Implications

Investors, who receive low postissue stock returns, and managers, who rapidly increase capital expenditures, appear to be too optimistic about the prospects of issuing firms. Analyst forecasts are a direct measure of expected postissue operating performance. Ali (1997) reports that the postissue earnings forecasts are systematically too optimistic. Healy and Palepu (1990), Brous (1992), and Jain (1992) find that analysts make only tiny revisions in their earnings forecasts when companies announce stock issues.[16] In addition, Korajczyk, Lucas, and McDonald (1991) and Cheng (1995) find some evidence that the market is surprised by future earnings announcements for issuers.

If analysts and investors overestimate the profit potential of issuing firms, is this partly because firms have "managed" earnings? Consistent with this view, Teoh, Welch, and Wong (1997) and Rangan (1997) report that issuers with high levels of discretionary accruals (which boost earnings relative to cash flows) have the worst subsequent stock returns. Presumably, some issuers attempt to manage earnings, raising the stock price, while others issue and invest after observing a stock price runup that the managers have not consciously attempted to manipulate. This latter interpretation is consistent with Lee's (1997) finding of a lack of massive insider selling for issuers.

Confounding effects and earnings management are not the only possible reasons for poor postissue performance. As emphasized by Jung, Kim, and Stulz (1996) and McLaughlin, Safieddine, and Vasudevan (1996), the cash inflow and reduced managerial percentage ownership associated with an equity issue may intensify agency problems and result in lower operating margins. If these increased agency problems are not fully anticipated by the market, they will be manifested in low postissue stock returns.

Our interpretation of the findings of this and other articles is that some, but by no means all, issuing firms are intentionally, and successfully, misleading investors. This is not the whole story, however. The most salient feature concerning firms' equity issuance behavior is that most firms issue equity after large stock price increases.[17] To manage earnings, companies must plan ahead, and either suppress earnings now to give a high growth rate in the future, or boost current earnings by borrowing against future earnings. If a company boosts current earnings in preparation for a stock offering, the firm exposes itself to the possibility that the stock price will decline due to general market movements before the firm has had an opportunity to issue overvalued equity. Our opinion is that while some firms do try to manage earnings with

[16] All three of these studies require *Wall Street Journal* announcement dates, and thus are biased towards larger firms relative to our sample. Furthermore, Healy and Palepu (1990) and Brous (1992) exclude Nasdaq issuers.

[17] Bayless and Chaplinsky (1991) report the results of a logistic regression predicting debt versus equity offerings from 1974–1983. The variables that have the greatest ability to predict equity issues are the prior market return and the prior individual stock return. Jung, Kim, and Stulz (1996) report the results of a logistic regression predicting debt versus equity offerings from 1977–1984. They find that prior excess returns and the market-to-book ratio at the time of issuing are important determinants of equity issues.

the idea of issuing equity, others merely take advantage of windows of opportunity that are largely outside of their own control (i.e., the nearly doubling of stock prices between August of 1982 and July of 1983), without any intentional earnings management.

In the windows of opportunity framework, advanced by Ritter (1991) and Loughran and Ritter (1995), firms issue equity when they are overvalued. This explains two patterns that Myers' (1984) pecking order theory cannot explain: i) issuers have low postissue stock returns, and ii) many firms issue equity when they apparently aren't constrained to. In other words, unlike the static pecking order story, where the ranking of choices between internal equity, external debt, and external equity is always the same, there is a dynamic pecking order. Sometimes the ranking of choices is external equity, external debt, and internal equity; when this is the ranking, a firm issues equity. See Stein (1996) for an elaboration.

The pecking order hypothesis predicts that firms issuing equity will have used up their debt capacity. Korajczk, Lucas, and McDonald (1990) find that debt ratios typically do not increase prior to equity issues, suggesting that strained debt capacity is not the primary motivation for issuing equity. The firms in our sample share this feature: only 49 percent of our sample issuers increased their debt ratio during the fiscal year ending immediately prior to the offering, and the median debt ratio prior to issuing is only 28 percent.[18]

The windows of opportunity framework asserts that when a firm is substantially overvalued it is likely to issue equity, taking advantage of the opportune time to augment what Myers refers to as financial slack.[19] In some years, few firms are overvalued, and there is little issuing activity. In other years, many firms are overvalued, and there is a lot of issuing activity, followed by disappointing operating performance and low stock returns for these issuing firms.[20]

The evidence on the investment and operating performance of companies conducting seasoned equity offerings in the US is similar to the evidence regarding initial public offerings (IPOs). Loughran and Ritter (1995) report that the stocks of IPOs underperform by 7 percent per year in the five years

---

[18] The debt ratio is defined as long-term plus short-term debt divided by the book value of assets, measured at the end of fiscal years $-2$ and $-1$. The mean debt ratio changed from 29.2 percent to 28.9 percent, while the median debt ratio changed from 27.4 percent to 27.7 percent. These numbers are consistent with those reported by Masulis and Korwar (1986, Table 4). The mean debt ratio for our matching firms changes from 26.8 percent to 27.4 percent, while the median changes from 24.6 percent to 25.3 percent.

[19] Jung, Kim, and Stulz (1996) find that in logistic regressions predicting whether a public issue will be debt or equity, the future excess stock return on an issuer does not help to reliably predict the type of issue. They view this finding as inconsistent with the windows of opportunity hypothesis.

[20] Overvaluations are measured both in a relative sense (a firm is overvalued relative to comparable firms at a point in time) and an absolute sense (a firm is overvalued relative to its past or future market value). Tests of the degree to which many firms are simultaneously overvalued are subject to the same problems with low power that exist in testing for whether there is excessive stock market volatility in a time-series (Shiller, 1989).

after an issue, whereas the stocks of firms conducting SEOs underperform by 8 percent per year. Jain and Kini (1994) and Mikkelson, Partch, and Shah (1997) report that the median IPO has a subsequent deterioration in its operating performance. Furthermore, the evidence on the investment performance of SEOs in the United Kingdom and Japan is virtually identical to the US patterns, as shown by Levis (1995), Cai (1996), and Kang, Kim, and Stulz (1996). These patterns in what are generally considered among the world's most sophisticated equity markets are consistent with equity markets in which misvaluations are important determinants of market prices and corporate financing choices.

## REFERENCES

Ali, Ashiq, 1997, Bias in analysts' earnings forecasts as an explanation for the long-run underperformance of stocks following equity offerings, Working paper, University of Arizona.

Asquith, Paul, and David W. Mullins, 1986, Equity issues and offering dilution, *Journal of Financial Economics* 15, 61–89.

Barber, Brad M., and John D. Lyon, 1996, Detecting abnormal operating performance: The empirical power and specification of test-statistics, *Journal of Financial Economics* 41, 359–399.

Bayless, Mark, and Susan Chaplinsky, 1991, Expectations of security type and the information content of debt and equity offers, *Journal of Financial Intermediation* 1, 195–214.

Brav, Alon, Christopher Géczy, and Paul Gompers, 1995, The long-run underperformance of seasoned equity offerings revisited, Working paper, University of Chicago.

Brous, Peter Alan, 1992, Common stock offerings and earnings expectations: A test of the release of unfavorable information, *Journal of Finance* 47, 1517–1536.

Cai, Jun, 1996, The investment and operating performance of Japanese SEO firms, Working paper, Hong Kong University of Science and Technology.

Cheng, Li-Lan, 1995, The motives, timing, and subsequent performance of seasoned equity issues, Unpublished Ph.D. dissertation, Massachusetts Institute of Technology.

Cornett, Marcia M., and Hassan Tehranian, 1994, An examination of voluntary versus involuntary security issuances by commercial banks: The impact of capital regulations on common stock returns, *Journal of Financial Economics* 35, 99–122.

DeAngelo, Linda, 1988, Managerial compensation, information costs, and corporate governance: The use of accounting performance measures in proxy contests, *Journal of Accounting and Economics* 10, 3–36.

De Bondt, Werner F. M., and Richard Thaler, 1985, Does the stock market overreact?, *Journal of Finance* 40, 793–805.

Dechow, Patricia M., and Richard G. Sloan, 1997, Returns to contrarian investment strategies: Tests of naive expectation hypotheses, *Journal of Financial Economics* 43, 3–27.

Degeorge, Francois, and Richard Zeckhauser, 1993, The reverse LBO decision and firm performance: Theory and evidence, *Journal of Finance* 48, 1323–1348.

Dreman, David, 1982, *The New Contrarian Investment Strategy* (Random House, New York).

Eckbo, B. Espen, and Ronald W. Masulis, 1995, Seasoned equity offerings: A survey. In R. A. Jarrow, V. Maksimovic, and W. T. Ziemba, Eds.: *Handbooks of Operations Research and Management Science: Finance* (North-Holland, Amsterdam).

Hansen, Robert S., and Claire Crutchley, 1990, Corporate earnings and financing: An empirical analysis, *Journal of Business* 63, 347–371.

Healy, Paul M., and Krishna G. Palepu, 1990, Earnings and risk changes surrounding primary stock offers, *Journal of Accounting Research* 28, 25–48.

Jain, Bharat A., and Omesh Kini, 1994, The post-issue operating performance of IPO firms, *Journal of Finance* 49, 1699–1726.

Jain, Prem C., 1992, Equity issues and changes in expectations of earnings by financial analysts, *Review of Financial Studies* 5, 669–683.

Jensen, Michael C., 1993, The modern industrial revolution, exit, and the failure of internal control systems, *Journal of Finance* 48, 831–880.

Jung, Kooyul, Yong-Cheol Kim, and René M. Stulz, 1996, Timing, investment opportunities, managerial discretion, and the security issue decision, *Journal of Financial Economics* 42, 159–185.

Kang, Jun-Koo, Yong-Cheol Kim, and René M. Stulz, 1996, The underreaction hypothesis and the new issue puzzle: Evidence from Japan, Working paper, The Ohio State University.

Kaplan, Steve, 1989, The effect of management buyouts on operating performance and value, *Journal of Financial Economics* 24, 217–254.

Kahneman, Daniel, and Amos Tversky, 1982, Intuitive prediction: Biases and corrective procedures, in D. Kahneman, P. Slovic, and A. Tversky, eds.: *Judgement Under Uncertainty: Heuristics and Biases* (Cambridge University Press, Cambridge).

Korajczyk, Robert A., Deborah Lucas, and Robert McDonald, 1990, Understanding stock price behavior around the time of equity issues, in R. Glenn Hubbard, Ed.: *Asymmetric Information, Corporate Finance, and Investments* (University of Chicago Press, Chicago, Ill).

Korajczyk, Robert A., Deborah Lucas, and Robert McDonald, 1991, The effect of information releases on the pricing and timing of equity issues, *Review of Financial Studies* 4, 685–708.

Lakonishok, Josef, Andrei Shleifer, and Robert Vishny, 1994, Contrarian investment, extrapolation, and risk, *Journal of Finance* 49, 1541–1578.

Lee, Inmoo, 1997, Do managers knowingly sell overvalued equity?, *Journal of Finance* 52, 1439–1466.

Levis, Mario, 1995, Seasoned equity offerings and the short and long-term performance of initial public offerings in the U.K., *European Financial Management* 1, 125–146.

Loughran, Tim, and Jay R. Ritter, 1995, The new issues puzzle, *Journal of Finance* 50, 23–51.

Masulis, Ronald W., and Ashok N. Korwar, 1986, Seasoned equity offerings: An empirical investigation, *Journal of Financial Economics* 15, 91–118.

McLaughlin, Robyn, Assem Safieddine, and Gopala Vasudevan, 1996, The operating performance of seasoned equity issuers: Free cash flow and post-issue performance, *Financial Management* 25:4, 41–53.

Mikkelson, Wayne H., M. Megan Partch, and Ken Shah, 1997, Ownership and operating performance of companies that go public, *Journal of Financial Economics* 44, 281–307.

Myers, Stewart C., 1984, The capital structure puzzle, *Journal of Finance* 39, 575–592.

Rangan, Srinivasan, 1997, Earnings management and the performance of seasoned equity offerings, *Journal of Financial Economics*, forthcoming.

Ritter, Jay R., 1991, The long-run performance of initial public offerings, *Journal of Finance* 46, 3–27.

Shiller, Robert J., 1989, *Market Volatility* (MIT Press, Cambridge, Mass.).

Spiess, D. Katherine, and John Affleck-Graves, 1995, Underperformance in long-run stock returns following seasoned equity offerings, *Journal of Financial Economics* 38, 243–267.

Stein, Jeremy, 1989, Efficient capital markets, inefficient firms: A model of myopic corporate behavior, *Quarterly Journal of Economics* 104, 655–669.

Stein, Jeremy, 1996, Rational capital budgeting in an irrational world, *Journal of Business* 69, 429–455.

Teoh, Siew Hong, Ivo Welch, and T. J. Wong, 1997, Earnings management and the underperformance of seasoned equity offerings, *Journal of Financial Economics*, forthcoming.

# [15]

THE JOURNAL OF FINANCE • VOL. LII, NO. 1 • MARCH 1997

# Equity Issuance and Adverse Selection: A Direct Test Using Conditional Stock Offers

JOEL F. HOUSTON and MICHAEL D. RYNGAERT*

**ABSTRACT**

We conduct a unique test of adverse selection in the equity issuance process. While common stock is the dominant means of payment in bank mergers, stock acquisition agreements provide target shareholders with varying degrees of protection against adverse price movements in the bidder's stock between the time of the merger agreement and the time of merger completion. We show that it is the degree of protection against adverse price changes and not the percent of stock offered in a bank merger that explains bidder merger announcement abnormal returns. This result is difficult to explain outside of an adverse selection framework.

FIRMS ARE OFTEN RELUCTANT to issue equity to fund new investments. A frequently cited rationale for this reluctance is that markets might interpret an equity issue authorized by managers with private information about a firm's value as a signal that the firm's stock is overvalued (Myers and Majluf (1984)). Consistent with this adverse selection scenario, firms generally experience a significant drop in their stock price when they announce that they are selling stock in a secondary offering,[1] and merger announcement returns are lower when bidding firms offer stock, rather than cash, as payment.[2] There are, however, alternative explanations for why share prices decline when firms issue equity. Firms issuing equity rather than debt may forego the discipline that debt imposes on managers (Jensen (1986)) or lose the potential tax advantages of debt financing. Additionally, firms issuing equity may face a downward sloping demand curve for firm shares (Loderer, Cooney, and Van Drunen (1991)). While these explanations are not mutually exclusive, testing the validity of any one explanation requires controlling for the alternatives.

In this article we conduct a unique test that isolates the impact of adverse selection in the equity issuance process. Our tests focus on the means of payment used in a large sample of bank mergers agreements during the period 1985–1992. Acquiring banks issuing stock to target bank shareholders offer varying degrees of protection to target shareholders against adverse private

---

\* Both Houston and Ryngaert are from the Graduate School of Business, University of Florida. We thank Chris James, David T. Brown, Mark Flannery, Charles Hadlock, and Subu Venkataraman for their helpful comments. Alison Miller and John Race provided valuable research assistance.

[1] For example, see Asquith and Mullins (1986), Masulis and Korwar (1986), and Korajczyk, Lucas, and McDonald (1991).

[2] For example, see Travlos (1987) and Brown and Ryngaert (1991).

information concerning the bidder's future share price. Some stock merger agreements provide target shareholders a fixed number of shares when the merger is completed. In these cases, a decline in the bidder's stock price prior to closing reduces target shareholders' compensation. Alternatively, many agreements condition the number of shares issued to target shareholders on the price of the bidder's stock shortly before the merger is completed. We refer to these agreements as conditional stock offers. In its most extreme form, a conditional stock offer provides target shareholders a fixed dollar amount of stock. If the bidder's stock price falls (rises) prior to the completion of the merger, the target receives additional (fewer) shares to maintain the same dollar level of compensation.

Since regulatory delays in banking mergers cause the average time to completion of a proposed merger to exceed seven months, a great deal of the uncertainty (and hence private information) about the value of the bidder and target will be resolved between the time of the initial merger agreement and when the deal is closed. Consequently, a conditional stock offer allows the bidder to offer the target firm stock in the merged entity *and* provide the target some degree of protection from post agreement revelations of adverse changes in the bidder's true value. This is of particular importance in bank mergers, because regulatory factors favor stock as a means of payment.[3] Hence, under-valued acquiring banks may view conditional stock offers as a substitute for a cash offer. In fact, such offers are common in bank mergers.

Our sample consists of 209 bank merger announcements where the mode of financing consists of cash, common stock or a combination of the two. For each agreement, we estimate the percentage of target merger compensation that is common stock. We also estimate the elasticity of the target's compensation with respect to the bidder's stock price at the time of each merger agreement. Since conditional stock offers frequently establish "caps" or "floors" on the number of shares to be exchanged, we use option pricing techniques to estimate this elasticity. If adverse selection contributes to share price declines associated with equity issues, then the stock market will respond more favorably when bidders announce a merger agreement where the value of target compensation is less sensitive to changes in the bidder's stock price. Consistent with the adverse selection hypothesis, we find that after controlling for other factors that are likely to influence the market's response to an acquisition, *including the percentage of stock in the offer*, abnormal returns to bidders are greater when target compensation has a lower elasticity with respect to the bidder's stock price. Furthermore, when we control for the protection an offer provides against adverse selection, the percentage of stock used to finance an acquisition has no incremental effect on the bidder's abnormal return.

By focusing on conditional stock offers, our article provides a novel test of the importance of private information and adverse selection in the method of payment choice. Past empirical work has examined whether the price reac-

---

[3] Factors that favor stock include capital requirements, long merger delays that make bidders unable to close a deal quickly with cash, and taxation of capital gains in cash offers.

tions of bidding firms differ for cash versus stock offers. The decision to use cash or stock, however, depends on factors besides private information. In contrast, whether a firm issues stock through a fixed exchange ratio offer or a conditional offer has little or no effect on firm free cash flow, firm capital structure, the supply of firm stock, or the tax treatment of the offer. Thus, it is difficult to explain our results outside of a private information framework.

While our evidence suggests that stock offers can be constructed to minimize the adverse selection concerns of target firms, fixed exchange ratio stock offers are still the most popular form of stock acquisition mechanism, despite the lemons problems they may create. Our final empirical tests address this issue. Relying on models that account for the fact that both the bidder and target may face adverse selection in a merger agreement (Hansen (1987), Eckbo, Giammarino, and Heinkel (1990), and Fishman (1989)), we argue that there are potential costs to the bidder that may arise from guaranteeing the target a fixed dollar compensation. We present evidence consistent with these models.

The article proceeds as follows. Section I discusses adverse selection and the means of payment. It includes how we estimate the elasticity of the target's compensation with respect to the bidder's stock price. Section II describes our sample. Section III presents descriptive statistics and Section IV presents regression results relating bidder abnormal returns to the degree of protection provided to target shareholders. Section V examines the factors that influence the extent to which targets are protected against the private information of the bidder. Section VI concludes.

## I. Adverse Selection and the Method of Payment in an Acquisition

The compensation received by bidder and target shareholders in a merger depends on the underlying value of the combined firm and the terms of the merger agreement. The underlying equity value of the combined firm (V) is the sum of three components: the stand alone equity value of the target (Vt), the stand alone equity value of the bidder (Vb), and any synergies that can be created by combining the two firms (S).

Assume that the bidder has private information about its own stand alone value (Vb). Adverse selection problems arise when the bidder offers the target compensation that could decrease in value if the bidder's stand alone value falls. The bidder can lessen adverse selection concerns by bearing more of the risk associated with shifts in its stand alone value. The terms of the merger agreement determine the allocation of this risk. The theoretical literature in finance (e.g., Hansen (1987) and Eckbo, Giammarino, and Heinkel, (1990)) has generally viewed this relative risk bearing as a cash versus stock proposition, in which "high" value bidders bear more risk by offering more cash and "low" value bidders bear less risk by offering more stock.

Consider an example where the target receives some present value amount of cash, C, along with a fixed percentage, $\alpha$, of the combined firm. The value of this offer to the target, TCOMP, and the value of the merger to the bidder, BCOMP, and the value of the combined firm, $V$ are:

$$\text{TCOMP} = C + \alpha(Vt + Vb + S - C) \tag{1}$$

$$\text{BCOMP} = (1 - \alpha)(Vt + Vb + S - C) \tag{2}$$

$$V = Vt + Vb + S = \text{TCOMP} + \text{BCOMP}. \tag{3}$$

Holding TCOMP and BCOMP constant, larger values of $\alpha$ and lower values of $C$ shift the risk associated with changes in underlying firm value from the bidder to the target. In fact, one measure of the relative risk being borne by the target is the percentage of total compensation paid to the target that is common stock:

$$\text{PCTSTK} = \frac{\alpha(V - C)}{C + \alpha(V - C)} \tag{4}$$

In this article, we are interested in a more general characterization of relative risk bearing that can be applied to any offer. We employ the percentage revaluation of the target's compensation with respect to the percentage revaluation of the bidder's compensation that is induced by a change in the stand alone value of the bidder, Vb. This elasticity, ELAST1, is defined as:

$$\text{ELAST1} = \frac{\partial \text{TCOMP}/\partial Vb}{\partial \text{BCOMP}/\partial Vb} \times \frac{\text{BCOMP}}{\text{TCOMP}}. \tag{5}$$

Presumably, bidding firms that are confident of their underlying value would be willing to assume greater exposure to shifts in Vb and provide the target with less exposure, resulting in a lower level of ELAST1. In the case where the number of shares in the offer is fixed:

$$\text{ELAST1} = \frac{\alpha(V - C)}{C + \alpha(V - C)}. \tag{6}$$

Note that in this case, ELAST1 equals the percentage of total dollar compensation in the offer that is common stock. Hence, a straight stock for stock exchange where the exchange ratio is predetermined will have an elasticity of one. For an all cash offer, the elasticity is zero.

For conditional stock offers where the number of shares issued is a decreasing function of bidder share price (and underlying firm value), the elasticity measure, ELAST1, prior to the merger's completion will be less than the percent of compensation that is attributable to stock. For a conditional stock offer where the target is guaranteed a certain dollar amount of stock, the elasticity measure equals zero. Conditional stock offers of this sort have the same protection as cash, provided that all of the bidder's private information at the time of the merger agreement is released prior to closing. However, this

*Equity Issuance and Adverse Selection: A Direct Test* 201

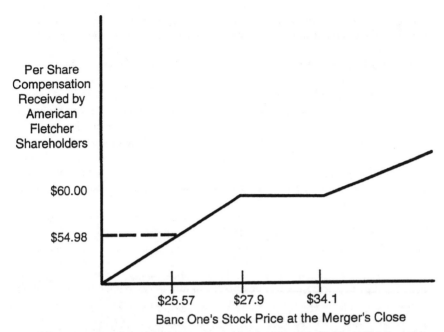

Per Share
Compensation
Received by
American
Fletcher
Shareholders

$60.00

$54.98

$25.57     $27.9     $34.1

Banc One's Stock Price at the Merger's Close

**Figure 1. Compensation schedule for American Fletcher shareholders.** This figure plots the per share compensation received by American Fletcher shareholders in their 1986 merger with Banc One Corporation, as a function of Banc One's stock price on the day the merger is completed.

type of offer is rare. For the vast majority of conditional stock offers, the initial merger agreement places restrictions on the number of shares to be issued.

In these instances, the value of target compensation, TCOMP, can be expressed as a long stock position in the joint company coupled with options, written and/or held with differing exercise prices, on the joint company's stock. The process by which we estimate ELAST1 can be demonstrated with a merger agreement from our sample.

In January 1986, Banc One entered into an acquisition agreement with American Fletcher. The agreement stipulated that Banc One would exchange a certain number of its common shares for each share of American Fletcher stock. The number of shares depended on the average Banc One share price, $P$, for a ten-day period ending six days before the merger closing. The exchange formula is given below:

| Number of Shares Exchanged | Price ($P$) Range for Banc One Stock |
|---|---|
| 2.15 shares | if $P < \$27.9$ |
| 60/(Banc One Share Price) | if $\$27.9 < P < \$34.1$ |
| 1.76 shares | if $P > \$34.1$ |

Figure 1 plots American Fletcher's compensation, TCOMP, as a function of Banc One's share price. If Banc One's price at closing had been between $27.9

and $34.1 a share, American Fletcher shareholders would have received $60 worth of Banc One stock for every share exchanged. If, however, Banc One's price went outside of this range, American Fletcher shareholders would have received a fixed number of shares, and their compensation would have been sensitive to any additional changes in Banc One's stock price.

The payoff plotted in Figure 1 is analogous to the payoff that an investor would receive from a strategy of: purchasing 2.15 shares of Banc One stock, writing 2.15 call options on Banc One stock (each with a strike price of $27.90) and purchasing 1.76 call options on Banc One stock (each with a strike price of $34.10). Of course, the price of Banc One stock will be based on the combined firm's underlying value. Consequently, the value of this package must be reexpressed as a long position in the combined firm's value, along with a short and long call option on the combined firm's value.[4]

To estimate the value of this compensation to American Fletcher shareholders, TCOMP, we use the Black-Scholes option pricing model. We use the six month T-bill rate as the risk free interest rate, and the time between the agreement date and eleven days before the merger actually closed as the time until expiration.[5] To estimate the volatility of the combined firm, we calculate the variance of the bidder and target's weekly continuously compounded stock returns, as well as the correlation of their weekly stock returns. These estimates are based on stock market returns over the interval 230 to 31 days before the first news story indicating that the target was a takeover candidate. The weights used to calculate the variance of the combined firm are based on the market values of the bidder and target five days before the first news story that the target was a takeover candidate.

Recalling that TCOMP is a long position in the combined firm's value, $V$, along with long and short call options written on $V$, we cannot solve for TCOMP without knowledge of $V$. Since TCOMP is a function of $V$ and $V$ = TCOMP + BCOMP, we solve for TCOMP and $V$ by fixing the value of BCOMP. To estimate BCOMP we use the bidder's stock market value two days before the merger announcement date less the estimated present value of dividends to be paid between the merger agreement and merger closing. This assumes that all synergies from the merger go to the target.

Finally, we calculate the change in the value of the target's compensation with respect to changes in the value of the stand alone bidder, $\partial TCOMP/\partial Vb$,

---

[4] Details of this calculation are available upon request.

[5] Eleven days before closing is the midpoint of the ten-day period during which the price of Banc One stock was averaged for the purposes of the merger agreement. For all agreements, we use the actual time between the merger agreement and the midpoint of the price determination period as the time to expiration with two exceptions. For merger accords where the time to expiration exceeded one year, we cap the time to expiration at one year. For cases where the merger was never completed, we use the average time to expiration of other conditional stock offers in our sample.

Equity Issuance and Adverse Selection: A Direct Test        203

again using option pricing techniques.[6] Plugging this and our estimates of BCOMP and TCOMP into equation (6), we calculate ELAST1 to be 0.627 for the Banc One/American Fletcher merger.

A complicating factor in the elasticity estimation is that many merger agreements have an additional clause that allows one or both parties to call off the merger if the price of the stock goes above or below some threshold value. For instance, in the American Fletcher merger agreement, there was a clause that allowed the American Fletcher board to call off the deal if the price of Banc One's stock fell below \$25.57 per share. However, unlike the other terms of the conversion formula, the contract did not require a new conversion ratio in the event the price fell below \$25.57. Our ELAST1 estimate assumes that any violation of this price threshold will be ignored. In fact, in this case, Banc One stock did fall below \$25.57, and American Fletcher proceeded with the previously agreed upon exchange ratio.

Nevertheless, such terms can protect target shareholders against a collapse in bidder share price, and occasionally terms are renegotiated based on violations of these thresholds. So, we calculate a second elasticity estimate under the assumption that American Fletcher shareholders would be "made whole" if the Banc One stock dropped below \$25.57. This assumes that they will get shares of Banc One worth \$54.98 (2.15 shares at \$25.57 a share). In this situation, bidders are providing target shareholders additional put options with a strike price equal to \$25.57. This additional downside protection is represented by the dashed lines in Figure 1. Including this "put protection" into the American Fletcher package, we get a new second definition of elasticity (ELAST2) with a value of 0.421. Arguably, for most deals, the "true" elasticity lies somewhere between ELAST1 and ELAST2, but using both measures allows us to check the robustness of our results.[7]

Three additional points are worth making. First, all conditional stock offers are not alike. While the type of offer outlined above is the most common, other types provide a dollar compensation floor and/or cap to the target. Second, some fixed exchange ratio stock offers also provide the target with back-out provisions that allow ELAST2 to be less than one. Third, bidders, as well as targets, occasionally have back-out options. For instance, in some fixed exchange ratio offers there are price ceilings that, if violated, give the bidder an option to back out. Furthermore, some offers that provide the target with more shares if the bidder's price falls allow the bidder to back out if it believes that its stock has been depressed too significantly and the number of shares to be issued is too high. In calculating ELAST2, we assume that the party with the back-out option can use it to their advantage. For instance, if a target was

---

[6] Since $dV/dVb = 1$, the quantity $\partial TCOMP/\partial Vb = \partial TCOMP/\partial V$. For the option components of the target compensation, the changes in value due to changes in Vb (V) fall out of the "hedge ratio" of these options.

[7] ELAST2 is likely to be biased downward for cases with a back-out clause because the target may not seek renegotiation if the price decline of the bidder was market related. In fact, a number of agreements with renegotiation clauses render the clauses inapplicable if the bidder's share price decline was accompanied by a large percentage decline in other bank stocks.

guaranteed $20 of stock, but the bidder could call off the transaction if its price fell below $20 per share, we assume that the target's compensation falls dollar for dollar as the bidder's price falls below $20 at closing. Given this possibility, we have four offers where ELAST2 actually exceeds ELAST1.

Furthermore, virtually all merger agreements allow either party to back out in the event of a material adverse change in either firm before the merger closes. In this sense, targets and bidders are protected against major events that adversely affect their merger partner. Thus, conditional stock offers might be viewed as protecting target shareholders against contingencies that are not easily classified as materially adverse.

Finally, all merger agreements stipulate that the target firm shareholders must approve the agreement. If, for instance, a decline in the bidder's share price significantly reduces the target's compensation, target shareholders can reject the merger. The ability of shareholders to reject the initial merger terms if they become "unfair" will tend to operate like a material adverse change clause. This possibility may blur the distinction between a conditional and fixed exchange ratio stock offer if mergers are terminated routinely and/or renegotiated because of changes in available information.

Two factors limit this possibility. First, in most agreements, target management agrees to use its best efforts to get shareholder approval. In a few cases, targets face a financial penalty if the deal is not approved. Second, a merger may be beneficial to the target even at a lower value than originally anticipated. Shareholder rejection in hope of more favorable terms assumes that the process of bid revision is costless and certain. Rejected bids are not always renegotiated. Furthermore, if shareholder rejections of initial merger agreements due to changes in available information were likely, then no differences would exist in how the market reacts to the means of payment and in what determines the means of payment. We demonstrate later that this is not the case.

## II. Data and Empirical Design

### A. *Description of Sample*

We collect a sample of initial bank merger agreements announced from 1985 through 1992 from three primary sources: a keyword search on Dow Jones News Retrieval, the bank mergers and acquisitions section of the Wall Street Journal (WSJ) Abstracts Index, and the mergers and acquisitions section in the New York Times (NYT) Abstracts Index. To insure full data availability, target firms must have at least 100 million dollars of assets and stock return data on the Center for Research in Security Prices (CRSP) tapes. To keep a relatively homogeneous set of bidders, we exclude bidders that are thrift institutions and restrict our analysis to friendly acquisitions.[8] We eliminate mergers that have to wait more than two years before they can be legally

---

[8] This eliminates institutions that are holding companies for savings banks and thrifts.

consummated, because a disproportionate number of such mergers are never completed. We also exclude "mergers of equals" from the sample because it is unclear which firm is the bidder. We define a merger of equals as a merger in which either the assets or the equity value of the smaller firm would constitute more than 45 percent of the combined assets or equity value of the two firms *and* the new board of directors will be composed of equal numbers of directors from each firm. We also eliminate one case where the acquirer simultaneously announced a stock issue of greater value than the acquisition itself.

For each remaining merger agreement, we try to obtain a copy of the initial merger agreement from 8K and proxy filings describing the merger terms. In many cases, we cannot get a full copy of the merger agreement. In these cases, we rely on descriptions of the deals reported in news stories or other SEC filings. Remaining agreements are only used if there are sufficient details about the merger's terms, the compensation is entirely common stock and/or cash (including cash equivalents like nonconvertible debt and preferred stock), and it is possible to estimate elasticity measures. Consequently, we exclude another twelve agreements because the compensation includes convertible stock, warrants, or payoffs that are pegged to the bidder's book value (rather than stock price).

The final sample consists of 209 offers. The sample contains 29 offers where no common stock is offered. These consist of 26 cash offers, one debt offer, one straight preferred offer, and one combination cash and straight preferred offer. There are 94 fixed exchange ratio stock offers, 60 conditional stock offers, 17 offers where the target received a combination of cash and common stock with conditional terms, and 9 offers where the target received a combination of cash and common stock with a fixed exchange rate. The breakdown of merger types indicates that the use of cash in bank mergers is rare compared to industrial mergers.[9] Regulatory and tax considerations may explain why there are fewer cash offers in banking, and why there is a need for close informational substitutes such as conditional stock offers.[10]

Of our 209 merger agreements, 151 were definitive agreements and 58 were preliminary agreements. There is more latitude to back out of or alter the terms of a preliminary agreement, although in our sample, the majority of preliminary proposals are adopted as definitive merger terms. Additionally, 184 of the merger agreements lead to an actual merger and 25 agreements are terminated.

---

[9] For example, Brown and Ryngaert (1991) find that cash is the means of payment in roughly 60 percent of industrial mergers in their sample between 1981 and 1986. A review of *Mergers & Acquisition* magazine shows that for the period 1987–1992, the ratio of cash offers to stock offers was about 5 to 1.

[10] Cash offers generally reduce the capital ratio of bidding banks, and subject target shareholders to capital gains taxes when the merger is completed.

## B. *Empirical Methodology*

To properly calculate the abnormal returns associated with each merger agreement we must capture any "information leakage" prior to the merger announcement. For each bidder and target we identify two dates: the agreement date and the leakage date. The agreement date for the bidder and target is the date of the initial agreement reported in the WSJ or NYT or the day after the first Dow Jones Newswire story if the merger agreement is not reported in the WSJ or NYT. The leakage date for the target is the first announcement that the target was a takeover candidate. We find this date by searching the Dow Jones News Wire, NYT index, and WSJ Index for the three months prior to the agreement date to identify any news story indicating that the company put itself up for sale, was in merger talks, or received a takeover proposal. If we find a story, we go back an additional three months to see if there is another prior story. The leakage date for the bidder is the first date that the bidder reveals that it is in talks with the target or offers to acquire the target. Note that the bidder's leakage date is never before the target's leakage date. Also, if there are no identifiable news leaks, the leakage date is the agreement date.

We use event study methodology to estimate abnormal returns for the bidder and target. Using continuously compounded firm and CRSP equally-weighted market returns, market model parameters are estimated over day $-230$ to day $-31$, where day 0 is the leakage date. One concern when calculating the abnormal returns for bidding firms is that their stock market performance prior to the acquisition is likely to be correlated with their choice of financing and elasticity offer. If, for example, bidding firms delay making high elasticity stock offers until share price-increasing good news about the firm is released, then we would expect to see positive intercepts (alphas) in our market model estimates for these firms. This may result in a downward bias in the abnormal returns for firms making high elasticity stock offers.[11] To correct for this potential bias, we replace alpha with the daily estimated return to risk-free investment multiplied by 1 minus the estimated beta from the market model. This is essentially a one factor return model with the daily abnormal return for firm $i$ on day $t$, $AR_{it}$, equal to

$$AR_{it} = R_{it} - (1 - \beta_i)R_{ft} - \beta_i R_{mt} \qquad (7)$$

where $R_{ft}$ is the continuously compounded return to firm $i$ on day $t$, $\beta_i$ is the estimated market model beta for firm $i$, $R_{ft}$ is the daily risk free return proxied for by the continuously compounded annual yield on a 6-month Treasury bill at the time of the merger agreement divided by the average number of trading days in a year, and $R_{mt}$ is the continuously compounded equally-weighted CRSP market return on day $t$.[12]

---

[11] We thank the editor for raising this potential bias issue. The fact that firms may experience a price run-up before an equity issue is discussed in Lucas and McDonald (1990).

[12] Although we use this particular abnormal return measure throughout the article, all the basic results in our study continue to hold when we use an abnormal return generated under the

The overall abnormal bidder and target returns are calculated by summing up the abnormal returns for four days before the leakage date through one day after the agreement date. We refer to these returns as BID6 and TAR6, since the window will be 6 days long if there is no information leakage. Similarly, we estimate abnormal returns from one day before the leakage date through one day after the agreement date and refer to these abnormal returns as BID3 and TAR3, since the windows will be 3 days long if there is no information leakage.

If adverse selection concerns are meaningful, we expect bidder abnormal returns to be negatively related to the elasticity measures, even when controlling for the percent stock in an offer. We also need to control for other factors that might influence bidder returns. If acquisitions tend to be value-reducing for bidders, then larger acquisitions might lead to larger price declines. So, we take the ratio of the target's stock market value five days before its leakage date to the bidder's stock market value five days before its leakage date to estimate the variable RELATIVE SIZE. Larger values of RELATIVE SIZE are expected to negatively influence bidder returns.[13]

The degree of observable competition for a target's shares has had a significant negative impact on the shares of successful bidders in industrial acquisitions (see Bradley, Desai, and Kim (1988)). We would expect the same for bank mergers. If the press accounts at the time of the merger agreement or in the 100 trading days prior to the announcement indicate that the target had received a bid from another entity or that another bank had sought permission to acquire more than 20 percent of the bidder's shares, then we assign that observation a value of one for a dummy variable called COMPETE and zero otherwise. In our regression analysis we interact COMPETE with RELATIVE SIZE based on the premise that larger highly competitive acquisitions will lead to a larger decline in the bidder's announcement window returns.

We also expect higher bidder returns from acquisitions that generate greater cost savings. Mergers that are "in-market" present greater opportunities to reduce costs by closing overlapping branch offices and redundant headquarter facilities. To capture the potential for cost savings, we create a variable called OVERLAP. We identify each subsidiary of the target and bidding bank, including whenever possible deals that either bank may have pending. Using the Rand McNally and Thomson Bank Directory, we identify how many branches each firm has in a given city. Let $n$ be the total number of cities that either bank has offices in, let $T_i$ denote the total number of offices the target has in

---

assumption of a standard market model with an estimated intercept (alpha) representing a benchmark return.

[13] In a study of industrial mergers, Asquith, Bruner, and Mullins (1983) find a positive relation between bidder merger returns and the relative size of the target to the bidder. Their sample, however, is made up of cases where the bidder's return from the merger was positive. Houston and Ryngaert (1994) document a negative link between bidder return and relative size for bank mergers.

city $i$ and let $B_i$ denote the total number of offices the bidder has in city $i$. OVERLAP is defined as:

$$\text{OVERLAP} = \frac{\sum_{i=1}^{n} \min(T_i, \, B_i)}{\sum_{i=1}^{n} B_i}. \tag{8}$$

OVERLAP can be viewed as the maximum level of overlapping offices that could be closed as a result of the merger relative to the current scale of the bidder's operations. Higher levels of OVERLAP are expected to result in higher bidder returns.

The relative performance of the bidder is also likely to affect the bidder's returns. One measure of the bidder's performance, which has been found to be significant in explaining abnormal returns in industrial mergers is Tobin's $Q$.[14] Higher bidder $Q$s lead to higher bidder returns. Arguably, the extent to which the bidder's $Q$ matters depends on the size of the acquisition. Therefore, we interact RELATIVE SIZE with a dummy variable which equals 1 if the bidder's market to book ratio of total assets exceeds the median market to book ratio for publicly traded banks on the 1993 COMPUSTAT Industrial and Research Tapes in the year prior to the acquisition announcement. If high performance bidders realize better returns on larger acquisitions, we would expect a positive coefficient on this interacted variable.[15]

### III. Descriptive Statistics

Table I provides descriptive statistics for the entire sample. We find that the announcement of a merger agreement results in the bidding firm realizing an average negative 2.3 percent abnormal return for the shorter window (BID3) and negative 2.4 percent for the longer window (BID6). By contrast target firms realize large positive abnormal returns. These results are consistent with other recent studies of bank mergers.[16]

Table I also shows that the large majority of acquisitions are financed with stock. The percentage of compensation coming from stock averages 81.9 percent. The elasticity of target compensation measures range from 0 to 1, and have an average level of 0.649 and 0.595 for ELAST1 and ELAST2, respectively. These numbers can be interpreted as follows: for the average acquisition, the target's compensation rises (falls) 0.649 percent when the bidder's stock price increases (decreases) by 1 percent. This calculation assumes that clauses that enable a deal to be canceled if the bidder's stock price crosses a certain level are not binding. If these clauses are assumed to lead to renego-

---

[14] See, for instance, Servaes (1991) and Lang, Stulz, and Walkling (1989). We thank an anonymous referee for suggesting that we include a measure of the bidder $Q$.

[15] We also consider, at the referee's suggestion, whether bidder abnormal returns might be explained by the percentage of stock held by the firm's officers and directors. The estimated coefficient on this measure (while controlling for the other variables) is routinely insignificant and including it in our regressions does not affect the nature or significance of any of the other results.

[16] See, for instance, Houston and Ryngaert (1994) and Neely (1987).

### Table I

## Descriptive Statistics for 209 Bank Merger Agreements During the Period 1985–1992

BID6 is the bidder abnormal return from four days before to one day after merger announcement, BID3 is the bidder abnormal return from one day before to one day after merger announcement, TAR6 is the target abnormal return from four days before the first merger news to one day after merger announcement, TAR3 is the target abnormal return from one day before the first merger news till one day after merger announcement. ELAST1 is the elasticity of the target's compensation with respect to the bidder's compensation assuming no renegotiation of merger terms if the bidder's price crosses a specified threshold, ELAST2 is the elasticity of the target's compensation with respect to the bidder's compensation assuming renegotiation of merger terms if the bidder's price crosses a specified threshold. PCTSTOCK is the percent of the target's merger compensation that is received as common stock, RELATIVE SIZE is the premerger market value of the target's equity divided by the market value of the bidder's equity, OVERLAP is the number of overlapping bidder and target branches divided by bidder branches, HIGH Q DUMMY is a dummy variable equal to one if the bidder has a market to book asset ratio greater than the median COMPUSTAT banking firm, and COMPETE is a dummy variable that equals 1 if the bidder faced observable competition in acquiring the target.

|               | Mean    | Median  | Maximum | Minimum |
|---------------|---------|---------|---------|---------|
| BID6          | −0.024  | −0.018  | 0.183   | −0.328  |
| BID3          | −0.023  | −0.015  | 0.142   | −0.256  |
| TAR6          | 0.204   | 0.197   | 0.858   | −0.539  |
| TAR3          | 0.177   | 0.174   | 0.687   | −0.538  |
| ELAST1        | 0.649   | 0.815   | 1       | 0       |
| ELAST2        | 0.595   | 0.675   | 1       | 0       |
| PCTSTOCK      | 0.819   | 1       | 1       | 0       |
| RELATIVE SIZE | 0.171   | 0.102   | 0.836   | 0.003   |
| OVERLAP       | 0.037   | 0.008   | 0.559   | 0       |
| HIGH Q DUMMY  | 0.689   | 1       | 1       | 0       |
| COMPETE       | 0.086   | 0       | 1       | 0       |

tiated terms (as described earlier), the target's compensation rises (falls) 0.595 percent for a 1 percent increase (decrease) in the bidder's stock price.

For the average merger agreement, the pre-announcement value of the target represents just over 17 percent of the bidder's value. Target operations overlap, on average, in 3.7 percent of the locations where the bidder operates. For 68.9 percent of the acquisitions, the bidder has an above median Q ratio. In 8.6 percent of the acquisitions, there were published press reports that an identifiable firm had made a competing bid for the target.

Table II divides the sample by the method of payment: cash, stock, or a combination of the two. For each type of financing, the mean six-day bidder weighted abnormal return is reported. The observations are weighted by the inverse of the standard errors from the estimated market models. The evidence suggests that the method of payment influences the bidder's abnormal return in a manner consistent with the adverse selection hypothesis. Bidders offering cash have less negative abnormal returns than those offering stock, and bidders that make conditional stock offers do better, on average, than bidders that offer a fixed number of shares.

Table II

## Mean Statistics for Selected Variables Grouped by the Mode of Acquisition for a Sample of 209 Bank Merger Agreements Among Publicly Traded Firms, for the Period 1985–1992

BID6 is the bidder abnormal return from four days before to one day after merger announcement, BID3 is the bidder abnormal return from one day before to one day after merger announcement. Percent Common Stock is the percent of the target's merger compensation that is received as common stock. ELAST1 is the elasticity of the target's compensation with respect to the bidder's compensation assuming no renegotiation of merger terms if the bidder's price crosses a specified threshold. ELAST2 is the elasticity of the target's compensation with respect to the bidder's compensation assuming renegotiation of merger terms if the bidder's price crosses a specified threshold. RELATIVE SIZE is the premerger market value of the target's equity divided by the market value of the bidder's equity, and the number of trading days between merger agreement and closing of merger is only calculated for completed mergers. The Fixed Ratio Stock mode is used when the target receives a fixed number of the bidder's shares, and the Conditional Stock mode is used when the number of bidder shares the target receives is a function of the bidder's share price.

| Mode of Acquisition | No. of Observations | WLS Mean 6-Day Return to Bidder: (BID6) | WLS Mean 3-Day Return to Bidder: (BID3) | Percent Common Stock | ELAST1 | ELAST2 | Mean RELATIVE SIZE | Mean Trading Days Between Agreement and Closing |
|---|---|---|---|---|---|---|---|---|
| Fixed ratio stock | 94 | −0.034 | −0.033 | 1 | 1 | 0.938 | 0.234 | 154.8 |
| Conditional stock | 60 | −0.013 | −0.011 | 1 | 0.536 | 0.455 | 0.133 | 170.0 |
| Fixed exchange ratio stock and cash | 9 | −0.023 | −0.037 | 0.698 | 0.698 | 0.662 | 0.209 | 200.9 |
| Conditional stock and cash | 17 | −0.002 | −0.007 | 0.636 | 0.184 | 0.177 | 0.052 | 188.4 |
| Cash, debt, and straight preferred | 29 | −0.008 | −0.006 | 0 | 0 | 0 | 0.102 | 194.4 |

Table II also illustrates the different levels of elasticity of target compensation for each offer type. In particular note that ELAST1 averages only 0.536 for pure conditional stock offers. Though not reported in the table, it is worth noting that there is considerable variation in these elasticities involving conditional stock offers. For the all conditional stock offer group, ELAST1 ranges from a minimum of zero to a maximum of 0.883. Interestingly, bidder returns appear to roughly correspond with the level of elasticity. Also notice that ELAST2 is only slightly less than ELAST1 for all categories of stock offers.

Table II reports two additional statistics of interest. First, we report the number of trading days between initial merger agreement and merger completion. The means are similar (and statistically indistinguishable at conventional significance levels) for conditional and fixed exchange ratio stock offers. More importantly, the 170 trading day interval for conditional stock offers leaves adequate time for uncertainty about the bidder's private information to be resolved before the merger's completion.[17] The results in Table II also indicate that the average relative size for conditional stock offers is similar to that found in cash offers, and considerably less than that found for fixed exchange ratio stock offers. The evidence on returns and size of acquisition suggests that conditional stock offers are used in circumstances similar to those of cash offers. These descriptive statistics also suggest that it is misleading to lump together conditional and fixed exchange ratio stock offers in analyzing the mode of acquisition.

## IV. Bidder Abnormal Returns and Adverse Selection

Tables I and II indicate that the average bidder realizes a negative abnormal return upon the announcement of an acquisition. However, there is considerable variation in the abnormal returns across the sample. Table III presents evidence relating bidder abnormal returns to the degree of protection the target receives against changes in the bidder's share price, as well as other factors that influence bidder abnormal returns. In Table III, ELAST1 is used as the measure of target sensitivity to changes in the bidder's share price. Table IV presents similar evidence using ELAST2.

To the extent the adverse selection hypothesis is correct, bidders with lower levels of ELAST1 and ELAST2, send a better signal to the capital markets, and therefore should realize, ceteris paribus, higher abnormal returns. When an elasticity measure is included with the percent of the offer that is stock, the coefficient on elasticity should continue to be negative and significant, with percent stock adding little explanatory power. In fact, if all relevant private information that the bidder has about the offer is revealed prior to the closing of the merger, then the percentage stock offered should have no explanatory power that is attributable to the private information revealed by the offer.

---

[17] Actually, the time for private information releases is slightly shorter because the price used to determine shares issued is generally an average of prices 5 to 25 trading days before merger completion.

**Table III**

## Regressions Relating the Bidder's Abnormal Return to the Mode of Acquisition and Other Characteristics of the Merger

Sample consists of all 209 bank merger agreements during the period 1985–1992. BID6 is the bidder abnormal return from four days before to one day after merger announcement. BID3 is the bidder abnormal return from one day before to one day after merger announcement. ELAST1 is the elasticity of the target's compensation with respect to the bidder's compensation assuming no renegotiation of merger terms if the bidder's price crosses a specified threshold. PCTSTOCK is the percent of the target's merger compensation that is received as common stock. RELATIVE SIZE is the premerger market value of the target's equity divided by the market value of the bidder's equity. OVERLAP is the number of overlapping bidder and target branches divided by bidder branches. RELATIVE SIZE* COMPETE is the relative size variable times a dummy variable that equals 1 if the bidder faced observable competition in acquiring the target, and RELATIVE SIZE*HIGH Q DUMMY the relative size variable times a dummy variable equal to one if the bidder has a market to book asset ratio greater than the median COMPUSTAT banking firm. The regressions are weighted by the inverse of the standard errors of the abnormal return estimates, and $t$-statistics are in parentheses.

| Dependent Variable | BID6 | BID6 | BID6 | BID3 | BID3 | BID3 |
|---|---|---|---|---|---|---|
| INTERCEPT | −0.004 | 0.002 | −0.000 | −0.003 | 0.000 | −0.000 |
| | (−0.54) | (0.30) | (−0.02) | (−0.54) | (0.09) | (−0.04) |
| ELAST1 | −0.037 | −0.028 | | −0.032 | −0.025 | |
| | (−3.45) | (−3.76) | | (−3.29) | (−3.78) | |
| PCTSTOCK | 0.013 | | −0.015 | 0.009 | | −0.015 |
| | (1.15) | | (−1.84) | (0.91) | | (−2.02) |
| RELATIVE SIZE | −0.095 | −0.098 | −0.117 | −0.078 | −0.080 | −0.096 |
| | (−3.29) | (−3.40) | (−4.01) | (−2.95) | (−3.05) | (−3.66) |
| OVERLAP | 0.091 | 0.087 | 0.082 | 0.071 | 0.069 | 0.064 |
| | (2.36) | (2.28) | (2.09) | (2.05) | (1.99) | (1.80) |
| RELATIVE SIZE* | −0.113 | −0.110 | −0.106 | −0.125 | −0.122 | −0.119 |
| COMPLETE | (−2.18) | (−2.11) | (−1.99) | (−2.62) | (−2.56) | (−2.42) |
| RELATIVE SIZE* | 0.072 | 0.074 | 0.074 | 0.052 | 0.054 | 0.055 |
| HIGH Q DUMMY | (2.49) | (2.58) | (2.51) | (2.01) | (2.08) | (2.05) |
| ADJUSTED $R^2$ | 0.178 | 0.176 | 0.134 | 0.186 | 0.187 | 0.147 |

The evidence in Tables III and IV strongly supports the adverse selection hypothesis. When elasticity is the only means of payment variable included in the cross-sectional regression of abnormal returns, there is a strong and statistically negative coefficient on each measure of elasticity. This result holds regardless of the length of the window used (3-day or 6-day) to calculate bidder abnormal returns. The point estimates suggest that bidder returns are more than three percent higher for offers providing targets full protection (elasticity equals 0), compared to offers with no protection (elasticity equal to 1).

Moreover, the results in Tables III and IV suggest that it is elasticity, not the percentage of stock, that influences abnormal returns. When both variables are included in the regression, the elasticity coefficient continues to be negative and significant, while the percent stock coefficient is positive but insignificant at the 10 percent level. When the only means of payment variable

Equity Issuance and Adverse Selection: A Direct Test          213

### Table IV
## Regressions Relating the Bidder's Abnormal Return to the Mode of Acquisition and Other Characteristics of the Merger Using an Alternative Elasticity Measure

Weighted least squares (WLS) regressions relating the abnormal return of the bidding banks from a sample of 209 publicly traded mergers, 1985–1992, to the mode of acquisition and other characteristics of the merger. BID6 is the bidder abnormal return from four days before to one day after merger announcement. BID3 is the bidder abnormal return from one day before to one day after merger announcement. ELAST2 is the elasticity of the target's compensation with respect to the bidder's compensation assuming renegotiation of merger terms if the bidder's price crosses a specified threshold. PCTSTOCK is the percent of the target's merger compensation that is received as common stock. RELATIVE SIZE is the premerger market value of the target's equity divided by the market value of the bidder's equity. OVERLAP is the number of overlapping bidder and target branches divided by bidder branches. RELATIVE SIZE* COMPETE is the relative size variable times a dummy variable that equals 1 if the bidder faced observable competition in acquiring the target, and RELATIVE SIZE* HIGH Q DUMMY the relative size variable times a dummy variable equal to one if the bidder has a market-to-book asset ratio greater than the median COMPUSTAT banking firm. The regressions are weighted by the inverse of the standard errors of the abnormal return estimates, and $t$-statistics are in parentheses.

| Dependent Variable | BID6 | BID6 | BID3 | BID3 |
|---|---|---|---|---|
| INTERCEPT | −0.004 | 0.000 | −0.004 | 0.000 |
| | (−0.53) | (0.09) | (−0.55) | (0.06) |
| ELAST2 | −0.035 | −0.029 | −0.032 | −0.027 |
| | (−3.24) | (−3.65) | (−3.27) | (−3.80) |
| PCTSTOCK | 0.009 | | 0.007 | |
| | (0.85) | | (0.74) | |
| RELATIVE SIZE | −0.092 | −0.095 | −0.074 | −0.076 |
| | (−3.12) | (−3.24) | (−2.76) | (−2.86) |
| OVERLAP | 0.092 | 0.089 | 0.073 | 0.071 |
| | (2.38) | (2.32) | (2.09) | (2.04) |
| RELATIVE SIZE* COMPETE | −0.118 | −0.114 | −0.129 | −0.126 |
| | (−2.26) | (−2.20) | (−2.69) | (−2.64) |
| RELATIVE SIZE* HIGH Q DUMMY | 0.070 | 0.072 | 0.051 | 0.053 |
| | (2.43) | (2.51) | (1.95) | (2.03) |
| ADJUSTED $R^2$ | 0.172 | 0.173 | 0.186 | 0.188 |

included in the regressions is percent stock offered, the coefficient on percent stock is negative and significant at the 10 percent level for the six day return regression and at the 5 percent level for the three day return regression. This evidence indicates that there is considerable variability in the information content of stock offers.[18]

[18] Arguably, the information content of a conditional stock offer also depends on how long it takes to complete the deal. If the deal is completed in a short period of time, a conditional stock offer will have an information content similar to that of a fixed exchange stock offer, whereas if the deal takes a long time to complete, its information content is more similar to that of a cash offer. To consider this effect, we create a new variable, TIMEINT, which is calculated as a weighted average of ELAST1 and PCTSTOCK. The weight is the number of trading days it takes to complete the deal divided by 127 (the number of trading days in a six-month period). If a deal took more than six months to complete, we assume that all of the bidder's private information was revealed, and

Other estimates in Tables III and IV deserve mention. First, there is a negative relationship between bidder abnormal returns and RELATIVE SIZE. This result suggests that bidders suffer more when they make larger acquisitions. Bidders that face competition in acquiring the target also realize lower abnormal returns proportional to RELATIVE SIZE. Also, consistent with Houston and Ryngaert (1994) the positive coefficient on OVERLAP suggests that bidders do better the greater the amount of overlap between the markets in which they and the target operate. Finally, we find a positive and significant coefficient on the variable which interacts RELATIVE SIZE with a dummy variable indicating whether the bidder's $Q$ exceeds the industry median for the year prior to the acquisition. This indicates that better performing banks realize higher abnormal returns when they make an acquisition.

The results in Tables III and IV are remarkably similar, suggesting that the results are robust with respect to the elasticity measure used. It appears that the option to back out of a deal if the bidder's stock price goes beyond a certain threshold does not materially affect the signal provided by the mode of acquisition. This probably reflects the fact that the majority of these options are exercisable only if there is a considerable change in the bidder's share price after the announcement of the acquisition.

Table V reports similar estimates for the subset of deals in which there was a definitive agreement, and for the subset of deals that were ultimately completed. Arguably, agreements that are preliminary in nature are not binding contracts. In fact, stock offers that are preliminary might be viewed as "conditional" offers in the sense that any decline in bidder stock value might lead to a renegotiation of terms before a definitive agreement is made. Similarly, the set of deals that are ultimately completed might be viewed as deals that the participants were more firmly committed to at their inception. The results in Table V, however, are similar to our previous estimates for the whole sample. The elasticity variable is again negative, significant, and roughly of the same magnitude as documented in Table III, while the percent stock variable has little explanatory power. Consequently, including canceled deals and nondefinitive deals in our sample does not appear to alter our conclusions.

As a final robustness check, Table VI presents regressions that restrict the analysis to offers that are exclusively stock. This eliminates any special influence that cash offers might have on the sample. Again, we find a strong negative relationship between bidder abnormal returns and the measures of elasticity. This result reinforces our previous results and highlights the uniqueness of our tests. Whether a firm issues stock through a fixed exchange ratio offer (with elasticity equal to 1) or a conditional offer (with an elasticity less than 1), has little or no effect on firm free cash flow, firm capital structure,

in these instances we set the weight equal to one, which sets TIMEINT equal to ELAST1. The results are qualitatively similar using TIMEINT, as opposed to ELAST1 as the explanatory variable. One drawback of using TIMEINT is that it somewhat arbitrarily assumes that all private information is revealed in six months (although we do obtain similar results using alternative benchmark periods). A second drawback is that it forces us to throw out deals that were not completed.

**Table V**

## Regressions Relating the Abnormal Return of Bidding Banks to the Mode of Acquisition and Other Characteristics of the Merger for Subsamples with Mergers with Definitive Agreements and Mergers that were Completed

Subsamples come from full sample of 209 bank merger agreements during the period 1985–1992. BID6 is the bidder abnormal return from four days before to one day after merger announcement. ELAST1 is the elasticity of the target's compensation with respect to the bidder's compensation assuming no renegotiation of merger terms if the bidder's price crosses a specified threshold. PCTSTOCK is the percent of the target's merger compensation that is received as common stock. RELATIVE SIZE is the premerger market value of the target's equity divided by the market value of the bidder's equity. OVERLAP is the number of overlapping bidder and target branches divided by bidder branches. RELATIVE SIZE* COMPETE is the relative size variable times a dummy variable that equals 1 if the bidder faced observable competition in acquiring the target, and RELATIVE SIZE* HIGH Q DUMMY the relative size variable times a dummy variable equal to one if the bidder has a market to book asset ratio greater than the median COMPUSTAT banking firm. The regressions are weighted by the inverse of the standard errors of the abnormal return estimates, and $t$-statistics are in parentheses.

| Sample | Mergers With Definitive Agreement (N = 151) | Mergers With Definitive Agreement (N = 151) | Completed Mergers (N = 184) | Completed Mergers (N = 184) |
|---|---|---|---|---|
| Dependent Variable | BID6 | BID6 | BID6 | BID6 |
| INTERCEPT | −0.010 | −0.007 | −0.004 | 0.003 |
|  | (−1.10) | (−0.95) | (−0.58) | (0.56) |
| ELAST1 | −0.036 | −0.029 | −0.039 | −0.027 |
|  | (−2.25) | (−3.05) | (−3.41) | (−3.38) |
| PCTSTOCK | 0.010 |  | 0.018 |  |
|  | (0.57) |  | (1.48) |  |
| RELATIVE SIZE | −0.090 | −0.092 | −0.102 | −0.106 |
|  | (−2.75) | (−2.81) | (−3.40) | (−3.51) |
| OVERLAP | 0.120 | 0.118 | 0.081 | 0.078 |
|  | (2.67) | (2.65) | (2.09) | (2.00) |
| RELATIVE SIZE* COMPETE | −0.104 | −0.102 | −0.230 | −0.224 |
|  | (−1.84) | (−1.80) | (−3.66) | (−3.57) |
| RELATIVE SIZE* HIGH Q DUMMY | 0.080 | 0.081 | 0.075 | 0.078 |
|  | (2.48) | (2.52) | (2.52) | (2.58) |
| ADJUSTED $R^2$ | 0.172 | 0.219 | 0.214 | 0.169 |

the supply of firm stock, or the tax treatment of the company. Thus, a more positive share price response to lower elasticity conditional stock offers is difficult to explain outside of a private information framework.

## V. Factors Affecting the Degree of Protection Provided to Targets

The above results suggest that if a bidding bank offers target shareholders a fixed number of shares rather than making a low elasticity conditional stock offer, target firms will assume that the bidder's stock is overvalued and attach a lower value to the offer. Nevertheless, stock offers with fixed exchange ratios

**Table VI**

## Regressions Relating Bidder Abnormal Returns to the Elasticity of Target Compensation and Other Merger Characteristics for a Subsample of 154 Merger Deals Entirely Financed with Common Stock During the Period 1985–1992

BID6 is the bidder abnormal return from four days before to one day after merger announcement. BID3 is the bidder abnormal return from one day before to one day after merger announcement, ELAST1 is the elasticity of the target's compensation with respect to the bidder's compensation assuming no renegotiation of merger terms if the bidder's price crosses a specified threshold, RELATIVE SIZE is the premerger market value of the target's equity divided by the market value of the bidder's equity. OVERLAP is the number of overlapping bidder and target branches divided by the bidder branches. RELATIVE SIZE* COMPETE is the relative size variable times a dummy variable that equals 1 if the bidder faced observable competition in acquiring the target, and RELATIVE SIZE* HIGH Q DUMMY the relative size variable times a dummy variable equal to one if the bidder has a market to book asset ratio greater than the median COMPUSTAT banking firm. The regressions are weighted by the inverse of the standard errors from the estimated abnormal returns, and the $t$-statistics are in parentheses.

| Dependent Variable | BID6 | BID3 |
|---|---|---|
| INTERCEPT | 0.006 | 0.006 |
|  | (0.61) | (0.64) |
| ELAST1 | −0.034 | −0.031 |
|  | (−2.93) | (−2.81) |
| RELATIVE SIZE | −0.103 | −0.094 |
|  | (−3.29) | (−3.23) |
| OVERLAP | 0.115 | 0.100 |
|  | (2.67) | (2.50) |
| RELATIVE SIZE* COMPETE | −0.118 | −0.131 |
|  | (−2.16) | (−2.54) |
| RELATIVE SIZE* HIGH Q DUMMY | 0.085 | 0.068 |
|  | (2.77) | (2.38) |
| ADJUSTED $R^2$ | 0.205 | 0.206 |

frequently are observed in bank merger offers, despite the lemons problems that can arise from such offers. This result therefore raises an interesting question: What determines the degree of protection that bidders provide target shareholders?

To address this question, we appeal to a model developed by Hansen (1987). Hansen shows how the medium of exchange is structured to reduce the costs of adverse selection when *both* the bidder and the target have private information. Cash offers resolve the lemons problem concerning the bidder's value, while stock offers reduce the lemons problem concerning the target's value. Hansen's model predicts that cash offers are more likely when the market value of the target is small relative to the bidder.

Hansen does not consider conditional stock offers. However, if most of the bidder's private information becomes public before the completion of the merger, conditional stock offers allow a bidder to avoid issuing undervalued shares in a fashion similar to cash offers. Thus, we predict that low elasticity offers (conditional stock offers and cash offers) are more likely when the target's market value is smaller relative to the bidder's market value—suggesting a positive relationship between elasticity and RELATIVE SIZE.

We believe that two other factors can explain the choice of offer elasticity. The greater the correlation of premerger stock returns, the more likely it is that the bidder will employ a high elasticity offer for two reasons. First, it is less likely that the bidder can mislead the target with respect to its private information. Large positive correlation in returns suggests that the bidder and target are affected by similar economic forces. Second, if stand alone bidder and target values tend to move together, then setting a fixed common stock exchange ratio (a high elasticity offer) makes more sense because it is more likely that the terms of the merger will remain "fair" to both parties at the time the deal closes. For instance, if a bidding bank establishes a fixed dollar acquisition price and then the stock prices of banks collapse (boom), the bidding firm (target firm) would have an incentive to find some means to back out of the deal. This kind of ex-post contractual squabbling can be avoided by setting the terms initially in a way that will diminish the probability that the terms will eventually become "unfair" in the eyes of either party. We measure the correlation of bidder and target stock returns using weekly stock returns in the period 230 to 31 trading days before the target was first "put in play."

There is also reason to believe that competition for the target might be important in determining the elasticity of the offer made. For instance, Fishman (1989) argues that in more competitive bidding environments, bidders will make offers that are less contingent on the value of the merged firm. Furthermore, bidders may wish to put forth a firm price for a company in a bidding contest so that the value of their offer does not fluctuate with their share price.

We formally test whether relative size, stock return correlation, and competition can explain the choice of elasticity of target compensation. One concern is that the dependent variables, ELAST1 and ELAST2, are constrained to be between 0 and 1. Ordinary least squares (OLS) estimates, while instructive, may be biased. To address this concern, we present double-sided Tobit estimates that constrain the dependent variable to be between 0 and 1.[19]

The first set of results in Table VII are estimates for all 209 agreements in our sample. Consistent with Hansen (1987), statistically significant coefficients on the relative size and correlation variables indicate that higher elasticity offers are more likely when the target is large and the correlation of bidder and target stock returns is high. This holds true regardless of the elasticity measure employed. While the coefficient on the competition dummy

---

[19] LIMDEP was used to generate the double-sided Tobit results. See Greene (1993) for a description of the problems that arise when dependent variables are either censored or truncated. In all cases the double-sided Tobit results are qualitatively similar to the unreported OLS estimates.

**Table VII**

## Double Sided Tobit Estimates of the Elasticity of Target's Compensation

Double-sided Tobit estimates the elasticity of the target's compensation for the entire sample of 209 bank merger agreements and a subsample of 154 all common stock offers during the period 1985–1992. RELATIVE SIZE is the premerger market value of the target's equity divided by the market value of the bidder's equity. CORRELATION is the correlation of the bidder and targets weekly stock returns over a 200 day window preceding the first news story indicating that the target was a takeover candidate, and COMPETE is a dummy variable that equals 1 if the bidder faced observable competition in acquiring the target. $t$-statistics in parentheses.

| Sample | Entire Sample (N = 209) | Entire Sample (N = 209) | Common Stock Only | Common Stock Only |
|---|---|---|---|---|
| Dependent Variable | ELAST1 | ELAST2 | ELAST1 | ELAST2 |
| INTERCEPT | 0.443 | 0.370 | 0.895 | 0.701 |
| | (4.18) | (5.25) | (10.12) | (12.37) |
| RELATIVE SIZE | 1.901 | 1.408 | 0.935 | 0.792 |
| | (3.84) | (4.59) | (2.64) | (3.62) |
| CORRELATION | 0.992 | 0.489 | 0.627 | 0.241 |
| | (2.63) | (2.02) | (2.14) | (1.30) |
| COMPETE | −0.399 | −0.322 | −0.333 | −0.303 |
| | (−1.62) | (−1.99) | (−1.70) | (−2.34) |
| Log Likelihood | −199.12 | −190.81 | −106.30 | −99.12 |

is of the correct sign, its significance is dependent on the elasticity measure used.

Table VII also presents results for the subset of firms where the method of payment is all stock. This is a better test of whether the choice of offer elasticity is dependent on private information concerns, because offers with cash in them may be driven, in part, by capital structure and tax concerns. The results are strikingly similar and again consistent with private information models of the means of payment. For the specification using ELAST1, the relative size and correlation coefficients are significant, while for the specification using ELAST2, the relative size and compete coefficients are significant.

## VI. Conclusion

This article examines how stock offers can be structured to mitigate adverse selection problems in bank mergers. In particular, we discuss how a bidder can provide a target with protection against price deterioration in the bidder's stock price between the time a merger is announced and the time it is completed. We show that bidders receive higher merger announcement returns when greater levels of protection are built into a merger offer. In fact, we show that it is not the percentage of stock offered in a merger that conveys private information about the bidder's value, but rather how sensitive the target's compensation is to changes in the bidder's stock price during the time it takes

*Equity Issuance and Adverse Selection: A Direct Test* 219

to complete the merger. We also demonstrate that the decision on how sensitive to make the target's compensation to bidder stock price changes is driven by factors that are largely consistent with adverse selection models of the method of payment. While our analysis has focused on one type of equity issuance in a single industry, our tests enable us to more completely isolate the effects of adverse selection. Consequently, our results provide support to earlier studies that have attributed declining firm value at the announcement of equity issuances to adverse selection.

## REFERENCES

Asquith, Paul, Robert F. Bruner, and David W. Mullins, Jr., 1983, The gains to bidding firms from merger, *Journal of Financial Economics* 11, 121–140.

Asquith, Paul, and David W. Mullins, Jr., 1986, Equity issues and offering dilution, *Journal of Financial Economics* 15, 61–89.

Bradley, Michael, Anand Desai, and E. Han Kim, 1988, Synergistic gains from corporate acquisitions and their division between the shareholders of target and acquiring firms, *Journal of Financial Economics* 21, 3–40.

Brown, David, and Michael Ryngaert, 1991, The mode of acquisition in takeovers: Taxes and asymmetric information, *Journal of Finance* 46, 653–669.

Eckbo, B. Espen, Ronald M. Giammarino, and Robert L. Heinkel, 1990, Asymmetric information and the medium of exchange in takeovers: Theory and tests. *Review of Financial Studies* 3, 651–675.

Fishman, Michael, 1989, Preemptive bidding and the role of the medium of exchange in acquisitions, *Journal of Finance* 44, 41–58.

Greene, William, 1993, *Econometric Analysis* (Macmillan Publishing Company, New York).

Hansen, Robert, 1987, A theory of the choice of exchange medium in mergers and acquisitions, *Journal of Business* 60, 75–95.

Houston, Joel, and Michael Ryngaert, 1994, The overall gains from large bank mergers, *Journal of Banking & Finance* 18, 1155–1176.

Jensen, Michael C., 1986, Agency costs of free cash flow, corporate finance, and takeovers, *American Economic Review* 76, 323–329.

Korajczyk, Robert, Deborah Lucas, and Robert McDonald, 1991, The effect of information releases on the pricing and timing of equity issues, *Review of Financial Studies* 4, 685–708.

Lang, Larry, René Stulz, and Ralph A. Walkling, 1989, Tobin's q and the gains from successful tender offers, *Journal of Financial Economics* 24, 137–154.

Lucas, Deborah, and Robert McDonald, 1990, Equity issues and stock price dynamics, *Journal of Finance* 45, 1019–1043.

Loderer, Claudia, John W. Cooney, and Leonard D. Van Drunen, 1991, The price elasticity of demand for common stock, *Journal of Finance* 46, 621–652.

Masulis, Ronald, and Anwar Korwar, 1986, Seasoned equity offerings: An empirical investigation, *Journal of Financial Economics* 15, 91–118.

Myers, Stewart, and Nicholas Majluf, 1984, Corporate financing and investment decisions when firms have information that investors do not have, *Journal of Financial Economics* 13, 187–221.

Neely, Walter P., 1987, Banking acquisitions: Acquirer and target shareholder returns, *Financial Management* 16, 66–73.

Servaes, Henri, 1991, Tobin's q and the gains from takeovers, *Journal of Finance* 46, 409–419.

Travlos, Nickolaos, 1987, Corporate takeover bids, the method of payment and bidding firms' stock returns, *Journal of Finance* 42, 943–963.

# [16]

Journal of Financial Economics 37 (1995) 3–37

# Asset sales, firm performance, and the agency costs of managerial discretion

Larry Lang[a], Annette Poulsen[b], René Stulz*[,c]

[a] *Chinese University, Hong Kong, Hong Kong*
[b] *University of Georgia, Athens, GA 30602, USA*
[c] *Ohio State University, Columbus, OH 43210, USA*

(Received May 1992; final version received February 1994)

## Abstract

We argue that management sells assets when doing so provides the cheapest funds to pursue its objectives rather than for operating efficiency reasons alone. This hypothesis suggests that (1) firms selling assets have high leverage and/or poor performance, (2) a successful asset sale is good news, and (3) the stock market discounts asset sale proceeds retained by the selling firm. In support of this hypothesis, we find that the typical firm in our sample performs poorly before the sale and that the average stock-price reaction to asset sales is positive only when the proceeds are paid out.

*Key words*: Asset sales
*JEL classification*: G3; L2

## 1. Introduction

Existing empirical evidence shows that asset sale announcements are associated with positive stock-price reactions. Alexander, Benson, and Kampmeyer (1984), Hite, Owers, and Rogers (1987), and Jain (1985) document significant average abnormal returns between 0.5% and 1.66%. The theory advanced in the

---

* Corresponding author.

Respectively, Reader, Chinese University of Hong Kong, Augustus H. 'Billy' Sterne Chair in Banking and Finance, University of Georgia, and Ralph Kurtz Chair in Finance, The Ohio State University, and NBER. We are grateful for useful comments from David Brown, Gailen Hite, Ravi Jagannathan, Michael Jensen, David Mayers, Robert McCormick, Craig Lewis, Jeffry Netter, Tim Opler, Eli Ofek, participants at seminars at Clemson University, New York University, the University of Michigan, the WFA meetings in San Francisco, the AFA meetings in Anaheim, and especially Harry DeAngelo (the referee).

literature to explain this empirical evidence, most explicitly by Hite, Owers, and Rogers (1987), is that asset sales promote efficiency by allocating assets to better uses, and sellers capture some of the resulting gains. With this view, which we call the efficient deployment hypothesis of asset sales, managers only retain assets for which they have a comparative advantage and sell assets as soon as another party can manage them more efficiently irrespective of their financial situation; stockholders benefit from asset sales equally of whether managers re-invest the proceeds or pay them out.

In this paper, we advance an alternative explanation for asset sales. We take as our starting point that management values firm size and control, so that it is reluctant to sell assets for efficiency reasons alone. For such management, a more compelling motivation to sell assets is that asset sales provide funds when alternative sources of financing are too expensive, possibly because of agency costs of debt or because information asymmetries make equity sales unattractive.[1] With this view, which we call the financing hypothesis of asset sales, the completion of an asset sale is good news about the value of the asset because if the value of the asset had turned out to be low, the sale would not have taken place. Further, one expects the market to discount proceeds of asset sales retained by the firm in the presence of agency costs of managerial discretion since shareholders do not capture all of the value of the asset sold.

Our main empirical results are consistent with the financing hypothesis of asset sales rather than with the efficient deployment hypothesis. First, we show that firms selling assets tend to be poor performers and/or have high leverage. In particular, for our sample, median net income normalized by total assets is insignificantly different from zero in the year before the sale, even though we exclude from the sample bankrupt firms and firms in default. This result suggests that the typical firm selling assets is motivated to do so by its financial situation rather than by the discovery that some other firm has a comparative advantage in operating the assets. Second, contrary to the efficient deployment hypothesis, we find that the stock-price reaction to successful asset sales is strongly related to the use of the proceeds. In our sample, the stock-price reaction to asset sales is significantly positive for those firms expected to use the proceeds to pay down debt, but negative and insignificant for firms which are expected to keep the proceeds within the firm.

Section 2 develops the financing hypothesis in greater detail and discusses the existing empirical evidence. Section 3 presents our sample of large asset sales. In Section 4, we investigate the characteristics of the firms in our sample and show that they are consistent with the financing hypothesis. In Section 5, we show that

---

[1] In addition, as argued by Boot (1992) and Weisbach (1993), management might be reluctant to sell because doing so might reveal that it made poor investment choices. Weisbach (1993) shows that divestitures are concentrated around management changes.

*L. Lang et al./Journal of Financial Economics 37 (1995) 3– 37*                    5

abnormal returns associated with asset sale announcements differ substantially between firms that have performed poorly and use the proceeds to repay debt and those that do not. Section 6 uses cross-sectional regressions to explore the robustness of our main results. Concluding remarks are presented in Section 7.


## 2. The financing hypothesis

The efficient deployment hypothesis assumes that management maximizes shareholder wealth. In contrast, the financing hypothesis assumes that management pursues its own objectives and, more specifically, values control and firm size. Since it values firm size, management has little incentive to sell assets unless it needs to raise funds and cannot do so cheaply on capital markets. Management may have to raise funds to reduce financial distress costs, to pay dividends to shareholders to prevent a takeover, or to undertake investments that it values but shareholders do not.

Why would selling assets be an efficient source of new funds? Consider a firm where management wants to raise funds to pursue its own objectives but cannot sell low-risk debt because the firm has high leverage and/or poor performance. Outsiders know that the firm wants to raise funds. Such a firm may find it expensive to use the capital markets for at least three reasons: First, it may face the underinvestment problem described by Myers (1977) or the asset substitution problem analyzed by Jensen and Meckling (1976). Second, raising outside funds may be costly because of the adverse selection costs modeled by Myers and Majluf (1984). Third, the cost of outside funds may be high because of agency costs of managerial discretion.[2] In particular, if management is expected to use new funds to pursue objectives of doubtful value, capital providers require a higher promised rate of return or restrictions on the use of funds.

Asset sales may provide a source of funds that managers find preferable to capital markets despite high transaction costs. First, informational asymmetries may be less important for the asset the firm wants to sell than for the firm as a whole. Second, if the firm's debt overhang is large, selling an asset may avoid the recapitalization costs that would have to be paid to raise funds on capital markets. Third, if management pursues its own objectives, selling an asset provides funds with potentially fewer restrictions on managerial discretion.

Of course, managers trying to sell an asset to obtain cheaper funds than on the capital markets may fail. The sale price they can obtain after shopping the asset may be too low to justify selling it, either because the asset is worth too little to outsiders relative to its value in its current use or because, as emphasized by Shleifer and Vishny (1992), a quick asset sale may require a large discount

---

[2]See Jensen (1988) and Stulz (1990).

because of limited liquidity. Hence, if the firm succeeds in selling the asset at
a price that makes the transaction worthwhile, this is good news about the
asset's value even if it is known that managers want to sell the asset to raise
funds.

If the intended use of the proceeds is a positive NPV project for the shareholders, and if the firm does not have a more advantageous source of funds,
a successful asset sale means that the firm can carry out the positive NPV
project with the cheapest available funds. For some firms, however, the sale
proceeds could be put to uses that do not increase shareholder wealth, so that
the good news about the value of the asset sold is tempered or negated by the
expectation that some of the proceeds will be wasted by management. For
instance, a firm whose core operations are suffering massive losses and should be
changed dramatically may sell assets to finance these losses to avoid making
necessary changes. Hence, for firms where agency costs of managerial discretion
are important, the stock market views asset sales where the proceeds are paid
out to debtholders or shareholders more favorably than those where the proceeds are kept within the firm.

## 3. The sample of asset sales and the use of the proceeds

To investigate the financing hypothesis, we have to identify the use of the
proceeds from asset sales, since this hypothesis specifies that the stock-price
effect of the announcement of asset sales is related to the use of the proceeds.
In this section, we describe our sample and our evidence on the use of
the proceeds. We investigate asset sales reported to the SEC in 8K forms
as identified through the NEXIS database.[3] NEXIS reports all 8K filings
from October 1988 but only selected abstracts are included from 1985 through
October 1988. The 8K form requires that the registrant furnish specific information if it or '... any of its majority-owned subsidiaries has acquired or disposed.
of a significant amount of assets, otherwise than in the ordinary course
of business'. Hence, asset sales reported in 8K forms are ideally suited to address
the issues raised in this paper, since the firm deems the sale to be both significant
and unanticipated. In particular, the sample selection criteria exclude asset
sales programs and make the sample more appropriate to investigate the
financing hypothesis.

We identify 151 asset sales taking place from 1984 to 1989 for firms which
have data available on the Compustat files. We want to study voluntary asset
sales and therefore eliminate firms that are in default, in a corporate control contest, in voluntary or involuntary liquidation, or that have filed for

---

[3]The NEXIS search used the key words 'asset' within ten words of 'sale', and 'divestitures'.

reorganization under Chapter 11.[4] Further, we omit all asset sales of less than $1 million. Finally, we eliminate all firms for which stock returns could not be found on the CRSP files for NYSE and AMEX stocks. Of the 151 asset sales, 93 sales made by 77 firms satisfy our additional criteria. The Appendix provides detailed information on each sale in our sample; the reader can refer to this Appendix when we mention specific sales in our discussion. The average number of asset sales per year (15.3) in our sample is substantially smaller than in the Jain (1985) sample, but substantially larger than in the Alexander, Benson, and Kampmeyer (1984) and Hite, Owers, and Rogers (1987) samples. We use as the announcement date the earliest of the following three dates: (1) the Wall Street Journal (WSJ) announcement date (44 cases), (2) the Dow Jones News Retrieval Service announcement date (25 cases), (3) the agreement date as reported by the 8K filing (24 cases).

Since we are interested in the differences between firms that are expected to pay out the proceeds and those that are not, we use information from the 8K filings, annual reports, the S&P Standard Stock Reports, and the WSJ to determine why the asset was sold and how management expects to use the proceeds. The sample has 40 asset sales by 35 firms with proceeds paid out to creditors and/or shareholders and 53 sales by 43 firms with proceeds retained by the firm (one firm makes one sale of each type). We call the sample of 40 sales the 'payout sample' and the sample of 53 sales the 'reinvest' sample throughout the paper. For 22 asset sales by 18 firms in the payout sample, information about the use of the proceeds is given by the 8K filing or press articles contemporaneous with the announcement.[5] For the other 18 asset sales in the payout sample, our sources describing the use of funds are later than the sale announcement. These sources are the annual report (12 times), an 8K filing subsequent to the announcement date (four times), or the S&P Standard Stock Reports (two times).

If the financing hypothesis applies to the sales in our sample, we would expect the proceeds paid out to be used to pay down debt rather than to distribute cash to shareholders. If a firm is excessively levered in management's eyes, management has a strong motivation to sell assets to reduce leverage and avoid possible costs of financial distress. In contrast, management that values size and control seems unlikely to want to pay out the proceeds to the shareholders in the absence of pressures from the market for corporate control. Evidence that

---

[4]Brown, James, and Mooradian (1993) study asset sales of firms in default. They find that asset sales of firms in default where the proceeds are paid out to creditors typically benefit creditors at the expense of shareholders.

[5]Of these 22 sales, there are 12 cases where the source for the announcement date is the WSJ or the Dow Jones Wire and the use of funds is given in the WSJ and four cases where the announcement date is the date of the 8K filing and the 8K form gives the use of funds. In the remaining six cases, the announcement is the Dow Jones Wire and the use of funds is from the 8K form filed on the same day.

management tends to pay out the proceeds to shareholders would seem consistent with the absence of agency costs of managerial discretion and supportive of the efficient deployment hypothesis which implies that management pays out to shareholders funds it cannot invest profitably within the firm. We have only five cases where there is evidence that management plans to pay some of the proceeds to shareholders: Allied-Signal, Culbro Corp., Federal Mogul, Koppers Co., and Union Carbide. Since we have only five observations where shareholders receive some of the proceeds directly, we cannot investigate this subsample separately in the following analysis and treat it as part of the sample of firms that pay out the proceeds. The results in this paper do not depend on these five observations.

Even when there is no indication that management expects to pay out part of the proceeds to shareholders, there could still be an indirect connection between asset sales and payouts to shareholders. For instance, management could sell assets to replenish liquid assets used for repurchases or to repay debt incurred to finance share repurchases; alternatively, it could change its mind about the use of the proceeds after the sale and repurchase shares. A careful reading of the case histories provided in the Appendix shows that the evidence in favor of an indirect connection is limited. After the sale, only two firms not paying out proceeds, John Fluke and Varo Inc., announced that they would undertake a stock repurchase. For ten firms paying out proceeds, there are repurchase announcements in the year before the sale. Six of these repurchases are targeted repurchases where the company buys out a major shareholder, raising suspicion of entrenchment.

There is some indication, though, that dividend payments may be affected by asset sales in our sample. Irrespective of the use of the proceeds, approximately twice as many firms increase dividends in the year after the sale compared to the 12 months before the sale (five relative to three for firms that pay out proceeds; 11 relative to five for those that do not). Two firms that pay out the proceeds decrease dividends in the 12 months before the sale and one in the following 12 months. In contrast, three firms that retain the proceeds reduce dividends in the year before the sale and one does so in the year following.

In our sample, firms provide a number of different reasons for selling assets. In some cases, they sell assets explicitly to reduce debt. In other cases, they give other reasons to sell assets, but still pay out the proceeds. If a firm sells an asset and pays out the proceeds, though, the asset sale typically reduces the firm's diversification. If the asset is an unrelated division, it necessarily does so. To avoid this mechanical relation between paying out the proceeds and greater firm focus, we explore separately management's motivation for the sale for the firms which retain the proceeds. For the 53 sales made by firms that do not plan to pay out the proceeds, the following reasons for undertaking the sales are given for at least five sales in our sample:

*L. Lang et al./Journal of Financial Economics 37 (1995) 3–37* 9

(1) *Focusing on core businesses.* For instance, Warner Communications Inc. sold Franklin Mint in 1984 because this business was not part of its core businesses. In total, we have 15 firms (21 asset sales) where this motivation is prevalent.

(2) *Selling unprofitable or slow-growing businesses.* An example of this is the sale of United Inns Inc.'s car wash business in 1988 for $17 million. Thirteen firms (14 asset sales) fit this explanation.

(3) *To finance acquisitions or expansion.* Primark Corp. sold its TV leasing business for $37.9 million in 1988 to generate cash for a pending acquisition. This explanation seems appropriate for six firms (nine asset sales).

It is noteworthy that many companies seem to sell assets while engaged in a program of acquisitions so that the asset sales provide cash for these programs, even though management may motivate the asset sale using different considerations, such as eliminating unprofitable divisions or focusing on core activities. These cases are certainly consistent with the view that management might be raising funds to pursue its own objectives. An example of such a sale is the sale by Canal Capital Corp. of its stockyard business for close to $7 million in 1989. The annual report mentions that the stockyard business was not profitable, but at the same time the firm had moved (according to its annual report) from a stockyard firm to a diversified firm interested in real estate development, trading securities, and investing in ancient art!

Table 1 summarizes the characteristics of the sales for our whole sample and for the two subsamples formed according to the use of the proceeds. It is immediately apparent that our sample selection procedure is successful in identifying asset sales that are significant for the selling firms. The median asset sale in our sample represents 23% of the value of the selling firm's equity. There is a significant difference (at the 0.01 level) between the median sale proceeds as a fraction of the equity value for firms that pay out proceeds (42%) and the other firms (13%). The difference in the size of the sale relative to equity is partly due to the fact that the median market value of equity for the firms in the reinvest sample is higher than for the firms in the payout sample. There is no significant difference, however, between the median book values of total assets of the two groups of firms. Finally, we report the average accounting gain or loss on sale, which turns out to be small for the typical firm regardless of the use of the proceeds. Evidence of an average accounting loss on sale would indicate that firms mostly sell losers and might be supportive of the efficient deployment hypothesis of asset sales.

## 4. Firm characteristics and the financing hypothesis

With the financing hypothesis, firms selling assets are firms for which raising funds on capital markets is likely to be expensive because of high leverage

10            *L. Lang et al./Journal of Financial Economics 37 (1995) 3– 37*

Table 1
The sample of 93 significant asset sales from 1984 to 1989

The sales are obtained from inspection of 8K forms. The accounting loss on the sale is from the 8K form. All other data are obtained from Compustat and CRSP tapes. The Compustat data are from the year preceding the asset sale. The market value of equity is for six days before the announcement date. *, **, and *** denote significance of the *t*-test for the difference in the means between the two subsamples at the 0.1, 0.05, and 0.01 levels respectively. (In parentheses we report the significance level for the median test.)

|  | Whole sample (93 sales) | Payout sample (40 sales) | Reinvest sample (53 sales) |
|---|---|---|---|
|  | Mean (Median) | Mean (Median) | Mean (Median) |
| Value of sale (million $) | 120.68 (32.50) | 129.04 (50.50) | 114.00 (22.00) |
| Market value of equity (million $) (**) | 904.78 (150.45) | 740.30 (110.00) | 1028.92 (292.64) |
| Value of sale/Value of equity **(***) | 0.69 (0.23) | 1.32 (0.42) | 0.18 (0.13) |
| Total assets (TA) (million $) | 1470.48 (348.93) | 1588.04 (348.93) | 1387.21 (366.05) |
| Value of sale/TA ***(***) | 0.11 (0.09) | 0.17 (0.13) | 0.07 (0.06) |
| Gain on sale/Market value of equity (**) | − 0.95% (0.19%) | 2.23% (1.41%) | − 3.25% (0.00%) |

and/or poor performance. In this section, we investigate the characteristics of the firms in our sample and whether they are consistent with the financing hypothesis. We also seek to understand how the firms that pay out the proceeds differ from those that do not, since the financing hypothesis implies that firms that pay out the proceeds will do so because of excessive leverage.

In Table 2, we provide data on the firms which made the 93 asset sales in our sample. Although we report both means and medians, we focus on the medians because the sometimes large difference between means and medians indicates that the distribution of the variables is not symmetric, and hence the medians are likely to be more informative about the typical sample firm. The median interest coverage is 2.53, but firms in the payout sample have a lower coverage ratio than firms in the reinvest sample. The median coverage ratio of firms that pay out the proceeds is 1.56, indicating that earnings for the typical firm exceed interest payments by 56%. In contrast, the median coverage ratio for the reinvesting firms exceeds 3. Hence, the typical firm paying out the proceeds is

*L. Lang et al./Journal of Financial Economics 37 (1995) 3– 37*          11

Table 2
Firm characteristics for a sample of 93 significant asset sales from 1984 to 1989

The sales are obtained from inspection of 8K forms. Managerial ownership is obtained from proxy statements. All other data are obtained from Compustat and CRSP tapes. The Compustat data are from the year preceding the asset sale. The market value of equity is for six days before the announcement date. The net of market abnormal return is the return on the firm minus the return on the market portfolio. *, **, and *** denote significance of the $t$-test for the difference in the means between the two subsamples at the 0.1, 0.05, and 0.01 levels respectively. (In parentheses we report the significance level for the median test.)

| | Whole sample (93 sales) | Payout sample (40 sales) | Reinvest sample (53 sales) |
|---|---|---|---|
| | Mean (Median) | Mean (Median) | Mean (Median) |
| (A) *Leverage characteristics of selling firms* | | | |
| Interest coverage (EBIT/Interest payments) (***) | 16.11 (2.54) | 0.98 (1.56) | 27.04 (3.38) |
| Short-term liabilities/TA | 0.32 (0.29) | 0.35 (0.28) | 0.30 (0.29) |
| Short-term debt/TA | 0.09 (0.05) | 0.11 (0.07) | 0.07 (0.04) |
| Long-term debt/TA * | 0.27 (0.21) | 0.31 (0.28) | 0.23 (0.20) |
| Long-term + Short-term debt/TA **(*) | 0.36 (0.31) | 0.42 (0.34) | 0.30 (0.23) |
| (B) *Performance characteristics of selling firms* | | | |
| Net income/TA (**) | − 0.01 (0.01) | − 0.03 (− 0.02) | 0.00 (0.01) |
| Operating income/TA (**) | 0.09 (0.10) | 0.07 (0.07) | 0.10 (0.12) |
| Cumulative net of market returns ( −250 to −5) (**) | − 6.25% (− 10.97%) | − 8.60% (− 14.45%) | − 4.48% (− 3.75%) |
| Tobin's $q$ **(*) | 0.83 (0.73) | 0.67 (0.67) | 0.94 (0.87) |
| Managerial ownership as a fraction of total equity (***) | 0.13 (0.08) | 0.17 (0.12) | 0.11 (0.05) |

close to being unable to pay interest out of earnings. The firms paying down debt seem to have a powerful motivation to sell assets, providing evidence consistent with the financing hypothesis.

For the full sample, the average ratio of the sum of short-term and long-term debt to the book value of total assets, 0.36, is larger than the average ratio of 0.28

12          *L. Lang et al./Journal of Financial Economics 37 (1995) 3–37*

in Bernanke and Campbell (1988) for the 1986 universe of Compustat firms, providing some evidence that our sample firms have above-average leverage. Using the ratio of the book value of long-term debt to the book value of total assets, the median test results in no difference between the firms that intend to pay out the proceeds and those that reinvest. There is also no evidence that firms paying out the proceeds have significantly more short-term debt or short-term liabilities. However, the ratio of short-term and long-term debt to total assets is significantly higher for firms that pay out the proceeds for the mean and the median.

The firms in the sample perform poorly before the sale. Their average net income is negative and their median net income is trivially small. Their cumulative net of market return, computed as their return minus the market's return over the period from day $-250$ to day $-5$, is negative. Their Tobin's $q$ is also low. In addition, the performance of firms paying out the proceeds is significantly worse than the performance of the reinvest sample. The payout sample has significantly lower net income to total assets and operating income to total assets. In fact, the typical firm in the payout sample loses money in the year before the sale. Cumulative net of market returns are lower for the payout firms at the 0.05 level. The firms in the payout sample also have a significantly lower Tobin's $q$ ratio than the firms in the reinvest sample, suggesting that firms that retain the proceeds have better investment opportunities.

Though asset sales by firms in distress have been studied in a number of recent papers (Asquith, Gertner, and Scharfstein, 1991; Brown, James, and Mooradian, 1993; Ofek, 1994), it is important to note that the firms in our sample were not selected because of distress or poor performance. Further, as explained earlier, we removed from the sample those firms that were bankrupt at the time of the asset sale announcement. Only one firm files a Chapter 11 petition in the year following the asset sale. Seven firms defaulted on their loans or restructured their debt in the year before the sale; four of these firms paid down debt from the proceeds. Two firms renegotiated loans in the year before the sale and both paid down debt with the proceeds. Two firms defaulted after the sale and both used the proceeds to pay down debt. Hence, the typical sale in our sample is not undertaken to cure a default or as part of a workout. The median firm is, however, a poor performer whose net income is just about zero and whose stock price is not keeping up with the market.

There is some weak evidence that being a takeover target makes it more likely that a firm will pay out the proceeds of an asset sale. In the 12 months preceding the asset sale, there is evidence of takeover activity for nine firms and five of these firms paid out the proceeds of the asset sale. Further, there is evidence of takeover activity for five firms following the sale and three of these paid out the proceeds.

The last row of Table 2 provides evidence on managerial ownership. If it turned out that managerial ownership for the firms selling assets and reinvesting

*L. Lang et al./Journal of Financial Economics 37 (1995) 3–37*          13

the proceeds is large, one might conclude that management's incentives are better aligned with shareholders' interests for these firms and hence be skeptical of the financing hypothesis. Table 2 shows that this concern is not important since the firms that reinvest the proceeds have lower managerial ownership than the firms that pay out the proceeds.

## 5. The stock-price effect of asset sales

In the previous section, we found that the firms selling assets are generally poorly performing firms with significant leverage. These results are supportive of the financing hypothesis. The financing hypothesis also predicts that the market discounts the proceeds of successful asset sales when the proceeds are reinvested. In this section, we investigate this hypothesis and compare the announcement abnormal returns for the payout sample and the reinvest sample. In most of the analysis of this section, we use the whole sample of firms paying out the proceeds even though for some firms the announcement of the use of the proceeds is made after the announcement of the completion of the sale. We therefore assume that investors have rational expectations at the time of the asset sale announcement, in the sense that, on average, they expect the proceeds to be paid out when a subsequent announcement to that effect is made. To the extent that the probability that such a statement will be made is less than one, the effect of the planned use of the proceeds on the announcement of the sale is reduced and our tests are less powerful.

In Table 3, we provide the cumulative market model prediction errors for two event windows around the announcement date.[6] The first window includes the day before the announcement and the day of the announcement. The second window includes the 11 days centered on the announcement day. For the full sample, our finding of a significantly positive cumulative average return of 1.41% for days − 1 and 0 is comparable to findings in earlier papers. We show, however, that this positive cumulative average return is due to the payout subsample. For this subsample, the cumulative average return for the short window is 3.92%. For the reinvest subsample, it is − 0.48%. The average difference between the two subsamples is 4.40% with a *t*-statistic of 4.21. The difference between the medians of these two subsamples is 2.24%. The evidence for the longer window is similar. This evidence is strongly supportive of the financing hypothesis and contrary to the prediction of the efficient deployment hypothesis that the use of the proceeds should not matter since management always maximizes shareholder wealth.

---

[6]The market model is estimated from 250 to 50 days before the announcement.

Table 3
Cumulative percentage abnormal returns for the whole sample and various subsamples for 93 asset
sales undertaken from 1984 to 1989

The cumulative abnormal returns are obtained from market model prediction errors. $z$-statistics are
given in parentheses for the means, $p$-values for the sign-rank test are given in square brackets, and
$p$-values for the median test are given in curly brackets.

|  | From day −1 to day 0 | | From day −5 to day +5 | |
|---|---|---|---|---|
|  | Mean | Median | Mean | Median |
| Whole sample (93 sales) | 1.41% | 0.72% | 2.80% | 1.70% |
|  | (3.61) | [0.15] | (2.80) | [0.02] |
| Payout sample (40 sales) | 3.92 | 1.90 | 5.65 | 4.42 |
|  | (5.93) | [ < 0.01] | (5.07) | [ < 0.01] |
| Reinvest sample (53 sales) | − 0.48 | − 0.34 | 0.65 | 0.25 |
|  | (− 0.43) | [0.50] | (0.34) | [0.94] |
| Difference between payout | 4.40 | 2.24 | 5.00 | 4.17 |
| and reinvest samples | (4.21) | {0.03} | (3.06) | {0.08} |

We see from Table 2 that firms paying out the proceeds are typically firms
that have poorer performance (as measured by net income, operating income, or
cumulative net of market returns before the sale) and higher leverage (as
measured by long-term plus short-term debt and by interest coverage) than
firms reinvesting the proceeds. This evidence raises an important question about
the results of Table 3: Could it be that the abnormal returns differ between the
payout and reinvest samples not because of the difference in the use of the
proceeds but because of the difference in the financial health of the selling firms?
A distressed firm could benefit from an asset sale irrespective of the use of the
proceeds because the sale removes financial constraints. To investigate whether
the positive abnormal returns of firms in the payout sample are due to financial
distress rather than to the use of the proceeds, we provide in Table 4 mean and
median cumulative abnormal returns for several subsamples of asset sales
constructed using various indicators of poor performance. In successive panels,
we classify firms as poorly performing if they (a) have negative news in the WSJ
asset sale announcement, (b) have negative net income in the year before the
sale, (c) have negative cumulative net of market returns for the period from 250
days to 5 days before the announcement, and (d) have a coverage ratio below
the sample median.

In all subsamples in Table 4, the cumulative average abnormal return is
higher for the firms classified as poorly performing. However, for the traditional
window of days − 1 and 0, the difference in cumulative average returns between
the firms in the poorly performing subsamples and the other firms is never

*L. Lang et al./Journal of Financial Economics 37 (1995) 3–37*                    15

Table 4

Cumulative percentage abnormal returns for subsamples formed according to firm performance indicators from a sample of 93 asset sales from 1984 to 1989

The cumulative abnormal returns are obtained from market model prediction errors. The net of market return is the firm return minus the market return. $z$-statistics for the means are given in parentheses, $p$-values for the sign-rank test are given in square brackets, and $p$-values for the median test are given in curly brackets.

| Subsamples (# of sales; # in payout sample) | From day −1 to day 0 | | From day −5 to day +5 | |
|---|---|---|---|---|
| | Mean | Median | Mean | Median |
| **(A) *WSJ announcement includes negative news*** | | | | |
| Includes | 2.31% | 1.01% | 5.07% | 4.00% |
| (50; 27) | (3.61) | [0.08] | (4.10) | [< 0.01] |
| Does not include | 0.37 | 0.80 | 0.15 | 0.25 |
| (43; 13) | (1.38) | [0.95] | (0.34) | [0.83] |
| Difference | 1.94 | 0.21 | 4.92 | 3.75 |
| | (1.67) | {0.27} | (2.78) | {< 0.01} |
| **(B) *Net income (year before the sale)*** | | | | |
| Negative | 2.12 | 0.85 | 4.38 | 4.19 |
| (37; 22) | (3.35) | [0.12] | (3.41) | [0.05] |
| Positive | 0.13 | − 0.93 | 1.27 | 0.87 |
| (45; 12) | (1.54) | [0.96] | (0.60) | [0.26] |
| Difference | 1.99 | 1.78 | 3.11 | 3.32 |
| | (1.11) | {0.27} | (2.50) | {0.12} |
| **(C) *Cumulative net of market returns for the period from day −250 to day −5*** | | | | |
| Negative | 2.15 | 0.35 | 5.42 | 3.81 |
| (53; 26) | (3.38) | [0.16] | (3.67) | [< 0.01] |
| Positive | 0.43 | 0.89 | − 0.67 | 0.07 |
| (40; 14) | (1.58) | [0.62] | (0.00) | [0.85] |
| Difference | 1.72 | − 0.54 | 6.09 | 3.74 |
| | (1.51) | {0.61} | (4.09) | {< 0.01} |
| **(D) *Coverage ratio (EBIT/Interest payments)*** | | | | |
| Below median | 1.62 | 1.00 | 3.76 | 3.17 |
| (42; 23) | (2.71) | [0.20] | (2.46) | [0.04] |
| Above median | 0.40 | 0.02 | 1.73 | 0.87 |
| (39; 11) | (2.08) | [0.90] | (1.47) | [0.24] |
| Difference | 1.22 | 0.98 | 2.03 | 2.30 |
| | (0.51) | {0.32} | (0.75) | {0.15} |

significant. For the longer window of days $-5$ to $+5$, the mean average abnormal return is significantly higher for firms whose WSJ announcement includes negative news, for firms with negative net income for the year before the sale, and for firms with negative cumulative net of market returns for the year before the sale. Firms with coverage ratios lower than the sample median have cumulative abnormal returns insignificantly different from firms with higher coverage ratios.

Table 4 shows that dividing the sample according to performance indicators is not as successful as dividing the sample according to the use of the proceeds. Unfortunately, though, it is obvious from Table 4 that there is substantial overlap between the firms in the payout sample and those that exhibit poor performance and/or financial difficulties. This overlap does not affect the interpretation of the results for the shorter window since there the only way to split the sample to obtain a significant difference between abnormal returns is to divide the sample according to the use of the proceeds. However, for the longer window, dividing the data on the basis of firm performance indicators yields the result that poorly performing firms have greater abnormal returns than the other firms. To understand better the impact of firm performance and use of the proceeds on the stock-price effect, we divide the sample into four mutually exclusive groups in Table 5. We define firms as poorly performing if they have negative net of market cumulative returns the previous year, negative net income over the previous year, and/or a WSJ sales announcement that provides some evidence of difficulties, such as negative earnings. For the 11-day window, asset sales have a significant positive average stock-price reaction only for poorly performing firms in the payout sample. The poorly performing firms in the reinvest sample have an insignificant positive abnormal return which is significantly lower than the poorly performing firms in the payout sample. For firms not in the poorly performing subsample, firms in the payout sample have a higher abnormal return than firms in the reinvest sample. The same results hold with the two-day window, except that healthy firms in the payout sample have a positive significant stock-price effect that is significantly lower than the poorly performing firms in the payout sample. Given that there are only seven firms in the healthy payout sample, such a result has to be interpreted with caution.

A concern with Table 5 is that the sample of poorly performing firms in the payout sample might be dominated by firms that are facing immediate financial difficulties, so that the positive average abnormal return reflects the ability of these firms to sell assets successfully and hence reduce their financial difficulties. To investigate this possibility, we divided the sample into firms with a coverage ratio (EBIT divided by interest payments) above the sample median and firms with a coverage ratio below the sample median. We then compared stock-price reactions for firms with a coverage ratio below the sample median in the payout sample to similar firms in the reinvest sample. We found that the 18 asset

*L. Lang et al./Journal of Financial Economics 37 (1995) 3–37*                17

Table 5
Eleven-day percentage abnormal returns for subsamples of asset sales formed on the basis of performance and use of proceeds from a sample of 93 asset sales from 1984 to 1989

Poorly performing firms are firms that have negative cumulative net of market returns for the period from day $-250$ to day $-5$, negative net income for the previous year, and/or a WSJ asset-sale announcement that provides some evidence of distress. For each cell, we report the mean, the median in parentheses, the $z$-statistic for the mean in square brackets, and in curly brackets the number of observations and the fraction of observations with a positive value. The lower right-hand cell gives the mean difference between troubled firms that pay out the proceeds and healthy firms that reinvest the proceeds.

|  | Poorly performing firms | Healthy firms | Difference |
|---|---|---|---|
| Sales in payout sample | 6.16 | 3.22 | 2.94 |
|  | (4.65) | (1.39) | [2.67] |
|  | [3.58] | [1.38] |  |
|  | {33;0.70} | {7;0.57} |  |
| Sales in reinvest sample | 1.16 | $-0.44$ | 1.60 |
|  | (1.15) | (0.21) | [1.00] |
|  | [0.80] | [$-0.60$] |  |
|  | {36;0.53} | {17;0.53} |  |
| Difference | 5.00 | 3.66 | 6.60 |
|  | [2.35] | [1.25] | [3.26] |

sales by firms with below-median coverage ratios in the reinvest sample have an insignificant abnormal return that is significantly lower than the stock-price effect for firms with below-median coverage ratios in the payout sample. Since the abnormal returns for firms that pay out the proceeds do not differ between firms with above and below-median coverage ratios, it is unlikely that the relation between abnormal returns and the use of the proceeds depends on the selling firm's financial situation.

In Table 6, we provide results for additional subsamples of interest. First, we show the average and median abnormal returns for the sale announcements where the source for the use of the proceeds is similar to the source for the announcement. This sample comprises sales where the announcement is reported on the Dow Jones wire or in the WSJ with a WSJ story that has the use of the proceeds or where the announcement date is the agreement date from the 8K filing with the use of the proceeds described in the 8K. These 16 observations have slightly higher mean and median returns than those reported for the 40 observations in Table 3, but the $z$-statistic is lower and the $p$-value of the sign-rank test is higher, possibly because of the smaller number of observations. Second, we show that, among the firms that do not pay out the proceeds, there is no evidence that there are subsamples of sales with average or median abnormal

18          L. Lang et al./Journal of Financial Economics 37 (1995) 3– 37

Table 6

Percentage cumulative abnormal returns for additional subsamples based on how information is released and on strategic reason for sale from a sample of 93 asset sales from 1984 to 1989

Cumulative abnormal returns are market model prediction errors for a sample of 93 large asset sales obtained from 8K forms from 1984 to 1989. The subsamples are constructed using information from press articles, the 8K form, the annual report, and the S&P Standard Stock Report. Simultaneous announcement means that the same source provides the announcement of the sale and of the use of the proceeds. The subsamples selected on the strategic reason for the sale use the announcement of the sale to select the strategic reason. These subsamples include only firms in the reinvest sample.

|  | From day $-1$ to day 0 | | From day $-5$ to day $+5$ | |
|---|---|---|---|---|
|  | Mean ($z$-statistic) | Median [$p$-value for sign-rank test] | Mean ($z$-statistic) | Median [$p$-value for sign-rank test] |
| Payout sample (40) | 3.92% (5.93) | 1.90% [$< 0.01$] | 5.65% (5.07) | 4.42% [$< 0.01$] |
| Payout sample; simultaneous announcement (16) | 4.98 (3.93) | 2.13 [0.19] | 7.76 (3.25) | 6.86 [0.04] |
| Focus on core; reinvest sample (21) | $-0.46$ $(-0.61)$ | $-0.34$ [0.60] | 0.50 (0.82) | $-0.56$ [0.93] |
| Sell unprofitable division; reinvest sample (14) | $-1.41$ $(-0.31)$ | $-0.42$ [0.43] | 3.88 (1.36) | 4.05 [0.07] |
| Finance acquisitions or expansions; reinvest sample (9) | 1.24 (1.44) | 1.03 [0.43] | 0.47 (0.01) | 0.25 [0.50] |

returns comparable to those of firms that pay out the proceeds when one focuses on the shorter window. For the longer window, there is no case where the $z$-statistic is significant when the firm does not pay out the proceeds, but the magnitude of the abnormal returns is fairly high in the case of the firms that sell an unprofitable division and retain the proceeds. In contrast, firms that sell assets to focus more on core operations but do not pay out the proceeds have very small abnormal returns in absolute value and for the short window both average and median abnormal returns are negative.

## 6. Explaining the cross-sectional variation in cumulative returns

### 6.1. Relative proceeds and stock-price reaction

The efficient deployment view of asset sales does not distinguish between poorly performing firms paying out asset sales proceeds and other firms selling assets. Since we document in this paper a sharp difference in the stock-price reaction between these firms, can our evidence be reconciled with the efficient

*L. Lang et al./Journal of Financial Economics 37 (1995) 3–37*      19

deployment view? One possibility that we have not explored so far is that the differences in stock-price reactions are driven by differences in the ratio of asset sales proceeds to the market value of equity. To understand this concern, note that Table 1 shows that firms paying out the proceeds have a significantly greater ratio of asset sale proceeds to the market value of their equity. Hence, if the seller's gain from selling an asset (the premium the bidder pays for the asset in excess of the asset's value when used by the seller), expressed as a percentage of the proceeds, is the same irrespective of the firm that sells the asset, one would expect a larger stock-price reaction for firms in the payout sample. However, in this case, the relation between the stock-price reaction and the use of the proceeds would be spurious. Regressions 1 and 2 of Table 7 show there is a significant relation between the stock-price reaction and the proceeds divided by the market value of equity. However, this relation does not explain the higher average abnormal return of the payout sample since the dummy variable that takes the value one for the firms that pay out the proceeds is significantly positive.[7] Regressions 1 and 2 are consistent with the argument of Shleifer and Vishny (1992) that, given the illiquidity of the market for asset sales, large asset sales are more likely to fail. We find that the completion of asset sales is better news for larger asset sales than for small asset sales.

Throughout the paper, we have assumed that the firm's financial situation is known, so that asset sales are informative about the asset's value rather than about the firm's need for funds. The literature on security issues generally emphasizes that they convey information about the true value of the firm's securities and its financial situation (see, for instance, Myers and Majluf, 1983, and Miller and Rock, 1983). The same could be true here: an asset sale could provide information that the firm's earnings are lower than expected or that it was not able to get attractive terms on financial markets. Mayers and Singh (1993) provide evidence that announcements of asset sale programs reveal information about a firm's financial situation.[8] It makes sense that program announcements would reveal mostly information about the firm's financial situation since, by definition, such disclosures reveal that managers plan to raise capital. In this paper, our sample is collected to include annoucement of sale

---

[7]All regressions of Table 6 are estimated using weighted least squares, where the weight is the reciprocal of the standard deviation of the residual of the market model regression.

[8]They find positive stock-price effects when the firm announces that it intends to use the proceeds to finance a stock repurchase and when the firm intends to reinvest the proceeds, and a negative effect when the firm intends to repay debt. The size of the effects they observe is similar to the size of the effects one would observe if the announcements were not accompanied by the announcement of asset sale programs: stock repurchase announcements have large positive effects, announcements of investments have small positive effects, and announcements of leverage decreases have small negative effects. See McConnell and Muscarella (1985) for evidence on investment announcements and Smith (1986) for a review of the stock-price reactions to financing announcements.

Table 7
Weighted least squares regressions of the abnormal return on firm and sale characteristics for
a sample of 93 asset sales from 1984 to 1989

The sales are obtained from inspection of 8K forms. Managerial ownership is obtained from proxy
statements. The accounting loss is from the 8K form. All other data are obtained from Compustat
and CRSP tapes. The Compustat data are from the year preceding the asset sale. (*t*-statistics in
parentheses below the coefficient estimates.) The net of market return for a firm is the firm's stock
return minus the market return. The dependent variable is the cumulative abnormal return
measured over the day of the announcement and the day before ( $-1,0$ ), or over the 11 days
overlapping the day of the announcement ( $-5, +5$ ).

| | Regression Sample size (Event window over which the abnormal returns are computed) | | | | | |
|---|---|---|---|---|---|---|
| | 1 81 ( $-1,0$ ) | 2 81 ( $-5, +5$ ) | 3 82 ( $-1,0$ ) | 4 82 ( $-5, +5$ ) | 5 79 ( $-1,0$ ) | 6 79 ( $-5, +5$ ) |
| Intercept | $-0.37$ ( $-0.44$ ) | 0.21 (0.16) | $-0.49$ ( $-0.43$ ) | 0.77 (0.46) | 0.31 (0.21) | 1.95 (0.89) |
| Payout proceeds dummy | 2.92 (2.11) | 4.01 (1.87) | 2.82 (2.25) | 3.85 (2.05) | 3.00 (2.24) | 2.88 (1.46) |
| Proceeds/Equity | 1.22 (2.54) | 1.38 (1.86) | | | | |
| Managerial ownership | | | | | $-2.54$ ( $-0.59$ ) | 7.27 (1.15) |
| Net income | | | 0.05 (0.01) | $-2.65$ ( $-0.20$ ) | | |
| Tobin's $q$ | | | | | $-0.23$ ( $-0.16$ ) | $-2.28$ ( $-1.10$ ) |
| Net of market cumulative returns from day $-250$ to day $-5$ | | | $-1.46$ ( $-0.79$ ) | $-9.35$ ( $-3.38$ ) | $-1.82$ ( $-0.93$ ) | $-7.67$ ( $-2.66$ ) |
| Long-term debt/ Total assets | | | 1.61 (0.42) | $-1.29$ ( $-0.23$ ) | | |
| Adjusted $R^2$ | 0.14 | 0.09 | 0.04 | 0.15 | 0.04 | 0.15 |
| *p*-value for *F*-test | $< 0.01$ | 0.01 | 0.14 | $< 0.01$ | 0.16 | $< 0.01$ |

completions outside of asset sale programs rather than announcements of asset
sales programs. If our sales primarily conveyed information about the firm's
financing requirements and hence the firm's financial situation, one would
expect larger sales to convey worse news since they imply that the firm needs
more funds. Hence, if our sales conveyed information about financing requirements, we would expect the coefficient on the proceeds in Table 7 to have the

*L. Lang et al./Journal of Financial Economics 37 (1995) 3–37*                21

opposite sign. In fact, the positive relation we find between abnormal returns and the size of the proceeds is the opposite of the negative relation found between stock-price effects and the size of security issuances.[9]

### 6.2. Abnormal returns and performance: A multivariate perspective

We investigated in Section 5 the extent to which the difference in abnormal returns can be explained by the fact that a successful asset sale is more important for the firms in the payout sample since these firms are generally in a worse financial situation and would face significant costs of financial distress without the successful sale. In that section, dividing the sample according to recent performance or the extent of financial difficulties does not lead to significant differences between subsamples for the shorter event window, but does so for the longer event window. It could be that our classification of firms as poorly performing or healthy does not capture a relation between performance and stock-price reactions that could be captured by regressing stock-price reactions on levels of performance measures. To investigate this, we relate abnormal returns to net income, net of market cumulative returns for the period from day $-250$ to day $-5$ and the debt–asset ratio in regressions 3 and 4.

The regression estimates in Table 7 confirm the earlier results that the higher abnormal return of firms in the payout sample cannot be explained by these firms having poorer performance or a more precarious financial situation. Whereas past stock returns are correlated with abnormal returns for the longer window, this effect does not explain why firms in the payout sample have higher abnormal returns since the payout dummy variable is significant for both windows. Further, regressing abnormal returns on past performance could lead to significant results when abnormal returns are estimated from market residuals because the intercept of the market model estimates depends on past performance.

Regressions 5 and 6 relate abnormal returns to net-of-market cumulative returns for the period from day $-250$ to day $-5$, Tobin's $q$, and managerial ownership. The financing hypothesis implies that there should be a negative relation between the stock-price effect and the degree of agency costs. We would expect abnormal returns to be higher for firms with higher managerial ownership (provided that management is not using its control of voting rights for entrenchment purposes). We also would expect high-$q$ firms to have lower agency costs of managerial discretion, so that the stock market would discount sales proceeds less for these firms. For the shorter window, these variables have no explanatory power whatsoever. For the longer window, these variables make

---

[9]See Korajczyk, Lucas, and McDonald (1990) for a review of the evidence on the determinants of the stock-price reaction to equity issues.

22          *L. Lang et al./Journal of Financial Economics 37 (1995) 3–37*

the dummy variable for the use of the proceeds insignificant. This is because they are correlated with the use of the proceeds. In a logistic regression not reported here, we find that firms with low managerial ownership or a high $q$ are significantly more likely to retain the proceeds, so that introducing these variables in the regression makes it more difficult to estimate the coefficient on the use of the proceeds precisely.

## 7. Conclusions

In this paper, we have shown that for a sample of large asset sales the stock-price reaction is significantly positive only for those firms that plan to pay out the proceeds. This evidence is inconsistent with the hypothesis that the market reacts favorably to asset sales simply because they lead to more efficient use of assets and the selling firm captures some of the benefit from the increased efficiency.

Our evidence is consistent with what we call the financing hypothesis. Under this hypothesis, management sells assets to obtain funds to pursue its objectives when alternative funding is either too expensive given its objectives or unavailable. On average, firms benefit from announcing successful sales because a successful sale means that the firm received enough money to make the sale worthwhile. Further, proceeds are discounted when retained by the selling firm because of agency costs of managerial discretion. In our sample, firms selling assets typically are poor performers and they are more likely to pay out the proceeds when they find it difficult to service their debt. The average stock-price reaction to asset sales is positive and it is significantly higher for firms that pay out the proceeds. We do not, however, find a direct link between abnormal returns and proxies for agency costs of managerial discretion.

This paper raises some questions which should be addressed in further research. We do not explore why managers might be reluctant to sell assets. Why is it that managers value size? Are they reluctant to sell assets because they do not want to acknowledge failure or is it that complex organizations cannot sell assets easily because of intrafirm relationships and quid pro quos? Though we are convinced that our evidence demonstrates the relevance of the financing hypothesis, it is also clear from our analysis and from our empirical results that the information conveyed by asset sales is difficult to evaluate because asset sales convey news about the value of the asset sold, the intended use of the proceeds and, possibly, the firm's financial health. Larger samples of possibly less significant asset sales might offer a way to disentangle these various effects with more precision and provide useful information on the relative importance of the financing hypothesis and of the efficient deployment hypothesis.

In conclusion, our sample suggests that the efficient deployment hypothesis is not as useful as prior studies might have suggested. Perhaps one could view our

*L. Lang et al./Journal of Financial Economics 37 (1995) 3– 37*          23

evidence as showing that firms seem more aware of their comparative advantage when they are short of funds than otherwise. If this is the case, though, it provides further support for the view that the agency costs of managerial discretion matter and that debt plays a useful role in disciplining management.[10]

## Appendix: Brief description of asset sales

The following material briefly describes the asset sales in our sample. Each sale was reported to the SEC in an 8K filing, indicating that the sale represented a '... significant amount of assets'. Information regarding each sale is gathered from several sources, including annual reports, 8Ks, the Wall Street Journal (WSJ), Dow Jones News Service, S&P Standard Stock Reports, and other news sources.

The source of the date of the first public announcement of the asset sale is indicated below in parentheses following the announcement date: WSJ indicates that the announcement was in the WSJ (we used one trading day before the WSJ story as the announcement date); DJ indicates that the story was reported over the Dow Jones News Wire but was not reported in the WSJ on the same or following date; agreement date indicates that the first public date related to the announcement was the date the sale agreement was signed, as reported in the 8K.

### Format of asset sale information

*Seller/Buyer*
Cumulative abnormal return ( −1, +1) in percent / announcement date (source of announcement date)
Price (in millions) / gain on sale (in millions)
Business of asset sold / business of buyer
Use of funds from sale / code [0 = strategic, 1 = cash paid out of firm through debt reduction and / or stock repurchase] / source of information on use of funds
Brief details (including information on payouts to stockholders through repurchases where applicable)

*Adobe Resources Corp. / Equitable Resources*
7.06 / 12/30/86 (DJ)
$22.4 / NA
Oil wells & land / natural gas
Reduce debt / 1 / annual report
Adobe Resources had a loss in the quarter around the sale due to lower oil prices. The asset sale occurred at the same time the firm called $55 million in convertible debentures and enabled Adobe

---

[10]See Jensen (1988) and Stulz (1990).

Resources to reduce its long-term debt to zero. The firm mentioned that the assets were not consistent with their long-range objectives. Stock repurchase: On 1/28/86, bought back a million shares for $12 million and may buyback 500,000 more. No indication of connection to asset sale.

*Airgas Inc. / Jackson Acquisition Company*
7.25 / 9/12/89 (DJ)
$70 / $32.2
Manufacturing / NA
Reduce debt / 1 / 8K
Airgas went public in 1986 and made several acquisitions over the following two years. This asset sale enabled the firm to reduce borrowings under a revolving credit facility by $50 million and was consistent with their long-term plan to emphasize gas distribution.

*Allied Signal Inc. (two sales) / (1) Lanesborough Corp. (2) Commerzbank AG*
(1) −3.59 (2) 4.77 / (1) 4/6/87 (WSJ) (2) 3/25/87 (DJ)
(1) $479 (2) NA / All discontinued operations gave $79 million gain.
(1) Electronics (2) electronics / (1) NA (2) NA
(1) & (2) Reduce debt, share buyback and investment in core businesses / (1) & (2) 1 / (1) & (2)
    Annual Report
Allied Signal was formed by the merger of Signal Cos. and Allied Corp. in 1985. These asset sales are part of a program to reduce debt and concentrate the new firm's assets in desired areas. Stock repurchases: the firm announced that proceeds from asset sales would be used to buy back shares but no additional information on number or price of shares available.

*American Barrick Resources / Peabody Coal Company*
−3.41 / 3/31/87 (agreement date)
$12.5 / NA
Coal operations / mining
Not profitable / 0 / 8K
Over the previous five years, this successful firm had grown into one of the largest North American gold producers, in part through acquisitions. This sale was its exit from unprofitable coal operations.

*American Brands / MacAndrews and Forbes Holdings Inc.*
2.19 / 7/25/86 (agreement date)
$14 / NA
Cigar maker / NA
Strategic / 0 / annual report
Faced with poor performance in the tobacco market, American Brands was engaged in a program of diversification and international expansion. The firm sold this tobacco unit as part of this plan.

*Amfac Inc. / Borden Inc. and Rabin Brothers*
−2.14 / 11/12/86 (WSJ)
NA / $20
Fisher Cheese Co. / diversified food companies
Strategic / 0 / 8K
Amfac sold Fisher Cheese Co. in an effort to streamline operations and strengthen its financial position.

*Armco Inc. / Kawasaki Steel*
1.02 / 3/24/89 (agreement date)
$350 / $109.4

Steel division / steel
Joint venture / 0 / WSJ, 8K
Kawasaki Steel (which had a 40% stake in the sold unit) purchased remaining interest as part of a joint venture with Armco.

*Artra Group Inc. / VWR Corp.*
8.11 / 8/8/89 (DJ)
$25.5 / −$16.5
Laboratory supply / photo supplies
Reduce debt, paydown bank loans / 1 / annual report
The firm sold several unprofitable assets that it had previously purchased as part of an expansion plan.

*Baker Hughes Inc. / Oy Tampella AB*
−2.25 / 3/13/89 (WSJ)
$130 / $0
Mining equipment / NA
Strategic / 0 / annual report
Baker Hughes was formed in 1987 as merger of Baker International and Hughes Tool Co. The sold division did not fit in with the long- run plans of the new company.

*Ball Corporation / TBG Europe*
−5.05 / 1/29/87 (WSJ)
$80 / $8
Glass and container manufacturing / joint venture
Joint venture / 0 / WSJ, 8K
The asset sale was a spinoff of Ball's glass container business into a 50–50 joint venture with a European firm.

*Banner Industries / Diamond Monitors*
−1.58 / 3/31/87 (WSJ)
NA / NA
Gas detection device manufacturing / NA
Restructuring to divest operations not meeting growth and profit objectives / 0 / 8K
In early 1987 the firm purchased Rexnord. This sale was part of a program to divest units not meeting the firm's growth and profit objectives.

*R.G. Barry Corp / Jumping-Jack Shoes*
2.08 / 9/23/85 (DJ)
$2.3 / −$1
Footwear division / footwear
Restructuring (strategic) / 0 / annual report
This asset sale is the last of a series of sales to downsize the firm and turn profits positive. Stock repurchase: the firm agreed in November 1984 to buy about 10% of its shares from the Streim family for about $2.3 million.

*Brown Group Inc. / Jepson Corporation*
−0.98 / 5/7/85 (WSJ)
$50 / −$9.3
Recreational products / NA
Strategic / 0 / annual report

This asset sale completed Brown Group's strategic withdrawal from the volatile, low-return recreational products business.

*Canal Capital Corp. / USK Acquisition Corporation*
−3.37 / 6/23/89 (DJ)
$6.875 / $2
Stockyard business / NA (former insider)
Not profitable / 0 / annual report
The sale of its stockyard operations reflected the fundamental change in the nature of this firm's business from a stockyard firm to a diversified firm including real estate development, trading securities, and investing in ancient art.

*Champion International Corp. / Stone Container*
−5.52 / 9/30/85 (WSJ)
$372.9 / $0
Paperboard mills, corrugated container and bag packaging plants / paperboard packaging products
Reduce debt / 1 / WSJ
This sale was part of Champion International's restructuring by selling assets to reduce debt incurred when it acquired St. Regis as a white knight.

*Craig Corp. / Bercor Inc.*
−0.05 / 12/27/85 (agreement date)
$1.61 / $0
Consumer electronics / NA
Cash for acquisitions / 0 / news reports, annual report
Craig Corp. sold assets of its consumer electronics division while at the same time developing an aggressive expansion policy that could lead to increased debt. Craig was retained as a consultant by the buyer. Stock repurchases: In October 1985, directors authorized repurchase of about $1 million worth of shares. No evidence that it was carried out.

*Crompton and Knowles (two sales) / (1) NCH Corp. & others (2) Univar Corp.*
(1) −0.23 (2) −2.14 / (1) 12/19/86 (agreement date) (2) 12/5/88 (agreement date)
(1) $14.7 (2) $11 / (1) −$0.92 (2) −$0.8
(1) Cleaning subsidiary (2) chemicals / (1) chemicals (2) chemicals
(1) Strategic / 0 / annual report; (2) cash for acquisitions (strategic) / 0 / annual report
These asset sales combined with acquisitions were part of management's strategy for improving long-term growth. Stock repurchases: In December 1986, redeemed all preferred shares in a private transaction for about $4.5 million. In October 1986, bought back 8% of common shares from largest holder. Amount paid not disclosed.

*Crown Central Petroleum / Amoco Corp.*
−1.97 / 11/12/87 (agreement date)
$166 / $62.7
Oil and gas exploration / oil and gas
Reduce debt / 1 / 8K
The company suffered from falling oil prices. It sold this asset to reduce debt and to concentrate on marketing and convenience stores instead of production.

*Culbro Corp. / American Maize Products*
11.74 / 12/31/85 (WSJ)
$65 / NA

Tobacco / NA
Strategic (also paid dividend of $45 million) / 1 / 8K
As part of its plan to reduce reliance on tobacco industry, Culbro sold its smokeless tobacco division and distributed the proceeds to shareholders as a special dividend.


*Di Giorgio / Bergen Brunswig Drug Co.*
0.00 / 5/29/86 (DJ)
$45 / $8.2
Drug division / drug distribution
Reduce short-term debt / 1 / annual report
To strengthen their balance sheet to support future growth, the firm took several actions to reduce debt, including the sale of this asset and the conversion of debt to equity.


*Divi Hotels NV / Palmer Group*
5.32 / 8/24/89 (WSJ)
$62 / NA
Hotels / real estate and hotels
Obtain cash for working capital and to pay down debt / 1 / WSJ
The firm sold several hotels after failing to obtain needed working capital in other ways.


*Ducommun Inc. / Arrow Electronics Inc.*
12.68 / 9/21/87 (WSJ)
$124 / −$10.5
Electronics distribution / electronic components
Reduce debt (Arrow Electronics traded $10 million of Ducommun's debt held by Arrow for the asset, paid $79 million cash used to reduce bank debt, and made up the rest in Arrow stock distributed to Ducommun shareholders.) / 1 / WSJ
Arrow Electronics paid $10 million in Ducommun debt, $79 million in cash and about $35 million worth of Arrow stock for this asset. Ducommun used the proceeds to lower its outstanding debt. The firm's performance had suffered due to slowdown in the semiconductor and space industries.


*EAC Industries / Chromalloy Compressor Technologies*
9.04 / 12/23/88 (DJ)
$11.5 / −$1.3
Jet and tank components manufacturing / NA
Reduce debt and focus on core hardware and related business / 1 / 8K
This firm had several unprofitable years and sold this asset (and several others) to reduce debt and concentrate on its core. In addition a group held a more than 10% stake in the firm.


*Electrosound Group Inc. (two sales) / (1) Audio Sub Inc. (2) Mitsubishi*
(1) −7.51 (2) −6.08 / (1) 3/10/89 (DJ) (2) 6/26/89 (WSJ)
(1) $2.5 (2) $1.5 / (1) $0.418 (2) NA
(1) Commercial duplicating (2) compact disk manufacturing / (1) NA (2) manufacturing
(1) strategic (2) strategic / (1) 0 (2) 0 / (1) annual report (2) annual report
The firm sold its commercial duplicating operation and ended a joint venture with Mitsubishi because they were unprofitable. This enabled them to concentrate on core businesses and reduce debt. Stock repurchase: In June 1988, Electrosound repurchased $1,080,000 worth of shares from Cinram Ltd. No evidence of connection to asset sale.

28          *L. Lang et al./Journal of Financial Economics 37 (1995) 3– 37*

*Enviropact Inc. / GSX Tank Management*
11.83 / 10/23/89 (DJ)
$5.4 / −$1.4
Pump drilling division / NA
Reduce debt, pay taxes and increase working capital / 1 / annual report
The firm sold these operations in mid-1989 to reduce debt and return to profitability.

*Equitec Financial Group Inc. / Hallwood Group Inc.*
3.69 / 10/18/89 (DJ)
$76.2 / NA
Real estate investment partnerships / real estate
Financial difficulties, need cash / 1 / annual report
This financial service firm was hit hard by the Tax Reform Act of 1986 and sold assets as part of an attempt to avoid bankruptcy.

*Federal Mogul / CMV Interamerica Inc.*
1.80 / 1/9/89 (WSJ)
NA / $8.3
Diamond blade manufacturing / blade manufacturing
Used part of proceeds to repurchase one million common shares and to create an ESOP as
   a defensive tactic against possible bidder Nortek Inc. / 1 / WSJ
This firm, in response to a threatened hostile takeover, refocused the firm on its core businesses by selling this division. It used part of the proceeds to repurchase 1 million shares and create an ESOP. Stock repurchases: The announced defensive repurchase of 1 million shares would cost about $51 million. In a standstill agreement in October, 1989, the firm repurchased $13.3 million worth of shares from Nortek.

*First City Industries Inc. / HB Holdings, subsidiary of Glen Dimplex Ltd.*
0.17 / 10/9/86 (WSJ)
$90 / $9.8
Hamilton Beach small appliances / Irish appliance maker
Used to repay debt / 1 / 8K
First City Industries reduced their long-term debt significantly through the sale of two operating units, including Hamilton Beach.

*John Fluke Mfg. Co. / N.V. Phillips*
−0.55 / 9/28/87 (DJ)
NA / −$7.9
Stock in European subsidiary for sale of electronic equipment / joint venture
Establishing joint venture / 0 / 8K
This firm and a European firm entered into a joint venture in which each would sell the other's products in their area. The asset sale consisted of the John Fluke's European sales division. Stock repurchase: In December 1986, the firm bought back about $20 million in stock from the Fluke family. In November 1987, the firm authorized repurchase of about $8 million. No evidence it was carried out.

*General Host Corp (three sales) / (1)Kraft (2) Management (3) American Salt Acquisition Co. (Mgt.)*
(1) 13.89 (2) −1.48 (3) 8.61 / (1) 6/4/87 (WSJ) (2) 6/22/87 (WSJ) (3) 2/1/88 (agreement date)
(1) $95.8 (2) $39 (3) $31 / (1) $87 (2) $0 (3) $0
(1) All American Gourmet Co. (2) Hickory Farms (3) American Salt / (1) food products (2) mgmt
   group (3) mgmt group

*L. Lang et al./Journal of Financial Economics 37 (1995) 3– 37*                    29

(1) & (2) Reduce long-term debt (3) cash for litigation settlement / (1) & (2) & (3) 1 / (1) & (2) WSJ (3) 8K

In the early 1980s, General Host began restructuring away from cyclical dependent industries to focus on retailing, nurseries, and crafts. The proceeds from these asset sales were used to reduce debt and were part of the continuing restructuring. Stock repurchases: General Host repurchased about $21 million worth of shares in an open-market buyback program in 1986. Through 1987 and 1988, the firm repurchased about $58.6 million worth of shares on the open market.

*Gleason Corp. / Diesel Kiki Co.*
− 5.56 / 4/22/89 (agreement date)
$18 / $7.725
Differential and gear manufacturing / NA
Strategic, termination of joint venture, selling interest to partner / 0 / Annual report
This asset sale is part of the firm's exit from a failed diversification effort.

*Goodyear Tire & Rubber Co. (two sales) / (1) Loral (2) International Paper*
(1) 2.51 (2) 2.17 / (1) 1/22/87 (WSJ) (2) 4/13/87 (WSJ)
(1) $640 (2) $70 / (1) NA (2) NA
(1) Aerospace (2) oil and gas division / (1) military electronics (2) paper manufacturing
(1) & (2) Restructuring, reduce debt incurred in repurchase of shares / (1) & (2) 0 / (1) WSJ (2) 8K

As part of a successful defense to a hostile bid, Goodyear sold several assets, refocusing the firm on its core tire and rubber business. As part of the defense, the firm repurchased 40 million shares, financing the repurchase with the sale of all non-tire assets. Stock repurchases: Firm paid approximately $2 billion for shares repurchased in defensive moves.

*Greyhound Corp. / Investor group*
4.92 / 12/23/86 (WSJ)
$255 / 30.1
Bus lines / NA
Not profitable / 0 / WSJ & annual report
Greyhound was unable to profitably cope with deregulation in the bus transportation industry and thus sold its unprofitable bus lines. Stock repurchases: Firm announced plans to buy back up to 8 million shares ($265 million) in June and September 1986.

*Grow Group / Nippon Oil and Fats*
1.38 / 7/13/89 (DJ)
$25.3 / $15
Paint production assets / paints and coatings
Reduce debt, general business purposes / 1 / 8K
Grow Group grew in the 1980s through acquisitions. However, earnings suffered. The asset sale enabled the firm to report a profit and reduce its high debt level.

*Gulf Resources & Chemical Corp. / Grace Petroleum*
2.62 / 9/18/89 (agreement date)
$25 / $0.4
Oil and gas / oil and gas
Cash for working capital and environmental costs and penalties / 1 / annual report
Gulf Resources & Chemical Corp. faced environmental cleanup and liability costs. To generate cash, the firm sold this and other assets.

*Harnischfeger Corp. / Century II, Inc.*
3.10 / 5/12/88 (agreement date)
$76.2 / $59.3
Construction equipment manufacturing / management buyout
Strategic -sold to MBO / 0 / 8K
The company decided to discontinue its construction equipment division and sold the business to a group of former managers.

*Helene Curtis Industries Inc. / PTI Holdings Company*
1.85 / 10/24/85 (DJ)
$12.5 / NA
Sealants and adhesives subsidiary / newly formed holding company
Strategic / 0 / annual report
The sale of the sealants subsidiary was consistent with Helene Curtis Inc.'s focus on personal care products.

*Inspiration Resources Corp. (2 sales) / (1) Minerco (2) Cyprus Corporation*
(1) 7.79 (2) −1.10 / (1) 12/3/85 (WSJ) (2) 7/1/88 (DJ)
(1) NA (2) $125 / (1) $10 (2) $26.7
(1) Oil and gas (2) copper / (1) mining (2) mining
(1) Restructuring (2) repay debt (retired all of bank debt) and general business purposes / (1) 0 (2) 1 / (1) 8K (2) 8K
(1) Given the poor economic conditions in the natural resources industry, the firm divested operations (purchased only a year earlier) and tried to remake the corporation in a way that significantly improved the prospects for profitability. (2) The firm's attempt to concentrate on agribusiness and away from cyclical metal resources continued with the sale of its copper division.

*Intermedics / Intermedics Intraocular Acquisition Corp. (First Chicago Venture Capital)*
−1.84 / 5/2/86 (agreement date)
$35 / 'substantial gain'
Intraocular lens subsidiary / venture capital group
Proceeds to pay off debt / 1 / annual report
The intraocular lens division was sold to First Chicago Venture Capital.

*International Thoroughbred / Greenwood Racing Inc.*
14.79 / 6/30/89 (agreement date)
$63 / NA
Race track / race track management - newly formed company
Reduce debt and obtain cash / 1 / annual report
This financially troubled firm sold its Philadelphia race track to repay debt and obtain needed cash.

*International Technology Corp. (two sales) / (1) Tenera, LP (2) GSX Chemical Services*
(1) 5.18 (2) −12.85 / (1) 10/12/88 (WSJ) (2) 4/11/89 (WSJ)
(1) NA (2) $84.9 / (1) NA (2) −$110.1
(1) Nuclear risk control (2) treatment and disposal division / (1) services to manufacturing (2) chemicals
(1) & (2) Strategic (focus on core) / (1) & (2) 0 / (1) & (2) 8K
(1) The sale of the nuclear risk control group is consistent with the continuing effort of the firm to direct its resources into the rapidly growing industrial risk assessment sector. (2) The sale was part of the firm's restructuring program to concentrate on growing subsidiaries.

*IU International Corp. / Paper Corp. of America, subsidiary of Alco Standard Corp.*
5.24 / 3/10/86 (WSJ)
$32.5 (total cash $106.7 with gain from terminating pension plan) / $21.6 with gain from terminating pension plan
Paper distribution operations / paper company
Broad restructuring and debt reduction effort / 0 / WSJ (restructuring seems to dominate debt reduction)
As part of a broad restructuring effort, IU International sold several operating units, including this and the bulk of its agribusiness operations and its macademia nut orchards. Over recent years, the restructuring has transformed IU from a complex enterprise serving a multitude of markets into a simpler and smaller company focused on a much narrower range of business activities.

*K-H Corporation (Fruehauf) / Terex Trailor Corp.*
18.11 / 3/28/89 (WSJ)
$231.3 / NA
Trailer manufacturer and shipyard / NA
Pay interest on outstanding debt, repay banks, working capital /1 / WSJ
In 1986, the firm underwent a management buyout. This asset sale was part of the resulting program to restructure the firm and pay down the debt with asset sales.

*Keystone Consolidated Industries / Fastener Five Acquisitions, Inc.*
– 3.08 / 1/16/89 (Agreement date)
$16 / – $17.6
Metal and plastic crafters / NA
Strategic (focus on the core) / 0 / Financial World, Feb. 1990
After losing money for most of the 1980s, the company earned $9.3 million in the first nine months of 1989 after extensive restructuring.

*Kollmorgen / PC Acquisition Corp.*
– 3.62 / 9/30/86 (WSJ)
$25 / $5
Photocircuits division / management group
Strategic / 0 / annual report
As part of a plan to concentrate on new markets in electronics, the firm sold its photocircuits division to a management group.

*Koppers Co. / NA*
1.70 / 12/13/85 (agreement date)
$160 / – $100
Ten different businesses / NA
Strategic / 1 / annual report
Koppers announcement of the sale of ten business units reflected its plan to reposition the company to increase earnings growth rate and raise its value to shareholders by concentrating on its construction materials and services and chemical-based operations. The proceeds were to be used to repurchase the company's preferred stock and some of its common shares. Stock repurchases: In June 1986, announced plans to redeem convertible preference shares for about $46.6 million. In December 1986, board approved repurchase of about 15% of common shares for about $135 million.

*Lee Enterprises Inc. / Henry/Benedek Broadcasting*
– 3.00 / 9/4/86 (WSJ)
$13 / $10
Radio station / broadcasting

Regulation / 0 / 8K
To avoid violation of FCC rules against ownership of television and radio stations in the same community, Lee Enterprises sold its ratio station in Omaha after acquisition of a television station there.

*Loral Co. / Opus Acquisition Corp.*
−1.14 / 3/26/89 (agreement date)
$455 / $5
Aircraft braking division / NA
Strategic / 0 / annual report
The sale of the aircraft braking division was part of the firm's goal of redeploying assets from slower growth to growing core activities, including growth through acquisitons. There were allegations of conflicts of interest in the sale to the firm's chairman.

*Morgan's Foods Inc. / Midwest Restaurants Concepts*
7.58 / 1/10/89 (agreement date)
$3.752 / −$4.013
Sizzler Restaurants / restaurants
Strategic, not profitable / 0 / 8K
The company sold 11 Sizzler Restaurants that had never achieved projected sales volume and had operated at a loss since their acquisition.

*National Intergroup Inc. (two sales) / (1) Norandahl Inc. (2) Werner Co.*
(1) −4.50 (2) −6.73 / (1) 9/13/89 (WSJ) (2) 10/27/89 (WSJ)
(1) $117.7 (2) $15 / (1) −$16.45 (2) −$2.5
(1) National aluminum (2) extrusion division / (1) aluminum (2) NA
(1) & (2) Strategic (concentrate on core) / (1) & (2) 0 / (1) & (2) annual report
These asset sales were part of the firm's exit from aluminum and steel to concentrate on the core distribution business.

*S.E. Nichols Inc. / Schreiber Wholesale Services*
11.70 / 5/24/89 (DJ)
$21 / $3.5
Wholesale distribution division / management buyout
Financial difficulties, need to reduce debt / 1 / S&P ASE stock reports
Nichols sold its F.R. Schreiber Co. subsidiary to a group of management investors. The proceeds were to be used to repay its revolving credit line and for working capital.

*Nicolet Instrument Corp. / AM International*
1.41 / 6/27/86 (WSJ)
$22 / −$9.4
Electronic instrument testing division / NA
Strategic / 0 / annual report
The firm was unable to operate this division profitably due, in part, to depressed market conditions. Its sale was accompanied by restructuring of the remaining product lines.

*Nicor Inc. / Adcor Drilling Inc.*
−0.29 / 9/2/86 (WSJ)
NA / NA
Drilling division / management buyout
Reduce debt through restructuring / 1 / annual report
After two years of sizable losses, the firm returned to profitability by divesting several unprofitable units, including this drilling division. The proceeds were used to reduce debt.

*Nortek Inc. / Duro Industries Inc.*
−6.71 / 12/30/85 (agreement date)
$20 / −$6
Textile processing / management buyout
Strategic / 0 / annual report
Although the textile processing division remained viable, the firm concluded that it no longer fit into Nortek's long-term plans due to foreign competition and low growth prospects.

*O'Sullivan Corp. / Vulcan Corp., Jones and Vining*
−3.31 / 6/4/86 (agreement date)
NA / $0.15
Rubber heel and sole operations / footwear
Strategic / 0 / annual report
O'Sullivan Corp. decided to get out of the rubber business and concentrate on its core businesses of vinyl sheeting and injection molding.

*Portec / Harsco*
−3.91 / 2/6/89 (DJ)
$9.1 / NA
Railway maintenance products / steel/metal works
Cut bank debt (in default) / 1 / 8K
The firm sold its railway maintenance products division and used the proceeds to repay its outstanding bank debt. The firm had been in default with its creditors until a debt restructuring in August 1988.

*Primark Corp. / C. Itoh and Co., Inc.*
8.51 / 9/21/88 (WSJ)
$37.9 / NA
TV leasing company / NA
Cash for pending takeover / 0 / WSJ
Primark sold its Telerent Leasing Corporation (providing TV leasing to the lodging industry).

*Professional Care Inc. (two sales) / (1) Tender Loving Care Health Service (2) Olsten Corporation*
(1) −35.02 (2) −3.41 / (1) 9/1/87 (DJ) (2) 7/22/88 (DJ)
(1) $3 (2) $2.4 / (1) $.3 (2) $.67
(1) Offices (2) offices / (1) health care (2) temporary services
(1) & (2) Cash for litigation settlement in medicaid fraud / (1) & (2) 1 / (1) & (2) 8K
The firm had several years of financial difficulties due to civil and criminal litigation charging medicaid fraud. These sales were part of an asset sale program used to pay litigation expenses and penalties.

*Punta Gorda Isles Inc. / Village Builders of Florida*
17.65 / 10/19/85 (agreement date)
$23 / NA
Real estate / real estate
Reduce debt and financial difficulties / 1 / 8K
Weak real estate conditions and a heavy debt burden had resulted in poor performance for this company since 1981. The proceeds from the sale of this marina project were used to further reduce its debt.

*Quantum Chemical Corporation / Henkel Corporation*
19.32 / 12/28/88 (WSJ)
$480 / $16.8

34          *L. Lang et al./Journal of Financial Economics 37 (1995) 3– 37*

Oleochemicals business / NA
Cash to repay bank loan that was used to pay dividend / 1 / WSJ
This asset sale was part of the firm's unusual recapitalization in late 1988. The firm used the proceeds from the asset sale and a debt issuance to repay a bank loan used to pay shareholders a $50 dividend and maintain the ability to continue their acquisition program. Stock repurchase: On 3/8/88, the firm announced a stock buyback plan valued at $246 to $273 million.

*Savin Corp. / Scriptex Enterprises*
4.82 / 1/13/87 (DJ)
NA / $1.9
New York and Long Island retail branches / retailer
Strategic (focus on the core) and streamline operations / 0 / annual report
This asset sale was part of the firm's program to streamline operations, focus on the core, increase efficiency and lower its breakeven point. The firm had restructured its debt to get out of default in the previous year.

*Service Resources Corp. (two sales) / (1) U.S. Banknote Company (2) Thomas L. DePetrillo*
(1) −4.94 (2) 13.14 / (1) 880829 (WSJ) (2) 890406 (DJ)
(1) $7.6 (2) $3.2 / (1) −$19.1 (2) 2.036
(1) Financial printing company (2) keyboard manufacturing / (1) financial printing (2) management buyout
(1) & (2) financial difficulties & pay down debt / (1) & (2) 1 / (1) WSJ (2) 8K
This financially troubled firm (in default on interest payments since 1987) sold these assets in an attempt to remain solvent.

*Sierracin Corp. / Valor Electronics Inc.*
7.12 / 860607 (agreement date)
$2.3 / $0
Power systems division / electronics
Strategic / 0 / annual report
The firm sold this asset to concentrate on growth-oriented businesses and core technologies.

*Talley Industries Inc. / TRW*
−16.93 / 2/6/89 (WSJ)
$85 / $37.5
Air bag division / industrial
Cash earmarked to repay debt / 1 / WSJ
The sale of the air bag division culminated the firm's two-year restructuring program of divestments and acquisitions.

*Tandy Brands Inc. (2 sales) / (1) Action Inc. and D. Motsenbocker (2) Grate Home and Fireplace Co.*
(1) −2.47 (2) 12.20 / (1) 4/10/86 (DJ) (2) 3/4/87 (DJ)
(1) $3 (2) $1.6 / (1) −$0.88 (2) −$9.3
(1) Western leather division (2) grate and fireplace division / (1) NA (2) home supplies
(1) & (2) Strategic / (1) & (2) 0 / (1) & (2) annual report
These sales were part of the company's restructuring program designed to enable the firm to concentrate resources on its remaining rapidly growing speciality retailing division.

*Morton Thiokol / Dow Chemicals*
−11.86 / 11/15/84 (WSJ)
$131 / $75.1
Household cleaner division / chemicals

Strategic (focus on the core) / 0 / annual report & WSJ
The sale of the household cleaning division to Dow Chemical for cash and the shares of the firm held
by Dow helped the firm concentrate on its other businesses and served as an antitakeover device
against Dow (the sale was accompanied by a ten-year standstill agreement).

*Total Petroleum Ltd. / Various buyers*
2.98 / 1/4/89 (WSJ)
$152 / $2
Oil and gas / NA
Strategic / 0 / annual report
The oil and gas operations in the U.S. did not offer sufficient prospects for future profitability.

*Tridex Corp. / Jordan Industries Inc.*
8.05 / 8/3/89 (DJ)
$9.9 / NA
Radio coaxial connectors division / NA
Redeem notes, working capital and acquisitions / 1 / WSJ
The firm used the proceeds to pay in full its outstanding indebtedness of $6.7 million to Heller
Financial and to end its credit facilities with Heller.

*Tribune Co. / Cooke Media Corporation*
1.66 / 12/10/85 (WSJ)
$176 / $176.7
LA Daily News (newspapers) / communications
Retire debt / 1 / WSJ
The proceeds from this sale plus the sale of four cable systems were used to retire debt that had been
incurred in the acquisition of a Los Angeles TV station.

*Union Carbide Corp. / Ralston Purina*
4.86 / 4/7/86 (WSJ)
$1415 / $304
Battery products division / diversified company
Proceeds used as special dividend (about $33.20 per share) / 1/ WSJ
These asset sales were part of Union Carbide's restructuring as a defense to a hostile bid from GAF.
In the restructuring, the firm repurchased 56% of its shares for cash and debt, and paid a large cash
dividend to shareholders. Stock repurchases: To ward off GAF, paid out $774.6 million in cash plus
about $2.6 billion in debt for 56% of shares. Also paid out the proceeds from sale of unit to
shareholders as a special dividend.

*United Inns Inc. / Hanna Car Wash*
−0.84 / 8/12/88 (DJ)
$17 / $2.2
Car wash business / car wash
Not profitable / 0 / annual report
This firm sold its unprofitable discontinued car wash division.

*U.S. Shoe Corp. (3 sales) / (1)  Edison Brothers Apparel Stores (2)  Freeman Shoe Co. (3)  Linen*
*Supermarket*
(1) 1.31 (2) 0.55 (3) 0.38 / (1) 4/29/87 (WSJ) (2) 5/11/87 (agreement date) (3) 6/9/87 (agreement
date)
(1) $44 (2) $41 (3) $4.6 / $7 on all three combined
(1) J Riggings (retailing) (2) mens shoe division (3) home front division / (1) shoes (2) shoes
(3) home products (1), (2) & (3) Strategic / (1), (2) & (3) 0 / (1), (2), & (3) annual report

U.S. Shoe sold a chain of apparel stores, its home products division and its mens shoe division to fund expansion of specialty retailing and optical retailing, as well as selective footwear opportunities.

*Varo Inc. / Varo Quality Semiconductor Inc.*
−0.30 / 12/24/85 (WSJ)
$14.8 / −$2.2
Semiconductors / management group
Unprofitable division / 1 / S&P stock reports
Varo sold its unprofitable semiconductor manufacturing subsididary and earmarked the funds to repay $7 million of short-term debt with the remainder for working capital purposes. Stock repurchases: Firm authorized repurchase of about $1 million of common stock on the open market.

*Vermont Research Corp. / Miltope*
−7.02 / 9/19/88 (WSJ)
$2.85 / $1.5
Disk drive manufacturing / computer
Unprofitable division / 0 / S&P ASE stock reports
Disappointing sales of a new disk drive led to the sale of a disk drive production facility and related technology.

*Warner Communications Inc. / American Protection Industries, Inc.*
0.37 / 12/13/84 (WSJ)
$162 / NA
Franklin Mint (collectible manufacturing) / newly formed partnership – Warner Communications
    retains stake
Strategic / 0 / annual report
Warner Communications sold several businesses to reduce corporate overhead, build upon continuing operations, improve balance sheet and refocus attention on its core businesses. Stock repurchases: Announcement on 3/19/84 that firm would buy back Rubert Murdoch's News Corp.'s shares for $180.6 million, ending a 15-week struggle for the company.

*Warner–Lambert Co. (three sales) / (1) Becton Dickinson & Co. (2) Cambridge Instrument Co.*
    *(3) Henley Group Inc.*
(1) 1.47 (2) 5.61 (3)  −2.45 / (1) 3/6/86 (WSJ) (2) 3/26/86 (DJ) (3) 4/25/86 (WSJ)
(1) $225 (2) $50 (3) $163.5 /  −$497 on all three combined
(1) Hospital products division (2) scientific instruments division (3) Imed / (1) health care (2) NA
(3) NA
(1), (2), & (3) Restructuring to focus on the core / (1), (2), & (3) 0 / (1), (2), & (3) 8K
As part of a review of operations and the changing business environment in the hospital supply industry, Warner–Lambert made the decision to write down and divest certain of its operations and to restructure and consolidate others. Stock repurchases: WSJ reports on 11/29/85 that firm plans to buy back 8 million shares, for about $352 million.

*Westinghouse Electric Corp. / Group of five telecommunications companies*
−1.51 / 12/23/85 (WSJ)
$1700 / $500
Cable company / telecommunications
Restructuring / 0 / 8K
This sale is part of Westinghouse Electric Corporation's restructuring program designed to promote growth as the leading participant in several markets. Stock repurchases: By March 1986, the firm had repurchased about 21 million shares for about $887.25 million.

## References

Alexander. G.J., P.G. Benson, and J.K. Kampmeyer, 1984, Investigating the valuation effects of announcements of voluntary corporate selloffs, Journal of Finance 39, 503–517.

Asquith, P., R. Gertner, and D. Scharfstein, 1991, An anatomy of financial distress: An examination of junk-bond issuers, NBER working paper no. 3942 (NBER, Cambridge, MA).

Brown, D.T., C.M. James, and R.M. Mooradian, 1993, Asset sales by financially distressed firms, Unpublished paper.

Bernanke, B. and J.Y. Campbell, 1988, Is there a corporate debt crisis?, Brookings Papers on Economic Activity, 83–125.

Boot, A., 1992, Why hang on to losers? Divestitures and takeovers, Journal of Finance 47, 1401–1424.

Easterbrook, F.H., 1984, Two-agency cost explanations of dividends, American Economic Review 74, 650–659.

Hart, O. and J. Moore, 1990, A theory of corporate financial structure based on the seniority of claims, MIT working paper no. 560 (MIT, Cambridge, MA).

Hite. G.L., J.E. Owers, and R.C. Rogers, 1987, The market for interfirm asset sales: Partial sell-offs and total liquidations, Journal of Financial Economics 18, 229–252.

Jain, P., 1985, The effect of voluntary sell-off announcements on shareholder wealth, Journal of Finance 40, 209–224.

Jensen, M.C., 1988, Agency costs of free cash flow, corporate finance, and the market for takeovers, American Economic Review 76, 323–329.

Korajczyk, R.A., D. Lucas, and R.L. McDonald, 1990, Understanding stock price behavior around the time of equity issues, in: R. G. Hubbard, ed., Asymmetric information, corporate finance, and investment (University of Chicago Press, Chicago, IL).

Lang, L., R.M. Stulz, and R.W. Walkling, 1989, Managerial performance, Tobin's $q$ and the gains from successful takeovers, Journal of Finance 44, 771–789.

Lehn, K. and A. Poulsen, 1989, Free cash flow and stockholder gains in going private transactions, Journal of Finance 44, 771–789.

Mayers, D. and V. Singh, 1993, Divestiture program announcements: Wealth effects, redistributions and the structure of corporate debt, Unpublished paper (Ohio State University, Columbus, OH).

McConnell, J.J. and C. Muscarella, 1985, Corporate capital expenditures decisions and the market value of the firm, Journal of Financial Economics 14, 399–422.

Miller, M. and K. Rock, 1985, Dividend policy under asymmetric information, Journal of Finance 40, 1031–1051.

Myers, S.C., 1977, The determinants of corporate borrowing, Journal of Financial Economics 5, 147–175.

Myers, S.C. and N.S. Majluf, 1984, Corporate financing and investment decisions when firms have information that investors do not have, Journal of Financial Economics 13, 187–221.

Ofek, E., 1994, Capital structure and firm response to poor performance: An empirical analysis, Journal of Financial Economics 34, 3–31.

Shleifer, A. and R. Vishny, 1992, Liquidation values and debt capacity: A market equilibrium approach, Journal of Finance 47, 1343–1366.

Stulz, R.M., 1990, Managerial discretion and optimal financing policies, Journal of Financial Economics 26, 3–28.

Weisbach, M.S., 1993, The CEO and the firm's investment decision, Unpublished working paper (University of Rochester, Rochester, NY).

# Part III
# The Role of Intermediated Finance

# [17]

## CORPORATE STRUCTURE, LIQUIDITY, AND INVESTMENT: EVIDENCE FROM JAPANESE INDUSTRIAL GROUPS*

### Takeo Hoshi
### Anil Kashyap
### David Scharfstein

This paper presents evidence suggesting that information and incentive problems in the capital market affect investment. We come to this conclusion by examining two sets of Japanese firms. The first set has close financial ties to large Japanese banks that serve as their primary source of external finance and are likely to be well informed about the firm. The second set of firms has weaker links to a main bank and presumably faces greater problems raising capital. Investment is more sensitive to liquidity for the second set of firms than for the first set. The analysis also highlights the role of financial intermediaries in the investment process.

## I. INTRODUCTION

This paper explores the empirical relationship between corporate financial structure and investment. Our analysis is based on the large body of theoretical work that shows that information problems in the capital market can have important effects on both financial structure and investment. We focus on a common theme of this work, namely that liquidity—the availability of internal funds—should be an important determinant of investment when there are information problems in the capital market. We find evidence to support this view.

This paper also presents evidence on the role of banks and other financial intermediaries in channeling funds into productive investment. Diamond [1984], among others, argues that banks serve as corporate monitors who bear the costs of becoming informed about their client firms and who ensure that they make

*We are grateful for helpful comments from Olivier Blanchard, Ken Froot, Fred Furlong, Robert Gertner, Glenn Hubbard, Carl Kester, Andrew Lo, Tim Luehrman, John McMillan, Jim Poterba, Julio Rotemberg, Andrei Shleifer, Masahiko Takeda, Robert Vishny, David Wilcox, Jeff Wooldridge, Stephen Zeldes, the referees, and seminar participants at the University of California (Berkeley and Davis), the Garn Institute, MIT, Michigan, the National Bureau of Economic Research, Northwestern, Rochester, Stanford, and the Western Finance Association Meetings. We thank the Nikkei Data Bank Bureau for generously providing us with the data and MIT's International Financial Services Research Center and the Olin Foundation for financial support. The views expressed in this paper are those of the authors and do not necessarily reflect the opinions of the Board of Governors or its staff.

The Quarterly Journal of Economics, February 1991

efficient business decisions. The evidence presented here is consistent with the view that banks indeed play such a role.

The basis of our empirical investigation is a panel data set of Japanese manufacturing firms. We focus on Japanese firms because they operate in an environment that appears to mitigate information problems in the capital market. The key component of this environment is the *keiretsu* or industrial group. This institution coordinates the activities of member firms and—most interestingly from our perspective—finances much of their investment activity. Much of the financing comes from the large city banks that form the core of each of the large groups: they are both creditors and shareholders of group firms. We argue in the next section that this close bank relationship is likely to mitigate information problems that typically arise when debt and equity are diffusely held and no individual investor has an incentive to monitor the firm. By contrast, there is another set of Japanese firms that are not affiliated with an industrial group. In general, these independent firms have weaker banking ties. As a result, they are likely to face greater difficulty raising capital.

Thus, it is relatively easy to distinguish between firms that are likely to face information problems and those that are not. Our analysis then compares the investment behavior of these two sets of firms. The basis of comparison is the importance of liquidity as a determinant of corporate investment. We compare firms in this way because essentially all models that posit some sort of information problem in the capital market predict that more liquid firms should invest more. These models also predict that liquidity is irrelevant when there are no information problems. Thus, our strategy is to see whether liquidity is a more important determinant of investment for independent, unaffiliated firms than for group firms with close banking ties.

This empirical test is based on the predictions of many models. Two prominent examples are Jensen and Meckling [1976] and Myers and Majluf [1984]. Jensen and Meckling argue that incentive problems raise the cost of external finance. Outside financing dilutes management's ownership stake, thereby exacerbating incentive problems that arise when managers control the firm but do not own it. Myers and Majluf stress information problems rather than incentive problems, but reach a similar conclusion. If managers are better informed than investors about a firm's prospects, the firm's risky securities will sometimes be underpriced, thereby raising the cost of external finance. In both cases, managers find it more attractive to finance investment with internal funds. Thus, for firms facing information and incentive problems, liquidity will be an important determinant of investment.

We are not the first to focus on the link between investment and liquidity. Meyer and Kuh [1957] is one early empirical study of liquidity effects; many other papers have built on their work. A standard criticism of these studies is that liquidity proxies for other unobservable determinants of investment, in particular the profitability of investment. High liquidity signals that the firm has done well and is likely to continue doing well. Thus, more liquid firms have better investment opportunities; it is not surprising that they tend to invest more.

One way around this problem is to control for the expected profitability of investment when determining the investment effects of liquidity. One can do this by using the forward-looking information in Tobin's $q$: the ratio of the market value of the firm to the replacement cost of its assets. The theory predicts that if liquidity constraints are unimportant, Tobin's $q$ should be the only determinant of investment. Not surprisingly, liquidity matters despite the inclusion of $q$.[1] Yet, skeptics remain unconvinced about the importance of liquidity constraints: they rightly point out that Tobin's $q$ is difficult to measure and that there are many other strong assumptions underlying the theory.

Fazzari, Hubbard, and Petersen [1988] suggest a more sophisticated approach to this problem. They divide firms according to their a priori beliefs about whether a firm faces information problems in the capital market and then test whether liquidity is more important for the firms where information problems are presumed to be severe. Their basis of comparison is corporate dividend policy, arguing that firms that retain more of their earnings are more likely to be liquidity constrained. Indeed, they find that investment is more sensitive to liquidity for firms that consistently retain a larger fraction of their earnings.[2]

As discussed above, we take a similar approach to this problem, dividing our sample into two sets of firms, independent firms for which we would expect liquidity to be important and

---

1. See, for example, Chirinko [1987].
2. Zeldes [1989] takes a similar approach to analyzing the effects of liquidity constraints on personal consumption by dividing his sample of individuals into a group with a low level of assets and one with a high level. As predicted, his structural Euler-equation approach detects liquidity constraints for the former group of individuals, but not the latter.

36          *QUARTERLY JOURNAL OF ECONOMICS*

affiliated firms for which we would not. The advantage of this approach is that even though the individual estimates of the liquidity coefficients may be biased (say because Tobin's $q$ is mismeasured), provided that the bias is to be the same for two sets of firms, the estimated difference in the coefficients will be an unbiased estimate of the true difference. Rejection of equality of the coefficient then indicates that the true effects of liquidity are more important for one set of firms. Indeed, the hypothesis of equality of the coefficients is easily rejected: liquidity is much more important for independent firms than for affiliated firms.

Much of the paper considers whether it is reasonable to assume that the biases in the liquidity coefficients are identical; it is conceivable that the estimates are more positively biased for independent firms than for affiliated firms. This would explain why investment appears to be much more sensitive to liquidity for independent firms. We explore three reasons why this may be so. We do not find support, however, for this hypothesis. Thus, we interpret our findings as evidence that group financing arrangements relax liquidity constraints.

Our work complements the large empirical literature that explores the interaction between capital structure and information problems. This work is relevant because many of the information-based models that predict the importance of liquidity also make predictions about capital structure. For example, Myers and Majluf predict that more liquid firms should invest more *and* that equity issues should be associated with a negative share price response. This is precisely what Asquith and Mullins [1986] find. Other studies find similar share-price movements to capital structure changes that are consistent with information-based models of capital structure and investment.[3]

By contrast, there is little empirical work on the role of banks in the corporate investment process. James [1987] is one exception, but his evidence is indirect. He documents a more positive share-price response for firms that announce that they have borrowed money from a bank than for firms that issue bonds. James interprets this finding as evidence that banks serve a monitoring function that public bondholders do not. Although this result is

---

3. In addition, there is a small literature that tries to explain capital-structure choices based on information problems in the capital market. See Auerbach [1985] and MacKie-Mason [1990].

consistent with our findings, there is clearly more work to be done on how banks affect firms' real business decisions.

The remainder of the paper is organized as follows. The next section describes the institutional features of Japanese corporate finance that enable us to analyze the effects of information problems on investment. Section III describes how we distinguish between independent and group firms and presents some sample statistics on the two sets of firms. In Section IV we discuss the rationale behind our approach, describe the data we use, and present the basic regression results. Section V considers alternative explanations of our results. We conclude in Section VI with a brief discussion of the implications of our work and speculation about some recent changes in Japaneses capital markets.

## II. INSTITUTIONAL FEATURES OF JAPANESE CORPORATE FINANCE

The purpose of this section is to provide a brief description of the important features of industrial groups. The six largest industrial groups—Mitsubishi, Mistui, Sumitomo, Fuyo, Dai-ichi Kangyo, and Sanwa—date back to the 1950s.[4] The first three emerged from the fragments of the prewar *zaibatsu* that were initially outlawed after the war. The second three were formed somewhat later and were initiated by the banks that now form the core of these groups. Most large companies in the 1950s developed some affiliation with an industrial group. Membership in these groups has been remarkably stable for over three decades.

The groups are both diversified and vertically integrated. For example, the Mitsubishi group has member firms in the automobile, beer, and chemical industries. By conservative estimates, 89 of the top 200 Japanese industrial firms have strong business connections to one of the six largest groups. These firms account for 40 to 55 percent of total sales in the natural resources, primary metal, industrial machinery, chemical, and cement industries.

In addition, affiliated firms do much of their buying and selling within their group. As an extreme example, Gerlach [1987] reports that Mitsubishi Aluminum sold 75 percent of its output to other group firms and bought all of its inputs from group firms. He also estimates that affiliated firms are three times as likely to do

---

4. There are numerous other smaller groups, but we focus on the six largest because the ties within these groups are strongest and the most financially oriented.

business with other firms in their group than with unaffiliated firms.

More interesting from our perspective, however, are the financial ties among group firms. The most important financial link is between group firms and the banks at the center of each of the six primary industrial groups. The banks in these six groups include the five largest in the world and nine of the top fourteen banks.[5]

Affiliated firms do a significant fraction of their borrowing from the banks in their group. This contrasts with unaffiliated, independent firms that are much more inclined to spread their borrowing around. It is also different from the borrowing patterns of large U. S. corporations that rely more heavily on the corporate bond market. In addition, until very recently, group banks (of which there are typically more than one) owned as much as 10 percent of the equity of member firms; often affiliated life insurance companies own large equity stakes as well.[6] Moreover, group banks often place their employees in key managerial positions of affiliated manufacturing firms, thereby easing the flow of information between banks and their client firms.

These close ties are likely to reduce the cost of capital of affiliated firms. Because banks own large equity stakes in member firms and lend considerable capital, they have strong incentives to get around the information and incentive problems typically associated with arm's-length capital-market transactions. This concentration of financial claims in the hands of a few banks reduces the free-rider problems that plague firms with diffusely held debt and equity.

Moreover, because affiliated banks are both shareholders and debtholders, firms have less incentive to take actions that benefit one class of investors at the expense of another.[7] The concentration of borrowing and the linkage of debt to equity also reduces the cost of financial distress because it reduces conflicts that arise among

5. These statistics come from the American Banker's 1989 survey, *The Top 500 Banks in the World*. For perspective, Citibank, the largest U. S. bank, was twenty-second in the world and less than half the size of the top four banks.
6. The Revised Anti-Monopoly Act of 1977 required banks to reduce their holdings of equity to no more than 5 percent by 1987. Note that in the United States the Glass-Steagall Act prohibits any equity ownership by banks.
7. Aoki [1984] makes this point. Interestingly, the capital structures of these Japanese firms resemble some U. S. firms that have used "strip financing" as part of a leveraged buyout: like Japanese banks, investors in these highly leveraged firms hold both its debt and equity.

investors when a firm is near default.[8] This reduction in the costs of financial distress enables firms to issue more debt. As a result, they receive the greater tax advantages of debt financing. They can also avoid the adverse-selection costs associated with equity financing.

There is some evidence that these factors, particularly the alleviation of conflicts among creditors are important. Suzuki and Wright [1985] have shown that in times of financial distress Japanese companies with strong bank ties are more likely to avoid bankruptcy proceedings than companies without close bank ties. One interpretation of this finding is that the concentration of debt and equity enables the bank to restructure the firm's liabilities without having to rely on the coordinating role of the bankruptcy courts.

There is also considerable anecdotal evidence to support this view. For example, Abegglen and Stalk [1985] cite the case of the automobile manufacturer, Mazda, which was in financial distress during the 1970s. As a member of the Sumitomo group, Mazda had close connections with the group's major bank. When the company got into financial trouble, one of the managing directors of Sumitomo's bank assumed the leadership of the firm and led it out of financial trouble. Indeed, according to Sheard [1985], a former head of the Sumitomo bank was quoted as saying, "We are always prepared to help out when a member firm is in trouble. We won't allow any group member companies to go into business failure." Sheard documents several other instances in which group banks bailed out affiliated firms.

In contrast, Sheard notes that weak banking relationships were an important factor behind the four largest Japanese postwar failures: Kojin, Eidai Sangyo, Osawa Shokai, and Rikkar. In each of these cases no bank was willing to step in and organize a workout. Indeed, in covering the Osawa Shokai bankruptcy, *Nihon Keizai Shimbun* (the Japanese financial daily paper) ran an article titled, "The weakness of not having a main bank" [Sheard, 1985].

In sum, close banking ties are beneficial for at least three reasons. First, because banks with large financial stakes in their client firms have the incentive to monitor these firms, information

---

8. See Bulow and Shoven [1978] and Gertner and Scharfstein [1990] for analyses of the conflicts that arise in situations of financial distress. In a recent paper [Hoshi, Kashyap, and Scharfstein, 1991] we document the importance of group relationships and close bank ties in mitigating the costs of financial distress.

and incentive problems are reduced. Second, conflicts among creditors are eased, particularly when a firm is in financial distress. This enables firms to take advantage of tax-favored debt financing. Finally, the placement of former bank employees in management positions at client firms can facilitate information flows between the bank and firm.

In many ways, the relationship between a group firm and its bank resembles the relationship between a division of a large firm and the central office: banks, like the central office, provide capital and managerial support, in exchange for which they get an ownership interest in the firm and some say in how it is run. Of course, the links in the group are considerably weaker,[9] and the firm still retains ultimate authority over its own operations. But those links are important. And unlike a conglomerate, where the divisions are not publicly traded, we can observe these links. Thus, our analysis may provide useful information about the structure of the firm that is otherwise difficult to observe.

### III. DISTINGUISHING BETWEEN INDEPENDENT AND GROUP FIRMS

The sample we analyze is a subset of the Japanese manufacturing firms that have been continuously listed on the Tokyo Stock Exchange between 1965 and 1986 and have fiscal years ending in March. We restricted the sample to firms with accounting years ending in March to simplify the construction of (tax-corrected) Tobin's average $q$, which we use in our regression analysis. We extracted most of the data from the Nikkei Financial Data tapes. The data construction is described in more detail in Hoshi and Kashyap [1990].[10]

Determining which firms are affiliated and which are independent is somewhat difficult. Several publications (*Keiretsu no Kenkyu, Industrial Groupings in Japan,* and *Nihon no Kigyo Shudan*) attempt to make this distinction. We chose *Keiretsu no Kenkyu's* classification scheme because it focuses on the strength of a firm's relationship to the financial institutions in the group: the propensity to borrow from group banks and insurance companies and the

---

9. We discuss this in more detail in subsection V.2 below.
10. These basic selection rules leave us with a sample of 353 firms. We drop 16 more firms for which the absolute value of $q$ exceeded 50 in any accounting year.

percentage of shares held by other group firms.[11] We use Nakatani's [1984] refinement of *Keiretsu no Kenkyu*'s classification
scheme which selects firms in the largest six groups and which
eliminates firms that switched groups. The latter restriction
ensures that we have a sample of firms with strong and stable
group ties.

It is important to keep in mind that group "membership" is
not clearly defined; there are no membership dues or cards.
Instead, it is best to think of a group as a network of business and
financial relationships of varying degrees and kinds. We have
chosen to focus on the financial aspects of group affiliation: in
particular, a firm's relationship with a major bank. It is best to
think of this as a *type* of group affiliation, rather than as a
*definition* of affiliation. Some firms in the sample do not fit *Keiretsu
no Kenkyu*'s definition; nevertheless, they may have close business
relationships with other nonfinancial firms in the group. And,
firms that are not considered part of the group may have very
strong ties to a main bank, although on average they are weaker.

The intersection of Nakatani's sample and ours leaves us with
121 group firms and 24 independent firms. According to *Keiretsu
no Kenkyu*, as of 1981, only 83 of the 859 nonfinancial firms listed
on the Tokyo Stock Exchange were completely independent of an
industrial group. Thus, the small number of independent firms in
our sample reflects the fact that there are few of them in the
Japanese economy. The remaining 192 firms analyzed in Section V
are hybrids of affiliated and independent firms.

Table I shows some relevant statistics for the two sets of firms.
More precise definitions of the variables are given in subsection
IV.2. All statistics are computed for the fiscal years 1977 to 1982.
As the table shows, gross investment normalized by the beginning
of period capital stock is about the same across the two classes. The
independent firms tend to invest slightly more, and their investment is more volatile. A similar conclusion holds for liquidity and
production. The liquidity-capital and production-capital ratios of
the independent firms are both larger and more volatile. Tobin's $q$
is slightly higher for independent firms. The most striking difference between the two sets of firms is that group firms tend to have

---

11. More specifically, *Keiretsu no Kenkyu* identifies a firm as being strongly
affiliated with a group if it meets one of the following criteria: one of the group banks
was the largest lender to the firm in three consecutive years and shareholdings in
the group exceed 20 percent; the largest lender provided at least 40 percent of the
firm's bank debt; there is a historical affiliation.

TABLE I
SUMMARY STATISTICS COMPARING GROUP AND INDEPENDENT FIRMS*

|  | Group firms | Indep. firms |
|---|---|---|
| Number of firms | 121 | 24 |
| Median $I/K$ | 0.130 | 0.148 |
| Mean standard deviation $I/K$ | 0.110 | 0.138 |
| Median cash flow/$K$ | 0.240 | 0.291 |
| Mean standard deviation cash flow/$K$ | 0.106 | 0.120 |
| Median production/$K$ | 7.23 | 7.79 |
| Mean standard deviation production/$K$ | 1.15 | 1.48 |
| Median Tobin's average $q$ | 1.04 | 1.23 |
| Median debt/equity | 0.97 | 0.66 |
| Median $K$ (millions of 1982 yen) | 13,037 | 13,388 |
| Median sales growth | 0.069 | 0.081 |
| Median short-term securities/$K$ | 0.145 | 0.116 |

*Medians are calculated for all firms over all years. Standard deviations are calculated on a firm-by-firm basis and then averaged. Investment, $I$ and capital $K$ are for depreciable assets; other variables are defined in subsection IV.2 of the text.

much higher ratios of debt to equity. The higher debt-equity ratio is consistent with the view that a close bank relationship reduces the cost of debt financing. The last three lines of the table show that the two types of firms are similar in several other ways. Independent firms are slightly larger and tend to have slightly higher sales growth; both types of firms hold roughly similar percentages of short-term liquid securities.

One might be tempted to use these statistics to support or reject the hypothesis that independent firms are liquidity constrained. For example, the higher volatility of investment by independent firms would appear to be consistent with this hypothesis, while their higher level of investment is not. We caution against such comparisons: none of the differences in the means of the relevant variables are statistically significant, and the comparisons do not condition on the other characteristics of the firms.

## IV. REGRESSION EVIDENCE

### IV.1. Estimation Strategy

Numerous studies dating back at least to Meyer and Kuh [1957] document a pronounced positive correlation between liquidity and investment at both the firm level and aggregate level. At first glance, one might try to interpret this finding as evidence of

CORPORATE STRUCTURE, LIQUIDITY, AND INVESTMENT    43

liquidity constraints. The now standard criticism of this interpretation is that liquidity proxies for an important omitted variable, namely the profitability of investment: when a firm's liquidity is high, it is likely to be doing well and so should have good investment opportunities. It is therefore not surprising that they invest more.

While there are many ways around this problem, the most popular approach is to use securities-market data to control for the value of investment opportunities.[12] Hayashi [1982] has derived conditions under which Tobin's average $q$, the ratio of the market value of the firm to the replacement cost of its assets, is sufficient to assess how much the firm should invest. These conditions are quite stringent: among other things, capital markets must be perfect; firms must use a constant returns-to-scale technology; and they must not have market power. Therefore, it should not be surprising that in investment regression equations that include liquidity and Tobin's $q$, both variables are significant. One interpretation is that liquidity constraints are important. However, it is also possible that Hayashi's conditions are not satisfied or that $q$ is mismeasured (which is not unlikely given that the denominator is constructed using accounting numbers).

We are sensitive to the ambiguity in the interpretation of the significance of variables other than $q$, and most of the remainder of the paper tries to resolve this ambiguity. As discussed in the Introduction, we follow the basic approach of Fazzari, Hubbard, and Petersen [1988]. Instead of estimating the effect of liquidity on investment for all firms, we separate firms based on our a priori beliefs about how liquidity should affect their investment. Studying Japanese firms is useful in this regard because there is a straightforward way of isolating firms for which liquidity should be important: it should matter for independent firms and not for affiliated firms. We test to see whether this is indeed the case.

This approach is useful even if the estimated coefficients on liquidity are biased. This is because the *difference* in the estimated coefficients is an unbiased estimate of the true difference as long as the biases are the same for the two sets of firms. It is conceivable that in classifying the firms as independent or affiliated, we

---

12. Alternatively, one can use the investment Euler equation to assess whether a neoclassical, perfect capital-market model can explain investment. Recent work by Whited [1990], Hubbard and Kashyap [1990], and others finds that this model alone is not sufficient; however, when the authors incorporate borrowing restrictions, they are capable of explaining investment behavior. This approach is similar to Zeldes' [1989] strategy for analyzing consumption behavior.

implicitly sorted them according to the size of their bias. For example, it is possible that firms with a high correlation between liquidity and unobservable investment opportunities are largely independent firms. In this case, a larger coefficient of liquidity for independent firms may simply be uncovering this fact. After presenting the basic results establishing that the estimated liquidity effects do appear to be more important for independent firms, we explore three reasons why the estimates for independent firms may be more biased. We do not find evidence along these lines.

### IV.2. Regression Equations

The regressions we ran include as regressors, one or more measures of liquidity, Tobin's $q$, and lagged production. To eliminate the effects of scale, we normalize the investment, production, and liquidity measures by the firm's capital stock in the beginning of the year. To remove firm-specific effects, we include a firm dummy; and to weed out macro shocks, we include a yearly dummy.

We use both flow and stock measures of liquidity. The cash flow measure is income after tax plus (accounting) depreciation less dividend payments.[13] This number records the net flow of cash into the firm during the period of investment. The stock of liquidity is more difficult to measure since we do not have precise data on firms' cash balances. We do, however, have data on firms' holdings of short-term securities. These are securities that the firm describes as readily convertible into cash. The vast majority of the firms in our sample hold these types of securities. We use the level of short-term securities at the beginning of the period to measure the stock of liquid assets the firm has when it decides on investment at the beginning of the period.

Our measure of Tobin's $q$ is the ratio of the market value of depreciable assets (debt plus equity minus the market value of nondepreciable assets such as land) divided by an estimate of the replacement cost of depreciable capital.[14] Tobin's $q$ is calculated at

---

13. It is not clear whether dividends are discretionary and thus whether they belong in a measure of liquidity. When we estimate our model including dividends, the results do not change. This is not surprising given the low and stable payout rates in Japan.

14. We briefly describe our procedure for calculating the data required to compute $q$. More details are contained in Hoshi and Kashyap [1990]. The market value of debt is estimated by dividing the reported interest paid by a market interest rate. The value of equity is straightforward to compute. Calculating the replacement cost of assets is more complex. In some cases the replacement cost is taken to

the beginning of the period. Gross investment is measured as the change in the stock of depreciable capital from the previous year plus capital depreciation during the year.

Finally, we include lagged production in the regressions, where production is defined as sales plus the change in final goods inventories. This "accelerator effect" is important in the empirical investment literature despite the lack of a compelling theory behind it.[15] One theoretical explanation for the inclusion of production is that liquidity effects are important; however, in this case it would be better to include lagged liquidity itself. Alternatively, Schiantarelli and Georgoutsos [1987] have shown that when firms have monopoly power lagged production should be related to current investment. We do not include production for these reasons, but instead do so as a practical matter. Since liquidity and production are correlated, if we were to exclude production, liquidity might proxy for accelerator effects that appear to have been important but that we do not fully understand. As we discuss below, however, the basic character of our findings does not depend on whether production is included.

The inclusion of $q$ and production are imperfect attempts to control for effects that are difficult to observe. We caution against a structural interpretation of the coefficients and, instead, rest our conclusions on the estimated differences in the effects of liquidity.

## IV.3. Regression Results

We report our basic results in Table II. The first column contains the results for the pooled sample of independent and group firms. The results indicate that $q$ alone does not adequately explain investment: the estimated effects of production and liquid-

---

be the asset's book value. This is done for liquid securities (such as cash) and for assets like goodwill and patents where no other option was feasible. We used a recursion technique to calculate the replacement cost of inventories and physical capital. We equate the market value of an asset to its book value in an initial period (March 1965) and then sum subsequent inflation-corrected flows to derive stock values of inventories and physical capital. Finally, we estimated the value of land in two steps. First, we multiply the acreage owned by each firm in a base period (March 1974) by a price for that period. We then update this measure using a recursion similar to the one described above. The special procedure for treating land was adopted because the alternative approach (using a recursion after setting the market value equal to the book value in a base period) led to implausibly low estimates of land values.

15. See Jorgenson [1971], who writes, "Real output emerges as the single most important determinant of investment."

TABLE II
INVESTMENT REGRESSION EQUATIONS*

| | All firms | Group firms | Indep. firms | Group firms | Indep. firms |
|---|---|---|---|---|---|
| Cash flow | 0.106 | 0.041 | 0.501 | 0.060 | 0.451 |
| | (0.032) | (0.033) | (0.084) | (0.035) | (0.083) |
| Short-term | 0.096 | 0.061 | 0.512 | 0.081 | 0.441 |
| securities | (0.025) | (0.024) | (0.085) | (0.026) | (0.081) |
| Tobin's | 0.006 | 0.007 | 0.007 | 0.011 | 0.003 |
| average $q$ | (0.002) | (0.003) | (0.004) | (0.003) | (0.004) |
| Production | 0.019 | 0.022 | −0.022 | ---- | ---- |
| | (0.003) | (0.003) | (0.009) | | |
| $\overline{R}^2$ | 0.391 | 0.432 | 0.458 | 0.362 | 0.435 |
| Number of firms | 145 | 121 | 24 | 121 | 24 |

*The dependent variable is investment in depreciable assets divided by the capital stock at the beginning of the period. Production and the liquidity measures are normalized by the capital stock. The regressions include yearly dummies and firm dummies and cover the fiscal years 1977–1982. Standard errors are reported below the coefficient estimates.

ity are statistically significant and positive. The estimated coefficient on $q$ is statistically significant, but small.[16]

The second and third columns of Table II report the results when we condition on whether the firm is part of an industrial group or is independent. The second column establishes that the coefficient of cash flow is small and statistically insignificant for group firms. The short-term securities variable is statistically significant as are production and $q$. The third column shows that cash flow, short-term securities, and production are statistically significant, while Tobin's $q$ is statistically insignificant.

The main result of the paper is that the estimated coefficients of both liquidity variables are much larger for the independent firms than for the group firms—eight to twelve times as large. The differences in the coefficients of cash flow and short-term securities are both statistically significant at the 1 percent confidence level.[17] We can easily reject the null hypothesis of equality of the liquidity coefficients.

Note that production appears to be much more important for

16. We do not give a structural interpretation to this coefficient, but if one wishes to, it can be viewed as implying implausibly large adjustment costs in investment. This is a common finding. See, for example, Summers [1981].

17. The $t$-statistic of the difference in the coefficients is 5.10 for cash flow and 5.11 for short-term securities. These are well above the cutoff point for the 1 percent confidence level.

group firms; the differences in the estimated coefficients are statistically significant. Given that we do not have a strong theoretical rationale for including production, this coefficient is difficult to interpret. To establish that the liquidity result is not driven by the inclusion of production, we drop it from the regression equation. The results are reported in the last two columns of Table II. These columns indicate that liquidity continues to be more important for independent firms despite the exclusion of production; the differences remain statistically significant at the 1 percent confidence level.

In our view, the regressions we report are the most sensible and straightforward. We did, however, estimate several other specifications to determine the robustness of our results. None of the conclusions was affected. In particular, we added more lags of liquidity and production to account for the possibility that it may take more than a year for investment to show up in the capital stock. We found no substantive difference in the results. We also included $q$ at the end of the period because cash flow that comes in during the period might contain information about future investment opportunities not contained in $q$ at the beginning of the period. The effect of this variable is small and insignificant, and it does not materially affect any of the other coefficients. In addition, we instrumented for cash flow using lagged values. The instrumental variables approach should wipe out the component of cash flow that is unpredictable given beginning-of-period $q$. This is another way of avoiding the problem that cash flow during the period contains information about investment opportunities not contained in beginning-of-period $q$. Again, none of the qualitative results were changed.[18]

We conclude this section by reporting the results for the remaining 192 firms in our sample, those that are neither independent nor affiliated. These firms can be classified into three subcategories. Two of the subcategories include firms that are hybrids of affiliated and independent firms. As one would expect, liquidity matters more for these firms than for affiliated firms, but less than for independent firms. The third set of firms are subsidiaries of group firms. Not surprisingly, their investment is not very sensitive to liquidity.

The first subcategory is comprised of 25 firms that have some

18. These results are reported in an earlier version of this paper issued as MIT Sloan Working Paper No. 2071-88.

connection to a major group, but may not have close financial ties with the group's banks. These firms are members of a group's President's Council which meets monthly to discuss broad business concerns facing the group. Membership is fairly prestigious and is generally restricted to firms with active business ties to other members of the group.

There are several reasons why President's Council firms may not have been included in Nakatani's list of group-affiliated firms. First, the firm may have joined the President's Council only recently or may have switched group affiliation. Alternatively, the firm may have been involved in some merger activity. Or, the firm may have a ceremonial appointment to the President's Council, but may not have any active affiliation with the group. Finally, it may have weak affiliation with the group's financial institutions.

Depending on the reason for exclusion, we have different beliefs about whether these firms have ready access to funds from group banks. Unfortunately, we do not know exactly why Nakatani excluded each firm from his list. Nevertheless, it is fair to assume that in general these firms have weaker ties to group banks. It is not clear, however, whether these firms also have weaker nonfinancial affiliations with other firms in the group.

The first column of Table III shows that the coefficient of cash flow is statistically significant for these firms while that of short-

TABLE III

INVESTMENT REGRESSION EQUATIONS FOR FIRMS WITH MIXED STATUS

|  | President's Council/not group firms | Quasi-indep. firms | Subsidiary firms |
|---|---|---|---|
| Cash flow | 0.406 | 0.245 | −0.082 |
|  | (0.162) | (0.042) | (0.049) |
| Short-term | 0.110 | 0.082 | 0.105 |
| securities | (0.072) | (0.033) | (0.0131) |
| Tobin's | −0.002 | −0.000 | 0.019 |
| average $q$ | (0.004) | (0.004) | (0.008) |
| Production | 0.032 | 0.012 | 0.022 |
|  | (0.008) | (0.004) | (0.007) |
| $\bar{R}^2$ | 0.408 | 0.227 | 0.582 |
| Number of firms | 25 | 152 | 15 |

*The dependent variable is investment in depreciable assets divided by the capital stock at the beginning of the period. Production and the liquidity measures are normalized by the capital stock. The regressions include yearly dummies and firm dummies and cover the fiscal years 1977–1982. Standard errors are reported below the coefficient estimates.

term securities is not. The difference between the coefficient of cash flow for President's Council firms and group firms is statistically significant at the 5 percent confidence level. The relatively large standard errors of the estimated liquidity coefficients suggest that there is considerable heterogeneity among these firms. It seems likely that for some of them liquidity is irrelevant while for others it is important. Given the various reasons these firms were not classified as affiliated, it is not surprising that we estimate this coefficient imprecisely. Nevertheless, the results are consistent with the idea that liquidity is more important for firms with weaker bank ties.

The second subcategory is comprised of 152 firms that are neither independent nor affiliated. Nakatani does not list these firms as strong group members, and none is a member of a group's President's Council; however, these firms are not sufficiently distanced from the six major groups to be called independent. It is also possible that some of these firms may be members of one of the minor industrial groups.

The second column of Table III shows that their investment patterns reflect this hybrid status. Liquidity is quite important for these firms; the estimated coefficients of the two liquidity measures are between the estimates for the group firms and the completely independent firms. The difference between this cash flow coefficient and those of independent and group firms is statistically significant at the 1 percent confidence level. The short-term securities coefficient is statistically significantly different from the coefficient for independent firms at the 1 percent level. There is no statistical significance in the difference of the coefficients for independent and quasi-independent firms. These findings suggest that the closer a firm moves to the group banks, the more easily a firm can attract funds to finance investment projects.

The final subcategory is comprised of the fifteen firms that Nakatani lists as subsidiaries of group firms. The third column of Table III shows that the coefficients of both liquidity measures are statistically insignificant. The difference between the cash-flow coefficients of the subsidiaries and independent firms, quasi-independent firms, and President's Council firms are all statistically significant at the 1 percent confidence level. The coefficient of short-term securities for this set of firms is statistically different from the coefficients for the independent firms, but not the others. Because these firms, at least through their parent companies, have access to group banks, it is reassuring to see that their investment is not particularly sensitive to their liquidity.

## V. Competing Explanations

Thus far, we are able to reject the hypothesis that the measured effect of liquidity is the same for independent and group firms. As long as the potential bias introduced by the omitted variable problem is the same for the two sets of firms, this amounts to rejecting the hypothesis of equality of the true liquidity coefficients. We interpreted this finding as evidence that independent firms face more binding liquidity constraints.

One might, however, explain our results by arguing that the estimated effects of liquidity are more positively biased for the independent firms than for the group firms. Thus, one can explain the observed pattern of coefficients even under the null hypothesis of no liquidity constraints. We begin this section by considering several reasons why the estimates may be more biased for independent firms and conclude by discussing the possibility that independent firms are overinvesting rather than underinvesting.

### V.1. Industry Effects

One possible explanation of our results is that independent firms may operate in high growth industries where current liquidity is likely to proxy well for the value of investment opportunities, whereas group firms may operate in low growth industries where liquidity is an uninformative proxy. This could induce a larger positive bias for independent firms than for group firms. We find no evidence to support this view.

Table IV shows the breakdown of firms by broad industrial classification. Given the small number of independent firms, comparison on a finer industry level is not informative. The distribution of firms across industry classes is roughly similar for independent and group firms. Thus, it appears that our classification scheme does not simultaneously sort firms by industry.

Even with this aggregated industry classification, regression analysis would be uninformative because there are too few independent firms. However, if we pool independent firms and quasi-independent firms—both of which showed a strong sensitivity of investment to cash flow—we can crudely gauge whether industry effects explain our results.

CORPORATE STRUCTURE, LIQUIDITY, AND INVESTMENT  51

TABLE IV
DISTRIBUTION OF GROUP AND INDEPENDENT FIRMS BY BROAD
INDUSTRIAL CLASSIFICATION

| Industries | Number of group firms (% of total group firms) | Number of indep. firms (% of total indep. firms) |
|---|---|---|
| Food, textiles, pulp and paper, clay, glass, and stone | 25 (21%) | 3 (13%) |
| Electric machinery and precision machinery | 26 (21%) | 6 (25%) |
| Oil, chemicals, rubber, and drugs | 24 (20%) | 6 (25%) |
| Steel and nonferrous metals | 18 (15%) | 3 (13%) |
| Autos and transportation durables | 7 (6%) | 1 (4%) |
| Machines | 16 (13%) | 5 (21%) |
| Miscellaneous and ship building | 5 (9%) | 0 (0%) |
| All Industries | 121 | 24 |

To conserve space, we briefly summarize our results. For group firms, the coefficient of cash flow is statistically insignificant in each of the seven sets of industries. In five of the seven categories the coefficient is small and precisely estimated. The only large coefficient is in autos and transportation durables, where there are only seven firms. In the electric machinery and precision machinery industries, the effect of cash flow is moderately large, but also is imprecisely estimated. On balance, there is no evidence that pooling industries is responsible for our finding that cash flow is only a minor determinant of affiliated firms' investment.

Analysis of the pooled sample of independent and quasi-independent firms shows that pooling industries also does not account for our findings on independent firms; in each industry group, the estimated coefficient of cash flow is relatively large. In six of the seven broad industry categories, cash flow is significant. In the remaining category, which includes the food, textile, pulp and paper, and clay, glass and stone industries, cash flow is statistically insignificant but seven times the point estimates for group firms. In each industry except autos and transportation durables, the point estimates are larger for the nonaffiliated firms. These differences are statistically significant in three industries.

Similar results hold for the coefficient of short-term securities. The point estimates are larger for independent firms in five of the seven industries. They are insignificant in each of the industries for group firms and significant in four of the seven industries for independent firms. The differences in the estimated coefficients are only significant in one of the industries. Thus, it seems that industry effects cannot explain our findings.

### V.2. Measurement Error

Another explanation of our findings is that the accounting measures of cash flow might be more polluted for group firms than for independent firms. This would be another situation in which observed liquidity provides less information about the value of investment opportunities for group firms than for independent firms. There are two reasons to believe that this might be the case. First, group firms' transactions with other group firms may not take place at market prices. Second, group firms may try to shuffle income across firms to reduce tax liabilities, smooth reported income, or fund investment where it is needed.

We find this class of explanations unconvincing for several reasons. First, the tax-reduction and income-smoothing explanation presumes a degree of strategic micro-management that is inconsistent with what we know about behavior within the group. There are undoubtedly enough product-market linkages among group firms to enable them to shuffle income. However, these firms are all publicly traded and independently managed. It is hard to believe that firms have an incentive to make themselves look bad to help other firms.

This explanation then depends on the existence of an institutional structure that would coordinate and enforce transfers among firms. Neither of the two obvious candidates, the President's Council nor the banks, appears to have undertaken this role. The President's Council meeting is described as a loosely organized gathering that does not deal with these types of details. Moreover, banks do not seem to engage in such aggressive management. As one Sumitomo executive put it [Gerlach, 1987], "We are a big company now, and cannot be run even from the President's office. How possibly could the President's Council or some other Sumitomo grouping do it?"

An explanation related to income shuffling is that the group is liquidity constrained as a whole and the bank or President's Council simply allocates funds within the group to firms with the most valuable investments. Thus, the group is similar to a conglomerate that decides how available cash is allocated among the various divisions, but the bank does not add to the liquidity of the group as a whole. Although this result is consistent with our findings, we do not find it compelling because it overstates the observed coordinating role of the banks and President's Council and understates the autonomy of these publicly traded companies.

It is difficult to explore this idea empirically, but one point is worth noting. If the group actively managed the income of its members, one might expect to see a significantly lower volatility of cash flow for group firms than for independent firms. This would follow if the group took income from unusually cash-rich firms and gave it to unusually cash-poor firms, thus smoothing the time series of observed cash flow. As Table I indicates, there is a small difference in the standard deviations of group and independent firms, but this difference is far from statistically significant. Thus, there is little evidence in the data to support this idea.

## V.3. Endogeneity of Group Membership

Another possible problem with our interpretation of the results is that group membership is endogenous; factors that lead a firm to avoid group membership might be correlated with factors that would make liquidity more informative about investment opportunities. A similar criticism has been suggested by Blinder [1988] in his comments on Fazzari, Hubbard, and Petersen's [1988] finding that low-dividend-paying firms exhibited a greater sensitivity of investment to liquidity than high-dividend-paying firms. It is possible that firms which retain most of their earnings do so because they have good investment opportunities that may not be observable by the market.

One might make a similar argument regarding the endogeneity of group membership. For example, it is possible that firms that do not join a group are those with particularly profitable investment opportunities. Thus, investment is more sensitive to liquidity because it is a better proxy for investment opportunities. We find this argument unconvincing for two reasons. First, most firms have been affiliated with group banks for more than 25 years. During the time of our sample, group affiliation was essentially fixed and independent of short- and medium-term fluctuations in financing needs. Moreover, firms may have wanted to join a group, but were prevented from doing so [Gerlach, 1987]. Second, there is no strong evidence that independent firms have performed significantly better during the sample period: investment, sales growth rates, and $q$ were not statistically different. Thus, it is unlikely that sorting firms on the basis of affiliation implicitly sorts firms on the basis of their growth opportunities. Moreover, any potential bias along these lines is dealt with by the inclusion of a fixed firm effect since these opportunities are not likely to change over the time of our sample.

Finally, we note that some have argued that these financing arrangements were established to allocate funds during a time of capital scarcity and rationing. The firms that joined groups were the ones that were the most liquidity constrained. If this is true, then it biases the results against us: in the counterfactual circumstance in which the group-classified firms did not join a group, their investment would be extremely sensitive to liquidity.

### V. 4. Overinvestment or Underinvestment?

As discussed in the Introduction, most models of financial structure and investment imply that information and incentive problems lead firms to underinvest. In contrast, Jensen [1986] and others have argued that if managers prefer growth over profitability, they may invest free-cash flow in negative net present value projects. In this view, the correlation between liquidity and investment is a symptom of overinvestment rather than of underinvestment. According to this theory, close bank relationships should mitigate this problem because banks can prevent their client firms from investing in unprofitable projects.

Lang and Litzenberger [1989] try to distinguish between the overinvestment and underinvestment theories by examining stock-price responses to dividend announcements of U. S. firms. According to both theories, stock prices should rise in response to unanticipated dividend increases. In models of asymmetric information that typically imply underinvestment, a dividend increase signals higher future cash flows; in the overinvestment theory the dividend distributions prevent managers from overinvesting. Lang and Litzenberger argue that if the overinvestment theory is correct, the share-price response should be larger for firms with poor investment prospects since these firms are more likely to be overinvesting. In contrast, asymmetric information models have no particular prediction concerning the relationship between a firm's investment prospects and the share-price response to its dividend increase. The authors find evidence consistent with the overinvestment theory: firms with poor investment prospects, as indicated by a low value of Tobin's $q$, exhibit a more positive share price response to a large dividend increase than do firms with a high value of Tobin's $q$.[19]

Lang and Litzenberger's finding suggests a way to distinguish between these two views for our sample of Japanese firms. Our results indicate that investment is highly sensitive to liquidity for independent and quasi-independent firms. The overinvestment theory predicts that the investment of firms with poor prospects should be more sensitive to their liquidity than the investment of firms with good prospects. Moreover, we would expect group firms with poor prospects to overinvest less because they are subject to bank monitoring. Thus, according to the overinvestment theory, the difference in the liquidity coefficients of the group and non-group firms should be larger for firms with poor investment prospects.

To explore these predictions, we divided the sample of firms into those with generally good investment prospects and those with poor investment prospects. As a proxy for a firm's investment prospects, we used average Tobin's $q$ during the sample period 1977–1982. Firms with a value of average Tobin's $q$ above (below) the sample median were considered those with good (poor) investment prospects.

The first column of Table V reports the regression results for the set of nongroup firms that includes both independent and quasi-independent firms. We pooled these firms because of the small number of independent firms (although this set of firms is now more heterogeneous in their estimated liquidity effects). In addition to the variables used in the previous regressions, we add two interaction terms: (1) cash flow times a dummy variable which equals one if $q$ is above the sample median; and (2) short-term securities times the same dummy variable. The overinvestment hypothesis predicts a negative coefficient for both interaction terms: investment should be less sensitive to liquidity for high $q$ firms.

The results indicate that the coefficients of the interaction terms are *positive:* the investment of high $q$ firms is more, not less, sensitive to the two liquidity measures. (Note, however, that the

19. This finding is consistent with dividend increases being more of a surprise for low $q$ firms. The authors attempt to distinguish between this explanation and the overinvestment explanation.

TABLE V
INVESTMENT REGRESSION EQUATIONS IN WHICH LIQUIDITY EFFECTS VARY WITH
TOBIN'S $q$*

|  | Nongroup firms | Group firms |
| --- | --- | --- |
| Cash flow | 0.137 | 0.102 |
|  | (0.058) | (0.065) |
| Cash flow* High $Q$ dummy | 0.205 | −0.080 |
|  | (0.072) | (0.075) |
| Short-term securities | 0.084 | 0.084 |
|  | (0.042) | (0.069) |
| Short-term securities* high $Q$ dummy | 0.040 | −0.025 |
|  | (0.058) | (0.073) |
| Tobin's average $q$ | 0.001 | 0.008 |
|  | (0.003) | (0.003) |
| Production | 0.011 | 0.021 |
|  | (0.004) | (0.003) |
| $\bar{R}^2$ | 0.243 | 0.431 |
| Number of firms | 176 | 121 |

*The dependent variable is investment in depreciable assets divided by the capital stock at the beginning of the period. Production and the liquidity measures are normalized by the capital stock. The regressions include yearly dummies and firm dummies and cover the fiscal years 1977–1982. Standard errors are reported below the coefficient estimates.

effect is imprecisely estimated for short-term securities.) This finding is inconsistent with the overinvestment hypothesis.

The second column of Table V reports the regression results for the sample of group firms. The coefficients of both liquidity measures are larger for the low $q$ firms, although the differences are not statistically significant. More importantly, the difference between the liquidity coefficients of the group firms and the nongroup firms appears to be larger for the *high q* firms. The largest (and the only statistically significant) difference is in the cash flow coefficients of high $q$ firms: the total effect is 0.342 for nongroup firms and 0.022 for group firms. This finding conflicts with the prediction of the overinvestment theory that the differences should be larger for low $q$ firms. Thus, on balance, we find no evidence to support the overinvestment hypothesis, and if anything our findings tend to reject it.

## VI. CONCLUDING REMARKS

In this paper we have presented evidence consistent with the view that information and incentive problems in the capital market have important effects on corporate investment. This evidence comes from the fact that investment by firms with a close relationship to a bank—those firms that we a priori believe can minimize these problems—is much less sensitive to their liquidity than firms raising their capital through more arms-length transactions.

Our results lend support to the view recently put forward by Greenwald, Stiglitz, and Weiss [1984] and Bernanke and Gertler [1989] that capital-market imperfections contribute to excessive output fluctuations. In this view, high current profits increase current liquidity, thereby generating investment and increasing future output and profitability. The results also suggest that a related transmission mechanism may operate through the banking sector: a reduction in bank liquidity makes it difficult for firms to raise capital from informed lenders, thus raising their cost of capital. As Bernanke [1983] has shown, the large fall in bank liquidity may help to explain the depth and persistence of the Great Depression.

The results may also suggest that the institutional arrangements in Japan offer Japanese firms an important competitive advantage. While international cost-of-capital comparisons are generally quite difficult to make, the evidence here documents that Japanese institutions may enable firms to mitigate capital-market imperfections. To the extent that the U. S. capital market has no analogous institutional arrangement, U. S. firms may operate at a disadvantage.

We advise caution in jumping to this conclusion. If the Japanese system is indeed more efficient, why do not U. S. firms rely more heavily on concentrated bank borrowing? One reason may be that the Glass-Steagall Act prohibits banks from owning equity in U. S. corporations. It may then be inefficient for a bank to exercise control over the firm without an equity stake since their objectives (presumably ensuring that their loan is paid back) will be very different from shareholders'. This line of reasoning suggests that Glass-Steagall has real efficiency costs.

An alternative view is that the Japanese system itself evolved out of a restrictive regulatory environment. It is widely believed that capital was scarce at least through the mid-1970s. This was exacerbated by government regulations that imposed interest-rate ceilings and limited the ability of firms to raise money abroad. In this environment of capital rationing it was very important for firms to form close relationships to banks, which were at the time the only source of capital. Thus, the firms that were able to form close ties to a bank were less liquidity constrained, although the economy as a whole may have been liquidity constrained.[20]

Interestingly, the Japanese government has been loosening its capital-market restrictions. Interest-rate ceilings have been raised to reflect market conditions; restrictions on corporate issues of debt and other securities have been relaxed; and firms can more easily raise foreign capital and issue domestic bonds. The result has been that firms have begun to loosen their ties to banks and now borrow much more from the corporate bond markets. In an environment where it is easier to raise capital directly from securities markets, there are less compelling reasons to have close ties to a bank. Our more recent work [Hoshi, Kashyap, and Scharfstein 1990] documents and tries to explain the move by some firms away from banks as their primary source of capital.[21]

This suggests that there are costs and benefits associated with close banking relationships. This paper is about the benefits; the costs are less clear. Of course, there are reserve requirements that raise the costs of funds to banks. And, if banks are to monitor firms, these monitoring costs will raise the costs of bank financing relative to directly placed debt. Finally, and perhaps most important, the control that banks exercise over firms may be unpalatable to corporate managers. Once alternative financing arrangements become available, managers may prefer to raise capital from more anonymous sources who will not exercise such control. While this may be in managers' interest, it may hamper firms' ability to raise capital. These issues are the focus of our current research.

UNIVERSITY OF CALIFORNIA, SAN DIEGO
BOARD OF GOVERNORS, FEDERAL RESERVE SYSTEM
MASSACHUSETTS INSTITUTE OF TECHNOLOGY AND NATIONAL BUREAU OF ECONOMIC RESEARCH

## REFERENCES

Abegglen, James, and G. Stalk, *Kaisha, The Japanese Corporation* (New York, NY: Basic Books, Inc., 1985).

20. Johnson [1989] documents a similar phenomenon in Germany during the hyperinflation of the 1920s. Bank deposits dried up because individuals kept most of their wealth in goods rather than in cash. Thus, capital was scarce, and preference was given to large firms with long-standing relationships to the banks. Smaller firms were therefore unable to get bank credit. Many of them went public during this period or were acquired by large firms.
21. See Diamond [1989] for an interesting model of the choice between bank debt and directly placed debt.

CORPORATE STRUCTURE, LIQUIDITY, AND INVESTMENT     59

American Banker, *The Top 500 Banks in the World,* 1988.
Aoki, Masahiko, " 'Shareholders' Non-anonymity on Investment Financing: Banks
    vs. Individual Investors," M. Aoki, ed., *The Economic Analysis of the Japanese
    Firm* (Amsterdam: North-Holland, 1984).
Asquith, Paul, and D. Mullins, "Equity Issues and Offering Dilution," *Journal of
    Financial Economics,* XV (1986), 61–89.
Auerbach, Alan, "Real Determinants of Corporate Leverage," in B. Friedman, ed.,
    *Corporate Capital Structures in the United States* (Chicago, IL: University of
    Chicago Press, 1985).
Bernanke, Ben, "Nonmonetary Effects of the Financial Crisis in the Propagation of
    the Great Depression," *American Economic Review,* LXXIII (1983), 257–76.
——, and M. Gertler, "Agency Costs, Net Worth and Business Fluctuations,"
    *American Economic Review,* LXXIX (1989), 14–31.
Blinder, Alan, Comment on "Investment and Finance Reconsidered," *Brookings
    Papers on Economic Activity* (1988), 196–200.
Bulow, Jeremy, and J. Shoven, "The Bankruptcy Decision," *Bell Journal of
    Economics,* IX (1979), 437–56.
Chirinko, Robert, "Tobin's Q and Financial Policy," *Journal of Monetary Econom-
    ics,* XIX (1987), 69–87.
*Corporate Statistics Quarterly* (Tokyo: Ministry of Finance).
Diamond, Douglas, "Financial Intermediation and Delegated Monitoring," *Review
    of Economic Studies,* LI (1984), 393–414
——, "Monitoring and Reputation: The Choice Between Bank Loans and Directly
    Placed Debt," unpublished paper, University of Chicago, 1989.
Fazzari, Steven, R. G. Hubbard, and B. Petersen, "Investment and Finance
    Reconsidered," *Brookings Papers on Economic Activity* (1988), 141–95.
Gerlach, Michael, "Alliances and the Social Organization of Japanese Business,"
    Ph.D. thesis, Yale University, 1987.
Gertner, Robert, and D. Scharfstein, "A Theory of Workouts and the Effects of
    Reorganization Law," unpublished paper, University of Chicago, 1990.
Greenwald, Bruce, J. Stiglitz, and A. Weiss, "Informational Imperfections and
    Macroeconomic Fluctuations," *American Economic Review Papers and Proceed-
    ings,* LXXIV (1984), 194–99.
Hayashi, Fumio, "Tobin's Marginal q and Average q: A Neoclassical Interpretation,"
    *Econometrica,* L (1982), 213–24.
Hoshi, Takeo, and A. Kashyap, "Evidence on q and Investment for Japanese Firms,
    *Journal of the Japanese and International Economies* IV (1990), forthcoming.
——, ——, and D. Scharfstein, "Bank Monitoring and Investment: Evidence from
    the Changing Structure of Japanese Corporate Banking Relationships," in R.
    Glenn Hubbard, ed., *Asymmetric Information, Corporate Finance, and Invest-
    ment* (Chicago, IL: University of Chicago, 1990), pp. 105–26.
——, ——, and ——, "The Role of Banks in Reducing the Costs of Financial
    Distress in Japan," *Journal of Financial Economics* (1991), forthcoming.
Hubbard, R. Glenn, and A. Kashyap, "Internal Net Worth and the Investment
    Process: An Application to U. S. Agriculture," NBER Working Paper, No. 3339,
    1990.
*Industrial Groupings in Japan* (Tokyo: Dodwell Marketing Consultants, biannual
    publication).
James, Christopher, "Some Evidence on the Uniqueness of Bank Loans," *Journal
    of Financial Economics,* XVI (1987), 217–36.
Jensen, Michael, "Agency Costs of Free-Cash Flow, Corporate Finance, and
    Takeovers," *American Economic Review Papers and Proceedings,* LXXVI
    (1986), 323–29.
——, and W. Meckling, 'Theory of the Firm: Managerial Behavior, Agency Costs
    and Ownership Structure," *Journal of Financial Economics,* V (1976), 305–60.
Johnson, Simon, "Inflation, Disintermediation, and Economic Activity," Ph.D.
    thesis, MIT, 1989.
Jorgenson, Dale, "Econometric Studies of Investment Behavior: A Review,"
    *Journal of Economic Literature,* IX (1971), 1111–47.
*Keiretsu no Kenkyu* (Research on Industrial Groups) (Tokyo: Keizai Chosa Kyokai,
    annual publication).

Lang, Larry, and R. Litzenberger, "Dividend Announcements: Cash Flow Signaling vs. Free Cash Flow Hypothesis," *Journal of Financial Economics*, XXIV (1989), 181–91.

MacKie-Mason, Jeffrey, "Do Firms Care Who Provides Their Financing?" in R. Glenn Hubbard, ed., *Asymmetric Information, Corporate Finance, and Investment* (Chicago, IL: University of Chicago, 1990), pp. 63–103.

Meyer, John, and E. Kuh, *The Investment Decision* (Cambridge, MA: Harvard University Press, 1957).

Myers, Stewart, and N. Majluf, "Corporate Financing and Investment Decisions When Firms Have Information That Investors Do Not Have," *Journal of Financial Economics*, XIII (1984), 187–221.

Nakatani, Iwao, "The Economic Role of Financial Corporate Grouping," in M. Aoki, ed., *The Economic Analysis of the Japanese Firm* (Amsterdam: North-Holland, 1984).

*Nihon no Kigyo Shudan* (Japanese Enterprise Groups) (Tokyo: Sangyo Doko Chosa-Kai, annual publication).

Schiantarelli, Fabio, and D. Georgoutsos, "Monopolistic Competition and the Q Theory of Investment," Working Paper 87/11, Institute for Fiscal Studies, United Kingdom, 1987.

Sheard, Paul, "Main Banks and Structural Adjustment," Australia-Japan Research Centre, Research Paper 129, 1985.

Summers, Lawrence, "Taxation and Corporate Investment: A q-Theory Approach," *Brookings Papers on Economic Activity* (1981), 67–127.

Suzuki, Sadahiko, and R. Wright, "Financial Structure and Bankruptcy Risk in Japanese Companies," *Journal of International Business Studies*, (1985), 97–110.

Whited, Toni, "Debt, Liquidity Constraints, and Corporate Investment: Evidence from Panel Data," Federal Reserve Board, FEDS Working Paper 113, 1990.

Zeldes, Stephen, "Consumption and Liquidity Constraints: An Empirical Investigation," *Journal of Political Economy*, XCVII (1989), 305–46.

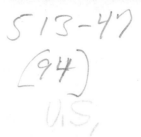

# [18]

THE JOURNAL OF FINANCE • VOL. XLIX, NO. 1 • MARCH 1994

# The Benefits of Lending Relationships: Evidence from Small Business Data

MITCHELL A. PETERSEN and RAGHURAM G. RAJAN*

### ABSTRACT

This paper empirically examines how ties between a firm and its creditors affect the availability and cost of funds to the firm. We analyze data collected in a survey of small firms by the Small Business Administration. The primary benefit of building close ties with an institutional creditor is that the availability of financing increases. We find smaller effects on the price of credit. Attempts to widen the circle of relationships by borrowing from multiple lenders increases the price and reduces the availability of credit. In sum, relationships are valuable and appear to operate more through quantities rather than prices.

IN A FRICTIONLESS CAPITAL MARKET, funds will always be available to firms with positive net present value investment opportunities. In practice, managers of small firms often complain of not being able to borrow enough capital at reasonable rates. Economic theorists (for example, see Stiglitz and Weiss (1981)) suggest that market frictions such as information asymmetries and agency costs may explain why capital does not always flow to firms with profitable investment opportunities. Developing on this theme, other economists (see Leland and Pyle (1977), Campbell and Kracaw (1980), Diamond (1984), Fama (1985), Haubrich (1989), and Diamond (1991)) describe how large institutional creditors can (partially) overcome these frictions by producing information about the firm and using it in their credit decisions. If scale economies exist in information production, and information is durable and not easily transferred, these theories suggest that a firm with close ties to financial institutions should have a lower cost of capital and greater

*Graduate School of Business, University of Chicago. Petersen thanks the Center for Research on Securities Prices while Rajan thanks the Graduate School of Business at the University of Chicago for funding. We thank Andrew Alford, Bob Aliber, Douglas Diamond, William Dunkelberg, Philip Dybvig, Anne Grøn, Oliver Hart, Steven Kaplan, Anil Kashyap, Randy Kroszner, Chris Lamoureaux, Mark Mitchell, David Rudis, and Rob Vishny for valuable comments. We thank René Stulz, the editor, and an extremely thoughtful referee for many valuable suggestions. We also benefitted from the comments of participants at the NBER Summer Workshop on Corporate Finance, the Finance Workshops at the University of Chicago and Washington University, St. Louis, the Financial Markets Group at the London School of Economics, and the Western Finance Association Meetings.

4                                    *The Journal of Finance*

availability of funds relative to a firm without such ties.[1] We term these ties relationships.

In recent years, a number of empirical studies have investigated the benefits of firm-creditor relationships. In a series of papers, Hoshi, Kashyap, and Scharfstein (1990a, 1990b, 1991) find that firms in Japan with close ties to their banks are less likely to be liquidity constrained in their investments than firms that do not have such ties. Furthermore, firms with close ties are more able to invest when they are financially distressed, suggesting again that banking relationships help overcome frictions impeding the flow of credit. For the United States, James (1987), Lummer and McConnell (1989), and James and Wier (1990) find that the existence or renewal of a banking relationship is a positive signal to the stock market. Shockley and Thakor (1992) find a similar effect for loan commitments.

Our paper differs from the ones cited above in that we use more detailed measures of the strength of firm-creditor relationships. Furthermore, we estimate the effects of relationships on both the availability and the price of credit. To the extent that we can do so accurately, we provide evidence on the precise channel or channels through which relationships benefit the firm.[2]

The data we use are from the National Survey of Small Business Finance collected by the U.S. Small Business Administration (SBA). The sample is well suited for our purposes. Only firms with fewer than 500 employees were included in the sample. The firms have a median size of book assets of $130,000 and median sales of $300,000. Since these firms are small, they are unlikely to be monitored by rating agencies or the financial press. As a result, there may be large information asymmetries between these firms and potential public investors. Furthermore, most of these firms are relatively young, with a median age of 10 years. In comparison, firms in the largest decile of New York Stock Exchange stocks have been listed for a median of at least 33 years. Since the youngest firms in our sample do not have much of a track record, a potential lender is uncertain about the competence and trustworthiness of the management, as well as the kinds of investment opportunities that could arise. If lenders remain at arm's length, management can indulge in pet projects, shift risk toward the fixed claim creditors, or otherwise misuse the borrowed funds. Some theorists have argued this is why small and young firms can rarely borrow in the public capital markets, and why we would expect firm-creditor relationships to be especially important in this sample (Diamond (1991)).

Apart from being an ideal testing ground for the theory, small firms are an important component of the national economy, producing 38 percent of gross

---

[1] Roosa (1951) appears to be the first to discuss the effect of bank-customer relationships in an environment with credit rationing. The recent theoretical developments discussed above have rekindled interest in the issue after a long hiatus. It should be noted that there are a few theorists who do not agree that stronger bank-creditor relations will always increase a firm's access to capital (for an example, see Blackwell and Santomero (1982)).

[2] Berger and Udell (1992), use the same data set as we do and find that a lender is less likely to demand collateral if a firm has had a long relationship with it.

national product (Dennis, Dunkelberg, and Van Hulle (1988)) and employing half of the work force (Brown, Hamilton, and Medoff (1990)). Some of these firms may be the industrial giants of the future. An important measure of the efficiency of a financial system is the extent to which such firms are nurtured and have access to the capital necessary for growth. This study is also a step toward understanding that process.

In the next section we discuss how, in theory, relationships can reduce frictions in the flow of capital from potential lenders to borrowers. This provides the basis for defining our relationship variables. Section II describes the borrowing patterns of small firms as they grow older and larger. Small firm borrowing is heavily concentrated among a few lenders, with banks being the predominant source. In Section III we examine the empirical determinants of the interest rate on the firm's most recent loan, and in Section IV the determinants of the availability of credit. This study provides evidence that relationships increase the availability and reduce the price of credit to firms. Furthermore, firms appear to reap the benefits of relationships more from increases in the quantity of finance made available by institutional lenders than through reductions in its price. Section V concludes with policy implications.

## I. Theories

In most markets, prices adjust to equate demand and supply. It has been argued that the capital market is special in that the interest rate need not always adjust to clear the market. Stiglitz and Weiss (1981) show that the rate charged, to an ex ante observationally equivalent group of borrowers, determines not only the demand for capital but also the riskiness of the borrowers. A higher interest rate either draws riskier applicants (the adverse selection effect) or influences borrowers to choose riskier investments (the incentive or moral hazard effect). If an increase in the interest rate increases the average riskiness of borrowers, lenders may optimally choose to ration the quantity of loans they grant rather than raise the rate to clear the market.

As discussed earlier, adverse selection and moral hazard may have a sizeable effect when firms are young or small, which may explain why they find it hard to raise money in the public markets. However, through close and continued interaction, a firm may provide a lender with sufficient information about, and a voice in, the firm's affairs so as to lower the cost and increase the availability of credit. We term this interaction a relationship. We now examine its various dimensions.

An important dimension of a relationship is its duration. The longer a borrower has been servicing its loans, the more likely the business is viable and its owner trustworthy (Diamond (1991)). Conditional on its past experience with the borrower, the lender now expects loans to be less risky. This should reduce its expected cost of lending and increase its willingness to provide funds. It is possible that the lender could obtain sufficient information on the firm's ability to service debt-like claims by observing its past interactions with other fixed claim holders like employees or prior creditors. If so, the age of the firm rather than the length of the financial relationship should determine the lender's cost and the availability of funds. Alternatively, the information generated within a financial relationship may not be observable (or transferable) to outsiders. If so, the length of the relationship should exert an independent influence.

In addition to interaction over time, relationships can be built through interaction over multiple products. Borrowers may obtain more than just loans from a lender, especially if the lender is a bank. Firms can purchase a variety of financial services from their lender and also maintain checking and savings accounts with it. These added dimensions of a relationship can affect the firm's borrowing in two ways. First they increase the precision of the lender's information about the borrower. For example, the lender can learn about the firm's sales by monitoring the cash flowing through its checking account or by factoring the firm's accounts receivables. Second, the lender can spread any fixed costs of producing information about the firm over multiple products. Both effects reduce the lender's costs of providing loans and services, and the former effect increases the availability of funds to the firm.

We have argued above that relationships can reduce the lender's expected cost of providing capital. Whether the cost savings are passed along in the form of lower loan rates, however, depends on how competitive the capital market for small firms is. The state of competition depends, of course, on the number of potential lenders in the market and on how informed they are. If, as discussed earlier, the information generated in prior relationships can be verified by potential new lenders, they can compete on par with the current lender. If the information cannot be verified by new lenders, the current lender acquires an informational monopoly over the firm. Greenbaum, Kanatas, and Venezia (1989), Sharpe (1990), and Rajan (1992) argue that this allows the current lender to extract the rents attributable to knowing that the borrower is less risky than average. Hence, if the information generated in the relationship is private to the lender and not transferable by the borrower to others, the relationship reduces the interest rate by less than the true decline in cost. Even though these theories imply that the effect of close firm-creditor ties on the cost of funds is ambiguous, in general, the availability of funds should increase.[3]

## II. Data

### A. Sample Description

The data in this study are obtained from the National Survey of Small Business Finances. The survey was conducted in 1988 and 1989 under the guidance of the Board of Governors of the Federal Reserve System and the

---

[3] If the (ex post) monopoly distorts the firm's investment incentives excessively, availability of funds could decrease (see Rajan (1992)). If the bank can freely dispose of its monopoly power, for example with loan commitments, availability will always increase.

*The Benefits of Lending Relationships* 7

**Table I**

**Distribution of Sample Firms by Industry**

This table contains the distribution of firms in our sample by the one-digit SIC code.

| Industry | Number of Firms | Asset Size (in 1,000s of Dollars) | | | | Firm Age (in Years) | |
|---|---|---|---|---|---|---|---|
| | | Min. | Mean | Median | Max. | Mean | Median |
| Mining | 26 | 30 | 3,129 | 464 | 32,317 | 12.5 | 7.0 |
| Construction | 447 | 1 | 708 | 103 | 12,000 | 14.2 | 12.0 |
| Manufacturing | 408 | 1 | 2,839 | 452 | 154,087 | 16.4 | 12.0 |
| Utilities and transportation | 117 | 7 | 1,778 | 275 | 62,983 | 13.3 | 10.0 |
| Wholesale trade | 344 | 1 | 1,671 | 302 | 35,945 | 15.1 | 12.0 |
| Retail trade | 930 | 1 | 589 | 114 | 22,820 | 12.2 | 9.0 |
| Insurance and real estate | 194 | 1 | 692 | 153 | 10,671 | 15.7 | 12.0 |
| Services | 938 | 1 | 591 | 82 | 69,073 | 13.8 | 10.0 |

SBA. It targeted nonfinancial, nonfarm small businesses which were in operation as of December, 1987.[4] Financial data were collected only for the last fiscal year. The sample was stratified by census region (Northeast, North Central, South, and West), urban or rural location (whether the firm was located in a metropolitan statistical area (MSA)), and by employment size (less than 50 employees, 50 to 100 employees, more than 100 employees and less than 500 employees (the maximum size in the sample)). The stratification was done to insure that large and rural firms are represented in the sample. The response rate was 70 to 80 percent, depending upon the section of the questionnaire considered.

There are 3,404 firms in the sample, of which 1,875 are corporations (including S corporations) and 1,529 are partnerships or sole proprietorships. Nearly 90 percent of these firms are managed by the owner or owners. Twelve percent are owned by women and 7 percent by minorities. Small firms are concentrated in businesses that require less capital assets. Nearly 28 percent of the firms in our sample are in the service industry. These firms are the smallest when measured on the basis of the book value of assets (see Table I). Another 27 percent of the firms are in the retail trade industry. The largest firms on the basis of book assets are manufacturing firms, which comprise 12 percent of our sample.

*B. Firm Borrowing Patterns*

Before turning to the impact of relationships on the financing of small firms, we describe the pattern and sources of borrowing for firms in our sample. The corporations are significantly larger than the proprietorships or partnerships. The mean book value of assets for corporations is $1.7 million

---

[4] Firms involved in the agriculture, forestry, and fishing industries, finance and insurance underwriting, or real estate investment trusts were excluded from the survey.

compared to $0.25 million for sole proprietorships and partnerships. Controlling for firm size, the corporations and noncorporations appear equally levered. The institutional debt-to-asset ratio (institutional debt excludes debt from the owners or their families) is almost identical—27 percent for corporations versus 24 percent for sole proprietorships and partnerships. These ratios conceal the large difference in the fraction of firms that have no debt. Twenty-eight percent of the corporations and 45 percent of noncorporations (sole proprietorships and partnerships) have no institutional borrowing.[5] Although more corporations have external debt financing, conditional on having institutional debt they have less leverage. The institutional debt-to-asset ratio, conditional on having institutional debt, is 43 percent for noncorporations versus 37 percent for corporations.

For firms with debt, Table II, Panel A shows the average borrowing from different sources when firms are grouped by size (book value of assets). The smallest 10 percent of firms in our sample borrow about 50 percent of their debt from banks.[6] Another 27 percent comes from the firm's owners and their families. The table shows that the fraction from personal (owner and family) sources declines to 10 percent for the largest 10 percent of firms in our sample. The fraction from banks increases to 62 percent for this group. There is no clear variation of borrowing with firm size for the other sources.

With the growing deregulation in the eighties, the distinction between banks and other financial institutions is perhaps not as clear as it once was. Therefore, we classify institutions as close if the firm obtains at least one financial service from it. Financial services include depository services—like providing checking and savings accounts—and services that provide the lender information about the firm's business—like cash management services, bankers acceptances, credit card processing, pension fund management, factoring, or sales financing. This classification attempts to capture how close the working relationship between the financial institution and the firm is. Approximately half of the institutional borrowing comes from close lenders. The fraction of institutional loans from close institutions increases from 0.45 to 0.62 as firm size increases.

Table II, Panel B describes the variation of corporate borrowing with firm age where age is defined as the number of years under current ownership.[7] The youngest firms (age less than or equal to 2 years) rely most heavily on loans from the owner and his or her family. These firms also use bank loans. In their initial years, their largest incremental source of funds is from banks, while they secularly reduce their dependence on personal funds. Eventually

---

[5] Firms may have unused credit lines—these would not show up in our loan volume data.

[6] We classify commercial banks, savings and loans associations, savings banks, and credit unions as Banks. Finance companies, insurance companies, brokerage or mutual fund companies, leasing companies and mortgage banks are classified as Nonbank Financial Institutions. We also have loans made by nonfinancial firms. The remaining loans consist of venture capitalist loans, loans from government agencies, and otherwise unclassified loans.

[7] We also measure age as the number of years since the firm was founded and obtained similar results.

## The Benefits of Lending Relationships                    9

### Table II
### Amount and Sources of Borrowing: By Size and Age

The first row is based on the smallest 10 percent of firms (book assets of less than $15,000). The asset percentiles are based on the entire sample ($N = 3,404$). The average debt is calculated for firms with debt only. The fraction of total borrowing, from different sources is described for firms that have debt. These percentages do not sum to 100 percent since the "not otherwise classified" category is not included. The $F$-statistic tests the equality of the means in each column. The last column contains the fraction of debt which firms obtain from close lenders. Close lenders are institutions which also provide the firm with at least one financial service. These include checking and savings accounts, cash management services, bankers acceptances, credit card processing, pension fund management, factoring, or sales financing.

#### Panel A: Sources of Borrowing: By Size

| Book Value of Assets ($1,000) | Assets Percentile | Percentage of Firms with Debt | Debt ($1,000) Mean | Debt ($1,000) Median | Fraction Borrowed from Each Source — Bank | Nonbank Financial Institution | Owner | Family | Other Firms | Fraction of Institutional Debt from Close Lenders |
|---|---|---|---|---|---|---|---|---|---|---|
| Less than 15 | 0–10 | 0.34 | 9 | 6 | 0.51 | 0.10 | 0.13 | 0.14 | 0.04 | 0.45 |
| 15–46 | 10–25 | 0.55 | 17 | 12 | 0.56 | 0.12 | 0.11 | 0.09 | 0.03 | 0.52 |
| 46–130 | 25–50 | 0.71 | 36 | 28 | 0.58 | 0.11 | 0.09 | 0.11 | 0.03 | 0.55 |
| 130–488 | 50–75 | 0.82 | 107 | 80 | 0.55 | 0.11 | 0.11 | 0.09 | 0.04 | 0.54 |
| 488–2,293 | 75–90 | 0.91 | 438 | 300 | 0.60 | 0.12 | 0.10 | 0.05 | 0.03 | 0.61 |
| Over 2,293 | 90–100 | 0.91 | 2933 | 1585 | 0.62 | 0.14 | 0.07 | 0.03 | 0.04 | 0.62 |
| $F$-statistic | | | | | 2.10 | 0.40 | 1.59 | 6.07 | 0.21 | 2.74 |
| $p$-value | | | | | 0.06 | 0.85 | 0.16 | 0.00 | 0.96 | 0.02 |

#### Panel B: Sources of Borrowing: By Age

| Book Value of Assets ($1,000) | Percentage of Firms with Debt | Debt ($1,000) Mean | Debt ($1,000) Median | Fraction Borrowed from Each Source — Bank | Nonbank Financial Institution | Owner | Family | Other Firms | Fraction of Institutional Debt from Close Lenders |
|---|---|---|---|---|---|---|---|---|---|
| Less than 2 | 0.79 | 648 | 40 | 0.49 | 0.09 | 0.10 | 0.17 | 0.05 | 0.52 |
| 2–5 | 0.77 | 395 | 61 | 0.54 | 0.12 | 0.14 | 0.11 | 0.03 | 0.60 |
| 5–10 | 0.77 | 334 | 53 | 0.58 | 0.11 | 0.10 | 0.09 | 0.04 | 0.57 |
| 10–19 | 0.74 | 410 | 54 | 0.63 | 0.12 | 0.08 | 0.05 | 0.03 | 0.57 |
| 19–30 | 0.71 | 695 | 96 | 0.60 | 0.14 | 0.10 | 0.04 | 0.04 | 0.55 |
| Over 30 | 0.59 | 912 | 128 | 052 | 0.15 | 0.10 | 0.06 | 0.04 | 0.50 |
| $F$-statistic | | | | 5.72 | 1.19 | 2.24 | 13.10 | 0.97 | 1.24 |
| $p$-value | | | | 0.00 | 0.31 | 0.05 | 0.00 | 0.44 | 0.29 |

10                                  *The Journal of Finance*

firms reduce their dependence on banks too. The fraction of borrowing from banks declines from 63 percent for firms aged 10 to 19 years to 52 percent for the oldest firms in our sample (see Table II, Panel B). This seems to suggest that firms follow a "pecking order" of borrowing over time, starting with the closest sources (family) and then progressing to more arm's length sources.[8] The fraction of institutional loans from close institutions is also consistent with this observation. Except for the first group, which contains firms which are larger than average, loans from close institutions decrease as the firm gets older, from 0.60 to 0.50.[9]

### C. Concentration of Borrowing

Another measure of the closeness of a borrower to its lenders is the concentration of the firm's borrowing across lenders. Table III, Panel A describes the average fraction of total firm borrowing that comes from the largest single lender when firms are grouped by size. The smallest 10 percent of firms who have a bank as their largest single lender secure, on average, 95 percent of their loans (by value) from it. By contrast, the largest 10 percent of firms obtain 76 percent of their loans from the bank. Thus, firms tend to concentrate their borrowing from one source, though this concentration decreases as firm size increases. As the table shows, such concentrated borrowing is not restricted to firms that have a bank as their largest lender. The same pattern appears no matter what the identity of the largest lender. Another way of measuring concentration is the number of sources from which a firm borrows. On average, the smallest firms tend to have just over one lender while the largest firms have about three lenders (numbers not in table).

Table III, Panel B describes the average fraction of total firm borrowing that comes from the largest single lender when firms are grouped by age. The high concentration of borrowing is still apparent in this table, but there is little variation with age. When the largest single lender is a bank, there is a slight decrease in dependency as firms age. In summary, the data show that small firm borrowing is highly concentrated. Firms diversify their sources as they become larger. It is less clear that age has any effect on diversification. Concentration of borrowing could be one measure of how close a firm is to its main lender. We will shortly describe other measures of closeness and their effect on the cost and availability of capital.

---

[8] The youngest 10 percent of firms in our sample borrow an amount equal to 0.32 of their book assets, while the oldest 10 percent of firms in our sample borrow only 0.15. The smallest 10 percent of firms in our sample borrow 0.22 of their book assets while the largest 10 percent of firms in our sample borrow 0.30 of their book assets. Thus, leverage decreases with age, but increases with size. A natural explanation for this is that young firms are externally financed while old firms finance via retained earnings. Larger firms may also be firms that have grown faster and have thus borrowed more.

[9] A regression shows that the fraction borrowed from close institutions is positively related to size and negatively related to the age of the firm. Both coefficients are statistically significant at the 5 percent level.

### Table III
## Concentration of Borrowing: By Size and Age

The results are reported by firm size, firm age, and primary source of debt. The asset percentiles are based on the entire sample and are the same as the ones used in Table II, Panel A. The first row contains information on the smallest 10 percent of the firms. The fraction of total borrowing from the largest single lender is reported by type of largest lender. The number of firms in each cell are reported in parentheses. The $F$-statistic tests the hypothesis that the percentage of borrowing from the largest lender is constant across the different size categories.

| Panel A: Concentration of Borrowing by Size | | | | | | |
|---|---|---|---|---|---|---|
| | | Fraction of Borrowing from Largest Lender | | | | |
| Book value of Asset ($1,000) | Asset Percentiles | Bank | Nonbank Financial Institution | Owner | Family | Other Firms |
| Less than 15 | 0–10 | 0.95 (51) | 0.93 (10) | 0.97 (12) | 0.93 (14) | 0.79 (5) |
| 15–46 | 10–25 | 0.93 (153) | 0.88 (31) | 0.92 (32) | 0.90 (26) | 0.88 (9) |
| 46–130 | 25–50 | 0.88 (359) | 0.81 (62) | 0.87 (52) | 0.84 (65) | 0.87 (17) |
| 130–488 | 50–75 | 0.84 (390) | 0.79 (72) | 0.74 (81) | 0.81 (65) | 0.85 (26) |
| 488–2,293 | 75–90 | 0.79 (296) | 0.74 (49) | 0.73 (38) | 0.81 (23) | 0.73 (15) |
| Over 2,293 | 90–100 | 0.76 (211) | 0.72 (43) | 0.75 (18) | 0.74 (7) | 0.71 (9) |
| $F$-statistic | | 19.98 | 2.61 | 6.16 | 1.79 | 1.44 |
| $p$-value | | 0.00 | 0.03 | 0.00 | 0.12 | 0.22 |
| Panel B: Concentration of Borrowing by Age | | | | | | |
| Less than 2 | 0–10 | 0.86 (150) | 0.80 (25) | 0.85 (25) | 0.89 (51) | 0.76 (16) |
| 2–5 | 10–25 | 0.85 (219) | 0.77 (43) | 0.82 (52) | 0.83 (44) | 0.86 (10) |
| 5–10 | 25–50 | 0.85 (347) | 0.76 (58) | 0.81 (53) | 0.83 (54) | 0.84 (24) |
| 10–19 | 50–75 | 0.85 (426) | 0.80 (71) | 0.80 (50) | 0.78 (30) | 0.88 (15) |
| 19–30 | 75–90 | 0.82 (216) | 0.84 (42) | 0.73 (34) | 0.77 (12) | 0.70 (10) |
| Over 30 | 90–100 | 0.80 (106) | 0.78 (28) | 0.83 (19) | 0.97 (9) | 0.83 (6) |
| $F$-statistic | | 1.51 | 0.62 | 0.96 | 2.10 | 1.25 |
| $p$-value | | 0.18 | 0.68 | 0.44 | 0.07 | 0.29 |

## III. The Cost of Capital

### A. Description of Loan Rates

In this section we examine the effect of relations on the firm's cost of debt. The data set includes the interest rate on the firm's most recent loan for 1,389 firms. The source of the loan is from institutions—a bank, a nonbank financial firm, or a nonfinancial firm—so that loans from the owner or her family are not included in this subsample. Banks are the dominant source of external capital, accounting for 82 percent of the loans in this sample. The interest rates average 11.3 percent with a standard deviation of 2.2 percent. This is 4.1 percent above the rate on a government bond of similar maturity, 2.4 percent above the prime rate at the time the loans were made, and 13 basis points below the yield on BAA corporate bonds (a basis point is one hundredth of a percentage point).

## B. Determinants of the Loan Rate

Before we turn to the role of relationships, it is important that we control for the underlying cost of capital as well as loan- and firm-specific characteristics that influence the rate. In the regression results below, we use the prime rate to control for changes in the underlying cost of capital. The prime rate includes the risk-free rate and a default premium for the bank's best customers. If these small businesses are not the bank's best customers, they will pay an additional default premium. We control for aggregate variations in this premium by including the difference between the yield on corporate

**Table IV**

**Borrowing Costs and the Role of Relationships**

The dependent variable is the interest rate quoted on the firm's most recent loan. Standard errors are reported in parentheses. In addition to the variables reported, each regression also includes seven industry dummies based on the one-digit SIC codes, three regional dummies, six dummy variables for the type of assets with which the loan is collateralized, and an intercept.

| Variable | (1) | (2) | (3) | (4) |
|---|---|---|---|---|
| *Interest rate variables* | | | | |
| Prime rate | 0.278* | 0.282* | 0.312* | 0.278* |
| | (0.030) | (0.030) | (0.035) | (0.030) |
| Term structure spread | −0.019 | −0.017 | 0.000 | −0.027 |
| | (0.083) | (0.083) | (0.100) | (0.083) |
| Default spread | 0.333** | 0.340** | 0.183 | 0.325** |
| | (0.149) | (0.149) | (0.175) | (0.149) |
| *Firm characteristics* | | | | |
| Log(book value of assets) | −0.254* | −0.264* | −0.255* | −0.259* |
| | (0.045) | (0.044) | (0.056) | (0.045) |
| Debt book assets | 0.005 | −0.015 | −0.051 | 0.001 |
| | (0.143) | (0.143) | (0.159) | (0.143) |
| Borrower is a corporation (0, 1) | −0.238*** | −0.229*** | −0.257 | −0.243*** |
| | (0.139) | (0.139) | (0.169) | (0.140) |
| Sales growth (1986–87)[a] | | | −0.585* | |
| | | | (0.301) | |
| Profits/interest[a] | | | −0.010* | |
| | | | (0.006) | |
| Mean 1987 gross profits/assets ratio in two-digit SIC industry | | | | 1.391** |
| | | | | (0.700) |
| Mean $\sigma$(gross profits/assets) between 1983–87 in two-digit SIC industry | | | | −0.771 |
| | | | | (0.681) |
| *Loan characteristics* | | | | |
| Floating rate loan (0,1) | −0.463** | −0.448** | −0.469** | −0.473* |
| | (0.181) | (0.181) | (0.222) | (0.182) |
| Bank loan (0, 1) | 0.238 | 0.216 | 0.341 | 0.248 |
| | (0.225) | (0.225) | (0.270) | (0.225) |
| Nonfinancial firm loan firm (0, 1) | −1.125* | −1.178* | −0.513 | −1.138* |
| | (0.360) | (0.361) | (0.430) | (0.360) |

## The Benefits of Lending Relationships                    13

**Table IV**—*Continued*

| Variable | (1) | (2) | (3) | (4) |
|---|---|---|---|---|
| *Relationship Characteristics* | | | | |
| Length of relationship (in years)[b] | 0.002 | 0.081 | 0.003 | 0.002 |
| | (0.006) | (0.059) | (0.007) | (0.006) |
| Firm age (in years)[b] | −0.014** | −0.227* | −0.011*** | −0.014** |
| | (0.006) | (0.078) | (0.007) | (0.006) |
| Information financial service (0, 1) | −0.089 | −0.087 | 0.057 | −0.087 |
| | (0.159) | (0.158) | (0.185) | (0.159) |
| Noninformation financial service (0, 1) | −0.097 | −0.101 | −0.134 | −0.104 |
| | (0.153) | (0.153) | (0.181) | (0.153) |
| Deposit accounts with current lender (0, 1) | 0.064 | 0.008 | −0.041 | 0.061 |
| | (0.182) | (0.186) | (0.225) | (0.182) |
| Number of banks from which firm borrows | 0.306* | 0.321* | 0.303* | 0.302* |
| | (0.085) | (0.085) | (0.096) | (0.085) |
| Herfindahl index for financial institutions | 0.042 | 0.033 | −0.024 | 0.033 |
| (1, 2, or 3) | (0.077) | (0.077) | (0.091) | (0.077) |
| Number of observations | 1,389 | 1,389 | 978 | 1,389 |
| Adjusted $R^2$ | 0.145 | 0.146 | 0.158 | 0.146 |
| Root mean squared error | 2.18 | 2.18 | 2.16 | 2.18 |

[a] When profits are negative, "Profits/interest" was coded as zero. Both "Profits/interest" and "Sales growth" are truncated at their 95th percentiles (76.0 and 1.0) to limit the influence of outliers.

[b] We replace length of relationship and firm age by the natural log of one plus the length of relationship and firm age in column 2. Thus the coefficient measures the change in the interest rate due to a one percent increase in the independent variable.

* Significant at the 1 percent level.
** Significant at the 5 percent level.
*** Significant at the 10 percent level.

bonds rated BAA and the yield on ten-year government bonds.[10] We also include a term premium, defined as the yield on a government bond of the same maturity as the loan minus the Treasury bill yield, to account for interest rate differences across different loan maturities. For floating rate loans this variable is set to zero. We estimate an ordinary least squares regression of the form:

Interest rate on most recent loan

$$= \beta_0 + \beta_1 \text{ Economy wide interest rate variables}$$

$$+ \beta_2 \text{ Firm characteristics} + \beta_3 \text{ Loan and lender characteristics}$$

$$+ \beta_4 \text{ Region and industry dummies}$$

$$+ \beta_5 \text{ Relationship characterestics} + \varepsilon. \qquad (1)$$

The regression that explains the variation in the rate quoted on the most recent loan is reported in Table IV, column 1. A significant fraction of the rate

[10] We obtain the yields on government bonds from the CRSP Fama-Bliss Bond Files. We obtain the yield on BAA corporate bonds from the Citibase database.

14                           *The Journal of Finance*

variation is explained by economy-wide factors. The change in the loan rate due to a change in the market rate is, however, significantly less than one. A one percent increase in the prime rate raises the loan rate by 28 basis points. The relative insensitivity of the loan rate is consistent with evidence from markets for consumer borrowing (see Ausubel (1992)). Increases in the default premium also raise the firm's borrowing rate. Each percentage increase in the spread between the BAA corporate rate and the long-term government bond rate raises the average loan rate by 33 basis points.

To control for variation in the loan rate due to the characteristics of the firm we include the firm's size (book value of assets), leverage, dummies for the firm's industry (coefficients not reported), and whether the firm is incorporated. The coefficient estimates for the firm characteristics are consistent with these variables being proxies for risk. Larger firms pay lower interest rates. A firm with assets of $740,000 (the 75th percentile) can expect to pay 0.59 percentage points less than a firm with assets of only $72,000 (the 25th percentile). Being incorporated lowers the interest rate by an additional 24 basis points.

To control for variation in the loan rate due to the characteristics of the loan we include dummies for whether it is a floating rate loan, for the kind of collateral offered (coefficients not reported), and for the type of lender making the loan. We also include regional dummies, industry dummies (coefficients not reported), and a measure of the Herfindahl index of the concentration of depository institutions in the area where the firm is headquartered.

## C. The Role of Relationships

Based on the discussion in Section II, we expect relationships to lower the lender's cost of lending to small firms. We estimate the effect of relationships on the interest rate charged. Implicit, therefore, in our analysis is the assumption that reductions in the lender's cost are passed on to the borrower in a lower rate. The first dimension of a relationship that we include is the length of the relationship between the borrower and its current lender. This should be a proxy for the private information the institution has about the firm. Firms who have been doing business with their lender for a short time should pay a higher rate. Of course, we must distinguish this effect from the fact that younger firms pay higher rates on their loans (Dennis, Dunkelberg, and Van Hulle (1988)). The length of the relationship and the age of the firm are correlated but not as highly as expected ( $\rho = 0.41$ ). When both variables are included in the regression, we find little independent importance for the length of the relationship (see Table IV, column 1). The coefficient is positive, but its magnitude is statistically zero ( $\beta = 0.002$, $t = 0.3$ ). Older firms, however, are charged statistically smaller interest rates; an additional year lowers the interest rate by 1.4 basis points or 0.014 percentage points ( $t = -2.3$ ).

The firm's reputation may not increase linearly with the age of the firm. The effect of an additional year of existence should decline with the age of the firm. To test for a possible nonlinear relation, we first estimate a separate slope for the firm age variable when firm age is less than 10 years (the median age). The coefficient is slightly larger, but the larger standard error means the coefficient is not statistically different from zero. We next replace the firm age and the relationship age by the log of one plus the age. This allows the marginal impact of age to decline. The estimates are reported in Table IV, column 2. The coefficient on the length of the relationship is again not significantly different from zero, while the coefficient on firm age indicates a declining impact of age. An additional year reduces the interest rate by 16 basis points if the firm has just been founded or acquired (age = 0), but only 2 basis points if the firm is 10 years old. To see the economic importance of this coefficient, a one standard deviation increase in the log of one plus the age of the firm reduces the interest rate it is charged by 0.19 percentage points. Later, we will compare the economic impact of relationship proxies on the interest rate with their impact on the availability of credit. An admittedly crude comparison is to calibrate these effects against a common standard, i.e., the effect of an increase in firm size. A one standard deviation increase in the size of the firm reduces the interest rate by 0.47 percentage points. Thus the effect of firm age on the interest rate is only 40 percent as large as the effect of firm size on the interest rate.[11]

The $R^2$ in columns 1 and 2 is almost identical, meaning that the data do not distinguish between a linear specification and a log linear specification. We also use the alternative definition of firm age as the number of years since the firm was founded rather than the number of years under current ownership. The coefficient on firm age drops by two thirds. The owner's reputation is apparently more important than that of the business.

The second measure we examine is the nonborrowing side of the firm's relationship with its current lender. In addition to borrowing, the firm may have checking or savings deposits with its current lender. Sixty-four percent of our sample does. The firm may also purchase financial services from the firm. As discussed earlier, these nonloan services can be used by the lender to monitor the firm. If these sources of information reduce monitoring costs or improve the accuracy of the lender's information, they should reduce the expected cost of such loans. We have already listed the financial services that might provide information to the lender (see Section II.B for a list of these services). In addition, the lender may perform services that arguably do not give it information—for example, providing change and night depository services. We code dummy variables for whether the firm had checking or savings deposits with the current lender, whether it purchased other informationally intensive financial services from it, and whether it purchased noninformational services.

---

[11] The figure of 40 percent is obtained by dividing the magnitude of the effect of a one standard deviation change in the log of one plus firm age on the interest rate (0.19 percent) by the effect of a one standard deviation change in firm size on the interest rate (0.47 percent).

That a firm obtains financial services from the current lender has no significant effect on the interest rate in our sample (see Table IV, column 1). Lenders who provide their customers with informationally intensive services charge a lower rate on their loans; however, the magnitude of this reduction is tiny (9 basis points). In addition, all three coefficients are statistically indistinguishable from zero.

Our third measure of the strength of the relationship is how concentrated the firm's borrowing is. From the results in Section II, it is clear that the firms in our sample borrow a significant fraction of their debt from a single institution. Even the largest firms in our sample borrow three quarters of their debt from a single institution (see Table III, Panel A). Firms may concentrate their borrowing with a lender to reduce overall monitoring costs, improve the lender's control, and cement their relationship. In these cases, concentrated borrowing should be associated with lower cost credit. Alternatively, firms may borrow from a single lender because it is their only source of credit. If so, then concentrated borrowing should be associated with more expensive credit.

We use the number of banks from which the firm borrows as a measure of borrowing concentration.[12] The firms in our sample borrow from no more than six banks, and the median firm borrows from only one bank. Eighteen percent of the firms borrow from more than one bank. We find that the rate paid by a firm increases by a significant 31 basis points when a firm increases the number of banks from which it borrows by one (Table IV, column 1). If we use the calibration method discussed earlier, the effect of the number of banks on the interest rate is about 53 percent of the effect of size.

As an alternative measure of concentration, we include the number of nonbank institutions from which the firm borrows. Increasing the number of nonbank institutions from which the firm borrows has no effect on the firm's borrowing rate. It is perhaps more plausible to think that ties between a firm and a bank are more indicative of a close relationship than ties between a firm and a nonbank. If so, this evidence suggests that the rate increases with a multiplicity of relationships rather than a multiplicity of creditors. In summary, a single banking relationship lowers borrowing costs, while multiple banking relationships are costly.

An alternative interpretation of the above result is that the number of banks is really a proxy for the firm's quality. Lower quality firms, unable to borrow additional money from their first bank, must approach other banks for additional capital. If so, the unwillingness of the original bank to extend the firm additional credit may be a signal of the firm's riskiness or quality, and the firm can obtain credit at a second bank only at a higher rate. In discussions with small business bankers, we were told there are several reasons besides quality why a firm may have multiple banks. Some banks specialize in the type of loans they make. Thus, a firm whose management wants to borrow with a line of credit against its accounts receivable may have

---

[12] We also consider the fraction of the firm's debt that is borrowed from its current lender. The results are qualitatively identical.

to approach a different bank than the one that made it a mortgage loan. Some firms borrow from multiple banks, so they can play the banks off against each other. Finally, some owners like the prestige of multiple banking relationships. To test the quality hypothesis, we divide the sample into those firms that have one bank and those that have more than one bank. We then search for differences between the two samples.

The firms with multiple banks are over twice as large as those with only one bank. As firms grow, they expand the number of banks from which they borrow. But these are not necessarily firms which are in the process of expanding (over) aggressively. The firms with multiple banks have lower sales growth (16 percent versus 35 percent).[13] They also have lower interest coverage (median profits/interest of 2.2 versus 4.3). These numbers suggest that the number of banks may be a proxy for lower quality firms. To test this hypothesis we include interest coverage and sales growth as additional explanatory variables in the interest rate regression (see Table IV, column 3). Both variables help predict the interest rate, and both are marginally statistically significant.[14] But the coefficient for the number of banks is only marginally lower than that in column 1. This suggests that the number of banks is not strictly a proxy for quality.

Finally, it is possible that since the data come from a survey of small businesses, many of which may not be audited, the profit figure is uninformative. While we do not have access to the names of the firms and cannot obtain more data on them, we know the two-digit Standard Industrial Classification (SIC) industry code for each firm. From COMPUSTAT, we extract the average gross-profits-to-asset ratio in 1987 for each firm's industry. We also calculate the standard deviation of the gross-profits-to-assets ratio between 1983 and 1987 for each COMPUSTAT-listed firm and obtain the average for the two-digit industry.[15] The first is a measure of profitability, and credit quality should increase with it. The second is a measure of risk, and credit quality should decrease with this variable. We report the results in column 4 of Table IV. The coefficients have the opposite sign to that expected. The interest rate is increasing in the average profitability and declining in the variability of profitability. Only the first coefficient is significantly different from zero.[16]

---

[13] For most variables the survey includes financial data only for 1987. It does, however, include sales figures for both 1986 and 1987. We use these numbers to calculate the firm's sales growth.

[14] Interest rate coverage will depend in part on the interest rate of the current loan. This endogeneity will bias the coefficient downward. Thus our estimated coefficient is probably more negative than the true coefficient.

[15] We only consider COMPUSTAT firms with book value of assets in 1987 below $150 million. We consider lead and lagged average profits, but these do not enter significantly.

[16] We examine this further by dropping loans where the interest rate was below the government bond rate. Presumably, these loans are made as part of a broader set of transactions and may not represent the true (relationship-adjusted) cost. The coefficients on average industry profits and standard deviation of industry profits reverse and have the expected sign, suggesting that loans to some poor quality firms—with low industry profits and high industry standard deviation of profits—are made at rates below the risk-free rate. Petersen and Rajan (1993) explore this issue in greater detail.

Not all of our proxies for the strength of firm-lender relationships are correlated with cheaper credit. That these variables do not all have a significant effect on the observed interest rate is consistent with three different theoretical explanations and an econometric one. The simplest one is that relationships do not matter much because all information is public or, at least, easily verifiable. If any potential lender can evaluate a loan's risk as accurately (and at the same cost) as the relationship lender there is no value to a specific relationship. A second possibility is that relationships do indeed have value, but rationed firms prefer greater availability of funds to a reduction in price. A third possibility is that the lender is not compelled by market forces to pass on the benefits via a lower interest rate. If the relationship confers a monopoly on the lender, this is what we would expect. The econometric explanation is that our measures may not capture the existence or strength of relationships.

## IV. The Availability of Credit

### A. *How to Measure the Availability of Credit*

We now estimate the effect of relationships on the availability of credit. If our proxies for relationships predict the availability of credit, then the econometric problem discussed above does not explain our interest rate regression. Furthermore, we may be able to distinguish among the theoretical explanations. Unfortunately, it is difficult to measure credit availability directly. The firm's debt ratio will underestimate the credit available to the firm—firms may have low debt ratios because the firm is liquidity constrained (a supply constraint) or because they have little need for external capital (a demand constraint).

The firm's debt ratio is simultaneously determined by the firm's demand for credit and the supply of credit from institutions. Thus regressions that use the firm's debt ratio as the dependent variable will suffer from a simultaneous equations bias. Changes in the debt ratio can be due to changes in demand for credit (the supply curve is observed) or by changes in supply of credit (the demand curve is observed). This statistical problem is apparent when we regress a firm's debt-to-asset ratio on characteristics of the firm. The results are reported in Table V. The dependent variable is total debt divided by assets. Credit availability should be greater for higher quality firms. Consistent with this intuition, large firms and firms in industries with high average earnings and low earnings volatility tend to have a high debt-to-assets ratio. However older firms and more profitable firms—which should be higher quality—have lower, not higher, debt ratios. The problem is we cannot tell whether older firms are rationed by creditors (a supply effect) or whether they have a lower demand for external credit. Since the coefficient estimates from this regression are not unbiased, we propose an alternative measure of the credit available to the firm.

Table V

## Determinants of the Firm's Debt Ratio

The dependent variable is total debt divided by the book value of assets. It has been multiplied by 100. Since the debt ratio is censored at zero we estimate the coefficients using a one-sided tobit model. Asymptotic standard errors are reported in parentheses. The regression also includes seven industry dummies based on the one-digit SIC codes.

| Variable | |
|---|---|
| Log(book value of assets) | 4.40* |
| | (0.56) |
| Profits/assets (%) | −0.99* |
| | (0.38) |
| Borrower is a corporation (0, 1) | 9.32* |
| | (1.99) |
| Firm age (in years) | −0.80* |
| | (0.09) |
| Length of longest relationship | −0.19** |
| (in years) | (0.08) |
| Herfindahl index for bank deposits | 3.57* |
| | (1.33) |
| Mean 1987 gross profits/assets ratio | 19.34** |
| in two-digit SIC industry | (8.92) |
| Mean $\sigma$(Gross profits/assets) between 1983–87 | −11.94 |
| in two-digit SIC industry | (9.48) |
| Number of observations | 3,233 |
| $\chi^2$ | 347.1 |
| ($p$-value) | (0.000) |

*Significant at the 1 percent level.
**Significant at the 5 percent level.

If institutions limit the credit extended to a firm, the firm will borrow from more expensive sources, so long as the returns from its investments exceed the cost of funds from those sources. Firms with unlimited access to institutional credit will never turn to the more expensive source. Therefore, with certain caveats discussed below, the amount borrowed from more expensive sources should measure the degree to which firms are supply constrained by institutions. More specifically, let the firm's rate of return on the marginal dollar invested be given by curve *JKE* in Figure 1. The firm should invest until the rate of return from the marginal dollar of investment equals the opportunity cost of capital. The firm has three sources of capital: internally generated cash flow (*OB*), borrowing from institutions (*BC*), and borrowing from an alternative source (*CD*).

The firm will exhaust its cheapest source, internal cash, before approaching the financial institutions. If institutions do not ration credit, the firm will invest to the point where the (increasing) marginal cost of borrowing from institutions (represented by curve *GN*) intersects the curve *JKE*. The firm will invest *OM*. If, however, institutions ration the amount of credit they offer the firm, say to amount *BC*, the firm only invests *OD*. Holding all else equal,

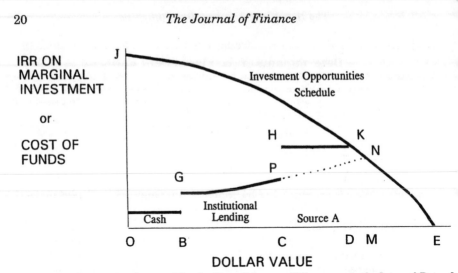

**Figure 1. Sources and uses of funds.** The solid curve *JKE* represents the Internal Rate of Return (*IRR*) on the marginal investment. *GP* is the marginal cost of institutional credit offered, while *HK* is the marginal cost of borrowing from *Source A*. *OB* is the amount of cash the firm has, *BC* is the amount borrowed from institutional lenders, and *CD* is the amount borrowed from *Source A*. *OD* is the total amount invested.

the amount *CD* that the firm borrows from the alternative source is then an inverse measure of the quantity of credit available from institutions. For *CD* to be an appropriate measure of institutional credit rationing, the marginal cost of borrowing from the alternative source must exceed the marginal cost of available institutional credit. If this is not true, the amount *CD* will be a function of the price financial institutions charge, as opposed to the volume of credit they are willing to offer. Also, the cost of borrowing from the alternative source should be relatively similar for firms within an identifiable class. Otherwise the amount *CD* will be a function of the specific firm's cost of borrowing from the alternative source.

What could the expensive source of credit be? Most of the firms in our sample are offered trade credit—short-term financing, which some suppliers provide with their goods and services.[17] We have data on the percentage of a firm's purchases that are made on credit, the percentage of this credit that is accompanied by discounts for early payment, the percentage of the discounts that are taken, and the percentage of trade credit that is paid late. In general, discounts for early payment and the penalties for late payment are substantial. They are meant to encourage the firm to pay on time. For

---

[17]Clearly, the trade creditor realizes a margin on the goods sold which is why she may be prepared to offer credit tied to the purchase of the goods even when others ration credit. Mian and Smith (1992) offer a variety of other reasons why trade creditors may do this. The manufacturer may find the collateral (merchandise) more valuable and easier to sell after repossession. Also, she may have a cost advantage in credit evaluation. Trade credit may be a method of price discrimination. Finally, there may be tax advantages if the financing qualifies as an installment loan. None of this suggests that trade credit is a cheap source of finance.

example, some firms in the retail business face the terms 10–2–30 (Smith (1987)). This is a discount of 2 percent if paid within 10 days (the "discount" date) and the full amount if paid in 30 days (the "due" date). Foregoing the 2 percent discount is equivalent to borrowing at an annual rate of 44.6 percent.[18]

Clearly, the annualized rate is not that high if firms are allowed to stretch repayments beyond the due date. Since the stated terms in an industry may differ from actual industry practice, we use our data to construct empirical measures of the actual stretch that firms face. Based on each firm's stock of accounts payable, we construct the days payable outstanding (DPO) for each firm, which is defined as 365 times the firm's accounts payable over its cost of goods sold. We report the DPO by industry in Table VI.[19] To estimate the potential stretch available to trade credit borrowers, we calculate the difference in the DPO between firms that regularly take the early payment discounts and those that do not. For each industry, we determine the median DPO for firms that take less than 10 percent of the discounts they are offered and the median DPO for firms that take more than 90 percent of the discounts offered. The difference between these two numbers is reported as the "Discount Stretch" in Table VI, and it is an estimate of how long firms that do not take discounts stretch their credit. For the retail industry it is 8.9 days.[20] Based on the standard terms, firms that do not take the discount are paying an additional 2 percent for 8.9 days of credit, which translates to an annualized interest rate of 129 percent.

A second way in which the firm can extend its trade credit financing is by paying late, i.e., after the due date. Clearly, the firm will incur both reputational and pecuniary penalties for paying late. For example, among gasoline wholesalers margins are so thin that a firm paying late may be forced to pay cash for future purchases and may be cut off from future supplies.[21] For each industry, we estimate the "Late Payment Stretch" as the difference between the median DPO for firms that repay more than 50 percent of their trade credit late and the median DPO for firms that repay less than 10 percent of their trade credit late. We find it to be 16.9 for the retail industry. Thus if the firm does not take the discount by paying on the tenth day and stretches the

[18] By taking the early payment discount, the firm is borrowing at 2/98 or 2.04 percent per 20-day period. Since there are 365/20 or 18.25 such periods in a year, this is equivalent to an annual rate of 44.6 percent ($[1 + 2/98]^{(365/20)} - 1$).

[19] We used two classifications for industry—the two-digit SIC code and the one-digit SIC code. We report only the broader classification in Table VI but use the two-digit SIC code in the estimates reported in Tables VII, VIII, and IX.

[20] Why is this number so low compared to the 20 days that should be the case if the discount terms are 2-10-30? A possible reason is that the discount date is not strictly enforced while the due date is, so that firms get discounts even if they pay after the tenth day (see Dun and Bradstreet (1970)). Another possible reason is that firms stretch entirely on the portion offered with discounts and not on any of the trade credit offered with net terms. If this is true (and we have no reason to believe that the firm should not stretch trade credit offered on net terms also), the stretch goes up to 8.9/0.3 = 30 days. This is an implicit interest rate of 27.9 percent, which is still higher than the highest interest rate on institutional loans in our sample (24.5 percent).

[21] Authors discussions with Mr. Chuck Patton, Credit Department, Amoco Oil Company.

## Table VI
## Days Payable Outstanding and Stretch by Industry

Days Payable Outstanding = 365 * Firm's Accounts Payable/Costs of Goods Sold. "Discount Stretch" is defined as the difference within the one-digit SIC industry between the median days payable outstanding for firms that take fewer than 10 percent of their early payment discounts and the median DPO for firms that take more than 90 percent of their early payment discounts. "Late Payment Stretch" is defined as the difference within the industry between the median days payable outstanding between firms that pay more than 50 percent of trade credit late and firms that pay less than 10 percent of their trade credit late. Due to the small number of observations in the utilities and transportation industry, we are not able to calculate the Discount Stretch or the Late Payment Stretch.

| Industry | Number of Firms | Days Payable Outstanding | | | Fraction of Firms Taking ≥ 90% of Early Payments Discounts | Discount Stretch (in Days) | Fraction of Firms Paying ≥ 50% of Trade Credit Late | Late Payment Stretch (in Days) |
|---|---|---|---|---|---|---|---|---|
| | | Median | Mean | Std Dev | | | | |
| Mining | 20 | 30.6 | 43.7 | 50.8 | 21.4 | 62.0 | 23.1 | 60.4 |
| Construction | 355 | 15.9 | 37.5 | 96.6 | 62.5 | 22.7 | 22.5 | 21.0 |
| Manufacturing | 356 | 27.3 | 43.8 | 83.3 | 42.3 | 14.9 | 24.6 | 18.4 |
| Utilities and transportation | 5 | 9.4 | 18.5 | 20.6 | 66.6 | — | 0.0 | — |
| Wholesale trade | 296 | 19.7 | 37.2 | 84.6 | 60.4 | 19.9 | 19.8 | 13.6 |
| Retail trade | 825 | 10.8 | 25.2 | 60.9 | 57.6 | 8.9 | 12.8 | 16.8 |
| Insurance and real estate | 69 | 0.0 | 207.2 | 1580 | 84.0 | 1.2 | 15.0 | 96.7 |
| Services | 60 | 4.7 | 16.5 | 26.3 | 56.7 | 16.5 | 12.0 | 0.0 |

payment out for 36.9 days (20 days plus the late payment stretch of 16.9), the implicit annual interest rate is 22.1 percent.[22] This is an underestimate of the true borrowing rate because it overstates the actual discount stretch that we estimate for the retail industry (8.9 days). It also underestimates the true borrowing cost because it ignores the reputational and pecuniary costs that missing the due date will impose on the firm. Despite these omissions, this interest rate is higher than 99.8 percent of the loans in our sample.

As a final way to document the true costs of financing a firm through delayed payment of its trade credit obligations, we calculate the percent of firms in an industry that take most of the early payment discounts (more than 90 percent) and the percent of firms that pay a significant fraction of their trade credits late (more than 50 percent). These numbers are reported in Table VI. That 58 percent of firms in the retail industry avail themselves of 90 percent or more of the discounts they are offered suggests that discounts are sizeable, and that firms that forego them are not getting cheap financing. Similarly, only 13 percent of firms pay more than 50 percent of their trade credits late, suggesting that the penalties for late payment are substantial. Furthermore, our conversations and previous work (Dun and Bradstreet (1970), Elliehausen and Wolken (1992)) indicate that discount terms are not specific to a firm, but are common practice throughout an industry. As these discounts and penalties are substantial and are industry specific and not firm specific, the fraction of trade discounts not taken or the fraction of trade credit paid late are good proxies for the amount *CD*.

## B. Trade Credit Data

In Table VII we present summary statistics for the data on trade credit. Larger (Table VII, Panel A) and older (Table VII, Panel B) firms make more of their purchases on credit, suggesting that the decision to offer credit seems to be firm specific. The percentage of credit offered with discounts for prompt payment, however, is invariant to firm characteristics like size and age. We test whether this percentage varies across age or size categories in Table VII. We cannot reject the hypothesis of a constant mean in either case ($p = 0.93$ for size and 0.63 for age). We also regress the percentage of discounts offered on several firm characteristics and 12 industry dummies. Only the industry dummies are statistically significant. It appears that once the decision to offer credit is made, discounts for early payment automatically follow if it is the supplier's policy. This evidence also seems to indicate that the size of the

---

[22] Neither measure of stretch is completely accurate. The discount stretch has the problems discussed in footnote 20, while the late payment stretch overestimates the stretch from the due date because it does not take into account the possibility that early payers may take substantially more of their discounts. Yet another measure of the stretch could be the difference in medians between those taking 90 percent of their discounts and those paying more than 50 percent late. In the retail industry, this is 19.4 days, which translates to a 46.2 percent annual rate.

## Table VII
## Trade Credit Usage of Firms: By Size and Age

Firms are grouped by size in Panel A and by age in Panel B. The number of firms in each cell are reported in parentheses. The F-statistic tests the hypothesis that the mean percentage is constant across the different size and age categories.

### Panel A: Trade Credit Usage of Firms: By Size

| Book Value of Assets ($1,000) | Asset Percentiles | Percentage of Purchases Made on Credit | Percentage of Trade Credit with Early Payment Discounts | Percentage of Offered Discounts Taken by Firm | Trade Credit Paid Late in Percent | Median Stretch for Firms (Measured from Last Day for Discounts)[a] | Median Stretch for Firms (Measured from Due Date)[b] |
|---|---|---|---|---|---|---|---|
| Less than 15 | 0–10 | 71.8 (203) | 33.2 (204) | 74.2 (122) | 18.0 (100) | −13.03 (108) | −17.91 (102) |
| 15–46 | 10–25 | 73.3 (366) | 31.4 (364) | 64.4 (245) | 21.2 (194) | −7.32 (245) | −10.71 (239) |
| 46–130 | 25–50 | 74.0 (639) | 32.7 (632) | 63.8 (457) | 19.8 (344) | −2.60 (445) | −5.86 (439) |
| 130–488 | 50–75 | 81.2 (694) | 32.8 (686) | 64.9 (539) | 21.7 (379) | 1.44 (473) | −0.81 (464) |
| 488–2293 | 75–90 | 84.8 (446) | 31.5 (433) | 68.3 (375) | 21.4 (260) | 6.59 (305) | 3.75 (308) |
| Over 2293 | 90–100 | 90.2 (298) | 34.1 (289) | 70.5 (278) | 21.0 (172) | 5.27 (214) | 2.85 (210) |
| F-statistic | | 25.65 | 0.27 | 2.17 | 0.56 | | |
| p-value | | 0.00 | 0.93 | 0.05 | 0.73 | | |

### Panel B: Trade Credit Usage of Firms: By Age

| Firms Age (Years) | Age Percentile | | | | | | |
|---|---|---|---|---|---|---|---|
| Less than 2 | 0–10 | 75.4 (299) | 33.6 (295) | 58.9 (224) | 25.1 (155) | −2.20 (208) | −5.86 (200) |
| 2–5 | 10–25 | 74.3 (414) | 32.2 (400) | 57.1 (295) | 23.7 (243) | 0.00 (282) | −3.16 (276) |
| 5–10 | 25–50 | 79.2 (623) | 30.4 (615) | 61.5 (457) | 22.1 (357) | −0.02 (400) | −2.97 (398) |
| 10–19 | 50–75 | 80.6 (689) | 33.3 (682) | 68.9 (539) | 18.4 (392) | 0.00 (470) | −2.71 (473) |
| 19–30 | 75–90 | 82.7 (377) | 33.4 (376) | 74.5 (308) | 18.6 (210) | 2.89 (260) | −1.22 (252) |
| Over 30 | 90–100 | 83.5 (244) | 34.1 (240) | 82.4 (193) | 15.8 (92) | 0.11 (170) | −0.72 (163) |
| F-statistic | | 6.47 | 0.69 | 14.89 | 4.09 | | |
| p-value | | 0.00 | 0.63 | 0.00 | 0.00 | | |

[a] For each two-digit SIC industry, the median DPO is obtained for firms availing of more than 90 percent of their discounts. This is subtracted from the DPO for the firm to obtain the stretch as measured from the last day for discounts.

[b] For each two-digit SIC industry, the median DPO is obtained for firms paying less than 10 percent of credit late. This is subtracted from the DPO

discounts offered for early payment are unlikely to be tailored to the specific customer.

The two variables of interest are the percentage of trade credit that is paid after the due date (which we call late payments) and the percentage of discounts for early payment that are taken (which we call discounts taken). Both variables are taken from the survey. Each is a proxy for the amount borrowed from the alternative source. A firm that makes more late payments or takes fewer cash discounts uses a greater amount of trade credit as a source of financing. As seen in Table VII, these two variables do not seem to depend strongly on firm size, but do depend on age. Late payments decrease from 25.1 percent for the youngest firms to 15.8 percent for the oldest firms. Discounts taken increase from 58.9 percent for the lowest age category to 82.4 percent for the oldest firms.

## C. Test of the Effect of Relationships on Credit Availability

To determine if relationships increase the availability of credit, we regress late payments and discounts taken against measures of the firm's investment opportunities, its cash flow, its debt, and various measures of relationships. The regression is of the form:

$$\text{Trade credits paid late}$$
$$= \beta_0 + \beta_1 \text{ Measures of investment opportunities}$$
$$+ \beta_2 \text{ Industry dummies} + \beta_3 \text{ Measures of cash flow}$$
$$+ \beta_4 \text{ Measures of relationships} + \varepsilon. \tag{2}$$

We include three measures of the firm's investment opportunities. Younger firms may have different investment opportunities than older firms. This may account for the pattern in Table VII, Panel B. Thus, firm age is one measure of investment opportunities. As discussed earlier, it is also a measure of the publicly available component of information. Investment opportunities could also depend on the firm's size (the book value of its assets). Finally, investment opportunities depend on the industry the firm is in, and thus industry dummies are included as explanatory variables. This will also control for differences in the price of trade credit financing across industries.

The firm's internal cash flow (normalized by book assets) is accounted for by including income after interest. While we do not have figures for depreciation, it ought to be a function of the firm's book assets which is already in the regression. We also include the ratio of outstanding institutional debt (i.e., total loans less family and owner loans) to book assets. This is a measure of the debt capacity the firm has already exhausted.[23] Finally we include a dummy for whether the firm is a corporation or not, because credit rationing

---

[23]An argument could be made for leaving debt out since if we perfectly control for investment opportunities, the level of trade credit used is an exact measure of the level of debt available. Leaving debt out of the regressions has no qualitative impact on the results.

should be greater for firms with limited liability. An owner-managed firm has a greater incentive to take on risky projects if it has limited liability.

We come now to the relationship variables. The first is the length of the longest relationship the firm has had with a financial institution. Second, we include a measure of how informed the firm's lenders are—this variable is the fraction of borrowing that comes from institutions that provide at least one significant financial service to the firm.[24] Third, we include a measure of how concentrated the firm's borrowing is—the number of institutions that account for more than 10 percent of the firm's borrowing. Finally, we include the Herfindahl index for financial institutions in the immediate area of the firm.[25] We cannot estimate our model with ordinary least squares since both dependent variables are expressed as percentages and are consequently censored at 0 or 100. The coefficients in a least squares estimate would be biased toward zero. We therefore estimate a tobit regression with two-sided limits.

## D. Findings

The regressions explaining late payments are reported in Table VIII. The investment and cash flow variables have the predicted sign. Older and larger firms do not make as many late payments. More profitable firms do not make as many late payments, though this effect is not statistically significant.[26] Firms that have taken on more debt are more likely to pay late. Finally, corporations make more late payments. We now examine the relationship variables.

The length of the longest relationship with a financial institution is both economically and statistically significant regardless of whether we use a linear specification for firm age and relationship length (Table VIII, column 1) or a log specification (Table VIII, column 3). It is instructive to compare the economic magnitudes of the age and relationship coefficients estimated here with those estimated in the rate regression. A one standard deviation increase in the log of one plus the firm age reduces the percentage of trade credits paid late by 1.35. A one standard deviation increase in the log of one plus the length of the relationship reduces the percentage of trade credits paid late by 2.05. A one standard deviation increase in size reduces the percentage of trade credits paid late by 1.48. Following our crude method of calibration (see Section III.C), firm age has about 90 percent of the impact that firm size has on the availability of credit while it has only 40 percent of the impact that firm size has on the price of credit. More interesting,

---

[24] These are either deposit accounts or the informational financial services defined above.

[25] The survey does not report the actual Herfindahl index. We know whether the Herfindahl index is less than 0.10, between 0.10 and 0.18, or greater than 0.18. Our variable is therefore coded as 1, 2, or 3.

[26] Profits could proxy for a firm's cash flow which should reduce the amount paid late, but it could also proxy for the profitability of a firm's investment opportunities which would increase the amount paid late. The predicted effect is thus ambiguous.

## The Benefits of Lending Relationships                27

### Table VIII
### Credit Availability and the Role of Relationships
### Dependent Variable: Trade Credits Repaid Late (%)

The dependent variable is the percentage of trade credits that were paid after the due date (paid late). The coefficient estimates are from a tobit regression with two-sided censoring. The dependent variable is censored at 0.0 and 1.0. Asymptotic standard errors are in parentheses. Each regression also includes seven industry dummies based on the one-digit SIC codes.

| Independent Variable | (1) | (2) | (3) | (4) | (5) | (6) |
|---|---|---|---|---|---|---|
| Log(book value of assets) | −0.662 | −0.542 | −0.753 | −0.678 | −0.533 | −1.580* |
| | (0.490) | (0.495) | (0.486) | (0.513) | (0.489) | (0.566) |
| Profits/book assets | −0.679 | −0.785 | −0.663 | −0.643 | −0.744 | 0.372 |
| | (0.753) | (0.754) | (0.753) | (0.782) | (0.750) | (0.916) |
| Debt from institutions/ | 4.853** | 4.902** | 4.888** | 4.463** | 5.775* | 5.932* |
| book assets | (2.040) | (2.038) | (2.045) | (2.108) | (2.045) | (2.310) |
| Firm is a corporation (0, 1) | 2.819*** | 2.857*** | 2.827*** | 3.248*** | 2.597 | 5.267* |
| | (1.635) | (1.633) | (1.638) | (1.726) | (1.632) | (1.936) |
| Firm age (in years)[a] | −0.142*** | −0.150*** | −1.531 | −0.181** | −0.140*** | −0.164*** |
| | (0.081) | (0.081) | (1.080) | (0.084) | (0.081) | (0.093) |
| Length of longest relationship | −0.155** | −0.152** | −2.299** | −0.165** | −0.150** | −0.177** |
| (in years)[a] | (0.069) | (0.069) | (1.089) | (0.070) | (0.068) | (0.078) |
| Debt from financial service | −5.576* | | −5.385* | −5.555* | −5.713* | −6.976* |
| provider (%) | (1.672) | | (1.678) | (1.748) | (1.663) | (1.907) |
| Debt from financial service | | −7.630* | | | | |
| provider (only one service) (%) | | (2.085) | | | | |
| Debt from financial service | | −3.895** | | | | |
| provider (multiple services) (%) | | (1.958) | | | | |
| Number of institutions from | 1.926** | 1.872** | 1.991** | 2.286** | 1.840** | 1.546 |
| which firm borrows | (0.900) | (0.900) | (0.901) | (0.946) | (0.897) | (1.043) |
| Herfindahl index for financial | −2.253* | −2.300* | −2.274* | −2.065** | −1.901** | −2.659* |
| institutions (1, 2, or 3) | (0.866) | (0.865) | (0.866) | (0.902) | (0.866) | (0.996) |
| Sales growth (1986–1987) | | | | −1.445 | | |
| | | | | (1.086) | | |
| Mean 1987 gross profits/assets ratio | | | | | −28.245* | |
| in two-digit SIC industry | | | | | (8.643) | |
| Mean σ(gross profits/assets) between | | | | | 22.677* | |
| 1983–87 in two-digit SIC industry | | | | | (7.851) | |
| Late payment stretch | | | | | | 0.012 |
| (in days)[b] | | | | | | (0.019) |
| Fraction of firms paying ≥ 50% of trade | | | | | | 84.997* |
| credit late | | | | | | (5.758) |
| Number of observations | 1,119 | 1,119 | 1,119 | 1,019 | 1,119 | 857 |
| $\chi^2$ | 83.5 | 86.2 | 80.7 | 86.3 | 96.6 | 127.1 |
| (p-value) | (0.000) | (0.000) | (0.000) | (0.000) | (0.000) | (0.000) |

[a] We replace length of relationship and firm age by the natural log of one plus the length of relationship and firm age in column 3. Thus the coefficient measures the change in the interest rate due to a one percent increase in the firm's age or the length of its longest relationship.

[b] For each two-digit SIC industry, the median DPO is obtained for firms paying less than 10 percent of credit late. This is subtracted from the DPO for firms paying more than 50 percent of credit late to obtain the late payment stretch.

* Significant at the 1 percent level.
** Significant at the 5 percent level.
*** Significant at the 10 percent level.

relationship length has about 138 percent of the impact that firm size has on the availability of credit while it has no impact on the price of credit.

Firms are less likely to pay late when their lenders are more informed. The coefficient on the fraction of debt from institutions that provide financial services is $-5.6$ ($t = 3.3$). If the provision of services is a good measure of the closeness of the lending relationship, then lenders who provide more services are closer and should increase availability even more. This is indeed the case (Table VIII, column 2). A firm can reduce late payments by increasing the fraction it borrows from an institution providing a single service ($\beta = -3.9$), but increasing the fraction borrowed from an institution providing two or more services has almost twice the effect ($\beta = -7.6$). Providing more information to lenders has little effect on the price of credit (see Section III), but it significantly increases its availability.

In Section III we found that concentrated borrowing is correlated with cheaper credit. It is also correlated with greater availability of credit. An increase of one in the number of institutions from which the firm borrows increases late payments by almost two percentage points (Table VIII, column 1). When banks and nonbanks are considered separately, the effect of an increase in the number of banks is statistically and economically more important than an increase in the number of nonbank institutions. The coefficients are 2.5 versus 1.8, although we do not report this regression in the table. Finally, following our calibration, the number of banks has 142 percent of the impact on the availability of credit that size has. Recall that in Section III, we found the number of banks to have only 53 percent of the impact that size has on the price of credit.

Interestingly, credit availability for firms in more geographically concentrated banking markets is significantly higher. A firm in the most concentrated area reduces late payments by 4.6 percentage points when compared to a firm in the most competitive area. By comparison, concentration of the local financial market has only a small and statistically insignificant effect on the price of credit (see Table IV). Petersen and Rajan (1993) explore this issue in greater detail. They argue that a possible reason banks help out small firms is because of the possibility that such firms generate significant future business when they grow. In return for a stake in the firm's future, the bank lends even when no one else will. Unfortunately, the firm cannot explicitly commit to giving the bank a stake, because banks in the United States are statutorily prohibited from holding equity in firms. This implies that the bank has to rely on an implicit promise that it will receive the firm's future business. In a concentrated market, such a promise is more credible because the firm has few options (until it grows large enough to approach arm's length markets). They find evidence consistent with such an explanation.

According to our hypothesis, firms could finance themselves with greater amounts of expensive trade credit, not just when institutions restrict their access to credit but also when they have better investment opportunities. A potential problem with our results is that we may not be measuring investment opportunities correctly. If firms with good investment opportunities are relatively young, have short relationships, and use multiple lenders to fund their investments, we would find that all three variables are correlated with our measures of usage of trade credit. Under the assumption that high-growth firms have above average investment opportunities, sales growth is a proxy for investment opportunities. If our relationship variables are better proxies for investment opportunities than for relationships, the inclusion of sales growth in the regression should reduce the magnitude of the coefficients dramatically. We report the coefficients in the fourth column of Table VIII. Two of the three relationship coefficients *increase* in magnitude. The coefficient on the fraction of debt from institutions that provide financial services decreases slightly. We find similar results when we use book assets to sales as a proxy for investment opportunities, suggesting that our relationship variables are not proxies for investment opportunities. We also include the industry mean profits and mean standard deviation of profits as defined in Section III. These coefficients have the correct sign and are statistically significant, but they do not change our estimates of the coefficients on the relationship variables (see Table VIII, column 5).

As a further check, we include in the regression proxies for standard industry practice in regard to paying late. If most firms pay late, paying late must not be very costly. Therefore the fraction of firms in the two-digit SIC industry paying more than 50 percent late is an inverse measure of the penalty for paying late. The Late Payment Stretch in the two-digit SIC industry is a second measure of the net benefit of paying late. Though we lose a number of observations when we include these two variables, the relationship coefficients are not significantly altered by these additions. Two of the relationship coefficients are higher and one is lower.[27] Thus the regression is robust to proxies for the costs and benefits of paying late.

The extent to which a firm takes cash discounts for early payment is an (inverse) measure of credit availability and should be driven by the same factors that make a firm avoid penalties for late payments. Thus, the regression with "discounts taken" as the dependent variable should be viewed as a test of the robustness of our results. We expect the coefficients on the relationship variables to have the opposite sign in comparison to the previous regression. The results are reported in Table IX and confirm our earlier results. Stronger relationships are correlated with greater credit availability. The only additional point to note in these regressions is that in column 6 of Table IX, we include the implicit interest rate calculated from standard terms

---

[27] We lose observations because we only include firms in industries with at least 10 firms. This restriction ensures our estimates of medians are reasonable. Ideally, we should define the Late Payment Stretch as the difference in DPO between firms paying 100 percent of their credits late and those paying 0 percent late. We use the definition in Section IV.A so as to get sufficient observations to estimate medians precisely in each group.

## Table IX
## Credit Availability and the Role of Relationships
## Dependent Variable: Offered Discounts Taken by the Firm (%)

The dependent variable is the percentage of early payment discounts that are taken by the firm. The coefficient estimates are from a tobit regression with two-sided censoring. The dependent variable is censored at 0.0 and 1.0. Asymptotic standard errors are in parenthesis. Except for column 6, each regression also includes seven industry dummies based on the one-digit SIC codes.

| Independent variable | (1) | (2) | (3) | (4) | (5) | (6) | (7) |
|---|---|---|---|---|---|---|---|
| Log(book value of assets) | 6.795* | 6.554* | 7.650* | 6.747* | 6.541* | 8.549* | 6.750* |
|  | (1.679) | (1.691) | (1.670) | (1.778) | (1.678) | (2.718) | (1.751) |
| Profits/book assets | 7.485* | 7.657* | 7.706* | 6.493** | 7.593* | 14.022** | 8.144* |
|  | (2.399) | (2.419) | (2.428) | (2.624) | (2.373) | (5.601) | (2.600) |
| Debt from institutions/ book assets | −14.178** | −14.326** | −14.825** | −16.020** | −15.736** | −34.934** | −14.326** |
|  | (7.161) | (7.168) | (7.217) | (7.437) | (7.184) | (13.736) | (7.353) |
| Firm is a corporation (= 1 if yes) | −9.913*** | −9.844*** | −9.811*** | −12.751** | −8.831 | −29.610* | −8.643 |
|  | (5.697) | (5.696) | (5.732) | (6.085) | (5.713) | (11.277) | (5.968) |
| Firm age (in years)[a] | 0.900* | 0.911* | 6.612*** | 0.972* | 0.899* | 1.085* | 1.003* |
|  | (0.246) | (0.246) | (3.474) | (0.271) | (0.246) | (0.392) | (0.254) |
| Length of longest relationship (in years)[a] | 0.904* | 0.901* | 17.154* | 0.878* | 0.884* | 0.598*** | 0.841* |
|  | (0.219) | (0.219) | (3.689) | (0.227) | (0.218) | (0.320) | (0.224) |
| Debt from financial service provider (%) | 5.655 |  | 4.415 | 5.875 | 5.919 | 10.517 | 5.650 |
|  | (5.667) |  | (5.705) | (5.969) | (5.660) | (9.670) | (5.817) |
| Debt from financial service provider (only one service) (%) |  | 10.159 |  |  |  |  |  |
|  |  | (6.939) |  |  |  |  |  |
| Debt from financial service provider (multiple services) (%) |  | 1.539 |  |  |  |  |  |
|  |  | (6.731) |  |  |  |  |  |
| Number of institutions from which firm borrows | −8.889* | −8.790** | −9.754* | −9.486* | −8.789* | −11.192** | −7.505** |
|  | (3.152) | (3.152) | (3.165) | (3.331) | (3.155) | (5.194) | (3.272) |
| Herfindahl index for financial institutions (1, 2, or 3) | 14.996* | 15.111* | 14.608* | 15.658* | 14.170* | 16.202* | 14.449* |
|  | (3.033) | (3.035) | (3.050) | (3.189) | (3.038) | (5.140) | (3.136) |
| Sales growth (1986–1987) |  |  |  | 1.254 |  |  |  |
|  |  |  |  | (3.744) |  |  |  |

**Table IX**—*Continued*

| Independent variable | (1) | (2) | (3) | (4) | (5) | (6) | (7) |
|---|---|---|---|---|---|---|---|
| Mean 1987 gross profits/assets ratio in two-digit SIC industry | | | | | 78.292** (33.676) | | |
| Mean $\sigma$(gross profits/assets) between 1983–87 in two-digit SIC industry | | | | | -69.090** (27.350) | | |
| Interest rate implied by trade credit terms in two-digit SIC industry | | | | | | -0.017 (0.063) | |
| Discount stretch (in days)[b] | | | | | | | -0.036 (0.190) |
| Fraction of firms taking $\geq$ 90% of early payments discounts | | | | | | | 146.60* (29.188) |
| Number of observations | 1500 | 1500 | 1500 | 1362 | 1500 | 545 | 1328 |
| $\chi^2$ | 194.1 | 195.3 | 185.7 | 183.1 | 202.8 | 76.7 | 216.5 |
| ($p$-value) | (0.000) | (0.000) | (0.000) | (0.000) | (0.000) | (0.000) | (0.000) |

[a] We replace length of relationship and firm age by the natural log of one plus the length of relationship and firm age in column 3. Thus the coefficient measures the change in the interest rate due to a one percent increase in the firm's age or the length of its longest relationship.

[b] For each two-digit SIC industry, the median DPO is obtained for firms taking more than 90 percent of discounts offered. This is subtracted from the DPO for firms taking less than 10 percent of discounts offered to obtain the discount stretch.

* Significant at the 1 percent level.
** Significant at the 5 percent level.
*** Significant at the 10 percent level.

of trade credit for the two-digit industry to which the firm belongs.[28] We lose two thirds of our observations, so these results must be interpreted with caution. We find that higher implicit rates have almost no effect on the percent of discounts taken. The coefficient is actually negative, but its magnitude is tiny. That the implicit interest rate has so little effect may imply that we are measuring it very inaccurately or that trade credit costs so much more than other sources that managers do not use it unless they have no other source of capital, an assumption implicit in our analysis.[29]

Clearly, our evidence that trade creditors lend when institutional lenders do not suggests that they have collateral, incentives related to the product they are selling, sources of leverage over the firm, or information that the institutions do not possess. Is it then possible that our relationship variables identify firms whose strong supplier relationship—and hence cheap trade credit—substitute for bank relationships and bank credit? For instance, suppliers may allow younger firms greater leeway in stretching out their trade credit repayments. If so, the negative correlation between age (or length of relationship) and the extent of late payments simply reflects the fact that the implicit cost of trade credit is lower for young firms. The data in Table VII, Panel B, however, do not support this explanation. The median stretch (as measured from the due date) for the youngest 10 percent of the firms is $-5.86$ days compared to a median stretch of $-0.72$ days for the oldest ten percent of the firms. Similarly, the median stretch for the smallest 10 percent of the firm is $-17.91$ days compared to a median stretch of 2.85 days for the largest 10 percent of the firms (see Table VII, Panel A). If, as suggested in Section IV.*B*, trade credit terms are uniform in an industry, it would imply that firms borrowing the most against trade credit are allowed considerably

---

[28] The terms were obtained from Dunn and Bradstreet's *Handbook of Credit and Collection* (1970). We obtained standard terms for 46 four-digit SIC industries which translated into 19 two-digit industries. We calculated the implicit interest rate assuming that the credit period began on the last day the discount could be used and continued till the day the payment was due (this assumption is consistent with our finding that the stretch in the retail and wholesale industry is somewhat smaller than the 20 days implied by the 2–10–30 rule). Whenever we had different terms for the same two-digit industry, we took a simple mean of the calculated implicit interest rates. The largest implicit interest rate (without considering those with cash terms where the due date and the discount date were the same) was 348 percent, and the lowest was 15 percent. The mean rate was 70 percent. The most common terms were 2–10–30, which were offered in 23 of the 46 four-digit SIC industries.

[29] Does the fact that firms borrow against trade credit even when the average implicit interest rate on the credit is 70 percent imply that the rate of return on the firm's marginal projects is higher than 70 percent? Clearly not. But as the following example shows, project indivisibility or nonconvexity is enough to rationalize the use of expensive trade credit. Consider a firm which has a $100,000 investment in equipment which will be liquidated at a fire sale price of $90,000 (see Shleifer and Vishny (1992)) if creditors get control rights over the firm. Further, assume a coupon payment of $5,000 is coming due. If the firm has no money to make this payment and no institution will lend more, it may borrow the $5,000 against trade credit to make the payment, in order to avoid the potential loss of $10,000 if creditors gain control. Even though the potential loss from project liquidation is only 10 percent of its value, the rate of return on the usage of trade credit is enormous. A similar point can be made for project initiations.

less stretch, and consequently pay considerably higher implicit interest rates on their trade credit borrowing. By contrast, interest rates on institutional loans are relatively less influenced by age and size (see Tables IV and X).

There is further evidence that trade credit is not meant to be a cheap substitute for medium-term financing. It is the practice in some industries for suppliers to finance buyers. The large volume of loans from nonfinancial firms in those industries is evidence of this. If supplier financing is explicitly intended to be medium term, we would not expect trade credit to be offered with discounts for early payment. This is indeed the case. Firms which have their largest source of loans from other nonfinancial firms were offered, on average, discounts with only 22.7 percent of their trade credit. By contrast, other firms are offered discounts on 32.9 percent of their trade credit. The difference in means is significant at the 5 percent level ($t = 2.4$). While trade credit may be the only source of finance when firms are young, the evidence that firms borrowing most on trade credit pay relatively the highest rates for it, and the evidence that suppliers who want to offer medium term credit offer explicit loans rather than trade credit, suggests that firms use trade credit out of necessity rather than choice.

A final possibility is that the relationship variables somehow proxy for firms in distress. If small, highly leveraged, and floundering firms are cut off by institutions (thus cutting short their relationship), and are forced to use trade credit, we would find a spurious negative correlation between the length of the relationship and the usage of trade credit. Are the firms using lots of trade credit necessarily distressed? The median firm repays 10 percent of its trade credits late. For firms paying more than the median late, the

**Table X**

**Average Interest Rates on Most Recent Loan**

The table contains the average interest rate on the firm's most recent loan categorized by the firm's book value of assets, the percent of trade credits paid late, and the percentage of early payments taken. The first row of the table contains the smallest firms, the firms that pay the largest percent of their trade credits late, and the firms that take advantage of the fewest early payment discounts.

|  | Percentiles Based on the Book Value of Assets | Percentiles Based on the Percent of Trade Credits Paid Late | Percentiles Based on the Percent of Early Payment Discounts Taken |
|---|---|---|---|
| 0–10% | 12.0 | 11.4 | 11.2 |
| 10–25% | 11.5 | 11.9 | 11.1 |
| 25–50% | 11.5 | 11.4 | 11.1 |
| 50–75% | 10.8 | 11.2 | 10.8[a] |
| 75–90% | 10.5 | 10.7 | 10.8 |
| 90–100% | 10.1 | 10.4 | 10.8 |

[a] Over 25 percent of the firms take all of the early payment discounts that are offered. Thus the groups 50–70 percent, 75–90 percent, and 90–100 percent are not distinct. Thus 10.8 percent is the average interest rate for firms taking more than the median percent of the early discounts which they are offered.

mean asset size is \$1.17 million, the mean profitability (as a fraction of assets) is 0.35, the mean sales growth is 0.25, and the mean debt-to-assets ratio is 0.32. This compares to a mean asset size of \$1.21 million, mean profitability of 0.44, sales growth of 0.19, and indebtedness of 0.26 for firms below the median. Only the debt levels are statistically different, though this may not reflect distress but simply that firms paying late are investing more (and hence are less profitable either because projects have not come on line or because they have greater depreciation tax shields) and using external financing. We also examine the difference between the age of the firm and the length of the longest relationship. If highly indebted firms are being cut off by their banks, leading to the spurious correlation suggested above, we should find the difference to be the highest in the case of the most indebted firms. Instead, we find that the longest relationship for highly indebted firms—firms with institutional debt above the median—is 1.3 years longer (relative to their age) than for firms with institutional debt below the median. Finally, Table X shows the average interest rate charged on the firm's most recent institutional loan. Firms using the most trade credit do not pay substantially more for their loans, suggesting indeed that we are measuring some form of credit rationing and not some spurious correlation arising from distress.

## V. Discussion and Conclusion

We began our empirical investigation by noting that borrowing by small firms is highly concentrated. Moreover, small firms borrow a significant fraction of their debt from lenders who provide them informationally intensive financial services. Are there benefits to concentrating borrowing and building relationships with a few lenders or is such concentrated borrowing costly? Our analysis indicates the former.

We find a small effect of relationships on the price charged by lenders. The length of an institution's relationship with the firm seems to have little impact on the rate. Similarly, the rate charged is insignificantly lower when the lender provides the firm financial services. We find that firms that borrow from multiple banks are charged a significantly higher rate. There are a number of potential explanations of this effect, other than that multiple sourcing weakens relationships, but we do not find strong support for any of them.[30]

It does not appear that the lack of explanatory power occurs because our proxies for the strength of relationships are faulty. Using similar proxies, we

---

[30] Conversations with bankers provide some casual support for the "weakening of relationships" explanation. One banker said that he invariably tries to be the sole lender. If the firm asking for a loan has a prior relationship with another bank, he usually insists on "taking out" the prior bank with part of the new loan. Being the sole lender improves his ability to control the borrower's actions. Another banker echoes these feelings, adding that firms tend to change banks primarily when their existing bank reaches its legal lending limits. In such cases, a firm occasionally insists on maintaining token ties with its old bank. He also feels that some small business owners have "outsize egos," leading them to believe that their firms are big enough to warrant multiple banking relationships, even though it is a costly practice.

find stronger effects of relationships on the availability of financing. The empirical results suggest that the availability of finance from institutions increases as the firm spends more time in a relationship, as it increases ties to a lender by expanding the number of financial services it buys from it, and as it concentrates its borrowing with the lender.

The results from the previous section rule out the possibility that relationships have no value. They also indicate that our proxies are indeed capturing some aspects of relationships. There are at least two theoretical explanations as to why the burden of adjustment to strong relationships falls on the availability of credit more than it does on price. First, if Stiglitz-Weiss credit rationing is indeed taking place, the firm's marginal returns from investment may be much higher than the price of credit. Therefore, if offered a choice, firms would prefer more, rather than cheaper, credit. Unfortunately, peripheral evidence on this hypothesis is decidedly mixed. When the SBA Survey asked firms about the most important characteristic of financial institutions, "interest rates and prices offered" was the most frequent response (27.3 percent) while "a willingness to extend financing" was in second place (23.8 percent). However, when asked about the least important characteristic of financial institutions, "a willingness to extend financing" was the least common response (5.6 percent) while "interest rates and prices offered" came next (10.8 percent).

The other theoretical explanation is that while the relationship reduces the lender's expected cost, it also increases its informational monopoly, so that cost reductions are not passed on to the firm. We cannot distinguish between these two possibilities.

The different effects on price and quantity may also stem from the organizational structure of lending institutions. In order to maintain adequate checks and balances in their business, financial institutions have fairly specific guidelines for loan pricing. It would be difficult, and perhaps defeat their purpose, for the institution to set these guidelines such that the loan officer's "soft" information about the firm can be embedded in the price. Given this structure, it may be much easier for the loan officer to use her knowledge to influence the loan amount and whether the loan is made at all, rather than the price.

Our study also throws additional light on another important public policy issue. A bank may have economic value because it screens out poor credits. But once the public credit market knows which firms are good (by observing firms that have had a long relationship), there is no externality imposed on the firms if the bank fails or is forced to contract its lending. On the other hand, if a bank generates substantial durable and nontransferable private information during the course of a relationship, there may be significant externalities when it fails or reduces lending commitments, because others cannot easily step into the breach (see Bernanke (1983)). Slovin, Sushka, and Polonchek (1993) provide evidence that banks may, in fact, serve as repositories of private information. They find that the impending insolvency of Continental Illinois Bank had negative effects and the FDIC rescue had positive effects on client firm prices. Our study adds to theirs by detailing the mechanisms through which the bank may acquire information about the firm, and how it passes on the benefits of this more intense monitoring back to the firm.[31] The public policy implication is that regulators should factor in the informational capital that will be destroyed when deciding whether to save a bank from liquidation.

Perhaps the most interesting conclusion of our study is that the apparent concentration of borrowing and the purchasing of financial services does not seem to make small firms worse off. Small firms may voluntarily choose to concentrate their borrowing so as to improve the availability of financing. Furthermore, we find that firms in areas where there are few bank-like institutions are less likely to be rationed. This accords with the notion in Mayer (1988) and Rajan (1992) that increased competition in financial markets reduces the value of relationships because it prevents a financial institution from reaping the rewards of helping the firm at an early stage. The policy implication is that these firms may best be helped if lenders can make their claims to the firm's future profits explicit; for instance, regulations prohibiting banks from holding equity could be weakened so that banks have an explicit long-term interest in the firms to which they lend.

[31] On its own, our study cannot fully resolve whether the information generated in a relationship is private or public. It is possible that the length of the relationship is a significant determinant of the availability of credit, not because the creditor has accumulated private information about the firm, but because creditors attempt to keep the business of their best credits as long as possible. The length of the relationship may then be a publicly available proxy, similar to the age of the firm, of a firm's creditworthiness. It is, however, harder to explain why availability increases as creditors come closer—where "closeness" is measured by the number of nonfinancial services they offer the firm—unless we accept that some private information is generated via these services. None of these services are so specialized or sophisticated that only "high-quality" managers would think of using them. Only a few of these services (banker's acceptances and letters of credit) force the bank to take on credit risk, and these commitments are usually short term and well secured so that the credit risk is minimal. It is hard to think of how the provision of these services could be a public signal of quality. It is, however, possible that the provision of these services helps tie the firm to its creditor in the long run, making the creditor more willing to extend funds.

## REFERENCES

Ausubel, Lawrence M., 1992, Rigidity and asymmetric adjustment of bank interest rates, Mimeo, Kellogg Graduate School, Northwestern University.

Berger, Allen, and Gregory Udell, 1992, Small firms, commercial lines of credit, and collateral, Mimeo, Board of Governors of the Federal Reserve System.

Bernanke, Ben, 1983, Non-monetary effects of the financial crisis in the propagation of the Great Depression, *American Economic Review* 73, 257–276.

Blackwell, N., and Anthony Santomero, 1982, Bank credit rationing and customer relation, *Journal of Monetary Economics* 9, 121–129.

Brown, Charles, James Hamilton, and James Medoff, 1990, *Employers Large and Small* (Harvard University Press, Cambridge, Mass.).

Campbell, Tim, and William Kracaw, 1980, Information production, market signalling, and the theory of intermediation, *Journal of Finance* 35, 863–882.

Dennis, William I., William C. Dunkelberg, and Jeffrey S. Van Hulle, 1988, *Small Business and Banks: The United States* (N.F.I.B. Foundation, Washington, D.C.).

Diamond, Doug, 1984, Financial intermediation and delegated monitoring, *Review of Economic Studies* 51, 393–414.

———, 1991, Monitoring and reputation: the choice between bank loans and directly placed debt, *Journal of Political Economy* 99, 688–721.

Dun and Bradstreet, 1970, *Handbook of Credit Terms* (Dun and Bradstreet, New York).

Elliehausen, Gregory, and John Wolken, 1992, The use of trade credit by small businesses, Mimeo, Board of Governors of the Federal Reserve System.

Fama, Eugene, 1985, What's different about banks?, *Journal of Monetary Economics* 15, 29–36.

Fazzari, Steve, Glenn Hubbard, and Bruce Petersen, 1988, Investment and finance reconsidered, *Brookings Papers on Economic Activity* 141–195.

Greenbaum, Stuart, George Kanatas, and Itzhak Venezia, 1989, Equilibrium loan pricing under the bank client relationship, *Journal of Banking and Finance* 13, 221–235.

Haubrich, Joseph, 1989, Financial intermediation, delegated monitoring, and long-term relationships, *Journal of Banking and Finance* 13, 9–20.

Hodgman, Donald, 1963, *Commercial Bank Loan and Investment Policy* (Bureau of Business and Economic Research, University of Illinois, Chicago).

Hoshi, Takeo, Anil Kashyap, and David Scharfstein, 1990a, Bank monitoring and investment: Evidence from the changing structure of Japanese corporate banking relationships, in R. Glenn Hubbard, ed.: *Asymmetric Information, Corporate Finance and Investment* (University of Chicago Press, Chicago).

———, 1990b, The role of banks in reducing the costs of financial distress in Japan, *Journal of Financial Economics* 27, 67–88.

———, 1991, Corporate structure, liquidity and investment: evidence from Japanese industrial groups, *Quarterly Journal of Economics* 106, 33–60.

James, Christopher, 1987, Some evidence on the uniqueness of bank loans, *Journal of Financial Economics* 19, 217–235.

——— and Peggy Wier, 1990, Borrowing relationships, intermediation, and the cost of issuing public securities, *Journal of Financial Economics* 28, 149–171.

Leland, Hayne, and David Pyle, 1977, Information asymmetries, financial structure, and financial intermediaries, *Journal of Finance* 32, 371–387.

Lummer, Scott, and John McConnell, 1989, Further evidence on the bank lending process and the capital market response to bank loan agreements, *Journal of Financial Economics* 25, 99–122.

Mayer, Colin, 1988, New issues in corporate finance, *European Economic Review* 32, 1167–1189.

Mian, Shehzad, and Clifford Smith, 1992, Accounts receivable management policy: Theory and evidence, *Journal of Finance* 47, 169–200.

Petersen, Mitchell, and Raghuram Rajan, 1993, The effect of credit market concentration on lending relationships, Working paper, University of Chicago.

Rajan, Raghuram, 1992, Insiders and outsiders: the choice between informed and arm's length debt, *Journal of Finance* 47, 1367–1400.

Roosa, Robert, 1951, Interest rates and the central bank, in *Money Trade and Economic Growth: Essays in Honor of John Henry Williams* (Macmillan, New York).

Sharpe, Steven, 1990, Asymmetric information, bank lending and implicit contracts: A stylized model of customer relationships, *Journal of Finance* 45, 1069–1087.

Shleifer, Andrei, and Robert Vishny, 1992, Liquidation values and debt capacity: A market equilibrium approach, *Journal of Finance* 47, 1343–1366.

Shockley, Richard, and Anjan Thakor, 1992, Information content of commitments to lend in the future: Theory and evidence on the gains from relationship banking, Discussion Paper No. 523, Indiana University.

Slovin, Myron B., Marie E. Sushka, and John A. Polonchek, 1993, The value of bank durability: Borrowers as bank stakeholders, *Journal of Finance* 48, 247–266.

Smith, Janet K., 1987, Trade credit and information asymmetries, *Journal of Finance* 42, 863–872.

Stiglitz, Joseph, and Andrew Weiss, 1981, Credit rationing in markets with imperfect information, *American Economic Review* 71, 393–410.

# [19]

THE JOURNAL OF FINANCE • VOL LIII, NO. 3 • JUNE 1998

# Does Corporate Lending by Banks and Finance Companies Differ? Evidence on Specialization in Private Debt Contracting

MARK CAREY, MITCH POST, and STEVEN A. SHARPE*

## ABSTRACT

This paper establishes empirically the existence of specialization in private-market corporate lending, adding a new dimension to the public versus private debt distinctions now common in the literature. Comparing corporate loans made by banks and by finance companies, we find that the two types of intermediaries are equally likely to finance information-problematic firms. However, finance companies tend to serve observably riskier borrowers, particularly more leveraged borrowers. Evidence supports both regulatory and reputation-based explanations for this specialization. In passing, we shed light on various theories of debt contracting and intermediation and present facts about finance companies.

MUCH OF THE RECENT RESEARCH on financial contracting and intermediation focuses on the distinction between private and public debt contracts. The central theme of this research concerns why, and to what degree, private market suppliers of credit are better suited than public creditors to finance "information-problematic" borrowers, or all but the least risky and well-known firms. Private market lenders are thought to have stronger incentives or greater ability to monitor borrowers (Diamond (1984, 1991) and Fama (1985)), or to be better positioned than public creditors to renegotiate contract terms or exercise control rights in the event of a problem (Berlin and Mester (1992), Rajan (1992), and Gorton and Kahn (1993)). Additionally, a valued reputation enhances private market lenders' ability to make credible commitments to act in good faith should a borrower experience problems (Chemmanur and Fulghieri (1994)).

Perhaps mainly for simplicity, almost all studies to date have analyzed generic intermediaries and private debt ("banks" and "bank loans"). Many important questions arise in corporate finance and financial intermediation, however, if different types of business lenders or private debt contracts are

* Carey and Sharpe are at the Federal Reserve Board. Post is at the Investment Company Institute. The views expressed herein are the authors' and do not necessarily reflect those of the Board of Governors or the Federal Reserve System. We thank the Editor, the referee, Mitch Berlin, Charles Calomiris, Richard Cantor, Ron Feldman, Rick Heyke, Joel Houston, Raghu Rajan, Rich Rosen, and participants in various seminars and conference sessions for helpful comments. We especially thank Margaret Kyle for excellent research assistance.

specialized to different borrowers, as practitioners often suggest. Why does specialization arise, and what can be learned about private debt in general by an examination of it? Which lenders and which types of private debt should a given borrower use? Are different capital or funding structures optimal for intermediaries with different lending specialties? How should different kinds of private lending be regulated, if at all? In wholesale restructurings of financial systems, should specialization in lending be preserved mainly within a single corporate structure such as a universal bank, in different organizations, or not at all?

This paper establishes empirically that specialization in private market corporate lending exists. Using a large microdata set with information on individual loans, we compare private market business lending by finance companies to that by banks. We test the hypothesis that their lending is effectively identical, with two specific alternative hypotheses in mind. One is that their borrowers differ along an asymmetric information dimension, as implied by the strand of literature which posits that banks in particular are unique in serving information-problematic borrowers (Fama (1985), James (1987), and Nakamura (1991)). We fail to reject the null of no difference. Given the extensive evidence that banks serve information-problematic borrowers, the implication is that *intermediaries in general* are special with respect to information, not banks in particular.[1] A second alternative is that bank and finance company borrowers pose different levels of ex ante observable risk, as measured by their leverage for example. We reject the null of no difference in borrower characteristics in favor of this alternative hypothesis.

Evidence on these matters is drawn from estimation of logit models that predict whether a borrower is served by a bank or a finance company. Common proxies for information problems (firm size, R&D to sales, market-to-book value, etc.) and observable risk (leverage, interest coverage, etc.) appear as explanatory variables. To buttress the logit results, and to provide a more complete portrait of competition and specialization, we also compare the distributions of many of these variables across lender types. Additionally, we compare loan purposes, types, spreads, and some nonprice terms. This evidence suggests that observable risk is the main dimension of specialization.

This pattern of specialization is not immediately explainable by modern theories of intermediation. We propose two explanations, both of which have support in practitioner lore, and offer evidence on their validity. One obvious possibility is regulation—perhaps bank regulators, in their efforts to limit excessive risk-taking, effectively limit banks' ability to serve high-risk bor-

---

[1] Other recent studies supporting this conclusion include Preece and Mullineaux (1994) and Billett, Flannery, and Garfinkel (1995), who find no difference in the reaction of borrower share prices to announcements of loans by banks and nonbanks, and Carey et al. (1993) and Kwan and Carleton (1996), who present evidence that insurance companies' private placement portfolios represent a form of information-intensive lending. The only recent studies examining finance companies or competition between finance companies and banks of which we are aware are those of Simonson (1994), Remolona and Wulfekuhler (1992), Cantor and Rodrigues (1993), and Gorton and Pennacchi (1993).

rowers. Our second explanation focuses on reputational factors. Even loans to lower-risk borrowers are frequently renegotiated (Kwan and Carleton (1995), and Beneish and Press (1993)) and such borrowers rely on lenders to be reasonable, that is, to refrain from extracting maximum rents when a covenant waiver or other change in terms is requested. A lender's reputation for reasonableness is thus a valuable asset, one that might be damaged if the lender is observed to frequently force borrowers into liquidation. Reputation costs might be reduced by specialization: High risk borrowers are served by lenders known to be tough and unbending, whereas lower-risk borrowers are served by those known to be gentle. Because we present no formal model of this mechanism, we view the explanation as speculative.

We present both formal and informal evidence on the validity of these explanations. For example, we compare the riskiness of lending by bank-affiliated finance companies and other finance companies, which differ along both regulatory and reputation cost dimensions. We find that borrowers at bank-affiliated finance companies are less risky than borrowers at other finance companies, which supports both hypotheses. We present a variety of other tests and evidence in an attempt to discriminate between the hypotheses, but various problems hinder identification. On the whole, however, the evidence points to a role for both regulatory and reputational factors in lending specialization.

In passing, the analysis provides evidence relevant to a variety of hypotheses about the operation of private debt markets. The hypothesis that easy access to the information in business checking accounts gives banks a unique advantage in monitoring borrowers (Black (1975), Fama (1985), and Nakamura (1991)) is not supported, at least for the corporate borrowers examined here, because finance companies monitor but do not offer checking accounts. There is some support for the hypothesis that a substantial share of lender liabilities in the form of demandable debt provides lenders with incentives to monitor (Flannery (1994), and Calomiris and Kahn (1991)) because a significant share of both bank and finance company liabilities is effectively demandable debt. Our findings also suggest that cross-selling is not the only factor behind borrower-lender relationships (Rajan (1992), Petersen and Rajan (1994), and Berger and Udell (1995)): Finance companies appear to have fewer opportunities to cross-sell but appear about as likely to be the "relationship" lender in multilender loans.

The analysis also has implications for recent narrow-banking proposals for restructuring the financial system. In such proposals, existing banks would be split into an insured depository with strict limits on the risk of its investments and an uninsured "finance company." Implicitly adopting the view that all information-intensive intermediaries are the same, proponents point to existing finance companies as evidence that there would be no disruptions to aggregate credit. Our evidence suggests that extant finance companies do not mimic bank lenders. Without a better understanding of the reasons they do not, it is premature to conclude that narrow banking would have little or no effect on the allocation of business credit.

An important caveat to our findings is that we examine only corporate loans, not small business or consumer loans. Thus, the findings may not apply to the latter because it is quite possible that contracting problems and lending practices and technologies differ for those sectors. Additionally, the specialization we observe is incomplete: Both banks and finance companies serve borrowers across the spectrum of risk. Even though the relative propensity of finance companies to lend to risky borrowers is much higher, in the aggregate banks probably serve more borrowers in all risk classes.

The remainder of the paper is in six parts. As characteristics of finance companies are not well known, we provide a brief profile in Section I. In Section II we describe the loan data. Section III reports results of logit models of the choice of banks versus finance companies as lenders and presents detailed comparisons of borrower leverage and cash flow. To uncover other possible dimensions of specialization, Section IV compares various characteristics of bank and finance company loans, including type, purpose, spreads, and some nonprice terms. Section V describes the regulatory and reputational hypotheses in more detail and presents evidence about their realism. Section VI offers concluding remarks.

## I. An Introduction to the Finance Company Industry

Finance companies include captive financing subsidiaries of nonfinancial corporations, general consumer and business finance companies, leasing companies, and factors, all of which are nondepository financial institutions involved primarily in extending credit to businesses and consumers. Because finance companies do not collect deposits, they are not constrained by bank regulations (unless affiliated with a bank), but they also do not have access to deposit insurance and the discount window. Historically, finance companies have been reputed to make high-interest loans to borrowers turned away by banks and to rely on relatively aggressive measures to ensure repayment. Those close to the industry argue that finance companies use different techniques for controlling risks than do banks and that these techniques are better suited to higher-risk classes of borrowers or different loan purposes.

At the end of 1995, finance companies had about $780 billion in assets, compared to commercial bank assets of about $4.5 trillion (Table I). The industry is concentrated, with the twenty largest finance companies holding two-thirds of all assets at the end of 1995. General Electric Capital Corp. (GECC), the largest firm, had $161 billion in assets, alone accounting for one-fifth of industry assets. General Motors Acceptance Corp., Ford Motor Credit, and Chrysler Financial Services together held another 27 percent of industry assets ($207 billion). Another twenty or so firms fall between $5 and $30 billion; beyond that, there is an uncertain number of firms that may be as small as $30 million.

Unlike commercial banks, which may only be owned by other banks or by regulated bank holding companies, ownership of finance companies is virtu-

### Table I
### Balance Sheet of Domestic Finance Companies, December 1995

This table reports estimated assets and liabilities of all U.S. finance companies. Data are from the Federal Reserve's monthly survey of finance companies (the G20 statistical release). Amounts are in billions of dollars. "Reserves for unearned income" represents unearned discounts and service charges on receivables.

| Assets | | Liabilities and Net Worth | |
|---|---|---|---|
| Receivables, gross | | | |
| Consumer | 233.0 | Bank loans | 15.3 |
| Business | 301.6 | Commercial paper | 168.6 |
| Real estate | 72.4 | Due to parent | 51.5 |
| Total | 607.0 | | |
| Less: | | | |
| Reserves for unearned income | (61.7) | Bonds, medium-term notes and other debt | 302.7 |
| Reserves for losses | (13.0) | Other liabilities | 165.1 |
| Receivables, net | 532.3 | Total liabilities | 703.2 |
| Other assets | 246.7 | Equity | 86.7 |
| Total assets | 779.0 | Total liabilities and net worth | 789.9 |

ally unrestricted. Indeed, among the largest firms in the industry, only a few are not wholly owned subsidiaries of other firms. The nature of ownership sometimes strongly influences finance companies' operations. Many of the captive finance subsidiaries of manufacturing or commercial firms exist almost solely to promote the sale of their parents' products, although some engage in a broader range of finance. Other finance companies, even though wholly owned, operate essentially as independent lenders and pursue a variety of portfolio strategies. The operations of finance company subsidiaries of domestic or foreign banking organizations may be constrained to some degree by regulation.

Finance companies rely primarily on the capital markets, their parents, or banks for funding. As shown in Table I, the largest fractions of their financing are from commercial paper, bonds, and medium-term note issuance. The commercial paper closely resembles demandable debt and may enhance finance companies' incentives to monitor their borrowers in the same way that short-term deposits are thought to influence banks' incentives to monitor (Flannery (1994), and Calomiris and Kahn (1991)). Alternatively, finance companies may issue commercial paper primarily to match the rate and maturity characteristics of certain assets.

Finance companies are less leveraged than banks. At the end of 1995, their aggregate equity-to-assets ratio was 11.1 percent, compared to about 8.3 percent for commercial banks. Moreover, finance companies' ratio may understate their true capital position because many of their parents, which have significant other assets, have implicitly or explicitly committed to support their subsidiaries.

## Table II

### Finance Company and Commercial Bank Business Credit

This table compares amounts of various types of business credit provided by finance companies with total C&I lending by banks. Amounts are in billions of dollars. Finance company business credit figures include securitized business loans and leases (most of which are in the auto-related category). "Auto-related" includes auto leasing to businesses and dealer floorplan finance. "Other" includes term loans and revolving lines of credit for retail and wholesale equipment finance and for other short- and intermediate-term business purposes. Finance company data are from the Federal Reserve G20 statistical release and bank data are from Call Reports except for offshore loans. In this table, commercial bank C&I loans include those made by foreign banks to U.S. firms but booked offshore (Nolle (1995)). The latest period for which an estimate of offshore loans outstanding is available is September 30, 1992. In computing the total for December 1995, we use the 1992 amount for offshore loans.

| | Finance Company Business Credit | | | | Bank C&I Loans |
| | Total | Auto-Related | Equipment Leasing | Other | |
|---|---|---|---|---|---|
| Dec 1985 | 149 | 51 | 38 | 61 | 564 |
| Dec 1990 | 270 | 69 | 95 | 107 | 805 |
| Dec 1995 | 328 | 85 | 131 | 112 | 871 |
| Growth 1985–95 (%) | 120 | 68 | 254 | 83 | 54 |

The composition of finance companies' business credit portfolios differs substantially from that of banks (Table II). Although total business credit at finance companies, at $328 billion, was about 38 percent of bank commercial and industrial (C&I) loans outstanding, $216 billion of this was either auto-related or equipment lease financing. Leasing and auto-related finance is a much smaller share of banks' business credit. Banks may be at a competitive disadvantage in these activities relative to the captives; additionally, bank regulations limit banks' ability to do certain types of leases.

The fact that a large share of finance company assets are lease-related is consistent with finance companies specializing in relatively high-risk finance. Sharpe and Nguyen (1995) provide evidence that lessees of fixed assets tend to be riskier than firms that acquire fixed assets outright, suggesting that lessors are more willing to bear the additional risk or can better manage it than other lenders.

Although the business credit portfolios of banks and finance companies differ on the whole, the $112 billion of "other" finance company business credit shown in Table II includes the corporate loans in our microdata sample, and here it is not clear that there are any differences. Moreover, practitioners perceive finance companies to be in direct and active competition with banks in providing such loans (Sherman (1993)). However, they often argue that finance companies utilize different monitoring and control strategies than banks. Finance companies are described as "asset-based" lenders and banks as "cash flow" lenders. In making a loan, an asset-based lender emphasizes collateral as a source of ultimate repayment whereas a cash flow lender relies more heavily on projected cash flow from operations. Asset-based lenders are said to monitor collateral much more closely after a loan is made.[2]

## II. Data

We analyze a sample of 14,735 loan agreements involving about 5,700 different U.S. business borrowers drawn from the November 1993 release of Loan Pricing Corporation's (LPC) Dealscan database, which at the time of the draw contained about 18,000 loans made from 1987 to early 1993. For the typical loan, the database includes the name and location of the borrower and the names of all lenders party to the loan contract at origination, the type, purpose, amount, and contract date of the loan, and information on price and some nonprice terms. The great majority of the loans are floating-rate loans. None of the loans are securities from a legal standpoint (data on private placements are collected separately), and very few are subordinated to other debt of the borrower.[3]

According to LPC, the great majority of the data were collected from commitment letters and credit agreements drawn from SEC filings. Especially in more recent years, some data were collected from news reports or through LPC's relationships with major banks. These collection strategies yield a database of mostly medium-size to large loans that are representative of the financing activity of publicly held or larger private firms, but no small business loans are included. The sample selection criteria appear unrelated to correlations between lender identity and loan or borrower characteristics (the primary focus of the empirical work). As shown in Panel A of Table III, the median full-sample loan is for $30 million and has a maturity of three years. Loan size is $250,000 at the 1st percentile and $1.5 billion at the 99th percentile.

About 56 percent of the loans involve only a single lender at origination, with the remainder involving multiple lenders. A variety of institutional types are represented, including U.S. and foreign commercial banks, savings and

---

[2] Some bank lending groups or affiliates of banks might themselves be asset-based lenders. However, some commercial bankers argue that bank supervisors fail to recognize or understand the distinct nature of asset-based lending and, as a result, may at times inappropriately classify such loans as nonperforming. Banking organizations may therefore be less likely to extend this form of credit.

[3] A substantial minority of the loan packages or "deals" involve more than one loan "facility" originated by the same borrower on the same date. A typical package might include a line of credit and term loan. In general, we conduct our analysis at the facility level, treating each as a separate loan, because deals involving multiple lenders do not always have the same set of lenders involved in all facilities. Our results are similar when analysis is done at the deal level.

We estimate that for year-end 1992, loan agreements in the database cover between one-half and three-quarters of all commercial and industrial loans outstanding by volume (but a far smaller fraction by number). We exclude from our sample loans to non-U.S. borrowers, the small number of loans made before 1987 or with a missing contract date, and those observations flagged by LPC as being based on unconfirmed information.

### Table III
### Loan Microdata Sample Characteristics

This table presents summary statistics for the full sample (all usable Dealscan loans) and for those loans with borrowers appearing in COMPUSTAT (Panel B). The latter subsample is used in the logit regressions reported in Section III. All dollar amounts are in millions.

|  | All | Single Lender | Multiple Lender |
|---|---|---|---|
| Panel A: Full Sample | | | |
| Number of loans | 14735 | 8229 | 6506 |
| Median loan size | 30 | 10 | 80 |
| Median term to maturity, months | 36 | 27 | 39 |
| Panel B: COMPUSTAT Sample | | | |
| Number of loans | 9145 | 5133 | 4012 |
| Median loan size | 25 | 10 | 75 |
| Median term to maturity, months | 36 | 25 | 37 |
| Median borrower sales | 232 | 108 | 566 |
| Median borrower assets | 219 | 91 | 566 |

loans, finance companies, insurance companies, investment banks, etc. We identify the type of each lender by matching names with corporate directory entries and databases maintained by the Federal Reserve. We then divide the lenders into three basic types: banks, finance companies, and other. We also determine the parentage of almost all the finance companies, classifying these into U.S. and foreign bank subsidiaries, nonfinancial corporation subsidiaries, financial corporation subsidiaries, and unknown. Where a loan involves multiple lenders, it is not uncommon for a variety of institutional types to be represented, but by far the most common mix is banks alone. Finance companies are next most frequently represented, being either the sole lender or a joint lender in about 10.5 percent of sample loans. The finance company participation share is relatively constant over the years of the sample, ranging from a low of 8.2 percent in 1987 to a high of 12.7 percent in 1989.

In cases where a loan involves more than one type of lender, several different classification schemes seem reasonable. Throughout the reported analysis, we classify any multiple-lender loan involving a finance company as a "finance company loan," regardless of the mix of other institutional types represented. Results are robust to other classification schemes, such as a requirement that a finance company be the lead lender. Of course, classification is unambiguous for the single-lender loans.[4]

We obtain borrower characteristics, such as leverage, by matching borrowers' names to firm names in the COMPUSTAT database, succeeding for about

---

[4] In an earlier version, we displayed all results separately for multiple-lender and single-lender loans, and results were qualitatively similar for the two subsamples (Carey, Post, and Sharpe (1996)).

half the borrowers and 9145 loans, as summarized in Panel B of Table III. Median loan size and maturity for this subsample are not far from full-sample values. The median COMPUSTAT sample loan is to a firm with $232 million in sales and $219 million in assets at the end of the fiscal year in which the loan is made. A relatively small number of financial and government borrowers in the full sample are excluded from this sample by construction.

## III. Lender Type Prediction Model Results

We estimate logit models of the form:

$$\text{Lender} = f(\text{Observable risk proxies, Information}$$
$$\text{proxies, Control variables}) \qquad (1)$$

where Lender takes the value 1 for finance company loans and 0 for bank loans. Control variables include dummies for the year of the loan, the industry of the borrower, and a dummy for observations where a missing value of R&D is set to zero. Table IV provides summary statistics for the right-hand-side variables, separately for bank and finance company loans.

Proxies for observable borrower risk include two measures of leverage, three measures of the level of cash flow and one measure of its volatility, and dummy variables for the stated purpose of the loan. Book leverage is the book value of debt divided by the sum of itself and book equity, whereas market equity replaces book equity in the market leverage measure. The three measures of cash flow are return on assets, return on sales, and interest coverage. The numerator of the three measures is earnings before interest, taxes, depreciation, and amortization (EBITDA). The denominator of interest coverage is interest expense, and total assets and sales are the denominators of the other two measures.[5] We measure the volatility of cash flow with a Z-score-based measure of the probability of negative cash flow, computed using the five-year mean and standard deviation of EBITDA. Sixteen different stated loan purposes that appear in the database are grouped and represented by four dummies.[6] As shown in Table IV, finance company

---

[5] Interest coverage and return on assets and sales are exceptions to our usual rule of measuring variables as of the end of the fiscal year in which the loan agreement was signed: Each is a three-year average, centered on the year of the loan. Results are generally robust to use of single-year values.

[6] "General purposes" includes working capital and "general corporate purposes" loans. "Recapitalization" includes debt repayment/consolidation, recapitalization, and debtor-in-possession loans. "Acquisition" includes general or specific acquisition program and LBO loans. The "miscellaneous" category includes securities purchase, stock buyback, and ESOP loans; trade finance, project finance, and real estate loans; credit enhancements; and commercial paper backups. None of the miscellaneous categories include a large number of loans.

**Table IV**

**Summary Statistics for Logit Analysis Independent Variables**

This table presents summary statistics for variables used in the logit analysis. Distributions of some variables are also plotted in Figures 1 to 4. Statistics are for the COMPUSTAT sample. Leverage is book value of total debt divided by total debt plus book value of equity. The market value of equity replaces book equity in the market leverage measure. EBITDA is earnings before subtraction of interest expense, taxes, and depreciation and amortization. Interest coverage is the ratio of EBITDA to interest expense. The probability of negative cash flow is a Z-score measure computed using the 5-year mean and standard deviation of EBITDA. Loan purposes are as stated in Dealscan, aggregated into the four categories shown.

| | Bank Borrowers | | Finance Company Borrowers | |
|---|---|---|---|---|
| | Mean | Median | Mean | Median |
| Panel A: Observable Risk | | | | |
| Leverage (book) | 0.502 | 0.496 | 0.718 | 0.745 |
| Leverage (market) | 0.376 | 0.349 | 0.536 | 0.540 |
| Interest coverage | 4.365 | 3.600 | 2.393 | 1.869 |
| EBITDA/assets | 0.119 | 0.126 | 0.097 | 0.116 |
| EBITDA/sales | 0.118 | 0.118 | 0.058 | 0.090 |
| Probability of negative cash flow | 0.117 | 0.011 | 0.150 | 0.043 |
| Loan purpose: Recapitalization | 0.222 | 0 | 0.420 | 0 |
| Loan purpose: Acquisition | 0.146 | 0 | 0.266 | 0 |
| Loan purpose: General purposes | 0.569 | 1 | 0.297 | 0 |
| Loan purpose: Miscellaneous | 0.063 | 0 | 0.017 | 0 |
| Panel B: Information or Control Problems | | | | |
| Log assets | 5.454 | 5.359 | 5.526 | 5.458 |
| Log sales | 5.434 | 5.404 | 5.661 | 5.596 |
| Market-to-book ratio | 1.394 | 1.175 | 1.198 | 1.021 |
| Sales growth (5 yr. avg.) | 0.304 | 0.121 | 0.268 | 0.070 |
| R&D-to-sales ratio | 0.017 | 0 | 0.010 | 0 |
| No. of years of COMPUSTAT data before loan | 8.554 | 10 | 7.900 | 10 |
| Panel C: Year and Industry Controls (dummies) | | | | |
| SIC 0000–3999 | 0.558 | 1 | 0.561 | 1 |
| SIC 4000–4999 | 0.140 | 0 | 0.098 | 0 |
| SIC 5000–5999 | 0.153 | 0 | 0.232 | 0 |
| SIC 7000–8999 | 0.149 | 0 | 0.109 | 0 |
| 1987 | 0.084 | 0 | 0.070 | 0 |
| 1988 | 0.174 | 0 | 0.179 | 0 |
| 1989 | 0.154 | 0 | 0.210 | 0 |
| 1990 | 0.156 | 0 | 0.115 | 0 |
| 1991 | 0.143 | 0 | 0.130 | 0 |
| 1992 | 0.181 | 0 | 0.191 | 0 |
| 1993 | 0.109 | 0 | 0.105 | 0 |

borrowers are substantially more leveraged than bank borrowers on average, but differences in cash flow are smaller and depend on the measure chosen.

We follow the literature in choosing proxies for information or control problems posed by the borrower. Smaller firms are commonly presumed to pose larger information asymmetries; we measure size by the natural logarithms of total assets or sales. The number of years up to the date of the loan that data for the borrower appear in COMPUSTAT is another proxy for the extent and history of widely available information about the borrower. Firms engaged in extensive research and development (R&D), those with relatively large growth opportunities, and those growing rapidly are thought to be relatively hard to monitor and control. The incentives and opportunities of such firms to expropriate wealth from lenders may shift rapidly. We measure these characteristics with the ratio of R&D expense to sales, the ratio of the firm's market-to-book value, and five-year average sales growth (ending with the year of the loan). Market-to-book is the ratio of the market value of common equity plus book debt to the book value of equity and debt. R&D expense is often missing in COMPUSTAT; we set such observations to zero, and then include a dummy in regressions for those observations in which it was originally missing (not shown in the tables, and never significant). Again referring to Table IV, the values of the information proxies appear rather similar on average for finance company and bank borrowers.[7]

### A. Observable Risk, Not Information Problems

Table V reports logit results for the choice between bank and finance company lenders. Independent variables include the proxies for observable risk and information problems as well as dummy variables to control for year and industry effects. The omitted loan purpose category is the general one, including general corporate purposes and working capital loans. The table reports coefficient values and $p$-values for standard two-tailed tests of statistical significance (in parentheses). Observable risk proxies appear in the top half of the table and information problem proxies appear below them.

Focusing on the first column, the main result is that observable risk proxies have significant predictive power for lender type, whereas information problem proxies have little power. Both book and market leverage appear in the specification in column 1, and in both single- and multiple-lender cases high-leverage firms are significantly more likely to borrow from a finance company than from a bank. The negative and significant coefficients on the EBITDA-to-sales variable imply that firms with poor cash flow around the time of the loan are also more likely to go to finance companies. Results for the loan purpose dummies indicate that finance companies are more likely than banks to make loans for what appear to be riskier purposes (restruc-

---

[7] The influence of outliers is limited by mechanically truncating most variables at the 1st and 99th percentiles (smaller or larger values are set to the values at those percentiles). For a few very noisy variables, such as interest coverage, truncation is at other values, such as the 10th and 90th percentile.

**Table V**

## Lender Type Prediction Logit Model Results, Primary Specifications

The logit model dependent variable is 1 if the lender is (or the lender group includes) a finance company and 0 if it is a bank (or if the group includes a bank but no finance company). *p*-values for two-tailed tests are in parentheses. Column 6 reports results when the sample is limited to term loans (TL), revolvers, and lines of credit (REV). Panel A presents coefficient estimates for proxies for observable borrower risk. Panel B displays estimates for proxies for information problems posed by the borrower. Estimated coefficients for control variables are not shown. Leverage is book value of total debt divided by total debt plus book value of equity. The market value of equity replaces book equity in the market leverage measure. EBITDA is earnings before subtraction of interest expense, taxes, and depreciation and amortization. Loan purpose dummies are from purposes stated in Dealscan, aggregated into the three categories shown, with general-purposes and working capital loans the omitted dummy.

| Independent Variable | Full Sample Specifications | | | | | TL+REV Only |
|---|---|---|---|---|---|---|
| | 1 | 2 | 3 | 4 | 5 | 6 |
| Panel A: Observable Risk | | | | | | |
| Intercept | −4.413 | −4.773 | −4.326 | −3.931 | −4.454 | −4.352 |
| | (0.0001) | (0.0001) | (0.0001) | (0.0001) | (0.0001) | (0.0001) |
| Leverage (book) | 2.256 | 2.562 | 2.282 | 2.731 | 2.682 | 2.317 |
| | (0.0001) | (0.0001) | (0.0001) | (0.0001) | (0.0001) | (0.0001) |
| Leverage (market) | 0.721 | 0.544 | 0.768 | | | 0.734 |
| | (0.1617) | (0.2236) | (0.1348) | | | (0.1726) |
| EBITDA/sales | −1.996 | | −1.729 | −1.622 | −1.045 | −2.156 |
| | (0.0001) | | (0.0001) | (0.0001) | (0.0002) | (0.0001) |
| Loan purpose: Recapitalization | 0.684 | 0.610 | 0.682 | 0.831 | 0.893 | 0.669 |
| | (0.0001) | (0.0001) | (0.0001) | (0.0001) | (0.0001) | (0.0001) |
| Loan purpose: Takeover | 0.816 | 0.799 | 0.846 | 0.772 | 0.687 | 0.782 |
| | (0.0001) | (0.0001) | (0.0001) | (0.0001) | (0.0001) | (0.0001) |
| Loan purpose: Miscellaneous | −0.973 | −1.106 | −0.890 | −1.061 | −0.945 | |
| | (0.0372) | (0.0170) | (0.0575) | (0.0223) | (0.0066) | |
| Panel B: Information or Control Problems | | | | | | |
| Log sales | −0.050 | −0.062 | | −0.051 | | −0.061 |
| | (0.1879) | (0.0619) | | (0.1316) | | (0.1142) |
| Log assets | | | −0.109 | | | |
| | | | (0.0054) | | | |
| Market-to-book ratio | 0.034 | 0.119 | 0.014 | −0.248 | | 0.086 |
| | (0.8214) | (0.2991) | (0.9262) | (0.0283) | | (0.5808) |
| Sales growth (5-yr. avg.) | 0.209 | 0.102 | 0.218 | 0.113 | | 0.176 |
| | (0.0694) | (0.3534) | (0.0577) | (0.3202) | | (0.1483) |
| R&D-to-sales ratio | −6.526 | −0.770 | −6.593 | −6.080 | | −5.994 |
| | (0.0309) | (0.7035) | (0.0302) | (0.0408) | | (0.0518) |
| No. of years of COMPUSTAT data before loan | 0.011 | 0.015 | 0.031 | 0.023 | | 0.002 |
| | (0.8278) | (0.7452) | (0.5441) | (0.6201) | | (0.9720) |
| No. of observations | 4207 | 5014 | 4207 | 4571 | 6544 | 3770 |
| Pseudo-$R^2$ | 0.14 | 0.13 | 0.15 | 0.14 | 0.13 | 0.14 |

turings and takeovers), whereas "miscellaneous purpose" loans (a category that includes commercial paper backups, trade finance, and "other" purposes) are more likely made by banks.

In contrast, there is little support for the hypothesis that the two types of intermediaries serve borrowers posing differing information problems. The coefficients for borrower size (as measured by the log of sales), market-to-book ratio, sales growth, and years of COMPUSTAT coverage are statistically and economically insignificant.

The coefficient on the R&D-to-sales ratio is negative and statistically significant, but this result is sensitive to specification, as shown in column 2, where cash flow is omitted. When EBITDA-to-sales is replaced by the probability of negative cash flow (not shown) R&D is again not significant. When the sample is restricted to firms below the median in size, again R&D is insignificant. When R&D intensity is represented by a dummy for firms with R&D-to-sales ratios above some threshold, such as 0.03 or 0.05, the coefficient is not robustly significant. Most importantly, inspection of the distribution of the R&D variable reveals that two-thirds of both finance company and bank borrowers report R&D expense as zero or missing. The distributions of nonzero values are similar across lender types. When we limit the sample to firms with a nonmissing value of R&D expense, the coefficient is insignificant. For some firms, R&D varies a lot from year to year, but when we use a three-year average of R&D to sales, results are qualitatively similar.

Column 3 of Table V reports results when firm size is gauged by the log of assets rather than the log of sales. Although statistically significant, the size of the coefficient is economically small. Its sign differs when logits are run separately for single- and multiple-lender loans. We take a closer look at this issue in Figure 1, which compares the size distributions of bank and finance company borrowers. The distributions are quite similar regardless of whether sales or assets (not shown) are plotted, confirming that firm size is not a powerful predictor of lender type and that both types of lenders serve borrowers across the size spectrum.

## B. Robustness

The qualitative results are robust to a wide variety of changes in specification. The remaining columns of Table V report a few variants of interest. In column 4, the market leverage measure is dropped from the model. Unsurprisingly, given the collinearity between market and book leverage, the resulting coefficient on book leverage is larger than in previous columns. Coefficients on other variables are largely unaffected, except market-to-book becomes negative and significant. We attribute the latter result to market-to-book's standing in for the marginal influence of market leverage relative to book leverage. Dropping the book leverage measure and retaining market leverage (not reported) yields similar results, except that market-to-book is insignificant. Dropping all the information proxies leaves coefficients and significance for the observable-risk proxies basically unchanged (column 5).

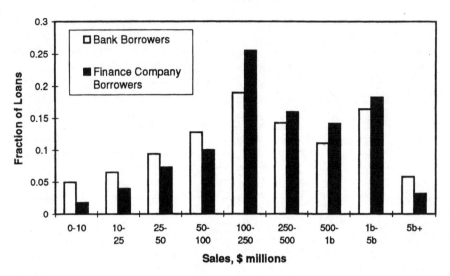

**Figure 1. Distribution of Borrowers' Annual Sales.** This figure compares the distributions of annual sales for bank borrowers and finance company borrowers. Sales are in millions of dollars, except that a "b" signifies billions of dollars.

Column 6 demonstrates that results for the full specification are similar when the sample is limited to lines of credit and term loans. Looking across the columns, it is clear that the information-problem proxies are either always insignificant or not robustly significant.

Other variations in specification (not shown) yield qualitatively similar results. A dummy for whether a borrower has public debt outstanding is significant only for some multiple-lender loan specifications, and even then the coefficient is economically small. Of three proxies for the extent of information problems recently proposed by Calomiris and Himmelberg (1995)—the ratios of cash to fixed capital, long-term debt to total debt, and sales to fixed capital—none are robustly significant. When the sample is restricted to rated firms and dummies for the various ratings are included, their coefficients are in line with the main results but generally insignificant unless leverage is dropped. When the sample is restricted to firms with leverage above 0.6, the results are qualitatively very similar. Proxies for the borrower's use of lease financing are not significant. Moreover, the results do not appear to be time-dependent—annual dummy coefficients are of mixed sign and significance, and show no particular pattern.

A previous version of this paper presents results separately for single- and multiple-lender loans. Coefficients on observable risk proxies are similar in sign and significance across the two subsamples, except that the takeover purpose dummy is significant mainly for multiple-lender specifications and the miscellaneous-purpose dummy mainly for the single-lender case. The split sample results offer further evidence of the information proxies' lack of predictive power: Coefficients on firm size proxies differ in sign across the two subsamples and significance is not robust, sales growth is never significant, and R&D to sales is significant only for single-lender loans.

We investigate the possibility that leverage acts as a proxy for the borrower's industry or asset composition. Inclusion in the logits of various combinations of SIC code dummies at the one- and two-digit levels leaves other results qualitatively unchanged, including the leverage results. Remarkably, when we interact book leverage with one-digit SIC dummies, almost all industry-specific leverage variables are significant and their coefficients are generally close to that for book leverage when it is included as a scalar. Using a joint test, we are unable to reject the hypothesis that all industry-specific leverage coefficients are equal to the value of the scalar coefficient on leverage. Thus it appears that the relationship between leverage and lender choice is similar across industries.[8]

When various measures of asset composition are included, such as the shares of inventory and receivables, fixed capital, intangibles, or cash in total assets, only the coefficient on the fixed capital share is robustly significant. In our regressions the variable carries a negative sign, implying that finance companies are less likely to lend to firms with a large share of assets in fixed capital, which we found surprising given the reputation of finance companies as asset-based lenders. Because this result is subject to a wide variety of speculative interpretations, we are reluctant to draw any conclusion from it.

### C. A Closer Look at Cash Flow and Leverage

The results for the leverage variables in Table V are quite strong and are extremely robust to changes in specification, but upon further investigation results for cash flow are indicative of a lesser degree of specialization. Table VI reports results for variants involving different measures of cash flow. Results in column 1 duplicate those in the first column of the previous table to make comparison easier. The information-problem proxies are included in the specification but are not reported to save space. EBITDA-to-assets and EBITDA-to-interest expense (interest coverage ratio) appear as alternative cash flow measures in columns 2 and 4, and the probability of negative cash flow appears in column 3. In column 5, interest coverage is replaced by dummies representing different ranges of the variable (coverage greater than 10 is the omitted dummy). The latter is an attempt to capture

---

[8] Stohs and Mauer (1996) find a positive correlation between borrower leverage and maturity of debt, raising the possibility that leverage acts as a proxy for loan maturity in our logits. The correlation between leverage and maturity in our dataset is positive (approximately 0.2). We normally omit maturity from the logits to avoid possible simultaneity bias. When included in the logits, maturity has a positive and significant coefficient, but other results are qualitatively unchanged.

Table VI

## Lender Type Prediction Logit Model Results, Specifications Focusing on Cash Flow

The logit model dependent variable is 1 if the lender is (or the lender group includes) a finance company and 0 if it is a bank (or if the group includes a bank but no finance company). $p$-values for two-tailed tests are in parentheses. The central panel presents estimates for various measures of borrower cash flow. Leverage is book value of total debt divided by total debt plus book value of equity. The market value of equity replaces book equity in the market leverage measure. EBITDA is earnings before subtraction of interest expense, taxes, and depreciation and amortization. Interest coverage is the ratio of EBITDA to interest expense. The probability of negative cash flow is a Z-score measure computed using the 5-year mean and standard deviation of EBITDA. Control variables and variables proxying for information problems are included in the specifications but not shown.

| Independent Variable | Full Sample Specifications | | | | |
|---|---|---|---|---|---|
|  | 1 | 2 | 3 | 4 | 5 |
| Intercept | −4.413 | −4.579 | −4.724 | −3.881 | −4.233 |
|  | (0.0001) | (0.0001) | (0.0001) | (0.0001) | (0.0001) |
| Leverage (book) | 2.256 | 2.170 | 2.401 | 1.697 | 2.103 |
|  | (0.0001) | (0.0001) | (0.0001) | (0.0008) | (0.0001) |
| Leverage (market) | 0.721 | 0.811 | 0.564 | 0.462 | −0.024 |
|  | (0.1617) | (0.1131) | (0.2188) | (0.3719) | (0.9645) |
| EBITDA/sales | −1.996 |  |  |  |  |
|  | (0.0001) |  |  |  |  |
| EBITDA/assets |  | −0.943 |  |  |  |
|  |  | (0.1648) |  |  |  |
| Probability of negative cash flow |  |  | 0.979 |  |  |
|  |  |  | (0.0010) |  |  |
| Interest coverage |  |  |  | −0.140 |  |
|  |  |  |  | (0.0001) |  |
| Coverage dummies: |  |  |  |  |  |
| = 1 if int. coverage < 0 |  |  |  |  | 0.242 |
|  |  |  |  |  | (0.5236) |
| = 1 if int. coverage 0–1 |  |  |  |  | 0.911 |
|  |  |  |  |  | (0.0117) |
| = 1 if int. coverage 1–3 |  |  |  |  | 0.538 |
|  |  |  |  |  | (0.0977) |
| = 1 if int. coverage 3–10 |  |  |  |  | −0.423 |
|  |  |  |  |  | (0.1783) |
| Loan purpose: Recapitalization | 0.684 | 0.709 | 0.602 | 0.672 | 0.657 |
|  | (0.0001) | (0.0001) | (0.0001) | (0.0001) | (0.0001) |
| Loan purpose: Takeover | 0.816 | 0.824 | 0.762 | 0.854 | 0.837 |
|  | (0.0001) | (0.0001) | (0.0001) | (0.0001) | (0.0001) |
| Loan purpose: Miscellaneous | −0.973 | −0.936 | −1.085 | −0.912 | −0.866 |
|  | (0.0372) | (0.0448) | (0.0194) | (0.0510) | (0.0644) |
| No. of observations | 4207 | 4207 | 4827 | 4202 | 4202 |
| Pseudo-$R^2$ | 0.14 | 0.14 | 0.13 | 0.14 | 0.15 |

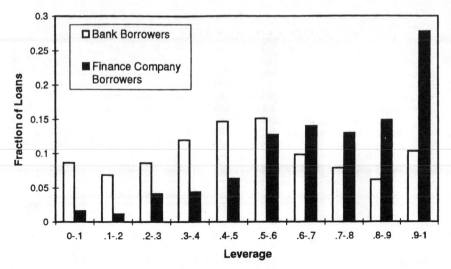

**Figure 2. Distribution of Borrowers' Book Leverage.** This figure compares the distributions of leverage for bank borrowers and finance company borrowers. Leverage is measured as the book value of debt divided by the sum of itself and book equity.

any nonlinearities in the interest coverage relationship. It may be that variations in interest coverage above some threshold value are unimportant.

The different proxies yield somewhat mixed results. Interest coverage and the probability of negative cash flow are significant, but EBITDA-to-assets is not. Further, when logits are run separately for single- and multiple-lender loans (not shown), the only measure significant in the single-lender case is EBITDA-to-sales. In designing the interest coverage dummies, our prior was that the coefficients would increase monotonically in magnitude for each step-down in coverage. This prior is only very weakly confirmed: Coefficients become more positive as coverage decreases to zero, but only the 0-to-1 coefficient is statistically significant, and the coefficient on the negative-coverage dummy is smaller in magnitude than that on the 0-to-1 coverage dummy.

Figures 2 to 4 display the distributions of book leverage and two cash flow measures for bank versus finance company loans. Figure 2 shows frequency distributions of borrower book leverage (total debt divided by total debt plus book equity). As this picture makes quite evident, finance companies serve higher-leverage borrowers to a much greater degree than banks. About half of bank loans are to firms with leverage less than 0.5, whereas only about one-sixth of finance company loans fall in that range. Conversely, more than half of finance company loans are to firms with book leverage exceeding 0.7.

On the other hand, Figure 2 also shows that the loan market is not completely partitioned by borrower leverage. Banks and finance companies com-

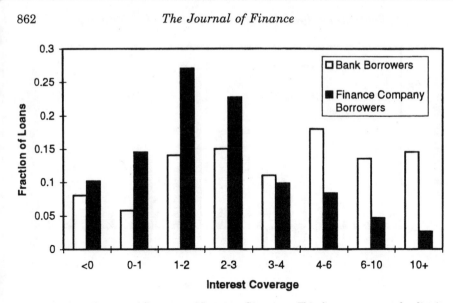

**Figure 3. Distribution of Borrowers' Interest Coverage.** This figure compares the distributions of interest coverage ratios for bank borrowers and finance company borrowers. Interest coverage is measured as EBITDA divided by interest expense. EBITDA is earnings before subtraction of interest expense, taxes, depreciation, and amortization.

pete across the spectrum of leverage even though their proportional presence in the high- and low-leverage segments differs.

Figure 3 shows the distributions of interest coverage ratios (EBITDA-to-interest expense) and Figure 4 shows the distributions of EBITDA-to-sales. According to the coverage measure, finance companies appear to focus on low cash flow firms. About one-quarter of the bank loans are to firms with high levels of coverage (ratios of 6 or above), whereas only 7 percent of finance company loans go to such firms. Conversely, more than 40 percent of finance company borrowers have coverage ratios between zero and two, about double the concentration of bank loans in that range. In contrast, the distributions of EBITDA-to-sales are much more similar across lender types. Thus, we conclude that the differences in the interest coverage distributions arise mainly from differences in borrower leverage, rather than differences in cash flow. The distribution of bank borrowers' cash flow does appear to be shifted a little to the right of the distribution of finance company borrowers' cash flow, but the differences are minor compared with the differences for leverage.[9]

---

[9] It is somewhat surprising that cash flow is a weak predictor relative to leverage because conventional wisdom among market participants often labels banks as "cash-flow" lenders and finance companies as "asset-based" lenders. It may be that such conventional wisdom has been based on univariate comparisons of interest coverage measures.

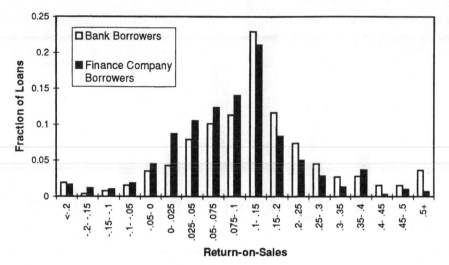

**Figure 4. Distribution of Borrowers' Return-on-Sales.** This figure compares the distributions of return-on-sales ratios for bank borrowers and finance company borrowers. Return on sales, a measure of cash flow, is measured as EBITDA divided by total sales. EBITDA is earnings before subtraction of interest expense, taxes, depreciation, and amortization.

## IV. The Scope of Specialization: A Comparison of Loan Characteristics

Finance companies appear to specialize in lending to firms with capital structures that make them riskier credits. Using the full sample summarized in Table III, this section presents comparisons of bank and finance company loans along a variety of other dimensions to add to the evidence of specialization by risk and to investigate whether their corporate lending is specialized in other respects. We compare loan types, purposes, maturities, incidences of secured status, and average interest rate spreads. We also examine the frequency with which finance companies operate in an agent or lead lender role in cases where loans involve both banks and finance companies. The comparisons reveal differences mainly in characteristics plausibly associated with observable borrower risk, consistent with this being the main dimension of specialization.

### A. Similar Loan Types, Somewhat Different Purposes

Table VII shows the distribution of loan types in the full sample for single lender facilities involving either (i) a bank or (ii) a finance company, and for multiple lender facilities involving either (iii) banks but not finance companies or (iv) finance companies and perhaps banks or other institutions. As can be seen from the first row, among single lender facilities, there are 822 loans made by finance companies and 7035 made by banks. A large percent-

**Table VII**

## Distribution of Loan Types for Banks and Finance Companies

In this table, the sample is the full sample of loans less those loans involving neither a bank nor a finance company and those involving mixtures of banks and other institutional types. The Line of Credit loan type includes revolving credits. Term loans and Bridge loans are loans for a fixed period, with Bridge loans typically being for relatively short periods between other financings. Demand loans have no fixed maturity and repayment may be demanded at any time. Standby letters of credit are lines of credit backing the borrower's promise to repay specific other liabilities, such as commercial paper. The Other loan category includes trade letters of credit, uncommitted guidance lines, and bankers acceptances. Multiple-lender, finance-company-participating loans include at least one finance company in the lending group and may include banks and other types of institutions in the group.

|  | Single Lender | | Multiple Lenders | |
|---|---|---|---|---|
|  | Bank | Finance Co. | Banks Only | Finance Co. Participating |
| Number of loans | 7035 | 822 | 5119 | 719 |
| Percent in category: | | | | |
| Line of credit | 57 | 51 | 66 | 49 |
| Term loan | 29 | 40 | 26 | 41 |
| Bridge loan | 2 | 4 | 3 | 5 |
| Demand loan | 5 | 2 | 0 | 0 |
| Standby letter of credit | 4 | 1 | 4 | 3 |
| Other | 3 | 2 | 0 | 2 |

age of loans made by both types of lender fall into the credit line or term loan categories. Although finance companies show a somewhat higher degree of relative specialization in the term loan category, particularly in the case of multiple lender loans, the distribution of both bank and finance company loans across contract categories is similar.

Table VIII categorizes loans by finance company parent type. For all four parent types, the two major categories of loans—credit lines and term loans—account for about 90 percent of the total. Moreover, the breakdown between credit lines and term loans does not point to major differences across parent types.

Table IX shows a breakdown by loan purpose for banks versus finance companies, a dimension along which there appear to be more substantial differences. Where there is only one lender, about 60 percent of bank loans are for either general corporate purposes or working capital, whereas less than 40 percent of finance company loans fall into this category. Finance company loans, on the other hand, show a higher concentration among restructuring-oriented purposes, such as acquisitions, leveraged buyouts, and debt consolidation. Among multiple-lender loans, such differences are a bit more pronounced. Additionally, finance companies are involved in very few commercial paper backups. These differences in purpose appear consistent with finance companies' specialization in higher-risk borrowers and loans.

## Table VIII
## Distribution of Loan Types for Finance Companies with Different Parent Types

In this table, the sample is limited to loans made by finance companies. To be included, multiple-lender loans must include at least one finance company in the lending group, but may include banks and other types of institutions in the group. Loans made by finance companies with unidentified parents are omitted. The small number of independent finance companies are included in the Other Financial Firm category. The Line of credit loan type includes revolving credits. Term loans and Bridge loans are loans for a fixed period, with Bridge loans typically being for relatively short periods between other financings. Demand loans have no fixed maturity and repayment may be demanded at any time. Standby letters of credit are lines of credit backing the borrower's promise to repay specific other liabilities. The Other loan category includes trade letters of credit, uncommitted guidance lines, and bankers acceptances.

| | Finance Company Parent Type | | | |
|---|---|---|---|---|
| | U.S. Bank | Foreign Bank | Nonfinancial Firm | Other Financial Firm |
| Number of loans | 349 | 480 | 362 | 160 |
| Percent in Category: | | | | |
| Line of credit | 54 | 50 | 44 | 59 |
| Term loan | 35 | 43 | 46 | 33 |
| Bridge loan | 7 | 3 | 2 | 4 |
| Demand loan | 3 | 1 | 1 | 0 |
| Standby letter of credit | 1 | 2 | 3 | 0 |
| Other | 1 | 1 | 4 | 4 |

Table X shows a breakdown of finance company loan purposes by finance company parent type. Finance subsidiaries of nonfinancial corporations make a smaller fraction of loans in the general corporate purpose/working capital category than other finance companies but, generally speaking, all the subsidiary types appear to make loans for a variety of purposes.

### B. Borrower-Lender Relationships

Recent research offers evidence that there is more to borrower-lender relationships than the cross-selling of credit and other products often mentioned by practitioners (Rajan (1992), Petersen and Rajan (1994), and Berger and Udell (1995)). We add to this evidence by examining the extent to which finance companies compete with banks for the agent or lead lender role where both types of institutions participate (Table XI). The lead lender likely has the primary relationship with the borrower because it has primary responsibility for negotiating terms and administering the loan after issuance. If relationships are an important part of private debt contracting, then finance companies ought to be in the lead in proportion to their market share. If instead, relationships are largely associated with cross-selling, banks should

**Table IX**

**Distribution of Loan Purpose for Bank and Finance Company Loans**

In this table, the sample is the full sample of loans less those loans involving neither a bank nor a finance company and those involving mixtures of banks and other institutional types. Multiple-lender, finance-company-participating loans include at least one finance company in the lending group and may include banks and other types of institutions in the group. ~0 indicates less than 0.5 percent.

|  | Single Lender | | Multiple Lenders | |
|---|---|---|---|---|
|  | Bank | Finance Co. | Banks Only | Finance Co. Participating |
| Number of loans | 7035 | 822 | 5119 | 719 |
| Percent in category: | | | | |
| General corporate purposes/working capital | 61 | 38 | 47 | 18 |
| Takeovers and acquisitions | 10 | 14 | 13 | 15 |
| Leveraged buyout | 4 | 13 | 6 | 22 |
| Debt repayment/consolidation | 14 | 26 | 22 | 26 |
| Recapitalization | 2 | 4 | 4 | 14 |
| Commercial paper backup | 1 | ~0 | 5 | ~0 |
| Other | 7 | 4 | 5 | 5 |

dominate the lead role because they offer a much wider array of products, with finance companies mainly acting as participants in loan syndicates.

Among the 661 loans in which both banks and finance companies are involved, finance companies are the agents almost 20 percent of the time and are coagents with banks 4 percent of the time. They are agents about in proportion to their dollar share in the 661 loans (27 percent, not shown in table). This suggests that finance companies are quite active in the lead lender role. Table XI also shows that finance companies' agenting is not confined to any particular type of loan. However, finance companies that are U.S. or foreign bank subsidiaries are somewhat more likely to be agents than others (loans involving bank subsidiaries are 55 percent of loans involving any finance company, but bank subsidiaries are the agent in 70 percent of finance-company-agented loans). Thus, the implied relationships in many cases may have been forged at the bank holding company level. On the whole, however, it appears that finance companies are lead lenders often enough to support assertions that private debt relationships involve more than cross-selling.

## C. Some Contract Terms

Table XII characterizes some price and nonprice terms for the full sample of loans, again broken out into single lender and multiple lender deals. The first row displays median spreads between the loan interest rate and LIBOR. Under an assumption of competitive loan markets and costless monitoring,

**Table X**

## Distribution of Loan Purpose for Finance Companies with Different Parent Types

In this table, the sample is limited to loans made by finance companies. To be included, multiple-lender loans must include at least one finance company in the lending group, but may include banks and other types of institutions in the group. Loans made by finance companies with unidentified parents are omitted. The small number of independent finance companies are included in the Other Financial Firm category.

| | Finance Company Parent Type | | | |
|---|---|---|---|---|
| | U.S. Bank | Foreign Bank | Nonfinancial Firm | Other Financial Firm |
| Number of loans | 349 | 480 | 362 | 160 |
| Percent in category: | | | | |
| General corporate purposes/working capital | 36 | 30 | 21 | 36 |
| Takeovers and acquisitions | 10 | 16 | 17 | 14 |
| Leveraged buyout | 19 | 13 | 22 | 13 |
| Debt repayment/consolidation | 29 | 28 | 21 | 28 |
| Recapitalization | 5 | 9 | 12 | 4 |
| Other | 1 | 4 | 6 | 5 |

this spread can be viewed as a measure of the residual riskiness of a loan after accounting for the mitigating effects of collateral, covenants, and other nonprice terms. To the extent that monitoring is costly and varies with underlying risk, this spread reflects compensation for monitoring as well as the riskiness of the loan.

For both single- and multiple-lender loans, the median spread charged on finance company loans is substantially greater than that for banks. Among single lender loans, the median spread on bank loans is 250 basis points, but for finance company loans it is about 400 basis points. The analogous difference in median spreads for multiple lender loans is also quite wide. Clearly, these figures are consistent with the view that finance companies lend to riskier borrowers on average.[10]

The remainder of Table XII presents statistics for maturity and collateral (almost none of the loans are subordinated). Finance company loans tend to. have longer maturities than loans involving just banks. For example, among single-lender loans, bank loan maturities average about two years, and finance company loans average about three years.

---

[10] Finance companies might also charge borrowers higher spreads than banks for any given level of risk. We attempt to control for differences in risk by computing the difference between spreads on loans to the subset of borrowers that are rated and spreads on similarly rated bonds, adjusted for differences in secured status. When such a measure is used, the differences are much less pronounced (not otherwise reported).

868                  *The Journal of Finance*

**Table XI**

**Who Is an Agent When Both Banks and Finance Companies Participate?**

In this table, the sample is limited to multiple-lender loans involving both banks and finance companies. The columns in the lower-right panel give, respectively, the percentage of such loans for which the lead lender is a finance company, a bank, or lead-lender status is shared by both banks and finance companies. Rows in the lower panel give results by loan type. The Line of credit loan type includes revolving credits. Term loans and Bridge loans are loans for a fixed period, with Bridge loans typically being for relatively short periods between other financings. Standby letters of credit are lines of credit backing the borrower's promise to repay specific other liabilities. No Demand loans or Other loan types appear in this table's sample.

|  | Number of Loans in Category | Finance Company | Bank | Both |
|---|---|---|---|---|
| Number of loans | 661 | 121 | 514 | 26 |
|  |  | Percentage in Loan Type Category | | |
| Line of credit | 329 | 20 | 76 | 4 |
| Term loan | 279 | 17 | 79 | 4 |
| Bridge loan | 31 | 19 | 81 | 0 |
| Standby letter of credit | 22 | 9 | 82 | 9 |

Single-lender bank and finance company loans are secured 70 and 92 percent of the time, respectively.[11] Smaller fractions of the multiple-lender loans are secured, with the difference between bank-only and finance-company-participating loans somewhat more pronounced. Clearly both types of lenders make secured loans very frequently, though finance companies do so more frequently than banks. This is consistent with findings of other research, which implies that riskier firms more frequently borrow on a secured basis (Berger and Udell (1990)).[12]

As noted in Section I, finance companies are often said to monitor collateral closely, whereas banks may obtain a lien on collateral assets but monitor less closely. We do not observe monitoring directly. However, one contracting technology that may be associated with more active monitoring involves limiting the total loan amount outstanding to some fraction of a

---

[11] The secured indicator we use differs from that in the LPC database, which yields an upward-biased estimate of secured proportions. The raw LPC indicator is missing for more than half the observations because LPC codes a loan as secured/unsecured only if LPC has explicit information about its status, but the typical unsecured loan contract simply does not mention collateral. We used information in a descriptive text field to identify loans for which LPC very likely saw the contract and set our indicator to "secured" if the original variable had that value, but "unsecured" either if the original so indicated *or* if the original was missing and the text field implied LPC saw the contract.

[12] One possible explanation for finance companies' more frequent use of secured debt is that lender-borrower agency problems are more severe for more highly leveraged borrowers, and collateral mitigates such problems (Stulz and Johnson (1985)).

**Table XII**

## Loan Terms: Spreads, Maturity, and Security

This table compares price and nonprice terms of loans made by banks and finance companies. In this table, the sample is the full sample of loans less those loans involving neither a bank nor a finance company and those involving mixtures of banks and other institutional types. Multiple-lender, finance-company-participating loans include at least one finance company in the lending group and may include banks and other types of institutions in the group.

|  | Single Lender | | Multiple Lenders | |
|---|---|---|---|---|
|  | Bank | Finance Co. | Banks Only | Finance Co. Participating |
| Median spread over LIBOR (basis points) | 250 | 402 | 163 | 275 |
| Median term to maturity (months) | 24 | 37 | 36 | 60 |
| Percentage of loans secured | 70 | 92 | 52 | 80 |
| Percentage of loans with borrowing base feature | 30 | 47 | 18 | 27 |

"borrowing base"—an appraised value of specified assets (often inventories and receivables). Loan agreements featuring a borrowing base need not be secured but usually are. We scan the Dealscan text field for indications that a loan features a borrowing base, and we construct an indicator using methods similar to those for the secured status indicator (footnote 11). Fractions of loans with a nonmissing indicator in each lender-type category that involve a borrowing base stipulation are shown in the last line of Table XII. As with secured status, both banks and finance companies use this technology frequently but finance companies more so.

Taken together, the comparisons of loan contract terms and lead lender status are consistent with the view that finance companies tend to make loans to observably riskier borrowers, but their corporate lending appears similar to that of banks in most other respects.

## V. Why Does Specialization Exist?

Why do finance companies tend to serve observably riskier borrowers? We offer evidence related to two explanations: (1) that regulation limits banks' ability to lend to risky firms; and (2) that banks avoid risky firms in order to preserve a reputation for reasonableness in renegotiations with borrowers. To shed light on these hypotheses, we perform a variety of tests in which we split finance companies and banks into various subsamples based on parentage. We also look at how finance companies' share of C&I lending has evolved over time, as well as the historical origins of finance company business lending. Although we present results of several *joint* tests of the hypotheses, our testing strategy is imperfect in that we can convincingly reject or confirm the *individual* hypotheses only if certain combinations of test results obtain—and we do not obtain them. On the whole, however, the results suggest that both regulatory and reputational mechanisms are important.

## A. The Hypotheses

Bank regulators, in their effort to limit excessive risk taking, may discourage banks from participating fully in the market for loans with high but manageable risk. For example, regulators may require banks to "classify" many high-risk loans. Even though collateral may limit exposure to losses on many such loans, regulators may require large loan loss reserves against them, with adverse consequences for regulatory capital and accounting measures of bank performance. It is not clear whether such supervisory action would affect only the insured commercial bank or be felt throughout the entire bank holding company (BHC), as holding companies and their non-bank subsidiaries are inspected and supervised by the Federal Reserve.[13]

Alternatively, specialization may be a by-product of a mechanism involving lender reputation as a solution to hold-up problems. Private debt commonly includes covenants that give lenders significant control rights, with some covenants limiting borrower actions in all states of the world and some giving the lender control when the borrower is in distress (Smith and Warner (1979), Berlin and Mester (1992), and Carey (1996)).[14] Borrowers naturally fear that lenders may extract rents in renegotiations, such as when a covenant waiver is needed (a hold-up problem), and thus prefer to deal with lenders with reputations for reasonableness. In this environment, it seems plausible that refusals to waive covenants and liquidations of borrowers, even when justified, could be costly to the lender's reputation. Of course, refusing waivers or forcing liquidation is most likely to be warranted for high-risk borrowers. Specialization may support conservation of reputational capital—high risk borrowers go to lenders with a reputation for being tough and, given their clientele, such lenders will be forced to liquidate borrowers and enforce covenants with high frequency. Low-risk borrowers go to other lenders, who are better able to maintain good reputations because liquidation and enforcement actions are rarely necessary.

It may be important that the two types of lenders be separate institutions if it is difficult for borrowers to distinguish reputations of different departments of the same bank, for example. Of course, there is no particular rea-

---

[13] A different element of regulation might also be responsible for specialization. U.S. bank holding companies are permitted to hold up to 5 percent of the voting stock of any firm and 20 percent more of all equity if nonvoting, but banks are permitted to hold equity positions in borrowers (straight or warrants) only as part of restructurings of troubled loans (though they may hold such equity for long periods). Finance companies in general face no such restrictions, and equity positions or warrants are anecdotally a common element of high-risk lending. Finance company subsidiaries of bank holding companies face limits on the amount of voting equity they can hold which are similar to the limits placed on the holding companies, but they may take warrants.

[14] The literature on financial distress (e.g., Gilson, John, and Lang (1990), Asquith, Gertner, and Scharfstein (1994), and Brown, James, and Mooradian (1993)) has examined the role of private lenders in restructurings and their propensity, relative to public bondholders, to relax covenants, restructure privately, or force bankruptcy. However, empirical work to date has not distinguished among different types of private lenders.

son that the low-risk lenders should be banks rather than finance companies—that would be a historical accident. Because this hypothesis is complicated, and we offer no model demonstrating the existence of such a mechanism, we view it as a speculation. But it does have anecdotal support, as does the regulatory hypothesis.

## B. Lending Specialization by Parent Type

Using logit regressions similar in structure to those presented in Section III, we model the choice of lender type for a variety of alternative pairs of types, focusing in each case on whether borrower risk differs. Results appear in Table XIII.

Under either hypothesis, borrowers at finance companies that are subsidiaries of U.S. bank holding companies should be less risky, on average, than borrowers at finance companies that are not affiliated with banks. The latter are not subject to bank regulation, and they have no bank affiliate with a reputation to be harmed by actions they take against borrowers. The hypotheses are jointly supported by column 1 of Table XIII, which shows that highly levered borrowers are significantly less likely to be served by a bank-affiliated finance company.

To test the reputational hypothesis more directly, we assume that a lender's name is a more important carrier of reputation than its affiliations. For example, suppose two finance companies are affiliated with banks, but one has a name similar to that of its affiliated bank (e.g, Citicorp Industrial Credit), whereas the other has a name very different from that of its bank affiliate (e.g., Heller Financial). If name is the primary carrier of reputation, borrowers may be more likely to mistake the actions of a similarly named finance company for those of the banking organization as a whole. Thus, tough actions by similarly named finance companies should impose more costs on affiliated banks than such actions by differently named finance companies, and similarly named finance companies should be less willing to lend to risky borrowers. Names should be unrelated to regulatory restrictions, however.

In column 2 of Table XIII, we split bank-affiliated finance companies into those with names similar to their parents' names and those with very different names. Strikingly, those with similar names tend to lend to less risky borrowers, consistent with the reputational hypothesis.[15]

---

[15] This result must be interpreted with some caution, however. Only a few sample BHC-affiliated finance companies have names very different from those of their parents. Heller Financial, a subsidiary of Fuji Bank, alone made more than 30 percent of the loans by such finance companies. When loans by Heller are dropped, the leverage coefficient in column 2 of Table XIII becomes insignificant, but of course power may be a problem due to the smaller sample size. Stripping down the specification to include only borrower sales, leverage, and year and purpose dummies increases the usable sample size, and in this specification the leverage coefficient is negative and significant whether loans by Heller are included or not.

**Table XIII**

**Lender Type Prediction Logit Model Results, Specifications Focusing on Reasons for Specialization**

The logit regression dependent variable varies by column. In column 1, the dependent variable is 1 if the lender is (lending group includes) a finance company subsidiary of a U.S. bank holding company (BHC), and 0 if it is (includes) a finance company not affiliated with a BHC. All loans not meeting these criteria (or meeting both) are omitted from the regression. In column 2 the sample includes only loans involving bank-affiliated finance companies; the dependent variable is 1 if the affiliated finance company's and bank's name are similar, and 0 if the names are different. In column 3, the dependent variable is 1 if the lender is (lending group includes) a U.S. bank-affiliated finance company and 0 if it is (includes) a U.S. bank that has a finance company affiliate. Estimated coefficients for control variables are not shown. Leverage is book value of total debt divided by total debt plus book value of equity. EBITDA is earnings before subtraction of interest expense, taxes, and depreciation and amortization. Loan purpose dummies are from purposes stated in Dealscan, aggregated into the two categories shown plus general purpose and working capital loans (the omitted purpose dummy). Miscellaneous-purpose loans were omitted from the samples to eliminate sparse-sample convergence problems related to purpose dummies. $p$-values of two-tailed tests are in parentheses.

| Independent Variable | 1<br>All Finance Co.<br>Loans<br>1 = U.S. BHC<br>finance co.<br>0 = nonBHC<br>finance co. | 2<br>BHC Finance Co.<br>Loans<br>1 = name similar<br>to bank's name<br>0 = different names | 3<br>BHC Affiliate<br>Loans<br>1 = U.S. BHC finance co.<br>0 = U.S. bank affiliated<br>with a finance co. |
|---|---|---|---|
| Intercept | 4.050<br>(0.0300) | 0.815<br>(0.6579) | −1.444<br>(0.2235) |
| Leverage (Book) | −2.919<br>(0.0016) | −2.293<br>(0.0013) | 0.516<br>(0.2833) |
| EBITDA/sales | 0.926<br>(0.5479) | 0.306<br>(0.8306) | −0.620<br>(0.4782) |
| Purpose: Recapitalization | −1.287<br>(0.0040) | −0.576<br>(0.1325) | 0.430<br>(0.1269) |
| Purpose: Takeover | −1.386<br>(0.0122) | −1.142<br>(0.0409) | 0.780<br>(0.0150) |
| Log sales | −0.745<br>(0.0001) | 0.138<br>(0.3468) | −0.250<br>(0.0012) |
| Market-to-book ratio | 0.183<br>(0.6431) | 0.426<br>(0.1670) | −0.292<br>(0.1987) |
| Sales growth (5-yr. avg.) | −1.180<br>(0.0031) | −0.197<br>(0.4956) | −0.700<br>(0.0439) |
| R&D/sales | −17.257<br>(0.0809) | 9.779<br>(0.4470) | −7.283<br>(0.1945) |
| No. of years of COMPUSTAT data before loan | 0.411<br>(0.0095) | 0.014<br>(0.9311) | 0.123<br>(0.2878) |
| No. of observations | 279 | 215 | 1207 |
| Pseudo-$R^2$ | 0.41 | 0.10 | 0.11 |

Direct tests of the regulatory hypothesis are more difficult to construct because bank regulation in the United States operates at both the bank and the bank holding company levels (holding companies and their nonbank affiliates are inspected by the Federal Reserve). Although in principle the standards are uniform, based on conversations with market participants, our prior was that bank examiners would be more likely to discourage loans to risky firms than inspectors of finance company subsidiaries of bank holding companies. However, as shown in column 3 of Table XIII, which compares loans by finance companies and affiliated banks, we find no difference in average riskiness. The coefficient on leverage has the expected sign, but is insignificant and relatively small in magnitude. Because this is a joint test of the regulatory hypothesis and our prior, however, it would be premature to interpret this as evidence against the regulatory hypothesis, as our prior may simply be wrong—perhaps bank-level and holding-company-level regulation is similar in practice as well as in principle.[16]

### C. Evidence from History

We attempt to shed additional light on the regulatory hypothesis by examining the time-series behavior of finance companies' share of aggregate commercial and industrial (C&I) lending and by considering some anecdotal evidence regarding finance companies' historical origins. If costs or restrictions imposed by bank regulators influence banks' share of aggregate C&I lending vis-à-vis finance companies, then shifts in banks' share of such loans ought to occur as regulations change. Figure 5 plots from 1970 to 1995 banks' share of the total of bank C&I loans and finance company "other business credit," the category of finance company receivables that most closely resembles bank C&I loans.

During this period, there were several changes in prudential bank regulation. In 1985, formal capital ratio requirements applicable to all U.S. commercial banks were first implemented. A few years later, the Basle Accord resulted in more and tighter capital regulation. In 1992, the FDIC Improvement Act imposed even tighter capital regulations. More generally, the banking crisis of the early 1990s led to intensive supervisory scrutiny of bank portfolios.

All of these developments are likely to have increased regulatory restraints on bank lending to riskier borrowers; the regulatory hypothesis suggests that such restraints should have decreased banks' share of the C&I loan market. However, Figure 5 shows only a modest decline in banks' share

---

[16] If BHC-wide regulation is responsible for specialization, finance companies affiliated with foreign banks should resemble U.S. bank affiliates because, technically, foreign bank subsidiaries are regulated like U.S. bank holding-company subsidiaries with respect to their U.S. operations. We ran a logit making this comparison and found that foreign bank affiliates tend to make loans to more highly leveraged borrowers. But again, the problem is that we are testing a joint hypothesis: It may be that foreign bank affiliates are treated differently by regulators de facto.

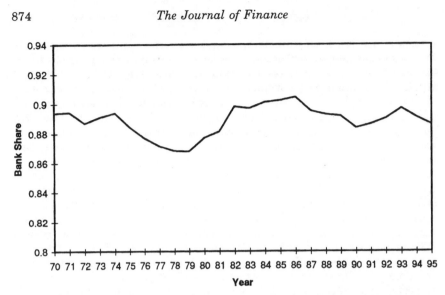

**Figure 5. Banks' Share of Total Bank and Finance Company C&I Lending.** This figure plots the variation over time in banks' and finance companies' relative shares of the aggregate market for commercial and industrial (C&I) loans to U.S. borrowers. Finance companies' share is one minus banks' share. Bank C&I lending includes loans made to U.S. borrowers by foreign banks and booked offshore (see McCauley and Seth (1992) and Nolle (1994) for estimates of the volume of such loans and for a discussion of the importance of making such adjustments).

of C&I lending since 1987.[17] The most notable shift in the bank share is the substantial dip during the mid to late 1970s and the subsequent recovery. This pattern is very likely a consequence of a decline and subsequent recovery in the availability of funding for bank lending. Regulation Q restrictions on deposit interest rates became a binding constraint with the rise in interest rates in the late 1970s, prompting outflows of bank deposits. The bank share of the loan market appears to recover as Regulation Q was phased out during the early 1980s. Although this suggests that finance companies' competitive position is influenced by bank regulation, Regulation Q funding restrictions, unlike prudential bank regulation, have no obvious implication for the relative risk characteristics of bank and finance company loan portfolios.[18]

[17] We ran some simple OLS regressions (not reported) of banks' share on dummy variables for the changes in capital regulation discussed above and some control variables for whether Regulation Q was binding. Results are quite sensitive to specification, but on the whole there is weak statistical support for capital regulation having an influence on banks' share.

[18] In passing, it is also notable that Figure 5 does *not* reveal any long-term trend toward a larger finance company share, as has often been claimed in popular accounts. This is mainly because the C&I loan statistics on which our ratio is based include foreign bank loans to U.S. nonfinancial borrowers, both onshore and offshore loans. As pointed out by McCauley and Seth (1992), Nolle (1994), and Boyd and Gertler (1993), failure to take account of such loans can seriously bias aggregate statistics.

Looking further back in history, if bank regulation is largely responsible for finance companies' specialization in lending to high-risk firms, one might expect the rise of finance companies to be associated with the advent of regulation, but that does not appear to be the case. Rather, the appearance of finance companies represented an improvement to the relatively incomplete structure of financial markets in the United States in the late 19th and early 20th centuries. At that time, many firms and individuals were poorly served by existing financial institutions and capital markets. The founder of one of the early finance companies (now CIT Group Holdings) recognized that many creditworthy producers and wholesalers of goods he met in the course of ordinary business—he managed a large department store—were unable to obtain financing from banks. These businesses economized on working capital by offering very large discounts for immediate cash payments for goods sold, with effective interest rates on the order of 100 percent per annum. CIT began offering credit at significantly lower effective rates of interest. Somewhat later, CIT and others offered to purchase consumer installment credit notes on cars and other goods, another market neglected by banks. At least to some extent, CIT's business opportunity appears to have resulted from the influence of the social mores of the time on finance: Many believed that installment lending was immoral, and that it would push consumers to financial catastrophe and result in a general economic contraction (see Wilson (1976)).

Taken as a whole, the formal and informal evidence offers some support for both the regulatory and reputational explanations of finance companies' specialization in serving higher-risk business borrowers. However, neither hypothesis alone appears to be able to explain all the facts. Regulation alone appears insufficient because the logit results only weakly support that hypothesis and the confirming historical evidence is also rather weak. Reputation alone as we have defined it also appears incomplete because the structure of the industry poses a puzzle for the reputation story: Why would a bank holding company set up a finance company at all, especially one with a similar name? The answers to such puzzles may well be associated with finance companies' broader activities (leasing, consumer lending, etc.) and thus more research on finance companies is needed to achieve a full understanding of their role in financial intermediation.

## VI. Concluding Remarks

Recent literature has emphasized that private debt contracts and the financial intermediaries which invest in private debt exist to address contracting problems that are difficult to solve using widely held and traded debt. In some of the literature, private debt is referred to generically, with the implication that it is all the same. Other research has suggested that banks in particular are special in their ability to efficiently evaluate and monitor borrowers.

This paper's evidence implies that neither of these simple views is adequate for a full understanding of private debt. It is private market intermediaries in general, not banks in particular, that are special; banks and finance companies appear to lend to equally information-intensive borrowers. However, all private debt and lenders are not the same. We find strong evidence of specialization within the private market, with finance companies tending to serve borrowers with higher observable risk, especially higher leverage. Coupled with the failure of the standard information problem proxies to predict lender type, this result appears inconsistent with purely information-based analysis of private debt.

Thus, the evidence implies that it is not enough to understand the public–private debt mix, a focus of some recent research (Diamond (1991) and Houston and James (1996)); the mix of varieties of private debt also matters. If contract restrictions and monitoring activity differ substantially across the varieties of private debt, different mixes in a firm's capital structure likely have different implications for corporate policy and public security holders.

We provide evidence supporting both regulatory and reputational explanations for the differing specializations of banks and finance companies in corporate lending, in the process providing formal empirical evidence that lender reputation plays a role in solving private debt contracting problems. However, more evidence is needed for a full understanding. In general, more research on the types of private debt and private lenders promises to advance understanding of the fundamentals of debt contracting, financial intermediation, and corporate finance.

## REFERENCES

Asquith, Paul, Robert Gertner, and David Scharfstein, 1994, Anatomy of financial distress: An examination of junk-bond issuers, *Quarterly Journal of Economics* 109, 625–658.

Beneish, Messod D., and Eric Press,1993, Costs of technical violation of accounting-based debt covenants, *The Accounting Review* 68, 233–257.

Beneish, Messod D., and Eric Press, 1995, Interrelation among events of default, *The Accounting Review* 70, 337–353.

Berger, Allen N., and Gregory F. Udell, 1990, Collateral, loan quality, and bank risk, *Journal of Monetary Economics* 25, 21–42.

Berger, Allen N., and Gregory F. Udell, 1995, Relationship lending and lines of credit in small firm finance, *Journal of Business* 68, 351–381.

Berlin, Mitchell, and Loretta J. Mester, 1992, Debt covenants and renegotiation, *Journal of Financial Intermediation* 2, 95–133.

Billett, Matthew Thayer, Mark J. Flannery, and Jon A. Garfinkel, 1995, The effect of lender identity on a borrowing firm's equity return, *Journal of Finance* 50, 699–718.

Black, Fischer, 1975, Bank funds management in an efficient market, *Journal of Financial Economics* 323–339.

Boczar, Gregory E., 1975, The evidence on competition between commercial banks and finance companies, *Journal of Bank Research* 6, 150–154.

Booth, James R., 1993, Loan collateral decisions and corporate borrowing costs, Working paper, Arizona State University.

Boyd, John H., and Mark Gertler, 1993, U.S. commercial banking: Trends, cycles, and policy, in Olivier Jean Blanchard and Stanley Fischer, eds.: *NBER Macroeconomics Annual 1993*, 319–367.

*Evidence on Specialization in Private Debt Contracting* 877

Brown, David T., Christopher M. James, and Robert Mooradian, 1993, The information content of distressed restructurings involving public and private debt claims, *Journal of Financial Economics* 33, 93–118.

Calomiris, Charles, and Mark Carey, 1994, Loan market competition between foreign and U.S. banks: Some facts about loans and borrowers, in *Proceedings of the 30th Annual Conference on Bank Structure and Competition* (Federal Reserve Bank of Chicago), 331–351.

Calomiris, Charles W., and Charles P. Himmelberg, 1995, Investment banking costs as a measure of the cost of access to external finance, Working paper, Columbia University.

Calomiris, Charles W., and Charles M. Kahn, 1991, The role of demandable debt in structuring optimal banking arrangements, *American Economic Review* 81, 497–513.

Cantor, Richard, and Anthony Rodrigues, 1993, Nonbank lenders and the credit slowdown, in *Studies on Causes and Consequences of the 1989–92 Credit Slowdown: Part I* (Federal Reserve Bank of New York), 251–317.

Carey, Mark, 1995, Are bank loans mispriced? Working paper, Federal Reserve Board, Washington, DC.

Carey, Mark, 1996, Financial covenants, private debt, and financial intermediation, Working paper, Federal Reserve Board, Washington, DC.

Carey, Mark, Mitch Post, and Steven A. Sharpe, 1996, Does corporate lending by banks and finance companies differ? Evidence on specialization in private debt contracting, Working paper, *Finance and Economics Discussion Series* 96-25, Federal Reserve Board, Washington, DC.

Carey, Mark, Stephen Prowse, John Rea, and Gregory Udell, 1993, The economics of private placements: a new look, *Financial Markets, Institutions and Instruments* 2, 1–66.

Chemmanur, Thomas J., and Paolo Fulghieri, 1994, Reputation, renegotiation, and the choice between bank loans and publicly traded debt, *Review of Financial Studies* 7, 475–506.

Diamond, Douglas W., 1984, Financial intermediation and delegated monitoring, *Review of Economic Studies* 51, 393–414.

Diamond, Douglas W., 1991, Monitoring and reputation: The choice between bank loans and directly placed debt, *Journal of Political Economy* 99, 689–721.

Fama, Eugene, 1985, What's different about banks? *Journal of Monetary Economics* 15, 29–36.

Fazzari, Stephen M., R. Glenn Hubbard, and Bruce C. Peterson, 1988, Financing constraints and corporate investment, *Brookings Papers on Economic Activity* 1, 141–195.

Flannery, Mark, 1989, Capital regulation and insured banks' choice of individual loan default risks, *Journal of Monetary Economics* 24, 235–58.

Flannery, Mark, 1994, Debt maturity and the deadweight costs of leverage: Optimally financing banking firms, *American Economic Review* 84, 320–331.

Gilson, Stuart C., Kose John, and Larry H. P. Lang, 1990, Troubled debt restructurings: An empirical study of private reorganization of firms in default, *Journal of Financial Economics* 27, 315–353.

Gorton, Gary, and James A. Kahn, 1993, The design of bank loan contracts, collateral, and renegotiation, NBER Working paper 4273.

Gorton, Gary, and George Pennacchi, 1993, Money market funds and finance companies: Are they the banks of the future?, in Michael Klausner and Lawrence G. White, eds.: *Structural Change in Banking* (Business One Irwin, Homewood, Ill.), 173–218.

Harris, Maury, 1979, Finance companies as business lenders, *Federal Reserve Bank of New York Quarterly Review* Summer, 35–39.

Houston, Joel, and Christopher James, 1996, Bank information monopolies and the mix of private and public debt claims, *Journal of Finance* 51, 1863–1890.

Houston, Joel, and Christopher James, 1995, Banking relationships, financial constraints and investment: Are bank dependent borrowers more financially constrained? Working paper, University of Florida.

James, Christopher, 1987, Some evidence on the uniqueness of bank loans, *Journal of Financial Economics* 19, 217–35.

Kwan, Simon, and Willard T. Carleton, 1995, The role of private placement debt issuers in corporate finance, Working paper, Federal Reserve Bank of San Francisco.

Kwan, Simon, and Willard T. Carleton, 1996, The structure and pricing of private placement corporate loans, Working paper, Federal Reserve Bank of San Francisco.

Mackie-Mason, Jeffrey K., 1990, Do firms care who provides their financing? in R. Glenn Hubbard, ed.: *Asymmetric Information, Corporate Finance, and Investment* (University of Chicago Press: Chicago, Ill.), 63–103.

McCauley, Robert N., and Rama Seth, 1992, Foreign bank credit to U.S. corporations: The implications of offshore loans, *Federal Reserve Bank of New York Quarterly Review* 17, 52–65.

Nakamura, Leonard I., 1991, Commercial bank information: Implications for the structure of banking, Working paper 92-1, Federal Reserve Bank of Philadelphia.

Nolle, Daniel E., 1994, Are foreign banks out-competing U.S. banks in the U.S. market? Working paper, Office of the Comptroller of the Currency, Washington, DC.

Papadimitriou, Dimitri B., Ronnie J. Phillips, and L. Randall Wray, 1994, An alternative in small business finance: Community-based factoring companies and small business lending, Public Policy Brief, The Jerome Levy Economics Institute, Annandale-on-Hudson, New York.

Petersen, Mitchell A., and Raghuram G. Rajan, 1994, The benefits of lending relationships: Evidence from small business data, *Journal of Finance* 49, 3–37.

Preece, Dianna C., and Donald J. Mullineaux, 1994, Monitoring by financial intermediaries: Banks vs. nonbanks, *Journal of Financial Services Research* 4, 191–200.

Rajan, Raghuram, 1992, Insiders and outsiders: The choice between informed and arm's-length debt, *Journal of Finance* 47, 1367–1400.

Remolona, Eli M., and Kurt C. Wulfekuhler, 1992, Finance companies, bank competition, and niche markets, *Federal Reserve Bank of New York Quarterly Review* Spring/Summer, 25–38.

*Secured Lender, The,* 1993, Asset-based lending is safe and sound lending, January/February 1976, 69–75.

Sharpe, Steven A., and Hien H. Nguyen, 1995, Capital market imperfections and the incentive to lease, *Journal of Financial Economics* 39, 271–294.

Sherman, Michael D., 1993, Survey of asset-based and other competitive lending activities, *The Secured Lender* November/December, 18–34.

Simonson, Donald G., 1994, Business strategies: Bank commercial lending vs. finance company lending, Working paper, University of New Mexico.

Smith, Clifford W., and Jerold Warner, 1979, On financial contracting: An analysis of bond covenants, *Journal of Financial Economics* 7, 117–161.

Stohs, Mark Hoven, and David C. Mauer, 1996. The determinants of corporate debt maturity structure, *Journal of Business* 69, 279–312.

Stulz, René, and Herbert Johnson, 1985, An analysis of secured debt, *Journal of Financial Economics* 14, 501–521.

Wilson, William L., *Full Faith and Credit: The Story of C.I.T. Financial Corporation, 1908–1975* (Random House, New York, NY).

Yelton, Barry D., 1993, Asset-based lending: An overview, *The Secured Lender* May/June, 22–31.

# [20]

# Trade Credit: Theories and Evidence

**Mitchell A. Petersen**
Northwestern University

**Raghuram G. Rajan**
University of Chicago

*Firms may be financed by their suppliers rather than by financial institutions. There are many theories of trade credit, but few comprehensive empirical tests. This article attempts to fill the gap. We focus on small firms whose access to capital markets may be limited and find evidence suggesting that firms use more trade credit when credit from financial institutions is unavailable. Suppliers lend to constrained firms because they have a comparative advantage in getting information about buyers, they can liquidate assets more efficiently, and they have an implicit equity stake in the firms. Finally, firms with better access to credit offer more trade credit.*

Trade credit is the single most important source of short-term external finance for firms in the United States.[1] Why do industrial firms extend trade credit when more specialized financial institutions such as banks could provide finance? There are many

We thank David Brown and Robert McDonald for helpful comments as well as seminar participants at Dartmouth College, the Federal Reserve Bank of Chicago, Federal Reserve Bank of New York, Harvard University, Hong Kong University of Science and Technology, Loyola University of Chicago, Notre Dame, Stanford University, University of Maryland, University of Wisconsin-Milwaukee, and the Western Finance Association. Rajan thanks the Center for Research on Securities Prices and the National Science Foundation for research support. Address correspondence to Mitchell A. Petersen, Department of Finance, J. L. Kellogg Graduate School of Management, Northwestern University, Leverone Hall, 2001 Sheridan Road, Evanston, IL 60208-2001.

[1] Rajan and Zingales (1993) report that accounts payable amounted to 15% of the assets for a sample of nonfinancial U.S. firms on Global Vantage while debt in current liabilities accounted for just 7.4%.

*The Review of Financial Studies* Fall 1997 Vol. 10, No. 3, pp. 661–691
© 1997 The Review of Financial Studies 0893-9454/97/$1.50

*The Review of Financial Studies / v 10 n 3 1997*

theoretical explanations for trade credit: Trade credit may provide access to capital for firms that are unable to raise it through more traditional channels. Suppliers may be better than specialized financial institutions in evaluating and controlling the credit risk of their buyers. If so, trade credit may be a way for firms with better access to credit markets to intermediate finance to firms with less access to credit markets. Alternatively, trade credit may allow suppliers to price discriminate using credit when discrimination directly through prices is not legally permissible. Finally, trade credit may be useful in reducing transaction costs or in providing assurances about the quality of the supplier's products. Unfortunately, there is very little systematic evidence about why trade credit is extended or which firms are the largest providers or users of trade credit. In this article, we shed some light on these issues.

The problem in testing theories of trade credit thus far has been the paucity of data. Databases like Compustat do not have the detail needed to test the nuances of the various theories that serve to distinguish them. In this article, we use a more detailed database compiled by the National Survey of Small Business Finance (NSSBF). This dataset focuses on small firms, which are more likely to face constraints on their ability to raise capital.

We find that suppliers appear to have some advantage in financing growing firms, especially if their credit quality is suspect. We conjecture three potential reasons for this. First, the evidence suggests these firms may be a source of future business, and suppliers are more willing to provide credit in anticipation of capturing this business. Second, suppliers may obtain the information they need at low cost from product market transactions, and perhaps from other suppliers. The information that suppliers use in monitoring and controlling repayment seems to be different from that used by financial institutions, perhaps because the nature of the credit is very different. Third, suppliers appear to rely on their ability to repossess and sell the goods against which credit has been granted.

The rest of the article is organized as follows. In Section 1, we flesh out the empirical implications of what we believe are the most important theoretical explanations of trade credit. In Section 2, we describe the data. Section 3 examines the determinants of trade credit granted by a firm, while Section 4 examines who receives credit. We conclude with a discussion of the results and suggestions for future research.

## 1. Trade Credit: Theories

We start with a brief description of the theories that have been proposed to explain the existence and use of trade credit. This list is not meant to be comprehensive. Rather, it reflects what we believe are the more plausible theories in the literature and the ones upon which our data can shed light.

## 1.1 Financing advantage theories of trade credit

The supplier may have an advantage over traditional lenders in investigating the credit worthiness of his clients, as well as a better ability to monitor and force repayment of the credit. This may give him a cost advantage over financial institutions in offering credit to a buyer [see Schwartz (1974) for an early exposition of the financing advantage theory of trade credit]. There are at least three sources of cost advantage.

**1.1.1 Advantage in information acquisition.** The supplier may visit the buyer's premises more often than financial institutions would. The size and timing of the buyer's orders also give him an idea of the condition of the buyer's business. The buyer's inability to take advantage of early payment discounts may serve as a trip wire to alert the supplier of a deterioration in the buyer's creditworthiness.[2] While financial institutions may also collect similar information, the supplier may be able to get it faster and at lower cost because it is obtained in the normal course of business.

**1.1.2 Advantage in controlling the buyer.** It may be in the nature of the goods being supplied that there are few economical alternative sources other than the supplier. If so, the supplier can threaten to cut off future supplies in the event of borrower actions that reduce the chances of repayment. This threat may be especially credible if the buyer accounts for a small portion of the supplier's sales. By contrast, a financial institution may have more limited powers; the threat to withdraw future finance may have little immediate effect on the borrower's operations. Furthermore, the financial institution's ability to withdraw past finance may be constrained by bankruptcy laws.

**1.1.3 Advantage in salvaging value from existing assets.** If the buyer defaults, the supplier can seize the goods that are supplied. The more durable the goods supplied, the better collateral they provide and the greater the credit the supplier can provide [see Mian and Smith (1992)]. Financial institutions can also reclaim the firm's assets to pay off the firm's loan. However, if the supplier already has a network for selling its goods, its costs of repossessing and resale will be lower than that of an institution. The advantage of suppliers over financial

---

[2] Theories of trade credit based on the seller having superior information to financial institutions or the seller using trade credit terms to sort buyers include Smith (1987), Brennan, Maksimovic and Zechner (1988), Biais, Gollier, and Viala (1993).

*The Review of Financial Studies / v 10 n 3 1997*

institutions will vary cross-sectionally depending upon the type of goods the supplier is selling and how much the customer transforms them. The less the goods are transformed by the buyer, the greater the advantage the supplier will have over financial institutions in finding an alternative buyer.[3]

## 1.2 Price discrimination through trade credit

Trade credit may be offered even if the supplier does not have a financing advantage over financial institutions because credit may be used to price discriminate [see Meltzer (1960), Schwartz and Whitcomb (1979), Brennan, Maksimovic and Zechner (1988), and Mian and Smith (1992)]. Since credit terms are usually invariant to the credit quality of the buyer, trade credit reduces the effective price to low-quality borrowers.[4] If this is the most price elastic segment of the market, then trade credit is an effective means of price discrimination. A natural reason why this segment's demand may be more price elastic is because it is typically credit rationed. If so, trade credit both lowers the effective price of the good and permits this segment to express its demand.

Another way of seeing this is to note that firms with a high margin (between sales and variable costs) for their product clearly have a strong incentive to make additional sales, but without cutting the price to existing customers. Since their profit on the next unit is higher, they would be willing to incur a positive cost to sell an additional unit, so long as it does not affect their previous sales. Under the assumption that antitrust laws prevent direct price discrimination, high-priced trade credit may be a subsidy targeted at risky customers. Creditworthy customers will find the trade credit overpriced and repay it as soon as possible. On the other hand, risky customers will find it worthwhile to borrow because trade credit may still be cheaper than the other sources they have access to.

A related version of this theory is that the supplier does not discriminate in favor of the risky customer solely because the customer's demand is more elastic in the short run. Rather, the supplier may have a long-term interest in the survival of the customer firm. This is especially true if the supplier has no potential substitutes for the customer. The supplier then factors in not only the net profit mar-

---

[3] Of course, if there are multiple creditors including financial institutions, bankruptcy laws may prevent a creditor from seizing particular goods unless the sale is on consignment, in which case this advantage may be irrelevant.

[4] Petersen and Rajan (1994) find that once the decision to grant credit has been taken, the credit terms seem to follow industry practice. They are usually not tailored to the particular borrower. Also see Smith (1980).

gin on current sales but also the present value of the profit margins on future sales when deciding whether to help the customer with credit. In other words, the supplier may want to protect the value of its implicit equity stake in the customer by providing it temporary short-term financing.[5]

### 1.3 Transactions costs theories

Trade credit may reduce the transaction costs of paying bills [Ferris (1981)]. Rather than paying bills every time goods are delivered, a buyer might want to cumulate obligations and pay them only monthly or quarterly. This will also enable an organization to separate the payment cycle from the delivery schedule. There are other versions of the transaction cost theory. There may be strong seasonalities in consumption patterns for a firm's products. In order to maintain smooth production cycles, the firm may have to build up large inventories. This has two costs: the costs of warehousing the inventory and the costs of financing it. Of course, the firm could lower prices in order to effect early sales. But there may be menu costs in doing this, as well as a loss in discretionary ability. By offering trade credit selectively, both across customers and over time, the firm may be able to manage its inventory position better [see, e.g., the classic Harvard Business School case, Harrington Corporation. Also see Emery (1987)]. The firm can thus reduce warehousing costs, especially if its customers have a better ability to carry inventory.

### 2. Data and Econometric Model

The above theories are hard to test without detailed firm-level data. Fortunately, the National Survey of Small Business Finances which we use contains detailed cross-sectional information on small firms. While these firms are much smaller than the typical firm on a database such as Compustat, some of the above theories are most applicable to small firms. A shortcoming of this survey is that with the exception of sales figures, all other data are available for only one year. This will limit the scope of our investigation. For instance, many of the testable implications of the transaction cost hypotheses pertain to the time series. To the extent that we do not have the data to test these theories, they should be considered part of the null.

---

[5] This argument is conceptually the same as that made in Petersen and Rajan (1995). In that model, banks in monopolistic credit markets were willing to subsidize borrowers with low interest rates since they expected to reap a return in the future by charging above-market rates to the firms that survived.

*The Review of Financial Studies / v 10 n 3 1997*

## 2.1 Sample Description

The National Survey of Small Business Finances was conducted in 1988–1989 under the guidance of the Board of Governors of the Federal Reserve System and the U.S. Small Business Administration. It targeted nonfinancial, nonfarm small businesses that were in operation as of December 1987.[6] Financial data were collected only for this fiscal year. The sample was stratified by census region (Northeast, North Central, South, and West), urban/rural location [whether the firm was located in a Metropolitan Statistical Area (MSA)], and by employment size [less than 50 employees, 50–100 employees, more than 100 employees, and less than 500 employees (the maximum size in the sample)]. The stratification was done to ensure that large and rural firms are represented in the sample. The response rate was 70% to 80%, depending upon the section of the questionnaire considered.[7]

There are 3404 firms in the sample, of which 1875 are corporations (including S corporations) and 1529 are partnerships or sole proprietorships. These firms are small. The median firm has a book value of assets of $130,000 and sales of $300,000. Nearly 90% of these firms are owner managed; 12% are majority owned by women and 7% by minorities. Nearly 28% of the firms in our sample are in the service industry. These firms are the smallest when measured on the basis of the book value of assets. Another 27% of the firms are in the retail trade industry. The largest firms on the basis of book assets are the manufacturing firms. Twelve percent of our firms are in the manufacturing industry.

One of the virtues of the NSSBF data is that it contains details that are not normally available in more commonly used datasets such as Compustat. The dataset not only includes information from the firm's balance sheet and income statement, but it is also a rich source of information on the current financing of the firm as well as the history of its interactions with financial institutions (i.e., length of relationships with financial institutions and whether the firm applied and was turned down for a loan in the last year). Firms report all outstanding financial obligations to financial institutions, nonfinancial firms, and individuals. Thus we know whether the firm has a mortgage, the unused portion of its line of credit (assuming it has one), and the interest rate on the firm's most recent loan. The dataset also reports some information about the type of financial institutions providing the firm with capital. For example, we know how long the firm has

---

[6] Firms involved in the agriculture, forestry, and fishing industry, finance and insurance underwriting, or real estate investment trusts were excluded from the survey.

[7] Firms were initially sent a series of worksheets that listed the financial information which the questionnaire would collect. The worksheets were followed by a telephone interview.

had a relationship with the financial institution and the services the institution provides.

## 2.2 Estimation strategy

We will attempt to verify some of the implications of the theories described earlier by examining the determinants of a firm's usage of trade credit. In addition to the standard proxies for trade credit usage, accounts receivable, and accounts payable, the NSSBF data provide us with proxies hitherto unavailable on a systematic basis. Even so, the lack of detailed data will necessitate some caution in interpreting the results.

When we view the firm as a supplier, its accounts receivable are a proxy for how much it lends its customers. When we view the firm as a customer, its accounts payable are its borrowing from its supplier. Thus we will examine both sets of trade credit relationships a firm has and treat the firms in our dataset first as lenders (suppliers) and then as borrowers (customers).

Although we refer to the level of the firm's accounts receivable as a proxy for how much it decides to lend, the level is not determined solely by the firm. A firm's accounts receivables are simultaneously determined by the firm's willingness and ability to extend credit, as well as the ability or desire of its customers to repay the amount when due. The former could be thought of as the supply of credit by the firm and the latter as the demand for credit by the customer (see Figure 1). When we regress a firm's accounts receivable on its financial characteristics in Section 3, we have not estimated a supply curve. The estimates are reduced form coefficients that include both supply and demand effects. For example, if we find that larger firms have higher accounts receivable, we could interpret this to mean that larger firms have better access to capital markets. Since they are less credit constrained they offer more credit to their customers (a supply effect). Alternatively, large suppliers may sell to small start-up firms with little access to capital markets. In this case, the credit demand by the customers of large firms is high. If they tend to repay their trade credit later than average, this would explain the higher level of accounts receivables for large firms. The ideal way to distinguish between these two effects (and possibly others) is to include information about both the supplier and customer in the model. In the absence of data on the customer, we cannot interpret the coefficients as structural. We still think it is possible to learn from the results, even given this problem.

The process of estimating trade credit borrowing by our firm is perhaps more informative (Section 4). The level of accounts payable is again determined simultaneously by both the credit extended to the firm by its suppliers as well as our firm's demand for funds. While

667

*The Review of Financial Studies / v 10 n 3 1997*

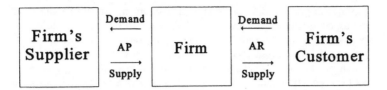

**Figure 1**
**The trade credit relationships**
The amount of trade credit extended between the firm and its suppliers will appear as the accounts payable on the balance sheet of the firm. The amount of trade credit extended between the firm and its customers will appear as accounts receivable on the balance sheet of the firm.

we do not have information on the firm's suppliers, we have a proxy for the quantity of credit supplied to the firm which is distinct from the firm's accounts payable. This is the fraction of the firm's annual purchases that are made on account. To understand why this may allow us to distinguish demand factors from supply factors, we have to consider credit terms in more detail.

Credit terms typically quote a discount date, a due date, as well as the amount of discount for payment by the discount date. For example, firms in the retail business quote trade credit terms as 2–10 net 30 [Smith (1987)].[8] This means the customer receives a 2% discount if their bill is paid within 10 days (the discount date) or they may pay the full amount by day 30 (the due date). These terms imply an escalating schedule of penalties. The customer gets what is effectively an interest-free loan until the tenth day. If the customer does not pay by the discount date, but pays on day 30, it is effectively borrowing over the next 20 days at an annual rate of 43.5%. If it does not pay by the due date, additional sanctions may be applied such as the eventual cutoff of supplies. These sanctions could raise the effective interest rate even higher.

Since there is no cost to accepting credit (at least until the discount date), the fraction actually purchased on account is relatively close to the fraction that is offered on account. This is the amount of credit voluntarily offered by suppliers. Thus when estimating the amount borrowed from suppliers, we will proceed in two steps. We first estimate the fraction of goods offered on credit to the firm, based on its characteristics. These estimates can then be used to predict the supply of trade credit to the firm. The second step is to note that the firm's accounts payable are a function both of the supply of trade credit and how long the firm takes to repay the debt. The former is proxied

---

[8] We do not know the actual discount offered, although we do know the fraction of credit purchases that have a discount associated with them.

for by the predicted value from the first regression, while the other variables in the regression control for demand factors. Holding the predicted supply of credit constant, greater demand for credit will appear as later payment and thus a higher level of accounts payable by our firm. We also use instrumental variables to estimate this equation and obtain very similar results. Whether we are able to distinguish the demand from the supply function is an empirical question we address below.

### 2.3 Data description: The use of trade credit by small and large firms

It is instructive to compare the use of trade credit by firms in our sample to the use of trade credit by larger firms in the much more widely used Compustat dataset. We calculate the accounts payable and accounts receivable to sales ratios by seven broad industry classifications for both our sample of small firms (NSSBF) and a sample of large firms (Compustat). To reduce differences induced by time we use Compustat data from 1987. The ratios are reported in Table 1. Small firms uniformly use less trade credit than the large firms. Firms in the NSSBF have accounts payable equal to only 4.4% of their sales, whereas for Compustat firms, accounts payable comprise 11.6% of their sales.[9]

Not only do the small firms borrow less through trade credit, they also extend less trade credit. The small firm accounts receivable:sales ratio is 7.3% versus 18.5% for Compustat firms. The difference in medians is similar (3.8% versus 16.1%). The greater use of trade credit by larger firms that is apparent in the aggregate numbers is also apparent in each of the industries. If small firms are more capital constrained we would expect them to extend less trade credit (smaller accounts receivables), but also borrow more through trade credit (have higher accounts payable). However, their desire to borrow through trade credit may not be matched by suppliers' willingness to lend. An analysis of which effect dominates is best left to the regression analysis. A final observation from Table 1 is that trade credit is not a net source of finance for most firms, large or small. Across the sample, trade credit is a net source of financing for about a third of the firms. The retail industry is the one exception. In this industry, trade credit is a net source of funds for over half the firms. The retail sector's low level of

---

[9] These averages are calculated including firms that report zero accounts payable (see Table 1). The fraction of firms with zero accounts payable is also reported in the table. Instead of standardizing by sales, we could have standardized by costs of goods sold. Using this standardization, small firms still have significantly lower levels of accounts payable. Accounts payable are 9.0% of cost of goods sold for the small firms and 18.9% of cost of goods sold for the large firms.

*The Review of Financial Studies / v 10 n 3 1997*

**Table 1**
**Accounts payables and receivables to sales ratios**

| Industry | Accounts payable/sales | | | Accounts receivable/sales | | |
|---|---|---|---|---|---|---|
| | Mean | Median | % Zero | Mean | Median | % Zero |
| Panel A: Small firms[a] | | | | | | |
| Mining | 6.1 | 4.6 | 23.1 | 9.9 | 6.9 | 30.8 |
| Construction | 5.4 | 2.5 | 25.7 | 10.4 | 7.8 | 14.8 |
| Manufacturing | 6.5 | 4.2 | 11.7 | 11.8 | 10.0 | 9.8 |
| Transportation/utilities | 3.8 | 1.9 | 31.5 | 8.1 | 6.5 | 17.6 |
| Wholesale trade | 7.0 | 3.8 | 15.6 | 8.1 | 7.0 | 6.2 |
| Retail trade | 3.9 | 1.7 | 26.6 | 3.0 | 0.4 | 39.6 |
| Services | 2.7 | 0.0 | 51.9 | 8.0 | 3.5 | 34.2 |
| Total | 4.4 | 1.8 | 30.9 | 7.3 | 3.8 | 26.5 |
| Panel B: Large firms[b] | | | | | | |
| Mining | 25.2 | 17.5 | 0.5 | 28.7 | 21.7 | 2.0 |
| Construction | 17.0 | 8.3 | 0.0 | 15.8 | 16.4 | 23.7 |
| Manufacturing | 9.8 | 7.4 | 0.4 | 19.1 | 17.0 | 0.6 |
| Transportation/utilities | 14.3 | 8.6 | 1.2 | 16.2 | 14.1 | 2.6 |
| Wholesale trade | 12.5 | 8.6 | 2.0 | 15.5 | 14.0 | 0.9 |
| Retail trade | 8.6 | 6.7 | 0.8 | 7.3 | 2.3 | 6.2 |
| Services | 10.6 | 6.5 | 1.1 | 22.4 | 19.4 | 3.7 |
| Total | 11.6 | 7.6 | 0.7 | 18.5 | 16.1 | 2.3 |

[a]This table is based on the National Survey of Small Business Finance. Firms in the agricultural (SIC 100–999) and financial sectors (SIC 6000–6999) were excluded. Ratios are expressed as percents.
[b]This table is based on the Compustat database. Firms in the agricultural (SIC 100–999) and financial sectors (SIC 6000–6999) were excluded. Ratios are expressed as percents.

accounts receivable may be the result of technological changes that have shortened the time it takes to collect (credit card) receivables. The growth of credit card usage will shrink the accounts receivables for retail firms. Accounts receivable have fallen monotonically as a fraction of sales from 9.4% in 1970 to 8.0% in 1980 to 7.3% in 1987.

We now examine the use of trade credit by small firms in greater detail. Even in our sample of small firms, borrowing on and extension of trade credit increases with firm size. Table 2 panel A shows the median accounts receivable:sales ratio when firms are grouped by industry and size. In all industries, the ratio increases with firm size. The median accounts payable:sales ratio also rises with firm size across industries (see Table 2, panel B). Thus, within the NSSBF sample, and between the NSSBF and Compustat sample, we find larger firms borrow and extend more trade credit.

The firm's purchases on account will be used as a measure of the credit it is supplied. We define annual credit purchases as the product of cost of goods sold and the fraction of purchases made on credit. We normalize this by the value of assets—because we want to draw a correspondence to leverage which is usually measured in terms of assets—and report medians in Table 2, panel C. There appears to be a weak positive relationship between credit purchases and size. Be-

Trade Credit: Theories and Evidence

**Table 2**
Trade credit offered and used by firms (by size and by industry)

| Book value of assets ($1000) | Asset percentile | Construction and mining | Manufacturing | Transportation | Wholesale (durables) | Wholesale (nondurables) | Retail | Services |
|---|---|---|---|---|---|---|---|---|
| Panel A: Accounts receivable[a] | | | | | | | | |
| Less than 15 | 0–10 | 0.00 (42) | 0.00 (17) | 0.00 (5) | 0.00 (7) | 0.02 (5) | 0.00 (54) | 0.00 (133) |
| 15–46 | 10–25 | 0.05 (86) | 0.02 (30) | 0.00 (7) | 0.05 (18) | 0.04 (12) | 0.00 (147) | 0.02 (167) |
| 46–130 | 25–50 | 0.07 (96) | 0.08 (52) | 0.03 (28) | 0.06 (36) | 0.06 (24) | 0.00 (288) | 0.04 (244) |
| 130–488 | 50–75 | 0.09 (102) | 0.10 (95) | 0.07 (33) | 0.08 (47) | 0.06 (36) | 0.01 (236) | 0.05 (215) |
| 488–2293 | 75–90 | 0.12 (54) | 0.12 (86) | 0.08 (22) | 0.09 (43) | 0.05 (40) | 0.01 (120) | 0.09 (83) |
| Over 2293 | 90–100 | 0.17 (33) | 0.12 (106) | 0.10 (13) | 0.11 (25) | 0.06 (28) | 0.01 (57) | 0.14 (42) |
| Panel B: Accounts payable to assets[b] | | | | | | | | |
| Less than 15 | 0–10 | 0.00 (42) | 0.00 (17) | 0.00 (5) | | 0.02 (12) | 0.00 (54) | 0.00 (133) |
| 15–46 | 10–25 | 0.02 (86) | 0.02 (30) | 0.00 (7) | | 0.12 (30) | 0.02 (147) | 0.00 (167) |
| 46–130 | 25–50 | 0.05 (96) | 0.05 (52) | 0.00 (28) | | 0.07 (60) | 0.03 (288) | 0.00 (244) |
| 130–488 | 50–75 | 0.08 (102) | 0.11 (95) | 0.02 (33) | | 0.12 (83) | 0.07 (236) | 0.00 (215) |
| 488–2293 | 75–90 | 0.14 (54) | 0.14 (86) | 0.04 (22) | | 0.16 (83) | 0.09 (120) | 0.03 (83) |
| Over 2293 | 90–100 | 0.18 (33) | 0.12 (106) | 0.05 (13) | | 0.17 (53) | 0.06 (57) | 0.03 (42) |
| Panel C: Credit purchases to assets[c] | | | | | | | | |
| Less than 15 | 0–10 | 2.54 (45) | 2.01 (12) | 0.00 (2) | 2.99 (9) | | 1.31 (28) | 0.00 (70) |
| 15–46 | 10–25 | 1.38 (68) | 1.10 (18) | 0.00 (4) | 1.77 (21) | | 1.02 (98) | 0.00 (117) |
| 46–130 | 25–50 | 1.36 (82) | 0.91 (47) | 0.00 (18) | 1.26 (49) | | 1.24 (200) | 0.00 (169) |
| 130–488 | 50–75 | 0.98 (83) | 1.25 (82) | 0.00 (29) | 2.07 (72) | | 1.36 (195) | 0.00 (158) |
| 488–2293 | 75–90 | 1.55 (47) | 1.42 (70) | 0.00 (23) | 2.00 (75) | | 1.43 (109) | 0.00 (68) |
| Over 2293 | 90–100 | 1.85 (27) | 1.33 (89) | 0.00 (11) | 2.03 (48) | | 1.85 (49) | 0.00 (41) |

[a]This panel describes the median accounts receivable:sales ratio for firms in the NSSBF. The number of firms in each cell is reported in parenthesis.
[b]This panel describes the median accounts payable to assets ratio for firms in the NSSBF. The number of firms in each cell is reported in parenthesis.
[c]Credit purchases are defined as the product of cost of goods sold and the fraction purchased on account. The panel describes the median purchases: assets ratio for firms in the NSSBF. The number of firms in each cell is reported in parenthesis.

*The Review of Financial Studies / v 10 n 3 1997*

cause of the nature of their business, both transportation and service firms make very few purchases, hence their credit purchases are also small.

## 3. Who Offers Credit?

### 3.1 The determinants of accounts receivable
We now test how the level of accounts receivable depends on the characteristics of the supplier. All the above theories would predict that firms that are more creditworthy and have greater observed access to institutional credit should offer more finance. The data confirms this in large measure, though there is some surprising new evidence. The use of trade credit as a means of price discrimination also suggests that the amount of credit offered should increase in the firm's margins. This is supported by the data.

**3.1.1 The supplier's access to financing.** In Table 3, we regress the firm's accounts receivable:sales ratio against proxies for the firm's own access to financing, the firm's characteristics, and its incentive to price discriminate. A summary of the data is reported in Table 4. Since the firm's ability to extend credit will depend upon its ability to raise funds in capital markets, we must control for the availability and cost of the firm raising capital. Both firm size and firm age are proxies for the credit worthiness of a firm. Typically, larger firms borrow more even though they have higher cash flows and fewer growth opportunities. This suggests that they are more creditworthy. The age of a firm indicates how long it has survived. It is an important proxy, especially in this sample, for firm quality and the firm's reputation with potential lenders.[10] Both variables should have a significant influence on the amount of credit extended by the firm.

This is indeed the case (see Table 3, column 1). A firm with $670,000 in assets (the 75th percentile) extends an additional 3.3% more of its sales in the form of accounts receivables as compared to a firm with $55,000 in assets (the 25th percentile). The effect is economically large for the median accounts receivable:sales ratio is 3.9% (see Table 4).

---

[10] In addition to being better credit risks themselves, older firms may also know more about their customers. In this case, older firms would face less risk in extending credit to their (long time) customers than younger firms. To test this hypothesis, we can separately control for the firm's age and the firm's age under current management. Only the latter variable is included in Table 3. A firm's age under current management is the empirically important variable in predicting the firm's access to capital [see Petersen and Rajan (1994)]. Thus, including the age of the firm can act as a proxy for the maximum amount of time the firm may have known its customers. Holding the time under current management constant and increasing the age of the firm lowers the firm's accounts receivable, which is inconsistent with this alternative hypothesis.

*Trade Credit: Theories and Evidence*

**Table 3**
**The determinants of accounts receivable**

| Independent variable | I | II | III | IV$^a$ | V$^b$ |
|---|---|---|---|---|---|
| Log(book value of assets) | .013* | .013* | .014* | .012* | .010* |
|  | (.001) | (.001) | (.001) | (.001) | (.003) |
| Log(1 + firm age) | .006* | .024** | .025* | .013 | .033 |
| (in years) | (.002) | (.010) | (.010) | (.009) | (.021) |
| Log(1 + firm age)$^2$ |  | −.004*** | −.004** | −.003 | −.007 |
| (in years) |  | (.002) | (.002) | (.002) | (.004) |
| Maximum available line of | .027* | .027* | .026* | .021* | .103** |
| credit/sales | (.006) | (.006) | (.006) | (.005) | (.051) |
| Net profits/sales | −.031* | −.033* |  |  |  |
|  | (.010) | (.010) |  |  |  |
| Net profits/sales |  |  | −.004 | −.009 | .023 |
| if positive, zero otherwise |  |  | (.013) | (.012) | (.042) |
| Net profits/sales |  |  | −.101* | −.105* | −.153* |
| if negative, zero otherwise |  |  | (.021) | (.020) | (.054) |
| Percent sales growth (86–87) | .032* | .033* | .033* | .004 | −.002 |
| if positive, zero otherwise | (.010) | (.010) | (.010) | (.009) | (.027) |
| Percent sales growth (86–87) | −.051* | −.053* | −.048* | −.030* | −.039 |
| if negative, zero otherwise | (.009) | (.009) | (.009) | (.008) | (.028) |
| Gross profit margin/sales | .016** | .060** | .056** | .117* | .201** |
|  | (.008) | (.028) | (.028) | (.030) | (.079) |
| (Gross profit margin/sales)$^2$ |  | −.043*** | −.045*** | −.118* | −.206** |
|  |  | (.027) | (.026) | (.030) | (.096) |
| Firm is in MSA (0,1) | .014* | .014* | .014* | .007** | .012 |
|  | (.004) | (.004) | (.004) | (.003) | (.009) |
| Wholesaler of durable goods |  |  |  |  | .001 |
| (0,1) |  |  |  |  | (.009) |
| Number of observations | 1805 | 1805 | 1805 | 1805 | 277 |
| Adjusted $R^2$ | 0.141 | 0.144 | 0.150 | 0.315 | 0.154 |

The dependent variable is the accounts receivable:sales ratio reported by the firm. The coefficients are estimated using ordinary least squares. Standard errors are in parentheses. Each regression has a constant whose coefficient is not reported. Firms in the financial industry (SIC 6000–6999) and the service industry (SIC 7000–8999) are excluded unless otherwise stated. When the distribution of a variable was highly skewed for high values, we recoded the highest percent of values to the 99th percentile of the distribution. Similarly if it was highly skewed for low values, we recoded the lowest percent of values to the 1st percentile of the distribution. These variables include accounts receivable to sales, net profits to sales, sales growth, and gross profit margin to sales.

$^a$40 two-digit SIC indicators are included in addition to the constant.
$^b$Includes only wholesalers (SIC codes 5000–5199).
*,**,***Coefficient significantly different from zero at the 1%, 5%, and 10% level, respectively.

**Table 4**
**Summary statistics**

| Variables | Mean | Median | Standard deviation |
|---|---|---|---|
| Accounts receivable:sales ratio | 0.066 | 0.039 | 0.083 |
| Log(book value of assets) | 12.18 | 11.96 | 1.93 |
| Log (1 + firm age) (in years) | 2.35 | 2.39 | 0.88 |
| Maximum available line of credit/sales | 0.06 | 0.00 | 0.09 |
| Net profit/sales | 0.10 | 0.05 | 0.23 |
| Percent sales growth (86–87) if positive, zero otherwise | 0.26 | 0.07 | 0.59 |
| Percent sales growth (86–87) if negative, zero otherwise | −0.04 | 0.00 | 0.11 |
| Gross profits/sales | 0.40 | 0.35 | 0.25 |

*The Review of Financial Studies / v 10 n 3 1997*

Older firms also extend more credit to their customers. However, the magnitude of the coefficient is smaller. Increasing firm age from 0 to 10 years old (the minimum to the median) raises the firm's accounts receivables by 1.4% of sales. The problem is we have not allowed for sufficient non-linearity in the relationship. Additional years add significantly to a firm's reputation early in its life, but have little effect later. When we include the square of the log of firm age (see Table 3, column 2), both age terms are statistically significant. Accounts receivable first increase with age and eventually fall. Accounts receivable peak when a firm is about 19 years of age. Once correctly specified, the effect of age doubles. When a firm matures from a startup to a 10-year-old firm, the credit it extends through accounts receivable rises by 3.5% of its sales. However the decrease in accounts receivable with age is not nearly as dramatic.[11]

While the above two variables proxy for the firm's access to external financing, we also have data on the maximum amount that can be drawn on the firm's line of credit (if it has one). This is strongly positively correlated with the amount of accounts receivable that a firm extends ($\beta_{\text{Max Line of Credit}} = 0.027$, $t = 4.8$). Interestingly, when we break this amount into the portion that has been drawn down already and the portion that is as yet untapped (regression not reported), the amount that has already been drawn down has an estimated coefficient of 0.028, while the amount that is unused has an estimated coefficient of 0.017. Thus the line of credit does appear, in part, to be directly financing accounts receivable.[12]

Surprisingly, net income, which is a proxy for internal cash generation, is negatively correlated with accounts receivable (see Table 3, column 1). We would expect that firms with more internal cash—higher profits—would be able to extend more credit to their customers. Conditioning on the other variables, however, profitable firms offer less trade credit. We will offer an explanation of this finding shortly.

---

[11] Another explanation of the eventual decline in credit offered with firm age is that the oldest firms in our sample are fundamentally different. Recall that to be in the sample, the firm has to have less than 500 employees. Thus, if a firm grew enough, it would not be in our sample. The really old firms are likely to be an adversely selected sample of old firms. Since they may also have higher costs of credit, sample selection and the cost of credit is enough to explain the age effect. We are careful to ensure that the results we highlight hold even when we restrict the sample to firms below 10 years of age where the effect of this selection bias is likely to be small.

[12] Analogous to this finding, Calomiris, Himmelberg, and Wachtel (1995) find that firms issuing commercial paper also offer more trade credit. So firms with access to short-term financing offer more short-term credit. We also include accounts payable (as a measure of trade credit borrowing) and the fraction of purchases made on credit (as a measure of the supply of trade credit). The coefficient estimates are positive and significant ($\beta_{\text{Payables}} = 0.056$, $t = 5.01$, $\beta_{\text{Purchases}} = 0.0002$, $t = 2.9$). The positive coefficients on payables and credit purchases are consistent with the idea that firms with greater access to financing extend more credit. However, the direction of causality between payables and receivables is debatable.

**3.1.2 Economic shocks.** Changes in a firm's sales may indicate shocks to the firm's operations and help us explain the coefficient on net profits. We include sales growth multiplied by indicators if positive and negative. Firms that have had positive sales growth offer slightly more receivables ($\beta = 0.032$, $t = 3.2$). The coefficient on positive sales growth is economically small.

Firms that have seen their sales decline, however, find their accounts receivable:sales ratios increase significantly ($\beta = -0.051$, $t = -6.0$). A firm whose sales drop by 30% (the average change for firms with sales declines), increases its accounts receivable:sales ratio by about 3% of sales.[13] Given that accounts receivable is short-term credit—the days receivable outstanding is less than 30 days on average—it is unlikely that the downward stickiness is because credit is offered before the collapse in sales and is not yet due. Rather, firms in trouble may use the extension of credit to attempt to maintain their sales. This leads to a possible explanation of why profits are negatively correlated with receivables. When we split profits up into positive profits and losses (Table 3, column 3), only losses are significantly negatively correlated with accounts receivable ($\beta = -0.10$, $t = -4.8$). Thus, firms making losses tend to extend more credit.

To explore this further, we separate losses into losses if the firm has positive sales growth and losses if the firm has negative sales growth. The coefficient on the former is almost twice as large ($\beta = -0.126$, $t = -4.579$) as the latter ($\beta = -0.072$, $t = -2.289$). So firms that grow fast (and generate losses in the process) seem to extend more credit and perhaps "buy" sales. But firms in distress (negative sales growth and negative income) also offer more trade credit. Some of the increase in credit extended by distressed firms may be involuntary. It is possible that debtors are less willing to repay a distressed firm. Since repayment is enforced by the threat of cutting off future supplies, such threats are less credible when the supplier is distressed. Also, a distressed firm may be less capable of legal action to recover its dues. The delay in repaying a distressed firm is a potential cost of financial distress that deserves further study.[14]

**3.1.3 Price discrimination—trade credit as a strategic tool.** Although our focus so far has been on whether a firm has the ability to

---

[13] This does not necessarily imply that the level of credit extended increases. Consider a firm whose initial accounts receivable:sales ratio is 7.3%—the average for firms in our sample. The regression results predict that a drop of 30% in the firm's sales is associated with the accounts receivable: sales ratio rising to 8.8%. Therefore, after sales drop by 30%, accounts receivable are now $0.103*0.700*$ initial sales, that is, 6.2% of initial sales. Accounts receivable have fallen, but only 15%.

[14] We also check that all our prior results are not driven only by distressed firms. We define a firm to be distressed if it has negative sales growth and negative net income. Dropping these firms or dummying them out does not qualitatively affect the coefficient estimates.

*The Review of Financial Studies / v 10 n 3 1997*

finance trade credit, our data allow us to test the price discrimination theory. It predicts that trade credit should be positively related to a firm's gross profit margin. The larger a firm's gross profit margin the greater its incentive to sell, and if necessary, finance an additional unit. We find a positive relationship (see Table 3, column 1) when only the gross profit margin is included ($\beta = 0.016$, $t = 2.0$). The correct specification is once again nonlinear (see Table 3, column 2). When the gross profit margin squared is included, the coefficient on the linear term rises from 0.016 to 0.060 ($t = 2.1$), while the coefficient on the squared term is $-0.043$ ($t = -1.7$). This implies that accounts receivable increase with gross profit margins until they reach about 70%. This is about the 90th percentile for gross margins in our sample. The effect is also economically sizable. An increase in gross margin from 0% to 35% (the median) increases accounts receivable by about 1.5% of assets.[15]

### 3.2 Robustness checks

At least part of the pattern of trade credit can be explained by differences in historical practices across industries [see Dun and Bradstreet (1970)]. To test whether our results are simply picking up historical accident, it is constructive to see whether they survive the inclusion of more-detailed industry dummies. In Table 3, column 4, we include 40 two-digit SIC dummies. This is the finest classification of industry contained in our data. Not surprisingly, the explanatory power of the regressions rises. However, the relationships discussed above are qualitatively unchanged. The economic significance of the gross profit margin is even greater when we control for industry. This is reassuring since gross profit margins differ significantly across industries and could therefore have proxied for unmeasured industry effects.

We have a large number of wholesalers in the sample. This group is further divided into those who sell durables and those who sell nondurables. By restricting the regression to this relatively homogenous group, we can check if the above results hold within group also. As the estimates in column 5 suggest, this is indeed the case.[16]

---

[15] We have argued earlier that firms with higher cashflow should be able to extend more credit. The gross profit margin is not merely a proxy for cashflow. Net income which is included in the regression is a better proxy. In fact, the correlation between the two is only 0.28.

[16] This subsample also enables us to test the "quality guarantee" theory. By this we refer to the argument that trade credit may serve as a warranty for product quality. Firms without reputations in the product market can attest to the quality of their goods by bearing the cost of financing them until such time as the buyer can ascertain quality for himself [see Smith (1987) and Long, Malitz, and Ravid (1994)]. This would imply that firms without a good reputation—that is, smaller and younger firms—offer more credit and that firms producing durables offer more credit than firms producing perishables. We include an indicator for wholesalers of durables. The quantity of credit offered by these merchants is both statistically and economically insignificantly different from those selling nondurables ($\beta = 0.001$, $t = 0.1$).

We also include an indicator if the firm is located in an MSA (regression not reported). A firm in an MSA extends significantly more credit ($\beta = 0.014$, $t = 3.8$). A potential explanation is that institutional lending is less available in the competitive metropolitan areas [see Petersen and Rajan (1995)] and therefore trade credit substitutes for it. Alternatively, the kind of information trade creditors obtain is less valuable in rural areas where everyone knows everybody else's business. Another possible explanation is that the penalties a creditor can exert on late payers is higher in rural areas, hence credit is repaid more promptly.

To summarize, we find evidence suggesting the cost and availability of finance to the supplier is an important consideration in determining whether credit is extended. This is consistent with any theory of trade credit. We do, however, find that higher gross margins are associated with higher accounts receivable, which is consistent with the price discrimination theory.

What was not predicted by any of the prior theoretical discussion is the greater extension of credit by firms with negative income and negative sales growth. Presumably such firms have higher costs of raising finance. If their extension of credit is voluntary, it suggests a different rationale for trade credit than any of the theories discussed so far. One explanation could be window dressing: managers of distressed firms make sales to low credit quality customers in order to keep the numbers up. Another could be that these firms try (but do not quite succeed) in signaling financial strength: strong firms offer credit and weakening firms attempt to imitate them.[17] Finally, if the extension is involuntary, it suggests a cost of financial distress little investigated in the literature.

## 4. Who Receives Credit?

We now move on to analyze who receives credit from their suppliers and for how long. This will enable us to better examine the relevance of the financing advantage theory. A firm's stock of accounts payable will depend upon both the amount of credit its suppliers offer as well as the firm's demand for trade credit. We divide our analysis into two steps. We start by examining how much credit the firm's suppliers offer the firm. We conjecture that a firm's creditworthiness should affect how much credit it is offered. But we will also test if

---

[17] A related conjecture (we thank David Brown for this) is that financially strong firms with deep pockets set trade credit standards in the industry so that the product-credit package puts financially weaker firms at a disadvantage. Such a conjecture begs the question of why the package cannot be unbundled by the other firms or customers, but suggests interesting avenues for future research.

*The Review of Financial Studies / v 10 n 3 1997*

factors that give the supplier a greater advantage in financing the firm influence how much credit it is offered.

## 4.1 Determinants of who is offered credit—purchases on account

### 4.1.1 Customer's credit quality.
We know the fraction of purchases that each firm makes on credit. Since the opportunity to purchase on credit and borrow interest free for a few days dominates paying cash, we expect all firms to borrow during the initial period.[18] Thus the firm's purchases on account should be an accurate measure of the credit offered to the firm. Since we do not know what fraction of a firm's cost of goods sold are purchases, we estimate the firm's credit purchases as the fraction of purchases made on credit multiplied by the firm's cost of goods sold. This variable is mismeasured because, in addition to purchases, the cost of goods sold includes other items. The most important of these is likely to be wages.[19] As the survey does not report wages separately, we include employment scaled by assets in our regressions to correct for the inclusion of wages in our dependent variable. As can be seen in Table 5, employment is strongly positively correlated with the dependent variable. Having controlled for wages, the remaining variation in the dependent variable should capture the variation in credit purchases from suppliers, which is what we are trying to explain.

The firm's credit quality may be especially important in determining whether it is offered credit. The explicit price of trade credit does not appear to vary with the customer's credit quality—customers in an industry get standard trade credit terms [see Smith (1987)]. If suppliers do not use prices—they do not charge lower-quality borrowers a higher explicit price—then they must use quantity restrictions. We therefore expect higher-quality firms to be offered more credit. This is indeed the case. Firms of observably higher credit quality—as measured by variables such as size and profitability—receive significantly more credit from their suppliers (see Table 5, column 1). This effect survives the inclusion of two-digit SIC indicators (Table 5, column 2).

We have identified at least three aspects of the financing advantage theory: the supplier has better information than financial institutions,

---

[18] Few industries offer discounts for immediate cash payment [see Dun and Bradstreet (1970)]. Most trade credit is advanced for a specific period of time. For example, payment may be due 10 days after the goods are delivered. Other trade credit is offered with a discount if the bill is paid prior to the due date. In either case, the implicit cost of the loan until the discount or due date is effectively zero.

[19] In general, firms do not borrow from their employees. An interesting historical exception can be found in Rogers (1994).

*Trade Credit: Theories and Evidence*

**Table 5**
**Trade credit supply: Purchases made on credit over assets**

| Independent variable | I | II[b] | III | IV | V |
|---|---|---|---|---|---|
| Proxy for wages | | | | | |
| Employees/assets ($10,000) | .200* | .247* | .366* | .199* | .174* |
| | (.042) | (.041) | (.068) | (.042) | (.043) |
| Firm credit quality | | | | | |
| Log(book value of assets) | .049 | .042 | .105** | .051 | .060*** |
| | (.033) | (.032) | (.048) | (.033) | (.033) |
| Net profits/assets | .326* | .326* | .420* | .325* | |
| | (.058) | (.055) | (.092) | (.058) | |
| Log(1+firm age) | .044 | .073 | −.353 | .044 | .078 |
| | (.196) | (.186) | (.272) | (.196) | (.195) |
| Log(1+firm age)2 | −.029 | −.039 | .031 | −.030 | −.037 |
| | (.043) | (.041) | (.061) | (.043) | (.043) |
| Firm is incorporated | .476* | .510* | .221 | .481* | .452* |
| | (.108) | (.103) | (.153) | (.108) | (.108) |
| Relationships with financial institutions | | | | | |
| Longest relationship with lender | −.015 | −.017 | .121 | −.018 | .003 |
| (in years) | (.066) | (.063) | (.098) | (.066) | (.065) |
| Risk premium on most recent loan | | | −.015 | | |
| (premium over treasuries) | | | (.024) | | |
| Firm denied request for loan | | | | −.213 | |
| in the last year (0,1) | | | | (.203) | |
| Relationships with suppliers | | | | | |
| Net profits/assets | | | | | .422* |
| (if profits > 0) | | | | | (.064) |
| Net profits/assets | | | | | −.844* |
| (if profits < 0 and sales growth > 0) | | | | | (.275) |
| Net profits/assets | | | | | .228 |
| (if profits < 0 and sales growth < 0) | | | | | (.433) |
| Liquidation costs[a] | | | | | |
| Percent of inventory which | −.725* | | −.661* | −.717* | −.709* |
| is finished goods | (.167) | | (.229) | (.167) | (.166) |
| Number of observations | 1644 | 1706 | 758 | 1644 | 1644 |
| $R^2$ | 12.0 | 21.2 | 15.4 | 12.0 | 13.0 |

The dependent variable is the firm's purchases on account divided by assets. Purchases on account is calculated as the percent of purchases made on account times the firm's costs of goods sold. The coefficients are estimated using ordinary least squares. Standard errors are in parentheses. Each regression includes one-digit SIC industry dummy variables (unless otherwise specified) and a constant whose coefficients are not reported. Firms in the financial industry (SIC 6000–6999) and service industry (SIC 7000–8999) are excluded unless otherwise stated. Due to low asset values 23 firms had extremely high ratios for purchase on account to assets. These observations were recoded to the 99th percentile of the distribution. We tested this approach by estimating the regression using a tobit with an upper limit of the 99th percentile of the purchase on account regression. The empirical results are qualitatively similar. Low asset values also caused some of the independent variables to be skewed. When the distribution of a variable was highly skewed, we recoded the upper percent of values to the 99th percentile of the distribution. These variables include operating profits to assets, employees to assets, and number of trade creditors to assets.
[a]Industry variables are calculated using 1987 Compustat data. Each variable was calculated for firms in a two–digit SIC code industry. These average industry values were then matched to the firms in the NSSBF.
[b] This regression includes 40 industry dummies, one for each two–digit SIC code in our dataset. The percent of inventory which is finished goods is based on industry averages and must therefore be dropped from this specification.
*,**,***Coefficient significantly different from zero at the 1%, 5%, and 10% levels, respectively.

the supplier has better control, and the supplier has a better ability to liquidate goods. We can test for each of these aspects.

*The Review of Financial Studies / v 10 n 3 1997*

**4.1.2 Relationships with financial institutions.** From earlier work [Petersen and Rajan (1994)], we know that relationships with financial institutions appear to increase the availability of finance from financial institutions to the firm. We use the length of the longest relationship with a financial institution to measure how much information, possibly private, the lender has accumulated about the firm. It is also a measure of the firm's reputation in debt markets [Diamond (1989)]. If suppliers rely on signals sent by prior relationships with lenders in their decision to offer credit, trade credit offered should increase with the strength of relationships with financial institutions. If, on the other hand, suppliers generate their own information, proxies for relationships with financial institutions should not matter.

A relationship with a financial institution does not increase the trade credit offered to a firm. The effect of relationship length on the supply of trade credit is economically tiny and statistically insignificant ($\beta = -.015$, $t = -0.2$). We also include the number of banks from which the firm borrows. A firm that concentrates its borrowing with a single lender will develop a stronger relationship with that lender. The coefficient on the number of banks from which the firm borrows is also small and statistically insignificant (regression estimates not reported). Even whether a firm borrows from a bank at all, a fact easily observable to the firm's trade creditors, has no effect on the supply of trade credit.

The interest rate a financial institution charges its customers should include all credit quality relevant information that the lender can observe and thinks is relevant. Suppliers may look to it as a superior source of information. As a proxy for this information source, as well as an additional measure of credit quality, we include the risk premium (the firm's interest rate relative to a treasury bond of comparable maturity) a firm paid on its most recent loan. Firms that pay higher risk premiums on their most recent loan do receive less credit from suppliers. However, the effect is small and not statistically significant (see Table 5, column 3). Finally, we include an indicator for firms that have asked for but have been denied credit by financial institutions in the last year. Firms that have been denied their request for a loan in the previous year are offered less on account. The coefficient is not statistically significant.[20] These results appear to rule out the possibility that suppliers rely on banks to monitor on their behalf.

---

[20] Firms that report they were denied a loan request in the last year may not be the best or the worst firms. The best firms are not denied, because they are good credit risks. The lowest-quality firms may not bother to apply for a loan they do not expect to receive. It is only firms of intermediate quality that apply for and are turned down for a loan. If this is correct, the proxy is noisy, which would explain why being turned down for a loan has a statistically insignificant effect on the amount of trade credit a firm is offered.

**4.1.3 Relationships with suppliers.** We explore the value to suppliers of investing in future relationships with their customers by examining the coefficient on profits in Table 5 more closely. Recall that suppliers offer more credit to profitable firms. When we estimate separate coefficients for firms making profits and firms making losses, we find the coefficient on negative net profits is negative ($\beta = -.551$, $t = -2.3$, regression not reported). So suppliers seem to offer credit to the most profitable *and* the most unprofitable firms. This suggests that they might have some advantage in lending to lower-quality credit risks who might otherwise be shut out off from institutional financing.

Both the financing advantage theory and the price discrimination theory suggest that trade credit should fall off for the lowest-quality credits. Why do suppliers seem eager to lend to the most unprofitable firms, when financial institutions are not? As argued earlier, one reason may be that a firm that is currently unprofitable may not remain so in the future. By investing in relationships with currently unprofitable but growing firms, a supplier may capture future profitable business from the firm.[21] To test this idea, we divide the net profit variable into three categories: firms with positive profits, firms with negative profits but positive sales growth, and firms with negative profits and negative sales growth. The results are reported in column 5. The last group are distressed firms, for whom low profits lowers the credit offered by suppliers.[22] By contrast, growing firms who are currently loosing money get more credit the lower their profits ($\beta = -.844$, $t = 3.1$). A possible explanation of this is that, first, suppliers have an increasing advantage in lending to poorer-quality credits, and second, they do so only if they anticipate that growth in future business will compensate them for the risks they are taking.[23] By lending to these apparently high-risk firms, suppliers can invest in the future viability and profitability of their customers.

---

[21] Banks in concentrated capital markets act in a similar way. They extend more credit to young firms than do banks in more competitive capital markets. The banks in concentrated capital markets anticipate correctly that they will be able to recoup their investment by charging higher rates when the firms expand and mature [Petersen and Rajan (1995)]. If suppliers have more market power over their customers than banks, they may be able to finance firms that banks cannot profitably finance.

[22] The coefficient on net profits for firms with negative profits and negative sales growth is positive, but not statistically different from zero. Neither is it statistically different from the coefficient on net profits for firms with positive profits. Pooling distressed firms with profitable firms has no effect on the explanatory power of the regression.

[23] An alternative explanation is that firms with positive sales growth are more likely in the long run to repay than firms with negative sales growth. While this may indeed be true for long-term loans, trade credit is so short term that the growth in sales should have little impact. The probabilities of default may be lower in the group with positive sales growth (though one could argue firms in this group are more likely to be cash constrained). This could explain the higher credit extended to the group with positive sales growth, but not why the credit extended increases as firms become more unprofitable.

681

*The Review of Financial Studies / v 10 n 3 1997*

Finally, we include an indicator if the firm is located in an MSA (coefficient not reported). These firms are offered more credit, though the coefficient is not statistically significant.

### 4.1.4 Liquidation costs.
The final source of financing advantage is the greater ability of suppliers (relative to financial institutions) to liquidate the firm's assets. Suppliers can repossess and resell goods to other buyers. But once the customer has transformed its inputs into outputs, they will be more costly for the supplier to sell and thus its competitive advantage over financial institutions in liquidating these goods is lost. As a proxy for the supplier's advantage in liquidating the borrower's assets we use the fraction of the firm's inventory that are finished goods. Since the NSSBF does not provide us with information on the composition of each firm's inventory, we use the average finished goods:total inventory ratio for Compustat firms with the same two-digit SIC code in 1987. The composition of inventory in an industry has a large effect on the credit that suppliers offer firms in our sample. A firm with only finished goods inventory, compared to zero finished goods inventory, will lower its purchases on account by 73 percentage points ($t = -4.3$).

To summarize our findings, suppliers do worry about the ability of the borrower to repay. In general, a firm with lower credit quality gets less credit. However, suppliers appear to support growing, cash-constrained firms with credit. Not only do the prospects of future profits give them a greater incentive to finance their customers, they may also have a financing advantage over financial institutions. Suppliers seem to use different criteria from financial institutions in assessing whether to offer credit. The availability of trade credit is not significantly related to the existence (or absence) of lending relationships with financial institutions. Finally, the ability of suppliers to liquidate collateral seems important. The lower the ratio of finished goods to inventory, the greater the amount of credit offered. Thus the financing advantage for suppliers appear to come from their low cost of information acquisition and their ability to more efficiently liquidate assets.

### 4.2 Determinants of who demands trade credit—accounts payable
#### 4.2.1 Supply of trade credit.
Having examined the supply of trade credit, we now turn to the determinants of a firm's demand for trade credit. Once a firm has purchased a good on credit, how long it waits (or can wait) before repaying will determine the level of the firm's accounts payable. An analysis of accounts payable can shed addi-

tional light on the financing advantage theory, though it will have no implications for the price discrimination theory.

We explain the firm's stock of accounts payable (normalized by assets) using the predicted supply of trade credit and proxies for the firm's demand for trade credit. We use the estimates from the previous section (Table 5, column 1) to calculate a predicted value of the purchases on account:assets ratio. Recall that this ratio is mismeasured to the extent that costs of goods sold include wages. We, therefore, subtract from the predicted ratio the firm's employee:assets ratio times the coefficient estimate of 0.200 for the employees:assets ratio estimated in Table 5, column 1.[24]

The firm's stock of accounts payable increases in our estimate of the purchases that are supplied on account to the firm (see Table 3, column 1). The coefficient estimate of 0.027 is economically large and statistically significant. This coefficient implies that an increase in the purchases:assets ratio from zero to the median of 1.38 increases the firm's stock of accounts payable by about 4% of assets.

**4.2.2 Demand for funding.** Conditional on the supply of credit, the amount by which firms stretch their accounts payable should be determined by their demand for credit in general and their demand for trade credit in particular. The variables that proxy for the firm's credit demand include measures of the firm's investment opportunities, asset maturity, liquidity, as well as access to credit from financial institutions.

Firms that are growing more quickly presumably have more investment opportunities. A proxy for this is the change in sales scaled by assets. The underlying relationship between the demand for trade credit and sales growth is nonlinear. Increases in sales raise the firm's demand for credit. Each additional dollar of sales increases the demand for trade credit by 1.2 cents.[25] To put this number in perspective, a firm's cost of goods sold averages 43% of sales in our sample. So firms finance about 3% of this with trade credit. However,

---

[24] Instead of including an estimate of the supply of trade credit in this regression, we could have included the purchases on account variable from Table 5 and then used instrumental variables to estimate the coefficients. This is done in column 2 of Table 6. In addition to the other variables in the regression (column 1), we used employees per thousand dollars of assets, whether the firm was incorporated, and the percent of inventory which is finished goods as instruments. These are the variables we used in Table 5 to estimate trade credit supply. The coefficient estimates in column 1 and 2 are similar.

[25] For twelve percent of our sample, 1986 sales are not reported. We code the change in sales equal to zero for these firms and include a dummy variable for whether 1986 sales are missing. If these observations are essentially new high growth firms, then we would expect their demand for trade credit to be higher than the trade credit demand from a firm with zero sales growth. We do not find this. Firms with missing sales have slightly lower demand for trade credit than a firm which reports no change in sales. The coefficient on this variable is not statistically significant. Thus coding the firms with missing sales as having zero sales growth is correct on average.

*The Review of Financial Studies / v 10 n 3 1997*

trade credit is short-term credit. If we recalculate this percent based on monthly sales (rather than annual sales) increasing by one dollar, then firms finance about 33% of their increased purchases with trade credit. The coefficient on sales declines is negative, but small in magnitude ($\beta = -0.004$). Firms whose sales fall have higher accounts payable, but only slightly more. Combined with the evidence from Table 5, this suggests that suppliers are willing to finance high sales growth firms by offering more credit.

In samples of large firms, investment opportunities are typically thought to decline in firm size and firm age. For small firms, it is less clear that this is the case, for certain projects may become viable only after the firm has acquired adequate assets and experience. Our estimates (Table 3, column 1) indicate that firm size and firm age are only weakly positively correlated with the firm's accounts payable. The strong positive relationship apparent in Table 2 between firm size and accounts payable therefore comes mainly from the fact that larger firms are offered more trade credit—presumably because they are better credit risks—not because they have greater demand to borrow from their suppliers (see Table 5, column 1; Table 6, column 1).

We also include a crude proxy for whether firms need credit. Firms in the dataset report whether they have applied for a loan or line of credit from a financial institution in the past year. Fourteen percent of the firms in our sample have. We find that loan applications are uncorrelated with demand for trade credit. If there are nontrivial costs of applying, the decision to apply may depend upon the firm's expected success in getting a loan. So a number of firms may need credit but may not apply. This may explain why we do not find a significant correlation.

It is unlikely that a firm will finance long-term projects with trade credit. Most firms match the maturity of assets and liabilities, and Diamond (1991) and Hart and Moore (1991) present rationales for this. A measure of a firm's demand for short-term financing is its short-term assets.[26] Firms whose assets consist mainly of current assets (excluding cash) demand significantly more trade credit. At the margin, 17% of the firm's current assets are financed by trade credit (see Table 6, column 1). Interestingly, cash holdings have no empirical effect (coefficient not reported).[27]

---

[26] The current assets ratio obviously varies dramatically across industries, ranging from a low of about 20% of assets in mining (SIC 1000–1499) and transportation and utilities (SIC 4100–4999) to a high of almost 60% in the wholesale trade industry (SIC 5000–5199).

[27] Firms with high cash holdings may have enough cash to not require accounts payable financing, or may have hoarded cash to repay accounts payable. It is not a priori clear which effect should predominate. The estimated coefficient on cash to assets is only 0.026 ($t = 1.1$).

*Trade Credit: Theories and Evidence*

**Table 6**
**Trade credit demand: Accounts payable over assets**

| Independent variable | I | II[b] | III[c] | IV | V |
|---|---|---|---|---|---|
| **Supply of trade credit** | | | | | |
| Predicted supply of trade credit/assets[a] | .027** | .029** | .085* | .027** | .028** |
| | (.013) | (.013) | (.019) | (.013) | (.013) |
| **Demand for capital** | | | | | |
| Δ sales (86–87)/assets if positive, zero otherwise | .012* | −.001 | .012* | .012* | .012* |
| | (.003) | (.008) | (.003) | (.003) | (.003) |
| Δ sales (86–87)/assets if negative, zero otherwise | −.004 | .007 | −.002 | −.005 | −.004 |
| | (.005) | (.006) | (.005) | (.005) | (.005) |
| 1986 sales missing (0,1) | .002 | −.001 | .002 | .002 | .005 |
| | (.014) | (.017) | (.014) | (.014) | (.014) |
| Log(book value of assets) | .005 | .004 | −.002 | .006** | .004 |
| | (.003) | (.003) | (.003) | (.003) | (.003) |
| Log(1+firm age) | .029*** | .036*** | .023 | .029*** | .029*** |
| | (.016) | (.019) | (.017) | (.016) | (.016) |
| Log(1+firm age)² | −.006*** | −.006 | −.004 | −.006 | −.006 |
| | (.004) | (.004) | (.004) | (.004) | (.004) |
| Current assets excluding cash/assets | .166* | .156* | .168* | .169* | .161* |
| | (.013) | (.018) | (.015) | (.013) | (.013) |
| Firm applied for loan during previous year (0,1) | .002 | .005 | .003 | .003 | .001 |
| | (.010) | (.011) | (.010) | (.010) | (.010) |
| **Credit availability** | | | | | |
| Net profits/assets | −.019* | −.021* | −.039* | −.019* | −.019* |
| | (.006) | (.007) | (.007) | (.006) | (.006) |
| Available line of credit/assets | | | | −.063* | |
| | | | | (.022) | |
| Firm denied credit request during previous year (0,1) | .012 | .019 | .010 | .012 | .012 |
| | (.017) | (.019) | (.017) | (.017) | (.017) |
| Log(1+longest relationship with lender) (in years) | −.011** | −.018* | −.009*** | −.011* | −.013* |
| | (.005) | (.006) | (.005) | (.005) | (.005) |
| Firm is located in an MSA | .017*** | .012* | .013*** | .017*** | .019* |
| | (.007) | (.008) | (.007) | (.007) | (.007) |
| **Price of trade credit** | | | | | |
| Percent of credit purchases offered with early payment discounts | | | | | .006 |
| | | | | | (.011) |
| Early payment discounts missing | | | | | −.035* |
| | | | | | (.010) |
| Number of observations | 1968 | 1588 | 1968 | 1968 | 1968 |
| $R^2$ | 14.9 | 20.0 | 17.6 | 15.3 | 15.6 |

The dependent variable is the accounts payable:asset ratio reported by the firm. The coefficients are estimated using ordinary least squares. Standard errors are in parentheses. Each regression includes five industry dummy variables and a constant whose coefficients are not reported. Firms in the financial industry (SIC 60000–6999) and service industry (SIC 7000–8999) are excluded unless otherwise noted. Low asset values also caused some of the independent variables to be skewed. When the distribution of a variable was highly skewed, we recoded the upper percent of values to the 99th percentile of the distribution. These variables include purchase on account to assets, operating profits to assets, employees to assets, and number of trade creditors to assets.
[a] Predicted trade credit supply is the estimated value of purchase on account over assets from Table 5, column 1. We adjusted our estimate of purchases on account by subtracting off 0.200 (the coefficient on employment over assets) times the value of employment over assets for each observation. This removed the mismeasurement in purchases on account caused by wages being included in cost of goods sold, but not purchases on account.
[b] This regression was estimated with instrumental variables. In addition to the other variables in the regression, we used employees per thousand dollars of assets, whether the firm was incorporated, and the percent of inventory which is finished goods as instruments. These are the variables that we used in Table 5 to estimate trade credit supply.
[c] This regression includes 36 industry dummies, one for each two-digit SIC code in our dataset.
*,**,***Coefficient significantly different from zero at the 1%, 5%, and 10% levels, respectively.

*The Review of Financial Studies / v 10 n 3 1997*

In addition to age and size, we also include dummy variables for each of the two-digit industries represented in the data to proxy for differences in industry investment opportunities in Table 3, column 3. This increases the magnitude and statistical significance of several of the estimate.

**4.2.3 Credit availability.** Having corrected for the availability of trade credit, the firm's investment opportunities, and the maturity of the firm's assets, we now investigate if the firm's liquidity position and the availability of credit from financial institutions affects the demand for trade credit. If it does in a significant way, this would suggest that trade credit financing is lower in the "pecking order" than internally generated cash [Myers (1984)]. The firm's ability to generate cash internally decreases its demand for trade credit.[28] Each additional dollar of monthly profits lowers the firm's demand for trade credit by 23 cents (= .019 * 12) and the estimate is significant at the 1% level. The statistically significant and negative coefficient for cash flow in the demand equation (see Table 6) and the statistically significant and positive coefficient in the supply equation (see Table 5) adds credence to our argument that the firm's purchases on account measures the credit offered to the firm by its suppliers, and that we have therefore distinguished the "supply for trade credit" equation from the "demand for trade credit" equation.

The firm's demand for trade credit may also depend upon its access to credit from financial institutions. We first examine several explicit measures. Four percent of the firms in our sample report were turned down for a loan or were approved for an amount less than they requested. Since we have also included an indicator if the firm applied for a loan, we can distinguish firms that applied and were granted a loan from firms that apply and get less than they demanded. The latter demand more trade credit, although the coefficient is not precisely estimated. As discussed earlier, this may be a biased measure of rationing because credit-constrained firms that do not expect to receive a loan may choose not to apply at all, making the proxy noisy.

The second explicit measure of rationing we consider is the availability of unused lines of credit. Almost one-third of the firms in our

---

[28] Theoretically, cashflow rather than profits divided by assets is the correct variable. However, the NSSBF does not report depreciation as a separate expense in the profit and loss statement. We could estimate depreciation as a fixed fraction of the firm's assets and add estimated depreciation to operating profits to get cashflow. However, since we then divide profits (or cashflow) by assets, this would only change the coefficient estimate but not the explanatory power of the regression or the variable. Alternatively we could estimate depreciation as a constant percentage of the firm's property, plant, and equipment. Using a depreciation rate of 10 percent raises the coefficient on cashflow to assets marinally.

sample have lines of credit they have not completely drawn down. We find that firms with larger unused lines of credit demand less trade credit. The coefficient (−0.063) is large (see Table 6, column 4). While firms appear to finance their short-term assets with short-term liabilities, they appear to treat institutional finance and trade credit as substitutes. Note that by including only the unused portion of the line of credit, we avoid picking up the accounting identity.

Petersen and Rajan (1994) find that relationships between firms and financial institutions relax credit rationing. If trade credit borrowing comes lower down in the pecking order than borrowing from close financial institutions, we should find that the strength of relationships with institutions is negatively correlated with demand for trade credit. This is exactly what the data show. We use the log of one plus the length of the firm's longest relationship with a financial lender to measure the strength of the lending relationships. Longer relationships with institutions correlate negatively with a firm's demand for trade credit.[29] An increase in the length of the maximum relationship from 0 to 10 years (the minimum to the median), lowers a firm's accounts payables by over 3% of its assets. This result implies that trade credit is relied on mainly by firms that are constrained by their institutional lenders. If a firm can secure enough credit from its financial institution, it does not stretch out its accounts payable as long, suggesting that borrowing from trade creditors, at least for longer periods of time, is a more expensive form of credit. Finally, firms demand slightly more trade credit in MSAs where institutional financing is weaker. Coupled with our observation from Table 5 that firms in MSAs are offered somewhat more credit, this suggests that trade credit substitutes for institutional finance in more competitive markets.

**4.2.4 Price of trade credit.** Thus far we have argued that suppliers do not vary the price of trade credit much. But does the demand for trade credit depend on its price? We do not know the specific terms a firm faces, but we do know what fraction of its credit purchases are accompanied by early payment discounts. In our sample, three-quarters of the firms report receiving early payment discounts on at least some of their credit purchases. The early payment discount should encourage firms to pay early and thus reduce their accounts payable, holding the supply of credit constant. To test the price elasticity of demand we include the percent of credit purchases offered with early payment discounts. The coefficient is very small and sta-

---

[29] The length of the longest relationship is also correlated with the firm's age. The correlation coefficient is 0.55 in our sample. However, the length of the longest relationship is not a proxy for firm age which is included in the regression.

*The Review of Financial Studies / v 10 n 3 1997*

tistically insignificant (see Table 6, column 5). This is consistent with the argument that missing early payment discounts is expensive and the decision to take advantage of early payment discounts is driven not by the implicit cost of this credit but instead by whether the firm has an alternative source of credit. Only credit constrained firms take advantage of this expensive form of credit.

## 5. Discussion and Conclusion

We now attempt to draw together the evidence we have accumulated on the rationale for trade credit. In the absence of confirmatory evidence, some of these conclusions may better be termed conjectures, and await future research.

As might be expected, suppliers offer more credit to firms of higher credit quality. But these firms use less trade credit if they have access to institutional finance. Coupled with the observation that suppliers provide strong incentives for firms not to extend the term of the offered credit by giving substantial discounts for prompt payment and strict penalties for late payment [see Petersen and Rajan (1994)], this suggests that trade credit is more expensive than institutional finance, especially if used for medium-term financing.

The desire of suppliers to restrict firms to short-term financing suggests an advantage in that type of financing over financial institutions. What is the nature of that advantage? One possibility is that creditors obtain information about the firm routinely, and at low cost, from their transactions with the firm. Of course, financial institutions also produce private information about the firms to whom they lend [Slovin, Sushka, and Polonchek (1993)]. Suppliers do not, however, appear to rely on information provided by lending relationships; measures of the strength of institutional relationships or the risk premium on institutional loans granted have little effect on how much trade credit a firm is offered. A reasonable conclusion from the data is that suppliers collect and use different information than financial institutions. The most valuable aspect of this information may be how current it is. By monitoring repayment and using discounts as a trip wire, suppliers get a quick read on a firm's financial and economic health [see Smith (1987)].

Suppliers appear to use this informational advantage in lending to firms of currently suspect credit quality (current losses) but with high potential for future business (high sales growth), as well as firms neglected by financial institutions. Why might suppliers continue extending credit to these firms when financial institutions do not? In addition to getting faster information about any deterioration of the firm's prospects, suppliers may continue to have a significant hold over the firm, so long as it continues production. This is unlike financial institutions whose control may be diminished by bankruptcy filings. Furthermore, suppliers can take added precautions such as making consignment sales when the customer's failure to avail of discounts or pay on time sets off a trip wire. Suppliers are in the best position to liquidate the goods they have sold the firm, provided it has not been transformed (and provided they are secured so suppliers can seize the goods). This may be why we find that the supply of trade credit increases in the extent to which inventories consist of raw materials.

In addition to having a greater ability to enforce repayment from risky firms, suppliers may also have greater incentive to offer credit than do financial institutions. When suppliers cannot discriminate by price, trade credit may be necessary to finance sales to those who cannot obtain credit from institutions. A supplier who cannot price discriminate has two margins with which to work: the price of credit and the price of the good. Thus the supplier's profit margin from a sale enables him to bear a lower profit or a greater loss on the credit than can a financial institution. We find that trade credit offered by a firm increases in the size of its margins on sales. Furthermore, if a firm and its supplier continue to transact in the future, the supplier has an implicit equity stake in the firm equal to the present value of the margins he makes on current and future sales of the product tc the firm. This may far exceed the implicit equity stake a financial institution may have because of the potential for future business, and may explain why suspect growing firms tend to be financed by suppliers.

In summary, we find from our analysis of small firms that suppliers may have a financing advantage, especially when a firm is financially troubled. Also, we have indirect evidence from the correlation between margins and receivables that a firm may offer trade credit as a means of price discrimination. A more direct test of the price discrimination theory would be possible if we knew the set of firms to which a supplier sold. If the set of firms had uniformly high credit ratings, there would be no need to offer credit. If they had uniformly low credit ratings, the supplier could simply lower the price and let financial institutions finance. It is only if buyers come with all manner of credit rating that trade credit becomes a viable instrument of price discrimination. This test awaits more comprehensive data.

The single most important step for future research is to examine the determinants of trade credit over time. This will permit more powerful tests of the financing advantage and transaction costs hypotheses. More detailed data (for instance, on the relationships between suppliers and customers) will allow researchers to investigate the price discrimination and quality guarantee hypotheses more fully. The role

*The Review of Financial Studies / v 10 n 3 1997*

of financially healthy suppliers in intermediating finance to growing firms as well as the implications for the transmission of monetary policy deserves further investigation. Finally, we show that firms with sales declines are forced to extend relatively more trade credit without getting any more support from suppliers. This points to a potential cost of financial distress that has hitherto not been investigated. Furthermore, it suggests that trade credit may be a strategic tool for deep-pocket firms to increase the minimum scale of staying in the industry. The scope for research is obvious.

**References**

Biais, B., Gollier, and Viala, 1993, "Why Do Firms Use Trade Credit?," mimeo, CEPR Conference, San Sebastian, Spain.

Brennan, M., V. Maksimovic, and J. Zechner, 1988, "Vendor Financing," *Journal of Finance*, 43, 1127–1141.

Calomiris, C., C. Himmelberg, and P. Wachtel, 1995, "Commercial Paper, Corporate Finance, and the Business Cycle: A Microeconomic Perspective," *Proceedings of the Carnegie-Rochester Conference Series on Public Policy*, 42, 203–250.

Diamond, D., 1989, "Reputation Acquisition in Debt Markets," *Journal of Political Economy*, 97, 828–861.

Diamond, D., 1991, "Debt Maturity Structure and Liquidity Risk," *Quarterly Journal of Economics*, 56, 709–738.

Dun and Bradstreet, 1970, *Handbook of Credit Terms*, Dun and Bradstreet, New York.

Emery, G. W., 1987, "An Optimal Financial Response to Variable Demand," *Journal of Financial and Quantitative Analysis*, 22, 209–225.

Ferris, J. S., 1981, "A Transactions Theory of Trade Credit Use," *Quarterly Journal of Economics*, 94, 243–270.

Hart, O., and J. Moore, 1991, "A Theory of Debt Based on the Inalienability of Human Capital," working paper, MIT.

Long, M. S., I. B. Malitz, and S. A. Ravid, 1994, "Trade Credit, Quality Guarantees, and Product Marketability," *Financial Management*, 22, 117–127.

Meltzer, A. H., 1960, "Mercantile Credit, Monetary Policy, and Size of Firms," *Review of Economics and Statistics*, 42, 429–437.

Mian, S., and C. W. Smith, 1992, "Accounts Receivable Management Policy: Theory and Evidence," *Journal of Finance*, 47, 169–200.

Myers, S. C., 1984, "The Capital Structure Puzzle," *Journal of Finance*, 39, 575–592.

Petersen, M., and R. Rajan, 1994, "The Benefits of Lending Relationships: Evidence from Small Business Data," *Journal of Finance*, 49, 3–37.

Petersen, M., and R. Rajan, 1995, "The Effect of Credit Market Competition on Lending Relationships," *Quarterly Journal of Economics*, 60, 407–444.

Rajan, R., and L. Zingales, 1993, "What Do We Know about Capital Structure: Evidence from International Data?," CRSP working paper, University of Chicago.

*Trade Credit: Theories and Evidence*

Rogers, F. H., 1994, "Man to Loan $1500 and Serve as Clerk: Trading Jobs for Loans in Mid-Nineteenth-Century San Francisco," *Journal of Economic History*, 54, 34–63.

Schwartz, R. A., and D. Whitcomb, 1979, "The Trade Credit Decision," in J. Bicksler (ed.), *Handbook of Financial Economics*, North-Holland, Amsterdam.

Schwartz, R. A., 1974, "An Economic Model of Trade Credit," *Journal of Financial and Quantitative Analysis*, 9, 643–657.

Slovin, M. B., M. E. Sushka, and J. A. Polonchek, 1993, "The Value of Bank Durability: Borrowers as Bank Stakeholders," *Journal of Finance*, 48, 247–266.

Smith, J., 1987, "Trade Credit and Information Asymmetry," *Journal of Finance*, 4, 863–869.

Smith, K., 1980, *Readings on the Management of Working Capital*, West Publishing, St. Paul, Minnesota.

# [21]

Journal of Financial Economics 39 (1995) 271–294

*613–36*

*('95)*

# Capital market imperfections and the incentive to lease

*(US)*

*G31*

*G32*

Steven A. Sharpe*, Hien H. Nguyen

*Federal Reserve Board, Washington, DC 20551, USA*

(Received September 1994; final version received April 1995)

## Abstract

This paper evaluates the influence of financial contracting costs on public corporations' incentives to lease fixed capital. We argue that firms facing high costs of external funds can economize on the cost of funding by leasing. We construct several measures of leasing propensity, plus some *a priori* indicators of the severity of financial constraints facing firms. We find that the share of total annual fixed capital costs attributable to either capital or operating leases is substantially higher at lower-rated, non-dividend-paying, cash-poor firms – those likely to face relatively high premiums for external funds.

*Key words*: Leasing; Asymmetric information; Capital structure
*JEL classification*: G31; G32; E22

## 1. Introduction

The corporate lease-versus-buy decision is typically analyzed under the Miller–Modigliani framework of financial structure irrelevance, that is, studies usually begin by invoking the assumptions of perfectly competitive capital markets with no transaction costs or information asymmetries. The popularity of this approach owes largely to the finance literature's emphasis on tax-related incentives (e.g., Miller and Upton, 1976; Myers, Dill, and Bautista, 1976). Indeed,

---

*Corresponding author.

The views expressed herein are the authors' and do not necessarily reflect those of the Board of Governors or the staff of the Federal Reserve System. We would like to thank George Fenn, Jean Helwege, Hamid Mehran, Michael O'Malley, James Schallheim (referee), and Clifford Smith for helpful comments.

272    *S.A. Sharpe, H.H. Nguyen/Journal of Financial Economics 39 (1995) 271-294*

a thorough characterization of just the tax implications of the lease-versus-buy decision and its interaction with a firm's overall capital structure, even under the assumption of complete markets, can be quite complex (Lewis and Schallheim, 1992).

On the other hand, the economics of leasing are widely recognized as going well beyond tax minimization strategies. Perhaps the most common set of motivations underlying the lease-versus-buy decision involve the use of leases to minimize transaction costs that arise when a firm expects the life of capital equipment to exceed its prospective usefulness (see, e.g., Flath, 1980; and Smith and Wakeman, 1985). The valuation of options embedded in leasing agreements is another fertile area of research (see, e.g., McConnell and Schallheim, 1983).

Perhaps some of the most interesting factors in the lease-versus-buy decision have received surprisingly little attention in the modern corporate finance literature. These are the 'financial contracting' motivations suggested by Smith and Wakeman but precluded by the complete markets framework. Such motivations arise when outside investors are less informed than firm insiders regarding ongoing operations or future prospects, or when conflicts of interest between classes of corporate claimants are costly to resolve. The influence of such financial market imperfections on corporate capital structure and financing policy has been the subject of extensive analysis (e.g., see review by Harris and Raviv, 1992), yet, little theoretical or empirical research in that area gives more than cursory consideration as to how leasing fits into that equation.

Similarly, much of the recent research on the behavior of capital expenditures – beginning with Fazzarri, Hubbard, and Petersen (1988) – examines the influence of capital market information imperfections on investment behavior. Here too, the option of leasing is virtually ignored, despite the fact that leased equipment now accounts for roughly a third of all equipment investment by business.

In this paper, we explore the role of leasing in alleviating financial contracting costs, and attempt to gauge empirically the influence of such costs on the propensity of public corporations to lease capital. We hypothesize that firms facing high costs of external funding may be able to economize on fixed capital costs by leasing. In particular, financing with a lease may reduce the premium on external funds that arises from severe asymmetric information (Myers and Majluf, 1984), or from agency problems that give rise to costly monitoring (Smith and Warner, 1979), or from underinvestment (Myers, 1977; Stulz and Johnson, 1985). To examine our hypothesis, we draw on commonly invoked identifying assumptions that firms which (i) pay little or no dividends, (ii) generate little current cash flow, or (iii) have low credit ratings face relatively high premiums for external funds. By estimating the effects of these proxies on the propensity to lease, we test the hypothesis that leasing lowers average capital costs for firms facing high premiums.

*S.A. Sharpe, H.H. Nguyen/Journal of Financial Economics 39 (1995) 271–294* 273

The empirical analysis employs Standard and Poor's Compustat data from 1985 to 1991. We define 'firm propensity to lease' as the fraction of a firm's total fixed capital costs – costs associated with the employment of property, plant, and equipment – that can be attributed to fixed capital on lease. Our estimate of the 'total lease share' of a firm's fixed capital costs is based on both income statement and balance sheet information, as it includes both capitalized and off-balance-sheet, or operating, leases. We also consider a narrower, somewhat more conventional measure of leasing propensity, which equals the proportion of property, plant, and equipment on the balance sheet that is attributable to capitalized leases.

We find strong support for the hypothesis that firms likely to face high financial contracting costs also have a significantly greater propensity to lease: the proportion of their total annual costs of fixed-capital usage incurred under leases is substantially higher than at firms relatively unhampered by such financial constraints. These results hold up even when controlling for firm size. Not surprisingly, the use of operating leases is negatively related to firm size, since firm size is likely correlated with financial, but also other, factors that influence the lease-versus-buy decision. On the narrower measure of leasing propensity, there is some, albeit weaker, evidence that financially constrained firms finance a greater share of their on-balance-sheet fixed capital via capital leases. Finally, all else the same, both measures of leasing propensity show more leasing by firms that appear to have lower current and future tax liabilities.

## 2. Background, analytical framework, and related research

This section begins with a brief description of leasing contracts, then lays out our theoretical arguments, and, finally, discusses previous research related to our central hypothesis.

### 2.1. Financial contracting rationales for leasing

Justifying any particular financial contracting cost argument as an inducement to lease necessitates a discussion of certain institutional features of lease obligations. A lease contract can be classified in one of two categories, depending on whether the lessor or lessee technically 'owns' the leased item, and what the attendant risks and benefits are. Ownership risks and costs include responsibility for casualty loss, wear and tear, and obsolescence, while ownership benefits entail the right of use, entitlement to gains from asset value appreciation, and ultimate possession of the property title. Whether or not a lessor retains ownership depends on whether it has retained a meaningful residual interest in the equipment under the lease agreement.

274        *S.A. Sharpe, H.H. Nguyen/Journal of Financial Economics 39 (1995) 271–294*

This dichotomy is complicated somewhat by the fact that the determination of ownership may differ, depending on whether it is made for financial accounting purposes or for legal and tax considerations. For financial accounting purposes, a lease is classified either as an operating or a capital lease. SFAS No. 13, 'Accounting for Leases', defines the criteria that differentiate operating and capital leases. Leases that do not substantially transfer the risks and benefits of ownership from the lessor to the lessee are classified as operating leases. In particular, a capital lease is defined by the following criteria: (i) ownership of the leased asset is transferred to the lessee by the end of the lease term; (ii) a bargain purchase option is available; (iii) the lease term is equal to 75% or more of the remaining economic life of the leased asset; or (iv) the present value of the minimum lease payments equals or exceeds 90% of the asset's market value.

At the inception of a capital lease, the lessee capitalizes the leased asset and records the corresponding debt obligation on the balance sheet. Subsequently, the lessee depreciates the leased asset and amortizes the debt liability. Thus, from an accounting perspective, capital leases closely resemble purchases by the lessee and, therefore, require disclosures similar to asset purchases. In contrast, operating leases represent off-balance-sheet financing for the lessee, and are reflected on the income statement as rent expense.

From a legal and tax point of view, when the lessor retains ownership, the agreement is said to be a 'true' lease; if not, it is a lease 'intended as security', and the lessor's claim is essentially viewed as a secured debt. Though our empirical analysis is based upon the financial accounting classification, the analytical arguments behind our hypotheses rest, in large part, upon the legal characteristics.[1]

Financial contracting rationales for the use of secured debt, as opposed to unsecured debt or equity, are offered by Smith and Warner (1979a) and Stulz and Johnson (1985). First, securing debt with a borrower's assets may be a cost-effective way of reducing asset substitution risks and may help to economize on lender monitoring costs. In addition, Stulz and Johnson demonstrate that a firm and its creditors can mitigate the underinvestment problem (analyzed by Myers, 1977) by allowing subsequent debt to be secured by the assets such borrowings can finance.

---

[1] The distinctions between true and nontrue leases are not stressed in our empirical analysis, owing to the fact that financial accounting data only distinguishes between operating and capital leases. However, basing our analytical arguments for leasing on the legal characteristics of leases ought not lead to major incongruencies with the empirical analysis. While the two classification systems do not yield a one-to-one mapping, the discrepancies are, in principle, minor. Operating leases are usually true leases, and most capital leases are likely to be treated as leases intended as security. Regardless, the main focus of our analysis is on differences between lease and nonlease financing, rather than the choice among types of leases.

*S.A. Sharpe, H.H. Nguyen/Journal of Financial Economics 39 (1995) 271–294* 275

The financial contracting advantages of a true lease may be even stronger than those for secured debt. One key difference between secured debt (or any other debt) and a true lease is in their treatment under a Chapter 11 bankruptcy filing. After filing for bankruptcy, the lessee has the option of either 'assuming' or 'rejecting' a true lease, that is, accepting or breaching all obligations entailed by the lease. If the lessee rejects an obligation, then the lessor may immediately recover possession of the equipment, re-lease or sell it, and file an unsecured claim against the lessee for economic losses incurred, including unpaid rents, late charges, and the present value of expected future rental shortfalls. In contrast, an automatic stay normally prevents secured creditors from repossessing their security after a bankruptcy filing.

If the financially troubled lessee chooses instead to assume the lease, and thus retain the equipment, the lessor is entitled to continue receiving compensation in accordance with the original lease agreement, since such obligations are classified as administrative expenses in the bankruptcy code. In fact, the lessor's entire claim, including delinquencies, late fees, and other damages suffered, is classified as an administrative claim that must be paid immediately or 'within a reasonable period' (Sweig, 1993).[2] Thus, when a true lease is not rejected, the lessor will continue to receive full compensation even after the lessee files for bankruptcy, while other outstanding creditor claims, including those of secured creditors, are accrued against the bankrupt firm with no assurance of being met.

By financing via true lease, as long as the leased asset is not returned prematurely to the lessor, the firm effectively puts the financial obligation on a par with other admininistrative expenses – such as employee and management compensation – that have a higher priority than normal debt. This aspect of a lease contract makes it a highly desirable financial contract in the presence of asymmetric information, since it would appear to put leasing at the top of the pecking order of external financing options. Apart from the potential for a few missed payments, under a true lease, the main risk borne by the lessor arises from the uncertainty of the value of the leased asset in the event that the obligation is rejected and the asset must be re-leased. In other words, much of the risk assumed by the lessor is only indirectly tied to the idiosyncratic, and perhaps concealable, aspect of the leasing firm's prospects.

---

[2]Not until the adoption of Article 2A of the Uniform Commercial Code in 1987 were the rights and remedies of lessor and lessee clearly defined (Zall, 1993; Strauss, 1991). Before Article 2A, there was considerable ambiguity about the criteria required for a lease to be treated as a true lease in bankruptcy. Article 2A has in effect broadened the definition of leases that meet the test of a 'true' lease.

276          S.A. Sharpe, H.H. Nguyen/Journal of Financial Economics 39 (1995) 271–294

## 2.2. Related empirical studies

Among previous analyses of the incentives to lease, Krishnan and Moyer (1994) is perhaps closest in spirit to our study. They hypothesize that leasing reduces bankruptcy costs in comparison to financing with ordinary debt, and argue that leases have all the advantages of secured debt and then some. As a consequence, leases should be more widely used by riskier, less established firms. This hypothesis is supported by their empirical finding that firms with lower and less stable operating earnings are more likely to lease. Nonetheless, their analysis examines the use of capital leases and ignores operating leases.

Other empirical analyses have attempted to gauge the effect of capitalized leases on overall debt capacity, but such studies fail to control for the underlying factors that determine debt capacity. Ang and Petersen (1984) examine the relation between the book value of capital leases and a firm's use of other debt. They find that leases are complementary to debt, that is, firms with leases also appear to have more nonlease debt (relative to book equity). As pointed out by Smith and Wakeman (1985), this result probably reflects the difficulty of controlling for debt capacity, that is, firms with higher debt capacity may also have (omitted) characteristics that make leasing relatively attractive. Bayless and Diltz (1988) control for such considerations by using an experimental setting in which banks are queried regarding the amount they would be willing to lend under various hypothetical circumstances. Bayless and Diltz found that, in the case of a term loan decision, banks did not treat outstanding capital leases and debt differently; however, leases had a somewhat negative relative effect on credit line decisions. They conclude that the fungibility of leases and other debt should generally depend upon the particular use for which the firm's other debt has been targeted.

Our empirical design controls for such considerations by reorienting the problem so that the firm chooses among contracts for financing services from fixed capital. That is, we begin by estimating the amount of fixed capital services a firm 'pays for' over a given year, and measure the proportion of those services acquired under lease agreements. Moreover, we use both operating as well as capital leases in our measures of firm 'leasing intensity'.

As previous researchers have pointed out, leasing gives rise to its own set of transactions costs and agency problems. Prominent among these is the lessee's reduced incentive to preserve the value of the leased asset through appropriate use and maintenance, since the lessee does not have a claim to the entire service life of the asset (e.g., Flath, 1980; Wolfson, 1985). Consequently, a firm's propensity to lease is a function of the type of capital required and the extent of leasing-related transactions costs associated with such assets. While it is difficult to control directly for such factors with the available data, we control for them indirectly by analyzing a firm's propensity to lease relative to other firms in its own industry.

*S.A. Sharpe, H.H. Nguyen/Journal of Financial Economics 39 (1995) 271-294*      277

## 3. Data and measurement issues

Firm level data used in this study are taken from the May 1993 Compustat files. Included in our panel are annual observations from 1986–1991 for firms on the active file for which 1985 data is available as well as firms on the research file that have data for 1985 and 1990. Foreign incorporated companies and a few industries are excluded.[3] We require that each observation have complete data for the relevant variables. After discarding observations with missing data, our sample contains an average of about 2000 observations per year. Firms are categorized into one of six industry groups by their primary SIC code (Table 1).

### 3.1. Leasing propensity

To measure the propensity to use capital leases, we calculate the capital lease share of property, plant, and equipment, or the proportion of fixed assets accounted for by capital leases. This is based on net book values reported on the balance sheet for both items:[4]

$$\frac{net\ capital\ leases}{net\ PPE}. \tag{1}$$

Due to off-balance-sheet financing of operating leases, reported fixed capital understates the stock of total property, plant, and equipment utilized in production processes. Therefore, the critical task is to quantify the relative importance of operating leases. We do this by comparing an estimate of the annual flow of rented capital services to an estimate of the annual flow of capital services implicit in the level of property, plant, and equipment reported on the balance sheet. The annual flow of services from noncapitalized leases is approximated by the amount of rental commitments due in one year on noncancellable, non-capitalized leases, as reported at the end of the previous year in a footnote to the balance sheet. The annual flow of capital services from balance-sheet capital is

---

[3]Aside from financials (two-digit SIC codes: 60–69) and utilities (49), excluded industries include those where real property or natural resources are a large portion of firms' capital (detailed property, plant, and equipment components were not disclosed) [petroleum refining (29), mining (10–14), agriculture and fishery (1–9)] as well as those where the main line of business involves leasing [auto repair (75), computer rental and leasing (73)].

[4]By accounting standards, capital lease assets (at cost) should always be greater than or equal to the corresponding liability, since the debt obligation is amortized over time. However, in about 5% of our observations, the disclosed lease asset is less than the debt obligation. This is probably because some lease assets are not reported separately, but are combined under the broader category of property, plant, and equipment, even though the corresponding liability may be fully disclosed. In situations where this occurs, the capital lease share of fixed capital is defined as the ratio of the capital lease liability (instead of asset) to net property, plant, and equipment.

proxied by the implicit rental cost of property, plant, and equipment, calculated as the sum of annual depreciation expense and the opportunity cost of holding property, plant, and equipment. Opportunity cost is estimated as the net book value of property, plant, and equipment times an opportunity rate. The on- and off-balance-sheet measures of capital services would be comparable if the interest rate used to represent the firm's opportunity rate was equal to the interest rate implicit in its operating lease payments. Since such data are not available, we use the firm's reported short-term average borrowings rate.[5]

The total annual flow of capital service costs associated with the use of fixed assets is therefore calculated as the sum of rental commitments, depreciation expense, and the opportunity cost of fixed assets:

$$total\ capital\ costs = rental\ commitments + depr\ expn + i*net\ PPE\,. \quad (2)$$

Using Eq. (2), we calculate our two key measures of leasing intensity, the 'operating lease share' and the 'total lease share'. The operating lease share is rental commitments divided by total capital costs:

$$operating\ lease\ share\ (OLS) = \frac{rental\ commitments}{total\ capital\ costs}\,. \quad (3)$$

The total lease share is the sum of the operating lease share and capital lease share, the latter calculated as the ratio of capital leases to total book PPE [from Eq. (1)], weighted by the share of total capital costs on the balance sheet:

$$total\ lease\ share\ (TLS) = OLS + (1 - OLS)*\frac{net\ capital\ leases}{net\ PPE}\,. \quad (4)$$

---

[5]We note that the short-term average borrowings rate is reported in Compustat for only about half of our observations. For firms where this is missing, we use the sample average interest rate reported that year by firms with the same bond rating. (Construction of our bond rating variable is described in detail below). Unfortunately, the reported interest rate appeared to be a somewhat noisy variable; for example, the incidence of outliers, such as values like 20%, was unrelated to either the bond rating or the year of observation. Consequently, we treated observations for which reported interest rates fell outside the interval between 6% and 15% as outliers and replaced such values with the sample average rate reported by firms with the same bond rating in the same year. After removing outliers, the average reported interest in the top-rated group was 1.5 to 2 percentage points lower than that for the 'unrated' sample group. For example, in 1991 AAA-rated firms faced a mean rate of 7.2%, while those without bond ratings faced a mean rate of 9.3%. In practice, outlier treatment had no effect on results. More generally, estimates from our leasing propensity models are largely unaffected by the set of interest rates chosen. For example, when we perform the calculations in Eqs. (2)–(3) using the end-of-year interest rate on AAA bonds as our estimate for every firm's opportunity rate, the results are quite similar.

*S.A. Sharpe, H.H. Nguyen/Journal of Financial Economics 39 (1995) 271–294*     279

## 3.2. Proxies for asymmetric information costs

To test our hypothesis that firms that face high costs of external capital owing to financial contracting costs are more inclined to lease, we construct several explanatory variables that act as indicators of a firm's information-cost related premium on external funds. Young, fast-growing, innovation-intensive firms are likely to have many investment opportunities. Such firms can face severe information asymmetry problems, and consequently may be forced to finance projects largely from retained earnings. Since firms that pay no cash dividends are likely to be among those most burdened by asymmetric information, a dummy variable equal to one for non-dividend-paying firms is used as an indicator for firms facing high capital market information costs.[6]

An alternative interpretation of our no-dividend indicator that is nonetheless consistent with our general hypothesis is suggested in Smith and Watts (1992). They argue that dividend payout should be lowest for those firms at greatest risk of facing the underinvestment problem. Firms with more growth opportunities 'can tolerate more restrictions on dividends before the expected benefits of controlling payout are offset' by the risk of triggering negative net present value investments. Thus, a finding that non-dividend-paying firms have a greater propensity to lease may alternatively be viewed as evidence that leasing helps to alleviate some of the expected costs associated with the underinvestment problem.

We develop two additional sets of proxies for gauging relative marginal funding costs. All else equal, firms generating poor cash flows probably face higher funding costs; in addition to providing cheap funds directly, greater cash flow enhances firm debt capacity. Our measure of cash flow is equal to the ratio of operating income to sales. We define cash flow as operating income before interest, depreciation, rent, and taxes. Rent expense is added back into cash flow in order to avoid creating a cash flow measure that is influenced by the choice of renting versus buying. In addition, the ratio is truncated at zero to avoid using a variable that is highly negatively skewed. Otherwise, large negative values appear for firms with low sales. Results are not sensitive to variations of the truncation point between zero and −1, or to the inclusion of a dummy indicating firms with cash flow ratios lower than the truncation point.

Finally, firms that have low-rated or unrated debt are probably closer to exhausting their debt capacity as well as their internal funding. Thus, they ought to face higher information- or agency-cost premiums on marginal financing.

---

[6]The use of low dividend payout as an indicator of the likelihood of facing financing constraints due to asymmetric information on investment is proposed, for example, by Fazzari, Hubbard, and Petersen (1988). Calomiris and Hubbard (1993) find historical support for this identifying assumption.

280						*S.A. Sharpe, H.H. Nguyen/Journal of Financial Economics 39 (1995) 271–294*

Based largely upon Standard & Poor's senior debt ratings, five indicator variables are used in a four-tier rating system with the fifth group being unrated firms. For companies without senior debt ratings, we use subordinated debt ratings if available. Failing this condition, we check for commercial paper ratings. Companies that do not have any such ratings are classified as unrated. The rating groups are partitioned according to: AAA through AA − (or A1 + for commercial paper); A + through A − (or A1 for cp); BBB + through BBB − (or A2 for cp); and BB + through D (or B, C, D for cp).

### 3.3. Other variables

Because firm size is correlated with the quality of outsider information about firms' operations and prospects, smaller firms are more likely to lease for financial contracting reasons. In fact, as evidence that firm size is negatively related to risk, Schallheim et al. (1987) find that yields charged on financial leases are higher for leases to smaller firms. If leasing reduced the information-cost premium on outside funds, then a decline in issuer size would be associated with an even steeper rise in yields on straight debt.

In addition, leasing propensity will be greater for smaller firms if there are significant nonconvexities, or indivisibilities, associated with the use of certain fixed assets. For example, smaller firms may not need an entire building. Also, such firms may face greater uncertainty on their future needs for any particular piece of capital equipment. Thus, leasing could minimize the transaction costs associated with resale. Larger firms are more likely to have alternative uses for equipment that is no longer needed in its originally intended use, and they may also have better developed mechanisms for remarketing equipment.

This alternative rationale for a firm-size influence on leasing propensity suggests some caution in interpreting size effects. We gauge firm size by the log of the number of employees. Since proportional changes in size might matter less once some threshold size is obtained, we allow for a more general functional form by including the square of size in those specifications where size is highly significant. Results are similar when the log of sales is used as the proxy of size. Using the standard measure of size – total assets – is inappropriate here because of its endogeneity. In particular, all else equal, firms that lease more will have a lower level of book assets. We choose the number of employees because, like assets, this is a measure of inputs to production, though, unlike assets, it should be roughly invariant to the leasing choice.

As we noted earlier, leasing is also motivated by tax incentives. Where the lessee faces a lower marginal tax rate than the lessor, both parties may benefit from a leasing-related transfer of tax shields to the lessor (see Brealey and Myers, 1984). This motivation might have been particularly influential under the tax code prior to the 1986 reform, as, in addition to providing for investment tax credits (ITCs), the code contained relatively generous tax depreciation rules.

*S.A. Sharpe, H.H. Nguyen/Journal of Financial Economics 39 (1995) 271–294* 281

Moreover, the influence of the pre-1987 tax code probably lingered for several years, as firms that had invested heavily during the early and mid-1980s only were able to fully utilize the associated deductions over time. In fact, about 75 of the firms in our sample – firms with a relatively high proportion of purchased, rather than leased, capital – continued to show ITCs on their balance sheets for several years after that benefit was eliminated on new inveştment.[7]

We construct two alternative proxies for a firm's tax status. First, we approximate a firm's tax rate with tax expense divided by pre-tax income; all else equal, firms paying little or no taxes should be more prone to lease. Ideally, we would like a measure of expected marginal tax rate (in the absence of lease financing). As an admittedly noisy proxy for this, we use the firm's average financial tax rate. The tax rate variable is truncated so as to fall between zero and one. It is set at zero for all firms with nonpositive tax expense, regardless of pre-tax income, and set at one for firms that have positive taxes and negative income. Coefficient estimates on the tax rate are largely unaffected by dropping observations characterized by such anomalies. Also, using realized future tax rates does not enhance the variable's explanatory power.

A better proxy of tax-motivated leasing incentives could be derived from tax-loss carry-forwards reported in the financial statements. Firms with significant tax-loss carry-forwards will be 'tax-exhausted' for a period of years, and thus unable to take full advantage of the tax benefits of ownership, including those from accelerated depreciation and investment tax credits. Since over two-thirds of the firms in any year have no tax-loss carry-forwards, and because of the highly skewed distribution of this variable for firms reporting a loss carry-forward, we employ dummy variables that indicate the presence of a 'high' or 'low' (versus 'no') loss carry-forward. Companies with tax-loss carry-forwards exceeding current year operating earnings (before depreciation, interest, and taxes) are placed into the high tax-loss carry-forward category, while those with positive loss carry-forwards that fail this criterion are labeled low tax-loss carry-forward firms. (We considered using the ratio of tax-loss carry-forwards to scaling variables such as operating income or sales, but, due to the highly skewed distribution of loss carry-forwards, this proved inferior to using dummies in the sense of having less explanatory power.)

To control for the characteristics of the property, plant, and equipment, we include industry dummies defined by broad industry categories or else use industry-adjusted values based on narrower, two-digit SIC industries. We also control for technological differences across firms by using a measure of capital

---

[7]As discussed in detail by O'Malley (1994), the implementation of the Alternative Minimum Tax in 1986 probably helped sustain tax-motivated leasing. That provision limited the extent to which firms could use depreciation (as well as other items) to shield income against taxes, a constraint which was binding for many capital-intensive firms.

intensity, the ratio of total annual capital costs [Eq. (2)] to the number of employees. The capital intensity of production processes may be negatively correlated with leasing intensity to the extent that firms that are more capital-intensive firms use specialized equipment that is less appropriate for leasing. Also, failing to control for differences in the capital–labor ratio may result in spurious estimated effects for variables such as operating earnings.

We also attempt to directly control for economic motivations arising in market environments characterized by a great deal of uncertainty. Firms in these environments could have asset needs that are unpredictable or temporary; leasing alleviates the problem of owning assets that are not expected to have productive use full-time. We construct a proxy for the anticipated variation in demand equal to the firm's realized variance of annual sales growth measured over the years during which the firm is in the panel. This variable should be positively related with the option value of a short-term lease, and should be correlated with (expected) instability of earnings. Thus, it can also proxy for tax-motivated leasing, as predicted in Lewis and Schallheim (1992).

Finally, because of inflation, measuring fixed assets at book value results in an underestimate of the true value of these assets, and hence an underestimate of capital costs. Consequently, leasing propensity measured as the lease share of total capital costs will be biased upward. This problem will be more severe for firms with older equipment. We construct a proxy for equipment age equal to one minus the ratio of net PPE to gross PPE. A firm with an entirely nonde-preciated stock of equipment will have zero for equipment age, while firms with mostly depreciated equipment will have values approaching unity for equipment age.

## 4. Empirical results

In this section, we begin by examining the means and correlations of our leasing measures and explanatory variables; then, we describe the empirical models and, finally, the model estimates.

### 4.1. Sample statistics and simple correlations

Mean values of firm leasing intensity are shown for the 1986 sample shown in Table 1, which groups firms by broad industry category and their size relative to the industry. The first measure of leasing intensity (col. 1) shows capital leases as a share of net property, plant, and equipment on the balance sheet. Numbers in square brackets are the fraction of firms reporting any capital leases. Except for the retail industry, where stores' square footage accounts for most of firms' fixed asset costs, capital leases usually account for less than 15% of net book property, plant, and equipment. Moreover, fewer than two-thirds of the nonretail

*S.A. Sharpe, H.H. Nguyen/Journal of Financial Economics 39 (1995) 271–294* 283

Table 1
Measures of 1986 leasing intensity: Means by industry and firm size

Capital lease share of PPE is net capital leases divided by net book property, plant, and equipment. Operating lease share of total capital costs equals current-year rental commitments divided by total capital costs, where total capital costs is the sum of rental commitments and an estimate of the implicit annual rental cost of net property, plant, and equipment. Total lease share of total capital costs is the sum of the operating lease share and the capital lease share of total capital costs, the latter calculated as the capital lease share of net PPE multiplied by one minus the operating lease share. Firm size classification is determined by dividing each industry into firms above and below the median size, as measured by the number of employees.

| Industry<br># companies | Capital lease share of PPE [% w cap. lease] | | Operating lease share of total capital costs | | Total lease share of total capital costs | |
|---|---|---|---|---|---|---|
| | Small | Large | Small | Large | Small | Large |
| Manufacturing 1167 | 0.10 [0.58] | 0.05 [0.61] | 0.27 | 0.16 | 0.34 | 0.20 |
| Transportation 63 | 0.05 [0.58] | 0.09 [0.87] | 0.32 | 0.16 | 0.36 | 0.23 |
| Communications 74 | 0.08 [0.53] | 0.01 [0.81] | 0.17 | 0.04 | 0.23 | 0.05 |
| Wholesale 135 | 0.13 [0.45] | 0.12 [0.68] | 0.34 | 0.27 | 0.43 | 0.35 |
| Retail 254 | 0.25 [0.81] | 0.24 [0.93] | 0.41 | 0.32 | 0.55 | 0.47 |
| Services 331 | 0.12 [0.64] | 0.07 [0.65] | 0.36 | 0.32 | 0.44 | 0.37 |

firms in our sample report any capital leases. The capital lease fraction of fixed assets tends to be higher for smaller firms (those with fewer than the industry median number of employees), although, in most industries, larger firms more frequently report a positive number for capital leases.

The second measure of leasing intensity is the operating lease share of total capital costs. Within each industry, operating leases account for a higher-than-average share of total capital costs for smaller firms, and in most cases, substantially more. Taken by industry group, the operating lease share ranges from a low of 4% for large communication firms to a high of 41% for small retail firms.

Statistics for the total lease share of total capital costs, the most comprehensive measure of leasing intensity, appear in the right two columns. The total lease share is generally 5 to 10 percentage points higher than the operating lease share, and the pattern across industry and size groups follows that depicted for the operating lease share. Finally, though not shown, the pattern of industry average total leasing shares shows little movement over time. However, there appears to have been some shifting toward operating leases from capital leases. (Two notable exceptions are in the transportation and communication industries; the average total lease share of large transportation firms grew about 7 percentage points, while that for small communication firms declined about 13 percentage points.)

Table 2 shows sample means and correlations among our measures of leasing intensity and explanatory variables (in 1986). Correlations are calculated using two-digit SIC industry-adjusted variables, that is, after subtracting 1986 industry mean values from each observation. Means are shown in the second column, correlations between measures of leasing intensity and explanatory variables are presented in the first three rows, and correlations among the explanatory variables constitute the remainder.

Since 'no dividend', 'no rating', and the two tax-loss carry-forward variables are all indicator (dummy) variables, their mean values equal the proportion of firms having such characteristics. Thus, 59% of our firms paid no dividends, 79% of them were not rated, and almost one-quarter of them had large tax-loss carry-forwards. The average number of employees reported by firms in our sample is about 800 (avg. firm size $\approx \ln[800]$).

The correlations suggest that, by all three measures, leasing intensity is positively related to the no dividend and no rating indicators, and negatively related to contemporaneous operating income (before rent expense). In addition, leasing propensity is positively correlated with the presence of large tax-loss carry-forwards and negatively correlated with the tax rate. Leasing propensities are negatively related to firm size and positively related to the variance of sales growth. This is consistent with the economic rationale related to the option value of leasing. Finally, our three indicators of information- or agency-cost premiums on marginal funding – the no-dividend and no-rating dummies and EBITDA/sales – all show substantial correlations with firm size, the tax-loss carry-forward indicator, and the tax rate, suggesting that these controls are potentially important for a convincing test of our hypothesis.

## 4.2. Regression models

Before examining the main hypothesis, we consider the subset of our information relating to capital equipment only on the balance sheet. In particular, we examine whether firms facing greater financial constraints are likely to lease a greater proportion of the fixed assets reported on their balance sheet. As noted earlier, such a test avoids what could be the most troublesome measurement problems. Strictly speaking, however, this test only makes sense if the operating lease option can be ignored when estimating the decision to purchase equipment outright or acquire it under a capital lease. In other words, the test presumes

Table 2

1986 sample statistics for variables: Means and two-digit industry-adjusted correlations

Correlations are calculated after subtracting 1986 two-digit industry mean values from each observation; those denoted with an asterisk (*) are significant at the 1% level (two-tail test). Capital lease/net PPE is net capital leases divided by net book property, plant, and equipment. Operating lease share equals current-year rental commitments divided by total capital costs, where total capital costs are the sum of rental commitments and an estimate of the implicit rental cost of net property, plant, and equipment. Total lease share is the sum of the operating lease share and the capital lease share of total capital costs, the latter calculated as the capital lease share of net PPE multiplied by one minus the operating lease share of total capital costs. No dividend (no debt rating) equals one if firm paid no dividend (was unrated) that year, and is zero otherwise. EBITDA is earnings before interest, taxes, depreciation, and rent expense. Tax rate is tax expense divided by pre-tax income. Large tax-loss carry-forward (CF) is one if firm had a tax-loss carry-forward exceeding current-year EBITDA. Firm size is the natural log of the number of full-time employees. Age of PPE equals one minus the ratio of net PPE to gross PPE. Capital intensity is total capital costs divided by the number of employees. Var(sales growth) is the variance of the annual change in ln(sales) from 1985–1991.

| | Sample means (N = 2024) | No dividend | EBITDA sales | No rating | Tax rate | Large tax-loss CF | Firm size | Age of PPE | Capital intensity | Variance sales growth |
|---|---|---|---|---|---|---|---|---|---|---|
| Cap. lease/Net PPE | 0.10 | 0.10* | −0.06* | 0.08* | −0.07* | 0.09* | −0.11* | −0.02 | 0.00 | −0.01 |
| Oper. lease share | 0.26 | 0.26* | −0.21* | 0.17* | −0.14* | 0.19* | −0.31* | 0.21* | −0.05 | 0.09* |
| Total lease share | 0.33 | 0.26* | −0.21* | 0.18* | −0.15* | 0.21* | −0.31* | 0.15* | 0.05* | 0.07* |
| No dividend | 0.59 | — | −0.23* | 0.33* | 0.17* | 0.28* | −0.56* | 0.00 | −0.06 | 0.11* |
| EBITDA/Sales | 0.12 | | — | −0.17* | 0.29* | −0.39* | 0.32* | −0.14* | 0.08* | −0.15* |
| No rating | 0.79 | | | — | −0.13* | 0.12* | −0.53* | 0.09* | 0.00 | 0.07* |
| Tax rate | 0.34 | | | | — | −0.15* | 0.26* | −0.02 | −0.01 | −0.10* |
| Large tax-loss CF | 0.25 | | | | | — | −0.38* | 0.13* | 0.07* | 0.16* |
| Firm size | 6.78 | | | | | | — | −0.11 | −0.14* | −0.16* |
| Age of PPE | 0.40 | | | | | | | — | −0.01 | −0.01 |
| Capital intensity | 0.12 | | | | | | | | — | 0.09* |

that the decision to acquire equipment under a capital lease is independent of the potential benefits of operating leases. Nonetheless, we explore the determinants of the capital lease share of property, plant, and equipment. Because many firms are observed to have no capital leases – capital lease share is truncated at zero – we estimate the determinants using a tobit specification, that is, we estimate Eq. (5) using maximum likelihood under the assumption of normality,

$$\frac{net\ capital\ leases_i}{net\ PPE_i} = \beta' x_i + u_i \quad \text{if} \quad RHS \geq 0,$$
$$= 0 \qquad\qquad \text{otherwise}, \tag{5}$$

where $x_i$ is a vector containing proxies for the firm's external funding premium as well as control variables, including six dummies for the industry groups.[8]

The results are presented in Table 3, in which estimates are shown for three separate years. The coefficient estimate of 0.03 on the no-dividend variable indicates that, all else equal, firms that fully retain their earnings have a capital lease fraction of property, plant, and equipment that is 3 percentage points higher compared with dividend-paying firms. In contrast, leasing propensity appears to have little relation to firm debt ratings. Perhaps surprising is the finding that leasing propensity is, if anything, positively related to cash flow (EBITDA/sales). Also, the coefficients on firm size and size-squared imply that the capital lease share is positively related to firm size for small and medium-sized firms. These latter two results suggest that it may be inappropriate to ignore the operating lease option when testing for the information-cost rationale behind leasing.

The significant positive coefficients on the high tax-loss carry-forward indicator and the negative coefficients on the tax rate in all three years suggest that capitalized leases are used more heavily by firms for which the tax benefits of ownership appear low. The strength of this result is somewhat surprising, in light of the ambiguous tax standing of capital leases and the finding by Krishnan and Moyer (1994) of no tax effects on the use of capital leases among a smaller sample of firms.

We examine the central hypothesis by modeling the cross-sectional pattern of the total lease share, or the proportion of total annual capital costs incurred under both capital and operating leases. Since, by construction, observations on this dependent variable vary over the interval between zero and one, we use a cumulative logistic transformation. The equation estimated is

$$\log\frac{TLS_i}{1 - TLS_i} = \beta' x_i + u_i, \tag{6}$$

---

[8]We also consider a logit specification using the indicator variable for the presence of capital leases, which yields similar results.

Table 3
Regression estimates of the capital lease share of PPE

Tobit regressions of net capital leases divided by net property, plant, and equipment, over three separate years (cross-sections). No dividend equals one if firm paid no dividend that year, and is zero otherwise. EBITDA is earnings before interest, taxes, depreciation, and rent expense. S&P rating is an indicator of the firm's senior debt rating, the omitted category being unrated firms. Tax rate is tax expense divided by pre-tax income. Large (small) tax-loss CF is one if firm had a tax-loss carry-forward exceeding (not exceeding) current-year EBITDA. Size is the natural log of the number of employees divided by 10. Capital intensity is total capital costs divided by the number of employees. Variance of sales growth is the variance of the annual change in ln(sales) over 1985–1991. Also included but not shown are one-digit industry dummies. $T$-statistics are shown in parentheses.

| Specification | 1986 | 1988 | 1991 |
|---|---|---|---|
| No dividend | 0.03 | 0.02 | 0.04 |
| | (2.02) | (2.06) | (3.42) |
| EBITDA/Sales | 0.01 | 0.12 | 0.11 |
| | (0.11) | (2.32) | (1.76) |
| S&P ratings: | | | |
| AAA to AA − | − 0.06 | − 0.03 | 0.01 |
| | ( − 1.55) | ( − 1.02) | (0.18) |
| A + to A − | − 0.01 | − 0.03 | − 0.03 |
| | ( − 0.42) | ( − 1.04) | ( − 0.93) |
| BBB + to BBB − | − 0.03 | − 0.02 | − 0.03 |
| | ( − 0.83) | ( − 0.71) | (0.92) |
| BB + to D | − 0.02 | − 0.02 | − 0.03 |
| | ( − 0.84) | ( − 1.39) | ( − 1.60) |
| Tax rate | − 0.06 | − 0.04 | − 0.04 |
| | ( − 2.68) | ( − 2.10) | ( − 2.11) |
| Small tax-loss CF | 0.04 | − 0.01 | 0.03 |
| | (2.04) | ( − 0.90) | (1.86) |
| Large tax-loss CF | 0.06 | 0.06 | 0.05 |
| | (3.61) | (4.44) | (3.63) |
| Firm size | 0.42 | 0.26 | 0.32 |
| | (2.56) | (2.08) | (2.32) |
| Firm size squared | − 0.25 | − 0.16 | − 0.20 |
| | ( − 2.18) | ( − 1.73) | ( − 1.97) |
| Capital intensity | − 0.01 | − 0.02 | − 0.00 |
| | ( − 0.43) | ( − 0.84) | (0.06) |
| Variance of sales growth | − 0.01 | − 0.01 | − 0.01 |
| | ( − 1.20) | ( − 0.60) | ( − 1.28) |
| # observations | 2024 | 2108 | 1978 |

288          *S.A. Sharpe, H.H. Nguyen/Journal of Financial Economics 39 (1995) 271–294*

where $TLS$ is the total lease share and $u_i$ is assumed to be normally distributed. In this specification, we control for a firm's industry by removing two-digit (year-specific) sample industry means from each variable and observation.

Regression results appear in Table 4, where three different specifications for 1986 are shown in the first three columns. In the second and third specifications, we omit either cash flow or firm size, respectively. We also report estimates of the complete specification for 1988 and 1991. In order to interpret estimated magnitudes as local derivatives, coefficients must be multiplied by a scaling factor, $\exp(\Sigma\hat{\beta}/\bar{x}_i)/(1 + \exp(\Sigma\hat{\beta}\bar{x}_i))^2$. However, since variables are demeaned by industry, regressor means are always zero, and thus the scaling factor equals 0.25.

Coefficient estimates indicate that non-dividend-paying firms are significantly more reliant on leasing, a result that is robust across all specifications. According to the first specification, we estimate that firms that pay no dividends have a total lease share that is 8 percentage points higher (0.32/4) than dividend-paying firms. Perhaps not surprisingly, omitting firm size from the model (specification 3) results in a larger dividend effect. A firm's reliance on leasing is also negatively related to cash flow (EBITDA/sales) in 1986, though not in later years. This is particularly evident in 1991, when the recession sharply reduced many firms' cash flows.

The third proxy for information cost differentials is a firm's bond rating. We find that firms with high bond ratings have a significantly and substantially lower propensity to lease. In fact, estimates suggest that, all else the same, the total lease share of firms in the highest rating category is 15 to 20 percentage points lower that that of the low-rated or unrated firms, while firms in the second-highest rating category fall in the middle.

Coefficient estimates on the large tax-loss carry-forward indicator, and on the tax rate in 1986, again appear to confirm that tax considerations are a significant motivation for leasing. It is interesting to note that the estimated effect of (large) tax-loss carry-forwards rises when cash flow is excluded; thus, cash flow may serve in part as a proxy for tax-related incentives to lease. Conversely, it is also possible that the tax-loss carry-forward variable picks up some of the cost-of-capital effect that cash flow is meant to capture.[9]

The influence of firm size is negative and significant. Moreover, the positive coefficient on the quadratic term suggests that size matters proportionately

---

[9]We also considered ITCs (on the balance sheet) as an indicator of tax-exhaustion. About 4% of our sample firms indicated having deferred ITCs in 1986 and fewer in later years. However, this variable is highly endogenous relative to the lease share (of outstanding capital), since the amount of a firm's ITCs should be closely related and caused by the amount of capital the firm had purchased (rather than leased). Indeed, we find that the lease share is negatively and significantly related to the presence of ITCs when an indicator for their presence is included in our regressions. In principle, we could sidestep the endogeneity problem by examining the effect of outstanding ITCs on the incremental, or marginal, lease-versus-buy decision, an approach that would be interesting, but is beyond the scope of this paper.

Table 4
Regression estimates of the industry-adjusted total lease share of total capital costs

The dependent variable is the logistic transform of the total lease share (TLS): $\log[TLS/(1 - TLS)]$. Total lease share is the sum of operating lease share and capital lease share of total annual capital cost, where total capital cost is the sum of current-year rental commitments and an estimate of the implicit rental cost of net property, plant, and equipment. Operating lease share is current-year rental commitments divided by total capital cost. The capital lease share is the capital lease share of net PPE multiplied by one minus the operating lease share. No dividend equals one if firm paid no dividend that year, and is zero otherwise. EBITDA is earnings before interest, taxes, depreciation, and rent expense. S&P rating is an indicator of the firm's senior debt rating, the omitted category being unrated firms. Tax rate is tax expense divided by pre-tax income. Large (small) tax-loss CF is one if firm had a positive carry-forward exceeding (not exceeding) current-year EBITDA. Size is the natural log of the number of employees. Variance of sales growth is the variance of the annual change in ln(sales) over 1985–1991. Two-digit industry means are subtracted from all variables.

| Specification | 1986 | | | 1988 | 1991 |
| --- | --- | --- | --- | --- | --- |
| | (1) | (2) | (3) | | |
| No dividend | 0.32 | 0.33 | 0.39 | 0.25 | 0.22 |
| | (5.28) | (5.53) | (7.30) | (4.39) | (4.08) |
| EBITDA/Sales | − 1.57 | | − 1.73 | − 0.61 | − 0.19 |
| | ( − 4.62) | | ( − 5.18) | ( − 1.62) | ( − 0.50) |
| S&P ratings: | | | | | |
| AAA to AA − | − 0.67 | − 0.82 | − 0.72 | − 0.66 | − 0.72 |
| | ( − 5.42) | ( − 6.29) | ( − 6.73) | ( − 5.13) | ( − 4.69) |
| A + to A − | − 0.18 | − 0.22 | − 0.24 | − 0.27 | − 0.33 |
| | ( − 1.93) | ( − 2.36) | ( − 2.90) | ( − 2.52) | ( − 3.15) |
| BBB + to BBB − | − 0.19 | − 0.19 | − 0.26 | − 0.09 | 0.05 |
| | ( − 1.70) | ( − 1.70) | ( − 2.49) | ( − 0.78) | (0.50) |
| BB + to D | − 0.00 | 0.01 | − 0.07 | 0.04 | 0.02 |
| | (0.02) | (0.10) | ( − 1.04) | (0.45) | (0.21) |
| Tax rate | − 0.17 | − 0.28 | − 0.24 | − 0.04 | − 0.10 |
| | ( − 1.82) | ( − 3.07) | ( − 2.65) | ( − 0.43) | ( − 1.25) |
| Small tax-loss CF | 0.09 | 0.09 | 0.08 | 0.01 | 0.06 |
| | (1.25) | (1.33) | (1.11) | (0.19) | (0.91) |
| Large tax-loss CF | 0.16 | 0.26 | 0.23 | 0.18 | 0.25 |
| | (2.49) | (4.16) | (3.54) | (2.87) | (3.77) |
| Firm size | − 0.20 | − 0.25 | | − 0.28 | − 0.36 |
| | ( − 3.23) | ( − 4.00) | | ( − 3.79) | ( − 5.50) |
| Firm size squared | 0.01 | 0.01 | | 0.01 | 0.02 |
| | (2.46) | (3.16) | | (2.97) | (4.35) |
| Age of PPE | 0.71 | 0.80 | 0.76 | 1.07 | 1.33 |
| | (4.54) | (5.01) | (4.85) | (6.42) | (7.78) |
| Capital intensity | − 0.46 | − 0.54 | − 0.38 | − 0.49 | − 0.58 |
| | ( − 2.06) | ( − 2.09) | ( − 1.87) | ( − 3.89) | ( − 7.23) |
| Variance of sales growth | − 0.01 | 0.00 | 0.00 | 0.00 | − 0.02 |
| | ( − 0.27) | (0.08) | (0.07) | (0.07) | ( − 0.42) |
| # observations | 2019 | 2019 | 2019 | 2107 | 1976 |
| Adjusted $R^2$ | 0.18 | 0.16 | 0.17 | 0.17 | 0.20 |

290        *S.A. Sharpe, H.H. Nguyen/Journal of Financial Economics 39 (1995) 271–294*

Table 5
Regression estimates of the industry-adjusted operating lease share of total capital costs

The dependent variable is the logistic transformation of the operating lease share (OLS): log[$OLS/(1 - OLS)$]. Operating lease share is current-year rental commitments divided by total capital cost, where total capital cost is the sum of current-year rental commitments and an estimate of the implicit rental cost of net property, plant, and equipment. No dividend equals one if firm paid no dividend that year, and zero otherwise. EBITDA is earnings before interest, taxes, depreciation, and rent expense. S&P rating is an indicator of the firm's senior debt rating, the omitted category being unrated firms. Tax rate is tax expense divided by pre-tax income. Large (small) tax-loss CF is one if firm had a positive carry-forward exceeding (not exceeding) current-year EBITDA. Size is the natural log of the number of employees. Capital intensity is total capital costs divided by number of employees. Variance of sales growth is the variance of the annual change in ln(sales) over 1985–1991. Two-digit industry means are subtracted from all variables.

| Specification | 1986 | 1988 | 1991 |
|---|---|---|---|
| No dividend | 0.30 | 0.20 | 0.15 |
| | (5.09) | (3.69) | (2.75) |
| EBITDA/Sales | − 1.46 | − 0.75 | − 0.23 |
| | ( − 4.22) | ( − 2.61) | ( − 0.61) |
| S&P ratings: | | | |
| AAA to AA − | − 0.57 | − 0.60 | − 0.71 |
| | ( − 4.95) | ( − 4.89) | ( − 4.72) |
| A + to A − | − 0.16 | − 0.29 | − 0.30 |
| | ( − 1.75) | ( − 2.69) | ( − 2.87) |
| BBB + to BBB − | − 0.10 | − 0.03 | 0.09 |
| | ( − 0.97) | ( − 0.29) | (0.88) |
| BB + to D | 0.06 | 0.10 | 0.06 |
| | (0.89) | (1.31) | (0.64) |
| Tax rate | − 0.10 | 0.06 | − 0.06 |
| | ( − 1.10) | (0.69) | ( − 0.78) |
| Small tax-loss CF | 0.02 | 0.05 | − 0.02 |
| | (0.26) | (0.76) | ( − 0.30) |
| Large tax-loss CF | 0.05 | 0.08 | 0.19 |
| | (0.81) | (1.32) | (2.93) |
| Firm size | − 0.29 | − 0.33 | − 0.40 |
| | ( − 4.62) | ( − 4.76) | ( − 6.21) |
| Firm size squared | 0.02 | 0.02 | 0.02 |
| | (3.97) | (4.04) | (5.21) |
| Age of PPE | 1.11 | 1.41 | 1.58 |
| | (7.26) | (8.65) | (9.53) |
| Capital intensity | − 0.46 | − 0.48 | − 0.57 |
| | ( − 1.97) | ( − 3.36) | ( − 7.41) |
| Variance of sales gowth | 0.02 | − 0.01 | 0.01 |
| | (0.52) | ( − 0.13) | (0.30) |
| # observations | 2023 | 2107 | 1977 |
| Adjusted $R^2$ | 0.17 | 0.17 | 0.21 |

more for small firms. For firms at the low end of the size spectrum, doubling in size is associated with a 5 to 7 percentage point decline in lease share. For firms in the range of 5000 employees (or a size of 8.5), doubling in size is associated with very little decline in lease share. Also, as predicted, we estimate that capital-intensive firms have a smaller total lease share. The positive coefficient on the control for equipment age suggests that the leasing share is substantially overstated because property, plant, and equipment is measured at book value. Finally, the variance of sales growth, our proxy for the option value of leasing, has no marginal predictive power for firm leasing propensity.

We estimate similar regressions for the operating lease share, or the proportion of total capital costs associated with rental commitments. As we show in Table 5, the estimated effects of most variables exhibit a pattern of results similar to those found for the total lease share. Again, low bond ratings and the policy of paying zero dividends are strong indicators of firms that are more reliant on leasing. One notable difference is that coefficients on the tax variables are substantially smaller and insignificant in 1988, and especially 1986, suggesting that prior to the implementation of the 1986 tax law, when the investment tax credit was eliminated, a lot of the tax benefits of leasing were obtained under longer-term capital leases.

Finally, we examine whether our framework produces similar inferences for within-firm changes in leasing propensity. We estimate our model for the total lease share – Eq. (6) – using three years of data (1986, 1988, and 1991) and a fixed effects estimator on firms with data in at least two of these years. Since it can take several years for marginal financing incentives to be reflected in a firm's average capital structure, coefficients generated from a within-firm estimator ought to be smaller than our estimates of the analogous cross-sectional effects. (Also, while the $R$-squares are much lower when compared with the cross-sectional regressions, mean squared errors in the panel (not shown) are about half the magnitude.)

Indeed, as the results in Table 6 show, the signs of estimated coefficients are generally consistent with results from the cross-sectional models (Table 4), although smaller in magnitude. The coefficients on the ratings indicators are about one-quarter the size of the earlier regressions. Nonetheless, the coefficient on the second-highest bond rating indicator remains at least marginally significant. The coefficient on the no dividend indicator is similarly reduced, but is significant. Within-firm behavior thus offers further support for our interpretation of cross-sectional findings.

## 5. Conclusions

In summary, we find strong evidence that a corporation's propensity to lease is substantially influenced by the financial contracting costs associated with

Table 6
Within-firm panel estimates of the total lease share of total capital costs using observations from 1986, 1988, 1991

The dependent variable is the logistic transformation of the total lease share (TLS): $\log[TLS/(1 - TLS)]$. Total lease share is the sum of operating lease share and capital lease share of total capital cost. No dividend equals one if firm paid no dividend that year, and is zero otherwise. EBITDA is earnings before interest, taxes, depreciation, and rent expense. S&P rating is an indicator of the firm's senior debt rating, the omitted category being unrated firms. Tax rate is tax expense divided by pre-tax income. Large (small) tax-loss CF is one if firm had a positive tax-loss carry-forward exceeding (not exceeding) current-year EBITDA. Size is the natural log of the number of employees.

| Specification | Model 1 | Model 2 | Model 3 |
|---|---|---|---|
| No dividend | 0.06 | 0.07 | 0.09 |
| | (2.10) | (2.19) | (2.86) |
| EBITDA/Sales | − 0.44 | | − 0.51 |
| | ( − 2.47) | | ( − 2.77) |
| S&P ratings: | | | |
| AAA to AA − | − 0.10 | − 0.11 | − 0.14 |
| | ( − 1.12) | ( − 1.14) | ( − 1.55) |
| A + to A − | − 0.08 | − 0.08 | − 0.12 |
| | ( − 1.51) | ( − 1.55) | ( − 2.25) |
| BBB + to BBB − | − 0.01 | − 0.01 | − 0.04 |
| | ( − 0.15) | ( − 0.11) | ( − 0.71) |
| BB + to D | 0.00 | 0.00 | − 0.03 |
| | (0.02) | (0.02) | ( − 0.67) |
| Tax rate | − 0.05 | − 0.06 | − 0.05 |
| | ( − 1.40) | ( − 1.96) | ( − 1.54) |
| Tax-loss CF | 0.01 | 0.02 | 0.02 |
| | (0.37) | (0.65) | ( − 0.67) |
| Firm size | − 0.13 | − 0.13 | |
| | ( − 4.87) | ( − 4.98) | |
| Age of PPE | 0.82 | 0.83 | 0.92 |
| | (7.61) | (7.72) | (8.59) |
| Year 1988 | − 0.05 | − 0.05 | − 0.07 |
| | ( − 3.77) | ( − 3.93) | ( − 5.09) |
| Year 1991 | − 0.01 | − 0.01 | − 0.03 |
| | ( − 0.33) | ( − 0.31) | ( − 1.67) |
| # observations | 5771 | 5771 | 5771 |
| Adjusted $R^2$ | 0.05 | 0.05 | 0.04 |

information problems. The main results concern the total lease share, or the percentage of firms' total annual costs of property, plant, and equipment use accounted for by capital or operating leases. After controlling for firm size and other factors, our estimates suggest that the total lease share of a low-rated firm that pays no cash dividends is about 25 percentage points higher than that of a highly rated dividend-paying firm. Not surprisingly, we also find that tax-related motivations help explain the relative propensity to lease.

Given that equipment under lease accounts for nearly a third of the total annual new equipment investment in the U.S. in recent years, the implications of these findings are clearly far-reaching. Our results suggest that a comprehensive analysis of corporate capital structure should not disregard the role of leasing, which serves as a means of alleviating financial contracting costs. Our results also suggest that microeconomic studies of fixed capital investment and its dynamics should consider the role of off-balance-sheet financing as reflected in rental expense. For example, our finding that leasing by small firms substantially exceeds that of large firms, particularly in manufacturing, suggests that current research focusing on the relative behavior of small- versus large-firm investment can generate misleading conclusions to the extent that these studies ignore the leasing option. Indeed, an examination of the dynamics of lease financing and equipment investment should prove fruitful in future research.

## References

Ang, James and Pamela P. Peterson, 1984, The leasing puzzle, Journal of Finance 39, 1055–1065.
Bayless, Mark E. and J. David Diltz, 1988, Debt capacity, capital leasing, and alternative debt instruments, Akron Business and Economic Review 19, 77–88.
Brealey, Richard and Stewart Myers, 1984, Principles of corporate finance (McGraw-Hill, New York, NY) 629–645.
Calomiris, Charles W. and R. Glenn Hubbard, 1993, Internal finance and investment: Evidence from the undistributed profits tax of 1936–1937, Working paper (National Bureau of Economic Research, Cambridge, MA).
Fazzari, Steven M., Glenn R. Hubbard, and Bruce C. Petersen, 1988, Financing constraints and corporate investment, Brookings Papers on Economic Activity 1, 141–195.
Financial Accounting Standards Board, 1976, Accounting for leases, Statement of Financial Standards No. 13 (FASB, Stamford, CT).
Flath, David, 1980, The economics of short-term leasing, Economic Inquiry 18, 243–255.
Harris, Milton and Arthur Raviv, 1991, The theory of capital structure, Journal of Finance 46, 297–356.
Krishnan, V. Sivarama and R. Charles Moyer, 1994, Bankruptcy costs and the financial leasing decision, Financial Management 23, 31–42.
Lewis, Craig M. and James S. Schallheim, 1992, Are debt and leases substitutes?, Journal of Financial and Quantitative Analysis 27, 497–511.
McConnell, John L. and James S. Schallheim, 1983, Valuation of asset leasing contracts, Journal of Financial Economics 12, 237–261.

Miller, Merton and Charles Upton, 1976, Leasing, buying, and the cost of capital services, Journal of Finance 31, 761–786

Myers, Stewart C., 1977, Determinants of corporate borrowing, Journal of Financial Economics 5, 147–175.

Myers, Stewart C. and Nicholas S. Majluf, 1984, Corporate financing decision when firms have investment information that investors do not, Journal of Financial Economics 13, 187–220.

Myers, Stewart C., David A. Dill, and Alberto J. Bautista, 1976, Valuation of financial lease contracts, Journal of Finance 31, 799–819.

O'Malley, Michael, 1994, The effects of taxes on leasing decisions: Evidence from panel data, Mimeo. (Federal Reserve Board, Washington, DC).

Schallheim, James C., Ramon E. Johnson, Ronald C. Lease, and John McConnell, 1987, The determinants of yields on financial leasing contracts, Journal of Financial Economics 19, 45–67.

Smith, Clifford W. and L. MacDonald Wakeman, 1985, Determinants of corporate leasing policy, Journal of Finance 40, 895–908.

Smith, Clifford W. and Jerold B. Warner, 1979, Bankruptcy, secured debt, and optimal capital structure: Comment, Journal of Finance 34, 247–251.

Smith, Clifford W. and Ross L. Watts, 1992, The investment opportunity set and corporate financing, dividend, and compensation policies, Journal of Financial Economics 32, 263–292.

Strauss, Robert D., 1991, Equipment lease under UCC Article 2A: Analysis and practice suggestions, Commercial Law Annual (Callaghan & Company, Atlanta, GA).

Stulz, René M. and Herb Johnson, 1985, An analysis of secured debt, Journal of Financial Economics 14, 501–521.

Sweig, Allan G. 1993, Why the equipment lessor will usually fare well in the bankruptcy of the equipment lessee, Presented in Conference on New Opportunities in Lease Finance (Institute for International Research, New York, NY).

Wolfson, Mark A., 1985, Tax, incentive, and risk-sharing issues in the allocation of property rights: The generalized lease versus buy decision, Journal of Business 58, 159–171.

Zall, Milton, 1993, The implications of UCC Article 2A, Equipment Leasing Today 5, Oct., 27–30.

# Name Index